Library of
Davidson College

Some Key Issues for the World Periphery

SELECTED ESSAYS

Other Titles of Interest

THE BALANCE OF PAYMENTS ADJUSTMENT PROCESS IN DEVELOPING COUNTRIES
S. Dell and R. Lawrence

STATE PETROLEUM ENTERPRISES IN DEVELOPING COUNTRIES
United Nations Centre for Natural Resources

TECHNOLOGY, EMPLOYMENT AND BASIC NEEDS IN FOOD PROCESSING IN DEVELOPING COUNTRIES
Edited by **C. Baron**

DEVELOPMENT PERSPECTIVES
V. V. Bhatt

MONEY AND MONETARY POLICY IN LESS DEVELOPED COUNTRIES
Edited by **W. Coats Jr. and D. R. Khatkhate**

ALTERNATIVE DEVELOPMENT STRATEGIES AND APPROPRIATE TECHNOLOGY
R. K. Diwan and D. Livingston

REDISTRIBUTIVE EFFECTS OF GOVERNMENT PROGRAMMES — THE CHILEAN CASE
A. Foxley, E. Aninat and J. P. Arellano

DEVELOPING COUNTRY DEBT
Edited by **L. G. Franko and M. J. Seiber**

LATIN AMERICA AND THE NEW INTERNATIONAL ECONOMIC ORDER
Edited by **J. Lozoya**

THE POLITICAL ECONOMY OF EEC RELATIONS WITH AFRICAN, CARIBBEAN AND PACIFIC STATES
Edited by **F. Long**

COST-BENEFIT ANALYSIS AND INCOME DISTRIBUTION IN DEVELOPING COUNTRIES
Edited by **J. D. MacArthur**

THE CHOICE OF TECHNOLOGY IN DEVELOPING COUNTRIES
J. Pickett

INTEGRATION OF SCIENCE AND TECHNOLOGY WITH DEVELOPMENT
Edited by **D. Babatunde Thomas and M. S. Wionczek**

TOWARD A NEW STRATEGY FOR DEVELOPMENT
Compiled by **Rothko Chapel**

SCIENCE, TECHNOLOGY AND ECONOMIC GROWTH IN THE DEVELOPING COUNTRIES
Edited by **G. E. Skorov**

Some Key Issues for the World Periphery

SELECTED ESSAYS

by
MIGUEL S. WIONCZEK
Senior Research Fellow, El Colegio de México, Mexico City

PERGAMON PRESS
OXFORD · NEW YORK · TORONTO · SYDNEY · PARIS · FRANKFURT

U.K.	Pergamon Press Ltd., Headington Hill Hall, Oxford OX3 0BW, England
U.S.A.	Pergamon Press Inc., Maxwell House, Fairview Park, Elmsford, New York 10523, U.S.A.
CANADA	Pergamon Press Canada Ltd., Suite 104, 150 Consumers Road, Willowdale, Ontario M2J 1P9, Canada
AUSTRALIA	Pergamon Press (Aust.) Pty. Ltd., P.O. Box 544, Potts Point, N.S.W. 2011, Australia
FRANCE	Pergamon Press SARL, 24 rue des Ecoles, 75240 Paris, Cedex 05, France
FEDERAL REPUBLIC OF GERMANY	Pergamon Press GmbH, 6242 Kronberg-Taunus, Hammerweg 6, Federal Republic of Germany

Copyright © 1982 Miguel S. Wionczek

All Rights Reserved. No part of this publication may be reproduced, stored in a retrieval system or transmitted in any form or by any means: electronic, electrostatic, magnetic tape, mechanical, photocopying, recording or otherwise, without permission in writing from the publishers.

First edition 1982

British Library Cataloguing in Publication Data
Wionczek, Miguel S.
Some Key issues for the world periphery.
1. Economic history - 1945-
2. Underdeveloped areas - Economic conditions
3. International economic relations
I. Title
330.9'172   HC59
ISBN 0 08 025783 6

Library of Congress Catalog Card no: 81-81336

In order to make this volume available as economically and as rapidly as possible the author's typescript has been reproduced in its original form. This method unfortunately has its typographical limitations but it is hoped that they in no way distract the reader.

Printed in Great Britain by A. Wheaton & Co. Ltd., Exeter

Contents

INTRODUCTION vii

List of Tables xiii

Part I MEXICO

1. Thirty Years of Incomplete Formal Planning, 1933-63   3
2. Economic Development and Political System   31
3. Foreign Investment in Mexico: Problems and Prospects   49
4. The State and the Electric-Power Industry, 1895-1965   65
5. The Consequences of Scientific and Technological Underdevelopment   89
6. Science and Technology Planning   109

Part II LATIN AMERICA

7. Development Research Problems in the Region   123
8. Latin American Growth and Trade Strategies in the Post-War Period   139
9. External Public Indebtedness and Sectoral Changes in Foreign Private Investment   167
10. Experiences of the Central American Economic Integration Programme and Their Relevance to East Africa   185
11. Towards a Common Treatment for Foreign Private Investment in the Andean Common Market   207
12. Pacific Trade and Development Cooperation with Latin America   237
13. Transnational Corporations in Latin America: Political and Economic Problems   253
14. Technology Transfer through Transnational Corporations   265
15. Science and Technology and External Dependency Relations   283

Part III GLOBAL PROBLEMS

16. Bilateral Resource Exploitation Arrangements between Less Developed and Industrialized Countries ... 295

17. Less Developed Countries and Transnational Corporations: Conflicts over Technology Transfer and Major Negotiable Issues ... 311

18. The Less Developed Countries' External Debt and the Euromarkets: The Impressive Record and the Uncertain Future ... 339

19. Science and Technology Planning in Less Developed Countries: Major Policy Issues ... 357

20. The Origins of the UNCTAD Code of Conduct for Technology Transfer ... 367

21. The UN Conference on Science and Technology for Development: Three Essays ... 377

22. A Diagnosis of Past Failures and Future Prospects of the New International Economic Order ... 393

23. What Can Be Done (If Anything) with the Brandt Report? ... 411

Name Index ... 425

Subject Index ... 427

Introduction

Identified by the publishers of this volume, Pergamon Press, as "one of the world's leading experts in economic underdevelopment", I am faced with the difficult task of clarifying with necessary restraint the origins of my limited expertise in that field.

I was born and had spent close to the first three decades of my life, including the whole Second World War, in Poland, a country pertaining — according to economic historians — to an "underdeveloped" part of Europe. I can hardly consider myself, however, a product of "underdevelopment" since I have learned relatively little about the nature of real underdevelopment while still living in Europe.

It is true that Eastern Europe's relative underdevelopment brought to the fore of discussion in Western economics at the close of the Second World War — through the seminal studies of Rosenstein-Rodan and Mandelbaum-Martin — the general issues of economic development. The East European "underdevelopment", as I do remember it from the thirties, had very little in common, however — both in quantitative and qualitative terms — with the underdevelopment of the Western world's colonial and post-colonial peripheries. Compared with most of today's Latin America, Africa and Asia, Eastern Europe and the Balkans were in the interwar period (1918-39) fairly advanced, albeit stagnant, economies and societies.

Thus, my upbringing in "underdeveloped" Europe and my intellectual background were not particularly helpful for my later inquiries into both the general and the specific problems of underdevelopment apart from one respect. The occupation of Eastern Europe by the Nazis in 1939-41 was followed by the abolishment by decree of all forms of formal education in the "conquered" countries so that they would become the Nazi empire's colonies. By closing down, among others, local universities the occupiers forced the local post-university generation, attracted to all sorts of informal underground higher learning institutions, to abandon for the duration of the war the traditional disciplinary approach to schooling.

People like Gunnar Myrdal insist that the persistence of the traditional mode of university education has been largely responsible for intellectual sterility of most of social sciences in modern times in Europe and elsewhere.

If there were some truth in these claims, then the Nazi destruction of formal education in sizable parts of Europe during the Second World War was perhaps a much lesser evil than it is generally thought. In countries like Poland, people engaged in illegal scientific and intellectual endeavours looked at the world not through the eyes of disciplines but of the clusters of issues considered relevant for the future after the expected disappearance of the war-time hell. Thus, the possibilities opened by informal postgraduate education combined with war-time moral values produced in certain parts of German-occupied Europe a generation of rather broadminded social scientists in lieu of unidimensional "economists", "political scientists", "historians" or "sociologists". Given the complicated and multidimensional nature of underdevelopment (and development as well), this integrated social science background which substituted the over-specialized expertise proved to be of considerable help for those like me who after the last world war had curiosity to look into the question of underdevelopment of the world peripheries.

The following chapter of my preparations for the study of underdevelopment consisted of seven years at the United Nations immediately after its birth (1946-53). While until the mid-sixties the United Nations was an overwhelmingly Western "social club", those early participants in the U.N. political and research activities who are still around will perhaps agree that the United Nations was at that time a highly interesting and inspiring place for the relatively young social scientist to be. As a matter of fact, the United Nations was the *only* place in the early post-war world, where in spite of rapidly growing conflicts between the Western "majority" and the socialist "minority", the conceptual framework started emerging around 1950 that would permit us later to consider global problems in global terms.

Few better instances of the learning process about the global approach can be recalled than in the U.N. Economic and Social Council's early post-war annual debates about the shape and the direction of the world economy. The fascination of these debates was closely related to the fact that the task of elaborating U.N. World Economic Surveys in the late forties and early fifties was in the hands of a particularly able group of political economists of many nationalities headed by a great heterodox Pole, Michael Kalecki. It was highly educating to be able to watch how that group of U.N. civil servants defended the fruits of their global economic research against attacks by the rather mediocre intellectually economic *aparatchiks* representing the respective largest "capitalist" and "socialist" establishments and their lesser allies. Both superpower establishments were unhappy reading the U.N. world economic surveys of these days, because they did not fall into category of either "friendly academic literature" or "enemy political propaganda". By dealing with the realities, the surveys were just embarrassing to both ideological camps.

It must be kept in mind, however, that these rather fierce, albeit small, battles were fought at the United Nations around 1950 in the midst of silence about the underdeveloped world. Underdevelopment was still not present formally at the United Nations agenda if only because its key world was the post-war reconstruction of the industrial world. Moreover, the political presence of the underdeveloped peripheries at the United Nations and elsewhere was limited at that time to a few historical "special cases" like Ethiopia or Thailand. The rest of the underdeveloped world, except in Latin America, was falling still within the terms of reference of the U.N. Trusteeship Council at best. In other words, those who spent some years with the United Nations prior to its physical settling for good on the Manhattan's eastside next to Hudson river, were still living in the political world of the (almost) Treaty of Versailles.

Introduction

The world outside the United Nations' "green house" was changing, however, imperceptibly but constantly. The change led to the discovery of the underdeveloped peripheries in the early sixties in the wake of what is also known as the decolonization process of Asia and Africa. The discovery took place almost a decade after my short and relatively happy life at the United Nations of the early post-war period. My coexistence with the United Nations came to an end at the beginning of the fifties after I had become aware that I was neither mentally nor emotionally suited to pass through life as an anonymous international civil servant, and after I had realized that once I had decided to do something else with myself I faced either the highly unenviable choice of going back to stalinist Poland or "choosing freedom" in Senator Joseph McCarthy's America. I did not do either, due perhaps to the lessons of the war in Europe. The war taught me, among other things, that real choices in life are not many and the correct ones involve untold risks. Moreover, it taught me that the successful implementation of the correct choices, i.e. the survival both in war and in peace, depends largely — given some personal luck — upon the individual's capacity of creating new options when the old ones expire.

In 1953, shortly after Joseph Stalin's death in Moscow but still long before Joseph McCarthy's political demise in the United States, I opted for unilateral non-aligned exit from the highly unattractive bipolar situation which was neither of my making nor my liking. In simple words, I moved down to (and later became a citizen of) Mexico. It is there — south of the industrialized north — where I started learning, some thirty years ago, about the many hardships and sins and the few virtues of underdevelopment.

In the last three decades — not as a cheerful tourist but as a sympathetic social scientist and sometimes a policy adviser — I have visited many times over most of the underdeveloped world except Southeast Asia (because of the war in Vietnam), South Africa (because of the apartheid) and the Persian Gulf (because of the lack of time). During these last thirty years I must have spent more than ten years in jobs and activities directly related to economic policy design and making at domestic and regional level and to international economic negotiations, first in Latin America and later in the context of north-south relations. I must also have attended literally hundreds of academic and intergovernmental meetings on the subjects which appear on the present broad north-south agenda: international trade and investment, economic co-operation among LDCs, food production and rural development, industrialization and technology transfer, transfer of financial resources, transnational corporations, etc. I had to deal with these matters in many different ways according to the occasion — as an academic, as a policy advisor, or as a straight negotiator. In the process I learned a lot about the patterns of behaviour and the goals of the "other parties" at these academic discussions, governmental bilateral encounters and multilateral negotiations. The "other parties" might have been at times domestic bureaucratic and political interests, and at other times foreign public or private groups or their instantaneous or longer-term coalitions. My earlier life in Europe and the United States, the prolonged visits to universities on both sides of the North Atlantic, and the extensive travels through the industrialized North, including Japan and the Soviet Union, were clearly of great help in understanding these "other parties", whether for analytical purpose or policy-directed negotiations.

During the second half of my life I proved to be as lucky as during the first one. Somehow I have never become a fully-fledged and full-time bureaucrat, whether international or national. All my international appointments were always *ad hoc*, advisory and of short duration, while on those numerous occasions when I held official positions in Mexico I always enjoyed an incredible degree of freedom. Instead of being provided with instructions for international meetings and negotiations, I was usually expected to know how to manage the difficult situations to the advantage of my country or my government, and by the mid-seventies — during various stages of the so-called north-south dialogue — to the advantage of the whole south.

The essays collected in this volume were written over the past twenty years, mostly but not exclusively in answer to external initiatives and invitations. Consequently, most, but not all of them, were originally published in learned journals and/or volumes of proceedings of respective international workshops, seminars or congresses. Since they represent only a fraction of my writings on underdevelopment at national, regional or global level, it goes without saying that the material for this book was chosen on the basis of its hopeful relevance for the sustained and multidisciplinary study of many facets of underdevelopment as can be found still today in the non-industrialized (yet) segment of the world economy. Across the volume as much as across the reality, some key issues repeat themselves constantly whether one looks at underdevelopment dynamically as a historical process or whether one analyzes it statically as the outcome of such process.

The volume's formal division into three parts (Mexico, Latin America and global problems) aims somewhat artificially at increasing the book's readability and at avoiding repetitions. Half-way through the volume, if not earlier, a patient reader will become aware that the book does not pretend to cover all important aspects of underdevelopment but only those of its key issues which attracted my particular attention over the past years of roaming through the twentieth century history of underdeveloped societies and not only through their present reality.

These key issues can be perhaps organized under the following general headings: (1) social and economic heritage of some underdeveloped countries (LDCs) like Mexico; (2) economic development strategies followed by the LDCs or their regional groupings in the post-war period; (3) recent industrialization's costs and benefits; (4) the role of the state in economic growth; (5) political and economic costs of foreign private investment and of external public indebtedness; (6) regional economic integration; (7) origins and consequences of scientific and technological underdevelopment; and (8) the so-called new international economic order. The selection of essays in this volume on all these eight major subjects should not be considered as reflecting my sustained encyclopedic interests but rather as coresponding to various subsequent stages of inquiry into the problems of underdevelopment, grouped around the clusters of issues.

During the first stage — in the fifties — superficially simple questions arose in my mind around the general question of what made some countries and regions underdeveloped compared with others? The search for even the preliminary answer to these questions forced me to study in some detail economic, political, social and cultural history of a few cases (on the national level — Mexico and on the regional one — Latin America). The study in turn led me to the conclusion that at the time of the beginning of the first industrial revolution in mid-eighteenth-century in Europe something happened in Mexico (then called New Spain) and Latin America (then called the Indies) which led them through the paths of political, economic, social and cultural change very much different from those followed by the so-called early industrializers. This particular turn, identified sometimes by social historians as the result of colonial heritage, not only deeply affected both internal and external relations of the individual underdeveloped non-European countries or their regions over the past 200 years, but it continued affecting them even in the late twentieth century in spite of the exogenous social shocks and the endogenous revolutions. My early excursions into the relatively distant past let me appreciate later and better the role of "colonial heritage" or "historical memory" as a crucial factor of the underdevelopment process. On the other hand, such appreciation of the non-tangible "anthropological" or "cultural" factors went accompanied by a lack of enthusiasm for most tools — and results as well — of the so-called modern quantitative analysis of underdevelopment (or the development), tools invented mostly in recent times in the so-called developed parts of the world.

Some superficial acquaintance with the historical evolution of Mexican and Latin American underdevelopment led me at the end of the fifties into the study of the problems arising from regional economic co-operation among underdeveloped countries. I worked in that field for about 10 years, attempting to answer — both for theoretical and policy purposes — first, the question about the pre-conditions of the successful regional economic co-operation among "unequal" national partners, and, later, the question of the reasons for dismal failures of all attempts at establishing institutional frameworks for regional economic co-operation in the LDCs. They failed in the post-war period not only in Latin America but also in Asia and Africa. My frequent travels through the three underdeveloped regions, and particularly my extensive stays in various parts of Africa, where regional integration schemes became fashionable in the mid and the late sixties, led me to the conclusion that all such schemes in the LDCs were condemned to fail for a rather simple reason: their promoters at national level were unable to solve satisfactorily from the viewpoint of all parties concerned the issue of the equal distribution of costs and benefits within such regional co-operation frameworks. This inability was due both to regional and extra-regional factors. Regionally, the greatest obstacle was arising from the exclusive fascination of the individual national governments with the issue of immediate trade and industrialization gains or losses arising from the establishment of regional trade blocks. In addition, other serious obstacles were emerging from the manipulation of these regional co-operation schemes by external actors, particularly foreign traders and investors whose profit maximization strategies were more often than not entering into conflict with regional co-operation goals.

After having dedicated almost a decade to all these problems, having been perhaps one of the first international experts asked to elaborate a scheme for economic unification of Africa within a common market after that continent's partial political decolonization of the early sixties, and after having surveyed all post-war attempts of economic integration in the three underdeveloped continents, I abandoned that field of inquiry and policy-making advice in the late sixties. It had occurred to me to leave behind a sort of intellectual testament in the form of a rather grim essay on the rise and decline of the Latin American economic integration, an essay reproduced so many times in so many places in the seventies, but it was decided to leave it out of this volume.

My next field of study for several years was the logical outcome of my earlier interest in the regional economic integration in the LDCs: it had occurred to me to look into the behaviour of the external agents of regional and national integration and disintegration according to the case — transnational manufacturing corporations (TNCs) in Latin America and elsewhere, transnational public and private financial intermediaries and related problems arising from external private and public indebtedness of the LDCs. Since international trade, industry and financing go hand by hand with

technology trade and moreover, since scientific and technological
underdevelopment is one of the most outstanding traits of general
underdevelopment, I am hardly aware when and how my interest shifted from
the TNCs into the field of technology transfer across the national borders
and particularly from the advanced to the underdeveloped countries. To that
last subject I have dedicated myself during practically the whole past
decade making inquiries at national level (in Mexico), regional level (in
Latin America), and in global terms (at various U.N. agencies and international
negotiations). As a matter of fact, I realize only now that about one-third
of the essays contained in this volume deal with the subjects of scientific
and technological backwardness and external dependency of the LDCs, subjects
that I consider one of the most pathetic reflections of past underdevelopment
and one of the principal obstacles to development in the future.

Any reader of these introductory remarks will suspect that after having
dedicated the seventies to the problems of scientific and technological
underdevelopment, I am presently directing my attention to some other field
of inquiry. Such suspicion is correct. Since the study of certain fields
leads us inexorably to other neighbouring areas, I have dedicated some time
and attention over the past few years to two specific subjects at which I
was unable to look earlier even in the most cursory way. These subjects are
respectively the energy problems of the LDCs after the "oil shock" of the
early seventies, and the frightening advancement of all sorts of military
technologies.

While still abstaining from writing on these most recent subjects of interest,
I am slowly coming to a preliminary conclusion that while the treatment of
the first of the two topics — energy — has been largely exaggerated both in the
advanced and the underdeveloped regions, the second topic does not receive
the treatment it deserves. Perhaps if the second volume of my selected essays
appears before the end of the eighties, I may have something relevant and
reasonable to say there on both subject matters, particularly on the second
one which looks more and more threatening to everybody and our whole planet
with the sudden extinction by, say, the year 2000. But before getting to
that magic year, let us get first in some orderly way to the end of the
eighties.

Mexico City, August 1981   M. S. WIONCZEK

List of Tables

1.1	Public and private investment in Mexico in selected periods, 1939-60	7
1.2	Participation of federal government administrative agencies and the rest of the public sector in public investment in Mexico in selected periods, 1939-60	7
1.3	Public investment by major categories in Mexico in selected periods, 1939-59	12
1.4	Financing of public investment in Mexico, 1941-58	18
1.5	Sectoral distribution of public investment in Mexico, actual (1959-61) and planned (1962-4)	20
1.6	Estimates of private investment in Mexico, 1962-4	22
3.1	Sectoral distribution of foreign private investment in Mexico, 1911-68	52
3.2	Book value of United States direct investment in Mexico, by major sectors, 1950-70	53
5.1	Remittance abroad of profits and related payments, 1961-5	96
5.2	Remittances of profits and payments for royalties and technical services, 1953-62	97
8.1	Regional differences within major indicators of economic growth in Latin America during the 1960s	140
8.2	Participation of manufacturing in GDP in Latin America, 1950-70	145
8.3	Changes in industrial structures in Latin America, 1955 and 1968	146
8.4	Exports of Latin American manufactures, 1962 and 1968	160
8.5	Exports of manufactures by selected Latin American countries, 1962 and 1969	160
9.1	Exports, imports, gross international reserves, external public debt and United States direct investment in Latin America, 1956, 1961 and 1966	180

List of Tables

9.2	New gross disbursements of foreign loans to the public sector, external debt service (amortization and interest), and external public debt of Latin America (including contracted but not disbursed), 1956, 1961 and 1966	181
9.3	Outstanding external public debt as a proportion of gross external current account revenue in Latin America	182
9.4	External public debt servicing as a percentage of gross current account external revenue in Latin America, 1956, 1961 and 1966	183
9.5	Book value of United States direct private investment in Latin America, 1956, 1961 and 1966	184
11.1	Estimates of current local expenditure of United States manufacturing companies in Colombia, 1957 and 1966	215
11.2	Value of exports by the Andean Group, 1966 and 1967	222
12.1	Japan trade with the world, Latin America, Australia, Canada and the developing market economies of Asia and Oceania, 1974-8	251
12.2	Distribution of Japan's trade by major regions	252
14.1	Distribution of United States-based TNC subsidiaries by sectors, 1968	268
14.2	Distribution of United States-based TNC manufacturing subsidiaries, 1968	269
18.1	Eurocurrency bank credits, 1972-6	343
18.2	Major LDC debtors to the Euromarket at the end of 1975	345
18.3	Reported end-users of Eurocredits to LDCs, 1971-3	348

PART I

MEXICO

CHAPTER 1

Thirty Years of Incomplete Formal Planning, 1933-63*

THE EARLY PERIOD, 1933-52

THE TERMS 'economic plan' and 'economic planning' appeared in Mexican political vocabulary in the mid-thirties. In the fall of 1933, in the midst of the Great Depression, the upper hierarchy of post-revolutionary leaders - under the prodding of younger intellectuals - drew up what received the name Plan Sexenal (Six-Year Plan). This was inspired in part by the policy of state intervention emerging in the more developed Western countries in response to the world-wide economic crisis and in part by what little was known in Mexico at that time about Soviet planning of the early thirties.

The Plan Sexenal was an economic plan in name only. In reality it was a general outline of economic policies to be followed after the change of administration in 1934, aimed in the first place at getting the country out of serious difficulties of external origin and, secondly, at encouraging economic development along the lines laid down at the end of the revolutionary strife by President Calles (1925-28), who still held effective power in 1933. It was produced jointly by federal government technicians and the Program Commission of the Partido Nacional Revolucionario (PNR) and was ratified by the PNR Second Convention, held in December 1933. The fact that the future president, Lazaro Cardenas, did not actively participate in its preparation suggests that it was principally a political document drawn up by the Calles group.

As a student of public administration in Mexico observed many years later:

> The Plan did not propose a financial program capable of supporting the remaining features, most of which called for increases in both federal and local government expenditures. . . . Neither is there evidence that

---

*This essay formed part of a comparative research project directed by Prof. Everett E. Hagen, Center for International Studies, Massachussets Institute of Technology, and appeared originally under the title 'Incomplete Formal Planning: Mexico' as Chapter VI in Everett E. Hagen (Editor), Planning Economic Development, Richard D. Irwin Inc., Homewood, Illinois, 1963.

the authors of the Plan seriously took into account the existing revenue structure or the possible methods of increasing such revenue, or that they understood the relationship between government expenditure and the general level of economic activity(1).

In addition, the *Plan Sexenal* did not provide for any practical tools for its implementation. At the time of its preparation Mexico did not have any economic or statistical agency that could undertake the studies necessary to translate the plan's general instructions into quantitative terms. Although the document implied an awareness of the need for annual economic programmes to complement the general framework of the plan, as well as for the periodic revision of its goals, it did not provide for the establishment of a federal agency for that purpose. It merely suggested that all these matters be taken care of by governing party organs.

On one occasion an attempt was made to eliminate this basic deficiency. In 1935 President Cardenas set up a special advisory committee (Comité Asesor Especial) composed of a number of ministers, a representative from the National Irrigation Commission, and the directors of the central bank and the Banco Nacional de Crédito Ejidal. This group was charged with coordinating national planning policies. However, after the fashion of many other interministerial groups created in following decades, the committee apparently did not function efficiently. Otherwise there would have been no need to establish a few years later in the Ministry of Internal Affairs (Secretaría de Gobernación) a technical office in charge of the plan. President Cardenas instructed this new agency to also draft another six-year plan for the duration of the following administration (1941-6).

In terms of concepts, but concepts only, the second *Plan Sexenal* represented an improvement over the first. A special introductory chapter, absent from the earlier plan, discussed at length problems related to concrete planning of governmental activities and coordination of the different governmental agencies, including coordination between federal, state, and municipal authorities. It suggested that the federal government delineate the plan of action in the economic field in quantitative terms and recommended the early establishment of a Supreme National Council in which all economic, social, political, and military forces would be represented. The Council's terms of reference were to be defined by legislative action of the Congress, but the body was to be only advisory in nature. It was left to the President of the Republic to decide 'the speed and the modalities for the implementation of the governmental program'. Finally, it was suggested that the authorities of the governing party revise and amplify the new programme in the light of experience acquired during the first *Plan Sexenal* and findings of the national census of 1940. All of these suggestions did not add anything new in practical terms. In very noteworthy degree the second six-year plan remained even more a paper plan than the first.

Even with only a sketchy knowledge of Mexico's modern political and economic history one can understand why the two plans consisted for the most part of pious exhortations and had very little practical effect. First, they were prepared without any knowledge of the planning methods applicable to a still very underdeveloped society suffering from a serious shortage on all levels of technicians and experts. Second, they were prepared by the outgoing administration in a country whose political system provides for the peaceful transmission of power within the governing (and for all practical purposes the only) party but makes no provision for continuity of economic policies except in the general sense of fulfilment of the spirit of the Constitution. Thus both the first and the second Plan Sexenal could have been binding on the incoming President only if the interest and objectives of the new regime had coincided fully with those of the previous one and providing that the general internal and external conditions had remained basically the same.

But this was not the case. For reasons not directly pertinent here, the Cardenas administration (1935-40) broke away from Calles' policies and turned toward the agrarian ideals of the revolution and the extreme nationalism for which the Great Depression and the behaviour of powerful foreign economic interests in Mexico were largely and jointly responsible. The Avila Camacho administration (1941-6), on the other hand, saw a return to the economic policies in force before the advent of Cardenas, a return made possible precisely because Cardenas had carried out reforms in land tenure, which partially solved the agrarian problem, and in nationalization of the petroleum industry. Controversy concerning nationalization had been a serious irritant in Mexico's relations with the outside world. Furthermore, the outbreak of the Second World War, by cutting the country off from external supply sources of manufactured goods, created excellent conditions for Mexico's speedy industrialization, since Mexico now possessed the technical and managerial skills necessary to produce many of the commodities no longer available from abroad. Industrialization, a national objective held in only secondary regard by Cardenas, was of great importance to Avila Camacho.

Contrary to a belief that still persists in many quarters, the Cardenas regime, bent upon agrarian reform and beset by enormous external problems, was not socialist if one defines socialist government as a political system aimed at the establishment of a centrally directed and state-controlled society. Cardenas and the radicals surrounding him made very little effort to revise, strengthen, or turn into law the national planning instrument they received from the Calles group in 1934. They probably would have had very little use for such an instrument even if it had been much more efficient and better designed technically. They simply took from the Plan Sexenal whatever suited their own priority list of social and economic goals and tried to implement those parts according to existing circumstances and available financial means. Since circumstances were very difficult and resources very limited, not much of what was proposed in the Plan Sexenal had been put into practice by 1940, except in the fields of irrigation and transportation.

The Avila Camacho administration had even less use for the following Plan Sexenal than the Cardenas regime for the first one, albeit for completely different reasons. In a manner of speaking, the Avila Camacho regime represented a return to normality; and it was a very prosperous normality indeed both because of the war-inspired boom in the external sector of the economy and because of the effects of the Cardenas reforms upon the economic and social structure of the country. At that time almost any private investment was yielding huge profits, and practically any public investment was highly productive. The public sector's revenue(2) increased rapidly from the depressed levels of the thirties, and for the first time since the pre-revolutionary era those who were governing Mexico could easily rationalize that what was good for the state was good for the private sector and vice versa. One should not forget that the Mexican economy grew during the war years at an annual per capita rate of nearly 5 per cent in real terms, a performance seldom matched except by programmes directed toward a war effort which mustered abnormal national energies. In these circumstances, orderly national planning seemed unnecessary. The 1942 decision of the Avila Camacho administration to establish a Federal Economic Planning Commission (Comisión Federal de Planificación Económica), a body whose accomplishments are somewhat obscure, had very little to do with planning. The Commission was supposed to gather facts and figures on the nation's industrial production, and it clearly responded to the growing need for an improvement in statistical information, whose dearth and inaccuracy undoubtedly hampered day-to-day operations of both public and private sectors.

When the time came in 1946 for another change of administration, economic expansion continued unabated but once again the term 'economic planning' was heard. The electoral campaign of presidential candidate Miguel Alemán introduced two novel elements with respect to the formulation of the economic policy programme for the incoming government. The first was that the aspirant to the presidency himself participated very actively in this endeavour. Secondly, the range of groups involved extended considerably beyond the usual government technicians and high members of the governing party.

During the twelve months preceding the 1946 elections round-table discussions were held in more than half the states and in all the urban centres of Mexico. At each meeting the candidate discussed a major national economic issue with representatives of local groups, including small farmers and trade union leaders, and thereafter regional problems were analysed. Important national issues were divided beforehand into four major groups: agriculture, industry, transportation, and the tourist trade. According to one of Alemán's chief advisers during his electoral campaign, Dr. Manuel Germán Parra, the future President did not want 'his detailed program of government to be the exclusive fruit of his personal experience, however broad, nor of the strictly technical point of view of a small group of experts in the various matters facing the country'(3). Unfortunately, whatever value the materials and opinions collected during the 1946 electoral campaign may have for future historians, they were not translated into any organized body of national economic policy or programmes, although three years later Dr. Parra insisted that the main findings of the nationwide debates were permanently retained in the presidential office to be used by the Chief Executive as his main reference work(4).

For all practical purposes the Alemán government represented a continuation of the Avila Camacho regime. The fear - quite common in Mexico at the war's end - of an economic recession in the United States and other industrial centres proved baseless; the demand for Mexican exports continued strong; the economic growth of the country during the war years resulted in a considerable expansion of the domestic market; and the economy found itself ready and able to finance the increasing amount of investment. In the private sector this investment was channelled to export commodity agriculture and industry, and in the public sector to all kinds of public facilities (or social overhead), including highways, railroads, large-scale irrigation, and electric power.

As Table 1.1 indicates, the government provided generous financial resources for these ends. Between 1946 and 1952 investment in the public sector, which was already 41 per cent of total investment, increased by some 50 per cent in real terms, a rate slightly higher than that of the increase in gross national product. The institutional structure of the public sector also underwent an important change. Whereas under the Avila Camacho administration the public sector consisted mainly of the federal government and a few major state enterprises (railroads, petroleum, and electric power), during the early post-war years various types of autonomous public agencies and state enterprises sprang up in great proliferation, all of them depending to some extent on federal government financial resources. There was also a change in the relative importance of the conventional administrative agencies of the federal government as direct investor as compared to the rest of the public sector. In the forties the capital outlays of autonomous public agencies and state enterprises were considerably smaller than direct investment by the federal government, but by the beginning of the 1950s they had increased to some 55 per cent of the investment of the public sector as a whole. (See Table 1.2).

TABLE 1.1. Public and Private Investment
in Mexico in Selected Periods, 1930-60

(Per cent of total gross investment; annual averages of the two-year periods)

	Public	Private
1939-40	39.6	60.4
1944-45	41.1	58.9
1949-50	42.1	57.9
1954-55	41.3	58.7
1959-60	40.1	59.9

Sources: Data for 1939-50 are from The Economic Development of Mexico: Report of the Combined Mexican Working Party, Baltimore, published for the International Bank for Reconstruction and Development by the Johns Hopkins Press, 1953; data for 1954-60 are from annual reports of Nacional Financiera.

TABLE 1.2. Participation of Federal Government Administrative Agencies
and the Rest of the Public Sector in Public Investment in Mexico
in Selected Periods, 1939-60

(Per cent of total public gross investment; annual averages of the two-year periods)

	Federal*	Rest of the public sector
1939-40	56.1	43.9
1944-45	60.8	39.2
1949-50	46.2	53.8
1954-55	44.9	55.1
1959-60	47.0	53.0

*Includes investment by states and municipalities, most of which is financed from federal budgetary resources.
Sources: Same as Table 1.1.

Early in the Alemán regime an initial attempt was made to subject this rapidly expanding and semi-autonomous part of the public sector to federal control(5). A law was passed at the end of 1947 empowering the Ministry of Finance to 'control and audit the operations of the decentralized agencies and concerns having state participation in order to keep informed of their administrative progress and ensure their correct economic performance, by means of a permanent system of audits and technical inspections'(6). A few weeks later the Ministry of Finance established the National Investment Commission (Comisión Nacional de Inversiones), an administrative entity charged with 'control, audit, and coordination' of current and capital budgets of some seventy-five autonomous agencies and state enterprises. This body never functioned more than formally, however, and another six years passed before the next (and this time more comprehensive) attempt was made to coordinate in some degree the investment activities in the public sector. By then other important reasons, both external and domestic, were added to the obvious political and administrative necessity for more effective control of the maze of instruments intervening and participating in the national economy in the name of the state.

First of all, in the final years of the Alemán administration, leading Mexican economists and some politicians realized that the economic growth experienced in the previous decade had been due to a very fortunate combination of circumstances that could hardly continue forever. The external boom for Mexican export commodities (which received a short-lived boost during the Korean War) was slowly tapering off. The easy and extremely profitable investment opportunities for the private entrepreneur were starting to become scarce, and, finally, there were certain initial indications that the very high yields from haphazard and improved public investment could not be expected to continue for long. Furthermore, the final phase of the public works programme, launched under the Alemán regime, had been financed to quite an extent by inflationary methods which were endangering the country's balance-of-payments position and at the same time fomenting internal social tensions.

THE INVESTMENT COMMISSION

When the new President, Adolfo Ruiz Cortines, took office in late 1952 he encountered a great many problems below the surface of prosperity. Federal finances were in bad shape; public agencies and enterprises were leading quite an independent life and were pressing continuously for new investment funds; inflationary pressures were on the rise; and the balance-of-payments position was shaky. A report prepared by the Combined Working Party of experts from the Mexican government and the International Bank for Reconstruction and Development, and available to the new President and his advisers, had this to say:

> The return from total investment in the next decade will depend on the extent to which official resources and (through appropriate policies) private funds are able to exploit the possibilities for offsetting lower immediate yields from increased outlays for public facilities, other long-term investments and maintenance and replacement of capital equipment. The task is different and more difficult than in the past when circumstances favored the selection of projects which yielded high returns from low outlays. In 1939-1950 Mexico did not need an agency to

coordinate investment in order to maintain a high rate of output. The Mexican economy has now reached a point where the uncoordinated selection of projects is no longer likely to bring the same results as in the past.

The time has come, therefore, when Mexico may want to abandon the project-to-project approach to economic development and look at the organic whole. This would not mean that a rigid 'plan' must be imposed from which no deviation would be permissible. On the contrary, it is important that shifts in the world situation or changed needs within the country be reflected quickly in economic policy. This requires that each project and economic policy must be justified by the extent to which it can contribute to economic development and that savings be directed into appropriate channels. In short, what is needed is a development program(7).

Things are never accomplished in full accordance with expert wishes and opinions. The Ruiz Cortines regime did not spell out the long-term development plan strongly suggested by the Working Party, but in the summer of 1953 (half a year after the change of government) the new President ordered the Ministries of Finance and Economy to prepare an investment plan for the public sector for the entire duration of the administration (1953-58). The plan was to be based upon information provided by all the ministries, autonomous agencies, and state enterprises regarding their individual investment programmes and their present and anticipated financial resources. All these data were to be transmitted to a newly created (or, recalling the 1947 attempt, one might say resurrected) Investment Committee (Comité de Inversiones) composed of representatives of the Ministries of Finance and Economy and designed to operate under the jurisdiction of the Finance Ministry, the central bank (Banco de México), and the national development bank (Nacional Financiera). According to officials who participated in its meetings in 1953/54, the Committee carried on its job of checking upon investment activities and programmes of the numerous federal and autonomous agencies so vigorously that it immediately ran into political difficulties. Consequently, it was transferred to the President's office and retitled. Thus for circumstantial and political reasons the Investment Commission (Comisión de Inversiones)(8) was born, an act which <u>ex post</u> may be considered as an important step toward the programming of public sector investment activities in Mexico.

The reorganized Investment Commission was to be responsible directly to the President and staffed with experts of his choice. Its expanded frame of reference included: (1) studying and passing judgement upon investment projects according to their importance for the immediate economic and social needs of the country; (2) making economic studies aimed at coordinating the priority, the volume, and the role of public investment with the objectives of economic, fiscal, and social policies; (3) submitting for the President's consideration a coordinated programme of public investment; and (4) suggesting to the President periodic adjustments in the investment programme in the light of new and unforeseen developments.

To help the Commission in its endeavours, all branches of the federal government, autonomous agencies, and enterprises with state participation were instructed once again to pass on to it information on investment programmes in progress as well as new projects under consideration and longer-term investment plans. At the same time, all the agencies were prohibited by presidential regulation from making any investment not previously submitted to the Investment Commission and approved by the presidency. The Finance

Ministry was to grant federal funds for investment purposes only when the Commission expressly approved the project in question.

From the very beginning the Investment Commission tried to establish as complete an inventory as possible of all publicly-financed development projects in the country and to rate them according to the investment criteria established by its staff. The criteria were: (1) the productivity of the project, or the ratio between the economic yield and the cost; (2) the social benefit; (3) the extent of coordination with other projects; (4) the degree of completion of projects under construction; (5) protection of the earlier investment in the case of projects already undertaken; and (6) the volume of employment generated by the project upon completion. Economic productivity and social benefit were assigned a greater weight than any of the other elements included in the overall priority index.

Having access to all general economic and technical data concerning publicly-financed projects in progress, in the preparatory stages, or under study, the Commission tried to check constantly the accuracy of the information against its own data collected through periodic field trips made by its technicians. The purpose of these informal inspection tours was not only to examine the progress of the works but also, in the case of newly planned projects, to gather additional data concerning the social (and probably also political) implications of new investment programmes, especially as regards the attitudes of the local population and the need for future investment in allied fields. One may safely assume that the Commission's technicians played an additional useful role by acting as a direct source of information for the presidency on the most pressing economic problems of outlying regions. This information served as a check on that received by the President through the more traditional channels: ministries, state and local authorities, and public development agencies and enterprises.

A few months before the beginning of each fiscal year the Commission received estimates from the Finance Ministry on the total federal resources available for investment; and the autonomous agencies presented the details of their capital budgets. These included information with respect to the anticipated origin of non-federal funds - for the most part the agencies' own resources plus foreign credits already available or under negotiation. On the basis of all these data (which together constituted the global investment programme for the whole public sector and indicated actually available total investment resources) the Commission drew up the preliminary plan for the distribution of federal funds among the multiple projects, agency by agency and project by project. Once the investment needs of the projects under construction were satisfied, taking into account the order of priority assigned to them in the Commission's inventory, the remaining funds were distributed among the new projects, again in accordance with the Commission's priority schedule.

Once the preliminary investment budget was ready, it was left to the President to make the final decisions and modifications in the light of his direct discussions with the Ministry of Finance, heads of other ministries responsible for capital investment programmes, and the directors of the major autonomous agencies. At this stage political considerations also presumable entered strongly into play, especially as regards the presidency's commitments to regional and local interests with respect to the early completion of given projects or the expansion of certain regional investment programmes.

After the investment programme was adjusted to the political realities of the day the Commission once again entered the field. It was now up to it to certify to the Ministry of Finance that a specified amount of federal funds had been committed for a given project or programme. Lacking such certification, no payments to agencies or private contractors working on specific projects could be made. The Commission's instructions were always quite precise and contained a great deal of technical information. A certificate of approval for a given project would describe all phases of the construction process and clearly define which was to be undertaken at that particular time. Where the building of a road was involved, for example, the Commission would list all the physical and technical characteristics of the work to be done during the year so that the disbursement of federal funds would correspond to that work only, subject to verification by documentary proof presented to the Ministry of Finance by the sponsoring agency.

Although the Commission was not legally empowered to supervise and control the overall investment performance of the federal dependencies, autonomous agencies, and state enterprises (in this last case investment funds were rarely supplied in their entirety by the Ministry of Finance), it was able to control these activities _de facto_ to quite an extent. This was made possible by having at hand the necessary financial and technical information on the progress of any particular public sector investment project and by being able to apply certain 'sanctions' to those agencies whose performance was poor in planning and executing their investment programmes. In the first place, undue delays in the execution of projects as a consequence of poor planning of management would affect the agency's position _vis-à-vis_ the Investment Commission when the time came the following year to ask for new appropriations. Secondly, a continuous record of poor performance, of which the Commission must have been aware, could have been brought informally to the President's attention with a resultant reshaping of the agency's administration. Since the competition for federal funds has always been very fierce, the Commission had an effective means of prodding the less efficient agencies in the direction of better performance.

The Investment Commission was criticized for not insisting from the very beginning on a mandate to set up overall priorities by sector for public investments and for having satisfied itself with the job of merely sorting out the investment projects prepared by the numerous state agencies and enterprises. It was said that this situation gave a privileged position to those agencies which because of good management and planning were able to submit a large number of well-prepared new project proposals, or to those officials or managers of state enterprises who had easier direct access to the presidency for reasons of internal politics. Consequently, as a rule more new top priority projects were in the Commission's files than could possibly be initiated in any given fiscal year. Very often the Commission was faced with the dilemma of determining what was more important: say, a multi-purpose river project or a first-class road linking a newly emerging production centre with neighbouring cities when both completely fulfilled the investment criteria set(9). Thus it was claimed that without participating in the preparation of the projects the Commission was free to decide which of them should be upgraded to be started immediately and which should be left for the future. But the final decision in these cases probably rested with the Chief Executive; besides, owing to a series of reasons, such situations appear to have been infrequent.

First, the Investment Commission started to operate in the midst of an uncoordinated investment programme. Hence one of its primary functions was to allot available funds in a somewhat more rational way among projects already in progress. It is estimated that more than three-fourths of the federal funds available each year for public investment were distributed among this group of projects. Here the Commission's role was limited in most cases to pushing some and slowing down others. Second, there was never an overabundance of new projects technically well prepared and ready for initiation. Third, as far as the sectoral distribution of public investment was concerned, there is evidence in Mexico's modern history of a certain continuity. Since the time of Calles, who might be considered the conscious initiator of the present phase of Mexican economic development, projects aimed at contributing directly to that development had preference over social investment. In addition, three fields always enjoyed the highest priority: irrigation, energy (electric power and petroleum), and transportation. At no time in the forties and fifties did they account for less than three-fourths of total public investment in Mexico. (See Table 1.3). Consequently all the agencies competing for federal funds knew from past experience what they might expect from the Ministry of Finance and what requests would be considered unreasonable by the Investment Commission and by the presidency.

TABLE 1.3. Public Investment by Major Categories in Mexico in Selected Periods, 1939-59

(Per cent of total gross public investment; annual averages of the two-year periods)

	Irrigation	Transport and Communications	Electric Power and Petroleum	Total
1939-40	13.4	52.9	15.1	81.4
1944-45	15.7	51.7	11.3	78.7
1949-50	13.5	39.3	22.4	76.2
1954-55	14.1	34.0	30.9	79.0
1958-59	10.4	39.1	29.0	78.5

Sources: Data for 1939-50, same as in Table 1.1; data for 1954-59 are as submitted by the Investment Commission to the International Bank for Reconstruction and Development.

In other words, in the annual process of presenting investment programmes to the Commission certain unwritten rules existed as to what share of federal investment funds would be forthcoming for any given sector, agency, or enterprise. All this served to make the bargaining process more realistic and limited the possibilities of preparation and presentation by interested agencies of outsized investment programmes which had no chance of approval.

The Investment Commission thus carried out functions beyond those enumerated in the 1954 decree, the expansion of its functions indicating that the Ruiz

Cortines administration considered this body both very useful and quite successful. The increasing role of the Commission was noted by outside observers. Published three years after the establishment of the Commission, the United Nations report on the agencies programming the economic development of Latin America declared that:

> The short-term approach that characterizes the work of the Commission is a consequence of its relatively brief experience and of the need to give a practical and immediate-use-value aspect to this beginning of planning, particularly to convince a certain type of government official not accustomed to curbs or hindrances in the relatively independent conduct of his office. This aim has been achieved, apart from the fact that to an increasing extent long-range economic considerations have been incorporated in the objectives originally set(10).

An International Bank Mission also commented on the Investment Commission's performance as follows:

> During the last three years the Commission has been able to formulate programs and direct public investment with increasing effectiveness. This success has been made possible by the new organization and the effective work of the Commission's staff. A prerequisite for the success has, however, been the careful fiscal and monetary policies followed by the Ministry of Finance and the Bank of Mexico. Without strict fiscal and monetary policies and without close collaboration between the Investment Commission on one side, and the Bank of Mexico and especially the Ministry of Finance on the other, it would not have been possible to control the over-all size of public investment as well as was done in 1955 and 1956(11).

By 1956 the Commission had been assigned additional functions: to conduct studies of the financial implications of public investment; to analyse general economic trends and to contribute to national economic policy planning aimed at integrating and justifying public sector investments; to make longer-term forecasts of investment needs by major sectors; and to study and analyse different aspects of public investment, such as its relation to economic development, impact on the private sector, and influence on the balance of payments.

The expansion of the Investment Commission's field of action apparently tied in with the growing inadequacy of domestic savings for financing public investment and the refusal of the federal authorities to return to the inflationary financing methods which characterized the final years of the Alemán administration. Consequently the need for external financing increased and with it the need for longer-term investment programmes, if only in the particular sectors which either through the federal government or directly were applying for foreign public and private loans. Thus the Investment Commission drew up its first two-year investment plan in 1956 (for 1957 and 1958), which served as the basis for negotiations with the International Bank and other foreign financial agencies with respect to new external credits for irrigation, energy development, and the transport system. The IBRD Mission that was invited by the Mexican government in 1957 to appraise this investment programme found it appropriate on the whole and concurred basically in its estimates of the financial resources available for public investment. The Mission commented, however, on the absence of longer-term studies on Mexico's public investment requirements. Noting that in some basic sectors of the Mexican economy, such as electric power and petroleum, studies of demand growth and investment requirements over longer periods had been made by interested autonomous agencies, the Mission suggested that studies of this type be conducted on a wide and more systematic basis and recommended that the Investment Commission play a leading role in their preparation. These in turn could be incorporated into five- or six-year development programmes of a general nature which could then be used as background data for much more detailed short-term investment programmes.

The growing importance of the Commission was due to four basic facts: (1) although it was a technical agency only, its highest officials had continuous access to the President - a tremendous advantage in a country whose political system centres on the person of the Chief Executive; (2) because of its technical nature and formally limited functions it could remain aloof from the mainstream of political and personal conflict daily in evidence in the executive branch of any government; (3) it became a depository and clearing house for vital economic information, only a part of which was available to other government agencies; and (4) through informal contacts with all the entities participating in public sector investment it was able to influence them without having to share the responsibility for setbacks encountered in the actual execution of individual projects(12).

The four years of the Investment Commission's operations under the Ruiz Cortines administration proved that the agency was fairly well adapted to Mexican political reality. It was not a revolutionary innovation. The limitations under which the Investment Commission operated were many. It was not a national planning or programming office because the initiative for setting goals for the whole economy did not originate with it. Neither was it empowered to formulate a national public investment plan of longer duration. The Commission was mainly an intermediary between the Ministry of Finance, the main source of public financial resources, and all the end users of these funds, be they ministries, autonomous agencies, or state enterprises. The Commission was never meant to become a superagency with jurisdiction over any of the existing ones, nor was it supposed to take over the Ministry of Finance's functions of fixing overall levels of public revenue and expenditure and acting as the final custodian and distributor of public funds. Neither was it meant to oversee and control the public non-federal sector as far as its general performance, policy, and investment management were concerned. It was a public interest watchdog only in the sense that it had a limited veto power over the overall investment programmes of the autonomous agencies and state enterprises by being able to deny them access to the federal funds on which practically all of them depended heavily.

THE MINISTRY OF THE PRESIDENCY

In the opinion of more than a few experts well acquainted with the activities of the Investment Commission under the Ruiz Cortines regime the agency's considerable success in comparison with earlier failures in the field of directing and channelling public investment was in large part responsible for the subsequent decline of its role. With the change of administration in late 1958, a new ministry was set up - the Secretaría de la Presidencia - designed to serve not only as liaison between the presidency and other federal agencies on political and economic matters(13) but also as the main economic coordination agency. Also ushered in by the incoming government, a new law on the functions of the executive branch empowered and enjoined the Ministry of the

Presidency to collect all data needed for the formulation of a general plan
of federal government expenditures and investments; plan public works and
their end use; draw up proposals for the promotion and development of regions
and localities; and plan, coordinate, and audit the investments of federal
authorities, autonomous agencies, and state enterprises(14). In other words,
the entire functions of the Investment Commission were transferred to the
Ministry.

The Commission itself, retitled the Public Investment Bureau, was incorporated
into the new Ministry as one of five bureaus, the remaining four being Planning, Supervision of Investments and Subsidies, Legislation, and Administrative Affairs. This peculiar structure of the Ministry, which placed functions
of distinctly dissimilar importance at the same organizational level, was
reputedly the outgrowth of administrative and personal considerations. The
former post of Director of the Investment Commission was considered too
important to be ranked any lower than immediately below the Minister and the
Undersecretary; on the other hand, it was felt that the newly created Bureau
of Planning was an experiment that did not merit a place higher in the hierarchy than that given to the reorganized Investment Commission. Consequently,
from the very beginning a curious dichotomy appeared as the result of the
coexistence of two parallel agencies independently occupied with two parts of
what is essentially a single whole: national planning and the management of
public sector investment. There is circumstantial evidence that the federal
officials responsible for the creation of the Ministry did not have a very
clear idea what they were trying to accomplish (in functional - not political - terms) by merging the Investment Commission with the Secretaría de la
Presidencia and balancing this decision with the establishment of the Planning Bureau.

The Presidential Resolution promulgated in mid-1959, instructing all the
federal dependencies, autonomous agencies, and state enterprises to formulate
an investment programme for the public sector for the period 1960-64, was
similar in many respects to the one issued six years earlier by the previous
President on the occasion of the establishment of the Investment Committee
as part of the Ministry of Finance. The new decree made reference to a
number of new social and economic objectives absent from the 1953 decree
(including, among others, income redistribution, priority attention to the
most backward parts of the national territory, and import substitution by
locally-produced goods), but its operational provisions differed very little
from those under which the Investment Commission functioned during the
previous administration. All public entities were ordered to provide information on their investment plans to the Ministry of the Presidency, which
would then 'proceed to study the programs, look to the most satisfactory
project coordination, and submit the coordinated 1960-64 public sector investment program, complete with priority ratings and sources of financing, for
the consideration of the Presidency of the Republic'. Individual investment
projects or programmes had to be accompanied by detailed plans for their
financing, 'specifying the origin and nature of the funds, be they budgetary
allocations, internal or external credits, resources belonging to the
decentralized organizations of state-controlled enterprises themselves, contributions from private sources', and so on.

Indirectly suggesting that under the previous regime not all the components
of the public sector had cooperated fully and willingly with the Investment
Commission, the 1959 regulation attempted to strengthen considerably the
sanctions against rebels. Not only was the Ministry of Finance prohibited

once again from providing federal funds for investments not expressly approved by the President but all the agencies were warned to refrain from seeking domestic and foreign credits without previous approval of the presidency. In addition, the Ministry of Finance was empowered to order the central bank, in the event of the use of credit for unapproved investment, to freeze the funds that each federal or autonomous agency and state enterprise was required to deposit there under the law; finally, the National Foreign Trade Bank (Banco Nacional de Comercio Exterior) was ordered to deny import permits for the public sector in the absence of documentary proof that they would be used for investments duly approved by the presidency. But once again, and notwithstanding the establishment of the Planning Bureau in the Secretaría de la Presidencia, the entire initiative with respect to the preparation of investment programmes was left to the agencies directly involved and no provisions were made for the longer-term planning of national economic policies or even of public sector activities by the new Ministry.

In fact, it took more than two years to put the Planning Bureau into motion, and as late as mid-1962 it was a very weak agency, weaker than either the old Investment Commission or its successor in the Secretaría de la Presidencia, the Public Investment Bureau. By that time the Planning Bureau had on its staff some twenty-five experts and auxiliary technicians who drew up or brought up to date a few sector programmes (for the steel industry and the development of tourist facilities in Mexico, among others) and a regional development programme for the Yucatán peninsula. Another regional plan for the southern part of the country (Chiapas, Tabasco, and certain portions of Oaxaca and Veracruz) was under preparation. However, since none of these was made public or offered for discussion outside the Ministry, it is not possible to pass judgement upon their merits. It is understood that the Yucatán development programme served as the basis for negotiation of an Inter-American Development Bank loan granted to Mexico in early 1962.

As far as integrated national planning is concerned, the Planning Bureau never really entered that field. Its answers to a questionnaire addressed to national planning agencies in the spring of 1962 by Professor Jan Tinbergen were extremely vague: 'Studies aimed at the quantification of [economic development] goals are currently being initiated'; 'goals have not been calculated by sectors of government or private activity although in certain instances specific objectives in quantitative terms have been set for 1964, but without having a definite place as yet within the national development plan already in process of preparation'; 'when national development plans are in readiness the [fiscal and economic policy] measures will be more closely coordinated as planning tools'; and so on.

The agency's ineffectuality was not necessarily its own fault. By using the term 'comprehensive planning' for the first time, the Presidential Resolution promulgated in the summer of 1961(15), the third year of the administration, was intended to define the field of action of the Planning Bureau but failed to provide for the centralization of national planning activities within the Secretaría de la Presidencia. The regulation only stipulated that the executive branch of the federal government 'through the ministries, departments of state, decentralized agencies, and enterprises having state participation <u>intensify</u> [italics added] its effort to . . . prepare national economic and social development plans, fixing concrete goals for the benefit of the community and outlining the means of achieving them'. The aims for accomplishment through these efforts were defined in very general terms: to detail the most adequate economic and social policy for accelerating the country's development; to calculate the amount, structure, and financing of national expenditure and investment; to formulate special development programmes; to plan the integral development of regions or localities; and to promote the consolidation of activities of public sector agencies among themselves and with state and municipal governments and private enterprise. In its own view the Secretaría de la Presidencia was clearly meant to be a kind of clearing house for all these endeavours and their general supervisor. Although it was empowered 'to set up procedures to govern the joint action of the public sector in the realization of these activities', there is no recorded evidence that the Ministry ever used this faculty in an orderly way.

Another Presidential Resolution, issued in March 1962, nine months after the mid-1961 decree, attests to the fact that the Secretaría de la Presidencia did not fulfil its functions and that top officials in the federal government finally realized that integrated national economic planning was not possible as long as the initiative was left to the independent judgement, good will, and public interest of dozens of major federal agencies, to say nothing of the continuously expanding list of enterprises with state participation. The new edict established an interministerial commission involving joint responsibility of the Ministries of Finance and the Presidency for the purpose of the 'immediate formulation of short- and long-term national economic and social development programs'(16). This new commission was also asked to estimate 'the amount, structure, and financing of the _domestic_ [italics added] expenditure and investment needed for the country's development to proceed at a satisfactory pace and in such a way as to make possible a steady improvement in the standards of living of the major sectors of the population'.

THE PLAN OF IMMEDIATE ACTION, 1962-64

Behind the initiative which led to the preparation by a group of Ministry of Finance experts of a short-term development programme covering the second half (1962-64) of the administration was the growing realization of the urgency to replace loose and only partially effective control and management of public sector investment with overall quantitative economic planning based upon clearly defined and coherent economic policy objectives. At least three readily discernible elements led to a departure from previous practices.

First, the fears expressed so convincingly at the beginning of the fifties by the Combined Mexican-IBRD Working Party unfortunately proved well-founded. Because - to paraphrase the Working Party's words - public resources and private savings (in the absence of appropriate overall policies and planning) were not able to exploit the potential possibilities for offsetting lower immediate yields from increased outlays for public facilities and other long-term investment, and because the deterioration in the external sector of the economy - also anticipated by experts for some time - actually started in the mid-fifties, Mexico's rate of economic development decreased considerably. As the population explosion gathered continuing momentum, the decline in the rate of growth of _per capita_ income took on disquieting proportions. In view of the persistence of this tendency, the claim that the slackening in economic growth was a temporary rather than secular phenomenon became increasingly untenable. An awareness of this fact, limited previously to small circles of professionally honest economists, spread to political circles and private enterprise as a result of the experiences of 1961, an extremely difficult year for the country's economy, both internally and externally. In that year two negative factors added their impact to the secular tendency mentioned above: stagnation in international commodity markets and the flight of domestic capital in response to a worsening of the Cuban crisis.

The second element which prompted a revision in attitudes toward planning was the increasing dependence of Mexican economic growth upon external resources, especially foreign public credits. External borrowings, as shown in Table 1.4, represented slightly more than 7 per cent of the total financial resources available to the public sector during the Second World War but accounted for over 15 per cent of public investment financing by the mid-fifties. This dependence increased steadily and led to the expansion of the external public debt (medium- and long-term) from some $500 million in 1955 to more than $1 billion in the early sixties. Consequently the debt service, which in the previous decade represented less than 10 per cent of foreign exchange earnings (defined as current exchange earnings minus foreign exchange expenditures for border trade and tourism), increased to 16 per cent by 1960/61, a very burdensome drain on the balance of payments for any country, even under the best of conditions(17).

TABLE 1.4. Financing of Public Investment in Mexico, 1941-58

(Per cent)

	1941-46	1947-52	1953-58
Federal fiscal resources	29.5	43.2	47.5
Current income of the public sector	25.8	25.1	25.4
Domestic credit	37.6	18.5	10.6
External credit	7.1	13.2	16.5
Total public investment	100.0	100.0	100.0

Sources: Data for 1941-51 were taken from The Economic Development of Mexico; Report of the Combined Mexican Working Party, Baltimore, published for the International Bank for Reconstruction and Development by the Johns Hopkins Press, 1953; data for 1952-58 originated in the Investment Commission.

It is difficult to determine to what extent this increasing dependence on external financing was a consequence of the reduction in foreign exchange earnings experienced by Mexico (in company with many other primary goods exporters) as a result of the international recession in commodity markets plus the government's refusal to return to inflationary development policies, and what measure of responsibility should rightfully fall to the absence of coherent programming of public sector investment. However, it did become abundantly clear that excessive recourse to external credit sources could in the long run create serious difficulties and still not solve the country's basic internal problems. Although the question of imposing limits on foreign indebtedness was not discussed openly in Mexico, evidence of a somewhat heightened awareness of the magnitude of the problem probably reflected a certain amount of prodding from the international lending agencies involved.

Some experts seemed to believe the dramatic increase in the capital-output ratio registered in Mexico was due not only to continuous government emphasis on industrialization and infrastructure investment but also to a considerable waste of investment funds, a concomitant of the unsatisfactory programming of public sector activities(18).

Finally, the international political framework changed considerably after the advent of the Kennedy administration in the United States. Together with all other Latin American republics, Mexico became a participant in the Alliance for Progress, which explicitly acknowledged a need for long-term planning for economic development(19). Subsequent to this change in United States attitudes and economic policies toward Latin America, similar but somewhat less obvious changes occurred in the practices of international aid agencies, which previously had not only been satisfied with the project-by-project approach toward economic development programming but had actually fostered such a procedure(20). This new atmosphere and Mexico's commitment under the 'Charter of Punta del Este' to submit her longer-term plan to Alliance for Progress experts for approval were probably as much responsible as the other factors mentioned earlier for abandonment of the obsolete, and even then none too effective, programming procedures followed in the fifties.

The 1962-64 plan, designated—in line with the precepts of the Charter of Punta del Este - the Plan de Acción Inmediata, aimed at attaining for the first half of the sixties a minimum annual growth in gross national product of 5 per cent, a rate equal to that of the fifties and equivalent to an annual increase in per capita income of slightly under 2 per cent. The planners estimated that to reach these goals it would be necessary to increase gross fixed investment from 15.5 per cent of the gross national product, its level at the start of the plan period, to 18.4 per cent by 1965.

This would involve a capital expenditure during the plan of about $6.4 billion as against slightly over $5 billion in the 1959-61 period. It was assumed that one half of the total would come from the public sector and that the other half would be mobilized by private enterprise. This important departure from investment patterns of the previous two decades, when some 60 per cent of gross fixed investment came from the private sector (see Table 1.1), was acknowledged by the authors of the plan: '. . . Because of the private investment lag and the recent incorporation into the public sector of some enterprises, such as the electric power plants, it would be difficult to restore, within the period covered by the Plan, the past ratios of private and public investment expenditure'(21).

The investment plan for the public sector was elaborated in the Secretaría de la Presidencia on the basis of individual medium-term capital expenditure programmes submitted by ministries, autonomous agencies, and state-owned or controlled enterprises. Presumably this plan was later revised by the working group of the Ministry of Finance, which adjusted the proposed allocation of public financial resources according to the general requirements of each of the major sectors of the economy. The distribution of public investment in 1962-64 was to differ considerably from that during the previous three-year period. (See Table 1.5).

Major changes in the distribution of public investment involved: (1) increased emphasis upon social investment (urban and rural social services, public health, education, and housing), which during the previous decade accounted for only about one-sixth of the state's capital expenditure; (2) a very large increase in agricultural investment - from some 10-12 per cent in the mid-fifties to about 18 per cent of the total under the plan; and (3) a relative decline in the importance of public capital expenditure for expansion and modernization of transport and communication systems.

TABLE 1.5. Sectoral Distribution of Public Investment in Mexico, Actual (1959-61) and Planned (1962-64)

(Per cent)

	1959-61	1962-64
Basic development	78.3	75.7
Agriculture	10.7	17.8
Electric power and petroleum	28.2	25.8
Transport and communications	36.1	28.6
Other	3.3	3.5
Social investment	18.9	23.4
Administration and defense	2.8	0.9
Total	100.0	100.0

Sources: Data for 1959-61 from Nacional Financiera; data for 1962-64 from Organización de los Estados Americanos, El desarrollo económico y social de México, México, D.F., October 1962.

These shifts can easily be explained. After the passage of two decades in which, on the one hand, public investment in infrastructure facilities dominated the thinking of the central government and, on the other, income distribution showed almost no improvement and the demographic explosion continued at an accelerated rate, the moment came when any further social investment would be extremely difficult to postpone although its developmental effect would be felt only over a period of years.

Another aspect of the Mexican economy which needed immediate attention was agriculture, or rather that part of it which produced for domestic markets. During the fifties, notwithstanding the large volume of public and private investment in export-oriented agricultural activities, the agricultural sector as a whole became the second slowest growing activity (after mining). The average rate of expansion of agricultural output declined from 6 per cent a year in the first half of the decade to about 3.5 per cent in the later fifties, reflecting not only the slack in demand for export crops but also the stagnation of traditional agriculture producing for domestic consumption. Under these conditions, and aware of the danger of inflationary pressures in a situation where the output of foodstuffs barely exceeded population growth, planners had to propose a considerable reallocation of public resources to this sector. Additional non-economic considerations were pressing in the same direction; many rural areas left out of the mainstream of economic progress had become focal points of serious socio-political tensions.

Finally, the need for public investment in transport and communications was declining, Mexico already possessed a very modern all-weather road system, one of the best in Latin America, and her railways had been largely modernized in the fifties. Thus the lowering of investment priority in this field would not create any serious obstacles to the country's overall development.

The distribution of public capital expenditure under the plan must have also been influenced by economic aid priorities set up under the Alliance for Progress, which had as an immediate objective the solution of Latin America's pressing social problems. Since the implementation of the 1962-64 plan depended to a considerable degree upon access to external credit, it was only logical that the planners gave high priority to social investment, especially education, public health, and housing.

In the previous decade close to 50 per cent of public investment in Mexico had been financed from fiscal resources of the federal government and 25 per cent from the current revenue of the rest of the public sector, whereas the remaining 25 per cent was financed in more or less equal parts by domestic credit and external medium- and long-term loans. The <u>Plan de Acción Inmediata</u> changed this pattern. It was expected that domestic non-inflationary resources would account for 50 per cent of the public financing needed (the federal government 25 per cent and the rest of the public sector another 25 per cent). The remaining half, equivalent to some $1.6 billion, or over $500 million a year, was expected to come from international financial institutions and various United States aid programmes under the Alliance for Progress. This projected inflow of external economic aid was almost double that actually received in the first three years of the administration. It was further assumed that because of the burden of servicing the external debt the new loans would be granted on much more liberal terms. It was presumably believed that the mobilization of such a large volume of long-term aid in a relatively short time would be facilitated by two facts: Mexico's outstanding past record in terms of political, economic, and monetary stability, and the country's special relations with the United States, largely due to its politically strategic position in Latin America. According to the planners, the only alternative to the availability of external resources of the magnitude outlined would be a return to the inflationary financing methods of the late forties. This solution, however, was firmly rejected as fully incompatible with the income distribution objectives of the 1962-4 plan.

The <u>Plan de Acción Inmediata</u> was the first national investment programme covering both the public and the private sector. It was extremely difficult to pass any judgement upon this part of the document not only because the complete text of the plan was still confidential at the time of writing but also because the statistical base available to planners was extremely weak and the country's experience with programming private investment practically nil. Although one should not exclude the possibility that the planners made some sample surveys of business investment intentions, it seemed probable that overall estimates of private capital expenditure in the plan period were residual and represented a gap between total investment needs dictated by gross national product growth goals and the public investment possible in the light of expected financial resources of domestic and external origin.

The official résumé did not throw any light upon the methods used to estimate the investment behaviour of the private sector in the period covered by the plan. The provisional figures for this sector (see Table 1.6) were accompanied only by a remark to the effect that manufacturing investment estimates

(40.6 per cent of the total) were based upon expansion plans and new projects in the leading industries known to the various business organizations.

TABLE 1.6. Estimates of Private Investment in Mexico, 1962-4

	US $ millions	Per cent
Agriculture	448.0	14.2
Manufacturing	1280.0	40.6
Construction	1040.0	33.0
Transport	304.0	9.6
Other	80.0	2.6
Total	3152.0	100.0

Source: Organización de los Estados Americanos, El desarrollo económico y social de México, México, D.F., October 1962.

According to the plan, private investment was expected to jump in the third year by some 20 per cent, presumably under the impact of heavy public capital expenditure in 1962 and 1963, to exceed the total volume of public investment for the first time since the end of the fifties. How it was to be achieved was not explained, but it was assumed that the increase in private sector investment would come from domestic sources. The year-to-year projections set the probable inflow of foreign private capital at $100 million a year, or only slightly more than in the years immediately before the plan period.

The planners indicated in a somewhat veiled manner that more efficient coordination of governmental policies directly affecting private business decisions would be of great assistance in the fulfilment of the private investment goals outlined, but they showed their awareness of shortcomings in this respect, stating with a frankness rather unusual for an official document that:

> Although the programing of economic aid and social development in Mexico has made considerable progress in the past two years, the combination of elements necessary to increase the efficiency of planning within the framework of a mixed economy does not exist as yet. Particularly, there is a great and urgent need for better understanding by the private sector of long-range objectives and general prospects for economic development. Private enterprise should begin studying different fields, especially manufacturing, for the purpose of coordinating its expansion plans in each field and with other sectors in order to secure full government cooperation in the implementation of private expansion programs(22).

In short, the implementation of the Mexican three-year plan, which was to be followed by a six-year plan (1965-70), would clearly depend, as in many other countries, upon greatly increased access to external public resources, the improvement of investment performance in the public sector, and the way in which the private sector would react to this innovation in Mexico's national endeavour. At the time of writing it was too early to say whether the plan's goals would eventually be reached or whether the plan would be reduced to an attempt at formal fulfilment of Alliance for Progress commitments. The recent history of the less developed regions abounds in competent and coherent development plans which have never been implemented because they lacked political support or have had to succumb to the overpowering weight of social and institutional obstacles.

CONCLUDING COMMENTS

From this brief account of Mexican experience in the field of economic development planning a few conclusions can be drawn. The first is that over the whole period of the country's modern (post-revolutionary) history and until 1961, conscious - albeit not too well organized - efforts were made by successive administrations to create conditions conducive to economic growth and to give priority to economic development over immediate social welfare. As stressed above, this continuity of endeavour did not preclude considerable changes in emphasis in the actual content of economic policies from one administration to another in response to political preferences and prevailing external circumstances. Consequently, Mexico's economy was subjected to successive policy shifts from broader to more limited state intervention, from good to not so good relations between the state and private enterprise, from inflationary financing to conservative and restrictive monetary policies, from emphasis on the use of domestic financial resources to growing dependence upon external borrowing for development. Nonetheless, during all three post-revolutionary decades no one in Mexico, among either the governing party or the governed, seriously challenged the basic idea of active state participation in the development process.

The second conclusion is that in her journey down a road studded with errors and omissions, Mexico since the thirties had made considerable progress toward general acceptance of another important idea: that a developing economy - especially one in the throes of a demographic explosion - needs overall programming and planning. This progress cannot be measured, however, in terms of actual performance by the planning mechanisms which functioned in Mexico during the period under study. With the possible exception of the Investment Commission under the Ruiz Cortines Administration in the fifties, the achievements of the agencies formally charged with directing the national economy toward the goals of development and general welfare were of limited practical effect. But it was their failure, together with the increasing complications of managing with reasonable efficiency a government apparatus comprising a formidable array of public agencies, that forced both the governing party members and public opinion (including some leading representatives of private enterprise) to give more and more weight to the arguments of the growing class of economic technicians (los técnicos). The latter in turn agreed that because of the inherent waste of scarce resources a traditional and pragmatic approach to development problems would not ensure the rate of growth needed in Mexico(23), even with the most liberal external aid for development purposes.

Successful economic planning is generally conceded to involve coordinated action at three separate stages: defining overall and accessible economic policy goals(24), elaborating a national plan, and administering the plan and controlling the performance of the different sectors of the economy. It may be useful therefore to explore the advantages and obstacles faced by

Mexico in each of these three activities.

The centralized structure of the Mexican political system, the continuation of power in the hands of the governing party, and the overwhelming role of the Chief Executive - all in addition to long experience in the field of promoting economic development - represented at least in theory a tremendous advantage for any regime attempting to define the aims of economic policy in such ways as to avoid contradiction(25). The fact is, however, that no one in Mexico had successfully arrived at such a definition.

The potential advantage of a strong central government, or, more accurately, of an extremely strong Chief Executive, was offset to quite an extent by a curious heritage from the Mexican past: the diffusion of political and economic power within and outside the government. The fact that for all practical purposes Mexico's president had no cabinet and all major issues were resolved directly between him and the minister or head of the department immediately involved, with very little coordination with other interested federal agencies, made it exceedingly difficult to achieve unity of action among all potential policymakers, to say nothing of reaching general agreement on what overall policy should be. This, of course, could be done if a strong Chief Executive had at his disposal a small group of policy advisers divorced from the context of the daily political struggle and was willing to support them against pressures exerted from various sources. The fact that the Investment Commission functioned fairly effectively in the fifties argued in favour of this contention, although once again it must be stressed that the agency was not a national planning body.

There can be no doubt that at the beginning of the sixties Mexico had at its disposal a sufficient number of economists and technicians thoroughly competent to prepare a good development plan for the national economy and its major sectors if the statistical base for such an endeavour was strengthened(26). This again was not a superhuman task, since the inaccuracies and scarcity of statistical information in Mexico were only partly due to deficient statistical methods and the difficulty of obtaining data from some of the more backward but important segments of the economy. The situation could be explained to quite an extent by the disquieting propensity of certain public officials to treat any statistical information as their private property on the plausible assumption that in the bureaucratic world he who knows more holds more power.

The presence of competent technical task forces within the public sector did not, however, dispose of the potential difficulties inherent in the fact that there were practically no well-qualified specialists in economics outside the government. This made any meaningful public discussion of general economic policy issues or of a given development plan difficult in the extreme, even assuming the plan's authors would be willing to enter into such a discussion. Although some might have defended the secrecy surrounding past activities of the Investment Commission on the grounds that they had to do with public sector investment of little direct concern to the rest of society, it was much more difficult to justify or explain the closed-door policy of the Planning Bureau and the lack of information regarding vital details of the <u>Plan de Acción Inmediata</u>, prepared under the auspices of the Ministry of Finance. Very few people appeared to realize that democratic planning is impossible unless people are educated to participate in its implementation. These attitudes were stranger still if one took into account the enlightened part played by public opinion in Mexico with respect to basic national economic issues and increasing acceptance by the private sector of the idea of comprehensive national planning along the lines followed in Holland, France, and Japan(27).

But the real and serious obstacles were related to the management of the development plan and control over the actions of different sectors of the economy and over the execution of regional development programmes. In the light of past experience it was extremely unlikely that Mexico could effect an orderly implementation of any such enterprise unless some basic and thorough reforms were made in public administration and in the legal and institutional structure of the public sector.

It seemed that in this respect Mexico badly needed three things: a civil service embodying concepts of security of tenure and of 'conflict of interest', a lifting of the veil of secrecy from the budgetary process, and bringing under effective federal control the innumerable state-owned or controlled autonomous agencies and enterprises. It has perhaps somewhat optimistically been assumed here that the private sector would be willing to cooperate in executing a development plan if only for two reasons: the stimulus given to the economy by a national plan would increase investment and profit opportunities, and the adoption of a plan would force the authorities to substitute formal and impersonal rules for the practice of solving issues and problems as they arose by recourse to administrative decisions as arbitrary as they were difficult to foresee.

Suffice it to recall that at the time of writing there were in Mexico fifteen ministries empowered by law to plan and execute their investment programmes, in company with six regional development commissions, a score of major autonomous agencies, and a few hundred state enterprises. Taken together, in 1959, the current budgets of some fifty major public agencies and enterprises alone almost equaled the entire federal budget, and their output represented nearly 6 per cent of the gross national product in that year. These official activities were not efficiently coordinated or controlled, despite numerous attempts to do so in the previous two decades(28). These circumstances provided many occasions for drains on the scarce financial resources of the federal government and, probably even more important, serious inroads on available managerial talents.

All this did not mean that coherent long-term planning of Mexico's economic development could not be achieved. It would be a rather difficult enterprise, however, because there were still many Mexicos: the Mexico of modern industrialists and of primitive capital accumulators in the best tradition of nineteenth-century capitalism; the Mexico of intellectuals of international renown and of illiterate Indian peasants; the Mexico of honest public officials and professionals and of unscrupulous politicians. Had it been otherwise, the country would no longer have been one of the world's many underdeveloped countries and the problem of <u>planning for development</u> would probably not even have arisen. It had arisen, however, and with great urgency; and to entertain the belief that planning from above without democratic participation by the country's population represents the best possible solution was to fall prey to delusion.

NOTES

(1) Wendell Karl Gordon Schaeffer, 'La administración pública mexicana', Problemas agrícolas e industriales de México (México, D.G.), Vol. 7, No. 1 (1st quarter, 1955), p. 291.

(2) The term 'public sector' refers to the conventional administrative agencies of government plus autonomous agencies and government corporations administering public enterprises.

(3) Conferencias de Mesa Redonda (presididas durante su campaña electoral por el Lic. Miguel Alemán, 27 de agosto de 1945-17 de junio de 1946), México, D.F., 1949, p. xxvi.

(4) Ibid., p. xxxvii.

(5) By 1947 there were seventy-five such agencies and enterprises and by 1959 their number exceeded 150. In late 1961 there were 375. See the Mexico City daily, Novedades, 17 October 1961.

(6) Ley para el control por parte del Gobierno Federal de los Organismos Descentralizados y Empresas de Participación Estatal, Diario Oficial, 31 December 1947; and a decree issued by the Ministry of Finance and Public Credit and published in the Diario Oficial, 31 January 1948.

(7) The Economic Development of Mexico: Report of the Combined Working Party. Published for the International Bank for Reconstruction and Development by the Johns Hopkins Press, Baltimore, 1953, pp. 151-2.

(8) 'Acuerdo que dispone que la Comisión de Inversiones dependerá directamente del Presidente de la República', Diario Oficial, 29 October 1954.

(9) According to a high official of the Investment Commission, this problem was being solved in the following rather pragmatic way: '. . . regarding the decision as to whether more roads should be constructed than dams, more dams than power plants, etc. . . . what has been done in our country has been to consider, on the basis of public investment need surveys, the damage that would be done if certain works were not constructed: for example, electric power restrictions in a given zone if an electric plant is not provided for in opportune time, or the shortage of fuel for industry in a specified area because of the lack of a refinery or adequate pipelines. It has been necessary to adopt this criterion in our country, in view of the limited investment resources available as compared to public works needs; for in this respect the objective consists of distributing whatever investment resources there are among the various sectors with the idea of avoiding economic bottlenecks. . . .' Gustavo Romero Kolbeck, 'La inversión del sector público', México - 50 años de revolución, Vol. I: La Economia, Fondo de Cultura Económica, México, D.F., 1960, p. 502.

(10) Enrique Tejera Paris, Introducción a la administracion pública en la política de desarrollo, Naciones Unidas, Programa de Asistencia Técnica, New York, 12 December, 1957, p. 11.

(11) International Bank for Reconstruction and Development, Mexico's Public Investment Program, 1957-1958, Washington, D.C., July 1957, p. 67.

(mimeographed).

(12) The obligation to control the individual investment programme fell upon the Ministry of Finance and the Ministry of National Property (Secretaría de Bienes Nacionales e Inspección Administrativa up to 1958, and Secretaría del Patrimonio Nacional afterwards).

(13) In previous administrations this function was performed by the President's Secretary, an official endowed with considerable power (although not having the rank of Minister of State) in view of the fact that there is no formal cabinet institution in Mexico. Heads of ministries are directly and separately responsible only to the President and hence should be considered the President's delegates in each ministry rather than members of government.

(14) The overall control of autonomous agencies and state enterprises was given to the ministry which exercised control over investment programmes, after 1958 the Secretaría del Patrimonio Nacional.

(15) 'Acuerdo Presidencial a las Secretarías y Departamentas de Estado para acelerar el desarrollo económico del país con base en criterios de planeación integral', 7 July 1961; reproduced in El Trimestre Economico, México, D.F., Vol. 28, October-December, 1961, pp. 782-4.

(16) 'Acuerdo Presidencial para crear la Comisión Intersecretarial', 1 March 1962, as published in the national press the following day.

(17) If the foreign investment directly and indirectly resulted in new exports which increased foreign exchange earnings by more than approximately 6 per cent above the level they would otherwise have attained, debt service equal to 16 per cent of increased foreign exchange earnings would be less burdensome than debt service equal to 10 per cent of the previous level of foreign exchange earnings.

(18) In the absence of thorough studies and because of the weakness of statistical bases, the capital-output ratio trend is a subject of wide controversy among Mexican economists. A recent investigation insists that the capital-output ratio declined in the post-war period. See Luis Cossio and Rafael Izquierdo, 'Estimación de la relación producto-capital de México, 1940-1960', El Trimestre Económico, México, D.F., Vol. 29, No. 116, October-December, pp. 634-44.

(19) The so-called 'Charter of Punta del Este' which set up the Alliance for Progress declared inter alia (Title II, Chapter II): 'Participating Latin American countries agree to introduce or strengthen systems for the preparation, execution, and periodic revision of national programs for economic and social development. . . . [These countries] should formulate, if possible within the next eighteen months, long-term development programs'. Inter-American Economic and Social Council, Special Meeting at the Ministerial Level, Punta del Este, Uruguay, 1961, Alliance for Progress; Official Documents, Pan American Union, Washington, D.C.: 1961, p. 5.

(20) Some Mexican economists who participated in the work of the Investment Commission in the fifties insist that by stressing this approach and circumscribing financial help to the foreign-exchange component of individual development projects international financial agencies made overall economic planning extremely difficult if not impossible.

(21) Organización de los Estados Americanos, Consejo Interamericano Económico y Social, El desarrollo económico y social de México (Informe presentado por el Gobierno de México a la Primera Reunión Anual del CIES), 2 October 1962, p. 34 (mimeographed).

(22) Ibid., p. 37.

(23) Very few experts in Mexico believe that even with planning and programming on a national scale the rate of growth registered in the forties (7 per cent per year) and the fifties (6 per cent per year) can be regained in the near future.

(24) As stated by Tinbergen: 'The word "planning" is often used to denote the technical elaboration of the means for the implementation of a policy which is considered as already given. This use of the word, however, obscures an important element in the concept of planning: far from being given a priori, an economic policy needs itself to be planned or, shall we say, designed'. Jan Tinbergen, 'Problems of Planning Economic Policy', International Social Science Journal (Paris), Vol. 11, No. 3, 1959, p. 351.

(25) This point is stressed in one of the few essays ever published in Mexico on the subject of planning: Sergio de la Peña, 'Introducción a la planeación regional', La planeación económica regional, Banco de México, S.A., Departamento de Investigaciones Industriales, México, D.F., 1960, pp. 127-28.

(26) Fairness demands that one record here a dissenting voice raised recently by a leading Mexican historian, who, when discussing the relationship between planned economic development and the political structures prevailing in Latin America, affirmed: 'The Latin American economist ordinarily is not a man of strong convictions, and one must concede that the idea of planned economic development cannot be brought to victory unless it is accompanied by conviction. . . . If the Latin American economist, generally speaking, only looks at a limited sector of the national economy; if his time and his energy are taken up by problems that are always trifling and always immediate; if, in short, he is not a man of strong convictions, should one be surprised that he is an ineffectual adviser of politicians and men in office, incapable of inculcating in them the idea of a planned economy, of igniting in them the spark of faith that would make them the standard bearers of the idea?' Daniel Cosío Villegas, El crecimiento económico programado y la organización politica, México, D.F., October 1960.

(27) Cosío Villegas shows extreme pessimism in this respect also: '. . . The idea and the purpose of channeling economic growth within a plan or program . . . do not at present enjoy sufficient popular support, or, to be more accurate, have no popular support at all. In addition - and despite vainglorious and repeated manifestations to the contrary - Latin American political parties and governing authorities are not sufficiently learned to comprehend this idea fully, embrace it, and make of it, in a manner of speaking, the central axis of their preachments and performance'. Ibid., p. 16.

(28) When introducing in the Mexican Congress a draft bill (subsequently shelved) at the end of 1961 calling for control over the public enterprises, Senator Rodolfo Brena Torres asserted: 'Heretofore [the decentralized sector of the federal public administration] has been like a mosaic put together with little regard for method and without the benefit of an integral approach.

The fact is that at that time there could be no method, nor overall vision, nor common mission of the decentralized agencies in the sense that there can be today'. Quoted in the Mexico City daily, Novedades, 28 December 1961.

REFERENCES

COSÍO VILLEGAS, DANIEL (1960), El crecimiento económico programado y la organización politica, Documento preparado para el Grupo de Trabajo sobre los Aspectos Sociales del Desarrollo Económico en América Latina, patrocinado por la UNESCO, Naciones Unidas y la CEPAL, México, D.F., (mimeographed).

DE LA PEÑA, SERGIO (1960) 'Introducción a la planeación regional', La planeación económica regional, Banco de México, S.A., Departamento de Investigaciones Industriales, México, D.F., (mimeographed).

The Economic Development of Mexico: Report of the Combined Mexican Working Party, (1953) Published for the International Bank for Reconstruction and Development by the Johns Hopkins Press, Baltimore.

FRIEDMANN, JOHN (Editor) (1959), 'The Study and Practice of Planning', International Social Science Journal (Paris), Vol. 11, No. 3, pp. 327-412.

INTERNATIONAL BANK FOR RECONSTRUCTION AND DEVELOPMENT (1957), Mexico's Public Investment Program, 1957-1958, Washington, D.C., (mimeographed).

JUNTA DE GOBIERNO DE LOS ORGANISMOS Y EMPRESAS DEL ESTADO (1959), Memoria 1959, México, D.F.

ORGANIZACIÓN DE LOS ESTADOS AMERICANOS (1962), El desarrollo económico y social de México, Documento presentado por el Gobierno de México a la Primera Reunión Anual del CIES al Nivel Ministerial, México, octubre de 1962, México, D.F.

─────── (1961), Organismos de planificación y planes de desarrollo en la América Latina, Documento informativo No. 8-ES-RE para la Reunión Extraordinaria del Consejo Interamericano Económico y Social al Nivel Ministerial, Uruguay, agosto de 1961, Washington, D.C., (mimeographed).

PARRA, MANUEL GERMÁN (Editor) (1949), Conferencias de Mesa Redonda, presididas durante su campaña electoral por el Lic. Miguel Alemán, 27 de agosto de 1945-17 de junio de 1946, México, D.F.

PRIMER SEMINARIO SOBRE DESARROLLO REGIONAL (1962), Mexico, 12 al 17 de marzo, Acta (mimeographed).

Revista de Economia (Mexico, D.F.) (1962), Vol. 25, Nos. 4, 5, pp. 105-96. Issues devoted to planning and economic development).

ROMERO KOLBECK, GUSTAVO (1963), 'Apuntes de las conferencias sobre la inversión pública en México', Dictadas en el Programa Técnico BID-CEMLA en septiembre de 1962, México (manuscript).

─────── (1960), La inversión del sector público en México - 50 años de revolución, Vol. I: La Economía, pp. 492-508. Fondo de Cultura Economica,

México.

SCHAEFFER, WENDELL KARL GORDON (1955), 'La administración pública mexicana', Problemas agrícolas e industriales de México (México, D.F.), Vol. 7, No. 1, pp. 209-314.

TEJERA PARIS, ENRIQUE (1957), Introducción a la administración pública en la política de desarrollo. Naciones Unidas, Programa de Asistencia Técnica, New York, (mimeographed).

YATES, PAUL LAMARTINE (1961), El desarrollo regional de México, Banco de México, S.A., Departmento de Investigaciones Industriales, México, D.F.

CHAPTER 2
Economic Development and Political System*

FEW COUNTRIES in the world matched Mexico's economic growth performance in the post-war period. In spite of a demographic explosion (an annual population increase of 3.4 per cent in the sixties), the average annual GNP increase of 6.5 per cent in real terms over the previous quarter of a century translated itself into an expansion of real per capita income of the order of 3 per cent a year. This, in turn, brought the level of per capita income in 1969 to over US $600 compared with a bare $100 on the eve of the Second World War and some $350 in 1960.

These achievements - it was officially maintained - represented the result of well thought out conservative monetary and fiscal policies which, by checking inflationary pressures rampant in Mexico in the forties and the early fifties, established an excellent climate for increased domestic savings and for both domestic and foreign private investment. The available statistics confirm these claims. Between 1960 and 1969 gross domestic savings increased from 15 to almost 18 per cent of GNP and gross domestic investment expanded even more - from 16 to 20 per cent of GNP - with the gap between total investment and total savings filled by public borrowing both at home and abroad and by foreign private investment. During the sixties Mexico's public external debt increased from US $800 million to over $3000 million and the book value of private foreign direct investment - about which curiously no official data are available - rose from $1400 million in 1960 to over $2750 million at the close of 1970.

Given the dynamic behaviour of the Mexican economy over the previous thirty years, the wisdom of the monetary, fiscal and financial policies and the resulting growth patterns should apparently not be questioned. However, they have been questioned within the country by a growing number of people and,

---

*This essay is based on a lecture delivered at the Conference on the Mexican Political System organized in April 1971 by the Institute of Latin American Studies at the University of Texas, Austin, and published in Spanish in William P. Glade and Stanley R. Ross (Editors), Críticas Constructivas del Sistema Político Mexicano, Vol. II, Institute of Latin American Studies, The University of Texas at Austin, Austin, 1973.

since the fall of 1969, by the then candidate for the Presidency, Luis Echeverría. Both dissident and official critics seemed to wonder whether the art of quantitative economic growthmanship as practised in Mexico had not approached the point of diminishing returns. Some more outspoken voices started claiming that these diminishing returns had been built into the Mexican economic growth model and political structures, resulting in the steady increase of social and political tensions after the late fifties.

For the sake of assuring speedy economic growth, the authors and executors of Mexican post-war models - from Miguel Alemán (1946-52) to Gustavo Díaz Ordaz (1964-70) - gave the highest priority to mobilization of domestic resources for <u>private</u> investment in industry, connected services and large-scale agriculture, but neglected small subsistence farmers and public social expenditure. Ideological declarations to the contrary, the state's role was to support and aid the private sector through investment in infrastructure and the provision of state-produced goods and services at subsidized prices. Given that Mexican society had one of the worst patterns of income distribution in Latin America and the highest population growth rate, this strategy led to a widening of the gap between the islands of modern economic growth and the poverty and stagnation of large parts of the Republic(1).

Few if any scholarly studies are available (in 1971) of the socio-economic effects of federal fiscal and budgetary performance in the 1960s(2). But although federal revenue grew, particularly after 1965, at an impressive rate in response to the general economic expansion, and federal expenditure also expanded rapidly becuase of the volume of domestic and foreign borrowing, two important facts must be considered: in Mexico the share of government revenue in GNP continued to be one of the lowest in the world (8-9 per cent) and no major fiscal reform had been launched for almost two decades(3). Consequently, public investment, required to support the private sector, became increasingly dependent upon the availability of external financial resources and private domestic savings, creating serious complications for the Treasury, on the one hand, and the country's balance of payments, on the other.

Fiscal policy, which historically played an unimportant role in Mexican economic policies, was largely replaced by a skilful financial game, despite gentle and sometimes not so gentle prodding from international lending agencies increasingly worried about the magnitude of Mexico's external obligations and the burden of their servicing upon the country's current foreign exchange revenues. Until the end of the Diaz Ordaz administration (November 1970), these proddings were being answered officially with the argument that any fast-growing, semi-developed economy must face a financial resources gap, particularly at the stage of rapid industrialization(4).

The case for better mobilization of domestic resources, particularly in the public sector, presented by some dissident economists during the 'stabilizing growth' period, however, could hardly be dismissed. The priority given during the sixties to encouraging private savings to the detriment of public revenue clearly had its drawbacks - both in an economic and a social sense. It is true that, contrary to experience elsewhere in Latin America, as a consequence of monetary stability, a high level of tariffs, and generous fiscal and other incentives offered to the private investor - domestic and foreign alike - the outflow of domestic savings was practically brought to a halt and foreign capital entered the country in large quantities. But the growing concentration of private wealth in the hands of a few major domestic and foreign financial industrial empires could hardly be considered a healthy phenomenon in the absence of any anti-monopoly legislation or of any attempts at curtailing the conspicious consumption of the relatively small number of beneficiaries of inward-directed industrialization.

With the passage of time, the serious degree of inefficiency of many private investment projects became clear. The limited size of a domestic market (probably not more than half the country's population of 50 million), added to the continuation of highly protective policies, permitted almost any enterprise in the industrial sector, whatever its efficiency, to reap very substantial profits from the much less than full utilization of existing productive capacity. While examples multiplied of wasteful uses of the scarcest factor of production - capital - few attempts were made to correct this. The cost of inefficient industrialization was paid by consumers, by subsistence agriculture and by the state. Those industrial firms which had failed even in the face of favourable official pro-industrialization policies, as a last resort had access to the state which, under the name of 'mexicanization', became the collector of all kinds of industrial 'white elephants'. The dice were obviously loaded against anybody but domestic and foreign investors in private industry.

The situation became even more complicated and burdensome for the masses because of the neglect in both public and private sectors of technological aspects of industrialization. As a result of the poorly designed educational system, the country became a mass importer of foreign technology which was rarely adapted to local factor proportions or size. Most of this technology was directed to satisfy the consumption preferences of the 'modern' high-income groups. The combination of high protection and extremely liberal industrialization incentives with the absence of local technological advancement led to intensification of difficulties on both the balance-of-payments front and in domestic public finances management, although this was difficult to detect because of the absence of reliable statistics. Moreover, mass imports of capital-intensive and consumption-oriented modern technology contributed much less than previously expected to the growth in industrial employment. While no data are available, it is quite likely that disguised unemployment had increased rather than declined during the sixties, not only in the rural but also in the urban sector.

With the fiscal system offering a premium upon rent from capital as against earned income, inevitably the lower-middle income groups and subsistence agriculture carried the main burden of financing economic growth in two ways: through excessive prices paid for low-quality domestic industrial products and by providing the Treasury with a considerable part of its revenue. While it is officially maintained that public current and capital spending had some redistributive effects upon unsatisfactory income patterns, as yet that particular claim has not been proven. Quite the contrary, some younger economists, educated abroad and well versed in modern economic theory, insist that the patterns of public revenue and expenditure policy accentuate rather than alleviate the highly uneven national income distribution(5).

Recent income distribution studies strongly suggest that, in spite of impressive post-war economic growth, some 40 per cent of Mexican families are - in relative terms - as badly off in the early 1970s as a quarter of a century previously. The richest 5 per cent, commanding about one-quarter of the country's wealth, are perhaps somewhat less rich than in the past. In other words, some income redistribution has taken place from the top income groups and the poorest sectors towards the urban middle classes, including the élite industrial labour unions. But while the growth of the middle classes is a promising phenomenon, the question remains as to whether they are growing fast enough.

Conservative fiscal policies brought additional difficulties. With the constant rapid expansion of current public expenditure, public sector savings practically stopped growing in the mid-sixties. Between 1960 and 1969 public sector revenues (including Federal District and all major government agencies and enterprises) increased (at current prices) almost threefold from US $1700 million to $4800 million, but public savings less than doubled, from $620 million to $1100 million. The result was a steady opening of the public investment-savings gap with the deficit in 1969 amounting to some 40 per cent of public investment. A considerable part of this gap was covered through the sale to the public, at attractive interest rates, of state development banks securities and through borrowing from the domestic commercial banking system. But strong pressures for increased borrowing abroad continued to dominate the scene through the sixties.

While, to a degree unmatched elsewhere in Latin America, Mexico had developed the art of diversifying foreign borrowing to cut down its costs, the gross amounts involved annually at the end of the previous administration were of such magnitude that no way could be found of completely escaping the curse of 'tied credits', which increased the real cost of loans very substantially over the extremely high interest rates prevailing in world capital markets. The resulting cost of public-sector imported capital goods and the growing burden of interest payments gave rise to serious preoccupations within and outside the public sector even before the administration of Luis Echeverría took office in December 1970.

It had also become clear that the public sector was not in a position to cut down on public investment, not so much because of the negative impact of such measures on the economy (in 1969-70 only one-third of total investment originated in the public sector), but because of the political and social repercussions of such a restrictive policy. During his pre-electoral campaign the new President committed his administration not only to an increase in public investment but also to further social overhead activities because of the omnipresent and growing economic and social disparities within the country.

The crucial issue at the beginning of the Echeverría administration was whether there was a way in which Mexico could get out of the trap of rapid economic growth with little general welfare. While there was a general consensus that the situation was largely due to the past sacrifising of social ends for the sake of rapid private capital accumulation and state-supported but largely privately-controlled industrialization, many difficult questions were posed. The first was whether it would be feasible to improve income distribution and increase employment if conservative monetary and fiscal policies were to continue. The alternative question was whether less conservative monetary and fiscal policies would not lead inexorably to inflationary pressures, with the subsequent pernicious effects on the social welfare of the low-income classes, on the one hand, and on the balance of payments, on the other. During its first four months the new government opted for an administrative approach to policy issues rather than for substantial economic reforms, making it difficult to judge which of the two possible roads the Echeverría administration would eventually take. But calls for overhaul of monetary, fiscal and public investment policies multiplied, because, among other reasons, social results of past policies contrasted heavily with the tenets of the ruling party and with the campaign promises and declarations of the new President.

In 1971 very little was known of the details of the economic policies of the new administration. During previous changes at the top it was customary for the new governmental team to dedicate its first year to working out a new policy mix in the light of the political and economic situation inherited from the previous administration. In practical terms, such a custom as a rule led to a year-long dip in levels of economic activity, aimed partly at correcting the public expenditure excesses of the final year of the outgoing administration. It seemed, however, that this 'presidential cycle', as it was called in Mexico, had been broken in 1970. First, Diaz Ordaz finished his term under signs of relative austerity. Second, his successor proceeded with his economic and social policy programme immediately after the elections in mid-July 1970. Consequently, the Congress found itself in December confronted with such an impressive list of legislative initiatives that, contrary to established practice, the congressional session had to be extended beyond the end of the calendar year. The new legislation was of two main kinds: amendments and revisions of laws of long standing, and laws establishing new administrative agencies to deal with problems apparently neglected in the past, such as promotion of foreign export trade and coordination of science and technology policies. In the field of fiscal policies, however, where there were strong expectations of more radical legislative changes, initiatives were limited to closing loopholes - some of them of importance - that were seriously affecting the size of federal revenue.

It appeared in 1971 that, following the tradition of the previous thirty years, the new administration did not intend to bring about a clear break with past economic policies, both for domestic and external reasons. Anyone with some knowledge of the inner workings of the Federal Government and public sector agencies and of past flaws in fiscal and financial management was aware of considerable room for improvement with respect to the mobilization of domestic financial resources for more socially equitable economic development. Such an improvement would depend upon the simultaneous introduction of many politically sensitive measures: substantial fiscal reform, curtailing tax evasion, the elimination of corruption, and more efficient control of public agencies' current and capital spending. Firm measures in the last three fields by themselves increase considerably the total tax yield and improve the overall public budget position, whereas fiscal reform was highly controversial politically. It may well be, therefore, that the new administration left the most difficult but basic task for later consideration.

Another problem discussed widely at the end of 1970, that of improving the efficiency of Mexican private investment, pampered by the state with an amazing range of special incentives and privileges - to an extent found in very few other countries - had not been treated very directly. The problem was not simple. In Mexico, the question was not how to increase the level of private savings, already very high, but how to cut conspicuous consumption and to modernize industry and the services sector for the dual purpose of taking a part of the heavy burden of industrialization off the shoulders of consumers and of improving the balance-of-payments position through export promotion. Many Mexican industries were almost, or could easily have become, competitive internationally if only the level of protection and the magnitude of rewards for inefficiency had been gradually diminished. In terms of the policy innovations of the new administration, the solution of this problem was divided into three parts, with priority given to balance-of-payments exigencies. First, a new export promotion agency was established with the status of quasi-ministry. Second, prospectively successful exporters of new commodities were offered an impressive set of special incentives. Third, some warnings were given that the state might deprive particularly inefficient industries of unduly high protection. But here again, as in the case of fiscal problems, direct confrontation with powerful domestic and foreign vested interests was studiously avoided.

It is a common sense proposition that an increase in public revenue, the better use of public savings and the modernization of entrepreneurial attitudes would go a long way toward diminishing all sorts of dislocations emerging in Mexico as the result of the public fiscal, financial and protective policy immobilisme of the previous fifteen years. The public investment-savings gap, the financial resources gap and the foreign trade gap represented different aspects of the same phenomenon - the continuation of policies designed a quarter of century before to start an industrialization process. But the Mexico of 1970 was a very different country from that of 1945. Broad economic policy adjustments were long overdue, but it was not clear if the adjustments to new social and political realities would be possible without a too radical departure from past economic policies and a subsequent adjustment of political structures. But even in a post-revolutionary one-party state, domestic economic policies cannot be managed and manipulated at will, divorced from the domestic political scene and the international political and economic framework.

THE MEXICAN POLITICAL STRUCTURES

It is difficult to neatly classify Mexico's political system according to the taxonomic schemes for one-party states proposed by foreign political scientists. While the system has its roots in the 1911-20 revolution, its birth cannot be explained exclusively as the sequence of the revolutionary upheaval. The period of domestic violence that lasted from 1911 to the mid-twenties was neither preceded nor accompanied (as occurred in revolutionary situations in other countries) by the emergence of a strong and coherent political movement endowed with a modernizing ideology aimed at combatting the interests of the ancien régime. Between 1911 and 1929, the year in which the one-party system was established under the name of Partido Nacional Revolucionario (PNR), the political life of the country was characterized by infights among multiple factions, led by numerous participants in the destruction of the Porfirio Díaz dictatorship. Leaving aside the general objective of the defence of the revolution against internal and external enemies, regional and personal interests of the revolutionary caudillos were at least as important as ideological considerations and institutional political forms.

Thus, unlike one-party systems in other parts of the world, the Partido Nacional Revolucionario emerged long after the death of the ancien régime. It appeared at the moment of the consolidation of personal power in the hands of Plutarco Elías Calles, the final victor over other contenders. Some Mexican political scientists even maintain that between 1911 and 1929 Mexico had a multi-party system but clearly these 'parties' had little to do with political party institutions as known in Western democracies. Loyalties were directed not to institutions or ideologies but to different jefes de la revolución who chose to expand the basis of their power by appealing not only to the military groups but also to various newly emerging social sectors (organized workers in the case of Venustiano Carranza and campesinos at the time of Alvaro Obregón).

The consolidation of the warring factions in the mid-twenties had been made possible by the violent disappearance of most major revolutionary figures and by Calles' unmatched ability to establish, first, informal armistices with different factions, and later, to bring these groups to full submission, while extending his power over the new national economic interest groups appearing in major urban centres. Given that the birth of the one-party system was due largely to the strong will of one man who held ultimate power in Mexico for more than ten years, it is difficult to accept the theoretical proposition of some foreign political scientists that strong one-party systems come into being when there is an explicit recognition of the difference between 'we' and 'they', accompanied by conflict between the two contending groups(6). It is no less difficult - following Huntington's taxonomy - to classify the Mexican political system as either exclusionary or revolutionary or to talk about the sequence of stages - transformation, consolidation and adaptation - that would institutionalize politically the revolution and result in the emergence of the established one-party system(7).

The Mexican one-party system at the time of its birth aimed at creating a relatively consensual society around vaguely defined national goals. Since this system did not arise from the previous revolutionary one-party system, it could skip with relative ease the difficult first stage of transformation and did not seem to face major problems at the consolidation stage (1929-45). While there are plenty of hair-splitting analyses of the importance of internal changes in party structure in 1938 under Cárdenas, when it took the name of Partido de la Revolución Mexicana (PRM), and again under Avila Camacho, these adjustments af the 'consolidation period' were not accompanied by major political upheavals. The only political crisis after 1929 had much less to do with the internal structure of the one-party system as established by its founder than with the relationship between the top party apparatus and the extension of the party into the sphere of the state that was the party and more than the party at the same time. Once the problem of conflict between party and state had been solved by the peaceful elimination of Calles from the political scene by Cardenas in 1935, no other basic issues troubled the Mexican system during the following thirty years.

How is it that, contrary to the historical experiences of many other one-party systems, where behind the facade of unity, the most serious crises periodically take place, leading in some cases to the degeneration of those systems into one-man dictatorships, the Mexican system found itself able to consolidate rather peacefully its power over the rapidly-modernizing society during almost forty years? The answer has to be sought not only in the confluence of post-revolutionary domestic conditions and the presence of real or alleged external threats, but also in historical experiences and the system of social and political values pervading Mexican policy since colonial times.

Whatever evidence exists of democratic multi-party yearnings of small intellectual élites after the demise of the Spanish empire, during the Reform period, and immediately before the revolution and in its early stages, Mexico had never known a political democracy as it had developed during the nineteenth century on both sides of the North Atlantic and in some other parts of Latin America. Mexico's political history can be described as a sequence of authoritative systems - when order was accompanied by some economic development - interrupted by periods of 'democratizing attempts' that ended in political chaos, civil strife and economic misfortune. Against this background, the one-party system, particularly coming in the wake of a major social and economic upheaval (the 1911 revolution) fulfilled Mexican society's desiderata and expectations fairly well. Moreover, the sheer magnitude of civil strife and the ensuing economic retrogression offered additional impetus for the appearance of a political consensus built around the exigencies of the return to normalcy within new social parameters and the broadly defined goals of economic progress.

This was not a particularly Mexican phenomenon, although authoritative experiences of the past had helped. There is historical evidence that a consensus based on 'peace, order and progress' has followed tragic episodes in many countries. In Mexico, while the revolution against the Porfirio Díaz dictatorship triumphed, both physically and economically Mexico had all the traits of a defeated country. As a rule, defeated countries need strong political systems and strong political leaders to start reconstruction and development. The historical memory of the relative advantages of authoritative systems and of the disasters of 'democratic experiments' turned the scale in Mexico toward general acceptance of a new modernized version combining one-man and one-party rule.

Calles showed political acumen in opting for a combination of both; political leaders after Calles' peaceful demise avoided the degeneration of the dual authoritative system into a series of one-man dictatorships. The solution of the succession problem, through periodical rotation of the holders of power at the state level, offered the Mexican system both flexibility and longevity. But even this ingenious innovation, absent in most other one-party developing countries, would not have assured the system its long-term viability if some other conditions had not been present. Two were perhaps decisive: first, Mexican society's long-standing nationalism resulting from the overwhelming presence of a powerful northern neighbour long suspected of inimical designs, and, second, values of political submissiveness which pervaded the society.

Historically, the sources of political and economic power in Mexico have always been regional and local, caudillos and caciques, the army, the clergy, large landowners, and domestic and foreign entrepreneurs(8). Directly or indirectly these power groups were responsible for decisions taken at the centre, whose political institutions had little to do with Western-type democracy. Given such historical influences, post-revolutionary society, particularly in peripheral areas, could not but welcome the emergence of a strong one-party and party-state that would at least check some particularly bad abuses of power by regional army commanders, local caciques, and would counteract exploitative acts of the clergy and large landowners. It was considered perfectly normal that the new political apparatus was built from above (while including representatives of campesinos and labour unions) and not from below. The masses did not expect full participation in political and economic decisions; they were willing to settle for some favours from the new holders of political power.

With respect to the consolidation period from 1929 to 1945, particularly relevant insights have been offered by Scott(9). The Mexican power élites of that period may be divided into two categories: the political élite that ran the party and the state and was composed of those whose power rested on the use of violence and the manipulation of political strength during the early post-revolutionary era; and the social and economic élite whose position of increasing power was directly related to their entrepreneurial successes during the Calles reconstruction period and again during the agricultural and industrial boom of the Second World War. By the PNR-PRM statutes and the unwritten rules of the game, the socio-economic élite was explicitly excluded from participation in the party and from holding governmental positions. There is evidence that while financial, industrial and commercial interests had established lines of communication with the state and high levels of government, relations between those involved in politics and in economic life were at arms-length, and continuously checked by higher echelons of the party. The only interesting development of that period was the disappearance of revolutionary military chieftains as active participants in the political system. Some of them died, others fell into disgrace after unsuccessful rebellions, and others moved into entrepreneurial activities, cashing in on earlier political connections.

This neat distinction between holders of political power and the economic élites became progressively more blurred in the mid-forties, for several reasons. First, a generational change took place within the political system: with few exceptions active participants in the revolution gave way to the first post-revolutionary generation raised and educated in the relatively peaceful Obregón-Calles reconstruction period. Miguel Alemán, elected president in 1946, was the first national leader whose active political life started after the chaos of revolutionary strife had subsided. Second, the job of running both the state and the economy became much more complicated, involving both political good sense and technical skills. The war-time boom, accompanied by the strengthening of entrepreneurial groups both in industry and commercial agriculture confronted the state and the party with new problems. Third, Mexican society of the mid-forties had changed: unlike the society of the twenties and thirties which was characterized by illiterate campesinos, relatively numerous but politically not very strong members of industrial labour unions, and the post-revolutionary military, all covered by the one-party system, facing relatively weak coalitions of local entrepreneurs, many of them survivors from pre-revolutionary times, involved in conflicts with foreign economic interests and living on the margin of the state and the new political system, the country now saw the gradual development of a complex society typical of a more industrial society but at the same time surrounded by socially and economically marginal subsistence campesinos and urban lumpenproletariat(10).

During the forties power relations between party and state, and the economic élites changed perceptibly. The relative role of the party as exclusive representative of the interests of the whole polity declined, while a new type of relationship developed between those sectors of growing importance, barred from participation in party life. During the Alemán administration high governmental posts were opened to members of the new economic élites who did not rise to power through participation in the party system. Also, the party became relatively less important and less emphasis was placed on ideology. The accent was instead placed on the rate of economic growth.

Political participation and social welfare were given low priority in the statutes of the party, whose name was changed again to Partido Revolutionario Institutional. While in the past state action appeared to reflect the party's programmes, now the party became the servant of the state whose field of action was much broader. Political and economic policy decisions no longer reflected attitudes of the three major sectors of the one-party system (labour, campesinos and loosely defined popular interests, mainly bureaucracy), but resulted from negotiations between official spokesmen for these sectors and the increasingly powerful economic élites organized outside the party system in <u>agrupaciones patronales</u>, acting jointly and separately through independent contacts with state authorities. While the birth of these organized pressure groups dated back to the end of the revolutionary period (Confederación de Cámaras de Comercio, Confederación de Cámaras Industriales and Confederación Patronal were established respectively in 1917, 1918 and 1929), they reached maturity as important pressure groups around 1945(11).

Moreover, new phenomena appeared. After 1945 not only did important spokesmen for non-party corporative bodies find their way into high governmental posts but, at the end of their tenure, ex-government and ex-party functionaries started crossing the previously strictly defined line between the political apparatus and the private sector, very often becoming successful leaders of the private business community.

These developments were not unexpected. In most non-socialist one-party states modernization through economic growth, urbanization and education brings about rapid diversification of social groups and the subsequent need for negotiation of their contending interests, with the state providing the political umbrella for such negotiations. Even if the state pursues the same economic growth model postulated by the revolution, the power relationship among interest groups - national, regional or local - changes. But if the state adjusts its economic growth model to changing economic power structures without being ready to abandon its 'revolutionary legitimacy', it is forced to dilute the ideological content inherited from more 'heroic' times while keeping the appearance of taking into consideration all possible interest groups. In many cases, this leads to a need to expand the organizational scope of the political system through inducing groups to nominally participate in the life of party and state. This results in the emergence of a corporative state where all major interest groups have a formal voice, while decisions favour those endowed with superior economic and political power.

Here a question arises as to why the Mexican system did not go all the way to a corporative state structure once an economic policy model clearly favouring the private sector (large financial, industrial and agricultural interests) was chosen in the forties. The most probable answer is that the system neither wanted to nor had to make such an open break with the past. Officially excluded from the party's organizational structure, private business became too strong to be included in it in terms of parity with the three traditional sectors. The all-inclusive party would have made negotiations among major factions impossible and might have threatened the ingenious political structure nursed carefully for over a quarter of century. Furthermore, such a move would have seriously brought into question the legitimacy of the party as the successor to the revolution. The incorporation into the one-party system of capitalist groups would have represented a very dangerous experiment carrying incalculable political risks.

On the other hand, the continuation of the earlier party structure - in spite of growing diversification of interest groups and the shift in their relative economic and political weight within society - did not create any risks. The system did not need to choose between including or excluding private sector interests because it solved the problem of succession within the one-party political structure relatively early. Given that this problem had been taken care of in the thirties, when the power of private economic élites was still

limited, the interesting and efficiently operating dual power structure
developed. In the long run, political power was kept in the one-party system;
in the short run - every six years - it was delegated to a particular group
within the party. The state was the extension of the party and vice versa,
but neither was able to hold absolute power indefinitely. This arrangement
permitted a degree of political and economic flexibility unknown in other one-
party systems by building into the Mexican political structure a complicated
combination of checks and balances unknown either in Western democratic
systems or in pure authoritarian states whether of right or left.

This also increased the power of both the party and the state to negotiate
with and manipulate the increasing number of interest groups. The party was
left with the task of dealing with, persuading, partially satisfying and
buying off - when necessary - the leaders of numerically large sectors of the
population. One of the primary responsibilities of the state was to negotiate
with the numerically small but economically powerful new interest groups
(bankers, manufacturers, merchants and foreign investors) and to continue
disarming potential opposition by coopting small dissident groups into the
party-state system, as long as the dissidents were not challenging the basic
validity of the system as a whole. While speculations abound, particularly
among foreign political scholars and economists, about the detailed nature
of the processes of major policy decision-making in Mexico, most of these
speculations are either widely off the mark or largely irrelevant because
they attempt to detect some peculiar personal patterns in these processes(12).

Key decisions on the presidential succession made on three grounds: the assurance of the continuity of the political system as a whole; the potential
ability of various contenders to deal with prospective short-term situations;
and the acceptability of the candidates to the broadest combination of interest groups within and outside the one-party system.

In the wake of the 'dance of millions' that characterized the Miguel Alemán
administration and brought Mexico to the brink of external and internal crisis,
an unimaginative administrator with a strong propensity to austerity, Adolfo
Ruiz Cortines, was elected. When in the latter days of that administration
the state and party faced growing labour unrest, the presidency was given to
a Secretary of Labour, not only an expert in his field but also endowed with
a certain charisma. When political clouds started gathering on the horizon
in the early sixties, the Secretary of Interior, Díaz Ordaz, received a mandate to deal with the situation. While Díaz Ordaz did not have a particularly
attractive personality or any charismatic qualities, he established his title
to the presidency as a tough and uncompromising man who would go to any length
to assure peace and order. After December 1970 the country was run by a new
President with impressive assets: youth, needed to establish contacts with the
new generation, contacts brutally broken by his predecessor in the fall of
1968; energy, needed to unravel the administrative mess inherited from two
administrations; and charismatic appeal which was effective with large sectors
of the population with traditional attitudes towards authority, not wanting
democracy but a leader to show them the way to a less difficult future.

In a one-party political system the party has to be 'all things to many
groups', while the representative of the system must be 'all things to all
men'. The degree of success in performing these tasks will depend not only
on the manipulative capacity of the holders of power but also upon the social
and psychological attitudes of the governed. As already mentioned, the task
of rulers in the past seemed to be easier in Mexico than in other one-party

countries because the sense of authority pervaded most relations - family, school, work group and government-political system(13). However, this relationship has, as Scott points out, some ambivalence. In Mexico it involves an exploitative and dominant exercise of power by those in authority, and rebellion-dependency reactions by those in subordinate roles. The recent history of ways in which the Mexican one-party system attempted to counteract difficult challenges seems to confirm this hypothesis.

Leaving aside the few unsuccessful rebellions against the post-revolutionary party and state (originated with military caudillos of the revolutionary period), the legitimacy of the new system was not seriously challenged after the establishment of the PRN by Calles in 1929, by which time the major post-revolutionary conflicts with the church, large landowners and foreign economic interests have been solved or alleviated. While minor conflicts abounded during the following thirty years, they were always peacefully or less peacefully solved. Most of them had economic and not political and ideological roots. They centred on the distribution of gains resulting from economic development, gains that were accruing in an increasingly disproportionate way to interest groups outside the formal political system. The absence of any major attack on the legitimacy of the one-party system and its performance not only confirms the persuasive presence of the authority syndrome but the skilful performance of the system itself. Most regional or nation-wide conflicts of an economic nature were defused. Those that were not, for example, some large labour strikes of 1936, 1943 and 1957-8 led to a general tightening of party control over labour, accompanied in the late fifties by severe punishment of the 'rebels'.

This absence of serious challenges did not have a healthy effect at the overall efficiency of the party and state. In the forties and fifties the party seemingly played a much less active role than in the earlier period of consolidation (1929-40). Its major functions were now fourfold: to resolve on regional and local levels immediate conflicts of interest whether political, economic or personal; to assure the flow of political information to the centre; to control the distribution of political spoils at lower levels; and to mobilize citizens for mass voting in presidential and congressional elections.

In brief, after 1945 the party became an appendix to the state rather than active co-participant in the power structure and political innovator. At times it almost seemed that the party was withering away without being replaced by any other articulated set of political structures. The apparent lack of challenge and the absence of threat bred political immobilisme and the ossification of the party. If self-inflicted withering away of the one-party system did not actually take place in Mexico, it is largely because, below the surface of the languid and relatively uneventful political superstructure, rapid economic growth was bringing nolens volens new tensions and conflicts, reflecting the modernization of the society.

Given the peculiarities of the economic growth model described above, this modernization started slowly but perceptibly to threaten the apparent homogeneity in outlook, political values and national ends, as presented to the society by official party-state programmes(14). It could not have happened otherwise. The emphasis on quantitative economic growth, the increasing participation in major policy decisions of the functional interest groups working outside the party structure, and the differentiation in rural and urban areas between the 'haves' and 'have-nots', as measured by income distribution, brought to a head local, regional and national conflicts with which the bureaucratized party-government structures could hardly deal efficiently.

There are reasons to believe that, from the late fifties, the party found itself unable to perform its most important function - that of informing the state at the centre of what was happening in the country and of implementing subsequent decisions. The emergence of the urban middle classes did not help to alleviate tensions, and conflicts started surfacing simultaneously in many places in the early sixties. In the traditional mix of rebellious-dependency reactions of social groups, rebellious attitudes started getting the upper hand over those of dependency.

No clear patterns of rebellion could be discerned. In some cases they were related to the exploitation of stagnant and poor regions by distant poles of industrial growth; in others the issues were political and reflected the growing inappropriateness of centralized nominations of new local authorities; in others violent confrontations occurred between new large landowners and small campesinos and rural landless labour.

With the advent of the Díaz Ordaz administration at the end of 1964, an attempt was made to revitalize party structures at the lowest levels in the name of 'internal party democratization'. This effort, associated with the name of Carlos Madrazo, nominated PRI chairman by Díaz Ordaz, lasted less than a year, ending in complete failure(15). This experiment offered a serious threat not only to the party's internal structure and outside vested interests but also to the basis of the Mexican political system: the dualistic coexistence of the official party and the state under the fundamental authority of the President of the Republic. Some observers maintained that Madrazo overplayed his hand, starting a double game, attempting to modernize the party and at the same time to gain enough personal followers to lead him later to the presidency. Madrazo's dismissal from chairmanship of the PRI did not solve any of the major problems arising from the immobilisme of political structures in the post-war period. The 1968 university conflict, that within a couple of months was transformed into the biggest national political crisis since the expulsion of Calles from Mexico in 1935, offers proofs for that assertion.

By the end of the sixties it was clear that the Mexican system was facing a new situation in which the continuation of the one-party system - in its relatively benevolent role in comparison with other authoritative systems - depended upon many innovative skills: the ability of both party and state to come to terms with a host of new actors that arose during modernization over the previous quarter of century. Mexican society witnessed, as Huntington has postulated for any modernizing society with a one-party system: the appearance inside and outside the political system of a new technical-managerial class; the development of a complex group structure, typical of a more industrial society, whose conflicting interests have to be accommodated within the political sphere; the appearance of a growing number of critical intellectuals apart from and, indeed, increasingly alienated from the institutionalized structure of power; and demands by local and popular groups for participation in and influence over the political system at various levels (16).

Some critics of the system postulated that the new situation called for basic restructuring of political life in Mexico and a peaceful transition from the

one-party structure to a mexicanized version of Western multi-party democracy.
But it seems that such political postulates missed the main issue. Whatever
degree of modernization of social structures took place in Mexico between
1945 and 1970, the political system in the early seventies showed no willingness to preside over its demise. Consequently, assuming that economic and
social modernization does not have to be automatically followed in one-party
systems by the emergence of multi-party structures, it seemed to be worth
looking at the options available to the Mexican system. Put in other terms:
what degree of political democratization and economic modernization could the
system afford without losing its character as exclusive holder of power.

Whereas no one could deny in 1971 the urgent need for mutual adjustment
between social modernizing forces and political structures heavily burdened
with the heritage of the pre-revolutionary past, the authority syndrome
characteristic of the society, and recent economic excesses and political
errors, one could assume that mutual readjustment between 'new' and 'old'
actors could only be made on terms acceptable to the holders of power. The
one-party system could hardly be written off as a weak and ageing actor. On
the contrary, the first months of the new administration showed its vitality
and flexibility in the face of a very complex and difficult situation. As
in the past, the main source of strength was the President. First, in
response to the emergence of a new, innovative, technical-managerial class,
the new administration gave high priority to incorporating this group both
into party and state organs even at the risk of alienating the intermediate
generation of politicians and <u>tecnicos</u>. Key party and state jobs were entrusted to people in their mid-thirties after decades in which the political
system was run by older people. Second, the development of the complex group
structure was attended to in political terms by the sometimes virulent public
attacks upon the preponderant influence of functional private interest groups
upon important economic policy decisions of previous administrations. The
improvement of the political balance between 'haves' and 'have-nots' was
advertized as a major goal. Third, the appearance of a critical intelligensia
was accepted as part of a liberalization of attitudes toward political criticism as long as it did not undermine the basic premises of the system. The
previous attitude of 'who is not with us is against us' was replaced by
another, 'who is not against us is with us'. Finally, demands by local and
popular groups for participation in and influence over the political system
were met with greater physical mobility of members of the political élite,
including the President. This style of political activity was introduced in
the pre-election campaign of 1969-70.

This new political style together with increased emphasis on national unity
and nationalist goals were aimed at stopping the process of increasing alienation of large sectors of the society from the political system that had
occurred during the previous two decades. In the light of findings on the
attitudes of politically and socially marginal elements toward the state and
nationalism in Mexico, the new strategy of 'modernization and democratization
from above' instead of Madrazo's 'democratization from below' seemed likely
to bring not only a considerable degree of psychic welfare to broad groups
of the population, particularly new migrants into the cities, but to revitalize the power basis of the Mexican political system(17).

CONCLUDING REMARKS

A United States political scientist noted some time ago:

> . . . a one-party system oriented primarily to economic development may find out that it can take care of demands only by decisions affecting the use of economic resources. Under such conditions many groups within the society may translate their aspirations into economic terms and then place an excessive strain on the limited resources of the country(18).

Given that excessive strain on limited resources was omnipresent in Mexico in the early seventies, that the number of interest groups had increased, and that demands facing the state and party received additional impetus from 'democratization from above' the economic policy tasks facing the new administration were immensely complicated. Given growing competition for resources - both in financial and real terms - on the one hand, and public investment-savings, financial resources and foreign trade gaps, on the other, the economic readjustment tasks facing the Mexican state were particularly difficult. This may have accounted for the pace of advances on the political front being more rapid than those related to economic problems.

The state possessed important assets: fiscal policy, management of state-owned enterprises, efficiency of the private industrial sector, foreign trade policies, and the management of long-term external obligations. But there was also powerful opposition from internal interest groups and serious external political and economic constraints. Assuming that somehow these obstacles could be overcome, it appeared in 1971 that short-run operational policy improvements followed by overall betterment of resource allocation in accordance with a new set of political priorities might go a considerable way toward the increase of social welfare within a context of fairly dynamic economic growth. This might also halt tendencies toward alienation from the system and uncontrolled politicization.

NOTES

(1)   On income distribution trends in Mexico, see particularly CEPAL, Estudios sobre la distributión del ingreso en América Latina, E/CN.12/770, Caracas, Venezuela, 29 March, 1967 (mimeo), Chap. 3,'Crecimiento económico y distribución del ingreso: el caso de México', pp. 183-228. A later, less critical version of the same study appeared in CEPAL, La distribución del ingreso en América Latina, Naciones Unidas, New York, 1970. Interestingly enough, the chapter on Mexico that in the earlier version run to some thirty-five pages was reduced here to only eight pages.

(2)   A widely quoted study, James W. Wilkie, The Mexican Revolution: Federal Expenditure and Social Change since 1910, University of California Press, Berkeley and Los Angeles 1967, stops at the year 1963 and is open to many serious methodological and factual criticisms.

(3)   While Mexico is nominally a federal state, both political and economic power is concentrated in the hands of the executive branch of the government. State and local fiscal and other revenues represent a fraction of total public revenues and state and local current and investment budgets depend almost wholly on the Federal Treasury.

(4) For a defence of the economic, monetary and financial policies, followed between 1950 and 1970, see Antonio Ortíz Mena, Desarrollo estabilizador - una década de estrategia económica en Mexico, Mexico, 1969. The author was Secretary of Treasury during two subsequent administrations, from 1958 to the fall of 1969.

(5) See Jesús Puente Leyva, Distribución del ingreso en un área urbana: el caso de Monterey, Siglo XXI Editores, México, 1969; Carlos Tello, 'Notas para el análisis de la distribución personal del ingreso en México', El Trimestre Económico (México), Núm. 150 (April-June, 1971) pp. 620-58, and Centro de Investigaciones Agrarias, Estructura agraria y desarrollo agrícola en México, México, 1970, Vol. I, Chap. 3, 'Tenencia de la tierra, producción e ingreso rural', pp. 262-551.

(6) Samuel P. Huntington, 'Social and Institutional Dynamics of One-Party Systems', in Samuel P. Huntington and Clement H. Moore (Editors), Authoritarian Politics in Modern Society - The Dynamics of Established One-Party Systems, Basic Books, New York and London, 1970, p. 13.

(7) Ibid., pp. 23 ff.

(8) Pablo González Casanova, La democracia en México, Ediciones Era, México, Chap. 2, 'Los factores del poder'. Similar attitudes towards sources of power and government in Mexican society were detected by Robert E. Scott in 'Mexico: The Established Revolution', in Lucian W. Pye and Sidney Verba, Political Change and Political Development, Princeton University Press, Princeton, New Jersey, pp. 330-95, and in an unpublished manuscript by Martin C. Needler, 'The Political Implications of Urbanization in Mexico'. It is also interesting to note that the only broad Mexican inquiry into the adequacy of the existing political system to Mexican social attitudes and economic development goals, promoted by a 'rebellious' politician-millionaire who held high official posts during the Carranza-Obregón-Calles period, Alberto J. Pani (Una encuesta sobre la cuestión democrática de México, Mexico, 1948), disclosed that some fifty early post-revolutionary leaders still alive in the late forties came to an almost unanimous conclusion that while the political system prevailing in Mexico had little in common with a Western democracy, it perhaps represented the 'second-best' solution particularly suitable to Mexican historical heritage and social structures.

(9) Robert E. Scott, Mexico: The Established Revolution, op. cit.

(10) On this subject, see Pablo González Casanova (1970), Sociología de la explotación, Siglo XXI Editores, México, and various writings of a leading Mexican sociologist, Rodolfo Stavenhagen.

(11) See for details, Marco Antonio Alcazar, Las agrupaciones patronales en México, Jornadas 66, El Colegio de México, México, 1970.

(12) Such exercises lead to ridiculous results when applied particularly to authoritarian one-party systems in socialist countries. But they also have an eerie quality when undertaken in much more open political systems such as the Mexican. One is bound to have a lot of fun when one reads, for example, long dissertations about how many people and who participate in the nomination of a new candidate of the official party of the presidency or what in fact 'the Revolutionary Family' is all about.

(13) See, Pablo González Casanova, op. cit.; Robert E. Scott, op. cit.; and Gabriel Almond and Sidney Verba, The Civic Culture - Political Attitudes and Democracy in Five Nations, Princeton University Press, Princeton, New Jersey, 1963.

(14) Rafael Segovia, 'El nacionalismo mexicano: los programas políticos revolucionarios (1929-64)', Foro Internacional, Vol. 8, No. 4, El Colegio de México, 1968.

(15) Thomas J. Bossert, 'Carlos A. Madrazo - The Study of a Democratic Experiment in Mexico', unpublished B.A. thesis, Woodrow Wilson School of Public and International Affairs, Princeton University, 1968.

(16) Huntington, op. cit., p. 33.

(17) For an analysis of socio-political attitudes of marginalized groups, see González Casanova, La democracia en México, op. cit.; Vincent Padgett, The Mexican Political System, Houghton-Mifflin Co., Boston, 1966: Robert E. Scott, op. cit.; and Thomas J. Bassert, op. cit.

(18) Lucian W. Pye, Aspects of Political Development, Boston, 1966, p. 73.

CHAPTER 3

Foreign Investment in Mexico: Problems and Prospects*

PAST conflicts, present attitudes and policies towards foreign private capital, and potential future frictions between Mexican society and foreign direct investment can hardly be understood without a brief overview of Mexico's political and economic history.

In the beginning of modern development there was exploitation of the very extensive sub-soil wealth of Mexico for the benefit of the Spanish metropole over three centuries of the colonial period. There followed the achievement of political independence from Spain in 1821 that, like the recent decolonization of Africa and Asia, did not affect in any substantial degree the country's social and economic colonial structure. Then there was a brief encounter with British private capital that went into Mexican mining in the 1820s to fill the void left by the disappearance of Spain as the exclusive market for Mexican precious metal exports. That encounter, accompanied by British loans to the newly independent country, ended in disaster both for the investors and the host country, due mainly to British attempts to inject advanced European technology into a primitive post-colonial economy. Almost half a century of political chaos and economic stagnation (1830-70) ensued, accompanied by the loss of a major part of Mexican territory to the United States and by endless foreign punitive expeditions and outright interventions on behalf of Mexico's creditors aimed at making out of Mexico an appendage to rapidly-growing European industrial economies.

Then came thirty years of political peace and economic development under the dictatorship of Porfirio Díaz (1880-1910) that opened the country to foreign private capital and technology, both European and American. The populist revolution of 1910 broke the back of Porfirian society, whose main pillars were, first, landed aristocracy, mercilessly exploiting the masses of Indian and mestizo population, and, second, foreign economic interests that had

---

*This paper was delivered at the Third Pacific Trade and Development Conference held in Sydney, Australia in August 1970, and published in Peter Drysdale (Editor), <u>Direct Foreign Investment in Asia and the Pacific</u>, Australian National University Press, Canberra, 1972. Reproduced also by kind permission of the University of Toronto Press, Toronto.

achieved, by the beginning of this century, the goal of making of Mexico an important source of raw materials (mining and tropical agricultural products) for the industrial countries of North America and Western Europe. There followed a period of political and economic reconstruction (1925-40) including agrarian reform, following one-and-a-half decades of savage civil war, and characterized by continuous overt and hidden conflicts between Mexico's post-revolutionary society and foreign private investors in mining, public utilities, transport and communications, conflicts that culminated in the expropriation of United States, British and Dutch oil companies in 1938.

The quarter of a century, 1945-70, is characterized by inward-directed heavily protected industrialization, broadly supported by the newly emerging domestic entrepreneurial groups and broadly-based nationalistic public opinion, and accompanied by the progressive elimination of foreign private investment still present in traditional sectors (extractive industries other than nationalized petroleum, public utilities, and transport and communications) through so-called 'mexicanization' procedures - that is, the total acquisition of foreign assets by the state or partial acquisition by domestic private capital.

The 'mexicanization' of traditional sectors was practically completed by the mid-sixties through two major decisions. In 1960, the Mexican state purchased two large foreign-owned electric-power companies that had become, in the late thirties, the centre of a serious conflict, due in part to the foreign companies' refusal to invest in generating facilities and their growing dependence, as electricity distributors in major urban areas, upon electric power produced by the state-owned Federal Electricity Commission(1). Moreover, in the mid-sixties, under new mining legislation, all foreign mining enterprises were forced to sell 51 per cent of their properties to Mexican domestic interests, with the state reserving to itself the right to extend new mining concessions to enterprises with 66 per cent of domestic capital. The new legislation affected, among others, the only dynamic sector of Mexican extractive industries (with the exception of the oil industry, owned by the state since 1938), sulphur mining, that made Mexico during the fifties the second largest world sulphur producer(2).

Ex post, these two important policy measures are easy to explain. In the case of the electricity industry, the failure of the state-run system of public utilities' regulation, on the one hand, and the inflationary excesses of the forties and the early fifties, on the other, had aggravated the conflict latent since the inter-war period and were related to the fact that both the state and large sectors of public opinion considered the adequate provision of electric power as a pre-condition for an industrialization drive. The breakdown of regulatory processes and the inflation of the forties made politically impossible an equitable increase in electric energy prices that would have satisfied the financial objectives of private electric energy producers and would have solved acute electric energy shortages faced by the Mexican economy after 1940. The growing technical skills of the state-owned Federal Electricity Commission, established on the eve of the Second World War, the increasing hostility of large sectors of society to foreign electric-power companies, coupled with the frustrations of their owners who considered themselves victims of public policies, made nationalization of the electric-power industry in 1960 the only alternative.

The mexicanization of the mining industry had a different rationale. Mexico was the single largest producer of silver and gold in colonial times and an important source of metals and minerals for industrial countries between 1880 and the onset of the Great Depression. In both periods that sector was fully-controlled by foreign interests. The appearance in the country after the revolution of resource conservation policies, aimed at securing a hold over mineral wealth for future industrialization, coincided with the shift of major United States and British mining companies to new sources of supply in South America and Africa. The contribution of mining to the Mexican national product and the share of Mexico in world metal and mineral markets continued to decline after 1929, with the exceptions of silver throughout the 1940-70 period and of sulphur in the fifties. It was in the late fifties, however, that the inward-directed industrialization drive brought about, on the one hand, the appearance of a rapid expansion of domestic demand for industrial raw materials, and, on the other, the state's dissatisfaction with traditional policies of foreign mining companies exporting unprocessed or semi-processed metals and minerals abroad. These two factors together with the growing import bill for intermediate metal goods represent the background to the mining legislation of the early sixties and the subsequent mexicanization of extractive industries. Except in the case of highly profitable sulphur mining, the state decision met with no obstacles from mexicanized foreign companies. Following the example of the electric-power companies, they used most of the proceeds from sales of their properties for investment in highly profitable manufacturing and ancillary activities in Mexico.

In the field of banking no need for mexicanization arose. The pre-revolutionary banking system, particularly that controlled by European interests, had effectively been destroyed by the revolution. The new banking system established in the inter-war period belonged, from the beginning, largely to nationals. Only one foreign commercial bank - a branch of the First National City Bank - was set up in Mexico on the eve of the Great Depression. In the early seventies it was still operating in the country but it accounted for less than one per cent of sight deposits of the whole banking system. Subsequent banking legislation barred the entry of foreign financial intermediaries into Mexico without - one must add - creating undue hardship to foreign enterprises operating in the remaining sectors. In the late sixties domestic financing of foreign enterprises exceeded 50 per cent of their total financial needs.

THE POSITION OF FOREIGN CAPITAL IN MEXICO

As shown in Table 3.1, foreign private investment had practically disappeared from the traditional sectors by the late sixties.

The magnitude of the shifts in sectoral distribution of foreign private investment in Mexico between 1910 and the late sixties had no parallel in any other Latin American country. At the end of the Porfirio Díaz era, of the estimated total of US $1200 million of foreign direct investment in Mexico, almost 80 per cent was in extractive industries, including petroleum, railroads and public utilities. Sixty years later only 6 per cent of the total estimated in 1968 at over US $2300 million was still in mining. Foreign investment had completely disappeared from petroleum, transport and public utilities, to be concentrated exclusively in manufacturing (75 per cent) and services other than banking (over 15 per cent). The shift that took place between 1950 and 1970 reflected, first, the progressive and peaceful takeover, mostly by the state, of traditional foreign investment in the name of economic independence, and second, the working of direct and indirect incentives available - under certain rules - to foreign manufacturing and service investment, incentives originally established in the forties to protect domestic entrepreneurial groups.

TABLE 3.1. Sectoral Distribution of Foreign Private Investment in Mexico, 1911-68

(Per cent)

Sectors	1911	1940	1950	1960	1968
Agriculture	7.0	1.9	0.7	1.8	0.7
Mining	28.0	23.9	19.8	15.6	6.0
Petroleum	4.0	0.3	2.1	2.0	1.8
Industry	4.0	7.0	26.0	55.8	74.2
Electric power	8.0	31.5	24.2	1.4	—
Trade	10.0	3.5	12.4	18.1	74.8
Transport and communications	39.0	31.6	13.3	2.8	—
Other services	—	0.3	1.5	2.5	2.5

Sources: For 1911: Cleona Lewis, America's Stake in International Investment, The Brookings Institution, Washington, D.C., 1938; for 1940-60: Banco de Mexico, S.A.; for 1968: estimates by the author. It should be noted that by 1911 foreign oil interests had just finished the first stage of their activities in Mexico; their participation in total foreign investment increased considerably during the revolution and reached its peak around 1925.

The fact that these incentives (including the rapidly-growing market, political and monetary stability, very high protection levels and a very liberal tax system) worked can be deduced from Table 3.2. While for the lack of other data the table covers only United States private direct investment in Mexico, which accounted for some 80 per cent of total foreign direct investment in the country at the end of the sixties, it reflects the sectoral distribution of all foreign direct investment flows in Mexico between 1950 and 1970.

One might surmise that the elimination of foreign private capital from the sectors in which it used to be historically a source of conflict and the entry of foreign capital in dynamic growth-inducing activities would guarantee the absence of future friction between foreign investors and the political and economic interest groups in modern Mexico as long as dominating local economic interest groups were assured some participation in the growing market via special state privileges and joint ventures. Strangely enough, although past situations of conflict had apparently been eliminated, the convenience or inconvenience of new foreign investment - in terms of political implications, resources gap relief, the balance-of-payments burden, the technological contribution - continued to be debated with an intensity similar to that which characterized discussion of traditional private foreign investment during the previous half-century. Outside official agencies which had decided not to publish any data on foreign investment except those pertaining to net financial flows which appear in the balance-of-payments statistics, the subject was discussed continuously and with highly emotional overtones. It is quite

TABLE 3.2. Book Value of United States Direct Investment in Mexico, by Major Sectors, 1950-70

(US $ million)

	1955	1960	1965	1968
Mining and smelting	154	130	140	125
Petroleum	15	32	48	38
Manufactures	274	391	756	1370
Public utilities	91	119	27	—
Trade	50	85	138	260
Other, including tourism	30	38	73	67
Total	614	795	1182	1860

Sources: For 1955: U.S. Investments in the Latin American Economy, U.S. Dept. of Commerce, Washington, D.C., 1957, and Survey of Current Business, U.S. Dept. of Commerce, August 1956; for 1960: Survey of Current Business, August 1961; for 1965: Walter Lederer and Frederick Cutler, 'International Investment of the United States in 1966', U.S. Dept. of Commerce, Overseas Business Reports, OBR 67-72, November 1967; for 1968: estimates of the author based upon unpublished partial United States and Mexican data.

probable that more rational approaches were hampered, first, by the extreme scarcity of reliable information, second, by the absence of scholarly studies of the sectoral composition of foreign investment, its profitability and real impact upon the balance of payments, and, finally, by doubts about the contribution of foreign capital to the technological progress of a society whose backwardness, in this respect, was directly due to its inadequately designed educational system. Given the particular characteristics of the Mexican political system, the absence of serious and publicly-available research strongly suggests that the issue of foreign direct investment was considered by the government as a politically highly sensitive subject. This seemed to be related in part to the outcome of official industrialization policies that resulted in a large-scale entry of foreign private capital into Mexican industry and services.

Official pronouncements on policies toward foreign direct investment offered the following broad policy guidelines. Basic sectors of the national economy, such as the oil industry, heavy petrochemicals, electric power, railways and communications were reserved to the state. Investment in agriculture and financial intermediaries was reserved to Mexican nationals; in other sectors (mining and manufacturing) the rule of domestic capital majority participation was applied to fields either closely linked with basic economic activities or considered of special importance for future industrial development. While no all-inclusive list of such activities was elaborated, some six important industries, such as steel, cement, glass and aluminium, among others, were declared as falling under the 51 per cent domestic ownership rule in July

1970; in all remaining fields, no limitations upon foreign private capital were imposed, except that it had to accept all legal obligations applied to domestically-owned enterprises. Unless it accepted domestic capital participation, it had to renounce access to fiscal and other privileges provided by the Law for New and Necessary Industries. Mexico was particularly interested in foreign investment projects that brought into the country new technology, created considerable sources of employment, and gave preference to the use of domestic physical inputs.

While these general directives, elaborated over two decades, might have looked forbidding to prospective investors by restricting considerably the participation of foreign private capital in Mexico's economic development, the inflow of new investment was larger than anywhere else in Latin America. Rapid industrial development, continuous diversification of domestic demand, and, finally, the extremely high level of profits in the private sector more than offset the apparently restrictive features of policy toward foreign private capital.

According to very preliminary estimates, the total book value of foreign private investment increased in Mexico from US $1080 million in 1960 to some US $2300 million by 1968; that is, it more than doubled in less than ten years. During the sixties, practically all new investment, reinvested profits and financial resources released by disinvestment in traditional sectors (especially in public utilities and mining) went into manufacturing and non-financial services, mainly commerce and tourist facilities. Between 1960 and 1968 the total book value of foreign direct investment in manufacturing grew from less than US $600 million to about US $1700 million and in the service sector (excluding financial intermediaries from which foreign investment was barred), from US $225 million to about US $400 million.

THE ROLE OF AMERICAN INVESTMENT

Because of the allegedly decisive contribution of foreign manufacturing investment to the solution of balance-of-payments difficulties and its presumably highly positive technological and welfare impact upon developing economies, the massive flow of foreign private capital into Mexican manufacturing and ancillary services is worth looking into closely. These alleged contributions were considered almost axiomatic by most of the literature from the advanced countries, and particularly by studies sponsored directly and indirectly by the United States Department of Commerce(3). Serious scholars had considerable difficulty in accepting these simplistic apologies(4).

In the case of Mexico, one had to work exclusively with data on the Mexican activities of United States-owned transnational manufacturing companies(5). A wealth of information on that subject was collected by Harvard Graduate School of Business Administration as part of a monumental study of United States transnational corporations, directed by Raymond Vernon(6). According to these data, Mexico occupied in 1967 third place in the world after Canada and Great Britain as a haven for American investment. There were 187 United States-based transnational corporate parent systems, accounting for over 70 per cent of United States direct manufacturing investment overseas and over 80 per cent of United States foreign direct manufacturing investment outside Canada. Of those 187 corporations, 179 entered Mexico through subsidiaries during the present century. The comparable figures for Canada and Great Britain were 183 and 180 respectively. In respect to the number of affiliates of these parent systems established over the same period, Mexico with 625 subsidiaries occupied the first place in Latin America and the fifth in the world after Canada (1697), Great Britain (1189), France (670), and Germany (632).

Because of mergers, sales to nationals or withdrawals, 162 out of 187 United States transnational manufacturing corporations were present in Mexico at the end of 1967 with a total of 412 subsidiaries. There were 255 subsidiaries in manufacturing (including assembling) activities, 31 in commerce, 14 in extractive industries, and 112 either in other sectors or unspecified by the Harvard researchers. Of the original 625 entries into Mexico before the end of 1967, 268 were newly-established subsidiaries, 225 involved acquisitions of existing firms(7), and the remaining 132 either appeared as separate new branches of existing subsidiaries or their form of entry into Mexico was unknown. Of 412 subsidiaries present in Mexico at the end of 1967, 143 were new entries, 112 acquisitions, and 109 were branches of subsidiaries established earlier. The mode of entry of the remaining 48 subsidiaries was not known. Some 56 per cent of the total were wholly owned by the parent system; 19 per cent had United States majority capital control and only 15 per cent had United States minority control. While the degree of foreign control of the remaining 10 per cent of subsidiaries could not be established, it is a fair assumption that half of them had majority control by the parent system. This would bring the percentage of Mexican subsidiaries of the 162 major United States transnational manufacturing corporations, fully-owned or with majority capital control, to some 80 per cent of the total.

The trend toward entry of United States-based transnational manufacturers into Mexico through acquisitions and the tendency toward full or majority control, measured in terms of flows, increased substantially in the period 1958-67. Compared with the first post-war decade (1946-57) the total number of entries jumped from 156 to 335, while the number of newly-established subsidiaries increased from 80 to 119 and that of acquisitions from 49 to 149. Looked upon in terms of stocks, a considerable number of mergers (presumably representing horizontal and vertical integration within the captive market) and an extension of activities into new fields could be detected in the behaviour of United States manufacturing companies' subsidiaries over the ten years of rapid industrialization in Mexico (1958-67). Of 178 subsidiaries established in Mexico after 1957, and existing ten years later as separate structures incorporated under local legislation, 34 were newly-established firms, 62 resulted from acquisitions, 73 were branches of other Mexican subsidiaries and the origin of the remaining 9 was unknown.

This brief overview would not be complete without mention of manufacturing industries in Mexico for which United States transnational manufacturing firms showed strong preference in the post-war years, particularly in the 1958-67 period. Of a total 315 United States entries into manufacturing in Mexico between 1946 and 1967, recorded in the Harvard directory, 99 subsidiaries, or close to one-third, were established in the chemical, pharmaceutical or cosmetics industries. The second place belonged to processed foods and beverages, with 65 entries; the third to the automotive industry including rubber products, with 34; and the fourth to domestic electric and electronic appliances including light electric machinery, with 26. These four industries represented over 70 per cent of all post-war entries of United States transnational manufacturing companies. All of them fell into the category of durable and non-durable goods, produced almost exclusively for the domestic market.

Under these circumstances one cannot be surprised if, of total sales in 1956 of United States manufacturing subsidiaries operating in Mexico, valued at US $643 million, 98.5 per cent (US $633 million) represented local sales and, ten years later in 1966, 87 per cent of total sales, valued at US $1480 million, represented sales in the domestic Mexican market(8). Except in the field of transportation equipment, where in 1966 sales of Mexican subsidiaries of two large United States automobile companies to their affiliates elsewhere amounted to US $149 million, total exports of all other United States manufacturing subsidiaries amounted to a mere US $38 million or 3 per cent of their total sales. They were composed as follows: sales to other affiliates of the same parent systems of US $15 million; exports to other clients in the United States of US $8 million, to Latin America of US $7 million and to other destinations of US $4 million(9). While at the close of the sixties exports of United States manufacturing newcomers to the Mexican border zone, adjacent to United States territory, expanded considerably, their effect upon the balance of payments was minimal since their activity was limited to assembling for re-export parts imported in bond, largely from the United States.

COSTS AND BENEFITS

This information strongly suggests that the post-war wave of foreign, mostly United States, manufacturing investment in Mexico represented a clear case of the kind, mentioned in Harry Johnson's essays, which takes advantage of high tariff barriers and gets, in addition, access to a wide array of state industrialization promoting measures, ranging from tax exemptions to open and hidden subsidies offered to the industrial sector as a whole. These take the form of generous provision of infrastructure financed from public funds and through sales below cost to private industrial enterprises of state-produced goods and services, such as energy and transport. The tariff protection element seemed to play a particularly important role in investment decisions of foreign private capital.

Whilst in comparison with other Latin American countries, Mexico has been considered a relatively lowly protected market with its foreign exchange rate reasonably close to equilibrium, studies of the level of Mexican tariff protection have undermined previous intuitive judgements based upon the concept of nominal tariff. Thus it has recently been found that the average Mexican level of _effective_ protection for manufactured goods is close to 50 per cent, varying from about 5 per cent for processed foodstuffs to over 100 per cent for consumer durables(10). Within this last group the automobile industry enjoyed an effective protection of 255 per cent. According to the same study, manufacturing industries, able to export some part of their output (from 5 to 10 per cent), received effective protection of 26 per cent; for those competing with imports the effective tariff was 73 per cent on the average and those that did not appear either on the export or import lists, 33 per cent. An effective level of protection for import-substitution industries close to 75 per cent could hardly be considered low. Its absolute level, which had probably increased in the previous decade, explained to a considerable extent not only the rush of foreign manufacturing enterprises into Mexico, but the coexistence of high profitability in manufacturing (within the range of 25 per cent a year on investment in fixed assets) with the use of about 60 per cent capacity on the average by the manufacturing sector. Inflexible protectionist policies coupled with the faulty design of the fiscal system and the absence of anti-monopoly legislation created in Mexico a framework conducive to the inefficiency of the domestically-owned industrial sector and a foreign direct investment situation, aptly described by Johnson in the following way:

> where the foreign direct investment has been attracted by protection or fiscal incentives, the profits earned may not be matched by a genuine contribution to increased output, and the servicing drain on the balance of payments constitutes a real burden on the economy. (Johnson in Drysdale (Editor), op. cit.)

While it is impossible to disagree with Johnson's observation that such a situation should be ascribed to governmental error in providing socially undesirable incentives to foreign direct investment rather than blamed on the foreign corporation per se, a further inquiry into the behaviour of the subsidiaries of transnational manufacturing companies in Mexico and the implications of this behaviour for the host economy and the Mexican political system is in order. This would help to define potential sources of conflict between a highly nationalistic Mexican society and foreign private investment, concentrated in dynamic industrial sectors.

This inquiry has to start by rejecting three major propositions. The first considers international capital flows as the transfer of a single factor of production which is missing in the recipient country and which complements existing factors. Once one replaces this proposition with another stressing that private capital transfers represent only a part of a package of capital, technology and managerial skills, the measuring of potential benefits or losses from foreign direct capital flows accruing to the host country while becoming more complicated, offers more fruitful answers(11).

The second proposition that must be discarded is that the flow of technology to developing countries (technology treated traditionally as an aggregate entity which, introduced as an index in the production function, 'augments' the availability of some or all other inputs in terms of efficiency units) takes place on a micro-economic level between two firms - the seller and the buyer - under competitive conditions(12). This proposition is as distant from the reality as the first, because of the emergence in the post-war world of a growing number of transnational manufacturing giants that, in the case of Mexico among others, represent an important vehicle of the transfer of packages of capital, technology and managerial skills.

Finally, the third major traditional proposition, of little if any use, is that the reported profitability of a subsidiary of a transnational corporation located in a developing host country, characterized by excessive protection and an oligopolistic market structure, is a correct accounting tool for measuring the foreign exchange costs and balance-of-payments effects of the operations of that productive unit. Paradoxically, the reported profitability of foreign subsidiaries and transfer of these profits abroad as compared with the inflow of new capital into a developing host country are used both against foreign private investment by its under-educated opponents in the developing world and, with some superficial degree of sophistication that takes into account the 'import substitution' and 'export creation' effect, by traditional apologists for foreign private investment. Instead of taking part in this spurious conflict between primitive accountants from 'the left' in developing countries and from 'the right' in capital exporting countries, one is forced to accept another novel proposition. Cost-benefit analysis of foreign direct investment must accept the reality of the package transfer, the monopolistic control of a large part of modern technology (both patented and unpatented) by transnational manufacturing corporations, and the effect upon the host countries of global profit maximization strategies of these large corporate bodies that, according to some projections, will account for more than one-half of world industrial production by the year 2000. Only then does one begin to deal with the real world(13).

Looking at Mexican experience between 1950 and 1970, one sees that of four major durable consumer goods industries, controlled almost completely by foreign private capital, three - chemicals and pharmaceuticals (including cosmetics of all sorts), automobiles, and domestic electric and electronic appliances - have certain common characteristics. They did not involve heavy initial investment outlays, they used relatively constant technology and, at the time of their entry into Mexico, depended heavily on imported inputs. In all cases the technology was tied to the provision of imported inputs through intra-parent system standardization of components (automotive and electric appliance industry) and by patents (the electric appliance industry and chemicals and pharmaceuticals). Under these circumstances, low capital investment needs, particularly at the assembly stage, considered along with the high income elasticity of demand in a society of rising middle classes (endowed with consumer preference patterns shaped by the proximity of the United States), the monopolistic control of tied technology by foreign manufacturing entrants, and tied sources of imported inputs, must have offered the parent systems, investing in a heavily protected market, extremely high profits that in no way could have been reflected in the balance sheets and profit-and-loss statements of the foreign subsidiaries in Mexico. They appear only in the profit-and-loss statements of the parent systems and this is why, among others, the parent companies' financial statements were generally published in consolidated form.

In fact, parent companies of transnational corporations showed no enthusiasm for disclosing the detailed results of overseas operations to their own shareholders at home either, as was pointed out in a survey made by the United States National Industrial Conference Board in early 1965. According to this study:

> more than 80 per cent of manufacturers surveyed earn money through exports, foreign licencing agreements or overseas manufacturing. About half have increased earnings from such sources in recent years. Yet few share the good news with their stockholders.
> Any reader of annual reports will find that vital information on foreign sales and earnings generally is lacking, buried in small print in footnotes or discussed in terms a layman cannot understand(14).

Reported subsidiaries' profits after local taxes, averaging in Mexico for the whole United States-owned manufacturing sector around 10 per cent a year, thus represented only the visible part of the profit iceberg accruing to parent companies through payments of royalties and 'technical assistance' and through intra-company pricing of imported inputs that were priced in relation to the local protection level and not sold by the parent company at their incremental cost. World-wide practices in this respect by chemical and pharmaceutical transnational corporations are too well-known to be discussed here(15). The key to the measurement of profitability of a foreign investment venture for the parent company remains the inter-company pricing permitted by high protective walls and control over tied-in technology(16).

These propositions explain, on the one hand, the extreme hostility of foreign manufacturing companies (and for that matter domestically-owned firms as well) to disclose to anyone but fiscal authorities any kind of financial information, and, particularly, any details of the cost structure in highly protected economies such as Mexico, and, on the other hand, the silent agreement between the state and the private sector to keep all this information secret. Under conditions of real or alleged scarcity of capital and technology and with a declared policy of economic nationalism, any breakdown of such 'gentlemen's agreements' on the secrecy of the internal financial operations of foreign-controlled enterprises might have many immediate and politically undesirable effects. First, it would destroy the 'good investment climate' for which Mexico has been famous; second, it would permit outside parties to quantify monopolistic rents accruing to foreign manufacturing investors through overpricing of technology and intra-company pricing of imported parts and accessories; third, it would throw serious doubts upon the whole development strategy, based upon heavy protection and additional industrialization incentives, that permitted these rents to foreign firms and offered a premium for inefficiency to many domestic producers, in the name of economic nationalism. Finally, it might raise a political storm in a nationalistic society and provide strong ammunition to the political left.

In the absence of any alternative development strategy, the Mexican government decided to face the challenge of the transnational manufacturing corporations in three indirect ways: by extending mexicanization pressures to new segments of the manufacturing sector; by forcing foreign-controlled industries to increase the use of domestically produced inputs; and finally, by linking the issuance of permits for imported inputs with the export performance of industrial enterprises. The results of the first two measures, in terms of balance-of-payments relief and consumer's welfare, were rather meagre. As one Mexican economist put it, when questioning both the way import substitution was fostered at that stage of Mexico's industrial development and the real effect of the mexicanization policies encouraging joint industrial ventures:

> (given the dominant technological position of transnational industrial corporations) the actual effect of import substitution policies is extremely paradoxical. While one of the objectives of such policies was to diminish the dependence of the Mexican economy upon world economic fluctuations, it has obviously stimulated strongly the growth of foreign investment in Mexico. . . . As a result of protectionist policies foreign corporations substituted trade by investment. . . . Following the example of other underdeveloped countries, our authorities have attempted to solve the paradox through a mexicanization policy; however, even under the best circumstances, this policy does not help to improve the competitive capacity of Mexican enterprises. It only results in that some already privileged Mexicans may participate in oligopolistic profits, associated with technological innovations whose availability and control had led foreign enterprises to invest in Mexico(17).

Forcing backward linkages upon such assembly activities as the automobile industry through a policy of increased integration into assembled units of domestic parts produced by new joint ventures brought rather disappointing results. While no study of the new auto parts and accessories industries was available at the time of writing, official policy, according to the automotive enterprises, the majority of which were fully foreign-owned, resulted in an increase in costs and a decline in quality standards. A preliminary survey

suggested, on the other hand, that most of the auto parts industry used
second-hand equipment brought mainly from the United States by foreign
partners, and paid very considerable fees on account of patents, trademarks
and technical assistance. Similar experiences were reported from other
industries subject to 'domestic integration' programmes, industries that,
because of local inability to adapt imported technologies to Mexican conditions and intra-company standardization of parts and accessories, depended
heavily on technologies acquired - again at a cost defined by the increased
protection level and the strong bargaining power of the sellers - from large
transnational manufacturing systems.

It is only the linkage of import permits to export performance of manufacturing firms that starts showing positive results by curtailing heavily the
possibility of monopolistic rents from the control of technology and over-
pricing imports of intermediate goods by the parent system. How large a
benefit this policy would bring was difficult to guess in 1970. It largely
depended upon Mexico's willingness to tackle, through fiscal measures and
new industrial property and patent legislation (current law was twenty-five
years old and completely outdated), the problem of the restrictive practices
of Mexican subsidiaries of foreign firms. Little if anything was known, for
example, about restrictive export practices (market division clauses) of
these subsidiaries. The only evidence that such practices were extensive
was an unpublished report on United States foreign investment in Mexico,
commissioned in 1969 by the National Chamber Foundation of Washington, D.C.
The report, based upon 122 answers to questionnaires sent to some 650 United
States-owned or controlled manufacturing enterprises, contained information
to the effect that one-half of the respondents (60) were enjoined from
exporting from Mexico by their parent companies.

Since both foreign and domestic industrial producers were interested, for
different reasons, in the highest level of protection possible, the Mexican
state that a quarter of a century previously gave political and economic
priority to industrialization practically at any cost to the consumer,
seemed thus to be somehow stuck with 'infant industry' policies. Although it
was easy to recognize that inward-oriented industrialization, heavily dependent an foreign capital and second-class foreign technology, was expensive in
terms of the foreign exchange burden and social welfare, any mention of the
need to lower protection levels was drowned by protests from powerful
coalitions of vested interests both foreign and domestic.

As long as Mexican industrial output was expanding at close to 10 per cent a
year and balance-of-payments problems could be taken care of by growing
tourist revenue, new foreign private investment and generous foreign public
and private lending extended to the public sector, no imperative necessity
could be seen in Mexico for a readjustment of crude industrialization policies
designed in the early post-war period. But in the late sixties the situation
began to change, though almost imperceptibly to the non-expert eye. The
balance-of-payments account was getting out of gear, the proportion of new
foreign investment to reinvested profits began to decline, the inability of
Mexican society to absorb and adapt foreign technology not tied to foreign
direct investment was becoming clear, while attempts to expand industrial
exports faced serious problems because of the low efficiency of the industrial
structure, the scarcity of international marketing know-how among domestic
firms, and restrictive export practices of foreign manufacturing subsidiaries.

Only then were questions raised about the performance of the industrialization model in force in Mexico since the end of the war and its social costs. A new generation of nationalist foreign-educated intellectuals questioned the generous treatment offered to foreign investment in key sectors, in spite of an apparently impressive web of restrictions and regulations aimed at mexicanization of manufacturing activities. Sophisticated questions were also asked about the technological and managerial contribution of foreign private investment and about the real meaning of mexicanization policies. While the managerial contribution of foreign direct investment seemed impressive, the costs of tied-in technology looked staggering when compared with those of non-tied technology that might be easily acquired in international competitive markets by domestic entrepreneurs if only they cared to search for it(18). As far as the results of private mexicanization of manufacturing and ancillary activities were concerned, there was a growing consensus that 'it is a tool used by the new middle class to accede to wealth and power'(19).

CONCLUSIONS

It would, however, represent a gross underestimation of the strength of Mexican political and economic nationalism to consider it as a mere outcome of the social stratification process that occurred in Mexico in recent decades and brought about the emergence of middle classes and the concentration of wealth recalling the industrial economies of the end of the nineteenth century. If one keeps in mind the highlights of Mexican political and economic history, presented at the beginning of this chapter, one is forced to accept that Mexican nationalism has very deep roots related to rather unhappy encounters with the advanced outside world over the past two centuries. Given the declared commitment of the political system to use industrialization as a major tool for increasing the country's independence from that outside world, and accepting at its face value the social content of the official post-revolutionary ideology, it is difficult to envisage the long-term continuation of a situation in which control of the dynamic new industrial sectors passes into foreign hands, or, at best, is shared by them with those members of the local middle classes that succeed in monopolizing wealth and power. Neither of these situations helps to resolve the problem of low efficiency in the industrialization process.

What kind of new long-run strategy would Mexico need not only to ensure continuation of her impressive economic growth performance over past decades, but also to translate this quantitative growth into increasing social welfare in a country with one of the worst income distribution patterns in Latin America and with one of the highest population growth rates? Such a strategy in respect of the contribution of foreign capital and technology to development would call for the following, among other things. First, it would require a sizeable but selective decrease in the level of effective protection in order to bring some degree of competition into monopolistic structures and increase Mexico's manufacturing export potential. It would also require the revamping of fiscal policies aimed at the abandonment of the whole array of superfluous incentives for 'infant industries' which long ago should have become, if not adults, at least adolescents. The knot that results in package transfers of foreign capital, technology and managerial skills, lending themselves to overt and covert abuses by foreign manufacturing enterprises would have to be unravelled. Finally, it would require a general and far-reaching reform of the educational system, the performance of which had led to the appearance of acute bottlenecks on the middle technical skills level and had curtailed severely the country's ability to select and to adapt to the economy's needs for untied technology available outside transnational corporate systems.

While all these proposals run against the interests of powerful vested interests, both domestic and foreign, the delay in their implementation might create within the not too distant future severe conflicts between foreign private capital and Mexican society and add to domestic political and social stresses originating in the past strategy of industrialization at any cost.

NOTES

(1) For details of the relations between Mexican state- and foreign-owned electric public utilities between 1900 and 1960, see Miguel S. Wionczek 'Electric Power - The Uneasy Partnership', in Raymond Vernon (Editor), <u>Public Policy and Private Enterprise in Mexico</u>, Harvard University Press, Cambridge, Mass., 1964, and Chap. 4, this volume.

(2) See my study of sulphur mining 'mexicanization' in Raymond F. Mikesell (Editor), <u>Foreign Investment in Petroleum and Mineral Industries</u>, Johns Hopkins University Press, Baltimore, 1970.

(3) For the most recent example of such treatment, see Herbert K. May, <u>The Effects of United States and Other Foreign Investment in Latin America</u>, The Council for Latin America, New York, January 1970, based upon partially released data of a long-overdue worldwide survey of United States foreign direct investment in 1966, made by the United States Department of Commerce the following year.

(4) See Johnson in Drysdale (Editor), <u>op. cit</u>., Chap. 1. See also Paul Streeten, 'The Contribution of Private Overseas Investment to Development', Pearson Conference, Columbia University, February 1970 (mimeo.) and Carlos F. Díaz Alejandro, 'Direct Foreign Investment in Latin America', University of Minnesota, 1970 (mimeo.).

(5) The term 'transnational corporation' lends itself to less confusion than 'multinational corporation' by making clear that these corporate giants are characterized by centralized control in the country of the parent and worldwide operations through manufacturing and other subsidiaries.

(6) All data used in the following section come from James W. Vaupel and Joan A. Curhan, <u>The Making of Multinational Enterprise - A Sourcebook of Tables Based on a Study of 187 Major U.S. Manufacturing Corporations</u>, Division of Research, Graduate School of Business Administration, Harvard University, Boston, 1969.

(7) Although no global data about both foreign and domestic acquisitions of Mexican firms are available for any period, the findings of a Canadian study strongly suggest that the entry of foreign firms into Canada through acquisition of domestic firms was of less importance between 1945 and 1961 in that country than in Mexico in 1958-67. For Canadian data, see Grant L. Reuber and Frank Roseman, <u>The Takeover of Canadian Firms, 1945-1961, An Empirical Analysis</u>, Special Study No. 10, Economic Council of Canada, Ottawa, March 1969.

(8) Figures for 1960 appear in U.S. Business Investments in Foreign Countries, U.S. Dept. of Commerce, Washington, D.C., 1960, p. 110, Table 22. The U.S. Department of Commerce 1956 census covered all United States manufacturing firms in Mexico with control of more than 25 per cent of its voting stock by the parent system. Figures for 1916 are taken from May, op. cit.

(9) May, op. cit., p. 32, Table 4. Even these figures may overestimate the exports of United States manufacturing subsidiaries from Mexico in 1966. The author of that study (based upon preliminary data supplied by U.S. Department of Commerce) made some adjustments to official United States figures, because the coverage of the 1966 worldwide census was limited to United States parent companies with majority of capital control and employing 100 or more people each. Figures quoted from May's study appear in his table under a heading 'presumptive exports'.

(10) Gerardo Bueno, 'The Level of Effective Protection in Mexico', in Bela Balassa (Editor), Effective Protection in Developing Countries, Johns Hopkins University Press, Baltimore, 1971.

(11) Examples of this 'conventional' approach can be found not only in official and private sector literature originating in capital exporting countries, but in periodical reviews of flows of financial resources to the developing countries published under the auspices of international agencies such as the OECD.

(12) For an excellent study of the unreality of this assumption, supported by a case study of the experiences of an underdeveloped Latin American country, Colombia, see Constantine V. Vaitsos, Transfer of Resources and Preservation of Monopoly Rents, paper submitted to the Dubrovnik Conference of Harvard University Development Advisory Service, May 1970 (mimeo.).

(13) According to a thoughtful student of foreign investment decisions affecting capital importing countries: 'economic theory does not pretend to mirror reality. It only claims, by a process of simplification, to isolate some significant strands in economic causal sequences, and to describe how these strands operate. Economic theory, therefore, is rarely right or wrong, it is only more or less useful, depending upon whether the necessary simplification constitutes a very large or very small deviation from reality. My conclusion, nevertheless, reached over a long period of time, was that the simplifying assumptions of classical economic theory represented so gross a departure from reality that the theory was an extremely inefficient frame of reference from which to observe, project and prescribe on the subject of capital investment'. Yair Aharoni, The Foreign Investment Decision Process, Graduate School of Business Administration, Harvard University, Boston, 1966, p. ix.

(14) New York Times, 11 April 1965, 'Foreign Data Held Lacking in Reports'.

(15) For details see volumes of Sen. Kefauver's hearings on administered prices of drugs held in the U.S. Congress in 1953-54, and Lord Sainsbury's report on the British pharmaceutical industry released by HMSO in London in September 1967.

(16) A neat theoretical analysis of this point can be found in Constantine V. Vaitsos, Transfer of Industrial Technology to Developing Countries Through Private Enterprises, Bogota, Colombia, February 1970 (mimeo.). Appendix 1.

(17) Carlos Bazdrech, 'Nuevas ideas sobre la inversión extranjera', Reunión Nacional para el Estudio del Desarrollo Industrial de México, Vol. 1, June 1970, p. 171.

(18) While no data about the foreign exchange costs of technology imports to Mexico are available, the Mexican Treasury found that some US $80 million were transferred abroad for 'technical assistance' in 1968 alone, only in large part to such 'industrialized' countries as Panama, Bahamas, Curaçao and Liechtenstein. For details, see 'Asistencia técnica del extranjero', Investigación Fiscal, Secretaría de Hacienda y Crédito Público (Mexico), No. 45, October 1969. This writer's report, written for the United Nations in 1968, discovered that between 1961 and 1965, the only period for which such data were available, remittances abroad of net profits by foreign companies, established in Mexico, increased by 20 per cent only, while overt payments on account of interest, royalties and technical assistance grew by 40 per cent. For details, see Miguel S. Wionczek, Arrangements for the Transfer of Operative Technology to Developing Countries - Case Study of Mexico, U.N. Economic and Social Council, E/4452/Add/3, March 1968 (mimeo.).

(19) Albert Breton, 'The Economics of Nationalism', Journal of Political Economy, (August 1964), p. 121.

CHAPTER 4

The State and the Electric-power Industry, 1895-1965*

THE AGE of electricity came very rapidly to Mexico, in the wake of its emergence in the United States and Western Europe in the last quarter of the nineteenth century. By the late 1890s electric plants were already providing energy to the country's mining activities and few industries and lighting to a few urban areas. The beginning of the present century witnessed impressive progress in the public utility field. Whereas in the United States a gross

---

*This essay is based on research on the relationship between public policy and private enterprise in modern Mexico, sponsored by the Center for International Affairs, Harvard University, and published in Business History Review (Cambridge, Mass.) Vol. 39, No. 4 (1965); a detailed monograph on the same subject appeared in Raymond Vernon (Editor), Public Policy and Private Enterprise in Mexico, Harvard University Press, Cambridge, Mass., 1964.

Detailed analytical studies on the growth of the electric-power industry in Mexico are extremely scarce and this scarcity contrasts with the wealth of material with strong ideological (anti-private power companies) content, published over the past forty years in Mexican professional journals, newspapers, and in the form of occasional pamphlets. Economic and financial information about the performance of the private companies is confined mainly to brief annual reports of the two major foreign-owned utilities bought out by the state in 1960: Mexican Light & Power Company, established at the beginning of the century, and American & Foreign Power Company, which started its Mexican operations in 1928. No study has been made of the state-owned, power-generating and distributing enterprise Comisión Federal de Electricidad, created in 1937. Among the principal sources on the electric-power industry in Mexico are: José Herrera Lasso, La industria eléctrica: lo que al público le interesa saber, México, 1933; Ernesto Galarza, La industria électrica en Mexico, México, 1942; Cristóbal Lara Beautell, La industria de energía eléctrica, México; Comité para el Estudio de la Industria Eléctrica Mexicana (CEE/MEX), Desarrollo de la industria eléctrica mexicana, México, a survey made available in a limited number of mimeographed copies for distribution among state officials and companies' executives in 1957; and Robert Peter Wolfangel, 'The History and Development of Private Electric Power Interests in Mexico', M.A. thesis, Mexico City College, 1961.

investment of some $275 million was devoted to electric-power generation and distribution between 1891 and 1900, British, Canadian, and United States interests spent around $75 million to the same ends in Mexico's smaller economy during the following decade. Between 1900 and 1910 nearly 150,000 kWs were added to the negligible generating capacity available in the country in 1900; more than forty plants were set up in major productive centres of the Republic; 10,000 people found employment in the new activity; and the main sectors of the Mexican economy were newly stimulated by the change from human and animal energy to mechanical power(1).

Between 1902 and 1906, five important British, Canadian, and United States companies entered the Mexican electric-power industry and became its backbone for the next forty years. Between 1905 and 1911, they set up four main systems in different parts of the country. The majority of the small Mexican-owned plants were purchased, integrated, and modernized by foreign investors. By the end of the Porfirio Díaz era, foreign firms also controlled the most profitable concessions for hydroelectric generation, having been granted these concessions by President Díaz or by purchasing them from their Mexican owners(2).

The interest of foreign concerns in Mexico's hydroelectric possibilities coincided with Díaz' and his advisers' desire to electrify the country. The Diáz administration was well informed about technological progress in Europe and the United States. In 1894, as the first large hydroelectric plants were set up in the United States, a Mexican decree revised a law of 1888 on jurisdiction over transportation rights to clarify the idea of federal control over national water resources. This decree introduced, for the first time, the legal concept of 'concession' with respect to the development of water resources. The Constitution of 1857 had left control over waterways partly to the states and municipalities; the decree of 1894 extended federal control to practically all existing river flows and gave the executive branch explicit authority to grant concessions 'for irrigation and production of power for industrial purposes'. The same decree established five-year tax exemptions for hydroelectric firms, tariff exemptions on imported equipment, and federal power to expropriate (with due compensation) properties of potential value for private development as electric-plant sites. Electricity rates were also made subject to federal approval.

Under these conditions, impetus to Mexico's power resources came from British and Canadian interests, while United States capital still preferred mining and railroad activities. British-controlled capital accounted for nearly 85 per cent of total foreign investment in electric-power generation and distribution between 1900 and 1910, as compared with 55 per cent in oil, 35 per cent in railroads, and 15 per cent in mining. United States participation was around 5 per cent in public utilities, 40 per cent in oil and railroads, and 60 per cent in mining(3).

In general, there was identity of interests between the electric-power industry developers and foreign investors in other sectors of the quickly expanding Mexican economy. Two of the most important men connected with the new activity already had wide interests in Mexico. Fred Stark Pearson, a Canadian and one of the founders of the Mexican Light & Power Company (operating in the central area of the Republic) was very active in prospecting and mining activities in northern Mexico. Weetman Pearson (later Lord Cowdray), the Briton who built public utilities in the oil-rich states of Puebla and Veracruz, had years of experience as a leading contractor for large public works undertaken by Porfirio Díaz(4).

The personal qualities of such men may explain the speedy arrival and expansion of the electrical age in Mexico. They were aware of the country's potential wealth and of the psychology of the rulers and the ruled. Their access to technology and capital in their home countries was matched by their excellent relations with the governing élites in pre-revolutionary Mexico, whose attitude toward foreign capitalists was one of far-sighted recognition of the benefits they were bringing to the still backward country. The Díaz regime did not discriminate against foreign capitalists, but it also took care of its national followers by freely granting them, under very liberal terms, concessions for the exploitation of hydroelectric power, most of which were rapidly sold to foreign interests. Speculation in these concessions reached enormous proportions at the end of the Porfirian period; they changed hands many times, and their final price was disproportionate to the cost of the other components of public-utility investment in Mexico at the beginning of the century.

Under Díaz the participation of domestic capital in the electric industry dwindled progressively, but the presence of Mexican nationals on the executive boards of the companies increased. This was probably another form of Díaz patronage, accepted and fostered by foreign managers anxious to count on the government's friendly attitude. Although by 1910 some shares in major electric-power companies were probably in the hands of influential Mexicans, the bulk of capital resources for the industry was raised abroad. Up to 1911, more than $60 million in bonds and common and preferred stock were placed in European, Canadian, and United States capital markets with no difficulty, as Mexican projects were thought sound and the abilities of their promoters were well-known.

The real profitability of these investments is controversial. Mexican sources maintain it was enormous from the very beginning, whereas foreign experts express serious doubts. Rippy concludes, for example, that British investment in Mexico 'turned out to be less profitable than in any other major Latin American country, and this was especially true of the capital invested in government bonds, railroads, real estate, and public utilities'(5). It is probable that electric-power investments under Díaz were less profitable than other ventures, but they were also much less risky than, say, mining activities.

This limited profitability was due to the fact that, although the Díaz government never enforced its veto power over rates as set up in the 1894 decree, and companies negotiated their contracts freely with private and institutional consumers under conditions of growing demand, the latter had serious collection problems with municipal authorities, and most of the energy was sold at cut rates to enterprises owned by the same groups that controlled public utilities.

Since these large consumers apparently received preference, small, domestic energy consumers had reason to believe (not only during the Díaz regime but until the post-revolutionary state started regulating activities of electric-power companies in the 1930s) that the Mexican public was subsidizing foreign-owned economic activities.

Consequently, the harmonious and reciprocally satisfactory coexistence of the public utilities and Díaz was spoiled in the final years of the pre-revolutionary period by conflicts between the companies and two classes of consumers whose demand for electric power was growing slowly but steadily: municipalities and small domestic firms. These conflicts first appeared when municipal lighting contracts were renewed and local authorities complained about deficient services and high rates. They received unqualified support from small industrialists and traders who, in fact, were paying the highest electricity rates of all and were being treated as second-class customers by the power companies. In the period 1906-10, these weak domestic entrepreneurial groups were the first to charge openly the 'foreign-owned monopoly' with exploitation of the Mexican consumer. The same language was to be used against foreign public utilities in Mexico thirty years later by Mexico's first nation-wide organization of small and medium-sized industrialists, the Cámara Nacional de la Industria de la Transformacion (CNIT)(6).

Intellectual dissenters soon joined the municipalities and domestic industrialists in their discontent. Andrés Molina Enríquez, an influential writer in the final years of the pre-revolutionary period, suggested, in 1905 and 1906, strengthening water resources legislation, limiting periods of concessions, standardizing tax exemptions, periodic revisions of electricity rates, levying taxes on public-utility companies in proportion to the rate level, and the use of the tax proceeds for subsidizing industrial development and irrigation. He also urged the setting up of a national plan for the utilization of hydraulic resources.

Molina Enríquez' views were echoed from quarters closely related to the científicos surrounding Díaz. Díaz took notice of these signs of discontent and in 1910, shortly before his fall, new water resources legislation was passed which followed Molina Enríquez' ideas of tightening the conditions for granting hydroelectric concessions.

These first signs of hostility were not taken seriously by the foreign companies. They thought that the benevolence and prosperity of the Díaz era could never end in a violent and abrupt manner. Their confidence is shown in that, even after Díaz' fall and the inauguration of Francisco Madero's short-lived government in 1910, the major electric companies continued their expansion policies.

It would be exaggerated to claim that foreign investors brought to Mexico, at the turn of the century, all the blessings of modern civilization, but it would also be unfair to condemn them unreservedly. They came in search of profits on their capital and experience and found and took full advantage of the opportunities afforded by a growing, laissez-faire economy. They came - they thought - to stay forever and, in their own way, they believed in Mexico's future. They made a large contribution to the growth of the country's economic infrastructure which, after the revolutionary upheaval, was to serve as a physical basis for the next stage of Mexico's modernization, coinciding with the international boom of the 1920s.

The revolution of 1910 and its issue of national survival deflected Mexico's attention for fifteen years from such comparatively minor problems as relations between foreign public-utility monopolies and electric-power consumers. But the pattern for further conflict was set. When the revolutionary upheaval ended in the mid-1920s, the private companies and the public resumed their respective roles. But the central government was destined to change its function. The state became first an arbiter between the two opposing groups, then a co-participant in productive activities, and finally - some sixty years after the coming of the electric age to Mexico - the exclusive owner of the electric-power industry.

During the revolutionary period foreign public utilities succeeded, in general, in preventing destruction of their installations. Nevertheless, their losses were substantial, and were made more painful by heavy obligations incurred in expansion and construction programmes begun late in the Díaz regime. Failure to meet bills during the long years of the civil war forced one public utility after another to suspend payments of dividends and service on its bonds and shook confidence abroad. But the owners and managers of the electric-power companies were not ready to give up.

Many Mexican sources confirm the industry's survival. After General Obregón took power in 1921, ambitious construction and expansion programmes were begun, which continued up to the early days of the Great Depression. The companies' optimistic attitude was fostered by the policy announcements of Obregón's successors, which emphasized the need to modernize and consolidate the economy within the new institutional structure, and by the continuance, in the electric-power field, of the laissez-faire conditions prevailing before 1910.

The great political debate surrounding adoption of the new Constitution of 1917 did not affect the electric-power industry. New legislation was passed which included water resources within the property of the nation, assigned jurisdiction over water resources and concessions to the Ministry of Agriculture and Development, and gave the Ministry of Industry and Trade control over technical aspects of the electric industry. But the framework for relations between the private sector and the state continued in force, unmodified. The electric-power companies took full advantage of this favourable situation, and, during the 1920s, the industry probably grew faster than any other sector of the economy. About one-fourth of the population, some 4 million people, became consumers of electric power, a high proportion bearing in mind the poverty of the majority of the country's inhabitants and their sparse distribution over a territory one-third the size of the United States.

The electric-power companies concentrated on expanding their productive facilities to cater to traditional production centres and the bigger urban areas. This attitude provoked discontent among the post-revolutionary Mexican government técnicos and intellectuals, but the complaints of the 1920s still assumed harmonization of the antagonistic interests of the companies and their customers through effective regulation, which should 'combine maximum convenience for the public with the greatest possible protection for the firms'(7).

President Obregón's establishment of the Comisión Nacional de Fuerza Motriz (CNFM), or National Power Commission, in December 1922, was the first real attempt at regulation of the industry(8). It was intended as an advisory body with broad terms of reference. Its founders were well-informed about developments abroad and hence the CNFM was instructed to prepare 'overall estimates of the industrial needs of the country and of the probable future demand for electric power in relation to the present state of development of national water resources'(9).

In operating terms, very little came of this first effort because the new official body faced serious administrative handicaps and the lack of cooperation and hostility of the companies. Yet the contribution of the CNFM to electric-power legislation should not be underestimated, since it drew up the legislation of 1926, which, for the first time, specified a series of general principles to be applied by the government in its relations with public utilities. If by the mid-1920s Mexico lagged behind more industrialized countries in the regulation of its electric-power industry, the decade of revolution was responsible.

Normality returned under President Plutarco Elías Calles (1924-28), and 1925 is considered to be the dividing line between the revolutionary period and Mexico's contemporary history. Though in this year President Calles met with difficult problems, external and internal, the técnicos in his entourage introduced a number of important policy measures, crucial for the future growth of the Mexican economy. Calles was considered abroad as a radical because he insisted on solving mainly agrarian and labour questions - the logical consequence of the revolution. But his conflict with the Church, his statements, and those of his closest collaborators reveal that this was not the case. In 1925, for example, the central bank, the Banco de México, and the national farm credit banking systems were created; the national irrigation commission was established; and a vast programme of public works was launched to improve and expand obsolete and severely damaged transportation and communication systems.

Following these major economic reforms came the adoption of the Código Nacional Eléctrico, or National Electric Code, on 30 April 1926. The CNFM had confirmed complete legal chaos and anarchy in relations between the government and foreign-owned public utilities, and to remedy this, as well as to correct the nature of the companies' behaviour toward their customers, the técnicos suggested legislation intended to fulfil two major purposes: to extend federal control to all stages of hydroelectric power generation and distribution, rather than just to the establishment of new electric plants; and to find a legal formula for federal jurisdiction over thermoelectric plants, which were still operating under state and municipal concessions and franchises.

The National Electric Code included a declaration of principles which would govern the industry and it stated that the power industry itself was to be considered a 'public utility'. Yet this represented only limited progress. No clear precepts were set forth as to how regulation and control would be exercised by the authorities. The vagueness and incoherence of the legislation of 1926 may have been because the Congressional politicians were not aware of legal quibblings and technical problems in relations between the state and the electric-power industry. But political considerations probably counted, for 1926 was a difficult year for Calles. It may well be that the President and his advisers decided not to complicate further their already complicated situation by provoking the foreign-owned public utilities, and left the question open for further study at a more convenient time. Such a decision would also explain in part why enforcement of the 1926 legislation was delayed for more than two years. The final decision in the summer of 1928, to bring some order into relations between the state and the public utilities must have been in response to the appearance of new vocal domestic pressure groups.

This new force consisted mainly of small industrialists and merchants who, for more than a quarter-century, had considered electricity prices unreasonably high. This class had grown in numbers and organized itself by the mid-

1920s, and sooner or later it was bound to find a common issue on which to test its strength. Cheap power was a perfect issue on many counts. First, electricity rates were considered to be exorbitant. Second, despite all the secrecy surrounding company records, the disparity between prices paid by large and small consumers had become widely known. Third, no known substitute for electricity was then available in the country. Fourth, the owners of the industry were foreigners, reputedly harvesting large profits from their operations, who, in addition, had easy access to external financial resources, in contrast with domestic entrepreneurs who were persistently short of investment funds.

The fight for cheap electricity seems to have originated with the textile industry, the biggest single consumer of electric power in the 1920s, with the exception of mining and petroleum(10). In strictly economic terms, the cost of power plays an insignificant role in total production costs for an industry such as textiles, but more than economics was at work here. The bitterness of the industrial-electricity users in Mexico must have been somewhat related to the especially vulnerable position of the foreigner who exercises monopoly power in a highly nationalistic environment. But because overall business was not only good but getting better every year, the companies again did not take the growing signs of dissatisfaction seriously. The generating capacity of all the major systems had increased by about 50 per cent and the behaviour of the companies between 1926 and 1930 was reminiscent of the good old days toward the end of the Porfirian era.

The ownership structure of the industry was changed, however, by a newcomer to Mexico, the United-States controlled American & Foreign Power Company, which brought to the country a large volume of new capital. This company, through the biggest financial operation - $70 million - in the history of Mexican public utilities until the industry's nationalization in 1960, became in 1928-9 the owner of all major generation and transmission facilities in Mexico, outside the Mexico City area. The optimism of this company in respect to the economic future of Latin America is indicated by its acquisition, between 1923 and 1929, of a score of enterprises in eleven different republics. Two reasons are given for these investments: relatively high rates of profitability abroad and threats of increased utility regulation in the United States. The American & Foreign Power Company followed up all expansion plans started under the previous management and immediately set additional programmes in motion. Thus, whereas the Mexican Light & Power Company's (controlled by Canadian and European financial interests) second stage of expansion ended in 1930, the newcomer kept on adding to its generation and distribution facilities for two years more, and in the case of the Puebla-Veracruz system even up to 1935, the year in which the self-financed growth of the private electric-power industry in Mexico was destined to end forever.

Neither the técnicos in the government nor the private power companies foresaw, in the fall of 1928, that the outbreak of the Great Depression would basically alter the nature of the relationship between the state and private enterprise all over the Western world, Mexico included.

The depression had a profound effect on both Mexico's government economic policies and Mexico's power industry, since all sectors of the economy were quickly affected by the developments in the United States and Europe. Mining, manufacturing production, and exports decreased in value and volume and Mexico's gross national product declined sharply. Electricity prices for middle and small consumers, however, did not undergo any change. The reason was, from the power companies' viewpoint, that since the demand for electric power in the mining and metallurgical sectors had suddenly dwindled, their revenue from the sale of electricity to middle and small consumers consequently increased in importance. The consumers, who had complained about the high cost of electricity during the economic recovery of Obregón's and Calles' administrations, felt even more abused now when the rates continued unchanged in spite of overall adverse economic conditions.

The conflict between the electric companies and the consumers and técnicos was coming to a climax. Consumer behaviour became increasingly violent, but the companies were still reluctant to yield to the public clamour for lower rates. The government remained inactive by not providing the means for enforcing existing legislation and abstaining from reform of Article 73 of the Constitution of 1917, without which the electric-power legislation of 1926-28 was on legal quicksand(11). The consumer resistance movement, spurred by foreign ownership of the companies, spread through the country and culminated in the creation, in late 1932, of the Confederación Nacional Defensora de los Servicios Públicos (National Public Service Defense Confederation), a nation-wide organization in which the técnicos and intellectuals joined forces for the first time with small industrial, commercial, and private consumers.

It is not easy to explain the inactivity of the Mexican government in the face of the disputes between consumers and utilities in the years from 1929 to 1932. It only intervened in a few individual cases and when the matter, because of the direct threat of the consumers to power company property, was about to get out of control. The rest of the time the two contenders were left to themselves to solve their problems in their own best way. The radical intellectual élite, however, continued to spur consumers on, using devious routes to keep the wave of protests against foreign-owned public utilities alive. Their main, if not clearly stated, objective was to wrest from the companies privileges inherited from the pre-revolutionary era, and to prevent the extension of company control over the water resources not yet incorporated in the large private generating systems. The técnicos considered that the country itself should control both its exhaustible resources, such as petroleum, and its renewable resources, such as water. If access to this potential wealth could be denied to the companies, either the state or domestic private capital might one day be in a position to exploit these resources for the country's direct benefit.

An opportunity to attain that end was offered by the passing, in August 1929, of a new Ley de Aguas de Propiedad Nacional (National Water Resources Law) which clearly sought to eliminate the possibility of private companies' getting hold of concessions for 'future use', and established a series of limitations all tending to widen state control over water resources. The same legislation defined priorities for the utilization of water resources and put their use by private electric-power companies at the very end of the list.

By the end of 1932 pressures for direct government intervention in the electric-power industry were getting out of hand. It was no longer simply a question of lower rates. A wave of nationalist radicalism had affected the country and undermined the faith of post-revolutionary intellectuals in the feasibility of building the economy along liberal lines with only moderate state intervention. Events abroad, such as the completion of the Soviet first five-year plan, showed to eager observers in Mexico that neither industrialization nor economic development was possible without an abundance of electric power, and that the development of electric power demanded that the problem should be handed over to the state, that is, to the técnicos. Some powerful voices in the United States, heard during the first Franklin D. Roosevelt campaign, lent support to the worst suspicions in Mexico regarding the anti-social behaviour of private electric-power companies all over the world(12).

Political circles now realized that the electricity issue could not be ignored, and President Abelardo Rodríquez, in the annual State of the Union Message on 6 September 1932, stated that the Ministry of Industry and Commerce had already begun to implement that part of the electric-power legislation applicable to its area of jurisdiction, above all in the sphere of rate control. As a result of this action, by the end of 1932, for the first time in the thirty-year history of the Mexican industry, the companies agreed in various localities to cut substantially their prices to medium and small consumers. But since the largest company, Mexican Light & Power, refused to cooperate (arguing that the legislation passed under Calles was unconstitutional), the administration asked Congress to pass an amendment to Article 73 of the Constitution that should expressly mention the electric-power industry as being under the jurisdiction of the federal government.

But all this - the government's actions and the companies' reluctance to admit a reduction of their earnings - was too little and too late for Mexican public opinion. In early 1933 the Confederación Nacional Defensora de los Servicios Públicos, having noted that Congress had delayed action on the constitutional amendment, called for nationalization of the power industry. Its attitude was strengthened by the publication, in March 1933, of Franklin D. Roosevelt's Looking Forward, a book which had a considerable impact in Mexico for it attacked the political power of the United States financial 'trusts', specifically public utilities. By mid-year, President Abelardo Rodríquez made known in an interview that 'in Mexico a project for the nationalization of all free electric-power resources is awaiting Senate approval'(13).

The government seemed finally resolved to act, and in the second half of 1933 things began to happen. The basic programme of the official party (Partido Nacional Revolucionario) outlining the economic policies of the government for the period 1934-39, known as the Plan Sexenal and sanctioned by Calles, the man who still held ultimate power in the country, included a section on the electric-power industry. The industry was declared to be of 'inherent social interest for the national economy' and two basic conditions were set for its development: the supply of electric power, instead of being governed by the companies' profit considerations, should be effected at a price low enough to enable agricultural and industrial enterprise to be developed by electric power; and the distribution system for electric power should branch out through the whole national territory, so that new regional producing centres would be developed and the formation of new industrial agglomerations facilitated.

This plan, ratified by the party in December 1933, added that in order to effect an adequate supply of electricity throughout the country 'the government will look to the formation of a national system of electric-power generation, transportation, and distribution, composed of semi-official enterprises and consumer cooperatives'(14).

That this was not just another declaration of principle is shown by the
following events: a tax on the generation of electric power was introduced;
the automatic five-year exemption from profit taxes for newly established
electric enterprises was rescinded; Article 73 of the Constitution of 1917
was amended to extend federal authority to all phases of the power industry,
including thermoelectric plants; and the President asked and received congressional authority to establish a Comisión Federal de Electricidad (CFE).
This new agency was to study appropriate planning programmes for the national
electrification system; undertake all types of operation connected with the
generation, transformation, and distribution of electrical energy; organize
semi-official regional and local electrical enterprises to produce, transmit,
and distribute electrical power at fair prices; and set up cooperatives of
electricity consumers aimed at supplying it under more favourable terms. In
fact, the CFE was not established until 1937, but the way for the government's
entrance into the electric-power industry had been cleared.

The expansion programme designed in the 1920s were completed by the private
electric companies between 1932 and 1935. Afterward, Mexico's power industry
was semi-stagnant till the end of the Second World War. Something less than
100,000 kWs were added between 1936 and 1945 to the country's total generating capacity of 610,000 kWs. Of this new capacity, the private utility companies created around 30,000 kWs in 1939, and another 40,000 kWs came from
installations set to work by the Comisión Federal de Electricidad (CFE) in
1944 and 1945. The average annual growth rate of the power industry over the
whole 1936-45 period was hardly more than 1 per cent and, as a result, Mexico
faced, by the end of the war, a critical power shortage. The lack of industrial equipment from abroad contributed to this standstill, but the real cause
was the cold war waged between the state and the companies since the mid-
1930s.

The framework for the modern regulation of public utilities in Mexico was set
up shortly before the beginning of the Cárdenas administration (1934-40),
under the pressure of several forces: Calles and his successors, técnicos,
intellectuals, and electric-power consumers. The Cárdenas administration,
which ended the conflict with the international oil companies by expropriating them in March 1938, showed at an early date that it also regarded electricity as a field of great urgency. It instructed the Ministry of National
Economy, the successor of the old Ministry of Industry and Commerce, to draft
an electric energy policy following the precepts of the Plan Sexenal, including a bill to consolidate federal control over the industry and to replace
the National Electric Code of 1926-8. The first draft of the Ley de la
Industria Eléctrica, completed before the end of 1936, was submitted for
comments to the electrical workers' unions, the President's main political
backing at the time, together with the rest of organized labour(15). Neither
this action nor the fact that President Cárdenas had submitted another proposal to the Congress, providing for new regulations on the expropriation of
private property, pleased the foreign-owned companies, for obvious reasons.

In view of earlier conflicts over the interpretation of the constitutional
clauses on federal-owned properties, and in spite of Cárdenas' assurances on
the meaning of the expropriation bill, public utilities executives became
suspicious. Their doubts increased with the rejection by the unions of the
electric-power law as too friendly to management. The expropriation bill,
in the companies' opinion, seemed also to suit everybody but the foreign
interests.

The political scene in 1937 was dominated by land reform and by the increasing dispute between the oil companies and their unionized workers. Land reform led the President to long absences from the capital and, on a trip to Yucatán, whose electric energy facilities were entirely limited to a few major cities, the Comisión Federal de Electricidad (CFE) was finally born. In his decree the President charged the new agency with 'organizing and directing a national system for electric-power generation, transmission, and distribution, based on technical and economic principles, on a non-profit basis, for the purpose of obtaining the greatest possible output at minimum cost, for the benefit of general interest'. The decree gave the CFE extremely broad powers, and as its terms of reference indicated, the fathers of the CFE, a small group of electrical engineers educated abroad, intended to create more than a state-owned electric-power company. Their aim was to set up a centralized agency which would take upon itself the task of the country's electrification and supervise and direct the activities of private companies in the electric field whenever such action was deemed advisable(16).

The establishment of an agency with a ridiculous budget of 50,000 pesos, smaller than the salary earned by a single public-utility executive, did not disturb the electric companies. They were preoccupied with the steady deterioration of the oil conflict and its possible repercussions for other foreign interests in Mexico. In the aftermath of the oil expropriation in the spring of 1938, the utilities officials considered the nationalization at any moment of their own properties a serious possibility. But even when their worry over possible expropriation was dispelled in August 1938, the government did not forget to pursue the goal of electric-power industry regulation.

A new and tightened-up draft of the Ley de la Industria Eléctrica, under discussion since 1936, was considered inimical to the companies' interest in respect to the rate-regulation mechanism and the concept of fair return on investment, points which in the opinion of the utilities executives were not adequately defined. Since the Ministry of National Economy refused to take the companies' viewpoints into consideration, they could only resort to President Cárdenas himself. United States Ambassador Josephus Daniels, upon express instructions from Washington, arranged an interview between Cárdenas and Curtis E. Calder, head of the American & Foreign Power Company, the details of which are unknown. The fact is that, after the Congress had approved a slightly amended Ley de la Industria Eléctrica at the end of 1938, the companies seemed reasonably content.

The law, modified in some respects at the end of 1940, became the basic legislation in the field, designed to control and regulate all aspects of the power industry and to promote its development as well until the industry was nationalized in 1960.

After the law was issued in 1939, the strain between the state and the companies diminished, and the latter responded to the growing demand for electricity by making minor additions to their generating capacity and distribution systems in the country. The year 1939 was the only one in the 1936-46 period in which the two large companies, Mexican Light & Power and American & Foreign Power, made new although small investments. Their expansion plans were abruptly suspended, however, when the first practical results of the new legislation became evident in 1940. Although the Deputy Minister of National Economy readily granted, in the late summer 1939, certain increases in rates asked for by Mexican Light & Power after the publication of the electric industry law, they were suspended a few months later on order from the President, demonstrating that rate-setting was, and would continue to be, governed by political as well as economic criteria.

Another six months and a change of administration were required for MEXLIGHT to get a reversal of the suspension and a rate increase of about 30 per cent. These increases were tied, however, to the condition of investing the additional proceeds in the expansion of generating facilities in Mexico City. By now, the relations between the state and the electric companies had been utterly damaged. The 1939-40 incident confirmed the latter's suspicions that there was 'a deliberate governmental policy to keep rates down, so that the federal authorities could eventually nationalize all the foreign private power interests'(17). On the other hand, government circles and large sectors of public opinion regarded the dispute as another proof that the companies' sole aim was to drain the country of its wealth by exacting exorbitant yields.

Meanwhile, the CFE was expanding its operations. Its budget was increased, first by bigger federal appropriations, then by additional proceeds from a special 10 per cent tax on the consumption of electric energy all over the country. The CFE undertook two immediate tasks: the construction of small plants in outlying areas devoid of electric-power facilities, and the development of the biggest untapped reserves of hydroelectric power in central Mexico, where in the early 1930s unexploited concessions had been rescinded. In 1944, the first major unit of the new facilities was inaugurated, and by the end of 1945 the CFE had a generating capacity of close to 50,000 kWs.

The second six-year economic plan, worked out in 1940 by the técnicos for the period 1941-46, was much more concrete with respect to the country's electrification needs than Plan Sexenal of 1934 had been. It provided for federal intervention in this field through:

(1) executing new electric-power projects in order to complete the national electrification programme;
(2) giving priority for generating facilities that would serve the greatest number of inhabitants per unit of investment;
(3) continuing study of the demand for electricity in the various regions so as to undertake necessary projects in the event these were not opportunely taken care of by private enterprises; and
(4) mobilizing budgetary resources, private savings, and all other means of financing to promote the country's electrification.

The CFE entered the 1940s in a setting which appeared to its directors particularly propitious for government-produced electric power. The five large systems owned by foreign interests had ceased to grow and, since they were not servicing new customers, they were restricting the electric-power supply. One of them, Compañía Hidroeléctrica de Chapala, serving Guadalajara, the second biggest industrial centre in Mexico, went bankrupt and was bought by the federal government from its United States owners in 1940.

The future industrial development of the country was seriously endangered. Since private companies abstained from new investment projects, the solution, as the técnicos saw it, was to mobilize domestic resources to finance an expansion of facilities to cope with deferred and expected demand. If private savings were not forthcoming they proposed to use those of the public sector supplemented by official external borrowing, presumably from United States government sources. Since domestic private savings were not attracted to this particular activity, the CFE felt itself to be the logical choice as the agency to conduct the national electrification programme. The CFE, however, though long on plans was short of funds until the mid-1940s. As a result, well before the end of the Second World War, serious shortages of electric power appeared all over the country, and by late 1945 they were so bad that the government had to seek emergency technical help from foreign engineers.

One of the papers drawn up in 1946 in connection with this foreign mission, by a Mexican government official, Oscar R. Enríquez (Director of the Bureau of Electricity in the Ministry of National Economy), after having analysed the relations between the state and the private companies from the early 1930s until the end of the war, came to the conclusion that

> . . . most of the blame for the present state of Mexico's electrical services rests on the authorities and officials who did not have sufficient foresight to measure and accurately evaluate the effects that the issuance of measures to control and regulate foreign firms would be likely to have on the nation(18).

It may be asked whether the problem was really that simple. Neither the state nor the private electric companies was the free agent they thought they were. The inability of each side, with its own vested interests, to fulfil the other's demands was only part of the picture. Additional complicating elements were the lack of government experience in the regulatory field and the traditional characteristics of the Mexican legislative structure, which confered broad discretionary powers on individual high officials.

Under normal conditions the regulation of private economic activities amounts to seeking a reasonable compromise between the conflicting interests of society and the private entrepreneur. Since the conditions under which the electric industry functioned in Mexico in the 1930s and 1940s were abnormal in the extreme, no reasonable compromise could have been reached. Even if the government had foreseen the companies' refusal to invest and had tried to do something about it, it was powerless to do so. Neither domestic private capital nor budgetary resources were available for the country's electrification. The concept of foreign developmental aid had not yet emerged, and international financial institutions did not exist. Consequently, during the Second World War Mexico could do little more than stand and watch the stagnation of her electric-power industry while her *técnicos* were drawing ambitious plans for the future. But, thanks to the establishment of the Comisión Federal de Electricidad in 1937, Mexico, at the end of the war, unlike most other Latin American republics, no longer had to rely solely on foreign-owned companies for an adequate supply of electrical energy.

After 1945 there was a great and sustained expansion of electric-power generation and distribution facilities in Mexico, the modernization of which brought electricity not only to urban centres but also to many outlying areas. Between 1945 and 1960, the installed electric-power capacity increased from 700,000 kWs to about 3 million. Annual power generation increased in the same period from 3.1 billion to 10.8 billion kWhs. This growth greatly reduced the relative importance of foreign-owned companies. Between 1945 and 1960, the CFE added more than 1 million kWs to its initial capacity of less than 50,000 kWs. The two large foreign companies, Mexican Light & Power and American & Foreign Power, increased their capacity by about 500,000 kWs. The rest of the industry contributed an additional 700,000 kWs. In 1945 the two foreign private companies had controlled 60 per cent of the total installed capacity; the CFE had accounted for 5 per cent; and the rest of the industry 35 per cent. By 1960 the CFE controlled about 40 per cent of total capacity; the two foreign companies together around 33 per cent; and the other service plants about 27 per cent.

In money terms, it can be estimated that of the total 1945-60 investment in the electric-power industry selling to the public, a little more than two-thirds (about US $100 million) was mobilized by the state-owned sector, and the rest (less than $200 million) by the two foreign private companies. The basic post-war change in the structure of ownership of installed capacity was not followed by similar changes in power distribution. The explanation lies in a working agreement between the state and the private power companies, whereby the CFE plants served the private companies first. From the inauguration of the first major CFE generating plant in 1944 until 1959, the energy purchases of the two foreign companies from the commission averaged 75 per cent of the commission's annual output.

Between 1945 and 1960 electric-energy consumption in Mexico increased at nearly 11 per cent a year, a rate almost double that of the increase in the gross national product. The diversification of the economy and the shifts in the location of certain economic activities ostensibly affected the pattern of power demand. Also, changes in the pattern of industrial power consumption proved that Mexican industrialization was progressing on all fronts. In 1945 the manufacture of capital goods absorbed only 30 per cent of the power bought by the industrial sector as against 70 per cent used in the manufacture of consumer goods. Fifteen years later these proportions were reversed. By 1960 the chemical industry alone accounted for one-fifth of the energy consumed by Mexico's industrial activities.

The expansion programmes were seriously limited in this period by the inability of the power industry as a whole to make profits and to mobilize additional resources in the domestic and private capital markets. In the case of the CFE, growth depended upon the availability of federal funds and upon the willingness of the World Bank to lend. The private electric-power companies also depended on the good will of Mexican and foreign credit institutions. When in the late 1950s these institutions started to reconsider their policies toward the private electric-power enterprises and, at the same time, the state was compelled to adopt more conservative financial and monetary policies, overall expansion of the industry slowed down perceptibly until the private companies were bought out by the state and rate policies were completely revised.

Although relations between the state and the private power companies under Miguel Alemán's administration (1946-52) were probably better than at any other time, the great impulse given the electricity industry in that period was mainly due to the government's willingness to provide ample financial support for all developmental activities, electrification included, without any very great regard for internal monetary stability or the balance-of-payments position. But Alemán's successor, Adolfo Ruíz Cortines (1952-85), had to swing the pendulum back and follow austere monetary and financial policies as a means of fighting inflationary pressures without bringing the country's economic development to a standstill. The success of such policies depended upon putting many economic activities vital to development - including the electric-power industry - on a more self-sustaining basis, with a view to reducing their growing dependence upon external and domestic credit.

The electric-power industry was obviously one of the first candidates for such reorganization, especially as the government had learned (through experience acquired by the CFE) that sustained expansion of electric-power facilities demanded very heavy investment, much greater than the state itself could handle. Therefore, in October 1953 a Comité para el Estudio de la Industria Eléctrica Mexicana was established, composed of officials drawn from the various governmental agencies concerned. This group, known as CEE/MEX, was instructed to study ways and means of financing the country's electrification and to present the federal authorities with a programme for action aimed at putting the electric-power industry on a sounder financial footing and bringing a greater measure of order to relations between the public and private enterprises operating in this field.

It took this mission about four years to fulfil its task, but the proposals of its very competent report have never been put into effect(19). That report confirmed what interested parties had intuitively known all the time: that legislation related to financial aspects of the electric-power industry, though effective for other countries, did not suit Mexico's needs and endangered the future of the industry. The committee considered that the state could not finance the industry's expansion and assumed that the adoption of some measures - a revision of legislation, an increase of electricity rates, and the improvement of the financial structure of the companies - would remove obstacles to mobilizing resources elsewhere. It affirmed that the necessary funds should be sought by raising new domestic private capital, by reinvesting profits, and by securing foreign loans. All this would be achieved by giving due assurances, in the financial and policy fields, to all segments of the industry, state-owned enterprises included. New legislation would have to be drawn up with the greatest possible clarity, and regulatory control of the whole power industry should be given to a new autonomous agency.

The CEE/MEX report produced a few secondary improvements in the relations between the state and the private power companies, helped to reorganize the American & Foreign Power properties under Mexican corporate law, and introduced some order into the companies' accounting procedures. But the report was somewhat naive in its discussion of the many non-economic factors largely responsible for the uneasy relations between the state and the foreign-owned utilities, and its recommendations were too dangerous to follow, from the official point of view. It suggested, for instance, that the CFE should be deprived of what the CFE itself and large sectors of public opinion considered one of the agency's most important *raisons d'être*: the function of planning, coordinating, and implementing national electrification programmes and policies. Nobody would have expected that the CFE give up those powers and accept the resurgence of the private companies as powerful and threatening competitors.

The sworn enemies of foreign-owned utilities, formerly the coalition of consumers, *técnicos* and other intellectuals, and trade unions, were now led by a newly organized class of smaller industrialists, grouped around the Cámara nacional de la Industria de Transformación (CNIT), with considerable political influence. The two CNIT slogans in the nationalistic battle against foreign capital were 'cheap power for national industry', and 'electric power development by the state'. The group was politically motivated and its thesis, presented at its annual meetings and in numerous publications, expressed the conviction that the interests of the Mexican state, industrialists, and individual consumers were constantly sacrificed for the benefit of a small group of foreign monopoly capitalists. The CNIT advisers insisted that the consumers should be given a voice, through CNIT, in the industry regulation, and in a revision of rates so that rich consumers would subsidize industry and the poorer classes. The more radical members of the CNIT called for immediate confiscation of the private companies' property, arguing that their profits over the years exceeded many times the initial investment. In its campaign against the private companies, the CNIT indicated that the power industry should also help the development of the country by buying its capital equipment and supplies in Mexico, which should, in turn, build a heavy electrical equipment industry.

The companies responded to these attacks by attempting to exert direct pressure upon the regulatory agencies and the higher government officials and by lobbying in Washington, where external credits were negotiated. They also brought very prominent Mexican and foreign personalities into their boards of directors, but these measures provided the companies' enemies in Mexico with highly effective political ammunition and contributed to creating resentment within the government itself.

By the late 1950s it became clear that the recommendations of the long-awaited CEE/MEX would not be acted upon. After the World Bank granted to Mexico in 1958 large foreign credit for power expansion, it became widely known that the CFE was preparing a new loan application for a still larger sum to finance its 1959-65 programme. Though well-informed people reported from Washington that international and United States agencies would demand that any new loans should be contingent upon the complete revision of the rate structure, government action in this field was not forthcoming. The process of periodic adjustment dragged along as before, and the state and the foreign-owned companies had come to a total impasse.

It was at that moment, according to a well-informed observer, that 'the big power companies seriously began to think in terms of selling out everything to the Mexican government, provided a fair sale value would be agreed upon' (20).

The nationalization - or 'mexicanization' as Mexicans like to call it - of the two major private companies was consummated peacefully between the spring and fall of 1960. It consisted of two separate financial operations, involving the transfer of property with a book value of $400 million. Later, in 1961, the government bought out the remaining privately-owned generating systems of marginal importance.

The first of the two major decisions came in April 1960, when the government acquired all the properties of the American & Foreign Power Company for a price of $65 million. At the same time, Nacional Financiera, the official development bank which took over the administration of the acquired properties, assumed all outstanding debts of the American & Foreign Power subsidiaries amounting to $34 million. The purchase price was in essence the same as the value which previously had been approved by the authorities as a basis for rate-making. The contract of sale stipulated a down payment of $5 million and the rest, including payment for constructions underway, was made payable in Nacional Financiera dollar obligations guaranteed by the government, maturing semi-annually over a period of fifteen years, and carrying an interest rate of 6½ per cent tax free. American & Foreign Power Company agreed to reinvest in Mexico in non-utility enterprises the amounts received from these Nacional Financiera obligations as they came due. A new

Mexican investment company, owned by American & Foreign Power, was established after the conclusion of the transaction, and between 1960 and 1965 made sizeable investments in various Mexican industries.

In the late summer of 1960 the properties of the Mexican Light & Power Company changed hands, but in a different way. By agreement, the government purchased directly from the Belgian holding company, Sofina, and from individual investors 90 per cent of the outstanding MEXLIGHT shares for a total of $52 million. This was a price somewhat higher than the stock-exchange quotations before the beginning of the negotiations. Besides, the Mexican government assumed the MEXLIGHT medium- and long-term debt amounting to $78 million. The government's initial cash outlays in both of these huge transactions were financed out of a loan granted to Mexico in March 1960 by the Prudential Insurance Company of America, the first long-term credit since the Porfirian era granted by a private, foreign financial institution without any conditions attached to its use.

The purchase of the two power companies was acclaimed in Mexico as a step comparable only to the land reform of the early revolution and the expropriation of the oil industry by Cárdenas in 1938. The President of the Republic himself, Adolfo López Mateos, set the tone of these national festivities in his 1960 State of the Union Message to Congress, declaring that the policy followed was directed 'to assure that the generation, transformation, and supply of electric power will be carried out by governmental institutions, organs of the Nation, through which, as always, the Mexican people - as ultimate authority - will be present', and that no harm had been done to any legitimate rights or interests. The companies themselves hailed the transfer as a fair, just, and equitable deal, though Mexican Light & Power executives explained their decision as a sheer necessity.

Very little has been officially revealed about the considerations which led to nationalization, but there is some evidence that the initiative came from the foreign utilities themselves. In the case of American & Foreign Power the move had been contemplated in the early 1950s, and some executives of the company went to Mexico in March 1960 with an offer to negotiate the sale of its properties to the Mexican government, since the company's problems and difficulties in the whole Latin American region seemed to be growing to unmanageable proportions. Those executives probably shared the view expressed in a leading United States utility journal in mid-1960, that 'it was believed in many quarters that in due time about all electric power supply will be government-owned and operated south of the Río Grande and as far as Punta Arenas'(21).

Though the power companies claimed that the federal government had planned for years to take over the industry, and though minority parties of the extreme left included in their election platform of 1957-8 a call for the industry's nationalization, and the left-wing of the official Partido Revolucionario Institutional asked at that time for the elaboration of plans for eventually taking over the public utilities by the state, neither the presidential candidate nor the official platform itself ever raised this issue in the 1958 campaign. These attitudes did not change even after the purchase of American & Foreign Power, and the handling of the negotiations indicates that the authorities wanted to keep the matter outside the political context, all of which suggests that the transaction involving American & Foreign Power properties was a fairly spontaneous deal in which the interests of both parties coincided for different, but mainly economic, reasons.

It is probable that after this operation the government realized that it might be convenient, both on economic and political grounds, to solve the remaining part of the problem by buying out Mexican Light & Power. This concern was apparently taken by surprise, as its overall position in Latin America was better than that of American & Foreign Power. Though MEXLIGHT executives acted as if nothing had happened, they evidently were impressed with the government's reasonable behaviour in the earlier transaction. The government, meanwhile, came under certain pressures because of events beyond the control of anyone in Mexico. These events had to do with Cuba.

In the summer of 1960 Mexico was dragged into the crossfire of the United States-Cuban conflict as a result of the seizure of Western-owned oil refineries by the Castro government and United States retaliation cancelling the Cuban sugar quota. The United States measures were interpreted as a sign that Washington was getting tough with Cuba, and not only on the Mexican left, but in the governing party as well, the opinion prevailed that the Cuban regime was being persecuted mainly on account of its hostility toward powerful private foreign interests. That attitude reminded many Mexicans of their own country's conflict with the oil companies in 1938, and voices were heard from influential figures in the Mexican Congress to the effect that in these difficult times Mexico's duty was to stand by Cuba. These statements, interpreted by conservative elements in the country as a sign of an official turn to the left, shook the country and threatened the political equilibrium dexterously fostered by successive presidents ever since the end of the Cárdenas administration. There were moments, in the summer of 1960, in which the situation was getting out of hand and seemed to be leading toward the polarization of political forces in Mexico into two blocs led respectively by pro-Cuban radicals and anti-Cuban conservatives.

At this juncture the situation seemed to demand the restoration of national unity around a bi-partisan issue. Nationalization of the electric-power industry provided that issue. The favourable reaction to nationalization by the major political groups from the extreme left to the extreme right vindicated the government's expectation. After the financial operation the image of national unity reappeared.

According to the statements of Finance Minister Antonio Ortiz Medina on taking over the Mexican Light and Power properties, the nationalization of the industry had been dictated by a number of considerations, but official declarations neither specified any details of the future structure of the integrated industry nor threw any light upon the role of the CFE in the new setup(22). In any case, nationalization did not lead to a sudden disappearance of past problems, nor did it bring a new unity of interest among government, labour, and consumers. It created a new conflict.

After 1960, the government had to cope with the tendency of the técnicos within the CFE to create a state within the state. Also the merger of the three separate electrical-workers unions into one, just as the integration of the industry itself, has been held in abeyance by political considerations. At the time of nationalization the electrical unions were organized in three separate sectors embracing respectively the major segments of the industry: Mexican Light & Power, American & Foreign Power, and the CFE. Through their political role and influence the unions had received from the foreign power companies wages and benefits unknown in other industries. In view of the fact that 'the industry now belonged to the nation', the unions made radical demands in 1960 for large increases in wages and fringe benefits, and workers' participation in the industry. All these suggestions were flatly rejected as demagogic outbursts of irresponsible union leaders. 'The government did not purchase the electric companies . . . in order to turn them over to the workers', said a Mexico City newspaper report in September 1960(23). When the pressure of union leaders did not yield, managers of the nationalized enterprises took a tougher line, warning workers not to expect any more in the future than existing legislation demanded. The new collective contract negotiations between the nationalized Mexican Light & Power and the Sindicato Mexicano de Electricistas in 1961 were scarcely different from the previous bitter negotiations with foreign management. Mutual recriminations and accusations were uttered and the final settlement was reached through the intervention of the Ministry of Labour. As a result the idea of the labour unification was dropped.

But one of the most important problems confronting the industry found solution within a little more than a year after nationalization. A special committee set up to study the financial implications of nationalization submitted its recommendations in late 1961 about rate changes, and in early 1962, the spokesmen for business, labour, and consumers declared them just, necessary, and unavoidable. In mid-January 1962, the system of rates was completely revised along the lines recommended by the special committee, and the government managed to do for itself what it could not allow the private companies to do, that is, to increase the overall level of rates(24). This upward readjustment of rates reopened to Mexico the door to external public borrowing for electrification. Less than half a year after the new rate schedules were put into effect, the World Bank granted Mexico the equivalent of $130 million to finance foreign exchange expenditures on a four-year investment plan worked out by CFE técnicos for the whole industry. With the use of these external funds and the industry's savings, some 1,400,000 kWs were added to the generating capacity all over the country between 1963 and 1965.

The problem of reorganization of the structure of the state-owned industry, still composed of three separate enterprises, was not raised until March 1965. Then, a few months after the inauguration of the Díaz Ordaz administration, a number of technical committees was set up by CFE with the participation of experts of two other companies 'mexicanized' in 1960 for the express purpose of unifying accounting procedures, standardizing technical norms, and coordinating construction and operation programmes. The official announcement carefully abstained from creating the impression that the work of technical committees represented a step toward establishing a national electric-power authority, although it was known that official legal experts were working on the first drafts of a new federal electric-industry law which would replace legislation still in force and dating from 1938. According to press reports previous to the establishment of the working groups by the CFE, technical studies calling for the interconnection of the eleven existing major electric-power producing systems, all belonging to the state and managed by three enterprises, had been terminated and the national electric-power grid was to be established before 1970 with financial support from the World Bank.

The state met the challenge of nationalization with the astuteness characteristic of seasoned politicians. The Mexican government could possibly have arranged the transaction with the two companies on much more favourable terms, but such a saving might have been costly to Mexico in terms of future hostility on the part of foreign business interests. Insofar as Mexico's liberal attitude toward the companies contributed to confidence in the country's political and economic future among foreign investors and in international circles, the price paid was well justified. Access to international financing resources was restored and the basis for future expansion of electric-power facilities vital for Mexico's sustained growth was assured.

The relations between the state and the private power companies witnessed several phases which gradually brought about encroachment on the 'sovereignty' of the companies and ascendancy of the public sector in the field. Starting with the 1930s, when public-utility regulation was first introduced into Mexico, all interested parties considered their mutual relations as a state of warfare. Therefore, while a large part of Mexican opinion was convinced that the nationalization of 1960 was the inevitable outcome of the battle with the companies, the latter regarded it as the final step of capitulation to a government long determined on taking over the industry.

Historical evidence does not support either of these opposite views. Nationalization was a logical solution to the impasse reached in the electric-power industry in the post-war period, but the reasons for it were more complex than the contending parties realized. Whereas their mutually hostile relations were dictated by factors beyond their control, the efforts at reaching compromise would have been successful only if two conditions could have been fulfilled: that the regulation of the utilities in Mexico could have been applied effectively and rationally; and that the long-term objectives of the private companies had coincided with the state's economic development targets.

The first difficulty in the field of utility regulation arose because such regulation is a highly complex legal and administrative process which could not be applied efficiently in Mexico, for it was patterned after the legislation in force in more advanced countries and did not suit Mexico's institutional traditions. The second, and even more important, difficulty stemmed from the impossibility of reconciling the companies' objective of getting maximum profits with the government's development goals, among which the country's electrification had a very high priority.

Looking back, it seems evident that the Mexican government could not allow foreign companies to adjust their rates upward considering their monopoly position and the formidable strength of Mexican nationalism. Nor was it possible to adjust rate revisions on a regional scale to conform to national development interests. The companies, in view of such a situation, refused to invest outside the traditional centres of demand for electric power. But the state was also aware of the importance of electrification for the country's development and had to expand power generation and distribution all over the country. Therefore, by mid-1960 the only way out of the impasse, from the point of view of Mexico's long-term interest, was to put the whole electric-power industry under direct government control. In this way, the relations between the state and the private electric-power industry ended the sixty-five-year presence of foreign-owned electric companies in Mexico.

NOTES

(1) For background, see J. Fred Rippy _Latin America and the Industrial Age_, New York, 1944, pp. 208-17; and James S. Carson, 'The Power Industry', in _Industrialization of Latin America_, edited by Lloyd J. Hughlett, New York, 1946, pp. 319-45. For U.S. investment data, see Melville J. Ulmer, _Capital_

in Transportation, Communications, and Public Utilities: Its Formation and Financing, Princeton, 1960, p. 548. Mexican figures are my own estimates.

(2) This essay is implicitly restricted to the hydroelectric-power industry because throughout the history of Mexico, thermal plants were of marginal importance in view of scarcity of coal. Except in the 1940s, when a limited number of thermal plants using petroleum fuel was constructed for servicing some major urban areas, thermal power has been limited to small plants built by industrial enterprises for their own use. In all such cases no issue of the relations between the state and the electric-power industry has ever occurred and consequently the author has left this subject untouched as beyond the scope of his main subject.

(3) Based upon estimates in the forthcoming volume on economic conditions during the Díaz era, in the series Historia moderna de México, edited by Daniel Cosío Villegas.

(4) J.A. Spender, Weetman Pearson, First Viscount Cowdray, 1956-1927, London, 1930.

(5) J. Fred Rippy, British Investments in Latin America, 1822-1949, Minneapolis, 1959, p. 47.

(6) Over the long stretch of time (especially in the inter-war period), in which the issue of 'low'prices for export-oriented mining and other activities versus 'high' prices for domestically-owned industrial enterprises and electricity used for household consumption, was an explosive political issue, no data were disclosed by the private power companies about their rate structure. Since rates were not effectively controlled by the state before 1938 and the setting of rates was considered the private matter of the power companies, they did not consider it mandatory to disclose details of the rate-fixing process. Consequently, no meaningful comparisons can be made with contemporaneous rates in the United States or other countries without additional painstaking research in the companies' records which are unavailable to outsiders. The companies' secrecy in this and other respects was one of the major points of friction between the state and the consumers, on the one hand, and the companies, on the other, for about one-quarter of a century. It is estimated that in the late 1920s and the early 1930s the disparity between prices of electric power paid by large mining and industrial consumers and those charged to commercial establishments, small industrial plants, and domestic consumers, ranged from 1 to 15, to 1 to 25. In the 1950s it was about 1 to 5.

(7) Comision Nacional de Fuerza Motriz: su organización, labores y tendencias, Pamphlet published by that official commission, México, 1924, p. 21.

(8) CNFM was set up as a permanent advisory body functioning as an agency at the two ministries, Agricultura y Fomento and Industria y Comercio, and was composed of public officials.

(9) Comisión Nacional de Fuerza Motriz, op. cit., p. 33.

(10) Before the 1910 revolution, more than half of the total energy sold was being used by mining and industrial enterprises which were owned in many cases by the same groups that controlled public utilities, and about one-third by public-lighting services, the rest being consumed by commerce and households.

The growing Mexican-owned textile industry took, by the mid-1920s, an increasing share of the consumption of electric energy for industrial, including mining, purposes.

(11) Article 73 limited Congress' authority in economic matters to mining, commerce, credit institutions, general means of communications, postal services, and water resources. Consequently, the only legal faculty in respect to the electric-power industry which the federal government had was that of issuing concessions for the use of water resources for the generation of electricity. Since the early 1920s, Mexican técnicos had insisted that because of the importance of electric power for economic development the scope of Article 73 should be extended by explicit inclusion of that industry among activities regulated by the state. The implementation of the National Electric Code of 1926 and the legislation of 1929 strengthening state control over national water resources ran into serious difficulties because the power companies claimed that both laws were unconstitutional. The Constitution was not amended accordingly until late 1933 because of domestic religious strife and external difficulties faced by Mexico under Calles, who held effective political power in the country from 1925 to early 1935, although his presidential period ended in 1928.

(12) Details of the Roosevelt power and utilities programme pursued during his governorship of the State of New York and his strong criticisms of the U.S. private power companies' behaviour, expressed during his 1932 presidential campaign (in speeches like the one made in Portland, Oregon on 21 September of that year), were reported extensively by the Mexican press and followed closely by técnicos.

(13) Interview granted to Ezequiel Padilla and published in El Economista, Mexico City, 10 August 1933.

(14) Plan Sexenal del Partido Nacional Revolucionario, 1934-9, quoted in Rodolfo Ortega Mata, Problemas económicos de la industria eléctrica, México, 1939, pp. 135-6.

(15) The first labour union in the electric industry was organized in 1914 at the height of revolutionary strife and by the mid-1920s the electrical workers were compactly organized in Sindicato Mexicano de Electricistas (SME). Until the early 1930s, the union was aloof from other labour organizations and denied its support to politically inspired labour activities during the Calles administration. From 1932 on, however, SME became one of the most aggressive labour unions in the country and went on long strikes against the power companies on the occasion of subsequent revisions of the collective work contracts and thus provoked Calles' open enmity. In mid-1935, during the conflict between President Cárdenas and ex-President Calles, which terminated in the expulsion of the latter from the country, SME threw its weight together with oil workers and with the rest of organized labour behind Cárdenas and was rewarded with the President's benevolent attitude during the rest of his administration. In the 1940s, a split in SME ranks and the appearance of Comisión Federal de Electricidad, whose labour was organized in the separate Sindicato de Trabajadores Electricistas de la República Mexicana (STERM), established a pattern dividing electrical workers into three separate unions.

(16) 'Ley que crea la Comisión Federal de Electricidad', Diario Oficial, 24 August 1937.

(17) Wolfangel, 'The History and Development of Private Electric Power Interests in Mexico', p. 80.

(18) Oscar R. Enríquez, 'Informe preliminar sobre la movilización de obras e instalaciones eléctricas existentes en México', Mimeographed report, Secretaria de Economia Nacional, November 1946.

(19) Comité para el Estudio de la Industria Eléctrica Mexicana (CEE/MEX), Desarrollo de la industria eléctrica mexicana, Mimeo, México, 1957.

(20) Wolfangel, op. cit., p. 68.

(21) Herbert Bratter, 'Latin American Utilities' Nationalization Proceeds Inexorably', Public Utilities Fortnightly (7 July 1960), pp. 1-15.

(22) In a speech in his capacity as new chairman of the board of the former MEXLIGHT on 27 September 1960, published in full in the Mexico City press the next day, Ortiz Medina cited increased demand for service and the lack of plans by the private companies to expand and a desire to end public-private controversies within the industry.

(23) Jorge, Davo Lozano, 'Problemas conexos a la nacionalización de la industria eléctrica de México', Excelsior, 8 September 1960.

(24) In early 1965 another considerable rate increase was introduced without any publicity whatsoever.

CHAPTER 5

The Consequences of Scientific and Technological Underdevelopment*

THE HISTORY of the economic development of industrialized countries shows that their present wealth and social welfare are due to a considerable extent to the longstanding support given both by the state and the private sector to education at all levels and to scientific and technological research. Moreover, students of the development process argue that countries which have entered the process of modern economic development relatively late have an advantage over those which started the industrial revolution between 1770 and 1870, since they can make immediate use not only of the scientific and technological knowledge accumulated over generations but also have access to the most recent advances. Furthermore, some social scientists claim that 'economic miracles' of the post-war period in both West and East Germany and in Japan were the result of the physical destruction, during the Second World War, of their antiquated productive and technological capacity, so that these had to be replaced by more modern structures of production. The schools of thought which consider that late entry into the modern process of development offers more advantages than disadvantages seem to accurately describe the experiences of the advanced countries. However, these theories do not fit the countries which have started the process of industrial development only very recently, such as Mexico whose modernization of productive structures has taken place only in the last forty years.

The difficulties which these semi-developed countries face in the transfer, adaptation and domestic diffusion of the results of scientific and technological progress accumulated throughout the world since the first industrial revolution indicate that the external availability of science and technology may be less important than such factors as domestic conditions adequate for the incorporation of foreign scientific and technological knowledge and the patterns of control of such knowledge in the advanced countries. In cases where the underdeveloped late entrants into industrialization are unable to or do not want to change socio-political attitudes inherited from their pre-industrial past, they are left defenceless - so to speak - against the

---
*This essay was published originally in Spanish in Miguel S. Wionczek (Editor), Presente y Futuro de la Sociedad Mexicana, Disyuntivas Sociales, Vol. II. México, Sep. Setentas, 1971, No. 5.

scientific and technological revolution taking place outside their borders.
Not only do they find it impossible to use modern science and technology for
their own development and modernization, but what is worse, in many cases
they are still acquiring through commercial channels inadequate or superfluous
foreign technology which increases rather than decreases their dependency.

Mexico's case is perhaps especially instructive. Anyone who has even a little
knowledge of the intellectual, scientific and technological history of Mexico
from the end of the colonial period to the beginning of the twentieth century
would hardly accept the notion that during that long period Mexico was a
'barbarian' country totally separated from the scientific and technological
advancement of Western Europe and the United States. In fact, in the last
decades of the colonial period and the first decades of independence, scientific and technological life in Mexico was not very different from that of
many countries on both sides of the North Atlantic.

In terms of degree of intellectual excellency, the scientific and technological élites of Mexico during that time were only surpassed by the two dominant
European societies - the British and the French - and were comparable to the
Spanish, Italian and even North American élites. When the history of science
and technology in nineteenth century Mexico is written, it will be discovered
that between 1780 and 1850 the country participated actively in the absorption
of scientific, technological and intellectual innovations from the rest of
the world, with a time-lag of some twenty years. Scientific activity is
evident from the scientific periodicals which appeared during the first half
of the last century in Mexico. The level of these journals has not been surpassed until recently.

The fact that Mexico was not technologically underdeveloped during the last
century in terms of access to relevant information is also evident from the
wealth of official reports of the time as well as from the literature on what
was then called 'material improvements'. This literature was a vehicle for
transmitting European and North American technological advances. Although
it is true that Mexican science and technology and the processes of scientific
and technological transfer from abroad were carried out in certain selected
fields, it may seem strange that in a country which was, socially backward,
and politically extremely conservative, as was Mexico before the revolution,
very considerable importance was given to science and technology. Whether or
not that knowledge was usefully applied is another story. But it is relevant
to note that at the end of the great popular upheaval the importance of science
and technology was downgraded for reasons still to be explained(1).

Between 1925 and recent years the potential benefit of science and technology
to the socio-economic development of Mexico was given very low priority.
This emerges from a survey of state and private financial resources spent in
this field and from a calculation of the human resources with a significant
scientific and technological background available in a country with a population of over 60 million. According to a survey carried out in 1965 by the
Academia de Investigación Científica, in that year Mexico only had 200 people
dedicated to pure science and approximately 1200 full-time technological
researchers(2).

Since a comparison between Mexico and those countries leading in scientific
and technological advances may seem unfair, one should compare Mexico with
other semi-developed countries. The results still do not seem impressive.
The number of people involved in scientific and technological effort in Mexico

is smaller – in relative and sometimes absolute terms – than in many other Latin American countries. For example, in 1967 the Mexican scientific and technological community had only published fourteen scientific books abroad, which puts the country in the category of Portugal and Bulgaria and behind Argentina and Brazil.

Until a few years ago Mexican society was not even aware of its scientific and technological backwardness. Very few people were aware of the urgent need to formulate a national scientific and technological policy and it was commonly thought that the problems of underdevelopment in these fields would more or less solve themselves automatically with the import of foreign technology available to the north of the Rio Bravo. The answer offered to those few people who were concerned at this state of affairs was that even though scientific and technological production in Mexico was small and disorganized, this situation was offset by the fact that Mexican scientists and technologists were immune to the 'brain-drain' which hampered other underdeveloped societies where efforts to create a scientific and technological structure were much greater. It was also pointed out that, with or without science and technology, the Mexican economy continued to grow at an incredibly high rate. The optimists or the unconcerned forgot that the absence of a 'brain-drain' did not reflect the idiosyncrasy of the Mexican who supposedly cannot live outside his country, but that it was rather a result of the deficiency at all levels of the educational system. Following the improvement in recent years of the training of local scientists and technologists inside the country and abroad, the 'brain-drain', especially in the case of the pure science, reached considerable proportions.

The impressive quantitative economic growth registered in Mexico, in contrast to the limited supply of scientists and technologists, and the overabundance of old-time politicians do not prove that science and technology are of marginal importance for Mexican development. They indicate something quite different. First, scientific and technological stagnation results in the almost prohibitive social cost of a development model based on the primitive accumulation of capital by the private sector and by the inefficient state and on the use of the almost unlimited supply of deficiently trained labour. Second, such stagnation also leads to growing and costly technological dependence on other countries. If from 1925 onwards the post-revolutionary governments had given the necessary support to domestic science and technology, the resulting rationality and efficiency would perhaps have lowered the social cost of growth and would have accelerated the rate of development. It would have also increased the independence of Mexico from the owners or hoarders of scientific and technological progress in advanced countries.

It is very easy to blame the acceleration of technological advance outside Mexico for the growing technological gap between Mexico and the advanced countries. There is no doubt, however, that this gap would be a lot smaller if the post-revolutionary political élites had recognized that verbal ideological battles against 'scientists' and the political manipulation and the cooptation of scientists and technologists seriously affect the efficiency of any society. The gap would also be smaller if they had accepted that individuals who have the necessary mental and moral aptitude for scientific and technological work need a minimum of prestige within society and also intellectual independence. Finally, the gap would have been smaller if the political élites had understood that scientific and technological research not only costs money but also cannot be subordinated to short-term political exigencies.

One of the things that capitalist and socialist societies share is that in both there is (for different reasons) a margin of freedom for research, and scientists and technologists live under decent conditions. In Mexico, on the other hand, until recently, these small intellectual groups were faced with the humiliating alternative of leading a life of sacrifice and self-denial or accepting unconditionally the rules of the political game. Among the reasons for this, one may mention:

(1) the anti-intellectualism - known under the more elegant name of pragmatism - of the post-revolutionary élites, resulting from the emergence of a national, regional and local leadership with a very limited educational background; the incorporation into the political system of the intellectuals willing to be coopted; and the deep distrust of the establishment for those unwilling to exchange their independence for second-class political participation;

(2) the deep deficiencies of the educational system built on the basis of verbal populism;

(3) the backwardness of the emerging entrepreneurial class which, though interested in the services of technicians willing to solve simple immediate problems, looked scornfully at serious scientists and technologists because their creative efforts did not represent short-term profit maximization for the entrepreneurs;

(4) the rapid stratification of the labour force, fostered by the political system, into two groups: the relatively small workers' élites (economically-privileged trade unions) and the great mass of unskilled labour; this stratification resulted in restrictive trade union policies within élitist trade unions, and the repudiation of technical education and technological research which could affect their privileges; and

(5) the apparently easy availability of seemingly simple technologies mostly from the United States.

Only after doubts about the unlimited excellence of the Mexican development model and of its Rostowian automatism were raised did concern over technological and scientific underdevelopment emerge. However, this concern came neither from the authorities in charge of education, nor from the scientific and technological community as a whole, nor from the entrepreneurs, the three social groups from which one might have expected - in other circumstances - intelligent, understanding and modernizing attitudes toward domestic scientific and technical effort to come. The reasons for this lack of concern seem to be closely related to the bureaucratization of the management of the educational system; the absence of an *esprit de corps* in the scientific and technological community, and the persistence of contempt for intellectuals among the new bourgeoisie.

Concern over the general underdevelopment of science and technology in Mexico came from other quarters: from politically uncommitted economists full of doubts about the future of the growth model based on import substitution at all costs, unaccompanied by expansion of the domestic market; from the new generation, still small in numbers of technologists and scientists who, during their studies abroad, became aware of the continuous progress of technology and modern sciences; and from owners of small and medium-scale industry threatened by the growing control of foreign technologies by oligopolistic foreign, domestic or joint enterprises. This heterogeneous coalition opened the debate in the sixties concerning the technological and scientific backwardness of the country and the urgent necessity of formulating, if not a scientific and technological policy, at least some priorities in that field.

As expected, lack of knowledge concerning the general problems and the newness of the debate itself caused considerable confusion and the spreading of some apparently nationalistic ideas which had little to do with a realistic nationalism. When Mexico's degree of scientific and technological dependency was discovered almost overnight, some well-meaning but desperate people called for its outright abolition through the creation of a 'truly Mexican' science and technology. Such proposals were made despite the fact that no country can afford to shut itself off from the stream of international scientific and technological discoveries. Another school of thought, represented by technocrats, proposed a less ambitious solution: the subordination of science and technology to immediate development needs. Without denying the apparent attractiveness of this line of argument it is easy to see its dangerous simplicity. First, it presupposes that a clear, detailed and coherent diagnosis of the developmental needs of the country, something like a master plan for socio-economic development, already exists. Second, it holds that science and technology is easily adaptable to centralized bureaucratic and administrative management. Disregarding the fact that, at present, no diagnosis of the social and economic long-term needs of Mexico exists, the experiences of other countries indicate that centralized management of a bureaucratic type, particularly in those societies with an initially low scientific and technological level, may suffocate rather than foster creative efforts in this field(3). The scientific and technological contribution to the solution of urgent problems depends mainly on previous accumulation of available knowledge and on its adaptability to the circumstances, not on bureaucratic pressures based on haphazard or short-term priorities.

The process of scientific creation and technological innovation is slow and risky and noone can guarantee the results beforehand. As well as small advances, the results of the effort of creative groups are important, more so than guidelines issued by a science and technology 'central committee'(4). They depend on long-term effort and not on the elaboration of emergency programmes(5). Moreover, as can be seen from the experiences of other countries which have managed to emerge from scientific and technological underdevelopment in the span of a few generations, success depends not only on the mobilization of human and financial resources for the solution of immediate, high-priority problems, supposing that such a mobilization is possible, but also on the positive attitude of society as a whole towards an intellectual effort. It also depends on a good educational system and on the capacity of the holders of political power to think about national long-term socio-economic problems.

The case of Japan, a country which perhaps achieved greater scientific and technological progress than any other in twenty-five years, is a particularly good example. Here is a society that has a high degree of national cohesion, has a surprisingly advanced educational system, values highly on the scientific and technological effort of both public and private sectors, and whose social mobility is based on creative effort and on the general acceptance of the thesis that education, technology and science form an indivisible package. In Japan all these factors work together. The high degree of social cohesion minimizes the potentially negative external scientific and technological influence which could lead the country along the path to superficial wealth and social welfare. The educational system generates human resources well prepared for difficult scientific and technological tasks. The prestige offered to scientists and technologists gives them a psychological lift and a sense of participation. The social mobility based on objective performance provides them with material incentives and, finally, the general acceptance of the indivisibility of education, science and technology creates a general framework in which scientific and technological priorities come from the producers and users of knowledge and know-how and not from bureaucratic decisions. One may ask how many of these conditions, necessary for continuous scientific and technological development, are present in societies such as Mexico.

TECHNOLOGICAL DEPENDENCY

Information on the technological dependency aspect of Mexican scientific and technological backwardness is very scarce. It could not be otherwise if one considers that until recently the state seemed to be unaware of the role of technology in development, while enterprises, whether public or private, international or domestic, continued to refuse to disclose any information on the modalities of the purchase of technology from abroad, considering the search for information on this subject as undue interference in their internal affairs.

The little that is known can be briefly summarized:

(1) While a key part of technical know-how used in Mexico comes directly from abroad, especially from the United States, in only a very few cases has it been adapted to local conditions.

(2) It is impossible to define which part of this know-how corresponds to the technology freely available on a worldwide scale and enters the country through the education of Mexicans abroad, books and other technical materials, and which part arrives incorporated in imported capital goods and intermediate products, or arrives directly associated with foreign investment.

(3) Circumstantial evidence shows that the most important transfer of foreign technology takes place at the enterprise level through contractual agreements.

(4) These agreements take the form of: (a) agreements on technical services, according to which an enterprise of a developed country provides technology and technical personnel services to an affiliated or independent company in Mexico; (b) agreements on patents, by which the granting enterprise gives the concessionary company certain rights to use patents, copyrights, inventions and non-patented techniques related to the manufacture and sale of products by the concessionary generally only for the internal market; (c) agreements on design and construction, according to which the foreign enterprise gives a local firm the technical and administrative know-how for the design and construction of installations which the latter may need.

Each of these three categories (agreements on technical services, granting of patent rights, and agreements on design and construction) is widely used by private and public local enterprises. Given that state-owned companies and those with a majority or minority public participation play a growing role in the present phase of Mexican industrialization, characterized by the establishment of heavy and intermediate industries, it is quite probable that the transfer of technology to the public and semi-public sectors represents a growing proportion of the total technology transfer with respect to its cost and its impact on the economy. However, the modalities of these transfers to the public sector are surrounded by the secrecy which encompasses all of its activities. However, this is not the place to discuss the reasons for that situation.

The intervention of the state in matters involving the transfer of foreign technology is limited to fiscal measures. According to legislation in force since the end of 1964, a distinction is made between payments made to nationals or to foreign non-resident enterprises for: (a) technical services and (b) royalties for granting patents and trademarks. In the first, payments are subject to a fixed 20 per cent tax retained at source; in the second, a progressive rate, which fluctuates between 3 and 42 per cent, is applied. The amounts paid for technical services and for patents to residents or foreign companies constituted according to Mexican legislation are deductible from the taxable income of the beneficiary, without restrictions of amount, and are considered as an integral part of the gross income of the physical person or enterprise residing in the country irrespective of ownership. No accelerated depreciation is applied to costs of research or to those of design incurred by national or resident companies. In other words, there are no special fiscal incentives to research.

Although more and more countries consider that agreements with foreign enterprises concerning the supply of technical services and granting of patent rights should be subject to approval by the authorities, this practice does not yet exist in Mexico(6). The only case where the state can intervene in these matters is that covering fiscal benefits conceded to new industrial enterprises under the Law for Development of New and Necessary Industries of 1955. Under this law enterprises that wish to obtain fiscal exemption from import and export tariffs and from the tax on corporate profits, during a period of from two to ten years, in accordance with the classification of each industry, must provide the pertinent authorities (Ministry of Industry and Commerce and Ministry of Finance and Public Credit) with information concerning their foreign personnel, the use of patented technology and the nature of agreements on payments for royalties, patents and services, amongst other things, clearly indicating if those contracts have been entered into with nationals or foreigners. Since the government has ample discretionary power with respect to the granting of exemptions provided by the Law for Development of New and National Industries, it is understood that petitions are rejected if stipulated payments for royalties, patents and technical services from abroad exceed 2 per cent of the sales of a new company. Although the fiscal benefits offered by this legislation are quite large, certain studies suggest that many companies abstain from asking for fiscal exemptions because of the complicated administration of the law and because a wide variety of information - considered secret by the enterprises - must be disclosed to the authorities without prior assurance of a favourable decision.

Other factors which indirectly restrict the scope of technical services agreements and management contracts with non-resident foreign companies are the general restrictive immigration policy applied in Mexico and the quantitative limitations imposed on the contracting of foreign personnel. These restrictions, which date back to the 1930s, are applied to all mercantile and industrial activities. It is compulsory for all foreign personnel, except for those resident foreigners who are considered as immigrants after working for the same enterprise for five consecutive years, to have a work permit, regardless of the duration of their services. As a study by the OECD pointed out, 'the Ministry of the Interior exercises considerable pressure on the foreign companies' to mexicanize their personnel as quickly as possible (7).

Careful reading of the documents and studies, both published and restricted, prepared by public agencies and economic and technological research institutes, has not revealed the existence of any research (prior to 1971) on the benefits of imported technology to the economy and society, the cost of the technology transfer or its effect on the balance of payments.

On the contrary, the availability of information on payments for technology transfer between foreign-owned or controlled companies operating in Mexico and foreign suppliers of technology diminished considerably after 1965 when the annual reports of the Banco de Mexico stopped publishing statistics on direct foreign investment, broken down into (a) net repatriated profits, (b) net reinvested profits and (c) remittances abroad of interest, royalties, etc. From data published for the five-year period 1961-5 one can deduce that remittances of interest, royalties, etc. grew more rapidly than the repatriation of net profits on direct foreign investments (see Table 5.1).

TABLE 5.1. Remittances Abroad of Profits and Related Payments, 1961-5

(US $ million)

Year	Remittances of net profits	Payments abroad for interest, royalties, etc.
1961	57.3	65.6
1962	56.4	66.7
1963	68.1	81.4
1964	90.0	95.9
1965	69.8	91.7

Source: Annual Reports of the Banco de México, S.A.

Information suggesting that this trend became even more pronounced in the second half of the 1960s may explain the disappearance from official reports of data concerning this subject. Thus in 1966 while the remittance of net profits on direct foreign investment amounted to US $16.4 million, payments abroad made by the same companies on account of interest, royalties, etc. amounted to $100.3 million. In 1967 the amounts were US $69.4 million and $133.8 million and in 1968 they were $89.2 and $156.2 million dollars respectively. In other words, while remittances of net profits from direct foreign investment grew by approximately 50 per cent in the short period between 1961 and 1968, payments of interest, royalties, etc. grew by approximately 120 per cent during the same period.

A comparison of remittances of net foreign profits made by branches and subsidiaries of foreign companies with the unofficial estimates of payments on account of royalties and other technical services, excluding interest payments, during the period 1953-62 (the only period for which there are fairly precise data on the second point) provides a very interesting picture (see Table 5.2).

TABLE 5.2. Remittances of Profits and Payments for Royalties and Technical Services, 1953-62

(US $ million)

Year	Remittances of net profits	Remittances of royalties and other payments for technical services
1953	56.9	14.7
1954	38.1	17.2
1955	48.7	12.7
1956	54.5	26.1
1957	47.8	29.2
1958	41.2	35.5
1959	59.1	34.7
1960	72.2	39.1
1961	57.3	42.6
1962	56.4	48.5

Source: Raúl Garduño García (1966), Ensayo sobre el crecimiento económico y la inversión extranjera (El caso de México: 1950-1964), UNAM, Escuela Nacional de Economía.

Extrapolating the figures from Table 5.2 to the period 1963-68 we can conclude that in 1968 the remittances abroad of foreign companies for royalties and technical assistance totalled approximately US $120 million, or eight times the amount paid scarcely fifteen years earlier. However, in reality, total Mexican foreign exchange expenditures generated by the purchase of technology abroad should be much higher due, among others, to several factors.

(1) It is quite probable that available data covers only contracts granting patent rights and technical services contracts between private enterprises with headquarters in the developed countries and their affiliates (branches and subsidiaries) in Mexico, although one should not exclude completely the possibility that these statistics may also encompass some similar contracts between enterprises in advanced countries and local firms.

(2) It seems doubtful that the costs of technology imported under contracts with foreign companies with regard to the design and construction of industrial plants are included since in many cases such costs are incorporated in imported capital goods and the corresponding foreign exchange remittances cannot be recorded separately.

(3) No data are available on payments for transfer of foreign technology to state-owned or controlled enterprises. Most probably, such payments appear in the residual 'errors and omissions' entry of the balance of payments on the current account.

(4) A study published in October 1969 by the Ministry of Finance and Public Credit estimated that total payments abroad by the private sector for technical assistance alone (excluding royalties) amounted in 1968 to US $67.2 million(8). It is quite probable that remittances for royalties were even higher than payments for technical assistance, if one includes royalties paid abroad by the public sector.

In view of these considerations, the figures corresponding to payments for foreign technology which appear above, together with the estimates for the most recent period, should be considered as very crude approximations rather than exact indicators of the precise amount of the remittances. Furthermore, changes in the distribution of foreign private investment by sectors which occurred in the fifties and sixties offer another indication of a trend to underestimate both the remittances for technology, actually or supposedly received by the branches and subsidiaries from their headquarters, and the total foreign exchange cost of technology imports(9).

Although the total value of private direct foreign investment in Mexico increased approximately three times between 1953 and 1968, from US $720 million to $2300 million, private foreign investment in two sectors which use relatively static technology - mining and electricity - decreased considerably due to the 'mexicanization' process. Leaving aside sectors which use relatively little foreign technology - agriculture, construction, domestic trade and other services, which jointly represented a quarter of total foreign private investment both in 1953 and in 1968 - one notices the rapid growth of foreign private investment in the sector which uses technology very intensively - manufacturing industry. The value of foreign investment in this sector increased more than seven times between 1953 and 1968, from US $225 million to $1715 million. Remittances abroad for royalties and other payments for technical services related to private foreign direct investment increased even more rapidly.

The existence of this kind of relationship between the rate of growth of the value of foreign investment in the key sector of the Mexican economy, on the one hand, and the remittances for technology transfer, on the other, suggests that there has been a high increase in the foreign exchange costs of technology per unit of new foreign manufacturing investments. Given that the rise in price of foreign technology is largely unaccompanied by qualitative improvement of output, it is very difficult to claim that such increase is exclusively due to internal factors which hinder the full utilization of imported know-how. Very little is known, however, about the degree of adaptation of foreign technology to the local availability of other production factors; the pricing of technology following the property relationship between the interested parties, and the modalities of the financial relationship between the Mexican economy and the advanced countries. What seems obvious is that Mexico is not in a position either to define its technology needs or to buy technology competitively on the international market.

A study of the real impact of the foreign technology transfer on Mexico's balance of payments should have been carried out long ago. Such a study should have taken into account not only the direct foreign exchange costs but also the indirect effects of the transfers on import substitution and export promotion. Some recent balance-of-payments projections apparently assume that future payments for technology made by foreign subsidiaries will increase in the next five to ten years at a much slower pace than to foreign private investments and net profits. There is little reason to accept the hypothesis that a process of technology substitution is already under way in Mexico and that the cost of technology per unit of new foreign investment is decreasing. It is much more probable that the rising total cost of imported technology will continue to exacerbate balance-of-payments difficulties, unless the utilization of foreign technology already available is managed better and the terms of future purchases are controlled. Obviously, these objectives are not attainable in the absence of a coherent national technology policy, and without a revision of the basis of the development model in force after 1940.

The urgency of a study of technology transfer emerges from the widespread conviction that Mexico pays too high a price for imported technology(10). Since no one seems to know exactly the real cost for the economy in general and for enterprises in particular of foreign technology acquired under the traditional modalities, nor what would be the cost of alternate technologies, nor how to evaluate their impact, the discussion revolves around several general and contradictory ideas.

(1) The country cannot abandon its objective of rapidly absorbing modern and new technologies and use instead 'second-hand' know-how because of long-term economic considerations, especially the need to diversify exports.

(2) Technological dominance, resulting from agreements which link access to new technologies to foreign private investment, is politically not acceptable.

(3) Through agreement with the state and the domestic private sector foreign private capital should plan its gradual withdrawal from industrial activities with relatively static technology or with easy access to non-proprietary know-how, activities in which consulting services to domestic firms would replace the investments controlled from abroad.

(4) Foreign capital must contribute to the development of applied research in the sectors with dynamic technology.

(5) Furthermore, the cost of foreign technology must decrease through external financial assistance and general liberalization of the terms and conditions of contracts on technical services, patents rights and design and construction negotiated between foreign technology owners and Mexican public and private enterprises.

The debate seems to reflect many of the legitimate complaints of a society subjected to rapid industrialization, faced with the technological power of more advanced countries and exposed to growing dependency on foreign technology(11). However, due to the absence of detailed studies of technological dependency and the unwillingness of the state to offer the necessary financial backing for scientific and technological activities, these complaints have a very limited value in the search for new solutions. Furthermore, they seem to forget that technical know-how is controlled, in one way or another, by the big private enterprises of advanced countries, mostly the transnational corporations which insist on exercising exclusive control over their know-how. One way to solve this difficult problem would be to implement in Mexico anti-monopoly measures with respect to technology transfer contracts, similar to legislation in force in the United States and Japan. In the absence of such measures, it would be quite unrealistic to insist, as proposed at a Latin American Symposium on Industrialization that: 'in many cases the collective importation of foreign technical know-how could be organized through domestic technological or technical assistance institutes, for industry as a whole or for specific industrial branches, which would disseminate technology received from abroad'.

DEVELOPMENTS IN THE LATE SIXTIES

In the late sixties there were some encouraging changes concerning Mexican government attitudes toward scientific and technological problems(12). In late 1967 a study sponsored by El Colegio de México demonstrated that national expenditure on scientific and technological research was ridiculously small (13). In October of that same year a Science and Technology Congress was organized in Mexico City to make an inventory of available teaching and research facilities and their performance. At the Congress, proposals were heard to establish a high-level committee which would formulate a national scientific and technological policy, determine priorities with respect to research and, in addition, estimate the necessary financial resources(14). Finally, when President Echeverría's administration took office in 1970, the National Science and Technology Council was created.

Until in mid-1970 under the auspices of the Instituto Nacional de Investigación Científica, the debate on scientific and technological needs was broadened, the subject was discussed mainly in terms of foreign technology costs versus the absence of domestic financial resources for scientific and technical research. While, on the one hand, the belief was gaining ground that foreign exchange expenditure on technology imports was exceedingly high, evidence continued to accumulate with regard to the rapid increase in the gap between Mexican expenditure on domestic research and development (R & D) and that of many other semi-developed countries. Thus, an El Colegio de México study disclosed that in 1964 approximately 150 million pesos (US $12 million) were spent in Mexico on scientific and technological activities and of this total scarcely 25 million (US $2 million) were destined for industrial research. In other terms, in the mid-sixties the country dedicated about 0.15 per cent of national income for pure and applied research, in comparison with an average of over 2 per cent in the developed world and 1 per cent in some developing countries. Taking into account per capita income differences, expenditures for scientific and technological research in Mexico only very recently represented, between one-sixtieth and one-eightieth of those of the industrialized countries. Even making adjustments in these rough global estimates for military and other special purposes R & D undertaken in major industrialized nations, one could conclude that the country was spending about one-twentieth of the amount necessary to reduce somewhat the scientific and technological gap between Mexico and the rest of the world. In these circumstances, the scientific and technological dependency of the rapidly industrializing economy had to increase very rapidly.

It is difficult to estimate the financial, economic and social costs of growing technological dependency by simply comparing the size of remittances for technology imports with meagre resources available for strengthening domestic scientific and technological capacity. Such a comparison assumes that both the state and the private sector not only purchase technology abroad under competitive conditions but are fully aware of the applicability of the imported technology to the needs of the productive process. It also assumes that domestic expenditures on science and technology are channelled in the best possible way. Both assumptions are not confirmed by the Mexican reality.

Leaving aside the problem of the 'fair price' of imported technology, one must insist that in the case of Mexico, as in that of other countries with a very low capacity to generate scientific and technological progress, there is no convincing evidence that the costs of purchasing technology correspond to the actual technology transfer. Furthermore, there is no reason to believe that the prices paid reflect international prices of the technology acquired. The only study available on foreign exchange expenditures for external assistance received by individual companies (a study carried out by the Ministry of Finance in 1969)(15) offers circumstantial evidence that the great part of the payments corresponds to the surreptitious outflow of the untaxed profits of foreign subsidiaries and also of some domestic firms. Thus, for example, the Ministry of Finance and Public Credit study showed that many payments for technical assistance were not covered by contracts with the alleged suppliers. The most extreme case is perhaps that of supermarket chains which allegedly received technical assistance from Panama.

Since the Ministry did not carry out a parallel study of payments abroad for royalties, very little is known about this aspect of Mexico's technology imports. There is circumstantial evidence, however, that in royalty transactions between foreign affiliates and subsidiaries and their respective home offices, the headquarters often set the price of technology in an arbitrary manner, independently of its value on the international market. On the other hand, there are clearly cases where the domestic company pays excessive royalties abroad. The first phenomenon is easily explained by the aim of a transnational corporation with branches in different countries to maximize global profits and not those of a particular branch. The second phenomenon is not difficult to explain either. In negotiations concerning purchase and sale of technology few domestic enterprises in underdeveloped countries have at their disposal ample information about the international technology market, particularly about the availability of alternative technologies. Furthermore, the relative financial weakness of these firms condemns them, on many occasions, to purchase technology tied to sources of foreign capital and intermediate goods. Finally, since these enterprises operate in a highly protected environment devoid of competition, the cost of imported technology is of little importance: it is just one of many costs to be paid by the final consumer.

The issue is complicated still further when a country like Mexico proceeds to diversify its productive structure through the progressive incorporation of national inputs. Such a policy brings about growing demand for foreign technology and converts domestic industries into satellites of foreign subsidiaries which produce finished goods. In many cases, new domestic industries dedicated to the production of intermediate goods depend almost exclusively on technology from big foreign companies already established in the country which are their main, if not exclusive, clients. The diversification and the expansion of industrial structure gives rise to a phenomenon similar to that which occurs at the beginning of the process of import substitution under high protective barriers. In the initial stage of the substitution process, former exporters to the currently well-protected market jump the barrier prohibiting imports by establishing themselves in the country, and compensate and sometimes overcompensate the loss of the export market with oligopolistic rents from production for the highly protected market. When the country passes to the stage of production of intermediate goods, the loss of profits from exports of these goods to the assembly affiliates is compensated for by the profits created by providing new industries with technology. Therefore, it is not strange that a large part of Mexico's technology imports comes from a single country whose investments represent approximately 80 per cent of total foreign private investments in Mexico.

There is no doubt that more efficient taxation, control of technological transactions and diversification of its sources would reduce the foreign exchange cost for technology transfer and eliminate illegitimate payments as well as restrictive business practices applied by the sellers of tied technology. However, the present scientific and technological backwardness of a country like Mexico puts heavy constraints upon these possibilities because any attempt to control the transfer of technology largely depends upon prior knowledge of the technological needs of a society. Moreover, to acquire appropriate foreign technology at competitive prices one must have a minimum of parallel know-how.

The task of lowering the cost of purchased technology and making correct choices in that field is especially difficult when the transfer of technology, as is the case in Mexico, takes the form of a 'package' which consists of the joint import of capital, capital goods and technology through direct foreign investment. The absence of control on the latter makes it impossible to ascertain the real cost for the importing country of the technology incorporated in machinery and intermediate goods which enter the country, together with the proprietary technology and technical assistance. The problem is further complicated by the fact that, especially in the case of joint companies with the participation of domestic capital, the so-called technological contribution is considered as a part of the financial contribution of the foreign investor. Since in the majority of cases the domestic partner is not in a position to estimate the financial value of the technological contribution from abroad, the conversion of technology inputs into a capital contribution is the object of negotiations in which the domestic entrepreneur is at a disadvantage. The foreign negotiator usually argues that it is only fair that the technology buyer participate equitably in the general expenses of pure and applied research incurred by its original owner. The argument seems convincing. The alternative for the domestic technology buyer is to incur heavy expenditure in creating his own technology, instead of acquiring that available abroad. In fact, the cost of this would be very high and sometimes prohibitive. However, the real problem does not lie here even though the technology owner has a genuine monopoly. While the cost of developing a technology afresh could represent high expenditures for its new user, the cession of already available technology by its owner involves for him only marginal costs(16). Therefore, the price of technology is the result (in the case of a technological monopoly) of the bargaining power of the purchaser and, in the case in which alternative technologies exist, of his knowledge of the international technology market. If the purchasing enterprise does not have such information and, for other reasons, is not in a position to freely choose from among the alternative technologies, it will be forced to accept the conditions of the owner of the desired technology.

In the real world the monopoly of technology is rare. It occurs mainly in sectors with very dynamic technologies, which are in small demand and have little application in countries with a level of development similar to that of Mexico. To strengthen his negotiating power the owner of technology will, however, almost always pretend that he offers an 'exclusive technology' and attempt to tie it by trademarks and other restrictive practices. However, the experience of Japan, which has had the greatest success in the mass purchase of foreign technology, has shown the ample availability of alternative technologies at the world level. The only way to gain access to these is to collect technological information on a global scale, a task which can only be carried out successfully by a state conscious that its function is not only to compile technological information but to disseminate it among interested domestic enterprises and to help them in negotiations with the foreign owners of technology.

Although it would be unrealistic to think that the government of a country like Mexico could follow the example of Japan, the Japanese experience suggests that Mexican purchasers of foreign technology will continue to be at a serious disadvantage vis-à-vis suppliers until Mexico's domestic scientific and technological capability is improved substantially. It is quite probable that the demands by developing countries that the owners of modern technology sell technological advances at a lower price will receive limited response. Neither will insistence by producing countries upon 'fair prices' have much effect. Irrespective of the social system and political ideologies, technology trade, as well as international trade in goods, is not regulated by ethical and moral precepts or by considerations of charity. The prices and other conditions of technology transfer depend on the relative strength of the negotiating parties.

CONCLUDING COMMENTS

The degree of scientific and technological advance can only be measured superficially by using data on national expenditures on these activities. According to these, the technological gap between the United States and other advanced countries will continue to grow constantly since the United States dedicates many more resources per capita to science and technology than any other country. However, it is doubtful if the United States can maintain its leadership in this field for very long because a large part of the scientific and technological effort is channelled into non-productive activities. Something similar is happening in the case of the scientific and technological effort of the Soviet Union which has achieved, for example, much success in space exploration without being able to increase its agricultural low productivity.

One can argue, similarly, that the size of per capita expenditure reflects correctly the scientific and technological progress of Mexico. Unfortunately, surveys have demonstrated that the major part of national spending on science and technology corresponds to so-called administrative expenditure. Additionally, there is an enormous proliferation of research institutes which rarely deserve this name since they are composed of a director and a couple of part-time researchers(17). The seriousness of the situation is confirmed by the fact that

> practically all the Ministries have some research department, despite the fact that in some cases these are mainly planning or economic study departments. . . . The Ministries account for 25 per cent of the total research personnel and of the total research budget of the country. However, after examining the number of publications, one finds out that these so-called research units have only contributed 4 per cent of the

published scientific material(18).

Thus bureaucratization and poor allocation of scarce financial resources for science and technology in Mexico seems to be even more acute in the public sector than in semi-autonomous scientific and technological institutions. As long as the situation does not improve, and it is obvious it will not improve by decree, it is difficult to see how the expansion of financial resources will lead by itself to an increase in the productivity of Mexican science and technology and a decrease of external dependency in this field.

The growing foreign exchange expenditures for the purchase of technology abroad only represent one of many aspects of another very serious national problem. This aspect, which has not been discussed sufficiently on a national level, is that while a considerable proportion of imports corresponds to superfluous technology which deforms instead of corrects patterns of consumption in an economy characterized by extremely bad income distribution, many technology imports enter the productive processes with minimum adaptation to the mix of domestic production factors. The lack of adaptation characterizes both technology transfers through foreign direct investment and the purchase of technology abroad by domestic enterprises.

The reasons for the use of complicated and labour-saving technology by foreign firms have been explained very clearly by Hans W. Singer:

> . . . the desire to maximize its profits from the expenditure on pure and applied research and technical know-how, as well as the interest in using a technology well known (by the headquarters) will lead the foreign firm to give preference to capital-intensive operations instead of using a large number of local workers. The machinery is already familiar and one can depend on it. . . . Local labour force is different and difficult to manage in the developing countries because of traditions and structures varying from those of industrialized societies where the transnational company was created. Therefore, the enterprise does not mind paying good salaries. In any case, they will still be low in comparison with the salaries paid in the home country of the headquarters. Under any circumstances, they will be equal to a small part of the total cost of an operation based on the intensive use of capital and will offer a good political investment for the foreign company. Finally, they will eliminate the danger of the labour union problems which may interfere in the effective use of the machinery. However, the foreign company will be much more reluctant to adjust its technology to the local situation and to start an operation based on the intensive use of labour. . . . A competent government is needed to harmonize the preference of the foreign company for the technology which it knows well with the needs of the host country which may consist of the creation of more employment(19).

The state's capacity to enforce the adaptation of technology to local needs should be particularly high in an economy of the Mexican type which offers all kinds of incentives to foreign direct investment, which acquires the major part of the technology from a single highly technologically advanced country (the United States), and which suffers serious unemployment and underemployment, resulting among other factors, from the demographic explosion unheard of in other parts of the world.

The fact that United States technology is particularly difficult to adapt to developing countries because the big United States enterprises are unwilling to take into account the mix of production factors characteristic of underdeveloped economies, is widely recognized(20). On the other hand, the fact that the state, the private sector, and Mexican society have a very limited capability for fostering the adaptation of foreign technologies to the development needs of the country and for using imported know-how for strengthening the domestic process of technological innovation is no less important. The starting point for overcoming scientific and technological backwardness is a self-critical acceptance that such backwardness is one of the characteristics of general underdevelopment, and in particular of educational underdevelopment. Education, science and technology form a whole, and as long as the deficiencies of the educational system are not attacked, social values not changed and political structures not modernized, the possibilities of scientific and technological progress will continue to be very limited. As a leading Mexican scientist has pointed out, the neglect of these problems during many post-revolutionary decades cannot be redressed by the effort of any single administration(21).

On this issue it is not enough to think in terms of the political and administrative cycle. One must keep in mind the future of the whole nation which depends on the state of its science and technology perhaps more than on the political games of the moment.

NOTES

(1) Although all the great revolutions, including those carried out in the name of reason, such as the French revolution of 1789 and the Russian revolution of 1917, produced a wave of anti-intellectualism once the <u>ancien régime</u> had fallen, the intellectual and scientific values, adjusted to the new social conditions, reappeared shortly. It seems that the Mexican revolution is somewhat different. During the fifty years following the destruction of Porfirio Díaz' rule no intellectual or scientific élites appeared in Mexico similar to the generation of Mora, Ortiz, Alemán and Otero after Independence, that corresponding to the reform movement (1850-70) or that of the 1890-1910 period. With a few exceptions, scientists and intellectuals of the post-revolutionary period adapted themselves easily to the demands of the bureaucratic power machine, or in other words, lost their innovating function within society. As for the 'technocrats', they generally opted for the role of servants of the state instead of society. The consequences are only now being felt. See numerous essays on this subject by Daniel Cosío Villegas in his <u>Ensayos y notas</u>, 2 vols., Editorial Hermes, México, 1966.

(2) José Luis Mateos Gómez, 'Estudio preliminar sobre la situación de la investigación científica y tecnológica en México y de algunas posibilidades de aumentar su ritmo de desarrollo', PRI-IEPES, National Meeting for the Study of Mexican Industrial Development, Naucalpan de Juárez, July 1970, Vol. III, pp. 374-86.

(3) See the article by Daniel Cosío Villegas, 'Institutos, consejos y controles', <u>Excélsior</u>, México, D.F., 15 January 1971.

(4) Particularly when the 'central committee', as Daniel Cosío Villegas notes in his essay quoted above, is composed of politicians whose encounters with scientific and technological problems are rather accidental.

(5) On this subject, see Emilio Rosenbluth, 'Investigación científica y

tecnológica: así que pasan seis años', PRI-IEPES, National Meeting for the Study of Mexican Industrial Development, Naucalpan de Juárez, July 1979, Vol. III, pp. 356-60.

(6) At the end of 1968 contracts between foreign technology supplying companies, and resident companies (subsidiaries and affiliates of foreign enterprises as well as joint and fully domestically-owned firms) were subject to government control for balance-of-payments reasons in, among other countries, Brazil, Chile and Colombia. The agreement on common treatment of foreign investments, approved in 1970 by member states of the Andean Common Market, established that licensing contracts for the use of foreign technology and for the exploitation of trademarks and patents would be subject to prior authorization in all member countries and such contracts were not permitted to contain restrictive clauses such as division of the markets, the obligation to use raw materials, intermediate goods and machinery furnished by the owner of the patents, etc.

(7) Angus Maddison, Foreign Skills and Technical Assistance in Economic Development, OECD Development Centre, Paris, 1965, p. 34.

(8) Ministry of Finance and Public Credit, 'Asistencia técnica del extrannero', Investigación Fiscal, México, D.F., No. 46 (October 1969).

(9) On sectorial changes in the location of foreign investment in Mexico, see Miguel S. Wionczek, 'La inversión extranjera privada en México: problemas y perspectivas', in M.S. Wionczek (Editor), La sociedad mexicana: presente y futuro, Fondo de Cultura Económica, México, D.F., 1973.

(10) This opinion is not limited to Mexico. In the report of the ECLA Latin American Symposium on Industrialization held in 1966 the question was raised 'how far, given the Latin American conditions, is it advisable to leave wide open the possibility of acquiring the know-how from abroad through licensing agreements', ECLA, Doc. E/CN/12/755, p. 112.

(11) Public discussions on this subject have strong political connotations. In a series of interviews published in late 1967 by El Día (Mexico City daily) on 'technological dependence and economic development', the majority of the participants - young university teachers - maintained that the more advanced countries impose technological dependency on Mexico as one of the new forms of controlling the patterns of the country's development. Similar opinions were voiced during public discussions prior to the establishment by the federal government, at the beginning of the Echeverría administration, of the National Science and Technology Council.

(12) Between 1935 and the end of the sixties the concern of the state with science and technology was expressed only in the establishment of several agencies whose impact was negligible. Recalling that the National Council of Higher Education and Scientific Research was established in 1935, the Coordinating Council for Scientific Research was created in 1942 and the National Institute for Scientific Research (INIC) appeared in 1950, the INIC report, released in July 1970, admitted that 'unfortunately, the scarce financial resources allocated to research institutes; their lack of authority to see that they function in a unified way and their lack of faculties to intervene in applied research; the absence of a 'critical mass' of scientists and technologists that would support official initiatives and, lastly the absence of a government science and technology policy, linked to social and economic

development, has determined that the actions of these agencies were of a very limited benefit for the country, despite their very best intentions'. Instituto Nacional de Investigación Científica, Política nacional y programas en ciencia y tecnología (Final Report), July 1970, (mimeo), p. 1.

(13) Victor L. Urquidi and Adrian Lajous, La educación superior, la ciencia y la tecnología en al esarrrollo económico de México, El Colegio de México, México.

(14) Eduardo Morales Coella, 'Ciencia, tecnología y desarrollo', Comercio Exterior, México, D.F., Vol. 17, No. 2, December 1967.

(15) Investigación Fiscal, op. cit.

(16) Constantino V. Vaitsos, Transfer of Industrial Technology to Developing Countries through Private Enterprises, Bogotá, Colombia, February 1970 (mimeo.).

(17) Ma. Luisa Rodríguez Salas de Gomezgil, Las instituciones de investigación científica en México, Instituto de Investigaciones Sociales, UNAM, Mexico.

(18) Ibid., p. 378.

(19) H.W. Singer, 'The Foreign Company as an Exporter of Technology', Bulletin of Institute of Development Studies, University of Sussex, Vol. 3, No. 1 October 1970, p. 11.

(20) See, for example, Richard D. Robinson, International Business Policy, Holt, Hart and Winston, New York, 1964, and Wickham Skinner, American Industry in Development Economics, John Wiley & Sons, New York, 1968.

(21) Emilio Rosenbluth, op. cit.

CHAPTER 6
Science and Technology Planning*

MORE than half a century after the revolution, Mexico still belongs to the underdeveloped world, with the majority of its rapidly-growing population subsisting in very precarious conditions. For years, historians, sociologists, political scientists, and economists have been trying to explain why the country has remained underdeveloped, but most general explanations are at best incomplete or partial, and at worst are based on unverified assumptions.

For a long time it was claimed in many quarters that the slowness of socially-acceptable development in Mexico was due to limited natural resources, a relatively small population dispersed over a very extensive territory, and a per capita income too low to generate sufficient savings to finance growth. However, more and more evidence is available that Mexico is not at all poor in natural resources, but rather that only a minute part of these resources has been surveyed and an even smaller portion is actually exploited. Nor can one speak of a shortage of human resources in a country with one of the highest demographic growth rates in the world and with the labour force increasing by about one million people a year. Moreover, with the present average annual income of about US $1000 and with the high concentration of income, it cannot be assumed that Mexico's potential savings are low.

Thus it would appear that the explanation for the persistence of Mexico's economic and social underdevelopment must be sought elsewhere. Without underestimating the difficulties arising from the nature of international economic relations between developed and developing countries, it is possible to maintain that among the most important causes are the absence of political modernization, the severely deficient social organization, the very poorly designed educational system, and scientific and technological backwardness. Together, these result in inadequate and inefficient management of the country's major problems.

---

*This paper was presented at the annual meeting of the American Association for Advancement of Science held in Denver, Colorado in January 1977, and published originally in Interciencia (Caracas), Vol. 2, No. 6, November-December, 1977.

MEXICO'S DEPENDENCY

The weakness of domestic scientific and technological activities reflects the backwardness and dependency of the Mexican exonomy. Mexico's rapid quantitative economic expansion, accelerated industrialization and scientific and technological development date only from the 1930s. It was at that time that university education was put on the list of priorities, together with official support for industrialization, thus creating conditions propitious for some scientific research unaccompanied, however, by similar efforts in the field of technology.

As a result, while scientific activities in the major universities registered some progress, the slow advance of applied research and development remained subject to deformations arising from the dependent and imitative industrialization process. In response to local technological backwardness, technology embodied in machinery or available through licensing of industrial know-how was imported massively, even though these imports very often did not respond to the needs of a country short of capital but with relative abundance of unskilled labour. Not only were technology imports demanded by industry and services linked to the production structure serving mainly urban groups whose preferences were formed by the consumption patterns of high income countries, but imported technology often required intermediate inputs not produced in Mexico, and at times even hindered the exploitation of some widely available renewable resources. The nature of technological links with the outside world changed little after the Second World War when Mexico's industrial structure expanded with the establishment of many intermediate goods industries and the appearance of the incipient capital goods sector.

Thus Mexico's scientific and technological dependency upon the outside world increased instead of diminished. Isolated attempts to rectify the situation by encouraging research and development (R & D) activities at the universities and in the public sector were not accompanied by the elaboration of a national policy on science and technology until very recently. Only with the setting up of the National Council for Science and Technology - CONACYT - at the beginning of the seventies, coinciding with worldwide recognition of the interrelationship between scientific and technological effort and the patterns and pace of economic and social growth, was the need for science and technology policy perceived in some quarters. Consequently, the National Science and Technology Council, in close cooperation with the scientific community, leading universities and representatives of public and private sectors, formulated in 1975/76 the first Science and Technology Plan, covering 1976-82 but within the framework of a longer-term R & D strategy. The contents of this Plan will be reviewed here at some length since they may throw some light upln the problems arising from scientific and technological backwardness of practically all developing countries.

SCIENCE IN MEXICO

The detailed survey of scientific and technological activities revealed that Mexico's R & D system, although having grown in the seventies faces formidable difficulties:

(1) It depends to an exaggerated degree on the development of science and technology in more advanced countries, thus limiting its output in many cases

to purely imitative quasi-research activities in fields in which serious indigenous R&D is badly needed, if only because many problems of underdevelopment are different from those facing developed societies.

(2) Financial resources available domestically for R&D are not only inadequate in comparison with those provided by industrialized countries, but also compared with R&D expenditures in some countries with a similar development level, such as the other larger Latin American republics.

(3) The science and technology system enjoys neither the quantity nor quality of human resources required, both in absolute terms and in comparison with many other countries of a similar level of development.

(4) Geographic and institutional concentration of science and technology institutional concentration of science and technology institutions is excessive. In 1973, research institutions located in or around Mexico City accounted for more than 80 per cent of total expenditures and personnel, and five institutions spent 45 per cent of the national R&D budget.

(5) The functional distribution of R&D expenditures is deficient. Almost 70 per cent of financial resources is spent on salaries and wages, while less than 15 per cent is available for purchasing equipment indispensable for serious research.

(6) Most R&D institutions lack a critical body of researchers. Only 3.5 per cent of the total of 400 existing research entities employ more than twenty people each, the minimum needed for relevant research in most fields.

(7) The development of science and technology is highly unbalanced sectorally and by disciplines with consequent neglect of very important areas of research. Resources for basic research are extremely scarce, and applied research and development is concentrated in those few sectors where the presence of the state is particularly great. Petroleum and energy, modern agriculture, medicine and health, and the intermediate goods industries absorb half of the financial resources available. Even in these fields, research is neither sufficient nor adequate to satisfy the country's specific needs for scientific and technological knowledge. Furthermore, R&D is neglected in such areas of great importance as subsistence agriculture, non-renewable resources, capital goods, transport and communications, urban development and housing, etc.

(8) Lastly, there are no permanent links between R&D effort and the educational and productive systems. Moreover, the structure of the science and technology system fosters a divorce between R&D and dynamic and technically complex productive activities. The weakness of technical diffusion and extension services obstructs the transmission of knowledge to the productive system, especially in non-commercial agriculture and the consumer goods industries(1).

Comparison of the existing situation with the country's probable R&D needs indicates that the science and technology system should expand its sphere of action considerably, both in quantitative and qualitative terms. It indicates, moreover, that future growth of the system and the relevance of R&D would depend largely on the formulation of a long-term overall development programme, badly missing in Mexico for _sui generis_ political reasons. In other words, the future of science and technology in Mexico seems to be contingent not only on an increase in financial resources for R&D and on more rapid training of human resources, but also on the integration of these efforts into a general planning framework. Given the nature of scientific and technological activities, the characteristics of the Mexican economic model, and the official ideology, such planning cannot be but indicative and participatory. In respect to science and technology, such planning should not only foster the expansion of R&D but aim at creating the practically non-existent demand for domestically-produced scientific and technological knowledge. Work on the Mexican science and technology plan demonstrated beyond doubt that in developing countries the mere supply of know-how does not create demand for it.

THE MEXICAN SCIENCE AND TECHNOLOGY PLAN

The Mexican science and technology plan is based on two premises: firstly, that the importance of science and technology for socio-economic development makes its longer-term planning an urgent necessity for any country; secondly, that the need for scientific and technological planning, while safeguarding freedom of research, is even more pressing in countries like Mexico, owing to the persistence of underdevelopment, the relative scarcity of the government's financial resources, and the magnitude of the still unsatisfied basic needs of the majority of the population.

The main objectives of the Science and Technology Plan were defined as <u>non imitative scientific development, cultural autonomy, and technological self-determination</u>. Scientific development should be understood here as the creation of a capacity for research in the exact, natural, and social sciences which would enable the scientific community to fulfil its social function and, at the same time, to participate meaningfully in the process of international scientific advancement. Cultural autonomy is an objective related to safeguarding certain societal values which are being lost in the process of industrialization in many developing countries. Lastly, technological self-determination is defined as the construction of a domestic capacity that would permit the demand for technology to be reoriented progressively to the extent needed toward local sources of technical knowledge, that would rationalize purchases of foreign technology, and that would help to assimilate and to adapt imported know-how, using it for the internal generation of technology.

The scientific and technological policy required to attain these objectives in the long run postulates that:

(1) Science and technology policies must be thoroughly integrated with the country's general development policy.

(2) The model of scientific and technological advancement must be adapted to the country's longer-term social and economic objectives.

(3) The adoption of an autonomous model for the advancement of science and technology in no way implies abandoning the selective use of externally generated scientific and technological knowledge.

(4) In the absence of a well integrated science and technology system the task of overcoming scientific backwardness requires a joint sustained effort on the part of the government, R&D entities, higher learning institutions and the productive system.

(5) Scientific and technological advancement demands a favourable environment that acknowledges its social value and particularly its contribution to the achievement of long-run national objectives.

(6) Attaining a degree of excellence in certain scientific fields until now little explored and developed elsewhere but of great relevance for the solution of the problems of underdevelopment is badly needed.

(7) Meaningful technological advance requires parallel and simultaneous activity on several fronts: in selected areas of conventional R&D practised in the advanced countries, in appropriate 'primitive' technologies of local origin, and in some specific fields where the dynamics of advanced R&D offer hope for major and early technological breakthroughs of social importance.

(8) Lastly, the science and technology system must have close links with the educational system and the economy.

Considering the state of underdevelopment prevailing in most R&D supporting activities and the urgent need to transmit R&D results to society for educational and productive purposes the Plan dedicates considerable attention to the problems facing the scientific and technological infrastructure, including training of high level human resources, diffusion and distribution of knowledge, information and statistics, engineering and consultancy services, production and maintenance of scientific equipment and instruments, and international scientific and technological cooperation. For each of these components of the system's infrastructure and its external linkages, the Plan attempts to determine long-term objectives and medium-term policy guidelines.

In respect to R&D itself, the Plan defines objectives and sets guidelines for problem-oriented research activities both in the exact and natural sciences and in social disciplines. In the field of applied R&D it develops technological policy guidelines for nutrition, agriculture and forestry, communications, urban development, industry, energy, renewable resources, construction and housing, medicine and health, educational techniques, and natural phenomena research. The Plan emphasizes that scientific advancement must be based not only on the recognition of university autonomy but on the state's commitment to guarantee the academic and research freedom necessary to foster scientific creativity. The specific scientific and technological policy guidelines are expected to be translated into institutional and sectoral programmes with the aid of some relatively simple interinstitutional mechanisms designed for that end. These mechanisms should be indicative, participatory, and flexible.

The Plan postulates that by 1982 expenditures on science and technology in Mexico should reach a total of 16,200 million pesos (US $1300 million at 1975 prices), i.e. almost three times the 1976 spending and slightly more than 1 per cent of GNP. The outlay for research and development alone should rise from 3090 million pesos (US $250 million) in 1976 to 9200 million pesos (US $735 million at 1975 prices) by 1982. A slight reduction in the government's share of total expenditures from its current level of 80 per cent to 75 per cent is assumed, along with a proportionate increase in private sector spending. Furthermore, planning offers medium-term targets for R&D support activities and a package of science and technology policy instruments aimed at increasing productivity of R&D. Finally, the setting up of mechanisms evaluating the progress of the Plan's implementation is considered.

The Science and Technology Plan proposes that policymaking be institutionalized through the permanent National Scientific and Technological Planning Commission, to be composed of high-level representatives of the federal government, decentralized agencies and public enterprises, higher education institutions, and science and technology users in the productive sector. The Commission would, first, coordinate and guide the preparation and periodic revision of science and technology policies, as well as of successive plans; and, second, guarantee a serious involvement in these tasks of the government itself, higher education institutions, the private sector, and scientific and technological community.

It is proposed that the Planning Commission would be supported by the Interinstitutional Science and Technology Committee, composed of the Consejo Nacional de Ciencia y Tecnología (CONACYT) and various key ministries in charge of allocating financial resources and of controlling their uses. The main function of the Committee would be to integrate the annual federal budgets for science and technology into the framework of financial targets and R&D guidelines set by successive science and technology plans. Together, the Planning Commission and the Interinstitutional Committee would form the basis of the permanent global planning mechanism for the science and technology system, planning closely interlinked with the socio-economic development strategy to be established by the federal executive.

A PERMANENT PLANNING PROCESS

The permanent planning process would comprise four phases:

(1) the formulation of a strategy for science and technology development within the country with a long-term perspective (20 to 25 years);
(2) definition of a medium-term (10 years) science and technology policy;
(3) formulation of successive indicative six-year science and technology plans;
(4) elaboration of institutional and sectoral general R&D and R&D support programmes for the duration of each plan.

Given the necessarily long period required for scientific and technological efforts to give tangible results, and considering its current underdevelopment in Mexico, unless science and technology planning works out a long-term strategy, it runs the risk of being reduced to an insignificant exercise with extremely limited effects. The need to define science and technology policy for ten-year periods only and to redefine it periodically is determined by the nature of scientific progress and technological change. Their speed is so great that science and technology objectives and policy guidelines must be revised from time to time, though not too frequently, in the light of worldwide developments. The need for formulation of successive six-year plans arises from the necessity for any realistic planning to take into account the political and administrative cycle of the country. Lastly, it is important that institutional and sectoral R&D programmes are worked out by the scientific and technological community itself so that R&D operative continuity is assured, its productivity is improved and the infrastructure facilities and financial and human resources are used more rationally.

The Science and Technology Plan would leave scientific and technological institutions free to define their short- and medium-term work programmes within the framework of policy guidelines and priorities established by consensus by the Plan itself. Institutional programmes are expected to contain eventually not only research and related activities' programmes for the duration of each plan, but also to outline in a general and preliminary way problem-oriented priority research areas for longer periods.

Institutional programmes would have to be coordinated by sectors, not to meet formal requirements of planning but because the scientific and technological policy guidelines presented in the Plan strongly indicate that the Mexican science and technology system will have to undertake in the coming years many multidisciplinary R&D activities that exceed the capabilities of any single institution. Linking institutional and sectoral programming with the formulation of the federal annual budget for science and technology is meant to enable a more efficient allocation of government financial resources and to insure their use in accordance with the policy guidelines of the Plan.

Although the very nature of scientific and technological planning requires it to be indicative, because R&D activities do not lend themselves to any other approach, various groups of participants in the science and technology system would have different degrees of commitment to the implementation of the Plan's global and sectoral guidelines.

Thus the Science and Technology Plan would be mandatory for the National Science and Technology Council. This would act as a technical advisor to scientific and technological institutions at their request, and at the same time would have to design its own R&D support programme for the duration of the Plan in those fields which other institutions were unable to cover because of insufficient resources, lack of infrastructure, etc. Thus within the framework of global science and technology planning, CONACYT would continue to foster certain activities which R&D institutions could not undertake by themselves. The Council's priority activities would continue to be: first, training of high-level personnel; second, setting up research centres in sectors lacking adequate institutional structure; and third, selectively promoting mechanisms needed to link science and technology with the educational and productive systems.

Government scientific and technological research institutions, centres, and units would have to accept a relatively strong commitment to the Plan's objectives, targets, and policy guidelines. The argument in favour of this commitment is rather simple. The Plan amounts to a federal programme, and the federal government is the direct source of funds for R&D activities undertaken within the public sector.

PRODUCTIVITY OF SCIENCE EXPENDITURE

Although the State and its enterprises account for some 60 per cent of national expenditure in R&D, in many cases the productivity of the government's direct expenditures in scientific and technological research is very low, due mainly, though not exclusively, to two factors. First, while there are few large research centres, such as the National Institute for Agricultural Research and the Mexican Petroleum Institute, whose contributions to national science and technology are unquestionably outstanding, there is in Mexico an excessive number of small research units which, because of size, budget, human resources, and bureaucratic problems, cannot be expected to make any relevant advances in the field. (There are in Mexico some 300 public sector R&D units each with three researchers or less. Second, many of the small units rarely count with formal research programmes and suffer from a lack of coordination, either internally within the institution they are attached to, or externally with other institutions carrying out similar research. If these small units are to increase their productivity and undertake more relevant research the government would have to involve itself explicitly in the implementation of the Science and Technology Plan by creating conditions which would permit these units to establish their programmes with a view participating in sectoral R&D planning.

Fortunately, these deficiencies are less conspicuous in the majority of R&D centres belonging to major higher education institutions. Consequently, and also in response to the concept of university autonomy, the Science and Technology Plan would be indicative for these research centres. Moreover, the Plan's broad research policy guidelines were drawn up and adopted by consensus, with wide participation by the scientific and technological community whose majority works at institutions of higher learning. These facts should make it relatively easy for major university R&D centres to formulate institutional research programmes within the Plan's general framework.

PRIVATE SECTOR PARTICIPATION

In view of the general lack of interest of business firms in R&D, the property structure of the industry, i.e. a strong participation of foreign capital in the technologically dynamic sectors, and a very marked preference both of foreign and local business for foreign technology, it is highly unlikely that the private sector will substantially modify in the short run its technological conduct. Consequently, the Plan contends that the government must implement fiscal, financial, and other mechanisms to stimulate private companies to develop their technological capacity, use research originating in the country, and augment their contribution to the domestic science and technology effort. It would also be necessary to design instruments which encourage large foreign-owned companies to adapt their technology to local conditions and requirements, since it is difficult to accept that they remain in a complete and perpetual state of dependence on foreign technology.

Nevertheless, even the best planning and implementation of scientific and technological programmes at institutional, sectoral, and national levels cannot guarantee the system's contribution to Mexico's development. The main limitation - contrary to some recent thinking in the industrialized world - is that science and technology by itself cannot solve major underdevelopment problems, although it may provide many elements essential to their solution.

In other words, as stated earlier, in order to take full advantage of the science and technology potential to help reach the nation's goals, science and technology policies would have to be coordinated with overall development policies. In operational terms, this means the creation of a number of direct scientific and technological policy instruments and the readjustment of existing economic policies that indirectly affect the functioning and development of the system.

One particularly urgent problem is the evaluation of the impact of industrialization policies on science and technology. Until now these policies, together with supporting fiscal, monetary, and foreign trade policies, have not taken adequate account of the need to accelerate scientific development or promote technological self-determination. In fact, many of these policies have a negative impact on science and technology objectives. The divorce between important economic policy instruments in force and the proposed science and technology policy instruments mainly originates in the fact that the design of the latter follows that of most economic policies that were elaborated when the relationship between scientific and technological activities, on the one hand, and socio-economic development, on the other, was not clearly understood. In summary, like many other developing countries, Mexico is facing the difficult and complicated task of integrating these two policy areas into a coherent whole.

LESSONS FOR UNDERDEVELOPED COUNTRIES

Independently from the degree of success which Mexico may have with the implementation of its Science and Technology Plan, the exercise of the plan itself offers many lessons to other underdeveloped countries.

The first amounts perhaps to the need to recognize that science and technology problems in the context of general underdevelopment differ basically from those encountered by science and technology in the advanced world. Thus advancement in this field in the underdeveloped part of the international economy can hardly be achieved by methods more or less successfully applied in the world's industrial centres. Since scientific and technological backwardness is part and parcel of overall underdevelopment, science and technology policies must be integrated into the general development policy framework. The absence of such a framework limits severely the relevance of any attempt to build up domestic scientific and technological capacity.

The second lesson is that a major obstacle for the advancement of science and technology in a country like Mexico originates from the divorce between local R&D activities and the educational and productive systems. Consequently, whatever knowledge is produced domestically is used neither for the improvement of the quality of education nor for productive purposes. Mexican experiences strongly suggest that the supply of internally-produced scientific knowledge and technical know-how does not create automatic demand for them, because demand is historically directed to the outside. Consequently, the advancement of science and technology in an underdeveloped country depends more upon the effort to establish links between the R&D system and the educational system and the economy than upon the simple increase in human and financial resources allocated for R&D. The acceptance of this proposition will make it easier to understand why a science and technology strategy proposed for underdeveloped countries by the advanced world and postulating the establishment of local modern scientific institutes more or less at random, while leaving applied R&D effort to traditional international transfer mechanisms, just cannot work. In the absence of demand for their output modern scientific institutes set up in underdeveloped societies wither away and become focal points of brain drain. At the same time, dependence on traditional technology transfer mechanisms leads to the emergence of advanced technology enclaves that perpetuate themselves in the context of general technological backwardness. The question here is not whether such technology transfers, for example through foreign-owned enterprises, are of any use in the absolute sense. They may be useful or useless depending on the presence of the absence of other vehicles for transfer and propagation of technical know-how in an underdeveloped society. Only a technological strategy designed to establish permanent links between technological imports and the domestic R&D system, on the one hand, and local R&D output and the educational and productive systems, on the other, can assure in the longer run meaningful technological modernization of a backward country.

The third point, originating in the previous two can be summarized as follows: the domestic science and technology system in an underdeveloped country must be defined not just as the sum of local R&D producing entities, but as the universe of all units dedicated to R&D, to R&D supporting activities and to intermediating between R&D institutions and those of higher learning as well as productive enterprises. The intermediation is not unidirectional - from those who produce knowledge to those who use it - but it should be visualized as a sort of two-directional triangular relationship. If science and technology policymakers in advanced countries seem to forget it, it is because they lack historical perspective. In all advanced societies the sort of triangular relationship between science and technology, education and production, absent in the backward societies, was built up slowly and - one has to admit - without any sort of planning, over the last two centuries. This statement also covers socialist societies. Contrary to widespread beliefs, they were not scientifically or technologically backward in pre-socialist times, particularly compared with the majority of underdeveloped countries today. The Soviet Union before 1917, Poland before 1945 and China before 1948 were quite advanced in comparison with most of Latin America, Africa and Asia of the mid-twentieth century. Thus to achieve scientific and technological advances in the underdeveloped world, one faces a difficult task of devising policy instruments affecting the broad R&D system as defined above and at the same time revising educational and economic policies in the light of scientific and technological effort.

The fourth major lesson of the Mexican exercise may perhaps be that we know little about the intrarelations, particularly in the context of underdevelopment, present inside of the continuum known as R&D. The simplistic proposition that every country needs to support in a similar way all parts of that continuum (because allegedly pure science is needed to prepare the ground for applied scientific effort, needed, in turn, for technological development) is open to many criticisms on logical, structural and historical grounds. Only by accepting our ignorance in respect to intra-relationships within R&D, agreeing that social functions of different parts of the R&D continuum vary considerably and relating the production of knowledge to some overall view of long-term social, economic and national objectives of a given society, is it possible to arrive at a very broad vision of national science and technology strategy for an underdeveloped country or region.

The final major point is that science and technology policy problems cannot be meaningfully handled just by scientists and technologists, if only because science and technology is not a specialized sector but affects every phase of social, economic, cultural and even political life. If we accept, furthermore, that science and technology is not socially neutral, we may arrive at the conclusion that planning scientific and technological endeavours is a very complicated matter in which 'wise men' from different walks of life, including wise politicians if available, should perhaps participate. This may be particularly true in the context of underdevelopment where it may well be that scientific and technological élites, while sometimes highly educated, are in other respects as backward as the societies in which they function.

Of course, many other important lessons might be drawn from the Mexican exercise. The purpose here was to draw attention to key issues arising at the planning stage. The problems of implementation of the Mexican Plan, assuming that it is going to be implemented which is still highly uncertain, will require separate analysis later.

NOTES

(1) These deficiencies are common to most of Latin American science and technology systems. For details, see Herrera (1972).

REFERENCES

CONSEJO NACIONAL DE CIENCIA Y TECNOLOGÍA (1976), Política nacional de ciencia y tecnología: Estrategia, lineamientos y metas and National Indicative Science and Technology Plan, English edition, CONACYT, Mexico.

HERRERA, A. (1972) 'Social Determinants of Science Policy in Latin America', Journal of Development Studies, Vol. 9, pp. 19-37.

PART II

LATIN AMERICA

CHAPTER 7

Development Research Problems in the Region*

> While the economic condition of countries is bad, men care for Political Economy, which may tell us how it is to be improved; when that condition is improved, Political Economy ceases to have the same popular interest.
> Walter Bagehot (1880), Economic Studies.

> The distinction between factors that are 'economic' and those that are 'non-economic' is, indeed, a useless and nonsensical device from the point of view of logic, and should be replaced by a distinction between 'relevant' and 'less relevant'.
> Gunnar Myrdal (1957), Economic Theory and Underdeveloped Regions.

THE PREOCCUPATION with economic research requirements for the less developed areas, and specifically for Latin America, has been with us for some time. The issue becomes progressively more urgent, however, in view of the fact that, in spite of proliferation of economic aid and technical assistance activities, socio-economic and political tensions in the underdeveloped areas continue to increase, suggesting that a considerable part of outside aid and domestic efforts is wasted because of our limited knowledge of the process of economic development under twentieth-century conditions.

In the past, various alternative development research agendas have been discussed at periodic interdisciplinary meetings in the western hemisphere, first among United States social scientists and economic aid dispensers and later with the growing participation of Latin American scholars. Thus one recalls, amongst others, a Conference on Research for the Improvement of Development Assistance Programmes and Operations, held at the Brookings Institution in Washington in early 1961(1) and a series of meetings on Latin American

---

*This lecture was delivered at an annual meeting of Directors of Development Training and Research Institutes organized by OECD Development Centre at Naples, Italy in September 1965, and published in Training and Research in Development, Development Centre of the Organization for Economic Cooperation and Development, Paris, 1967. The author would like to express his sincere appreciation to Victor L. Urquidi, El Colegio de Mexico for his penetrating comments on an earlier draft.

studies, appointed by the American Council of Learned Societies and the Social Science Research Council, and held in Santiago, Chile, Stanford, California and Rio de Janeiro in 1962, 1963 and 1965 respectively. In a way, the OECD Development Centre's annual meeting of directors of research and training institutes represents an extension of those regional gatherings on to a global scale. Consequently, the contents of this paper are directed mainly to economic and social research practitioners outside the western hemisphere, for the purpose of stimulating discussion about the similarity or difference in problems faced by development research workers in different parts of the world.

DEVELOPMENT RESEARCH IN LATIN AMERICA

The problems as seen from Latin America may be summarized as follows:

(1) Our present knowledge of the economics, politics, sociology and psychology of development is gravely deficient and, because of the complexity of the development process, it is difficult to expect that even the most serious gaps in the understanding of its nature can be closed in a short time. For the purpose of understanding the development process attempts - following the traditional division of social sciences - to isolate and analyse separately its multiple facets often turn into futile or misleading intellectual exercises, unless the results are incorporated into a larger whole. As one American scholar put it with great wit, everyone concerned with development problems

> has to be a highly exceptional person. He must be cultured and cross-cultured. He must be disciplined and interdisciplined. He must be well-stocked with empathy and antifreeze. He should be a model himself, and he should know about model-building, institution-building, stadium-building and body-building(2).

Such characters are unfortunately in short supply anywhere, both in advanced countries and underdeveloped areas.

(2) Research on the economic and social development process in Latin America seems to be somewhat behind that undertaken in other underdeveloped areas, in spite of sustained and valuable efforts by UN agencies, independent Latin American and United States research centres, and individual scholars within and from outside the region. This lag can be explained to some extent by the fact that during the three decades preceding the Cuban revolution, Latin America was in many ways for scholars from advanced countries a continent where presumably little had been happening and whose study, except by anthropologists and experts in international comparative law, brought very little intellectual and academic prestige. As far as Europe was concerned, its disappearance from the political scene in Latin America at the beginning of the century brought about the progressive extinction of intellectual interest in the area. Latin Americans, when left to themselves in the social sciences, until the early forties followed the universalist traditions of European universities of the beginnings of the present century. Although it would be unfair to claim that no contributions to the understanding of problems of economic (especially industrial) development could be found in Latin America during the inter-war period, the fact remains that such contributions originated only in a few countries and remained relatively unknown to the region itself and to the rest of the world. Only recently have they been rescued

from oblivion by historians of Latin American economic thought and ideologies.

(3) Because the recent wave of interest in Latin American development problems, especially prevalent in the United States, which followed rather than preceded the extension of the 'cold war' to the region, a considerable sector of Latin American intellectuals looked upon this outside interest with suspicion, assuming, rightly or wrongly, that many research projects, organized by and directed from the advanced countries, serve principally <u>political</u> interests of their sponsors and not necessarily the development objectives of Latin America, as seen from the region itself. These lingering and sometimes openly stated suspicions, reflecting the progressive radicalization of Latin American intellectual élites, made even more difficult than in the past communication between scholars from Latin America and the rest of the world. This communication has never been easy, on the one hand, because of the differences in cultural backgrounds and educational systems and, on the other, because of the wide divergence of attitudes in backward and advanced nations toward the role which the social sciences should and do play in the relatively poor and transitional societies as opposed to the affluent ones. As the concern of Latin American social scientists, in their great majority, is centred on social and economic change and immediate policy problems, they can hardly subscribe to a proposition widely defended in the advanced societies that social sciences, including economics, are politically neutral. For very many Latin American intellectuals such 'political neutrality' is a cover for the defence of ideologies in force in affluent societies inimical to the interests of the underdeveloped world. To ascribe such attitudes exclusively to Latin American Marxists and neo-Marxists would be an oversimplification.

(4) Development research in Latin America is hampered not only by the tenuous statistical information and limited knowledge of historical growth experiences of individual countries, due in part to the fact that the economic history of Latin America continues to be one of the neglected research fields both within and outside the area. It is also complicated by growing doubts held by Latin American economists and economic policymakers concerning the economic theory elaborated in the more developed Western countries. This 'traditional' theory is considered by many as inapplicable to the Latin American 'special case'. The reasons for this rejection are multiple, as suggested by discussions on the subject in Latin American economic journals(3), but the debate itself can hardly be described as a struggle between Latin American structuralists and monetarists, as some people believe. It raises basic philosophical and ideological questions, such as what economic theory is about and what is or should be its function in present world conditions? It can hardly be said that dissatisfaction with the state and role of economic theory, as elaborated in the advanced societies, comes only from people intellectually unable to digest its refined points. The leaders of the 'revolt' - practically without exception - mastered advanced economic theory at the best universities in Europe and North America. The difficulty lies, one would suspect, in the past and present experiences with economic policies within the region and even more with economic policies <u>towards</u> the region, based upon or defended with theoretical arguments taken from neo-classical economics and from the leading international propagators of 'conventional wisdom', the latter usually designed to fit the sponsors' policy ends. These practitioners of economic theory, with very limited knowledge of transitional societies but well represented in many high policymaking places in advanced countries, and in Latin America as well, are responsible more than anyone else for the progressive breakdown in communications between Latin American social scientists and economists and their counterparts outside the region.

Given the advanced stage of disenchantment in the area with political, economic and intellectual status quo, it is hardly surprising to follow, for example, the results of the Congress of Economics Faculties of Latin American Universities, held in Mexico City in 1965. The majority of participants, representing a rather broad spectrum of political opinions, after having reached agreement that 'the development theory formulated in the Western industrial countries neither explains in a satisfactory way the problems of Latin American development nor can serve as a basis for a policy able to solve successfully these problems', recommended as a matter of great urgency the elaboration of a Latin American economic development theory 'better adjusted than the "traditional theory" to the region's reality'. Whatever intellectual and scientific merits such recommendations may have, they represent an understandable reaction to the misuse and abuse of the economic theory elaborated in advanced societies in the fight against socio-economic change in tension-ridden Latin American societies.

(5) Conditions for economic research in Latin America are also made difficult by discontinuities in the application of research for economic policy purposes. Although a sort of general agreement exists in the region that economic and social research should be directly policy-oriented, transmission mechanisms between Latin American economists and policymakers continuously fail. If this happens, it is not, as ideologists from the extreme left maintain, because all Latin American policymakers are primitive and perverse political animals dutifully serving wrong causes. It is perhaps due to the fact that so many brilliant Latin American economists have one foot in their own societies and another in the advanced countries, where they not only learned their trade but also absorbed certain prestige values of limited validity in the Latin American reality. Consequently, there is a discontinuity in rapport between rank-and-file graduates from Latin American economic faculties, who as a rule received a rather mediocre professional education, on the one hand, and the highly sophisticated but thin foreign-educated élite, gravitating in most cases towards international or regional economic organizations, on the other. The exposure of this élite to the prestige structure and values in force among social scientists, and especially economists of the advanced countries(4), with special stress on theorizing and overspecialization, makes transmission of the useful body of knowledge to the less fortunate members of the profession rather difficult. Since the élites attempt to play at the same time two perhaps incompatible roles, that of high priests of a 'hermetic science' and of ideological leaders of their respective societies, the results are confusing at times. While the more fortunate followers of these small élites receive, in most Latin American economic institutes, specialized training in advanced tools of economic analysis, these tools break down when confronted with day-to-day reality, which obviously encompasses a whole array of highly relevant non-economic factors, often left out from the training in economics because of their belonging to other 'lower' social sciences. Anyone with some knowledge of public sectors in Latin America, which absorb almost the totality of young economists, remembers innumerable encounters with these technicians whose mobility within the society becomes extremely limited as a result of their overspecialization and whose professional skills cannot be fully exploited for policy purposes because of the same overspecialization. This professional narrowness of lower-level technicians leads in public life to their being left behind by many less technically competent but more politically minded people better adjusted to the rules of the game in underdeveloped societies. The same narrowness of professional attitudes does not help in the field of research, whose fragmentation in small disjointed projects characterizes the work of

many research institutes in the area.

The second major discontinuity is visible in the relationship between members of the professional élite, whether economists or other social scientists, and the actual economic policymakers. Because of the propensity of occupants of the highest level of an intellectual prestige pyramid to communicate only among themselves and because of their real, but not apparent, lack of interest in practical policy matters, policymakers are held in deep disdain. Consequently, many members of the élite are often both poor advisers and deficient research project designers and directors, assuming that, as it is claimed, their research is policy-directed. A considerable part of research undertaken in Latin America, whether on a national or a regional level, when presented to policymakers in the form of final recommendations is either not comprehensible to the recipients or too difficult to implement, because once again non-economic but relevant factors or considerations were left out. Latin American economic policymakers faced with reports and recommendations, offering only one (and probably the best from the viewpoint of economic analysis) solution, are often forced to run for advice to members of their bureaucratic entourage whose professional competence may be quite questionable but who can at least be understood. As a result, reports and studies, made with a large input of skills and money but not used for economic policy purposes, pile up with little visible effect upon the economic policy itself, even if conditions are propitious for what Hirschman calls 'reform-mongering'.

RESEARCH NEEDS AND PRIORITIES

The following cursory evaluation of past and current research and of research needs and priorities in Latin America implies acceptance of two assumptions, obviously open to challenge from many quarters. First, in view of the scarcity of resources available - in human and not only in financial terms - and the urgency of bringing more rationality into economic policy processes in Latin America, policy-oriented research should continue to have priority over pure scientific inquiry. Second, an interdisciplinary approach to research is desirable if our goal is to reduce progressively areas of ignorance on the interrelationship between political, social, cultural and economic aspects of Latin American development. Even in the case of pure economic research more pragmatic attitudes are in order. Theoretical propositions arising from intuitive knowledge of Latin America's problems must be tested against reality more rigorously than in the past.

Fortunately this last proposition finds more and more supporters in the advanced countries themselves. A recent worldwide survey of the contributions to economic growth theory makes a very eloquent plea in the same direction. Stating that one should not underestimate the scientific contributions of this theory in the past twenty-five years, the survey agrees that it is probable that the point of diminishing returns may have been reached

> Nothing is easier than to bring the changes on more and more complicated models, without bringing in any really new ideas and without bringing the theory any nearer to casting light on the causes of the wealth of nations. The problems posed may well have intellectual fascination. But it is essentially a frivolous occupation to take a chain with links of very uneven strength and devote one's energies to strengthening and polishing the links that are already relatively strong(5).

The same preoccupation about the growing divorce between economic theorizing and reality emerges from similar survey of developments in the theory of international trade, where hope is expressed that the seventies will see some important theoretical advances

> as the theorists pick up the impressive and paradoxical doctrines and the piecemeal arguments of the critics - arguments which are often based on close observation or sound instincts about the real world - and systematize and relate them to the body of received doctrine(6).

What we know about the nature of the Latin American development process and the magnitude of the difficulties involved is largely due to the efforts of the UN Economic Commission on Latin America in the fifties and sixties. Its research and its 'doctrine', as known through numerous Prebisch writings and ECLA studies, have been criticized both inside and outside Latin America for lack of scientific rigour and for many internal contradictions. It has often been said that the ECLA 'doctrine', build around the concepts of the division of the world economy into an advanced centre (or a group of centres) and backward peripheries, the uneven distribution of the benefits of technological progress, the secular deterioration of the terms of trade of primary producing countries and of the subsequent chronic external disequilibrium, affecting in a decisive way growth prospects for Latin America, has been constructed on a series of questionable _a priori_ assumptions. The ECLA programme of economic policy action, calling for import substitution, accelerated industrialization and regional economic integration has been no less challenged, especially outside the area, as running counter to traditional theoretical welfare maximization concepts. ECLA programming and planning techniques have not escaped harsh criticisms on both theoretical and practical grounds.

But looking at the ECLA doctrine and research efforts from a broader perspective, based as they are on direct observation of the real world or sound intuition, they nevertheless provide people working in the social sciences in Latin America with valuable insights into the nature of _real_ problems facing the region. As Victor L. Urquidi put it, whether one is ready or not to accept many parts of ECLA 'doctrine' and its research methods, one must recognize that thanks to that UN regional commission's Secretariat

> a consistent set of ideas has progressively emerged, at least within Latin America, that serves the long-run interests of economies with structures similar to those of Latin American countries . . . [and] ECLA studies have not only been of great use to individual countries of the region by stimulating studies and research projects at the national level, but also represent the most important antecedents for the Alliance for Progress and the present work of the UNCTAD on problems of relations between the advanced and the underdeveloped sectors of the world economy(7).

In other words, ECLA research with all its theoretical and conceptual shortcomings has had a germinal effect in Latin America in respect both to understanding the nature of the region's underdevelopment and the functioning of the world economy. It was only in the sixties that in developed countries the idea gained ground that the evolution of the advanced sectors of the world economy might not be understood properly 'in isolation from the sectors that are less developed'(8). ECLA staff, particularly Prebisch, were largely responsible for this breakthrough in understanding of pressing world economic problems. It is obviously a high priority task for economists in the more developed regions to attempt to test ECLA 'doctrine' against their accumulated knowledge of problems in other underdeveloped areas and to see to what extent some basic tenets of this 'doctrine' could be incorporated into the theory of growth and the dynamic theory of international trade, both of which badly need to be incorporated in turn into a larger whole. The matter cannot be disposed of easily by sermons and admonitions of some once highly estimated theorists. Neither can it be taken care of by frequent irrelevant comments originating with scholars from the lesser-known universities in advanced countries.

RESEARCH METHODS AND PERSONNEL

Although ECLA doctrine is accepted with certain reservations by a large sector of modern Latin American economists and other social scientists of the post-war generation, relatively little is being done in Latin American national economic research centres to transform this 'doctrine' into a body of homogenous economic theory. Wherever in the region research work is done based on ECLA precepts, it amounts mainly to the use of ECLA economic analysis and programming techniques to support policy solutions in such sectors as planning, industrial programming and external trade.

The reasons for such partial approaches are manifold. First, of a score of research and training institutes scattered throughout Latin America, but concentrated mainly in five countries, namely Argentina, Chile, Colombia, Mexico and Venezuela, relatively few have been able to undertake long-term research programmes with clearly established sets of priorities, adequate organizational arrangements, and necessary manpower and financial resources. In the mid-sixties most of the institutes are still primarily dedicated to training and, as was pointed out in a report on a visit to Latin America (undertaken in 1965 by an official of the OECD Development Centre) this training consists mainly of improving the level of general economic education in the area and not in preparing potential researchers in the social sciences(9). Second, the demand for highly trained economists coming from the public sectors and international organizations is strong in most Latin American republics and at the same time, neither teaching nor scientific research offer incentives, whether of a financial or prestige nature, comparable to those available in other fields. Thirdly, the politicization of Latin American intellectual élites is not conducive to mobilizing experienced social scientists for long-term research purposes. A Latin American economics graduate - with exceptions, of course - if he is in agreement with the political set-up in his country, will either enter into government service, with possibilities of a relatively rapid political career, or join private business groups, with immediate financial rewards. If he disagrees with the regime, he may go for a while to a university not only to teach but to influence politically the younger generation, but will have little time or interest for research. If the political climate becomes unbearable, he will emigrate to an international organization, hoping for an early return to his home country after some political upheaval.

Under these circumstances, possibly with the sole exceptions of Argentina and, a few years previously, Chile, adequate human resources are not available for longer-term research purposes, although the general betterment of levels of education, increasing social mobility, and the growing stream of young economists returning home after post-graduate work at the universities in the advanced countries, have been improving prospects in this area since the mid-fifties. Thus, it seems that, whereas various Latin American countries have substantial numbers of potential researchers in some specialized fields, the critical shortage still persists at the highest level. There is an acute lack of people with both high professional and organizational abilities who could - assuming greater financial support - launch broadly-conceived research projects or strengthen the research side of existing economic development institutes.

Any well-organized presentation of research ventures current in the mid-sixties in Latin America is difficult, because most of the institutes, even when located in the same country, are possessed of a considerable degree of independence and their respective research programmes reflect both professional preferences of their directors and the pressure for studying immediate problems, forthcoming from the national public agencies which co-sponsor or offer some additional funds to the research institutes. In some senses, many Latin American research institutes play a dual role as consultants to government agencies, first, and as academic research centres, second. Since the order of priority for studies required by state agencies is as a rule unpredictable and under Latin American political conditions changes constantly, the mapping out of some research patterns within a country and for the region as a whole is not an easy task.

Thus the list of research projects in Argentina, Brazil, Chile, Colombia, Mexico and Venezuela covers such varied subjects as improvement of national accounts, production-functions, agricultural projections, consumer budgets, export and import capacity, intra-territorial balance-of-payments, projections of water or electric-energy requirements for the next decade, research in economics of education, socio-economic analysis of a key economic region, operational research in selected industries, economic effects of urbanization, etc. The only common feature in the research programmes of most institutes, and probably more valuable in the long run than many concrete research projects themselves, is the increasing emphasis on elaboration and improvement of statistical data, a task of extreme urgency all over Latin America. But even in this field most institutes follow very varied approaches in respect to methodology, leaving to ECLA and other regional institutions the difficult task of establishing meaningful comparisons between various national statistical series. Attempts to bring some conceptual methodological order in the field of Latin American statistics have brought as yet very limited results, as can be seen from a cursory comparison of such series as the balance-of-payments accounts, national income statistics, or even relatively simple foreign trade series. It is clear that such a deficient state of Latin American statistics makes extremely difficult any attempt to organize economic and social research on a comparative, regional scale and casts doubts upon the validity of global surveys of the Latin American economy, based necessarily on largely estimated aggregates. Interestingly enough, there does not seem to exist any direct relation between the quality of the statistical data and the level of economic development or social advancement. Some relatively backward and small republics have often at their disposal much better statistical basic series than countries with the characteristics of a European society or those witnessing rapid and sustained economic growth and the rise of professional classes.

Although a lack of cooperation between research institutes at the national level and among institutes in the area as a whole still characterizes Latin America, certain promising trends have appeared. They are stimulated both from outside and find expression in a growing, but still limited, number of joint or parallel research projects, launched in various countries

simultaneously in specific well-defined fields. In the region itself, the
initiative comes principally from ECLA and its Economic and Social Planning
Institute, which has undertaken a number of projects in cooperation with
national research institutes on subjects such as real income comparisons for
the region as a whole, the role of agriculture in Latin American development,
sectoral studies of Latin American industrialization prospects, projections
of the demand and supply of petroleum and petroleum products in the area, etc.
These projects differ considerably from previous ECLA research practices
where research on a regional scale was done in a centralized way on the basis
of data provided to the ECLA Secretariat by national governments.

It may well be that the scarcity of financial resources, faced by all UN
agencies, is partially responsible for this very welcome change which brings
national research institutes into the mainstream of regional economic problems, but the emergence of the Latin American Free Trade Zone and the Central
American Common Market is also important. Similar attempts to mobilize
national research institutes for multinational research efforts can be discerned in the Inter-American Development Bank and even in the Organisation of
American States, although the OAS seems to follow a practice of parcelling
out some research to those Latin American research institutes which are known
for their 'political respectability'. It is too early, however, to pass any
judgement on the result of these first attempts to multilateralize and regionalize research effort in Latin America, since no major projects, managed
jointly by a regional institution and a group of national institutes, have
been completed as of the summer of 1965.

RESEARCH ON LATIN AMERICA

United States research on Latin American economies is still done in a haphazard way notwithstanding the increasing number of institutions and researchers and the growing magnitude of funds dedicated to the area. Research on
Latin America is being done in many places: (1) within the leading development
research institutes at top United States universities, dealing either with the
underdeveloped areas as a whole or with some specific aspects of global underdevelopment; (2) in a dozen centres, institutes, or programmes, devoted specifically to Latin American research located as a rule also at the major United
States universities(10); (3) in another dozen private research and consulting
firms, located mainly in Washington, and working principally on a contractual
basis for United States government agencies and large corporations; and,
finally, (4) by some individual experts on Latin American economic affairs
holding chairs at universities without special interest in the region, who
nevertheless foster their own professional interests among their post-graduate
students, as suggested by a growing number of doctoral theses on Latin America,
listed annually in The American Economic Review.

Leaving aside a considerable volume of allegedly economic literature meant to
squeeze into a few hundred pages a full diagnosis - both politically loaded and
'cold war' tinted - of Latin American ills under attractive titles of, let us say,
'Strategy for the Americas' or 'Economic Development with Freedom', the
remaining serious literature on Latin American economic development followed
until very recently, with few exceptions, certain rather well-defined patterns
in respect both to topical and geographical areas of interest. Among the
favourite subjects were monetary and financial systems and policies, analysis -
in traditional terms - of Latin American inflationary processes, and of
obstacles to foreign investment in the area, and case studies of the economic

development experience of the major Latin American republics, covering as a rule a couple of decades. This last topic seems to attract candidates for doctoral degrees in economics and political science, suggesting a considerable amount of intellectual and scientific naivety on the part of their authors, obviously unaware of the paucity of first-hand research material and the complexity of the subject itself. Lately, a couple of new topics have emerged. Amongst economists the Central American Common Market has become very fashionable and many demographers have been attracted to the subject of demographic aspects of Latin American economic development.

In respect to area priorities, and again leaving aside the 'cold war' subject of Cuba, on which numerous books have appeared in the United States without a trace as yet of any serious analysis of either pre-Castro or post-Castro Cuban economic development experiences, Central America, including the colonial economies of the formerly European-owned Caribbean Islands, seems to have a considerably greater fascination for United States social scientists and economists than the South American republics. Interest in Mexico, a country which became the subject of a rapidly multiplying number of inquiries within the framework of topical priorities mentioned earlier, strongly suggests that a large part of the United States scholarly community believes or suspects that a detailed knowledge of the Mexican development experiences in the past few decades will throw substantial light on problems faced by the rest of Latin America. The writer, for one, does not believe in the validity of such an approach as long as research on Mexico follows traditional topics and traditional lines of economic thought. Only when outside researchers start directing their attention to the obstacles to economic development still faced by Mexico in spite of its impressive economic growth during the past quarter of the century, will some valuable insights be gained into problems faced by the rest of the area, where conditions for economic and social development do not exist such as were created in Mexico by the revolutionary upheaval of 1910-21, which destroyed the fabrics of the semi-feudal society and the foreign-oriented economy.

Economic research by United States scholars on South America concentrates on Argentina and Brazil with some, perhaps growing, attention to four middle-sized republics, more advanced than the rest of the area: Chile, Colombia, Peru and Venezuela. The smallest or the most backward countries: Bolivia, Ecuador, Paraguay and the six Central American republics, considered individually, are still primarily left to anthropologists and sociologists of primitive cultures, as if no process of rapid socio-economic change were occurring in these parts of the region, perhaps with intensity greater than in the more economically advanced countries. The exception to this negligence by outside economists toward the most backward parts of Latin America, where the reciprocal impact of dual economies on dual societies can be observed at a close range, especially in respect of the disruptive or destabilizing effect of economic development in a primitive society, is represented by growing interest in the Brazilian northeast, explained probably not only by the sheer size of this depressed area but by its weight in Brazilian society.

One could hardly consider as important, on the other hand, part of the research on problems of the least developed parts of Latin America - numerous surveys and studies of their limited industrial potential made by regional organizations and by United States private consulting firms under contract to government agencies or private foreign corporations. Most of these studies are prepared for the immediate clients and are not published for general distribution. As one major research and consulting institute, working under an AID contract in a certain South American country put it, the purpose of its industrial studies is to 'determine the types of industries best suited to the country, identifying foreign concerns willing to invest in these industries, and provide the necessary background information to the foreign concerns'. Such research, independent from its value as source material for future students of the economies in question, can hardly meet with enthusiastic cooperation from Latin American scholars, economists and social scientists.

Until the early sixties economic and social research on Latin America was conducted - with very few exceptions - separately within Latin America and in the United States, being based upon somewhat different sets of motivations. Only recently was some kind of rapport established between Latin American research institutes and their United States counterparts, so much stronger in terms of staff and financial resources. The joint projects, launched or initiated by those few United States scholars with some empathy towards Latin America and Latin American economic development objectives (so that they do not come to Latin America to tell its intellectual élite what it should do to attain post-haste with the use of orthodox text-book formulae, the bliss reigning in advanced capitalist economies and are not considered outright agents of foreign governments or large private corporations) are probably the most useful in a long-run approach to the region's economic research needs.

Such joint projects as Brookings Institution's study of Latin American key industries from the viewpoint of their possible participation in regional economic integration or that launched by the University of Oregon with Resources for the Future, Inc. on the relationship between host countries and foreign mining companies operating in Latin America seem to have received full cooperation from both scholars and policymakers in the region because of a happy combination of factors. First, they represent joint ventures with participation of research institutes of various Latin American countries, where similar skills and research effort are provided by the parties concerned, with United States scholars offering economic research techniques, and Latin Americans' actual knowledge of the field of research with its political and other non-economic implications. Secondly, the projects address themselves to problems not only fascinating intellectually but considered in Latin America as of great importance for direct economic policy ends, thus assisting development in the fullest sense. Thirdly, they do not abstain from entering into politically-sensitive issues, thus breaking with a tradition, loathed all over Latin America, of some international organizations located outside the area, which taking a cue from interested governments and also, for reasons and philosophy of their own, consider most of the real issues so politically sensitive that they deserve only to be treated in confidential memoranda for circulation at the highest political level with little effect on actual economic policy.

Whenever the joint research ventures are followed up by the establishment of more permanent institutional links, exchange of research staff and financial help for the build-up of local research and training institutes, these initiatives are readily accepted by the Latin American scholarly community, as witnessed by the mobilization of local skills for research under arrangements in which, for example, the University of California participates in Brazil, Chile and Venezuela. Once it has been proven that a foreign researcher is not working with the cold objectivity of an early explorer of tribal customs in Melanesia, or is not coming on an intelligence mission to learn the socio-economic topography of potential enemy territory, wide possibilities of cooperation emerge. The success of some joint ventures, led by people of intellectual integrity independently of their nationality, suggests that it is probably the most efficient way in which common knowledge of the Latin American development process can be enriched.

Nevertheless, a word of warning that communication between Latin American and outside scholars is breaking down progressively, mentioned in the early part of this paper, has to be repeated here. This breakdown has been reinforced by research projects, born in the heads of some global strategists outside Latin America, and devoid of any political sensitivity, as suggested by results of the so-called Camelot Project(11). This research venture, suspended after a political scandal in Argentina and Chile, was launched by a large United States university under sponsorship and financing of the United States Defense Department. The outline of the project, circulated by the university among leading sociologists in Argentina, Chile, Colombia, Peru and Venezuela, announced a study into 'the potential for internal war' in Latin American countries. The same outline explained that the need for the projected inquiry was based on the new emphasis given to 'the United States Army's role in the overall United States policy of encouraging steady growth and change in the less developed countries of the world'. The same introductory paper suggested that the purely military concept of counter-insurgency required a deeper understanding of the processes of economic and social change and that independent sources of information were needed from Latin American social scientists to obtain more data on the 'social problems of insurgency'. The United States Army, the university circular added, 'has an important mission in the positive and constructive aspects of nation-building as well as responsibility to assist friendly governments in dealing with active insurgency problems'. The reaction of Argentinian, Chilean and other Latin American intellectuals to the terms of the project was one of dismay and disbelief, and some social scientists came under sharp criticism from the extreme left and ultranationalist circles for accepting such research grants. It was felt that Project Camelot had dealt a sharp blow to future cooperation between Latin American and United States scholarly communities and indeed foreign scholars more generally.

SUGGESTIONS FOR RESEARCH

Whatever the future of relations between Latin American and outside scholars and research centres, the agenda for economic research for Latin America is almost limitless, if one assumes that the purpose of such research is to maximize opportunities for an optimal, but relatively peaceful, transformation of Latin American societies into politically and economically viable concerns. Since we are intuitively aware that this transformation is hampered by many non-economic factors such as, for example, the demographic explosion in Latin America and the new technological revolution in advanced countries, there is an urgent need for a major and organized research effort in the field of what Colm and Geiger termed (at the Brookings Institution Conference in 1961) 'development studies', to be undertaken by independent non-governmental research institutes with possible participation of experts from both the developing and advanced countries but without pressures and limitations imposed by government agencies and international organizations.

During the early sixties in Latin America, practically everybody preached the need for development planning, without agreement ever being reached about how to go about planning in transitional societies. Although short-, medium- and long-term plans were elaborated under the auspices of the most august international expert groups, the fact remains that Latin American economic planning - to repeat Hagen's remarks made at the OECD meeting on training, held in Washington in 1964 - is neither imperative nor indicative. It is a largely decorative exercise. Without a comprehensive, detailed and objective appraisal of repeated failures of numerous plans, elaborated in many cases in the most elegant and competent way by mathematically-minded theorists, one will get nowhere and the point may be reached when the word 'planning' will become a meaningless expression for those large segments of Latin American public opinion which expect from planning so much in terms of increased economic and social welfare. Available research source materials, which might throw considerable light on the reasons for the failure of Latin American economic plans, but are considered in many places as either restricted or classified documentation, weigh, one is told on good authority, several tons. Should not then a brief moratorium be announced in Latin America on further efforts to refine planning and programming techniques and stock be taken instead of what went wrong, where, and why, when the plans passed from the boards of planners to development planning practitioners for implementation.

If, as suspected, national development planning, as understood by experts, is still impossible in many backward societies, should not one, instead of forcing meaningless plans upon them, dedicate available human and financial resources to research on obstacles to or prerequisites of the planning processes in Latin America, and once these obstacles and prerequisities are thus defined, offer to policymakers advice on how certain major obstacles can be cut to manageable size and how basic prerequisites for national planning can be established? In cases where such economic policy exercises prove unrealistic, should one not suspend comprehensive planning attempts and accept less impressive goals, such as good preparation of individual development projects or sectoral programmes with a hope that they will have some beneficial effect on the economy and the society?

Such a pragmatic approach to development needs would lead immediately to research on many politically-sensitive issues. It would involve first and foremost an objective confrontation of the actual results of development policy programmes with the results of economic policies toward the region followed by the advanced countries. Such a confrontation, undertaken jointly by Latin America and non-Latin American scholars, would necessarily have to redefine the concept of economic and financial aid, the concept which - as a perusal of reports released in advanced countries about the flow of external resources to underdeveloped regions attests - measures aid in purely accounting terms. The inquiry would also have to delve deeply into the contribution of foreign private investment to economic development, problems subject to basic controversy and on which the literature is scanty(12). Furthermore, this inquiry would have to deal in detail with costs to Latin American economies of the transfer of modern technology, which is an obvious condition of economic development, a subject about which practically nothing is known inside and outside of the region. It would also have to occupy itself with other aspects of external economic relations of Latin America, knowledge of which is limited to literature, not fully comprehensive, provided by ECLA and UNCTAD's economic staff.

If one descends from regional research to the national level, the list of subjects practically untouched by Latin American and foreign researchers is not less impressive. We know relatively little about the respective roles in Latin America's modern economic development process of the state and the private sector, and even less about income distribution patterns and their effect upon the development or stagnation of different national economies.

We know practically nothing about the present and future impact of accelerated demographic growth, on the one hand, and of labour-saving investment taking place in the dynamic productive sectors, on the other, upon the economic development in the region. Similar examples could be multiplied.

This paper has tried to demonstrate that on the Latin American side human and financial resources for development research are very limited both in absolute and relative terms. The situation is more promising in the advanced countries, although there the human base for development research seems to be much weaker than the available financial resources. The latter, one would suspect, are wasted in considerable quantities because of traditional attitudes toward development research and the development process itself among many of the dispensers of funds.

All this does not mean that one should try to correct all things at once, elaborate a comprehensive research agenda for Latin America and then attempt to distribute respective assignments to available research institutions or potential research leaders. Crash programmes often end with a crash and the development process in Latin America, as elsewhere, hardly lends itself to a centralized research approach.

In the process of economic policymaking in developing societies, the role of an adviser is often - contrary to his public image - limited to that of foreseeing in time and eliminating, if possible also in time, the probability of major policy disasters, and also diminishing to reasonable proportions wastage in allocation of available resources. In the field of development research such a minimalist approach might also have considerable practical advantages. Following this line of reasoning, one might suggest that a major disaster would occur if communication between scholars from the advanced and the underdeveloped regions should finally break down. It is still avoidable, if a common effort is made to limit the invasion of Latin America by pseudo-experts from the advanced countries with highly developed superiority complexes. The second step would amount to giving more emphasis to the building of research institutions in Latin America. Third, and last, the idea of research on Latin America from the outside without local participation still prevailing in many universities and development institutes in advanced countries should be abandoned in favour of joint research programmes or projects led by groups of scholars of different nationalities and representing various disciplines. As long as leaders or participants in these projects from the advanced countries prove their intellectual integrity, as has been demonstrated many times in the past, they may count on the full cooperation of their Latin American colleagues, whose ability to judge such integrity should not be underestimated.

Once the danger of a major general disaster is eliminated, one might dedicate efforts to diminishing wastage in allocation of available research resources by weeding out research projects and proposals with superficial intellectual fascination but with little bearing upon the urgent development needs of the region. This suggestion should not be construed as an attack on the freedom of scientific inquiry or a call for research censorship. It represents rather a plea for a commonsense approach, badly needed in a situation where resources are visibly limited, needs seem to be practically endless, and socio-economic tensions continue to increase.

NOTES

(1) The Brookings Institution, Development of the Emerging Countries - An Agenda for Research, Washington, D.C., 1962.

(2) Robert E. Asher, Development of Emerging Countries, op. cit., p. 215.

(3) See contributions to this debate in a Chilean journal Economía, Vol. 22 (1st, 2nd-3rd quarters, 1964) and a Mexican journal El Trimestre Económico (Vol. 32, No. 126 (1st quarter, 1965) by Anibal Pinto, Osvaldo Sunkel, Dudley Seers, Carlos Hurtado and E. Patricio Silva.

(4) See the uninhibited essay of J.K. Galbraith, The Language of Economics, Fontana, New York, December 1962.

(5) F.H. Hahn and R.C. Mathews 'The Theory of Economic Growth: A Survey', The Economic Journal, Vol. 74, No. 296 (December), p. 890.

(6) W.M. Corden, Recent Developments in the Theory of International Trade, Special Papers in International Finance Section, Department of Economics, Princeton University, Princeton, N.J., March 1965, p. 65.

(7) Victor L. Urquidi, Nuevas consideraciones sobre la investigacion economica de América Latina, paper presented to Rio de Janeiro conference on the status of social sciences in Latin America, April 1965. (Translation from Spanish by M. Wionczek).

(8) Hahn and Mathews, op. cit., p. 891.

(9) François van Hoek, Formation et recherche en matière de développement économique en Amérique du Sud, OECD Development Centre, Paris, 5 May 1965 (mimeograph).

(10) The Universities of California, Columbia, Cornell, Harvard, Tulane, Vanderbildt, Wisconsin and Yale, among others, had some sort of Latin American institutes or research programmes in the mid-sixties.

(11) Details of Project Camelot and its effect are taken from a cable from Buenos Aires by Henry Raymont, entitled 'US is Due to Drop Study of Latin Insurgency', published in The New York Times, 8 July 1965. It may be worth noting that 'who is doing research for what purposes' in Latin America is perhaps as important from the viewpoint of communication and final research results as the subject of research itself. The US Department of Agriculture organized a few years ago a series of detailed studies by Latin American experts on the future structure of demand and supply of agricultural commodities in selected Latin American countries, including Brazil, Chile, Colombia, Mexico and Venezuela. The project did not encounter difficulties anywhere and judging by preliminary information will yield extremely useful and enlightening results both for the countries under study and for United States agricultural policymakers.

(12) In spite of many decades of flows of US private capital into Latin America, for example, a US political scientist and economist had to admit recently that 'we have little knowledge of the political significance of sources of local [Latin American] unfavourable attitudes [toward foreign private capital] - whether they arise from misinformation and ignorance . . . ,

or whether they reflect a basic clash in economic and political ideology, or whether they stem from a genuine conflict in economic interests between foreign investors and the host country', Leland Johnson, <u>US Private Investment in Latin America: Some Questions of National Policy</u>, The Rand Corporation, Santa Monica, California, July 1964, p. 9.

REFERENCES

BROOKINGS INSTITUTION (1962), <u>Development of the Emerging Countries - An Agenda for Research</u> (with contributions by Robert E. Asher, Everett E. Hagen, Albert O. Hirschman, Gerhard Holm, Theodore Geiger, Arthur T. Mosher, R.S. Eckaus, Mary Jean Bowman, C. Arnold Anderson and Howard Wriggins), Washington, D.C.

van HOEK, François (1965), 'Formation et recherche en matière de développement économique en Amérique du Sud', OECD Development Centre, Paris, 5 May 1965 (CD/F/1073), unpublished mimeograph.

MASSAD, Carlos (1964), 'Economic Research in Latin America', <u>Social Science Research on Latin America</u>, Charles Wagley (Editor), Report and papers on a Seminar on Latin American Studies in the United States held at Stanford, California, 8 July - 23 August 1963, Columbia University Press, New York, pp. 214-42.

PAN AMERICAN UNION (1961), <u>The Teaching of Economics in Latin America</u>, Studies and Monographs, I, Organisation of American States, Washington, D.C.

URQUIDI, Victor L. (1965), 'Nuevas consideraciones sobre la investigacion economica en América Latina', Unpublished paper presented at an interdisciplinary meeting on the state of social sciences in Latin America, held in Rio de Janeiro, 27-9 May 1965, under auspices of Social Science Research Council and Centro Latinoamericano de Investigaciones en Ciencias Sociales.

U.S. DEPARTMENT OF STATE (1964), <u>Research Centres on the Developing Areas</u> paper prepared for the Agency for International Development by the External Research Staff, Washington, D.C. (November).

CHAPTER 8

Latin American Growth and Trade Strategies in the Post-War Period*

THIS paper attempts a general assessment of Latin American foreign trade performance in the recent past and particularly of the role of export growth in the present and future economic development of that region because as the prospectus for the Fifth Pacific Trade and Development Conference postulated, the economic growth of developing areas depends very much upon their export expansion. Under present conditions of the world economy and trade this expansion in turn poses problems of shifts in policies from import substitution to export promotion and of determination of proper industrial priorities for export. Moreover, whatever shifts are made and priorities defined on a country or a regional level, the final results of the new trade and development policies will largely depend upon trade policies and structural adjustments in advanced countries.

Covering these topics for the Latin American subcontinent as a whole is not an easy task. Latin America may seem a more or less homogeneous unit, considerably more developed than either Africa or the eastern and southeastern rim of Asia extending from Korea to Pakistan. But a closer look strongly suggests that Latin America is hardly more than a geo-political and geo-economic concept. Twenty-five economic indicators for Latin American republics (excluding Cuba and four ex-British colonies in the Caribbean that have gained independence – Jamaica, Trinidad, Guyana and Barbados), contained in Table 8.1, disclose that regional quantitative averages hide, in practically every respect, tremendous differences within the region.

As shown in the table, populationwise the region comprises giants like Brazil (90 million in 1969) and mini-states like Panama (1.4 million); the annual demographic growth rates vary from 3.8 per cent in Costa Rica to 1.1 per cent in Uruguay; the average annual GDP growth oscillated in the 1960s between 8 per cent in Panama and -0.3 per cent in Haiti; the per capita product ranges (1969) between US $980 in Argentina and US $98 in Haiti; population employed in agriculture accounts for close to 67 per cent of the labour force in

---

*This paper was presented at the Fifth Pacific Trade and Development Conference held in Tokyo, Japan in January 1973, and published in Development and Change, Sage Publications Ltd., The Hague, Vol. 5, No. 1, 1973-74.

TABLE 8.1. Regional Differences within Major Indicators of Economic Growth in Latin America during the 1960s

	Average	Highest	Lowest
Population (19 countries)(millions 1969)	13.6	90.6 Brazil	1.4 Panama
Annual growth rates of GNP (1959-69)	5.4%	8.0% Panama	1.1% Uruguay
Annual population growth (1960-69)	2.9%	3.8% C. Rica	1.3% Uruguay
Annual per capita growth rate of GNP (1960-69)	2.5%	4.8% Panama	-0.3% Haiti
GDP per capita 1969	514 Dls.	980 Dls. Argentina	98 Dls. Haiti
GDP per employed person (at 1960 prices)	1,269 Dls.	2,628 Dls. Argentina	216 Dls. Haiti
Percentage of population employed in industry and basic services 1969	—	36.9% Argentina	12.3% Honduras
Rate of growth of industrial output (1959-69)	6.4%	9.3% Nicaragua	0.9% Uruguay
Percentage of population employed in agriculture 1969	—	66.9% Honduras	15.6% Argentina
Rate of growth of agricultural output (1959-69)	3.5%	5.4% C.Rica	1.4% Uruguay
Average annual changes in consumer prices (1960-69)	—	47.1% Uruguay	0.4% El Salvador
Participation of agriculture in GDP 1969	17.3%	45.9% Haiti	7.8% Venezuela
Changes in the relative participation of industry and basic services in GDP between 1960 and 1969	—	37.7% Honduras	-2.2% Venezuela
Changes in the relative participation of employment in agriculture between 1960 and 1969	—	-22.2% Venezuela	-3.8% El Salvador
Changes in the relative participation of employment in industry and basic services between 1960 and 1969	—	15.6% Panama	-6.9% Ecuador
Participation of capital and intermediate goods in total industrial output 1969	—	60.1% Argentina	8.1% Guatemala
Direct taxes as percentage of the total tax revenue 1967-68	—	67.6% Venezuela	22.5% Guatemala
Ratio between government savings and public investment 1967-68	—	123.8% Ecuador	7.1% Bolivia
Investment coefficient of GDP 1969	19.6%	23.7% Paraguay	5.0% Haiti
Participation of net foreign financing in total investment, average 1967-69	7.1%	43.4% Dom.Rep.	-1.4% Uruguay
Participation of public sector in total fixed investment, 1969	—	58.6% Chile	17.2% Uruguay
Export coefficient of GDP, average 1967-69	10.7	39.0% Panama	6.1% Brazil
Import coefficient of GDP, average 1967-69	9.8	32.6% Honduras	12.3% Honduras

Source: ECLA, Economic Survey of Latin America, annual issues corresponding to the years 1964-71.

Honduras and only 15.6 in Argentina; annual price increases in the 1960s differed from 47.5 per cent in Uruguay to 0.4 per cent in El Salvador; investment coefficients as percentages of GDP were in 1969 as high as 23.7 per cent in Paraguay and as low as 5 per cent in Haiti. Finally, in respect to the importance of foreign trade for individual economies, at one end of the spectrum are countries such as Brazil with about 6 per cent of exports and imports as ratio of GDP, and at the other Panama with an export coefficient of 39 per cent and Honduras with an import coefficient of 32.6 per cent.

Traditionally, the subcontinent is considered as a conglomerate, composed of three large and semi-developed economies (Argentina, Brazil and Mexico), a half-dozen intermediate developing countries (like Venezuela, Colombia, Peru or Chile) and about a dozen republics that, in spite of the large territorial size of some (Bolivia or Paraguay), represent the hard core of Latin American underdevelopment. In fact, however, the picture is much more complicated. The region includes semi-industrial and also heavily agriculture-based economies rapidly growing in conditions of relative financial stability and more or less solid structural balance-of-payments positions; stagnant semi-industrial and agricultural economies with high degrees of inflation and increasing external sector constraints; economies with similar productive structures but highly dependent in some cases on public domestically-financed investment and in others on private foreign capital; dynamic as well as stagnant economies with different degrees of dependence on foreign trade; economies with fairly developed financial structures along with those lacking rudimentary networks of financial intermediaries, etc.

If additional economic indicators at the national level were included in Table 8.1, one would face a whole universe of socio-economic development models, starting with highly centralized socialist or semi-socialist economies, passing through those with a large degree of state intervention and participation and ending with almost free-market economies. Combining the characteristics of economic structures, political and economic policy instruments and social objectives, one would discover in Latin America an even more impressive array of socio-economic performance. In terms of historical comparison, and using such indicators as literacy and income distribution, one finds societies clearly still at the beginning of the present century, side by side with those whose degree of modernization is somewhat similar to that reached by the industrial countries between the two world wars. Moreover, even in the most advanced Latin American republics in respect of level of <u>per capita</u> income, it is easy to detect the socio-economic intra-regional and intra-sectorial dualism - the presence of dynamic growth poles and depressed areas together with the coexistence of modern and traditional low productivity activities in each major economic sector.

Only when these deep differences among and within Latin American republics are clearly established can one search for similarity in their economic development patterns in the past twenty-five years, with particular stress upon the behaviour of the external sector. Between 1945 and 1970 Latin America as a whole - but with different intensities and degrees of success reflecting the inequalities in development levels - tried successively three development strategies: import-substituting industrial policies on the national level, regional trade integration, and development of manufacturing for extra-zonal markets. The instruments, mechanics and results of each of these stages will be briefly commented on in this paper.

IMPORT-SUBSTITUTION ORIENTED INDUSTRIALIZATION: POLICIES AND PROBLEMS

Modern quantitative economic history is a very recent social discipline, largely cultivated in advanced countries where the wealth of long-term statistical data series have been discovered, processed and analysed(1). Such economic history has not yet been written for Latin America as a whole, although the first valiant attempts that go back to the colonial times of the region and of major countries and end with the analysis of post-war developments have seen the light in recent years(2). The difficulties of writing an economic history of modern Latin America can be deduced from the introductory remarks of this paper. Fortunately, literature on the import-substituting industrialization period is fairly abundant and of relatively high quality, although as a rule it covers only experiences of the 1945-70 period(3).

This does not mean - as some believe - that import-substituting industrialization started in Latin America during the Second World War. Its beginnings can be traced back in Brazil to the third quarter of the nineteenth century and in Argentina and Mexico to the 1880s. Thus it followed by some twenty-five to thirty years the import-substituting industrialization model adopted in Europe and the United States in the mid-nineteenth century, transfigurated there after a period of initial industrialization ended, around 1900, into industrial specialization among all advanced countries. The early-comers in import-substituting industrialization (continental Europe, the United States and later British white dominions and Japan) aimed at breaking the hold of the British industrial empire over the world economy. Late-comers such as Latin America attempted in turn to break out of the world division of labour that became consolidated in the early part of the present century, leaving for this subcontinent, Asia and Africa the role of suppliers of foodstuffs and raw materials and importers of manufactured goods from the North Atlantic area.

While long-range historical analysis falls beyond the scope of this paper, it may be pertinent to recall that while Latin American industrialization in the 1880-1914 period did not amount to much, it received strong impetus from the First World War, the Great Depression and the Second World War when, because of severe dislocations of the international economic system, the subcontinent faced concurrently extreme shortages of imported consumer manufactures and the slow but constant demand for such goods, particularly in the rapidly growing urban areas. It is common knowledge, however, that in Latin America import-substituting industrialization became a deliberate and principal policy tool only after the end of the Second World War. As ECLA literature of the 1950s insisted(4) and later studies have proved(5), after 1945 Latin America, together with the rest of the underdeveloped world, faced relatively slow growth of world demand for its traditional exports and consequently was forced into alternative economic strategies promising more dynamic growth, particularly in the face of a demographic explosion and large migrations of labour from rural to urban areas.

For the purpose of creating a modern industrial structure that was to diminish Latin American dependence upon the world economy, a surprisingly large number of policy instruments were put to work in Latin America in the 1950s. In his critical appraisal of the import-substituting industrialization experiences of the subcontinent, Werner Baer mentions protective tariffs and/or exchange controls; special preferences for domestic and foreign firms importing capital goods for new industries; preferential import exchange rates for industrial raw materials, fuels and intermediate goods; cheap loans by public development

banks for favoured industries; state financing of infrastructure designed to
foment industrial activities; and the direct participation of government in
certain industrial sectors, especially heavy industry, which in some cases was
considered 'politically strategic', and in other sectors where no private
financial resources, domestic or foreign, were available(6). While this list
of policy instruments is far from complete, it is interesting to note, first,
that it contains almost exclusively financial, fiscal and monetary measures;
second, that it looks very similar to the array of policy instruments used by
the early-comers in the United States and continental Europe a century ago;
and third, that while it puts emphasis on capital accumulation in the private
sector (by effects of protection and open and hidden state subsidies to the
manufacturing sector), very little has been done in respect of improvement of
domestic human capital and technological infrastructure. According to leading
students of economic growth performance in advanced countries, these two
factors are largely responsible for the acceleration of growth rates in the
developed world during the past twenty-five years(7).

In view of the unequal development levels and the varying size of domestic
markets, the results of import-substituting industrialization differed considerably in Latin America. While no clear pattern of a coherent economic
development strategy can be discerned even in the major countries of the area,
the promotion of new industries was in most, if not all, cases indiscriminate,
the mix of policy instruments largely improvised, and the appearance of new
manufacturing activities reflected as a rule the existing demand profile
defined by two major non-economic factors - inherited income distribution
patterns and the demonstration effect of consumption patterns in advanced high-
income countries upon the upper- and middle-income sectors of Latin American
societies.

In respect of overall import-substituting industrialization performance, three
major patterns can be discerned in the region. In the small and most of the
intermediate underdeveloped republics import substitution has never passed the
consumer industries stage(8); in others, like Argentina, Chile and Venezuela,
according to David Felix:

> . . . the initial industries are generally consumer goods or building
> materials products with a relatively simple technology and a low capital
> requirement per worker and per unit of output. Then they are followed by
> consumer goods industries requiring a more sophisticated technology and
> larger capital outlay, shading subsequently into industries producing
> relatively complex consumer durables, steel, engineering and chemical
> products(9).

Only in Brazil and Mexico was some kind of strategy adopted by the state aimed
at maximum vertical integration: the simultaneous promotion of final consumer
goods industries (generally in private hands) and intermediate and capital
goods (owned or heavily subsidized by the state).

In the face of heavy protection, faulty fiscal systems, high consumption
coefficients of the upper and middle-level income sectors and the haphazard
allocation of resources among new manufacturing activities, it is hardly surprising that the political, welfare and financial price of the Latin American
import-substituting strategy of the 1950s and 1960s was much higher than had
been expected by ECLA ideologists of the early post-war period, who had claimed
that import-substituting industrialization would bring to Latin America
greater economic and _ipso facto_ political independence from the advanced world.

ECLA's early position could be defended by pointing out that that regional brains trust did not postulate the autarkic industrialization on the national level that eventually prevailed in the region, and that ECLA was not in the position to foresee the changes in the world's industrial production structure due to the intensity of technological progress and the successful emergence of giant transnational industrial corporations. According to the ideological father of that development strategy, Rául Prebisch, it was about to be exhausted by the late 1960s

> The possibilities of intensifying the rate of substitution in recent years exclusively on the basis of domestic markets depends in large part upon the costs which each country would be willing to incur. This cost has been generally very high in the past. And also speaking in general terms, it is quite possible that it will be very much higher when it involves the intermediate and capital goods industries on which import substitution will be based in the future(10).

Did any substantial changes occur in the position of the manufacturing sector in Latin American economies between 1950 and 1970 if one assumes that, in spite of efforts in the field of regional trade, cooperation in the sixties and attempts after 1965 to produce manufactures for export to the advanced countries, the main post-war strategy concentrated on import-substituting industrialization? Available data do not suggest such deep changes.

Tables 8.2 and 8.3 strongly suggest that the progress of import-substituting industrialization ran rather rapidly into heavy difficulties in Latin America. Between 1950 and 1970 the manufacturing output participation increased from about 19 per cent to only 25.6 per cent of the region's GDP. Only in five countries (Argentina, Chile, Brazil, Mexico and Peru) had it exceeded 20 per cent by 1970, while in the rest of the region it hovered on the average around 16 per cent of GDP. Annual growth rates of industrial product, while obviously higher than those of the growth of the whole economy, declined perceptibly, from 6.8 per cent in the 1940s to 6.3 in the fifties and 5.4 in the sixties, suggesting the Prebisch-mentioned exhaustion of import-substituting industrialization on the national level. As should have been expected, because of its concentration on final consumer non-durables, that strategy debilitated rather than strengthened the Latin American position in world trade and created serious pressures on trade balances with the outside world. Latin America's participation in world exports declined from 10.6 per cent in 1950 to about 5 per cent in 1970, while import coefficients continued unchanged: the value of imports of goods and services represented 10.2 per cent of GDP in 1948-49 and 9.9 per cent twenty years later(11).

Moreover, there are reasons to believe that import-substituting industrialization did not help to any extent to solve or even alleviate socio-economic problems facing Latin America in the post-war period. Its costs were paid in part by agriculture and in part by the urban consumer, leading to further deterioration of intra-country income distribution.

Furthermore, import-substituting industrialization was unable to contribute in a tangible way to improvement of the employment problem. While the industrial product of Latin America expanded in the fifties and sixties at the average rate of 6 per cent, industrial employment grew between 1950 and 1968 by only 2.8 per cent, resulting in the accentuation of these major socio-economic difficulties: growing unemployment and underemployment in rural areas, large and growing migration of part of the surplus agricultural labour

TABLE 8.2. Participation of Manufacturing in GDP in Latin America, 1950-70

	1950	1960	1970[1]
Argentina	28.9	31.3	35.7
Bolivia	12.0	10.7	13.2
Brazil	16.5	23.4	24.7
Columbia	14.2	17.0	18.9
Chile	16.7	18.8	25.5
Ecuador	16.0	15.7	16.9
Paraguay	19.4	17.3	18.6
Peru	14.6	17.7	22.9
Uruguay	17.4	21.2	22.3
Venezuela	9.6	11.6	11.9
Mexico	18.4	20.5	23.2
Panama	8.2	12.6	17.3
Costa Rica	12.1	12.9	19.6
El Salvador	5.7	7.3	17.1
Guatemala	10.0	10.6	14.0
Honduras	8.5	12.1	15.7
Nicaragua	8.0	9.8	15.9
Latin America[2]	18.9	21.8	25.6

[1] Preliminary.
[2] Includes estimates for Haiti; excludes Cuba and Dominican Republic.

Sources: 1950 and 1960: ECLA, Economic Survey of Latin America, 1964, Table 161; 1970: ECLA, Economic Survey of Latin America, 1970, preliminary individual country data.

force to the cities, and tremendous expansion of urban underemployment in low-productivity traditional service activities.

On the other hand, import-substituting industrialization created or strengthened monopolistic rents accruing to 'domestic' industrial firms, many owned by foreign interests. Moreover, it increased the international indebtedness of the region. The total external debt of Latin America (public debt and foreign direct investment) grew between 1950 and 1969 from US $9600 million to US $35,000 million; the service of that debt in the same period increased from 18.5 to 37.0 per cent of total foreign exchange income originating in Latin American commodity exports(12). Finally, the expected technological modernization of the Latin American productive structure did not take place. Instead the 'prematurely old' industrial sectors emerged.

One of many attempts to evaluate the success and failures of import-substituting industrialization in Latin America, and particularly in Brazil, offers the following verdict

> Hindsight makes it easy to point out specific mistakes, even to suggest some modifications in policy that clearly would have avoided the greatest inefficiencies. It is much harder to compare actual results with those

TABLE 8.3. Changes in Industrial Structures in Latin America, 1955 and 1968

(percentages)

	1955		1968	
	Consumer non-durables	Others[1]	Consumer non-durables	Others[1]
Argentina	52.2	41.8	39.8	60.2
Bolivia	82.5	17.5	71.4	28.6
Brazil	52.5	41.8	41.9	58.1
Colombia	69.3	30.7	63.2	35.8
Chile	57.1	32.9	47.5	52.5
Ecuador	75.8	24.2	65.5	34.5
Paraguay	n.a.	n.a.	n.a.	n.a.
Peru	66.7	3.3	57.3	42.7
Uruguay	62.3	37.7	61.3	38.7
Venezuela	52.6	47.4	48.0	52.0
Mexico	52.9	47.1	41.2	58.8
Panama	75.8	24.2	73.7	26.3
Costa Rica	n.a.	n.a.	n.a.	n.a.
El Salvador	n.a.	n.a.	n.a.	n.a.
Guatemala	94.2	5.8	91.9	8.1
Honduras	n.a.	n.a.	n.a.	n.a.
Nicaragua	n.a.	n.a.	n.a.	n.a.
Dominican Rep.	94.6	5.4	85.7	14.3

[1]Other = consumer durables, intermediate and capital goods.

Source: ECLA, Economic Survey of Latin America, 1970, Table 14.

that might have come from some totally different policy that would not have included industrialization(13).

Such a statement, however, begs the question since it would most probably have been impossible to postulate for post-war Latin America or any other part of the developing world an economic policy that would have totally excluded industrialization. Not only has industrialization been part and parcel of economic growth everywhere since the first industrial revolution in Great Britain in the mid-eighteenth century, but any alternative development policy would have been rejected in Latin America not only on economic but also on political grounds. Thus, the question cannot be reduced to postulating ex post other development venues but should try to ascertain why import-substitution industrialization efforts spent themselves so rapidly without bringing the results expected ex ante(14).

This rephrasing of the issues involved forces us to summarize the multiple criticisms of Latin American post-war quasi-autarkic industrialization(15). The abundant literature on the subject makes it possible to distinguish between the two groups of critics whom Baer classifies conveniently: 'market critics' and 'structural critics'.

Leaving aside the particularly conservative economists within the first school that have seen something wrong in the region's post-war industrialization because it has been running against the principles of worldwide comparative advantage, the 'market critics' see the following drawbacks in the import-substituting industrialization model:

(1) across-the-board promotion of manufacturing activities without regard even to potential comparative advantages and emphasis on autarky;
(2) disregard of economies of scale;
(3) abuse of 'effective' rates of protection;
(4) attempts - in the case of major countries - to foster and maximize vertical industrial integration;
(5) anti-economic allocation of investment resources, particularly by the state, at cost to the agricultural sector;
(6) failure to stimulate traditional exports and diversify the export structure along with progress of the industrialization process; and
(7) the negative impact upon industrial employment of price distortions between sectors, due to the fact that no incentives were created to adopt labour-intensive production techniques.

The 'structuralist critics', on the other hand, stress the following negative aspects of the model:

(1) its effect upon income distribution is already very bad - except in a few southern Latin American republics - resulting in the increase of income concentration and severely braking the growth of demand for industrial products after import-substituting industries have been established;
(2) neglect of potential domestic demand in agriculture and low-income groups employed in the service sectors due, among other reasons, to the implantation of import-substituting industries that produce goods saleable only to high and upper-middle income groups;
(3) strong regional concentration of industry and income for the sake of external economies not only in the three major republics (Argentina, Brazil and Mexico) but also elsewhere, increasing regional income inequalities and reinforcing economic dualism;
(4) indiscriminate inputs of advanced technologies from industrial countries without any serious attempt to adjust them to factor proportions prevailing in Latin America, thus introducing 'technological' unemployment in societies cursed by an almost unlimited supply of labour; and
(5) absence of a clear policy toward foreign private investments that resulted in foreign investors' accumulating monopolistic rents from industrialization fostered under high, if not excessive, protection in small-size markets, inviting oligopolistic practices.

Some criticisms of the two schools represent the formulation of similar drawbacks and deficiencies of the model in different conceptual languages. But in general terms, one is tempted to acknowledge that the 'market school' shows particular preoccupation with the resource allocation results of import-substituting industrialization, while the 'structuralists' criticise the model for almost blindly following industrialization policies of other societies in earlier periods. Practically no consideration is given - they insist - to the socio-economic peculiarities of the Latin American region in the second half of the twentieth century and to social welfare objectives. As the growing number of Latin American economists was willing to admit in the late 1960s, the social costs of the post-war industrialization model were very high, the results amounted to quantitative economic growth instead of economic development, and the region as a whole found itself facing the 'structural lock' situation, characterized by high excess productive capacity, intrasectoral and intraregional imbalances, extremely high prices of industrial goods, and the stagnation of demand closely related to the low absorptive capacity of labour by the manufacturing sector. Consequently, some 'structural critics' add, after two decades of industrial effort, Latin America found itself more dependent than at any previous time on the outside advanced countries, both financially and technologically. Attempts to diminish that dependence have been largely abortive.

While the 'structural school' critique is fairly convincing, it is only fair to state that Latin Americans realized rather late, perhaps as late as the mid-sixties, that there is no such thing as 'easy industrialization'(16). As Bruton, Sideri, and others point out, import substitution as a strategy of Latin American development was to a very large extent arrived at by default, could hardly be described as a development strategy in the sense of a selection of alternative policies aimed at a well-defined objective and, moreover, was based upon the theoretically rather shaky assumption that the import structure of a country was the best indicator of what that country should start producing, given the composition of its factors of production and the available technology. This last assumption left aside two important questions: what kind of socio-economic reality did the import structure reflect? and was the available technology - mostly transferred indiscriminately from abroad - not only the most adequate but the only one available on the international technology market? In early ECLA literature, which theoretically underpinned import-substituting industrialization as practised in Latin America since the fifties, these issues have hardly ever been raised.

The neglect of these two issues: backwardness of the social structures and the lack of technological policies on national and regional levels, has been largely responsible for the very meagre results, not only of Latin American import-substituting industrialization of the post-war period, but also of the two following development models, based first in the 1960s on the regional economic and trade integration model, and after that on industrialization for export to more advanced parts of the world.

REGIONAL ECONOMIC AND TRADE INTEGRATION: THE DISAPPOINTING RECORD OF THE 1960s

In the mid-fifties ECLA technocrats and many economists and reformist politicians started having second thoughts about the longer-term results of the import-substituting industrialization strategy followed by individual Latin American countries after 1940. Consequently, as a corollary to that development strategy, regional economic integration based upon trade liberalization was postulated(17). According to this new strategy, a Latin American Common Market would stimulate the abandonment of patterns of traditional primary commodity trade with industrialized countries, the argument used earlier by import substituting industrialization proponents; moreover, it would help to modernize the Latin American economies by forcing them to specialize within the framework of an expanded and protected regional market. The general ECLA proposition was phrased convincingly:

> Latin America's basic long-run development problems can be solved only if the following fundamental fact is recognized: Latin America, however great assistance it receives, however high the rate at which its exports expand -

and they cannot do so very rapidly - will be unable to carry out its development plans, will be unable even to regain the rate of growth achieved in the ten post-war years, unless it makes a sustained effort to establish within its own territory the capital goods industries of which it is in such urgent need today, and which it will require on a large scale during the next quarter of the century. . . . In order to produce these capital goods and develop all the intermediate goods industries required to launch these highly complex dynamic industries . . . Latin America needs a common market(18).

While accepting ECLA's general development thesis, some individual political figures also saw in economic integration an important vehicle that would permit them to redress somewhat the lack of balance in hemispheric political relations.

Beset by foreign trade problems, lacking external capital assistance and moved by the idea of spiritual and cultural unity, Latin Americans found the proposals for regional economic cooperation attractive. Between 1958 and 1960 the Central Americans established their common market. At the same time, in a parallel but geographically broader movement, six South American republics (Argentina, Brazil, Chile, Paraguay, Peru and Uruguay) and Mexico opted for a free trade zone scheme that would - it was hoped - evolve during the 1970s into a common market covering the whole subcontinent. Drawing upon the example of Western Europe, both schemes accented trade liberalization as a vehicle for regional division of labour. The Central American arrangement provided for the creation of a common market by 1966 for all but a few commodities. The Latin American free trade zone was to be set up by 1972, through annual product-by-product tariff negotiations.

The Central American regional cooperation scheme provided not only for commercial but also for financial, monetary, fiscal and industrial cooperation. In the early 1960s an impressive array of institutions supporting the common market emerged in the area, among them a regional development agency (the Central American Integration Bank), a monetary council, a clearing house, and an industrial research institute. While these agencies worked with relative efficiency, coordination of major economic policies, particularly with respect to the siting of new industries and the common treatment of foreign investment, proved very difficult. The inability to reach agreements in the key field of industrial cooperation, partly because of an absence of national economic planning mechanisms in Central America and partly because of the opposition of powerful external political and economic interests, proved in the late 1960s to be the major source of CACM's difficulties.

The LAFTA agreement (known as the Montevideo Treaty) was less specific in respect to non-commercial cooperation mechanisms. However, it did commit the participating countries - whose initial number of seven increased to eleven by 1968 - 'to facilitate increasing economic integration and complementary economies' by making 'every effort to reconcile their import and export regimes, as well as the treatment they accord to capital, goods and services from outside the Area'. Furthermore, the Montevideo Treaty envisaged 'progressively closer coordination of the corresponding industrialization policies' through agreements 'among representatives of the economic sectors concerned'. Very little, however, was achieved in these fields during the first ten years of LAFTA's life. No regional agreement about the coordination of foreign trade and industrialization policies was reached. Neither was it found possible to agree upon a common treatment for private foreign capital. Only some agreements designed to make industrial developments complementary, by specialization of production in individual industrial branches with concomitant freeing of trade for their output, were signed. While some degree of cooperation was achieved in respect to the multilateral clearing of regional trade balances and maritime transport, these agreements had very little impact upon the expansion of intra-LAFTA trade and no effect whatsoever upon the acceleration of regional economic growth.

The achievements of CACM and LAFTA have been measured mainly by the growth of trade within their respective areas. Consequently, in the mid-1960s it appeared that the Central American Common Market was an unqualified success, whereas the Latin American free trade zone was making slow and hesitant progress. In fact, trade within Central America responded to the establishment of a common market with amazing dynamism. Regional trade flows, measured in terms of imports, increased from US $37 million to US $250 million between 1961 and 1970, or by about 35 per cent a year. About two-thirds of intra-Central American trade consisted of manufactured, mainly consumer goods, suggesting - on the surface - a significant diversification of zonal commerce and the progressive though limited impact of the common market upon the region's production structure.

LAFTA's trade achievements were much less impressive. The signing of the Montevideo Treaty was followed by several years of relatively rapid intra-regional trade expansion, partly in response to early progress in tariff negotiations - 70 per cent of all bilateral tariff concessions granted between 1961 and 1970 corresponded to the first three years of LAFTA's existence (1961-63). By 1970 intra-LAFTA import trade exceeded US $1300 million (11 per cent of the member countries' total import trade) as compared with US $600 million (8 per cent) in 1961. The regional trade of some newcomers to intra-Latin American trade - Mexico, Peru and Ecuador - grew very rapidly from the low levels registered at the end of the 1950s. The bulk of commercial exchange continued to be concentrated in the three southern republics - Argentina, Brazil and Chile - which had a long tradition of reciprocal trade and still accounted in 1970 for close to two-thirds of intra-LAFTA commercial exchange. In spite of the impressive number of tariff reductions (exceeding 11,000 by the end of 1970), very little was achieved in respect to regional trade-product diversification. In 1967 foodstuffs and other primary products, traditionally exchanged by South American republics prior to LAFTA appearance, still represented something like 70 per cent of intra-LAFTA trade. But the biggest setback to LAFTA was that while regional trade continued to grow and exceeded 11 per cent of the total of LAFTA's foreign trade in 1970, trade expansion did not tangibly affect the productive structures of member countries. They continued to be dominated (in respect of primary activities) by traditional trade relations with the outside world; on the national level, in manufacturing and in industry-supporting sectors (energy, transport and infrastructure), the road of inward-directed and import-substitution based policies was largely followed by all LAFTA members.

Thus, it seems that while the rapid setting up of a common market in Central America helped to accelerate trade and growth within that small area (until the issue of equal distribution of integration benefits broke CACM's back in the late 1960s), the trade liberalization measures of the Montevideo Treaty were too weak to produce a similar effect within LAFTA. But not only LAFTA became progressively paralysed at the close of the 1960s; the CACM ran into even more serious difficulties as the result of the 1969 Honduras-El Salvador war, with Honduras withdrawing from the common market arrangement in late

1970, and Costa Rica facing the most serious payment problems with the rest of the area.

An Overview of CACM's Drift into Disaster

A close analysis of CACM's experiences suffices to suggest that the positive impact of common market arrangements of a traditional type upon the economies of its underdeveloped member countries has been heavily overrated. In the absence of joint or even national long-term development policies, particularly in industrial and fiscal fields, the establishment of a common market brought relatively little real growth to Central America, all the impressive figures on intra-area trade notwithstanding. Some sources estimate that only 1 per cent of the annual 7 per cent average growth rate in Central America in the sixties resulted from common-market-induced activities(10). The setting up of a regional trade barrier considerably higher than the previous tariffs of the individual countries did not lead to serious industrialization but rather to the rapid expansion of various types of 'final-touch' industries in the integrated area. Many consumer goods imported in finished form before 1960 were subsequently imported in parts or at intermediate stages of production. After undergoing final processing (only bottling or packing in some extreme cases) they circulated in the whole region as 'Central American' manufactures until the El Salvador-Honduras crisis; they continued to do so with the exception of the trade flows suspended between these two countries after the summer of 1969.

The high regional protection offered to finished goods, the low tariffs extended to raw materials and intermediate products, the race of CACM member countries for 'new industries', together with the oligopolistic structure of the market, led to a statistically impressive expansion of intraregional trade in manufactured goods - from US $18 million in 1961 to US $225 million in 1970 - at considerable economic and social cost to the area. Among the economic costs of this particular type of regional integration were a rapidly growing bill for imports of capital and intermediate goods from third countries at 'administered transfer prices'; a steep decline in fiscal revenues; high prices of new regional 'manufactured goods', and exorbitant profits accruing mainly to foreign-owned manufacturing enterprises which moved massively into CACM once they became aware of the profitability of new ventures under that scheme. To make matters worse, the haphazard industrialization that followed the emergence of CACM led to political complications by accentuating differences in intraregional development levels. Most of the new 'final-touch' industries settled in the more advanced countries - Guatemala and El Salvador - which, followed by Costa Rica, became the principal exporters of manufactured goods to the area. Since the liberalization of agricultural trade proved an intractable issue, the two least developed members - Honduras and Nicaragua - found themselves in an uncomfortable situation. They became markets for expensive manufactures from the rest of the region while being unable to increase tangibly their intraregional exports of traditional non-competitive agricultural commodities.

As long as the overall balance-of-payments position of central America was satisfactory, relatively few complaints about the growing imbalance in regional development and trade were heard. But by the mid-1960s the area found itself facing a major payments problem vis-à-vis the outside world. The rapidly growing import bill was due both to CACM industrialization and to the high level of imports of luxury goods. The latter reflected the extremely unequal income distribution in the area, symptomatic of its social backwardness. Subsequently, the CACM scheme provoked heavy criticism from its less developed members. The unequal distribution of benefits accruing from integration became the key issue, and Honduras and Nicaragua began to press the rest for special concessions. The conflict was exacerbated when attempts to deal with regional balance-of-payments difficulties, through tariff surcharges on most imports from third countries and an equalized consumption tax on a large list of luxury commodities of regional origin, met with opposition from Costa Rica, dictated by purely domestic political considerations. In early 1969 Nicaragua, which had accumulated a sizeable commercial deficit within the region and was unable to export agricultural goods to neighbouring countries, introduced - without warning and in clear contravention of the CACM treaty - levies on regional imports. It lifted them only after the other members ratified the pending regional protocols. The most important of these was a protocol for the equalization of fiscal incentives, its absence in the original treaty having permitted the initial free-for-all fight aimed at attracting foreign industrial investment at almost any cost to the economy.

Shortly after the Nicaragua-induced crisis had been resolved, war between El Salvador and Honduras in the summer of 1969 put the entire future of CACM into question. Although some sort of political peace was restored to the region in early 1972, the CACM stopped functioning, although trade flows in the area continued except between El Salvador and Honduras. Honduras formally withdrew from the market. The long-simmering conflict of economic interests between the more developed CACM members (Guatemala, El Salvador and Costa Rica) and the poorer ones (Honduras and Nicaragua) reinforced nationalist attitudes in individual countries. Negotiations to keep CACM alive did not seem to lead anywhere.

While the issue of equal benefits for all CACM member countries might somehow be resolved, another issue continued to overshadow the area. Both the Central American left and many local conservatives insisted with growing vehemence that whatever gains from CACM might accrue to the region, foreign industrial investors were the principal beneficiaries of the common market arrangement. Given the force of nationalism in the underdeveloped countries, such a frame of mind could hardly be considered conducive to an orderly future for the Central American scheme for economic integration, especially in view of the fact that, ten years after the setting up of the common market, the area was socially and politically as backward as before.

LAFTA's Irrelevance for Latin American Development

LAFTA has also not been successful. Disenchantment with its performance began even before the rate of growth of intraregional trade started to decline in the second half of the 1960s. From 1964 onwards a number of attempts to accelerate implementation of the non-commercial commitments of the Montevideo Treaty members were made by the main proponents of regional integration, including the then President Eduardo Frei of Chile, Raúl Prebisch, and Felipe Herrera, the head of the Inter-American Development Bank. These initiatives led to the establishment of LAFTA's Council of Ministers and indirectly to the conference of American presidents, held at Punta del Este in the spring of 1967. But after two meetings the Council of Ministers apparently ran out of ideas, while the Punta del Este presidential declaration calling for the establishment of a Latin American common market by 1980 was quietly shelved. External and regional political and economic difficulties proved stronger than the superficial idea of Latin American solidarity.

LAFTA's inability to proceed on schedule with the original commitments of the Montevideo Treaty was finally admitted openly in mid-December 1969 at the Ninth Annual Conference of LAFTA's Contracting Parties held in Caracas, Venezuela. The protocol signed on that occasion postponed, from 1973 to 1980, the establishment of a free trade area between eleven Latin American republics; it slowed down the pace of tariff negotiations by committing each LAFTA member country to making annual tariff cuts equivalent to only 2.9 per cent (formerly 8 per cent) of the weighted average of duties applicable to all imports; and it suspended the implementation of the so-called common list of products freely traded until at least 1974, the date by which negotiations toward a 'new stage' of LAFTA were to begin. It is no secret in Latin America that the Caracas Protocol represented a victory for the three major countries (Argentina, Brazil and Mexico), who lost interest in all but the purely commercial aspects of regional economic integration and who assumed - perhaps correctly - that the point reached in tariff cuts assured them enough room for export expansion in the area for some time without forcing them to undertake any non-commercial commitments toward the less-developed LAFTA members. Significantly, the Caracas Protocol made only token reference to a common market by resurrecting two rather nebulous articles of the Montevideo Treaty that called for 'creating conditions favourable to the establishment of a Latin American Common Market' and 'adapting [LAFTA] to a new stage of economic integration'. The Protocol fixed no deadline for the setting up of a Latin American common market.

While there were many reasons for LAFTA's disappointing performance and the clear lack of enthusiasm for a common market, some were particularly important. One was the ambitious geographical scope of LAFTA. In the name of a Latin American community of interests, economies of all sizes and levels of development were put under one roof. In spite of highly publicized declarations of regional solidarity, events proved that each of the three groups within LAFTA (the industrial 'giants', Argentina, Brazil and Mexico; the middle group, led by Chile, Colombia and Venezuela; and the most backward republics, Bolivia, Ecuador and Paraguay) faced specific problems which hardly lent themselves to joint action. All the major conflicts that arose in LAFTA involved the economic relations among these three groups. The poor members and the middle group insisted, quite correctly, from the beginning that they were getting little, if anything, from the regional free trade scheme and were, in fact, running the risk of becoming markets for the industrial surplus of the 'big three'. And while Argentina, Brazil and Mexico were obviously interested in markets in neighbouring countries, their dependence on exports to the rest of LAFTA was not large enough to force them to grant these unilateral commercial and other concessions for which the less fortunate republics asked persistently. Argentina made it clear that its interest in LAFTA and any future regional common market was strictly limited by considerations of domestic economic development. Although Brazil and Mexico abstained from making public statements on their future LAFTA policies, their position was basically similar. It is interesting to note that in the recent past Brazil shifted its interests in Latin American outlets for its manufactures to Africa.

While differences in economic development levels between the LAFTA subgroups have been the main reason for its disappointing performance, a second obstacle had its roots in flaws in the ECLA doctrine that served as the rationale for the establishment of a Latin American free trade zone in 1960. ECLA claimed that the Latin American countries had to integrate because import-substitution on a national level had run its course by the mid-1950s. But the post-LAFTA experience of the 'big three' showed that inward-directed national industrialization programmes can continue in some parts of Latin America for a considerable time without an increase in the level of protection but not without additional political and economic costs. In response to the differentiation of domestic demand for industrial inputs and final goods, new manufacturing establishments continued to spring up in Argentina, Brazil and Mexico ten years after ECLA's warning that this type of industrial growth was running into a blind alley. It may be mentioned in passing that this vertical integration was heavily controlled by foreign direct investment(20). Eventually these large republics may encounter the difficulties predicted by ECLA, but as long as the constraints upon industrialization for the home market were not too severe and some outlets for manufacturing exports were found elsewhere, none of the three countries saw a manifest necessity to support LAFTA fully(21).

A very incisive survey of LAFTA's problems(22) points out that the nationalist ideology present in the three major LAFTA countries does not explain fully their arms-length attitude vis-à-vis the regional integration scheme. It correctly stresses that any expansion of the trade liberalization programme beyond the limits reached by 1967 would have in fact negatively affected vested interests of large domestic industrial sectors that might have become exposed to competition both from other larger LAFTA members and from less-developed republics. To avoid such competition, local industrial interests (and many foreign-owned manufacturing firms) opted for so-called 'industrial complementary agreements' that have some characteristics of sectoral cartels. The attractiveness of these agreements from the viewpoint of the industries involved consists of the fact that they include only some countries, are exempt from the application of the most-favoured-nation clause to other LAFTA members (with the exception of the least-developed that cannot offer competition) and, finally, can be denounced at short notice if the gentlemen's agreements among participants are broken by one of the parties. Such deviation from the original programme of regional trade liberalization to sectoral cartel-like arrangements suggested that the rationalization of productive structures through regional competition was further away than many thought. The progress along the alternative route of industrial specialization through regional industrial planning was even less probable in view of the complete lack of interest of major LAFTA members in regional economic planning.

The possibilities of continuing inward-directed industrialization in the middle group of countries were considerably more limited. This may explain in part their interest in an Andean subregional common market, a project under negotiation after 1966 and translated into a formal treaty, signed at Cartagena, Colombia in July 1969 by Bolivia, Colombia, Chile, Ecuador and Peru. At the last moment Venezuela opted out of the Andean scheme, proving that the private sector in that republic believed that national industrialization programmes were still feasible in most places regardless of market size, extent of natural resources, and the high cost of modern technology. Industrial entrepreneurs in Venezuela were very vocal in their opposition to the Andean scheme, predicting a major national disaster if Venezuelan borders were to be opened to the 'cheap labour' products of neighbouring countries. There was little reason why industrial interests in Venezuela should have thought otherwise in 1969-70. After all, they were reaping very handsome profits behind high protective barriers, and, in traditional and conservative Latin America, profits and national interest are easily equated. Only after abrogation of the United States-Venezuela trade treaty under which, in exchange for special treatment

for Venezuelan oil, Venezuela granted special tariff concessions to United
States goods, did Venezuelan interest in the Andean common market increase.
It seemed quite possible that during 1973 this would be translated into
Venezuela's adhesion to the Andean scheme.

Paradoxically, the third major obstacle to regional economic cooperation arose
from some improvement in international commodity trade, registered in the
second half of the 1960s under the impact of conditions of economic boom in
the advanced countries. Contrary to pessimistic ECLA predictions, external
demand for Latin America's traditional commodities improved considerably.
Although the rate of expansion of the region's exports lagged behind that of
trade among industrial countries, the results were better than expected.
Between 1963 and 1970 Latin America's commodity sales increased by 50 per cent
from US $9180 million to US $13,810. If Venezuela's oil exports, which
behaved sluggishly over the period, are excluded, the seven-year increase in
export revenue of the region amounted to almost 70 per cent. The improvement
of the export picture made internal industrialization efforts much easier in
domestic political terms than the alternative regional trade liberalization
or a negotiation of regional industrial cooperation schemes that might have
affected cretain powerful domestic and foreign interest groups in individual
countries. As at other times and in other places, once the atmosphere of the
external sector crisis that was hanging over Latin America in the 1950s and
the early sixties seemed to dissipate, longer-term problems were conveniently
forgotten(23).

The priority given by the capital-exporting countries to the practices of tied
public loans and of private suppliers' credits in lieu of untied public
foreign aid only strengthened the propensity of Latin American countries to
think in terms of national inward-directed development and industrialization.
Whatever their external payments situation might have been, Latin American
republics were swamped in the 1960s with offers of external credit for individual industrial projects involving imports of capital goods. These offers
were readily taken up, with the result that the duplication and overlapping
previously characteristic of primary activities in the region was extended to
the industrial sector. With new high-cost, foreign-financed, self-contained
industrial plants springing up even in the most backward countries, economic
and industrial regional integration became more rather than less difficult to
attain.

The absence of coordinated aid policies toward Latin America among donor
countries, and United States lack of interest in supporting LAFTA politically
and financially, created another important obstacle to integration(24).
Through its aid agencies the United States gave financial support to CACM
from the very start. CACM members agreed in turn to accept the 'proper' rules
of the game by abstaining from any interference with 'free market' forces and
foreign investment. Moreover, the possibility of a political challenge to
the United States from the Central American scheme for integration was
virtually nil, while acceleration of growth within the area was considered
by the United States as a possible means of lessening socio-political tensions
in a strategically important part of Latin America.

The United States' attitude towards LAFTA was more ambivalent. In the 1950s
she gave no support to Latin American integration efforts, even if only
because initiatives came from the ideologically suspect ECLA. With the emergence of the Alliance for Progress in 1960 her position began to fluctuate
between a 'hands-off' policy and one of 'neutral benevolence'. Only in 1965

did the United States begin to express qualified support for Latin American
integration. In the winter of 1966-7 and prior to the conference of American
heads of state, President Johnson offered aid for the readjustment of those
economies that might be affected in the process of the gradual establishment
of a regional common market. But Congress refused to support the executive's
offer, and in any case the amount of aid offered was considered by most Latin
Americans to be ridiculously small.

This aid, informally promised, never materialized. The United States claimed
that Latin America's lack of interest in implementation of the Punta del Este
agreement made any external financial help superfluous. The Latin American
countries, in turn, pointed out that they would perhaps be ready to take
Punta del Este common market proposals more seriously if only the United States
had not backed out of its promises. Obviously, this was mere verbal shadow-
boxing. Both the United States and Latin America put the matter of broad and
serious regional economic integration low on their list of priorities, and
both were fairly satisfied with the traditional, bilateral methods of hemispheric aid distribution. Given the attitudes prevalent in the United States
Congress in the late 1960s, the executive branch could hardly ask - even if
it would have liked to - for additional funds for supporting integration.
Moreover, in a period of declining aid, the maintenance of bilateralism was
not at all unattractive to aid-receiving countries. Each hoped that it would
somehow get more than the others because of its 'special' relationship with
the powerful donor. Moreover, since the earmarking of certain funds for
integration might have affected the amount of bilateral aid available, no
Latin American country was willing to press for financial assistance for
integration. Thus traditional aid distribution patterns continued, while both
Latin America and the United States found themselves in the comfortable position of being able to blame each other for the failure of the agreements
arrived at by the heads of state in 1967.

The final major obstacle to LAFTA's efficient functioning and its evolution
toward a regional common market arose from the growing conflict between Latin
American middle classes and intellectuals and foreign private investment,
particularly the transnational corporations(25). In many Latin American
quarters it was feared that, because of their managerial and technological
power, these corporations would reap the major benefits from integration and
in the process destroy many weak domestic industries(26). In principle, these
problems might have been solved by regional harmonization of policies toward
foreign private capital, and by special financial and technical assistance on
a regional scale to domestic industries. In practice, the harmonization of
such policies on a regional scale seemed a forbidding task. Less developed
LAFTA members claimed that the introduction of equal regional treatment for
foreign investment would result in its concentration in the few large
countries. The latter, in turn, insisted that offering the poorer republics
the right of more liberal treatment for foreign capital, on top of unilateral
regional trade concessions, would result in swamping Latin America with manufactured goods assembled by foreign firms in the less-developed republics.
Unable to resolve this particular regional dilemma, LAFTA members - with the
exception of the Andean group - continued to maintain highly varied national
foreign investment policies geared mainly to individual industrialization
needs. Thus, on the regional level a curious argument emerged: while each
country talked about the dangers of foreign domination of the free trade zone
or a future common market, only foreign investment located outside one's own
national territory was considered as a threat. And once local foreign-owned
enterprises became somehow the extension of national economic power,

negotiating battles were fought by the host-countries to give them access to neighbouring markets. Under such conditions the elaboration of a regional foreign investment policy was more than a forbidding task. It was an impossible exercise.

The Andean Common Market: Achievements and Prospects

It may well be that the Cartagena Agreement of May 1969 that set up the Andean Common Market, with the participation of Bolivia, Chile, Colombia, Ecuador and Peru, offers a way out of the difficulties blocking the progress of LAFTA and CACM. The Agreement is considered to be an extension of the Montevideo Treaty and not a separate international legal instrument. It is built around an assumption, proven correct by the experiences of the two previously launched schemes, that efficient progress towards economic integration among developing countries cannot be based on more or less automatic trade liberalization, but must attempt to solve from the very beginning such important issues as the problem of equal distribution of benefits arising from industrialization (i.e., provide for harmonized distribution of new important industrial projects), that of common trade and investment policies vis-à-vis the rest of the world, and also that of a strong regional institutional framework with some degree of supernational power.

In respect to a trade liberalization programme, the subscribers to the Cartagena Agreement took the middle way between the complicated system of annual negotiations of trade concessions product-by-product, embodied in the Montevideo Treaty, and the immediate freeing of most of the subregional trade - at the price of a considerable increase of external protection - provided by the CACM treaty of 1960. After prolonged and sometimes dramatic negotiations, the five Andean countries opted for a flexible, albeit firm in respect to the timing of subsequent liberalization moves, programme with rather few and moderate escape clauses. Complete freedom for most intra-Andean trade was to be achieved within ten years or not later than the end of 1980. Freedom of intraregional trade meant the elimination of not only tariff barriers but quantitative restrictions as well, including those that might arise from exchange controls and import licensing measures practised by most of the member countries.

The trade liberalization programme started with the adoption of the standstill principle, prohibiting the introduction of new restrictions of any kind in regional trade after the coming into force of the Cartagena Agreement at the end of 1969. Furthermore, it provided for positive steps toward full trade liberalization within the ten-year period: trade in goods included in sectoral complementation agreements, such as those governing the petrochemical industry and other heavy manufacturing, would be freed at the pace specified in such agreements, involving as a rule new industrial activities. Trade in some 100 products originally included in LAFTA's Common List, covering mostly agricultural goods with some degree of processing, was freed shortly after the entry into force of the Cartagena Agreement, and trade in goods not produced in any member country of the common market was freed totally in February 1971. Duties on all other commodities entering intra-Andean trade were to be reduced every year by 10 per cent of the starting duty, defined as the lowest duty for each product in force at the end of 1969 in Colombia, Chile or Peru, but in no case exceeding 100 per cent ad valorem. During 1970 all duties were brought down to the lowest duty applied in either of the three 'major' countries, with 10 per cent cuts from that level starting at the end of 1971, so that by the end of 1980 they would reach zero. The Cartagena Agreement provided for quite limited exception clauses that principally took the form of rather modest lists of exceptions in respect to trade in manufactures. Agricultural trade liberalization also provided for some escape clauses. Finally, the problem of the less-developed countries, Bolivia and Ecuador, was resolved by postponing their obligations to introduce annual across-the-board tariff cuts until 1975, although their own exports to be more advanced Andean countries would benefit from a programme of liberalization started by Colombia, Chile and Peru at the end of 1971. Moreover, the production of some goods under sectoral complementation agreements might be reserved for Ecuador and Bolivia by common agreement. The Andean Development Corporation, established in January 1968, was also expected to give some preferential treatment to the two poorer countries with respect to the provision of financial resources for infrastructure and manufacturing.

A common external tariff was to be established in two steps: by the end of 1975 a minimum common external tariff should be established; and five years later all member countries were expected to complete the transition to the same tariff, the level of which, however, was not set by the Cartagena Agreement. As in the trade liberalization programme, Bolivia and Ecuador would have more time to fulfil their obligations with respect to a common external tariff.

While the Andean agreement committed member countries to harmonization of industrial and agricultural programming, integration of physical infrastructure, and financial and monetary cooperation, the elaboration of adequate measures was left to the common market authorities, composed of a Ministerial Commission and a technical secretariat (known as Junta de Cartagena), made up of three members with their own staff and charged with acting only on behalf of Andean community interests. Most of the Commission's decisions required the affirmative vote of four out of five members. The drastic limitation of the veto power within the Commission, together with the obvious need to arrive at decisions agreeable to all parties concerned, led to the introduction of a healthy practice of continuous negotiation between the Junta and the respective governments in advance of the formal meetings of the Andean Commission.

Within the first three years of their existence, the Andean Common Market authorities did not run into any major difficulties in agreeing - within the time schedules provided by the Cartagena Agreement - upon a number of important regional decisions. The agreements related to the first stage of trade liberalization, including that of setting the level of duties in the region from which automatic reductions started at the end of 1971, the minimum common external tariff, and immediate freeing of trade in commodities contained in LAFTA's Common List. They also covered a list of industries to be affected by regional industrial programming (including petrochemicals, steel and the automotive industry). The Common Code for Foreign Capital and Technology was in force in the region after the end of June 1971 and in mid-1972 the first industrial agreement was reached for the metal-working industry(27).

To many outsiders, it might have seemed strange that the Andean Common Market seemed to be making substantial progress in spite of growing disparities in the political and economic structures of its member countries. At the time of the Cartagena Agreement negotiations in 1967-9, all members of the common market scheme were governed by liberal or left-of-centre political groups committed in varying degrees to laissez-faire economic policies. By the mid-seventies the group comprised at least two major countries (Chile and Peru) that chose leftist, although somewhat different, political and economic policies. The fact that these developments did not seem to affect the workings of the common market may be explained in two opposite ways: the 'socio-political' innovators did not want to burn the bridges to the rest of the embryonic Latin American-Pacific economic community; alternatively, the steady deterioration of world conditions for the developing countries, as perceived by Andean political and economic élites, created a new cohesion independent of the respective ideologies practised at national levels.

Each of these hypotheses seems to work in favour of the Andean Common Market, although it is too early in 1973 to indulge in prophesies about its long-term success. The hardest decisions related to implementation of regional industrial policies and harmonization of national policies in fiscal and monetary fields still lie ahead. But if the Andean Common Market scheme fails, it will be evident that an economic integration programme in Latin America or some parts of that subcontinent is not possible.

NEW STRATEGY: EXPORTS OF MANUFACTURES TO ADVANCED COUNTRIES

In the light of obstacles facing import-substituting industrialization and the meagre results of regional economic integration described in this paper, the Latin American region started around 1965 to play with another strategy emphasizing production of manufactures for sale in advanced countries. This strategy, in the words of an ECLA study

> would reflect the emergence of a new 'international division of labour' this time in the field of manufactures. Latin America would export those products in which the developed countries would be losing their interest in the light of evolution of demand and technological change. Latin American manufactured exports would thus complement other more technologically sophisticated goods produced by the advanced countries(28).

Latin American manufacturing export performance, stimulated by the coming into force - except in the United States - of an UNCTAD-sponsored general preference scheme for entry into the advanced countries of less developed countries' manufactures and semi-manufactures, has not yet been evaluated in detail, although some literature on the subject has become available(29). The scant evidence suggests that (a) Latin American manufactured exports grew during the 1960s more rapidly than the region's exports as a whole; (b) these exports were concentrated in the three major republics (Argentina, Brazil and Mexico); and (c) their participation in the GDP and total trade of the region was still below that of many countries of similar or even lower development levels in Asia. Between 1962 and 1968 the total manufactured exports of Latin America (excluding petroleum products and semi-processed non-ferrous metals) increased threefold: from US $280 million to US $905 million. Their destination and origin are shown in Tables 8.4 and 8.5.

Additional estimates for 1970 for such countries as Brazil, Colombia, Mexico and Peru indicate that these trends continued and that the rate of acceleration increased, particularly in Brazil and Mexico. In these two countries manufactured exports (excluding petroleum products and semi-processed raw materials) amounted in 1970 respectively to US $580 million and US $405 million. Available projections for 1971-5 suggest annual growth rates in manufacturing sales abroad of Brazil at the average of 30 per cent and of Mexico at 20 per cent(30).

TABLE 8.4. Exports of Latin American Manufactures, 1962 and 1968

(US $ million)

	Total	Developed market economies	Socialist countries	Latin America	Other LDCs
1962	279	176	5	79	12
1968	905	444	20	421	20

Source: UNCTAD, Study of Manufacturing Trade in Developing Countries, 1970.

TABLE 8.5. Exports of Manufactures by Selected Latin American Countries, 1962 and 1969

(US $ million)

	1962	1969	Annual percentage increase 1962-9
Mexico	107.1	379.7	19.8
Brazil	85.5	244.2	16.2
Argentina	95.6	207.7	11.7
Colombia	7.5	26.3	19.6
Chile	12.9	22.7	8.4
Uruguay	14.8	20.2	4.5
Paraguay	14.4	18.3	13.5
Honduras	5.3	17.9	15.1
Cuba	6.3	10.5	7.5

Source: Ibid.

These statistics should be treated with caution. Because of the heavy participation of transnational corporations in this trade, there is partial evidence to the effect that a large part of these exports was considerably underpriced (31). Moreover, in the case of Mexico, the data most probably include exports of United States-owned assembly plants located in the Mexican northern border zone. As long as data about local value added in Latin American manufactured exports are not available, it is hard to judge the degree of their real impact upon changes in productive structures of individual countries and their respective balance-of-payments positions. Comments made in the previous section about the growth of 'trade in manufactures' within CACM made such studies imperative.

An interesting policy-oriented study about the manufacturing export potential of Latin American countries suggests that room for additional expansion is considerable(32). Starting from the assumption that to devise such policies, it is necessary to understand whether and how the share of manufactures in a country's total exports is related to certain supply characteristics, a survey was made of the actual and 'expected' export performance of some seventy advanced and developing countries with the use of a multiple regression analysis on the basis of cross-sectional data. While the weakness of the study consists of not taking into consideration worldwide demand characteristics and trade policies of advanced countries (especially non-tariff trade barriers), it shows that over the period of 1960-8 only in three Latin American republics (Chile, Peru and Nicaragua) did actual shares of manufactures exceed the 'expected' shares. In twelve others, including Argentina, Brazil and Mexico, manufactured exports were below the 'estimated' shares.

As both actual and 'expected' shares of manufacturing exports include semi-processed metals, and considering that Chile and Peru are major exporters of these commodities, one arrives at the conclusion that in all Latin America manufacturing export potential has been used only fractionally. The study admits its limited value: almost 40 per cent of variation between actual and 'expected' manufacturing exports could not be explained by that sort of analysis and 'a large part of "unexplained" variations may reflect among other factors [like endowment of natural resources], the various forms of impediments and trade stimuli that are in existence on national and supranational level'(33).

An attempt to explain some of these impediments related to import-substituting industrialization policies and regional economic integration difficulties has been made in previous sections of this paper. A thorough analysis of obstacles to exports of Latin American manufactures arising from trade policies of developed countries would imply writing another paper.

FINAL COMMENTS

Whatever external obstacles exist to rapid expansion of Latin American manufactured exports, their presence does not invalidate our general proposition that the absence of coherent internal and regional economic policies in post-war Latin America resulted in the high cost of import-substituting industrialization, the lack of acceleration of economic growth through regional economic integration, and the limited results of the strategy based upon high priority for manufactured exports. While the conflict of objectives between import substitution and regional trade cooperation looks obvious, no such conflict seems to exist in the case of economic regionalism and manufacturing for worldwide exports.

In fact, it has been demonstrated that a regional industrialization policy would have helped immensely the objective of manufacturing for export(34). A study of fourteen products in six industrial branches, aimed at quantifying their costs under conditions of working for a Latin American area in optimum or near-optimum patterns of location, disclosed that in practically all cases such patterns of production would be competitive with imports from any developed country. The study suggests, furthermore, that 'whenever output moves to the levels where economies of scale operate, as it would for many commodities in a Latin American common market, and transportation costs are significant, production costs would permit competition with developed countries even without tariff protection'(35).

Given that many Far Eastern developing economies, the less developed countries of Southern Europe and Israel in the post-war period did better in terms of economic growth and export trade than Latin America(36), there are reasons to believe that the rather disappointing Latin American performance has largely been due to political, social and technological backwardness and not to traditional productive factor endowment. If it is true, as Linder postulated, that export possibilities depend upon the size, structure and growth of domestic demand(37), and as Georgescu-Roegen noted, that without changes in the domestic demand profile, an industrializing low-income country runs rapidly into 'structural lock' dilemma(38), then it is relevant to stress that all the Latin American post-war economic strategies studiously avoided internal socio-economic structural changes, including the improvement of human resource quality and of modes of social organization. This would lead us back to Simon Kuznets' dictum that 'the cause of economic growth is knowledge' and to Maddison's proposition that 'the basic problems of an economic growth policy . . . are not technical but political and institutional'.

NOTES

(1) The most outstanding examples of this literature are the contributions of Simon Kuznets, Modern Economic Growth Rate, Structure and Spread, Yale University Press, New Haven, 1966; W.G. Hoffmann, The Growth of Industrial Economies, Manchester University Press, Manchester, 1958; Alexander Gerschenkron, Economic Backwardness in Historical Perspective, Harvard University Press, Cambridge, Mass., 1962; Charles P. Kindleberger, Economic Growth of France and Britain, 1851-1950, Harvard University Press, Cambridge, Mass. 1964, and E.J. Hobsbawm, Industry and Empire, Weidenfeld & Nicholson, London, 1968.

(2) For example, Stanley J. and Barbara H. Stein, The Colonial Heritage of Latin America - Essays on Economic Dependence in Perspective, Oxford University Press, New York, 1970, and various authors, La historia económica en América Latina, Vol. I, Situación y métodos, Vol. II, Desarrollo, perspectivas y bibliografia, Collection of essays presented at the 39th International Americanist Congress, Lima, 1970, SEP/SETENTAS, Mexico, 1972.

(3) The major contributions in this field are represented by ECLA, The Process of Industrialization in Latin America, New York; ECLA, Economic Survey of Latin America, 1970, New York, 1971; Keith Griffin, Underdevelopment in Spanish America - An Interpretation, George Allen and Unwin Ltd., London, 1969; Santiago Macario, 'Protectionism and Industrialization in Latin America, Economic Bulletin for Latin America (Santiago), Vol. lo, No. 1 (March 1965); Albert O. Hirschmann, 'The Political Economy of Import-Substituting Industrialization in Latin America' in A Bias for Hope - Essays on Development and Latin America, Yale University Press, New Haven 1971 pp. 85-113; S. Sideri, 'The Industrial Development Deadlock in Latin America: From Import Substitution to Export Promotion?', Development and Change, 2, Vol. 3, No. 2 (1971-2), pp. 1-17, and Werner Baer, 'Import Substitution and Industrialization in Latin America: Experiences and Interpretations', Latin American Research Review, Vol. 7 (Spring 1972) pp. 95-122.

For an analysis of import substitution experiences of major Latin American republics, see among others, books and articles by Carlos F. Díaz-Alejandro, David Felix and Aldo Ferrer (on Argentina); Werner Baer, Paul G. Clark, Nathaniel Leff and María Conçeicao Tavares (on Brazil) and Roger Hansen, Leopoldo Solis and Clark W. Reynolds (on Mexico). References to some studies of the same problems in Central America, Chile, Colombia and Peru can be found in Werner Baer's review essay quoted above.

(4) See, on this point, among others, ECLA, The Economic Development of Latin America and Its Principal Problems, United Nations 1950; ECLA, International Cooperation in the Latin American Development Policy, United Nations; 1954 and Raúl Prebisch 'Commercial Policy in the Underdeveloped Countries', American Economic Review, Vol. 49 (1959), pp. 251-73.

(5) Among abundant literature on this subject, see, for example, Don Humphrey, American Imports, The Twentieth Century Fund, New York, 1955; Bela Balassa, Trade Prospects for Developing Countries, Richard Irwin Inc., Homewood, Ill., 1964, and UNCTAD, Trade Prospects and Capital Needs of Developing Countries, New York, 1968.

(6) Baer, 'Import Substitution and Industrialization', p. 98.

(7) Simon Kuznets, Economic Growth of Nations: Total Output and Production Structure, Harvard University Press, Cambridge, Mass. 1971; Edward F. Denison (assisted by Jean-Pierre Poullier), Why Growth Rates Differ: Post War Experience in Nine Western Countries, The Brookings Institution, Washington, D.C. 1967; Angus Maddison, Economic Growth in the West - Comparative Experience in Europe and North America, The Twentieth Century Fund, New York 1964, among others. While Kuznets is widely known for his statement that 'the cause of economic growth is knowledge', the Maddison study postulates that '. . . the basic problems of an economic growth policy . . . are not technical but political and institutional', p. 22.

(8) In the Caribbean and Central America even that stage has not been reached. Imports of consumer goods were substituted by and large by assembly activities with fractional domestic value added. For an analysis of this 'spurious' industrialization process see, among others, Miguel S. Wionczek, 'The Central American Common Market' in Peter Robson (Editor), International Economic Integration, Penguin Modern Economic Readings, Penguin Books, London 1971, and Philipp C. Schmitter, Autonomy and Dependence as Regional Integration Outcomes, University of California Institute of International Studies, Berkeley 1972.

(9) David Felix, 'Monetarists, Structuralists and Import-Substituting Industrialization: A Critique', in Werner Baer and Isaac Kerstenetzky (Editors), Inflation and Growth in Latin America, Richard Irwin Inc., Homewood, Ill. 1964, p. 383.

(10) Raúl Prebisch, Transformación y desarrollo, Fondo de Cultura Económica, México 1971, p. 101.

(11) For details, see Joseph Grunwald and Phillip Musgrove, Natural Resources in Latin American Development, Johns Hopkins Press, Baltimore, 1970.

(12) For details, see ECLA, Economic Survey of Latin America, 1971, Vol. I, Latin American and World Economy: Some Prospects and Trends, New York, June

1972, mimeographed.

(13) Joel Bergsman and Arthur Candal, 'Industrialization, Past Successes and Future Problems' in Howard S. Ellis (Editor), The Economy of Brazil University of California Press, Berkeley and Los Angeles 1969, p. 47, as quoted by Baer, 'Import Substitution'.

(14) Not all literature on the subject is thoroughly pessimistic. While insisting that 'the fact that import-substituting industrialization can be accommodated relatively easily in the existing social and political environment is probably responsible for the widespread disappointment with the process', Hirschmann concludes that his exploration 'has made it possible to discern avenues toward continued industrial growth that remain open to the late latecomers', 'The Political Economy', p. 123.

(15) Particularly useful in this respect are the Baer and Sideri review articles referred to earlier, and various chapters of ECLA, Economic Survey of Latin America, 1970, and Economic Survey of Latin America, 1971 that introduce into the analysis of Latin American post-war industrialization strategy two earlier neglected factors: world-wide technological change and transnational corporations.

(16) For more details, see Sideri, 'Industrial Development Deadlock', particularly pp. 2-8, and Henry J. Bruton, 'The Import-Substitution Strategy of Economic Development: A Survey', The Pakistan Development Review, Vol. 10, No. 2 (Summer 1970), pp. 125-40.

(17) In addition to mountains of ECLA, LAFTA and SIECA technical documentation, made public in the sixties, persons interested in the subject might find it useful to consult the following studies of the Latin American economic integration process: Sidney Dell, Problemas de un mercado común en América Latina, CEMLA, México, 1959; Victor L. Urquidi, Trayectoria del mercado común latino-americano, (CEMLA, México, 1960; Sidney Dell, Trade Blocks and Common Markets, Alfred A. Knopf, New York, 1963; Bela Balassa, Economic Development and Integration, CEMLA, México, 1965; Donald B. Baerresen, Martin Carnoy, Joseph Grunwald, Latin American Trade Patterns, The Brookings Institution, Washington, D.C., 1965; Miguel S. Wionczek (Editor), Latin American Economic Integration, Frederick A. Praeger, New York, 1966; Sidney Dell, A Latin American Common Market?, Oxford University Press, London, 1966; Miguel S. Wionczek (Editor), Economic Cooperation in Latin America, Africa and Asia, M.I.T. Press, Cambridge, Mass., 1969; Roger D. Hansen, Central America: Regional Integration and Economic Development, National Planning Association, Washington, D.C., 1967; James D. Cochrane, The Politics of Regional Integration: The Central American Case, Tulane University Press, New Orleans, 1969; William G. Demas, The Economics of Development in Small Countries with Special Reference to the Caribbean, McGill University Press, Montreal, 1965; Havelock Brewster and Clyve Y. Thomas, The Dynamics of West Indian Economic Integration, University of Jamaica Press, Kingston, Jamaica, 1967; Osvaldo Sunkel (Editor), Integración y política económica, Universidad de Chile, Santiago de Chile, 1970; Joseph Grunwald, Miguel S. Wionczek and Martin Carnoy, Latin American Economic Integration and US Policy, The Brookings Institution, Washington, D.C., 1971 and Christopher Garbacz, Industrial Polarization under Economic Integration in Latin America, Bureau of Business Research, The University of Texas, Austin, 1972.

(18) ECLA, The Latin American Common Market, United Nations, New York, 1959,

p. 1.

(19) Donald H. McLelland, The Common Market's Contribution to Central American Economic Growth: A First Appriximation', in Ronald Hilton (Editor), The Movement Toward Latin American Unity, Frederick A. Praeger, New York, 1969.

(20) For details, see ECLA, Economic Survey of Latin America, 1970, Part IV, Special Studies, 'The Expansion of International Enterprises and their Impact on Latin American Development', and Miguel S. Wionczek, Inversión y technología extranjera en América Latina, Joaquin Mortiz, Mexico, 1971.

(21) The potential conflict between the UNCTAD scheme for preferential treatment of manufactures produced by semi-developed countries and the regional trade integration schemes among the developing countries has been pointed out in Grunwald, Wionczek and Carnoy, Latin American Economic Integration.

(22) David Ibarra, 'Notas sobre la integración latinoamericana', Comercio Exterior, (Mexico) Vol. 21, No. 11, (October 1971).

(23) Improvement of the Latin American external sector in the late sixties was largely an illusion. The public foreign debt of the region doubled between 1961 and 1969 from US $8800 million to US $17,600 million and the cost of servicing that debt grew in the same period from US $1250 million to US $2200 million. In 1969 a number of Latin American countries (including the three major ones) spent over 20 per cent of their gross revenue on current account on servicing external public debt. See UNCTAD, Debt Problems of Developing Countries, Santiago, Chile, TD/118/Add. 6 December 1971, (mimeo.).

(24) For details, see Miguel S. Wionczek, 'Latin American Integration and United States Policies', in Robert W. Gregg (Editor), International Organization in the Western Hemisphere, Syracuse University Press, Syracuse, N.Y., 1968, and Grunwald, Wionczek and Carnoy, Latin American Economic Integration.

(25) For details, see Wionczek, Inversión y tecnologia extranjera en América Latina.

(26) There is growing evidence that these fears are well-founded. For the latest findings, see Fernando Fajnzylber, 'Estrategia industrial y empresas internacionales - Posición relativa de América Latina y Brasil', ECLA, Rio de Janeiro, November 1970 (mimeo); Hector Vazquez Tercero (Editor), Inversiones extranjeras directas en México, Comité Bilateral de Hombres de Negocios México-Estados Unidos, México 1970; Roland E. Müller 'Foreign Investment in Latin America', The American University, Dept. of Economics, Washington, D.C. 1971 (mimeo); Carlos F. Diaz Alejandro 'Direct Investment in Latin America', in Charles P. Kindleberger, The International Corporation - A Symposium, M.I.T. Press, Cambridge, Mass. 1970, pp. 319-44.

(27) The longer-term objectives and strategies of the Andean Common Market are analysed in Junta de Cartagena, Bases generales para una estrategia de desarrollo subregional, 3 vols., Lima, March 1971 (mimeo).

(28) ECLA, Economic Survey of Latin America, 1971, Vol. III, Special Studies, New York, 1972, (mimeo), p. 87.

(29) In addition to ECLA's document quoted in the previous footnote, see ECLA, Economic Survey of Latin America, 1970, New York; UNCTAD, Study of

Manufacturing Trade of Developing Countries, 1970, Report of the UNCTAD Secretariat, Geneva, December 1970, TD/B/C.2/102 (mimeo); and R. Banerji and J.B. Donges, Economic Development and the Patterns of Manufactured Exports, Kieler Diskussionbeiträge 16, Institut für Weltwirtschaft, Kiel, January 1972.

(30) For Brazil estimates see IBRD, Current Economic Position and Prospects of Brazil, Vol. III, Brazil's Exports of Manufactures, Washington, D.C., 1971 and for Mexico, local unpublished data.

(31) According to a survey of over 100 Latin American foreign-owned manufacturing firms, mostly subsidiaries of transnational corporations, their exports - within the respective corporate systems - to other Latin American countries and the rest of the world are underinvoiced by an average 50 per cent in comparison to prices obtained by other Latin American firms exporting on the open market. For details, see Ronald E. Müller and Richard Morgenstern, The Impact of Multinational Corporations on the Balance of Payments of LDCs: An Econometric Analysis of Pricing of Export Sales, Washington, D.C., 1972 (unpublished manuscript).

(32) Banerji and Donges, Economic Development.

(33) Ibid., p. 16.

(34) Martin Carnoy (Editor) Industrialization in a Latin American Common Market, The Brookings Institution, Washington, D.C.

(35) Ibid., pp. 69-70.

(36) Economic Commission for Europe, Some Aspects of Manufacturing Development in Southern Europe: Production, Trade and Transfer of Technology, Geneva, October 1971, TRADE/254 (mimeo); and Centre for Industrial Planning, Plan for the Development of Industry in Israel, 1969-1975, Ministry of Industry and Commerce, Jerusalem, February 1971.

(37) Staffan Burenstam Linder, An Essay on Trade and Transformation, Almquist & Wiksell, Uppsala, 1961.

(38) Nicholas Georgescu-Roegen, 'Structural Inflation-Lock and Balanced Growth', Economies et Sociétés, Cahiers de l'ISEA, Geneva, Vol. 4, No. 3 (1970).

CHAPTER 9

External Public Indebtedness and Sectoral Changes in Foreign Private Investment*

THE PURPOSE of this paper is to supply data allowing quantification of Latin America's external economic dependence and clarification of its consequences for future development of the region. The paper will briefly analyse one aspect of dependence, that is, the changes which occurred in the region's external financial relations during the ten-year period, 1956-66.

In general terms the author agrees with the analysis of the Latin American situation presented by the prestigious Chilean economist, Osvaldo Sunkel, in an inquiry into national development policy and external dependence(1). According to Sunkel's thesis, the ideological choice between socialist revolution or the condition of 'branch countries' of the large industrial powers, which has been offered to Latin American nations for some time, only seems acceptable to small minorities in Latin American societies. In view of the strength of current nationalism, Latin American majorities consciously or subconsciously wish for some kind of socio-economic development which includes certain features of the two apparently antagonistic economic systems, without being a copy of either of them(2).

The conclusions of Sunkel's study are optimistic. He expresses the conviction, based on his analysis of socio-political changes taking place within Latin American societies, that it would be feasible to design and implement a broad and coherent programme of economic measures of various kinds which would reduce Latin America's external dependence in the longer term. As we would expect, among the proposed measures figures the introduction of fundamental changes in the traditional pattern of external financial relations of Latin American countries, especially those with private foreign capital.

---

*Paper presented at the second General Assembly of the Latin Americal Social Sciences Council (CLASCO) held in Lima, Peru in October 1968. Published originally in Helio yaguaribe, Aldo Ferrer, Miguel S. Wionczek and Teotonio Dos Santos, La dependencia político-económica de América Latina, Siglo XXI Editores, Mexico, 1970, and reproduced by kind permission of Consejo Latino-Americano de Ciencias Sociales, Buenos Aires.

There are reasons to assume that the present system of financial relations
between Latin America and the developed countries has limited possibilities
of lasting. Its main weakness stems from the fact that it contributes little
towards solving the area's urgent problems of underdevelopment, counter to a
generalized criterion in high-income countries. Yet however well one may be
aware of the drawbacks presented by this type of financial relations, and
despite Latin America's efforts to introduce urgent changes, intellectual
answers to the phenomenon of financial dependence can hardly convert themselves alone into the desired changes.

The feasibility of adjusting international financial relations depends more
upon the real relations of power. Taking this to be true, a double question
immediately arises: has the degree of Latin America's financial dependence on
the outside world been growing or decreasing, and if it is growing, what are
the reasons for and consequences of this?

Owing to a series of factors which Sunkel expresses as a 'first sign' of
dependence, the two main aspects of Latin America's financial relations with
the industrial centres - public foreign indebtedness and private foreign
investment - have been studied in depth relatively little in the region. What
little is known we owe to international agencies and to interest in the subject
shown by a few foreign scholars. On the other hand, among the power élites
and the intellectuals of a considerable number of Latin American countries
the attitude seems to prevail that solving the problems of external public
indebtedness is the almost exclusive responsibility of the respective finance
ministries and monetary authorities.

This subject in turn, given the scarcity of rigorous Latin American analyses
of the behaviour of foreign investment, continues to be the main bone of contention in political and ideological discussions between supporters and
enemies of the participation of private foreign capital in the region's
development. We are witnessing a situation in which the myths created in the
countries of origin of foreign investment are clashing with other myths
created by Latin American ideologues(3).

It is obvious that it would be much more worthwhile for the region to try to
adopt more rational attitudes towards the role which foreign capital (credits
to the public sector and private foreign investment) could and should play in
Latin American development. Yet policymaking, which should be preceded by a
rational analysis of reality, seems to be a complicated task. It would
include as a prior condition the adoption of a series of domestic economic
policy measures which would affect the superficial stability of the power
relationship between the traditional incumbents of power, and which in the
short run would damage the interests of some of them(4). While the custom
of blaming the outside world for all the problems of Latin American development pays political dividends and helps to perpetuate the domestic socio-
economic status quo, there appears to be no motivation to experiment with new
economic policies which really would reduce the region's external dependence.

EXTERNAL PUBLIC INDEBTEDNESS AS A SUBSTITUTE FOR DOMESTIC REFORMS

Only a small number of Latin American scholars appears to have realized that
Latin America's external public indebtedness has reached dramatic proportions,
both in absolute terms and in terms of the burden of its service on the present
and future availability of financial resources provided by the export of goods

and services to the rest of the world. To support this affirmation, statistical tables are presented in the appendix, supplemented by data from the ECLA(5) the IBRD(6) and the IMF(7).

The available statistical material shows that:

(1) During the period 1957-66 Latin America's external public debt with a maturity of one year or more (including loans and credits negotiated but not disbursed) tripled, from US $4100 million at the end of 1956 to $12,600 million at the end of 1966. Furthermore, if the public sector's short-term debts and certain credits without government guarantee are included, the total public foreign indebtedness of Latin America would have exceeded $15,000 million at the end of 1966.

(2) In spite of the heavy increase in Latin American earnings from merchandise exports between 1961 and 1966 (from US $8200 to 11,000 million), the ratio of service of the public foreign debt to current account revenues in Latin America rose from 5 to 15 per cent over the period. In absolute figures, servicing of the external public debt (amortization and interests) increased by more than four times between 1956 and 1966, from $400 million to around $2000 million. In 1966 the three larger countries (Argentina, Brazil and Mexico) spent between 20 and 30 per cent of their current account revenues on servicing this debt. Three of the four medium-sized republics (Chile, Colombia and Peru) used between 10 and 15 per cent of their earnings from the sale of goods and services abroad for the same purpose.

(3) In the mid-sixties the region found itself in both a paradoxical and dangerous situation, as the servicing of the external public debt exceeded new inflows of credits and loans to the public sector. In other words, the volume of new loans was already insufficient to cover financial obligations on the public foreign debt contracted previously.

(4) In spite of various operations carried out to consolidate the foreign debt of Argentina, Brazil, and Chile, and partly as a result of the accumulation of interest on outstanding debts and the growing cost of new credits, the region's foreign debt structure (in terms of average life and interest rates) did not correspond to the servicing of indebtedness foreseeable in the near future. According to an estimate by the author, twelve Latin American republics (Argentina, Bolivia, Brazil, Colombia, Costa Rica, Ecuador, El Salvador, Guatemala, Honduras, México, Nicaragua and Peru) whose public foreign debt exceeded US $10,000 million at the end of 1966 (80 per cent of the region's total debt), had payments obligations of $7500 million in the following five-year period (1967-71) for servicing their public foreign debt. More than half of the outstanding debt of these twelve countries had maturity periods of less than five years at the end of 1966.

These simple data, which cover only the external liabilities of the public sector and not the total external liabilities of Latin American economies (which include private direct foreign investment and the foreign indebtedness of the private sector), confirm that the area's dependence on world financial centres is growing rapidly. In fact, if the high-income countries and international organizations were to decide to suspend flows of new financial resources to Latin America and to demand the payment of already contracted obligations, the region would face a crisis comparable to that of the 1930s. Thus the outside world has to provide new resources so that Latin American countries can continue to settle earlier debts. Nevertheless, the relationship is far from symmetrical. The region's creditors could survive relatively easily a moratorium declared by the Latin American republics, but the same can hardly be said of the latter.

To state that Latin America's financial dependence on the outside world has reached astonishing proportions leads us nowhere. It is much more illuminating to pose the question: how has this part of the world, in the brief space of ten years, come to this situation?

Given the performance of the export sector in the sixties, traditional explanations which use the development resources gap and the conditions of world trade seem unsatisfactory. They were valid during the 1950s, when the region's capacity to import decreased considerably owing to the stagnation of international trade in primary products. Nevertheless, in the first half of the 1960s Latin American export earnings showed a considerable improvement, rising from US $5675 to 8325 million, or by around 50 per cent from 1961 to 1966 (excluding Venezuela). It would appear that the region's terms of trade also improved, although only slightly, over the same period. However, the region's external public debt grew by some $5000 million, without the improved performance of the export sector and the heavy inflow of foreign credits to the public sector leading to a speeding up of Latin American development. In fact, the GNP growth rate remained the same in 1960-65 as in the previous five-year period (4.6 per cent annually in real terms), which is lower than the 5 per cent annual growth recorded between 1950 and 1955.

It helps very little to blame such disappointing results on circumstances foreign to Latin American economic policy decisions. The fact that Latin America, like other developing regions, did not have the foreign resources which it might have been able to absorb, nor terms of assistance which would have allowed it to cover its servicing without balance-of-payments difficulties, only partly explains the situation. It would appear that the slow growth recorded by the Latin American economies, with one or two exceptions, was due not only to the high income countries' financial policies towards Latin America but also to the latters' domestic economic policies.

In spite of theses to the contrary defended by representatives of the power élites of the hemisphere, Latin America has been unable, through the unwillingness of the great majority of governments in the region, to introduce structural changes in its economies which would have allowed an appreciable increase in domestic savings and improved its use efficiency, above all in the public sector, and which at the same time would have created favourable conditions to improve the use efficiency of external savings. No proof exists that the use of private savings became more efficient, in spite of their growth, achieved at the expense of a very deficient distribution of income. The difficulties do not stem from the fact that intellectuals and technicians have scarcely realized what conditions are necessary to speed up the development process.

In general it is agreed that due to existing conditions - underemployment of the factors of production, the apparent scarcity of savings, and constraints imposed by the limited absorptive capacity for technological change - the possibilities of sustained development depend to a large extent on the rise in marginal rates of savings, the fall of the capital-output ratio, and the general modernization of educational systems. But given the socio-political circumstances prevailing in Latin America, it seems impossible to achieve these objectives. Among the obstacles to be overcome the following stand out:

the government's lack of interest in curbing the luxury consumption of high-income groups; the demonstration effects of consumption patterns which predominate in the developed countries; the extremely high rates of population growth, which bring with them heavy burdens on the current expenditure of the public sector; the need for the latter to keep absorbing at least a part of the surplus labour force at the expense of decreasing efficiency of the state apparatus; the political inability of the state to harmonize public capital expenditure with that required in industrializing and modernizing the primary sectors; and finally, autarkic industrialization policies, when the import-substitution process on the national scale has in many cases reached the stage of diminishing returns.

If this description corresponds to Latin American reality and is not just a caricature, it is easy to reconstruct recent international financial developments without having to resort to a detailed quantitative analysis. First, from the beginning of the sixties, a considerable and perhaps growing part of available import capacity was wasted in importing luxury consumer goods or producer goods to satisfy such alleged consumer needs by domestic production. Second, the public sector did not succeed in raising the marginal rate of savings to an appreciable extent. Third, owing to its inability to elaborate long-term development programmes and improve the selection, formulation, execution and exploitation of new development projects, neither was it possible to lower the capital-output ratio(8). Thus the region had to suffer the consequences of policies which promoted luxury consumption and investment.

Having used the savings provided by exports in an inefficient manner, and having been neither able nor willing to increase the efficiency of investment realized with domestic resources, Latin American states in general had no alternative but to resort to external savings under terms dictated by their owners. The fact that a growing proportion of external public indebtedness took the form of bilateral loans, banking credits, and suppliers' credits (at the end of 1966 nearly half of the public external debt of Latin America consisted of loans from private sources and onerous suppliers' credits) shows that these external resources were used indiscriminately. Yet in this case too it would not be fair to blame external events. For completely different reasons, a certain union of interests grew up between borrowers and lenders. In exchange for the onerous political and financial terms which they accepted, the borrowing countries bought the freedom to continue postponing the review of their development policies, as this could affect powerful established national interests.

On account of the complex systems of guarantees and insurance in force in all the countries which provided capital to the developing regions, the lender countries, with no risk whatsoever on their part, secured high profits both on financial operations and export markets(9). The existence of this quid pro quo partly explains the wall of secrecy which surrounds Latin America's problem of external public indebtedness.

Thus it is feasible to conclude that Latin America has used a large part of its capacity for indebtedness as a substitute for domestic structural reforms, with the compliance of the outside world. If the magnitude and structure of the region's external public debt are borne in mind, serious doubts arise as to the possibility (set out by Sunkel) of introducing significant changes in the financial relations between Latin America and the 'centre' (using Prebisch's terminology), by Latin American initiative. If, as would appear, power élites in the area do not have negotiating power vis-à-vis the world's financial centres, nor real interest in improving the use of domestic savings, then Latin America's process of economic development must reflect the interests of the central countries more than those of Latin American societies. The former have given little proof of understanding the nature of the obstacles which hinder the region's development.

It matters relatively little if this lack of comprehension is due to neo-imperialist purposes, as some insist, or represents nothing more than a lack of vision of world problems in the advanced countries. It is worth noting, however, that the behaviour of Latin America's power élites has not helped much to raise the level of understanding, which in the late fifties seemed to be appearing in enlightened sectors of public opinion in high-income countries. On the contrary, owing to their unwillingness to act on the domestic front, Latin Americans have given support to powerful foreign groups which clearly consider it to their advantage to defend the <u>status quo</u> in international economic relations. The ease with which the majority of Latin American countries have accepted, and even favoured, the increase in their external economic dependence, in exchange for the sovereign right (in the name of so-called political independence) to adjust (or not) domestic policies to the needs of an economic development with social content, represents beyond any doubt an important - though secondary - factor responsible for public indifference in the northern hemisphere to the development problems of the southern peripheries.

Due largely to their own errors of omission, and not only as is usually maintained to the perversity and hostility of the outside world, Latin America faces a complicated situation. On the one hand, while prospects for the export sector show signs of weakening once more, Latin American countries need some $2000 million a year to pay the service on their external public debt. On the other hand, the developed countries are cutting down flows of international economic aid and toughening its terms, and advising underdeveloped regions that, in view of the lack of support by high-income countries for governmental foreign aid programmes, they should '. . . rely more on private enterprise as a source of credits and foreign investment'(10).

This advice represents a return to the attitudes of the forties and fifties which appeared to be overcome, and which obviously do not solve the financial resources problem. The serious thing about the reappearance of such attitudes is that twenty years previously Latin America's external public debt hardly reached a quarter of the total in the sixties, the region's population was 100 million less, and in those days the second technological and industrial revolution, which during the fifties and sixties fundamentally changed the face of the earth, had hardly begun.

SECTORAL CHANGES IN FOREIGN PRIVATE INVESTMENT AND EFFECTS ON LATIN AMERICA'S DEPENDENCE

Debates on the role of foreign private investment in Latin America's economic development and on how this investment affects the region's external dependence suffer from much confusion, since in general they are given an ideological character. On the one hand, Latin American public opinion is subject to domestic and foreign propaganda, endowing private enterprise, independently of the structure of ownership, with an impressive number of economic, social and ethical virtues which allegedly make it a highly effective agent of economic development and social welfare. On the other hand, spokesmen for left-wing political groups present a completely opposing image to the public: private enterprise seems to act within society in an almost diabolical manner, with its nature and behaviour in Latin America, at least, having not changed at all since the early stages of capitalism. This confusion increases even more when the ideological debate tackles the issue of private foreign enterprise, opposed not only by supporters of radical change in Latin America's productive systems, but by the nationalist intellectual élites and paradoxically by some of those traditional elements in the domestic private sectors whose behaviour recalls Dickens' tales of British capitalism in the first half of the nineteenth century. The existence of these coalitions against foreign private investment, made up of completely heterogenous elements committed to continual conflicts between themselves on other fronts, shows that the problem has many facets.

The economic aspects of foreign investment in Latin America themselves seem complicated and have been studied very little. Moreover, a first glance at the problem offers a panorama full of apparent contradictions. In the case of the United States, the region's main supplier of private capital, official policy entrusts private enterprise with the main role in aiding Latin American economic development. In order to promote private investment in Latin America, the United States government has organized a very impressive apparatus of all kinds of incentives, from fiscal incentives and guarantees against various risks to the financing of feasibility studies for new private investment projects. But to judge from the numerous references made in the United States and Latin America to the slow but steady reduction in new United States private investments in the region, these incentives do not appear to have given the hoped for results. This phenomenon supposedly has its origin in the unsatisfactory climate for foreign investment, in monetary instability, and in political tensions as opposed to the attractions which the high-income countries on both sides of the North Atlantic offer to the potential investor. Considering these circumstances, it would be logical to expect the conflict in Latin America between foreign investors and local societies to be weakened. Paradoxically, the opposite has happened.

Clearly both the United States and Latin America are responsible for the confusion and growing vehemence of the political and ideological conflict, in which data and statistics are used indiscriminately to defend opposing points of view. The confusion is due to the fact that foreign private capital is nearly always talked about in terms of large aggregates, as if it were homogeneous from the viewpoint of its influence on host economies. As it is not so, it is relatively easy to destroy both those theses opposing any type of foreign investment, and those which see in it the answer to the majority of Latin America's problems. Both schools of thought suffer from an oversimplification of concepts.

In view of the absence of a rational debate on the multiple effects of foreign investment behaviour on developing economies, it may be useful to review trends in the distribution of this investment by the main subregions and productive sectors of Latin America. Perhaps in this way some preliminary conclusions can be drawn as to the participation of foreign private capital in Latin America's development process. Consequently, the apparent paradox of the decline in new investment flows to the area, and, as many insist, the growing predominance of foreign private capital in the economies of the region may be cleared up. To this end, a few observations are in order on the consequences of the change which has occurred in the distribution of foreign investment by subregions and sectors, both for the area's balance-of-payments and for the possibility of reducing foreign dependence in its economic development.

Unfortunately, detailed data on the total value of direct foreign investment in each country are not available, nor do complete data on its distribution by sectors seem to exist. Therefore, one has to resort to data on United States direct investment, even though in some South American republics European capital makes up a considerable part of total foreign investment(11). Nevertheless, it does not seem that the absence of detailed data on foreign private capital from countries other than the United States changes the general trends, which can be described as follows (see also Table 9.5):

(1) Contrary to the opinion generally held outside Latin America, available data do not indicate that the value of United States direct investment (a crude but useful indicator of the degree of economic power of foreign corporations within Latin American economies) has been negatively affected by political tensions which followed it, monetary instability, or the supposedly unsatisfactory climate for private investment. On the other hand, the value of such investment flows to the area has been proportionately much less than that going to other regions. Nevertheless, the total value of these investments in Latin Americal grew from around US $6000 million to nearly $10,000 million, or around 70 per cent, during the ten years, 1957-66. Considering the small size of new inflows of United States capital, it is fair to assume that the investment was financed mainly with the profits of existing firms, depreciation funds, and with the growing use of Latin American domestic savings mobilized by foreign financial intermediaries.

(2) Over the same period considerable changes occurred in the geographical distribution of United States investment, with the relative share of South America (including Venezuela) falling in favour of middle America-Mexico, Central America and Panama. All this appears to reflect differences in the rates of economic growth of these two large subregions, and changes in the distribution of foreign investment by productive sectors.

(3) The fact which stands out in this process is the pronounced, growing transfer of United States investment (and one must assume the same for that from other sources) from traditional activities (mining, petroleum, transport, electricity, and tropical agriculture) into new sectors (manufacturing, commerce and finance). Scarcely ten years previously the value of United States private investment in primary export activities and public services was estimated at somewhat over $3000 million, half the total value of United States investment in Latin America, with the rest corresponding to manufacturing (including petroleum refining), commerce, tourism and finance. In 1966, whereas the value of United States investment in traditional sectors was estimated at $3800 million, the value of investment in manufacturing and services (excepting transport and electricity) rose to some $6000 million, double the investment in the same sectors in 1956. Most of the increase in traditional investment took place at the end of the fifties and was related to petroleum exploitation in Venezuela. On the other hand, the region experienced a disinvestment in public services and tropical agriculture.

(4) The rise in the value of United States investment in manufacturing, commerce and services was extremely rapid. In the industrial sector it grew from US $1250 to 3075 million (almost 150 per cent); in commerce, from $350 to 1150 million (over 200 per cent); and in the sector of financial intermediaries, from $300 to 800 million (over 150 per cent). In industry,

commerce and banking, the process accelerated after 1960, with United States investment showing special dynamism in industrial activities in Argentina, Central America, Colombia and Mexico; in the commerce sector in Brazil, Central America, and Venezuela; and in finance throughout the region (except Mexico, where participation of foreign capital in the finance sector is prohibited by law).

It is relatively easy to find explanations for the apparent loss of interest in Latin America shown by foreign corporations which traditionally operated in the region, and, on the other hand, the great awakening of interest in the region by firms which had recently established themselves in the modern sector. In the extractive industries, including petroleum, the world scene had changed radically in the post-war period. The discovery of rich new mineral deposits in other parts of the world, the expansion of mining activities in the industrialized countries, the revolution in exploration technology and transport, and low world demand for industrial raw materials combined to reduce the relative importance of Latin America's mineral resources to the transnational companies. Moreover, in the face of the abundance of industrial raw materials and the beginnings of the era of relatively peaceful coexistence between the two large power centres - the United States and the Soviet Union - Latin America's mineral wealth began to lose its importance as a stragegic reserve of American corporations.

The approval given by the large mining companies to 'joint production' agreements in Mexico and Chile merely expressed a rational reaction by these corporations, from the point of view of their economic objectives, to political pressures reflecting traditional Latin American nationalism. This nationalism, born in the period of scarcity of resources, did not take into account changes in supply of technology and the availability of natural resources on a world scale. Hence it insisted that national control of this economic sector was the first step towards independence from the outside world.

Such a position can be defended in countries which have succeeded in diversifying their economies and entered the phase of diversified industrial development based on considerable and recent inputs of domestically-produced raw materials. But for the industrially less advanced economies the objective of 'recovering' natural resources in exchange for transnational corporations domination of their modern sectors seems of very doubtful value. In general, in resource-rich countries outside Latin America, such as Canada and Australia, concern about external dependence arises more through fear of foreign control of manufacturing and finance than of that of the mining industry.

In Latin America we have witnessed the surprising phenomenon of a coincidence of interest, albeit for different reasons, between foreign enterprises traditionally devoted to the exploitation of natural resources and countries which play host to them. The former gradually cut down their activities, while the latter, under pressure from public opinion, helped them in their task by 'nationalizing' the mining industries. Something similar appeared to be happening in the tropical agricultural sector, at least in Central America and the Caribbean. Given the depressed situation in international markets for plantation agriculture products, foreign enterprises were transferring their property to nationals. They kept control over the marketing of products such as cotton, sugar, and tropical fruits, since distribution operations offered substantial profits without the risks which characterize agricultural production.

The foreign investors' departure from public services in the region, which is more evident than their relative lack of interest in mining, had another explanation. In inflationary situations, and due to social pressures on the state, legal systems aimed at regulating public service tariffs ceased to operate(12). Consequently, the degree of profitability of public service enterprises was so unattractive compared to profit margins in other sectors that the only reasonable thing to do from the foreign investors' viewpoint was to try to sell their property to the state. In Argentina, domestic control of public services was achieved in the 1940s by using the country's international currency reserves, which could have been used for industrialization. In the fifties, the process of 'recovery' of the public services from foreign hands extended to nearly all the region. While this process did not harm the economic interests of the old owners of the nationalized enterprises, yet it affected the domestic and external financial position of their new owner, the state. As the proceeds from the sale of these public service enterprises were reinvested immediately, in most cases, in the modern sectors of the respective economies, the cost of the operations, once more in the majority of cases, was met with external credits negotiated by the public sector. In other words, Latin American states helped foreign investors to increase their domination of local economies.

The first part of this paper put forward a somewhat bold hypothesis that a considerable part of the external indebtedness of Latin America's public sector had served as a substitute for domestic structural reforms, through the use of external financial resources. The experiences of the public services sector support this hypothesis. The insistence of Latin American governments on keeping low tariffs for these services in an inflationary climate, which led to the mass transfer of transport and electricity activities to the state, can hardly be defended as a measure to redistribute income or assist industrialization. Apparently there are no studies of the incidence of low costs for public services in the distribution of income in Latin America, and if there were, they would very probably have shown a regressive effect. On the other hand, Latin American industry would have been able to absorb the periodic adjustments in charges with no difficulty whatsoever if the services had been made more efficient.

The problem of fixing public service rates has nevertheless acquired a very special political character. Unable to take more serious measures of economic policy or lacking interest in adopting them, the state accepted the role of alleged defender of the masses against supposed exploitation by foreign-owned public service enterprises. This position also offered the advantage of distracting public attention from the real effect which the inflationary process had on the relative economic position of different income groups. Thus, besides converting itself into the symbol of defence of national interests by setting fixed rates for transport, electricity and other public services, the state became the symbol of defence of the welfare of the urban proletariat. Yet the resulting psycho-political satisfaction was not free of real costs. The proof of this lies firstly in the balances of former public service companies in Latin America, which transferred their activities to much more profitable sectors with great financial success, and second, in the effect which the nationalization of public services had on the external indebtedness of the public sector.

The inter-sectoral transfer of foreign private investment which took place partly explains the low level of new external capital inflows to the region. The high profitability of industrial, commercial and financial enterprises

was another factor in the paradoxical picture in which the rapid growth of
the value of foreign investment in the region contrasted with the small flows
of new capital. In the United States official reports stressed that not only
was the low level of profitability, together with the heavy risks, the main
obstacle to the flow of private capital to the developing countries, but also
that the profits of enterprises established in Latin America were lower than
in other parts of the world. These assertions are contradicted by what is
known, even superficially, about Latin American reality.

Due to excessive protectionism, the quasi-monopolistic structure of the market, the generosity of government incentives to industry, and the close integration of industrial firms with financial intermediaries, the profits of
domestically-owned firms in the modern sectors of the region's economy are
extremely high. One does not have to study the balance sheets of industrial,
commercial and banking enterprises to prove this assertion. One need only
glance at the national accounts of any country or consult data on income distribution. Thus it seems impossible to accept without reservation the results
of the periodic studies originated in the United States Department of Commerce
on United States investment abroad, according to which the average annual
profits of North American firms in Latin America (excepting petroleum) were
of the order of 7 to 8 per cent of invested capital. If this were really so,
Latin America would not have experienced the transfer of traditional investments to the manufacturing and services sectors; neither would the region
have seen the rapid growth of the value of these investments, the inflows of
new foreign capital being relatively small.

Here one reaches the crux of the problem. There is no doubt whatsoever that
the concentration of foreign private investment in the modern sectors of Latin
America's economies aided the import-substitution process, and helped to
increase the availability of foreign exchange through new exports, to create
employment, and to expand technology transfer. Yet it is still to be demonstrated that these contributions are comparable to the weight of foreign
investment on the different economies, and to their potential future burden
on the area's balance of payments. Furthermore, studies will have to take
into account the growing strength of nationalism in Latin America, and the
reactions of powerful groups of domestic entrepreneurs in each country who
do not want to see themselves displaced by foreign investment, notwithstanding
its modernizing effect on existing productive structures. Economists and
political scientists from both within and outside the area should study not
only the long-term economic consequences of the growth of foreign investment
in the dynamic sectors of Latin American economies, but also the region's
political capacity to absorb this investment. Apparently, here we are witnessing another paradoxical phenomenon. Whereas Latin America's dependence
on external financial and technological services continues to grow, its
political capacity to absorb them, in the conditions which govern the international transfer of capital and technical knowledge to the less-developed
countries, is falling as a result of socio-political stagnation.

GROWING EXTERNAL FINANCIAL DEPENDENCE VERSUS PRINCIPLES OF
ECONOMIC NATIONALISM

The data presented above seem to suggest that Latin America's external financial dependence increased greatly from the mid-fifties. Whereas the region's
gross national product rose around 60 per cent, Latin American external
liabilities (the external public debt and direct foreign investment),

estimated in a fairly conservative manner, grew by 125 per cent - from $10,000 million to £22,500 million - excluding public sector short-term debts, the commercial indebtedness of private enterprises, and private investments from outside the hemisphere. The servicing of these liabilities increased from $1300 million to 3200 million, or 150 per cent, and in 1966 represented around 25 per cent of Latin America's current account proceeds. Even if the task of calculating the capacity for servicing external liabilities, which among other factors depends on the GNP growth rate, the capital-output ratio, and average and marginal savings rates, becomes impossible for a region of over twenty different economies, it can be affirmed that the ratio of servicing external liabilities to current revenue in Latin America far exceeded prudent limits. Consequently, the area's growing external financial dependence was accompanied by acute vulnerability to possible fluctuations in international markets for goods and services of Latin American origin.

The rapid accumulation of external liabilities can be partly explained by, first, the growing real cost of the financial resources received by the public sector as external aid - if we include in this concept all types of loans and credits received from the private sectors of high-income countries - and, second, by inter-sectoral changes in foreign investment distribution. Viewing the problem from within Latin America, the situation reflected the opposition of local power élites to a more efficient use of domestic savings and to the modernization of social and productive structures by internal efforts. While external public indebtedness was used by the state as a substitute for domestic reforms, the task of modernizing the private sector was put in the hands of foreign private investment, while at the same time foreign capital, in exchange for its high profits, was expected to accept the rules of the game which supposedly reflected the national interest. In these conditions, it is difficult to see how foreign capital was going to satisfy the nationalist principles which strove to reduce the degree of external dependence of the Latin American republics.

NOTES

(1)   Osvaldo Sunkel, 'Politica nacional de desarrollo y dependencia externa', Comercio Exterior, Mexico, March and April, 1968.

(2)   This is not the place to go into the subject of the degree of antagonism between the two systems. One essay on this subject which stands out for its lucidity is: Ralph K. White, 'Socialism and Capitalism: an International Misunderstanding', Foreign Affairs, New York, January, 1966.

(3)   See my essay, 'La inversión privada norteamericana y el desarrollo de Mesoamefica', Comercio Exterior, México, August, 1968.

(4)   The nature of the phenomenon of apparent stability is masterfully described by Claudio Véliz in the introduction to his book Obstacles to Change in Latin America (London, 1965):

> In spite of its reputation for frequent and violent political upheaval, perhaps the principal contemporary problem of Latin America is excessive stability. There exists in the region a resilient traditional structure of institutions, hierarchical arrangements, and attitudes which conditions every aspect of political behaviour and which has survived centuries of colonial government, movements for independence, foreign wars and

invasions, domestic revolutions, and a confusingly large number of lesser palace revolts. More recently it has not only successfully resisted the impact of technological innovation and industrialization, but appears to have been strengthened by it.

(5) CEPAL, El financiamiento externo de America Latina, New York, 1964.

(6) Inter alia, Dragoslav Avramović and Associates, Economic Growth and External Debt, Baltimore, 1964 and S.R.N. Badri Rao, Cambios recientes en la deuda pública externa de los países latinoamericanos, CEMLA, México, 1964.

(7) Various volumes of IMF, Balance of Payments Yearbook, particularly volume 19 (1967-68).

(8) For details, see various evaluations of development plans by Organization of American States experts under the Alliance for Progress.

(9) See, on this subject, various studies by international organizations, inter alia, IBRD, Supplier Credits from Industrial Countries to Developing Countries, Washington, D.C., April, 1968. As shown in another study of Pakistan's experiences, the phenomenon described extends to all developing regions, not only Latin America. Mahbub ul Haq, 'Tied Credits - A Quantitative Approach', in J.H. Adler (Editor), Capital Movements - Proceedings of a Conference held by the International Economic Association, London, 1967.

(10) In an inquiry into public attitudes in high-income, both free-market and socialist, countries The New York Times (9 August 1968) wrote that: 'as a result of the disenchantement in those countries by the results of economic aid programmes, the United States and other Western countries advise the developing countries to rely more on private enterprise as a source of credits and foreign investments'.

(11) Whereas in Mexico and Central America, United States investment in 1966 represented more than 80 per cent of foreign private investment, in other countries its share varied from 40 per cent (Brazil) to a little over 70 per cent (Venezuela). But it must be pointed out that, for example in the case of Brazil, the distribution of both United States and European investment by sectors was the same both in 1956 and 1966.

(12) For details on Mexico, see Miguel S. Wionczek, El nacionalismo mexicano y la inversión extranjera, Mexico, 1967.

STATISTICAL APPENDIX

TABLE 9.1. Exports, Imports, Gross International Reserves, External Public Debt and United States Direct Investment in Latin America, 1956, 1961 and 1966[1]

(US $ million)

	1956	1961	1966
1. Merchandise –			
a) exports f.o.b.	8,072	8,218	11,040
b) excluding Venezuela	5,853	5,766	8,327
2. Merchandise –			
a) imports c.i.f.	6,489	7,389	9,720
b) excluding Venezuela	5,320	6,296	8,389
3. a) Official gold and foreign exchange reserves	3,196	2,705	3,180
b) Excluding Venezuela	2,257	2,125	2,404
4. a) External public debt	4,128	7,758	12,573
b) Excluding Venezuela	3,895	7,370	12,119
5. a) External public debt service	454	1,113	1,985
b) Excluding Venezuela	441	889	1,964
6. a) United States direct private investment	5,838	8,166	9,853
b) Excluding Venezuela	4,009	5,149	7,175
7. a) Servicing of United States direct private investment[2]	840	910	1,261
b) Excluding Venezuela	420	451	805

[1] Excluding Cuba.
[2] Including foreign firms' payments abroad of interest, royalties, and other services.

Sources: 1, 2, 3: International Monetary Fund;
        4, 5 : IBRD and IMF, Balance of Payments Yearbook for 1966, national data.
        6, 7 : United States Department of Commerce, Survey of Current Business.

TABLE 9.2. New Gross Disbursements of Foreign Loans to the Public Sector, External Debt Service (Amortization and Interest) and External Public Debt of Latin America (Including Contracted but not Disbursed), 1956, 1961 and 1966

	1956			1961			1966		
	ND	AI	PD	ND	AI	PD	ND	AI	PD
Argentina	49	18	687	540	252	1670	97	428	1888
Bolivia	2	3	91	3	14	182	8	13	293
Brazil	161	180	1380	526	246	2238	515	573	3201
Colombia	50	39	278	92	74	475	46	93	1013
Costa Rica	4	3	41	5	5	76	42	22	142
Chile	33	50	379	179	118	752	256	128	1260
Dominican Republic	—	—	3	—	—	5	32	2	172
Ecuador	9	6	74	19	12	107	18	13	198
El Salvador	4	1	27	10	3	46	15	8	80
Guatemala	1	2	18	13	4	65	16	14	83
Honduras	—	—	4	2	3	30	6	4	70
Mexico	88	92	491	340	205	1172	569	543	2236
Nicaragua	4	4	30	6	4	41	22	9	107
Panama	1	1	17	8	2	58	12	6	102
Paraguay	3	2	23	2	3	31	12	4	84
Peru	36	29	216	28	38	286	122	94	892
Uruguay	6	11	146	5	10	136	16	10	258
Venezuela	4	13	233	63	124	388	36	21	454
	455	454	4128	1841	1113	7758	1840	1985	12,573

ND: New disbursements;   AI: Amortization and interests;   PD: Public debt

Sources: For 1956 and 1961, IBRD statistics published in S.R.N. Badri Rao (1964) *Cambios recientes en la deuda pública externa de los países latinoamericanos*, México, CEMLA; for 1966, national data.

TABLE 9.3. Outstanding External Public Debt as a Proportion of Gross External Current Account Revenue in Latin America

(Percentage of total outstanding external debt (a) over foreign exchange inflows (b))

	(a) as at 31 December 1961 (b) average 1958-60	(a) as at 31 December 1966 (b) average 1963-65
Argentina	159	122
Bolivia	337	299
Brazil	159	200
Colombia	128	149
Costa Rica	78	108
Chile	160	187
Dominican Republic	4	93
Ecuador	72	109
El Salvador	40	42
Guatemala	55	41
Haiti	82	98
Honduras	42	31
Mexico	82	122
Nicaragua	49	71
Panama	52	49
Paraguay	54	156
Peru	72	123
Uruguay	82	112
Venezuela	13	18
Total	86	113

Sources: See Table 9.2.

TABLE 9.4. External Public Debt Servicing as a Percentage of Gross Current Account External Revenue in Latin America, 1956, 1961 and 1966

	1956	1961	1966
Argentina	1.6	21.1	23.8
Bolivia	3.8	21.9	9.6
Brazil	11.5	16.1	30.4
Colombia	5.4	12.8	14.0
Costa Rica	3.6	5.0	13.4
Chile	9.5	22.3	13.0
Dominican Republic	n.a.	n.a.	1.2
Ecuador	4.9	8.5	6.4
El Salvador	1.1	2.3	3.8
Guatemala	0.2	3.1	5.4
Haití	9.6	–	n.a.[1]
Honduras	–	3.8	1.3
Mexico	6.7	12.8	25.5
Nicaragua	5.5	4.7	5.1
Panama	0.9	1.4	2.3
Paraguay	14.2	6.1	6.2
Peru	8.2	6.5	10.5
Uruguay	5.0	4.5	4.0
Venezuela	0.5	4.7	0.8
	4.9	11.2	15.1

[1] n.a. not available

Sources: IMF, Balance of Payments Yearbook, various volumes.

TABLE 9.5. Book Value of United States Direct Private Investment in Latin America, 1956, 1961 and 1966

(US $ million)

	Total	Mining & smelting	Petroleum	Manufacturing	Public utilities	Trade	Others
Total 1956	5838	860	1768	1241	551	351	1067
Mexico	690	166	17	321	93	74	19
Central America, incl. Haiti, Panama and Dominican Republic	610	10	58	33	145	24	331
Venezuela	1829	20	1411	78	37	74	209
Argentina	333	–	–	161	54	35	83
Brazil	810	–	112	470	151	48	29
Colombia, Chile, Peru	1445	655	150	132	60	78	370
Other	121	–	20	46	11	18	26
Total 1961	8166	955	3087	1674	489	754	1207
Mexico	822	130	48	414	29	97	104
Central America, incl. Haiti, Panama and Dominican Republic	934	45	116	38	165	180	390
Venezuela	3017	30	2441	196	33	186	131
Argentina	635	–	50	283	–	28	274
Brazil	1000	14	92	543	198	137	26
Colombia, Chile, Peru	1587	736	300	158	48	106	239
Other	171	–	40	42	16	30	43
Total 1966	9853	1028	2902	3077	360	1158	1328
Mexico	1244	108	42	797	29	153	115
Central America, incl. Haiti, Panama and Dominican Republic	1475	54	316	108	198	355	444
Venezuela	2678	40	1922	293	19	253	151
Argentina	1031	–	100	652	–	41	235
Brazil	1246	58	69	846	38	182	53
Colombia, Chile, Peru	1938	756	356	338	50	150	288
Other	241	12	97	43	26	21	42

Sources: For 1956, adjusted data based on United States Department of Commerce U.S. Business Investments in Foreign ... for 1961, Survey of Current Business, August, 1962; and for 1966, Survey of Current Business, Sept., 1966.

CHAPTER 10

Experiences of the Central American Economic Integration Programme and their Relevance to East Africa*

IN PRESENT-DAY Africa there is general agreement upon an urgent need for industrialization as one of the basic means to accelerate economic development. At the same time there is a growing awareness that, because of the size of markets, the absence of managerial and entrepreneurial skills and the high cost of modern technology, the great majority of independent African states are not in a position to undertake industrialization efforts on a national scale. Consequently, numerous attempts are being made to bring about in various African subregions some measures of trade, cooperation and industrial integration. Among these schemes are the East African Common Market, the setting up of Maghreb institutions for economic cooperation, the Central African Customs and Economic Union, the projected Free Trade Area in West Africa and proposals for a larger Eastern African Common Market.

The experiences of other developing regions strongly suggest that one of the most difficult problems of economic integration is that of equitable multinational distribution of its benefits and burdens, especially in the industrial sector. Consequently, this paper analyses in some detail two concrete subregional industrial policy mechanisms: the Central American Regime for Integration Industries and the East African Kampala Agreement on allocation of industries on a regional basis. In the light of the failure of these two schemes, the final part of the paper offers some preliminary proposals which, it is expected, will help in elaborating mechanisms adaptable to African conditions.

THE CENTRAL AMERICAN REGIME FOR INTEGRATION INDUSTRIES

The Regime for Integration Industries is an important part of the economic integration mechanism set up in 1958 through the Multilateral Treaty on Free

---

*This paper was written for the Symposium on Industrial Development in Africa organized by the UN Ecomomic Commission for Africa in Cairo, Egypt in January-February 1966, and published in <u>East African Economic Review</u> (Nairobi), Vol. 2, New Series No. 1 (June 1966) and No. 2 (December 1966).

Trade and Central American Economic Integration. The Regime was joined by four Central Emerican republics (El Salvador, Guatemala, Honduras and Nicaragua) at the time of the signature of the Multilateral Treaty, and joined later by Costa Rica. The Multilateral Treaty itself, while creating a free trade zone for a defined list of commodities of domestic origin, considered trade liberalization and regional industrialization as two key aspects of the integration process and consequently contained a specific commitment of the member countries that

> with a view to promoting industrial development consistent with the purpose of this Treaty, the Contracting Parties shall adopt, by mutual agreement, measures designed to further the <u>establishment or expansion of regional industries</u> [italics added] directed towards a Central American common market and of particular interest to the economic integration of Central America(1).

The subsequent General Treaty on Central American Economic Integration, signed in 1960 and adhered to later by Costa Rica, transformed a limited free trade zone into a Central American common market, and dedicated to the issue of industrial integration even more attention. It endorsed the Agreement on the Regime for Central American Integration Industries; called for the establishment of the Central American Bank for Economic Integration (CABEI) 'as an instrument for the financing and promotion of a regionally-balanced, integrated economic growth', providing that CABEI members might not use its credit facilities unless they ratified the 1958 Regime for Integration Industries; and committed member countries 'with a view to establishing uniform tax incentives to industrial development . . . to ensure as soon as possible a reasonable equalization of the relevant laws and regulations in force'. The Charter of the Central American Bank for Economic Integration declared that the purpose of the institution 'shall be to promote the economic integration and balanced economic development of the member countries' and that its activities will be primarily designed to promote and finance, <u>inter alia</u>

> projects for long-term investment industries of a regional character or of importance for the Central American market which will help to increase the supply of goods available for intra Central American trade or for such trade and the export sector. The Bank's activities shall not include investment in essentially local industries(2).

Thus, within several years after the start of the regional integration programme, five Central American republics supported a series of interrelated legal instruments and regional institutions aimed at expanding zonal trade, financing new regional infrastructure and industrial projects, promoting the inflow of external capital resources and coordinating other activities important for the acceleration of regional industrialization. In addition to the 1960 General Treaty, the Regime for Integration Industries and the regional development bank, the most important elements of the integration scheme were: the equalization of import duties and charges (1959), uniform tax incentives for industrial development (1962) and a regional industrial research institute (ICAITI) dating from the mid-fifties.

Most of these regional integration instruments and institutions worked satisfactorily. During the seven years following the signature of the first Multilateral Treaty intra-Central American trade (imports <u>cif</u>) increased more than fivefold from US $20 million in 1958 to some US $105 million in 1964. Its participation in the region's global foreign trade increased from less than 5

to over 20 per cent. By the fall of 1965 the five countries' customs union
was in existence for all practical purposes and an external uniform common
tariff covered 97 per cent of foreign trade items. The structure of intra-
zonal commercial transactions underwent considerable diversification - in
1964 manufactures accounted for 40 per cent of the regional interchange.
Trade fluctuations, characteristic of the past and reflecting the marginal
and seasonal character of intra-regional trade until the end of the fifties,
largely disappeared. Upon the establishment in 1961 of a multilateral payments clearing house, a large measure of cooperation among monetary authorities and private banking systems had been achieved. The integration bank,
well-endowed with zonal and external resources and backed financially by the
Inter-American Development Bank and United States aid agencies, extended
during its first four years of existence credits totalling US $34 million to
public and private projects 'of interest to the integration programme'. The
trade liberalization process resulted in an increase of domestic and foreign
investment in the area. It is tentatively estimated that the inflow of
foreign capital induced by the emergence of the Central American Common Market
amounted in 1961-64 to a not negligible total of US $100 million. All this
contrasts with extremely slow changes in the industrial structure of the area,
still mainly limited as in the mid-fifties to light consumer goods, and the
absence of new dynamic industrial projects serving the whole zone and the
unimpressive performance of the Regime for Integration Industries. Thus, a
series of questions arises: is the issue of equitable distribution of industries in an integrating multinational area of paramount or only secondary
importance; was the idea of the distributive mechanism as conceived in Central
America well thought out; did the failure of the Regime for Integration Industries have any negative effect upon the economic development of the area,
and, finally, can other developing areas preparing their own regional integration schemes learn anything from the Central American experience?

The idea of the Agreement on the Regime for Integration Industries originated
in the early fifties with UN Economic Commission for Latin America (ECLA)
experts who had several objectives in mind: (1) to encourage or induce the
establishment or expansion of industries which might require immediate free
access to the entire regional market in order to operate under reasonable
economic and competitive conditions; (2) to promote the utilization - more
rational than in the past - of available capital, technical skills and natural
resources; and (3) to ensure that industrial development was distributed with
relative equity throughout the region. ECLA technicians, without whose assistance the Central American integration programme would never have started,
were well aware of the historical record of intra-area political and economic
fights, squabbles and friction after the break-up of the Spanish colonial
empire in the early nineteenth century, and of failure of numerous previous
attempts to bring about some degree of political and economic unification
into what for a short time, almost 150 years previously, was one political
unit - the Central American Republic(3). They were not less aware of the lack
of economic viability in terms of modern economic development of the five
minuscule and underdeveloped countries; considerable differences in per capita
income and resource endowments; the foreign-oriented character of five agricultural economies strongly linked to that of the United States, the major
market for their primary produce and the major supplier of consumer and investment goods; the lack of economic complementarity if considered in static and
not developmental terms; and the absence of commercial and financial links
within the area. Finally, they suspected and were afraid that with the growth
of trade in response to the progressive disappearance of intra-zonal custom
barriers, serious friction would arise in the long run among member countries

because of three possible effects of the trade liberalization programme: (1) losses of government revenues as an increasing volume of goods would enter each country from the others duty free; (2) a negative impact upon existing light consumer goods industries in more underdeveloped countries as they would begin to face competition from the same industries in other member countries, and (3) concentration of the activities induced by a free trade regime in a few existing industrial centres in the more developed republics, offering better external economies than the others. In the minds of ECLA technicians and more sophisticated members of Central American political and economic élites, pushed towards regional economic cooperation by deterioration in the traditional export sector after the short-lived international commodity markets boom during the Korean War, the viability of the regional integration scheme would have depended to a very considerable extent upon an adequate solution to one complicated but crucial problem: the way to distribute with relative equity the benefits and burdens of economic integration among prospective members of the Central American Common Market.

Since the economies of the area were by-and-large free enterprise economies and the local political élites had rather a conservative outlook, any attempt to introduce in Central America in the late fifties - whether on a national or regional level - planning or state economic *dirigisme* would have been futile. Thus a scheme was thought out leaving existing productive facilities to more or less grow spontaneously under the influence of market forces, but opening a way to a 'rational allocation of resources' in new heavier and and intermediate industries. Because of the size of individual national markets, such manufacturing enterprises were absent in Central America in the fifties. Consequently, the 1958 Regime defined as 'integration industries' those which would 'comprise one or more plants which require access to the Central American market in order to operate under reasonably economic and competitive conditions even at minimum capacity'. According to subsequent market surveys this definition would apply to such industrial branches as fertilizers, insecticides and fungicides; pharmaceutical products; tyres and tubes; paint, varnishes and dyes; glass, plastic and metal containers; pulp and paper products; rolled steel; petroleum refining, and artificial fibres, among others.

The Regime offered a number of benefits and protection to firms designated to operate as 'integration industries'. The first and foremost was immediate free access to the whole Central American market, while similar products of other firms - entering the area afterwards without benefit of this special agreement - would receive the same treatment only after ten years through successive gradual reduction of tariffs by 10 per cent a year. Enterprises designated as 'integration industries' would also enjoy ample fiscal incentives in the countries where they might decide to establish themselves, obtain sufficient external protection to make products competitive with imported goods and receive priority as suppliers to governments and other stage agencies.

The designation of an 'integration industry' would take the form of a protocol signed and ratified by all member countries. This would specify the location of the industry, the minimum capacity of the plant and the conditions under which additional plants would be distributed in case of a growing zonal demand; the quality standards of the products; the measures 'deemed convenient for the protection of consumers'; the regulations in regard to the participation of Central American capital and the level of the common external tariff to be set to protect each 'integration industry'. To ensure equitable distribution of these industries in the area it was agreed that 'the Contracting States shall not award a second plant to any country until all the five Central American countries have been assigned a plant in conformity with the protocols'.

The initiative in respect to 'integration industries' was to come from individuals or corporations and not from governments or regional integration authorities. Applications were to be presented, with all pertinent information, to the Secretariat of the Central American Industrial Integration Commission to be created under the Central American Economic Council, the top regional integration agency. Applications would be acted upon through the signature of a protocol only after a favourable technical opinion were received either from the Central American Research Institute for Industry (ICAITI) or 'from any other person or body that Commission considers competent'. Such advice would have to cover all major technological and economic aspects of each project and, in particular, the longer-term market prospects for an industry applying for the Regime's benefits.

The outline of the scheme made it clear that, acting upon the initiative of ECLA advisers, the five Central American republics thought it advisable to reserve the regional market for <u>single</u> enterprises in certain industries to avoid situations where the mushrooming of several small-scale and high-cost plants competing with each other in a small regional market and putting a heavy drain on resources in short supply (such as capital, skilled labour, managerial talents and technology) would perpetuate the industrialization pattern existing in light consumer goods fields. Furthermore, it was expected that through opening the way towards both horizontal and vertical integration of new heavier industrial activities to be declared 'integration industries' and which might be composed of one or a group of plants, the Regime would foster both product specialization and the appearance of relatively large-sized plants. It was hoped that, assuming parallel development of infrastructure facilities, such firms might become within reasonable time the area's development poles, which in turn would attract ancillary industries and new tertiary activities to each member country. Thus, given a reasonable economic location of these new industries in terms of varying natural resources endowments, availability of labour and technology, and the principle of multilateral negotiations on their distribution, the danger of industrial agglomeration and concentration in some areas could be avoided, a danger ever present under the conditions of complete freedom of localization available to any industrial activity ready to enter the Central American market. The clause of the Regime providing in somewhat obscured language for distribution of 'integration industries' by rounds of negotiations took into account not only their potential effect upon employment and income in member countries and future intra-zonal trade flows, but also the high political prestige attached to industrialization. In a way, the Regime represented an attempt to introduce into the area a <u>multilateral industrial licensing mechanism</u> responding to both economic and political considerations. Its final aim was to avoid political friction which might arise if one or two countries, presumably Guatemala and El Salvador, were to become centres of regional industrial growth, leaving traditional primary activities to the least developed members of the group, Honduras and Nicaragua.

The Regime clearly reflected a belief held by the majority of Latin American economists and by ECLA as well that a free play of market forces in developing countries can hardly promote industrial development at the necessary speed and, besides, by increasing existing gaps in development levels, can bring

serious political complications. Without dismissing market mechanisms, ECLA
experts thought it advisable to subject them both in the Central American
integration schemes and in the Latin American Free Trade Association established in 1960, with the participation of eight South American countries and
Mexico, to a series of corrective measures in the form of regulations, special
concessions, exceptions from the traditional free trade rules, etc. In Central
America a very detailed distribution scheme for new industrial activities had
been elaborated by ECLA staff sometime before the Multilateral Treaty had been
signed in 1958. This scheme fell through, however, because of the inability
of the Central American governments to agree upon its details, not without
the interference of national and foreign vested interests. In consequence,
the 1958 Agreement on the Regime for Integration Industries was drafted in
general terms and in somewhat obscure language and was open to conflicting
interpretations.

When in late 1961 informal negotiations on implementation of the Regime started
at the first meeting of the ad hoc Working Group on Industrial Development
held in Managua, Nicaragua, the politics of the distribution of the integration industries and not the economics became the main issue. The purpose of
the meeting was to select the first round of integration industries and draw
up necessary protocols. With official delegations of four out of five Central
American republics present (Guatemala, Honduras, El Salvador and Nicaragua)
and no practical experience available from anywhere, the meeting was very much
a trial-and-error affair. A big step forward came with the amicable preliminary selection by each country of one integration industry. Guatemala chose
the already existing tyre and tube plant, El Salvador, copper wire extrusion,
Nicaragua, caustic soda and insecticides, and Honduras, a small chemical industry project based on imported basic petrochemicals with an option to substitude within six months a glass container plant. In the opinion of some
observers, this meeting proceeded with considerable disregard for the economics of industrialization. The general attitude seemed to be that if a government chose a particular integration industry, encouraged by prospective or
actual local and foreign investors, then there would be no discussion of the
wisdom of the decision but only of details of the protocol to be signed
jointly at a later date. Virtually no use was made of existing ECLA industrial studies to relate individual projects to the needs of the region,
except in the sense that each project obviously needed access to the whole
regional market. Little attention was given to the economics of location
and only one participating country pressed in vain for a general discussion
of longer-run aims and objectives of the Regime for Integration Industries.

The meeting showed, on the other hand, the preoccupation of member countries
with the issue of foreign capital's role in the 'integration industries' and
with the principle of their equitable distribution throughout the area. It
became evident - and was confirmed in the following years - that the Central
American countries would insist on majority participation of capital originating in the area in all new major manufacturing enterprises and that the least-developed countries of the grouping would insist on the principle of negotiations by 'rounds', whereby each country would receive a similar number of
projects. The discussion also disclosed that the less-developed republics
considered the equitable distribution in terms of the size of investment
involved in each project, a criterion difficult to defend on the basis of
economic analysis. In addition, it became evident that 'integration industries' would receive a high level of protection, following demands from the
interested investor groups. The economics of industrial integration were
closely intertwined with the politics of economic cooperation and any attempt

to divorce them might have put a heavy strain on the orderly functioning of the Central American Common Market scheme.

The Regime did not, however, make spectacular headway in following years. Although the first protocol signed by five governments in 1963 declared a tyre and tube plant in Guatemala and a caustic soda and insecticide plant in Nicaragua as the first Central American 'integration industries', two years later in the fall of 1965 the protocol had still to be ratified by one of the five member countries, Honduras. Some progress towards its entry into force was made by the assignment to that country of the flat glass industry project and the signature of the corresponding protocol at the Fifth Meeting of the Central American Economic Council held in November 1965 in San Salvador. The decision to assign to Costa Rica another tyre and tube plant continued to be a matter of controversy and El Salvador gave up its insignificant metallurgical industry project.

On the other hand, in 1963 the signatories of the Regime for Integration Industries created another regional industrial promotion mechanism partly contradictory to the Regime itself and called a special system for promotion of new productive activities. It provided for periodical joint elaboration of a list of new Central American manufactures to be granted special tariff protection in the area from the moment they supplied at least 50 per cent of regional demand. The two lists approved between 1963 and 1965 include, among others, certain glass products, electric bulbs, sanitary paper and sulphuric acid. The new scheme aimed at eliminating monopolistic implications of the 1958 industrial agreement, but its performance was hardly more impressive than that of the 1958 Regime.

The failure of the Regime for Integration Industries to act as a dynamic factor in Central American economic integration was admitted by one of the leading ECLA experts in regional economic affairs, Carlos M. Castillo, who nevertheless defended a thesis that the achievement of balanced regional industrial growth through a joint development policy represented the basic precondition for success of the Central American Common Market. According to Castillo, various instruments incorporated in a series of regional integration mechanisms, including the 'integration industries' regime:

> fit well into the process of balance and development. They are indispensable rather than incompatible components in this process. The need for uniform tax incentives to industrial development and the equilibrating action of a selective policy with respect to investment on the part of CABEI are generally accepted. <u>As for industries regime so far it has not been possible to arrive at a working consensus for its application</u>'. [italics added](4).

The absence of a working consensus in respect to the Regime for Integration Industries reflected in some way the inability of Central American countries to change industrial structure in the area and to pass from the stage of light consumer commodities to that of industrial complexes producing certain heavier manufactures. This phenomenon, in turn, could hardly be explained by the size of the newly emerged market and the lack of factors of production, except technology. Thus the persistence of the traditional industrial structure was probably due not only to strictly economic factors but also to socio-political conditions within and outside the area.

The Central American Regime for Integration Industries has been subject to a detailed critique by many outsiders, including United States aid agencies operating in the area. The main counter-arguments centre on its allegedly producing uncertainties among potential investors which inhibit industrial investment in the area and thus retard economic growth; the arbitrary process of designating 'integration industries' involving a clear danger of political favouritism; the monopolistic implications of the scheme; its superfluity in view of the parallel existence of the Central American Bank for Economic Integration and of uniform tax incentives, supposedly easier to administer than the industrial regime itself, and, finally, its interference with the 'decision of the market place'(5).

At a somewhat higher level of sophistication, the Regime for Integration Industries has been criticized because of its basic assumption that economies of scale are decisive for the industrialization of developing countries in view of the shortage of capital and of the effect of these economies of scale on unit costs and prices. It was alleged that under monopolistic or oligopolistic conditions stimulated by the Regime prices would be fixed in relation to available tariff protection and not on the basis of costs and consequently no increase in consumer welfare could be expected. Contrarywise, an alternative policy of free entry of any industrial firm into the Central American Market, together with a joint effort to build up regional infrastructure, would give - it was maintained - much better developmental and welfare results. Such a policy would eliminate the danger of 'administered prices' and permit new productive facilities to take full advantage of external economies created by an expanded transportation network, a regional electric-power grid, a free flow of skilled labour, more advanced financial services, etc.(6).

In view of the extremely limited progress of the Regime for Integration Industries, a discussion of the relative advantages of economies of scale and external economies in a Central American integration programme remains a purely academic exercise. There is no evidence available that the Regime kept away potential investors nor that it did not permit actual industrial investors to take advantage of external economies emerging from public investment in infrastructure in each member country and on the regional level. The fact remains that industrialization patterns hardly changed in Central America between 1958 and 1965.

As far as the Regime itself is concerned available information strongly intimates that the negative attitude of the United States is partly responsible for its failure to take off. It is known, for example, that the United States government, which in 1960 committed considerable aid resources to the Central American economic integration programme both directly through the Agency for International Development and by loans to the CABEI - did not limit itself to disapproval of the scheme. According to an authority with direct access to United States foreign aid agencies:

> both the Inter-American Development Bank [partly financed with US money] and the Agency for International Development have refused the use of their funds loaned to the Central American Bank for Economic Integration for loans to firms designated as 'integration industries' and, therefore, given preferential treatment within the Central American Common Market(7).

Such strong opposition to the Regime is explained by the rejection by the United States Department of Justice of its monopoly clauses; the negative attitudes of some United States corporations whether with enterprises in the region or considering setting up new industrial ventures there; and the fear of the United States Department of State of difficulties with the foreign aid programme in Congress in case public funds were used to finance a scheme clearly interfering with the free enterprise philosophy(8). It would be too simple, however, to blame this denial of financial resources for the failure of the Regime.

Given the political and economic weight of the United States in Central America, one might have expected United States negative attitudes to cause the disappearance of the Regime, but it did not wither away. An explanation that it was kept alive but dormant by the Central American republics to please its authors, ECLA experts, on the one hand, and to demonstrate independence from external pressures, on the other, looks very ingenious but far from convincing (9). It is more probable that some kind of silent agreement was reached between Central American countries and ECLA experts that, however badly designed or wrongly timed the Regime for Integration Industries might have been in 1958, it could become in the future a useful industrialization instrument. With the progress of regional cooperation in non-industrial fields, it seemed that a growing number of Central Americans was coming around to the ECLA position that balanced growth and equitable distribution of industrialization benefits would in the long run - once the intensive industrialization programme was underway - represent the best guarantee against the disruption of integration by coalitions of domestic and foreign vested economic interests in each country taking a strongly 'nationalistic' line and trying to get the lion's share of Common Market benefits.

In retrospect it seems that the Regime was not well designed and was wrongly timed for reasons beyond the control of its authors. Since no other similar experiences were available elsewhere, it was an experimental exercise. Its main weaknesses were the passive role it ascribed to the Common Market authorities in designating 'integration industries', its cumbersome procedures and its limiting - in fact if not in word - of the concept of integration industries to single enterprises unrelated to the global industrialization needs of the area. But these weaknesses reflected not only the actual stage of Central American industrialization at the time of the 1958 Multilateral Treaty's signature(10). They also reflected the absence of basic data about long-term demand and supply trends outside the agricultural and light consumer goods sectors; the non-existence of industrial planning whether national or regional; the extreme shortage of domestic entrepreneurial skills and, finally, the lack of experience in integration-supporting institutions such as the regional industrial research centre (ICAITI), which in the late fifties led a very precarious life. Nor did the interested governments, as the 1961 meeting of the ad hoc Working Group on Industrial Development clearly demonstrated, understand clearly what the General Treaty and the Regime for Integration Industries tried to achieve in the industrial field and how the productive structure of the region would be affected by a relatively rapid trade liberalization. This explains the choosing at random by Common Market members of four unrelated and, from the viewpoint of the area, insignificant industrial projects for the first round of negotiations. A continuation of multilateral negotiations on similar projects would never be of more than marginal importance for regional industrialization, but the meagre performance of the Regime did not invalidate its two basic premises: that the unnecessary duplication of high-cost small industrial plants and the agglomeration of new manufacturing activities in some member countries would be harmful to the integration process taking place within a political framework which assumed a continued existence of five separate and sovereign states for a long time to come.

Some new economic and non-economic factors appeared on the Central American scene suggesting that although still dormant, the revised and expanded scheme might be a useful means of assuring the balanced development of intermediate and capital goods industries capable of supplying the regional market with inputs, whose imports from the outside world were limited by Central America's slowly growing import capacity. It might also be that the Regime, containing a specific clause in respect to the participation of domestic and regional capital in the 'integration industries', was the only mechanism able to dispel growing preoccupation - both in the public and private sectors - about the undue share of benefits from integration falling into the hands of foreign industrial enterprises. Paradoxically, this preoccupation was the result of Central American economic growth registered after 1958 and of the emergence of new domestic entrepreneur groups in response to socio-political change sparked by the integration movement.

These groups with access to capital resources previously transferred abroad or invested in land could not, however, by any means match financial and technological resources available to large international corporations entering the potential market, similar in size to that of the middle-sized Latin American republics such as Colombia, Chile and Venezuela(11). Although during the first stage of integration the 'forces of the market place' worked largely in favour of foreign manufacturing enterprises, leading to growing friction and the appearance of Central American economic nationalism, they had a considerable demonstration effect upon Central American entrepreneurs. When the process of regional import substitution in light consumer industries came to an end, both domestic and foreign capital started competing for industrial opportunities in the field which would clearly fall under the Regime for Integration Industries. If the scheme were adjusted to new conditions, were to receive technical support from the regional industrial research institute in the form of well-elaborated concrete projects linked with national industrialization plans and attractive in each particular case to groups of investors from various Central American countries, the governments of the region might reconsider their lukewarm attitudes and start negotiating distribution of such projects throughout the Common Market. In such a case, negotiations would cover not, as in the past, individual plants of marginal importance for regional industrialization, but larger industrial projects jointly financed by Central American entrepreneurs and meant to reestablish some equilibrium in the area between regional and extra-zonal capital and at the same time distribute major projects among all member countries. The fact that ICAITI together with CABEI organized in mid-1965 the first regional meeting on investment opportunities, pointing out the economic feasibility of some seventy new industrial projects, suggested that the Regime for Integration Industries might face a chance of an early revival if adequately revised.

THE KAMPALA-MBALE AGREEMENT

The second case which throws considerable light on the difficulties of multilateral arrangements providing for equitable distribution of benefits and burdens in a regional economic integration scheme in the context of developing countries is that of the still-born Kampala-Mbale Agreement, negotiated by the three members of the East African Common Market (Kenya, Uganda and Tanzania) between April 1964 and January 1965. Although the agreement never entered into force and only its principal points were made public officially by the Tanzanian Minister of Finance in mid-1964(12), enough is known about this scheme and subsequent developments to warrant a detailed discussion of the reasons for its failure.

It is not accident that negotiations leading to the Kampala-Mbale agreement started almost immediately after the last British territory in East Africa, Kenya, achieved independence in December 1963. As the voluminous literature on the trials and tribulations of the East African Common Market established in the twenties suggests, East African élites, British civil servants in the East African Common Service Organization (EASCO) and international experts and missions visiting the region with growing frequency in the post-war period were in agreement on two major points: (a) that differences between the development levels of the three former territories were not only considerable but steadily increasing, and (b) that the distribution of gains from the Common Market arrangement was heavily weighted in favour of the most developed member, Kenya. Here the consensus of opinions among experts ended, because no generally acceptable measure of the distribution of gains in an economic integration scheme had been elaborated and the traditional way of measuring benefits or losses from integration exclusively by the trade flows had serious theoretical shortcomings. Three alternative and divergent opinions in respect to East African Common Market results can be discerned: (a) Kenya was the greatest net beneficiary of the union, but the other two countries also got some benefits - although much smaller and perhaps marginal - from participation in the arrangement, mainly through the spread effect of Kenyan industrialization in the less-developed neighbours, their access to Kenya's growing market for certain primary goods and external economies offered to Uganda and Tanzania through joint common market services in fields such as transportation and communications(13); (b) Kenya was the greatest beneficiary, Uganda on balance gained rather than lost and Tanganyika suffered slight <u>net loss</u>(14); and (c) Kenya gained from the common market <u>at the cost</u> of its much poorer neighbours. Although there is no available factual evidence supporting the third position it cannot be dismissed lightly. Its wide and uncritical acceptance in political circles in the Federal Republic of Tanzania explains to a considerable degree Tanzania's policy towards the East African Common Market.

These three evaluations link the unevenness of the distribution of benefits to the advantages of Kenya in respect to the location of new industrial activities, advantages gained because of British economic policies in East Africa in the colonial period. A paper written in 1963 by a Ugandan economist, unaware of problems which faced ECLA economists attempting to build a viable common market in Central America at the same time, describes succinctly the nature of the difficulties arising in both areas:

> The location of industry is determined by a complex of historical and economic factors. In a <u>laissez faire</u> economy where market forces govern economic activity, industries will gravitate towards areas which possess certain economic advantages. These include, inter alia, proximity to markets for the products, availability and cost of new materials, an efficient and developed system of transport, availability of cheap and skilled labour and of other economic overheads - electric power, banking commercial and financial services. In general, areas which are relatively more developed tend to possess these economic advantages. This tendency for new industries to be concentrated in relatively developed areas <u>gathers momentum as development proceeds</u> [italics added] with the result that large areas of the economy will fail to feel the impact of the growth generated by the existence of the customs union. This is especially true of underdeveloped areas which are characterized by the existence of a few pockets of development surrounded by vast areas scarcely touched by

market forces(15).

In the light of the failure to restore intra-regional balanced development through fiscal compensatory measures, suggested before East African independence by the Raisman Commission (officially known as the United Kingdom Colonial Office Economic and Fiscal Commission for East Africa(16), the three governments immediately after the British withdrawal made a serious attempt to establish a new framework attenuating political and economic frictions inherited from the colonial past. The Kampala scheme, as subsequently revised and approved in Mbale in January 1965 by the heads of state of the three nations after nine months of difficult negotiations, provided for dealing with the inequitable distribution of gains from the Common Market - as reflected in <u>intra-territorial trade imbalances</u> - with five measures:

(1) immediate action with respect to certain inter-territorially connected enterprises aimed at shifting their productive activities in such a way as to increase production in a deficit country and thereby reduce imports from a surplus country;

(2) agreement as to the immediate allocation of certain major industrial projects;

(3) application of a system of quotas and suspended quotas whereby exports from surplus countries would be progressively reduced, and local production increased in the deficit countries according to the building up of the productive capacity of the deficit country;

(4) increased sales from a country in deficit to a country in surplus; and

(5) early agreement within the East African Common Market on a system of incentives and equitable allocation of future industrial activities among the three countries.

Although the Kampala-Mbale Agreement established an immediate link between regulation of regional trade flows and distribution of new industrial enterprises throughout the region, it seems that it gave first priority to the problem of allocation, understandably enough because of general expectations of the rapid inflow of foreign investment into the Common Market area and the high political prestige attached to industrial projects by each member country. Thus, in respect to immediate channelling to the rest of the area of certain firms having productive facilities in more than one country (cigarettes, footwear, beer and cement), Kenya and Tanzania agreed to promote a shift of some of their production lines to Tanzania because of that country's large trade deficit with Kenya. Similar joint persuasive action was expected to be followed by Kenya and Uganda. Immediate allocation of certain minor industries covered aluminium, bicycle manufacture, electric light bulbs, radio assembly and manufacture, nitrogenous fertilizers and motor vehicle tyres and tubes. It was agreed that these industries will be distributed under the territorial Industrial Licensing Ordinance(17) on the basis of an exclusive licence to a firm operating in the agreed territory. Tanzania was allocated the manufacture of aluminium sheets and foil; tyres and tubes; and radio assembly and parts production. Uganda received the sole rights for the production of bicycles and fertilizers and Kenya was left with the manufacture of electric light bulbs and possibly neon and fluorescent tubes. Finally, it was agreed that the problem of the future allocation of industry and differential incentives for new industrial activities would be studied by a regional committee of industrial experts. This committee would draw up lists of 'East African industries' according to one of two alternative definitions of their economic feasibility: (1) only if a given industry would have had access to the entire regional market or (2) only if it would have needed access to a market larger than that of any one country in East Africa. When examining a possible distribution of these regional industries, particular regard was expected to be given also to the need for an equitable distribution within the region and the industrial location of new projects.

In the fall of 1965, less than a year after the revised version of the Kampala Agreement had been approved in Mbale, the scheme had already been considered a dead letter in East Africa. Events in each of the three countries had overtaken the interested parties and the whole future of the East African Common Market became highly doubtful in spite of joint efforts to save at least its backbone, EASCO(18).

Difficulties in implementing the Kampala Agreement arose from the day of its signature and reflected the interplay of many internal and external factors. The agreement represented a considerable immediate sacrifice on the part of Kenya and it was signed by that country under the understanding that not only would the East African Common Market and EASCO continue but, in particular, that there would continue to be a single common currency in the area. The East African Currency Board, supposed to be converted into a single central bank for the three countries at an early date, actually disappeared from the scene in the spring of 1965 when Tanzania unilaterally established its own state bank in charge of currency issue and separate monetary policy, which led, in turn, to a decision by the two remaining countries to end the common currency arrangements in the area in 1966. Under these conditions, Kenya, at least, was no longer legally bound by the Kampala Agreement. But Tanzania's decision to have its own monetary policies was only one of many developments leading to the progressive deterioration of regional economic cooperation. Shortly after the Kampala scheme had been set up and before its ratification (which never took place) Kenya unilaterally withdrew its original approval to allocate to Tanzania an automobile assembly plant as a consequence of an offer from a group of local and foreign investors to build such a plant in its own territory. This relatively small incident forced prolonged multilateral negotiations of a revised list of allocated industries, injected a large measure of bitterness into Kenya-Tanzania relations and was largely responsible for Tanzania's putting into motion, in mid-1965, the second part of the Kampala Agreement providing for the imposition of quota restrictions in case of persistent trade imbalance with other member countries of the East African Common Market. Such trade imbalance was supposed to be cured by the switch of some productive activities by enterprises with plants in various East African countries and by the orderly implementation of the Agreement on allocation of major industries. Since neither of these schemes started working immediately, the patterns of trade hardly changed, increasing the grievances of Tanzania and Uganda. The seriousness of the situation for the future of the East African Common Market could hardly be described better than in a brief report written in early August 1965 from Dar-es-Salaam by an outside observer:

> President Nyerere explained why Tanzania had found it necessary to impose trade restrictions on Kenya. Speaking at the opening session of the Central Legislative Assembly he said that Tanzania had waited, following the Kampala Agreement last year, for ratification by the three East African Governments.

As the months went by without ratification Tanzania felt she had no option but to take action on her own, though in accordance with the principles agreed in Kampala. It therefore decided to impose temporary quotas on certain Kenyan imports with the sole object of promoting their production in Tanzania. This was an indication that Tanzania was taking only the very minimum action and then only when it became imperative for her own development. President Nyerere said that it was important to realize that even if the quotas cut imports from Jenya by as much as 2 million pound sterling annually, which was unlikely, Tanzania would still be the largest national importer of Kenyan goods(19).

Although there were many reasons to sympathize with Tanzania's urgent development needs, there was no doubt that when one member of a regional economic integration programme finds it necessary to threaten or apply trade reprisals to another, the situation is hardly propitious - politically or otherwise - for an orderly and continuous expansion of cooperation in commercial, industrial and other fields. The future of the East African Common Market seemed to be further complicated by the absence of any progress in respect to uniform regional treatment of foreign investment which - given the overall economic underdevelopment of East Africa - would have to provide a major share of financial resources for industrialization. In this respect East Africa witnessed a race of three countries both to attract foreign industrial investment under almost any conditions and to find new markets outside the region for their respective manufacturing output. In early 1965 the Kenya Parliament passed a foreign investment protection law, whose generosity could hardly be excelled and which aimed at attracting foreign capital both from sterling and other hard currency areas to, among others, tourist facilities, transportation, mining, and the agricultural machinery industry(20). A national licensing system for foreign-owned ventures was set up at the Kenya Treasury, suggesting that any regional agreement on uniform tax incentives was further away than at any time in the past. Uganda on its part 'amid the growing deterioration of the East African Common Market . . . has begun to look elsewhere in Africa for people to do business with'(21) and its Government was reported to have ordered the Ministry of Commerce and Industry to organize trade missions to Rwanda, Burundi, Congo and Sudan to find new outlets for Uganda's growing industries in view of the trade restrictions progressively imposed by Tanzania. Thus, instead of growing coordination of economic policies and the strengthening of institutional links and regional authorities, one witnessed the progressive disintegration of efforts to form a common market.

The fate of the Kampala Agreement demonstrated that industrialization policy which, under certain conditions could be the greatest potential source of economic and social gains given close East African integration, became the most important source of economic tension within the region, with the possibility that the three countries might resort to 'beggar-your-neighbour' import substitution policies. Judging by the experiences of smaller Latin American republics with a level of overall development similar to that of each of the three East African republics, in about five years, if they finally decided to 'go it alone', no additional substitution of imports would be feasible, independently of all possible national tax incentive laws aimed at attracting foreign investment and of all efforts to find outside outlets for manufacturing output. This would apply not only to Tanzania and Uganda but to Kenya as well, which because of the common market arrangements moved ahead of the two other countries, accounting in 1962 for some 45 per cent of manufacturing employment in the region, 60 per cent of gross product in industrial activities and over 75 per cent of inter-territorial exports of non-food manufactures. Whereas Kenya was the biggest gainer from the regional arrangement, the break-up of the common market would inexorably make all three countries net losers in a new situation and retard national economic development which would have been possibly only through raising dramatically total investment in the region.

Without forgetting political difficulties between the three members of the East African Common Market after independence, which in part have their roots in the three distinct political and economic policies followed by the colonial authorities in pre-independence days, one is forced to conclude that the major reason for the failure of the Kampala Agreement was that it established a close link between the distribution of industrial projects and the problem of persistent imbalances in visible intra-territorial trade. Although the institution of quota systems applicable to imports from surplus to deficit countries was probably considered by the largest deficit country, Tanzania, as the only weapon at its disposal to force Kenya (principally) to abide by the terms of the Agreement, the link was based on a wrong assumption that the distribution of new industrial activities would immediately result in a radical change in the patterns and flows of trade. The obvious lag between the decision to allocate the majority of new plants or branches of existing enterprises to the less developed members of the common market and the appearnace of new trade flows, a lag which in any part of the world would last several years, was obviously disregarded and, consequently, at the first sign of stress in mutual economic relations, the restrictive and not expansive part of the mechanism was put into motion. Thus the signatories of the Kampala Agreement got the worst of all possible worlds - inter-territorial trade imbalances diminished somewhat but at the cost of an overall decline, while no benefits of accelerated regional industrialization accrued to the region. Whatever immediate gains such development might have brought to Tanzania and Uganda by forcing some industries to establish themselves in their respective territories, it resulted, in fact, only in the substitution of their imports for those from the rest of East Africa instead of fostering the regional substitution of imports for those from the rest of the world, a primary objective of any economic integration scheme undertaken in the context of underdevelopment for the purpose of industrialization.

Additional reasons for the failure of the Kampala Agreement were the inability of the interested parties to incorporate in it any instruments of regional industrialization policy other than licensing arrangements. Such potential instruments include: (1) close cooperation in building up infrastructure conducive to economic and industrial integration; (2) strengthening already available mechanisms for consultation among finance ministers in respect to industrial tax incentives; (3) formal agreement on uniform customs protection for new enterprises considered as 'regional industries'; and (4) agreement on the role of national state-owned development corporations in respect to regional industrial projects. In these matters, at least, in spite of its forty years of existence, the East African Common Market seemed to be much behind the Central American integration scheme set up less than a decade previously.

The final weakness of the Kampala Agreement originated not in the national economic policies of the signatory governments but in the international conditions under which underdeveloped countries - jointly or individually - try to implement their industrialization policies and programmes. Since exporters from industrial countries to underdeveloped regions in Africa and elsewhere are covered by their own governments against any kind of risks involving sales

of the most liberally defined capital goods, growing competition for external
markets develops with very little regard for the viability of developing economies. In the face of increasing barriers to traditional exports of consumer
goods, reflecting the industrialization ambitions of newly-independent
countries of Africa, the manufacturing and commercial interests of the advanced countries were willing and ready to jump these barriers in one of two
ways: either by setting up productive facilities whenever enough protection
was offered or by selling equipment to local manufacturers or national development corporations wherever risks of direct investment were too large or the
size of the market did not warrant direct involvement. In both cases, these
external interests became allies of domestic groups unaware of a longer-run
lack of viability in an industrialization process limited exclusively to
national frontiers and of the high price paid for that type of self-defeating
industrialization. The ability of a small underdeveloped country to sell
almost any protection to attract a foreign industrial firm and the willingness
of advanced countries to offer unilateral industrial credits as long as they
were tied to exports of specific goods represented probably the single major
external obstacle to economic integration schemes in the poor regions, by
effectively blocking attempts to elaborate regional integration policies.
Future work on subregional economic cooperation in Africa will have to take
serious account of these partly political and partly economic facts.

PROSPECTS FOR REGIONAL ECONOMIC INTEGRATION

The failures of the Central American Regime for Integration Industries and of
the Kampala Agreement on regional licensing of industries point toward a
great practical difficulty in elaborating and implementing schemes for a
politically acceptable and economically viable distribution of industrial
activities among underdeveloped participants in a regional integration scheme.
The principal lessons of the Central American and East African experiences
are: (1) the distribution of benefits of the integration scheme, whether a
free trade zone, a customs union or a common market, cannot be left to the
free play of market forces as they do not operate efficiently in an underdeveloped environment; (2) the equitable distribution of new industries
cannot be attempted in isolation from other aspects of the integration process. On the other hand, taking into consideration institutional weaknesses
present in underdeveloped areas and the persistent shortage of skilled administrative and entrepreneurial resources one can hardly put too much confidence
in full-scale regional economic planning or in the harmonization of national
industrial policies. In most cases, whether in Africa, Asia or Latin America,
national development plans exist only on paper and national industrial policies
amount to a series of improvizations imposed upon the governments by domestic
difficulties and external economic problems.

This diagnosis should not be construed, however, as a flat denial of the possibility of fostering regional industrialization in developing areas. It
attempts rather to defend the proposition that the achievement of some measure
of multinational cooperation in this field calls for a slow creation of <u>minimum</u>
conditions for <u>limited</u> cooperation and coordination among a limited number of
neighbouring countries and not for grandiose plans for integrating dozens of
countries upon a hopeful but unrealistic assumption that a large number of
countries without any previous integration experience will somehow harmonize
their divergent economic policies and pool their natural and capital resources.
This last position greatly underestimates the force of economic nationalism
and the power of vested interests. As demonstrated in Latin America, both

within LAFTA and in the much smaller Central American Common Market, economic integration amounts to a slow, complicated and painstaking process of building up step by step regional institutions and cooperation mechanisms and of creating political support both in the public and private sectors to assure the functioning of such multinational economic arrangements.

The success of industrial integration would thus depend to a considerable extent upon the previous emergence of an overall institutional framework, preferably in the form of a customs union, providing for gradual freeing of practically all trade - with possibly special arrangements for agricultural products - but not equating the benefits of integration with the balance of trade flows. The introduction of such a concept would tend to balance the commercial interchange at the lowest and not highest potential level and eliminate the dynamic long-run effect of regional trade on development prospects of the area. Assuming - and this is doubtful - that the regional trade balance and not the overall trade position of each country vis-à-vis the rest of the world is an objective worthwhile pursuing, the correction of possible regional trade disequilibria should be left to non-trade mechanisms and success in this field will obviously depend on a regional investment policy. Such a policy is possible either when economic integration is fairly advanced, which is not the case of emerging free trade zones or common markets in developing countries, or when the capital-exporting rich countries show readiness to support fully and on a multilateral basis a given integration experiment. The second condition has not been fulfilled as yet. Under these circumstances it is left to participating underdeveloped countries to work out a limited regional investment policy by means of the following steps:

(1) first identifying productive sectors which could take advantage of available external economies and potential economies of scale offered by the multinational market;

(2) elaborating a series of concrete projects within these sectors;

(3) agreeing upon a regional uniform system for customs protection and tax incentives so as to avoid cut-throat competition for scarce production factors among prospective domestic and foreign investors;

(4) putting jointly at the disposal of potential investors certain development finance facilities; and

(5) setting up a permanent regional negotiation mechanism distributing periodically throughout the area new projects of regional interest.

Such a limited regional investment policy implies the early establishment, in addition to a free trade or common market general treaty, of a few important legal instruments mentioned above under (3); and, furthermore, the availability of a regional development bank or corporation and a regional industrial research institute. This last institution is probably decisive since any attempt to allocate regionally not yet existing industries in expectation of favourable responses from potential investors, or to distribute projects one by one when submitted by private interested parties is bound to end in failure, increasing political friction and recriminations. The negotiations on equitable distribution of new industrial projects in a multinational set-up represent the last and not the first step of a limited regional investment policy and their success or failure will depend upon the number and quality of projects. Here, the importance of a regional industrial research organization and its ability to elaborate concrete feasibility studies become clear. If a group of countries embarking on an economic integration venture cannot assure the relatively effective functioning of such a regional body, then any talk about regional industrial planning or harmonization of national development plans, which involve much bigger organizational and operational effort, represents a clear case of self-defeating although well-sounding mass delusion.

It is sometimes maintained that the allocation of new productive activities among a group of developing countries is an extremely difficult exercise on economic grounds, because of the alleged unavailability of external economies except in a few selected places. But anyone acquainted with the present conditions in respect to infrastructure and natural resources endowment in Central America and East Africa and having some idea of modern technology can hardly accept such a pessimistic proposition. As an expert on economic integration problems put it

> except in industries tied closely to highly specific natural resources that are expensive to ship, the advance of modern technology has greatly reduced the natural advantages of siting manufacturing activities in one place rather than another. By now, the advantages of one site over another are largely man-made rather than nature-made. And if advantages are made by man, they can also be changed by man in accordance with rational and deliberate planning criteria(22).

Leaving aside aluminium smelting, the iron and steel industry and a few others, scores of possible industrial projects, and practically all of them in the field of consumer durables and intermediate manufactures, could be located alternatively in many places both in Central America and East Africa. If this is so then in the final analysis, the success of industrial distributive mechanisms must depend on the broad availability of projects, and the failure of past mechanisms cannot be ascribed to the limitations of possible locations but to the shortage of well-prepared projects and the scarcity of financial and entrepreneurial skills. If a broad range of feasibility studies and well-elaborated projects - whose preparation could be financed with funds from the UN Special Fund, the World Bank or regional development institutions such as the African Development Bank - were undertaken, the field would be cleared for putting into motion the multinational negotiation mechanisms in each integrating area.

The rules of those negotiations would have to take into consideration two important facts: (1) although there must exist a number of alternative locations - acceptable on economic analysis grounds - for any given project in a multinational region, the least-developed countries have lesser possibility in that respect than the more developed; and (2) even given high quality projects, there is no assurance that all of them would attract potential investors whether from within or outside the area. Consequently, negotiations about distribution of a sizeable 'bunch' or projects would have to provide for the right of first refusal to the least-developed members of the group under an assumption that practically any regional industrial project can be fitted into the structure of the most developed partner. Secondly, once the allocation is agreed upon, members of the integration scheme acting as a group would invite tenders from potential investors for individual approved projects. Only if, within previously agreed terms, no interested private investors appeared would the regional development corporation undertake the establishment of the project with capital participation of member countries and under management of nationals of the country to which the project had been allocated. Even in this last case, provision would have to be made for the regional corporation to disinvest itself of the enterprise once a prospective buyer were found. This provision tries to avoid tying to industrial projects scarce capital resources, badly needed in any underdeveloped area for social overhead investment.

It may well be that some variant of this scheme should be tried on an experimental basis in one of the proposed common market arrangements in Africa. In the opinion of this writer, the future of these integration programmes depends to a considerable degree upon the successful introduction of a scheme which would assure all members some kind of participation in the industrialization process. In the absence of such a scheme, prospects for ambitious regional industrialization programmes starting from the top and not from the project level are bleak.

NOTES

(1) Multilateral Treaty on Free Trade and Central American Economic Integration (Tegucigalpa, 10 June 1958) Article XXI, reproduced in United Nations, Multilateral Economic Cooperation in Latin America, Vol. I. Texts and Documents, New York, 1961, pp. 17-23.

(2) Agreement establishing the Central American Bank for Economic Integration (Managua, 13 December 1960), Article 2 b, reproduced in United Nations, ibid., pp. 26-32.

(3) For details, see Thomas L. Karnes, The Failure of Union-Central America, 1824-1960, The University of North Carolina Press, Chapel Hill, 1961.

(4) Carlos M. Castillo, Growth and Integration in Central America, Frederick A. Praeger, New York, 1966, p. 125.

(5) US AID, 'Comments on the Regime of Integration Industries of the Central American Common Market', Memorandum, Washington, August 1963.

(6) Joseph Pincus, 'Algunos efectos de la integracion economica centroamericana en los precios de consumo' (Some effects of the Central American Integration on the Consumer Prices), July 1962 (mimeo.).

(7) Raymond F. Mikesell, 'External Financing and Latin American Integration' in M.S. Wionczek (Editor), Latin American Economic Integration, Frederick A. Praeger, New York, 1966.

(8) James D. Cochrane, 'US Attitudes Towards Central American Economic Integration', Inter-American Economic Affairs (Washington, D.C.), Vol. 18, No. 2, Autumn 1964. In respect to the second point Cochrane wrote that, 'Although there is no evidence that US investors have expressed any disapproval of "integrated industries" to government officials, it is quite possible that this has been privately expressed. The fact that "integrated industries" has several features which might be objectionable to US investors may, even in the absence of other pressures, have influenced the position taken by the United States Government', ibid., p. 85.

(9) This explanation is offered by James D. Cochrane in another essay,

'Central American Economic Integration: The "Integrated Industries" Scheme', Inter-American Economic Affairs, Washington, D.C., Vol. 19, No. 2, Autumn 1965, p. 70.

(10) The replacement of the 1958 Multilateral Treaty by the 1960 General Treaty creating a common market complicated legal aspects of the Regime. Under the earlier treaty it was easy to offer exclusive tariff protection for new industries, since free trade covered selected commodities only. Under the General Treaty, when the signatory countries committed themselves to free trade in practically all products and to establish a common external tariff by mid-1966, the offer of special tariff treatment for plants designated as 'integration industries' might be considered as a step backward from the global commitment of the Central American countries as long as one took a traditional attitude that a common tariff in a customs union should not be higher than previously in individual countries. This is clearly not the case in respect to the needs of integration schemes in developing regions where new industries emerging after the establishment of a custom union have the right to be considered 'regional infant industries' eligible for protection.

(11) For an analysis of problems arising from the clash between Latin American economic nationalism emerging within the framework of economic integration schemes and foreign private capital, see Miguel S. Wionczek, A Latin American Point of View', in Raymond Vernon (Editor), How Latin America Views the US Investor, Frederick A. Praeger, New York, 1966.

(12) Press Release of the Tanganyika High Commission in London, 16 June 1964, 'Extract from the Budget Speech of the Hon. Paul Bomani, Minister of Finance, delivered to the National Constituent Assembly [in Dar-es-Salaam] on 16 June, 1964' (mimeo.).

(13) Benton F. Massell, East-African Economic Union: An Evaluation and Some Implication for Policy, The Rand Corporation, Santa Monica, California, December 1963, seems to lean towards this school of thought, although he also states that 'it is not possible to determine whether Uganda and Tanganyika are made better or worse off as a result of economic union', p. 96.

(14) Dharam Ghai, 'Territorial Distribution of Benefits and Costs of the East African Customs Union', Kampala, 1963.

(15) Dharam Ghai, ibid., p. 3.

(16) One might still defend such a redistribution mechanism by arguing that the Raisman Commission proposals were not distributive enough. But the problem still does not disappear on two grounds: (1) fiscal revenue compensation proposals address themselves mainly to the issue of net gains and losses from the customs proceeds from the foreign trade of the area under conditions of intra-trade liberalization; (2) assuming that a formula were found to measure correctly all gains and losses from an integration scheme, it would be difficult to envisage as politically palatable net transfer of aid for development from one underdeveloped but relatively better off country to another more underdeveloped for the sake of probable, but not certain, future gains from integration for all parties concerned.

(17) The Industrial Licensing Ordinance was introduced in the three East African territories in 1948 for the purpose of encouraging 'the orderly establishment and setting up of new industries to the best advantage of East Africa

as a whole while providing protection to consumers and workers' (Part II, Section 3(2)). According to one source ' . . . the industrial licensing system rapidly became a means for preventing competition [from Uganda and Tanganyika] with plants already established in Kenya' and 'not unnaturally, the latter two countries became unwilling to agree to the addition of any new industries to the licensing schedule under such conditions', Sidney Dell, Trade Blocs and Common Markets, Alfred A. Knopf, New York, 1963, p. 238. The Raisman Commission concluded that by 1960 the system served very little useful purpose in relation to the industrial development of East Africa as a whole.

(18) In the early fall of 1965 the EASCO Authority decided to establish a commission comprising three high officials from each country and an independent chairman to inquire into ways and means of salvaging the Common Market and preserving regional common services. The commission was to report to the three governments by 1 May 1966.

(19) 'Tanzania Trade Curbs on Kenya', a cable from Dar-es-Salaam published in The Financial Times, London, 11 August 1965.

(20) Elisabeth Gillett, 'Kenya Offers Incentives to Lure New Investment', The Journal of Commerce, New York, 22 January 1965.

(21) Lawrence Fellows, 'Uganda Looking for New Markets' (a cable datelined from Kampala), The New York Times, 31 July 1965.

(22) Sidney Dell, A Latin American Common Market? Oxford University Press, London, New York and Toronto, 1966, p. 69.

CHAPTER 11

Towards a Common Treatment for Foreign Private Investment in the Andean Common Market*

My paper on external indebtedness and sectoral changes in foreign investment in Latin America(1) offered a brief outline of changes which took place between 1958 and 1967 in the sectoral distribution of United States direct investment in Latin America, including the Andean region. This analysis revealed the stagnation of private foreign investment in the traditional sectors (mining and smelting, oil and public services) and the dynamic behaviour of direct foreign investment as a whole both in the subcontinent and in the region. In the Andean Group (Chile, Peru, Colombia, Bolivia and Ecuador), United States investment represented perhaps 75 per cent of total foreign investment in the so-called dynamic sectors: manufacturing industry and related services such as commerce and banking. Let us look closer at its behaviour in the context of subregional integration plans.

According to the Cartagena Agreement, which created the Andean Common Market in 1969, and high-level political statements such as the Bogota Declaration (1966) and the Lima Declaration (1969), Andean subregional cooperation has three major objectives: (1) acceleration of the industrialization process throughout the area; (2) equal participation by all members of the Andean Common Market in that process; and (3) a decrease in the political and economic dependence of the subregion on industrialized world centres. For this to be achieved, harmonization of the treatment of foreign investment in the dynamic sectors would have to be given greater priority than the establishment of common treatment for foreign capital in the traditional sectors. Although one cannot disregard the importance for the Chilean and Peruvian economies of foreign private investment in the extractive sectors, the concentration of efforts on the establishment of a common regional treatment for sectors such as mining, which seems to be of secondary importance to Colombia and Ecuador, could cause serious regional political problems. Furthermore, it could increase the risk of a race throughout the region to secure foreign investment for the industrial sector and related activities, which would become more

---

*This background study was prepared in 1970 for the Secretariat of the Andean Common Market as part of preparations for the drafting of Decision 24 of the Cartagena Agreement, and published originally in Spanish in El Trimestre Económico (Mexico), Vol. 38 (2), No. 150, April-June 1971.

attractive to private foreign capital with the establishment of the Andean Common Market (ACM), in a similar way to what happened to other multinational economic integration programmes elsewhere.

Whether or not one accepts the premise of the great need in the short and intermediate term for the establishment of a common treatment for foreign private investment in the dynamic sectors, it seems obvious that the so-called harmonization of the treatment of direct foreign investment in the ACM is not solely a legal problem. In this case the purely legal approach is inadequate not only because of the political and economic implications of direct foreign investment in developing countries, but also because the Andean subregion does not count with national legislations which could cover all aspects of foreign capital activities. Moreover, there are serious doubts as to whether it would be feasible or correct to create general policy instruments concerning foreign investment in view of the fact that, as past experiences suggest, foreign private capital cannot be considered a homogeneous factor. Its political and economic impact varies according to its sectoral location. Problems of regulation, control and investment incentives vary according to the kind of activities the foreign investor is engaged in, particularly in the case of large transnational corporations.

Despite the fact that the countries of the Andean Group, like other Latin American countries, have created certain instruments to control or to encourage foreign investment according to the needs of the moment and the ever-changing political and economic situation, be it domestic or international, certain common attitudes toward foreign capital can be detected in the region. These attitudes reflect balance-of-payments difficulties, on the one hand, and on the other, the new priority given to productive sectors related to development through industrialization.

These common attitudes toward the presence of foreign private capital in the dynamic sectors of the Andean economies can be summarized as follows:

(1) The rejection of the participation of companies fully controlled by foreigners in the basic industrial sectors, such as the iron and steel industry or heavy petrochemicals;

(2) A general preference for joint ventures instead of the branches or affiliates of foreign companies;

(3) A growing awareness of the importance of foreign, jointly owned and domestic industrial enterprises as potential suppliers of foreign exchange through exports of their products;

(4) Disappointment with the technological contribution made by already established foreign industrial companies, due, among other things, to the very high cost of such contributions; and

(5) Concern over entry into the region of powerful international financial intermediaries.

The countries of the Andean Group have tried to translate these attitudes into legal or other types of measures not necessarily well integrated. Registries of foreign investment have been established in some countries as a means of controlling the remittances of profits and the expatriation of invested capital. State-owned companies have been created or expanded in the basic industrial sectors. Various administrative measures gave clear preference to joint ventures. Special incentives were provided for those foreign companies which promised to search for export markets. Payments for technology transfer from abroad were beginning to be regulated. Finally, barriers were established in some countries to avoid excessive use of domestic financial resources by foreign commercial and industrial companies.

However, all these measures taken separately at a national level and very difficult to harmonize regionally, were based on an old-fashioned premise. They assumed that negotiations between the country receiving the foreign capital and the foreign company interested in establishing itself in that country, would be bilateral, with the government of the host country at an advantage as legal owner of the potential market and so able to impose its conditions on the foreign investor through a combination of regulations and incentives.

In reality it does not appear to be like this. The negotiating power of an underdeveloped country with a limited domestic market is quite weak due to three factors: the desperate need to obtain capital as well as technology from abroad; limited experience concerning the negotiating process; and the fact that in the majority of cases the host government does not negotiate with a traditional foreign company which produces certain goods or services in its country of origin and also wishes to produce them in the negotiating country but instead the government deals with transnationals. Especially in Latin America, where United States transnationals predominate, the negotiating power of the supplier of capital and technology is greater than that of the recipient country government. The transnational has many more options concerning the use of its financial and technological resources than does the country which wants to obtain these production factors through investment by private foreign interests. In other words, a large transnational company is able to take its decisions with much more freedom than an underdeveloped country which often has political and economic sovereignty only in appearance.

Given that the characteristics and conditions of foreign private investment reflect the relative negotiating power of the two parties, there is a strong case for, first, the national coordination of policies relating to foreign investment in the dynamic sectors and, second, the coordination of these policies among a group of underdeveloped countries which decide to embark on economic integration.

The absence of such national and regional coordination of policies toward foreign investment in the sectors directly linked to industrialization, not to be confused with attempts to draw up general laws on foreign investment which are of doubtful usefulness, has serious disadvantages for both the individual country and for a group of countries in the process of integration. In the first case, a country runs the risk that the foreign company will successfully get round all regulatory attempts and make use of all the advantages it receives. In the second case, the risk is even greater. Manipulation by the companies of authorities of the different countries of the group will cause political friction which can ultimately paralyse the process of regional cooperation or subordinate it to extra-regional forces. This is what has happened with the various attempts at economic integration in Africa and in the Central American Common Market.

To establish a common treatment for foreign investment in the dynamic sectors of the economy of the Andean Group, especially in the industrial sector, one must analyse the behaviour of foreign manufacturing companies in the region.

Comparison of their behaviour with the individual country policies concerning foreign investment will show how far these policies have achieved their objectives and to what degree they can be used as a basis for a future common treatment of foreign investment in the region. This task is particularly difficult due to the absence of studies at a national level, the secrecy which surrounds the Latin American operations of the large transnational companies, and, finally, the fact that existing national legislation does not necessarily reflect the real situation. It is widely known that in Latin America many of the problems related to foreign investment are solved in a casuistic and administrative manner without reference to existing legislation and in response to the 'power of persuasion' of transnational companies making the investment.

A BEHAVIOURAL PROFILE OF SUBSIDIARIES OF UNITED STATES TRANSNATIONALS IN ANDEAN GROUP COUNTRIES

Despite the great concern felt in Latin America, in particular in the Andean Group, over the growing presence and dynamic expansion of subsidiaries of United States and European transnationals, there is little data for the assessment of their role in the various economies of the region. On the one hand, there are no national studies of this problem and, on the other, data published periodically by the United States Commerce Department concerning direct foreign investment from that country, do not make a distinction between the United States owned or controlled companies which have investments in a single Latin American country and those which are part of corporate transnational systems (companies which, through their subsidiaries, operate in a considerable number of countries on several continents).

Fortunately, studies carried out at Harvard Business School(2) provide information on the growth, the manner of entry, the system of ownership and the distribution within the industrial sector of the subsidiaries of the United States transnationals in Colombia and Peru. Unfortunately, there is no information from that source on Chile despite the fact that, according to the information from the United States Commerce Department, American investment in the production of manufactured goods in Chile has also grown rapidly. Thus, while the book value of United States investment in Colombia's manufacturing sector increased from US $77 million to $193 million (by 150 per cent) between 959 and 1968 and in Peru from $21 to 63 million (by 225 per cent), in Chile the value of North American investment in that sector grew from $31 million in 1959 to $96 million in 1968 (by over 200 per cent). In each of the three countries the pace of growth of United States investment in manufacturing was faster than in any other important economic sector.

COLOMBIA

According to information gathered by Harvard Business School(3), at the end of 1967 seventy-two United States transnational companies (USTNCs) with a total of 150 subsidiaries were operating in Colombia. If all the subsidiaries which established themselves in Colombia after 1901 were included there would be a total of eighty-eight USTNCs in that country in 1970, with a total of 196 subsidiaries. However, due, for example, to withdrawals from the market, sales of foreign firms to nationals, changes of ownership at headquarters and mergers of USTNCs as well as of their subsidiaries in Colombia, the total number of the subsidiaries which operated in that country at the end of 1967 was considerably smaller than the total number of all the subsidiaries established there between 1901 and 1967. Of the seventy-two USTNCs in Colombia at the end of 1967, with a total of 150 subsidiaries, the great majority were located in the manufacturing sector (sixty USTNCs with ninety subsidiaries). In commerce there were eleven USTNCs with fourteen subsidiaries and in the mining industry one USTNC with one subsidiary. Furthermore, the same seventy-two USTNCs had forty-five subsidiaries in Colombia engaged in otherm mostly unidentified, activities.

Up to the end of 1945 only ten USTNCs entered Colombia. Their headquarters were mainly engaged in producing consumer manufactures. The number of newcomers in terms of their headquarters increased to nineteen between 1946 and 1957 and to forty-four between 1958 and 1967. Up to 1945 it would seem that every USTNC owned one subsidiary in Colombia (as assembly plant in most cases). In the post-war period the number of subsidiaries started exceeding the number of new USTNCs. Between 1946 and 1957, twenty-nine manufacturing subsidiaries were set up in the country and between 1958 and 1967 the number increased by seventy-seven. Taking into account the non-manufacturing subsidiaries which established themselves in Colombia from 1950 to 1970, there is reason to believe that in the late sixties the practice by USTNCs of creating a group of subsidiaries in different sectors of the economy, once the headquarters had taken the decision to enter Colombia, had become increasingly widespread. This phenomenon suggests that the strategy of the USTNC global systems was different in 1970 from what it was before 1946. In many cases they now attempted to achieve not only close integration between headquarters and subsidiaries, but also between subsidiaries of the same corporation in the country. This, in turn, suggests that the USTNCs which operated in Colombia in the sixties, had diversified their scope of action and tried to complement their manufacturing activities with commercial and other ancillary services. However, we lack information on the degree of such vertical and horizontal integration of USTNC subsidiaries in any Latin American country, including Colombia.

As far as the form of entry into Colombia was concerned, until 1958 almost all subsidiaries were newly established companies. However, of the seventy-eight subsidiaries set up in Colombia between 1958 and 1968, only twenty-seven were completely new, sixteen were purchasers of locally established firms and twenty emerged as subsidiaries of existing subsidiaries. The form of entry of the remaining twenty-seven could not be identified.

Concerning the patterns of ownership of the 150 USTNC subsidiaries in Colombia at the end of 1967, eighty-four were entirely controlled by the headquarters. The headquarters had a majority participation in thirty-four subsidiaries and a minority participation in only fourteen. While USTNC participation in the remaining fourteen subsidiaries was not known, the patterns observed in other parts of Latin America, suggest that they were also in most cases companies with complete or majority control by their respective headquarters.

Of ninety USTNC subsidiaries existing in the manufacturing sector only twenty had domestic capital participation(4). The fact that all these manufacturing joint-ventures (30 per cent of the subsidiaries which entered Colombia between 1958 and 1967) were set up during that period suggests some progress in this respect. However, USTNC headquarters accepted minority participation only in few cases (seven subsidiaries).

Of the 123 USTNC manufacturing subsidiaries which appeared in Colombia between 1901 and 1967 (thirty-three of which disappeared in the same period), thirty-four belonged to USTNCs whose main activity was the chemical and pharmaceutical industry; twenty-four to the food and beverage industry; fourteen to the metal industry; eleven to the automotive and related industries (rubber), and eight to the oil industry (refining), making a total of ninety-one (75 per cent of the total) corresponding to these five industrial branches. Of the thirty-four chemical and pharmaceutical subsidiaries, twenty-three were established between 1958 and 1967 and of the twenty-four food and beverage subsidiaries sixteen were set up during the same period. The same pattern of sectoral concentration accompanied by a rapid increase in the number of subsidiaries in the sixties is seen in the remaining three industrial branches. In the two industries where the presence of USTNCs is especially evident (chemicals and pharmaceuticals and the food industries), a significant proportion of the new entries took the form of acquisition of domestic firms. Fourteen of the thirty-four chemical and pharmaceutical subsidiaries were the result of acquisitions, almost all after 1958. Fourteen of the twenty-four food industry subsidiaries were also formed in the same way.

This information indicates that in Colombia the USTNCs can hardly be considered as active agents of the diversification of industrial structure and technological modernization. In most cases they are not leaders in the field of industrialization but followers who have entered established industrial activities once the growth of internal demand and the high degree of protection created very attractive investment opportunities. If the same did not happen in other industries which produce non-durable consumer goods, such as textiles and cosmetics, it was because of the presence of strong domestic business groups and their relative independence with respect to imported technology.

Among the USTNCs with subsidiaries in Colombia, those which are predominant have (1) a relatively small technological research programme at headquarters; (2) low advertizing intensity in the United States; (3) little product diversity both in the United States and abroad; and (4) limited geographical diversity. In other words, many of the USTNCs with subsidiaries in Colombia do not carry out similar activities widely outside of the United States and the developing countries. In the more advanced countries (in Europe, for example) such industrial branches are in the hands of domestic companies or non-American transnationals whose knowledge of the production process and of marketing leaves little room for USTNCs and their subsidiaries.

The distribution of USTNC subsidiaries in Colombia by industrial branches shows that they produce almost exclusively for the internal market, as proven by the meagre data gathered by the United States Commerce Department. Unfortunately, there are no historical series in this respect, although data are available for 1957 and 1966. In 1957 all sales by foreign-owned or controlled manufacturing enterprises (and not only of USTNC subsidiaries included in the Harvard Business School survey) were directed to the Colombian domestic market. During that year, these sales - excluding refined oil products - totalled US $107 million.

By 1966 the value of sales by USTNCs in Colombia increased to US $358 million, of which $107 million corresponded to chemical and pharmaceutical products; $55 million represented processed foods; $31 million electrical machinery (probably electric and electronic home appliances assembled in the country); $21 million metal products (office furniture, etc.); and $144 million other products (including automobiles, parts and accessories). Of this same total

$320 million (almost 90 per cent) came from local sales; $24 million from sales to branches of the same companies abroad; $7 million from exports to other Latin American countries; and $10 million from exports to the United States and elsewhere. Of the subtotal of $38 million (exports from Colombia), more than half ($20 million) represented processed foods and chemical and pharmaceutical products sold to other branches abroad. While the final geographical destination of these sales is unknown, available data suggest a certain degree of transnational integration of some USTNC subsidiaries in Colombia. It is probable, however, that only a small proportion of exports in the non-durable consumer goods categories go to neighbouring countries.

Given the productive capacity of these companies in Colombia as well as the balance of payments of the country, these exports play a marginal role. Of total Colombian exports worth $510 million in 1966, those made by United States-owned or controlled manufacturing companies represented only 7.5 per cent.

In countries which export private capital it is insisted that the benefits of private foreign investment, 'one of the main factors for development and industrialization', lie in its positive effects on the balance of payments, the importation of new technology and job creation in the host countries. Supposedly, investment leads to a net inflow of capital from abroad, saving foreign exchange through the process of import substitution and encouraging exports. In the following paragraphs a preliminary attempt will be made to ascertain how many of these gains accrued to Colombia through the activities of USTNC subsidiaries in the sixties.

In trying to estimate the contribution of new capital from the United States to the expansion of United States-owned manufacturing activities in Colombia, whose book value increased between 1958 and 1967 by $116 million, one is faced with serious statistical and accounting problems. According to data published by the United States Commerce Department, the inflow of new United States capital to Colombia's manufacturing sector totalled $67 million during the period 1960-8, $41 million corresponded to reinvestment of profits and the remaining $8 million presumably came from other sources such as long-term intra-company loans, local sales of stock, or perhaps the revaluation of assets. However, this statistical series is difficult to match with other information published by the Commerce Department, according to which the total profits of USTNCs in Colombia between 1960 and 1968 (after deducting local but before deducting United States taxes) amounted to $74 million, and the net income of the same subsidiaries (excluding reinvested profits but including dividends and interest remitted abroad after local tax deduction) amounted to $50 million. Thus United States manufacturing companies reported that their reinvestment of profits in Colombia in the period 1960-8 were $41 million (according to the statistical series concerning the main sources of financing) or $24 million (the difference between their total and remitted profits)(5).

Thus, while no detailed local study is available, serious doubts arise concerning the validity of the information furnished to the United States Commerce Department by the Colombian subsidiaries of United States companies. These data are usually used, however, to calculate the contribution of private foreign investment to the total savings of the recipient country. Any serious analysis is further handicapped by the fact that, according to the same United States agency, the profitability of United States investment in Colombia's manufacturing is very low. Measured in terms of total profits over the book value of United States investments, their profits in the Colombian manufacturing sector reached an average of 6.4 per cent annually between 1960 and 1968, compared with the interest rate of at least 16 per cent a year registered in the Colombian capital market. It is difficult to accept such a low profitability for foreign subsidiaries not just because it does not agree with levels of profits on investment of domestic manufacturing firms but also because it makes it impossible to explain the growing interest shown by USTNCs in entering well-defined Colombian industrial branches(6).

A study carried out some time ago by the Stanford Research Institute of California(7), established as factors responsible for the decision of foreign investors to choose a country for investment - in addition to the official attitude favourable to private foreign capital - (1) the hope of relatively high profits; (2) prospects for the penetration of a new market; (3) the security of sales behind a tariff wall; (4) the anticipation of the entry of competitors; and (5) the development of a new industry. Other important factors, to judge from the experiences of TNCs throughout the world, have included the establishment of a base for exports, the availability of skilled labour, low labour costs and the existence of an adequate infrastructure. However, according to the Stanford Institute study, in Latin America the second group of factors was of marginal importance.

Considering that in Colombia the process of domestic substitution of finished consumer goods imports lasted for several decades and that foreign - in this case United States - capital did not in general dedicate itself to the development of new industries, it is reasonable to suppose that the growing participation of United States companies in Colombia's manufacturing sector reflected two main factors: their anticipation of relatively high profits and their interest in jumping the barrier created by import prohibition, the very measure which assures high profits.

If this were so, then the thesis that exports of private capital to the manufacturing sectors of countries like Colombia represent a highly positive contribution to the balance of payments, technological advancement and employment expansion is not supported by the evidence. In the first place, the total earnings of foreign-owned manufacturing companies, and particularly of USTNCs which operate in the less-developed countries, are much greater than those to be found in the official statistics of the capital-exporting countries, in this case the United States. From the point of view of the global system of a USTNC, its total earnings from a subsidiary, for example, represent the sum of the net earnings declared by the subsidiary, the payments received by the USTNC for technology transfer and the earnings from the export of capital goods and intermediate products by the headquarters to the subsidiary. The low level of declared earnings at the subsidiary level may be compensated for many times over by the payments for technology (existent or non-existent, or theoretically free but in fact tied) and by overcharging by headquarters for goods and materials exported not only for the construction or expansion of production or assembly plants but also for the production of final goods. The fact that any investigation into foreign investment in Latin America runs into a wall of secrecy at the company level with regard to cost accounting suggests that many strange things happen in this field.

A study by the Council on Latin America(8), based on statistics from the census of the United States Commerce Department made in 1966, comes to a surprising conclusion: almost all of the current expenditure of USTNCs in Colombia takes place in the country itself. The study's estimates of current local expenditure (see Table 11.1), would appear to be extremely exaggerated if we

TABLE 11.1. Estimates of Current Local Expenditure of United States Manufacturing Companies in Colombia, 1957 and 1966

(US $ million)

Expenditure	1957	1966
Material, supplies and local services	61	209
Wages and salaries	18	69
Taxes	9	23
Interest	1	9
Not identified	6	13
Total of local expenditure	95	324

Source: Council on Latin America.

consider: (1) the value of the total sales of the companies, estimated for 1957 at $107 million and for 1966 at $358 million; and (2) the degree of dependency of a considerable number of the foreign manufacturing subsidiaries in Colombia on imported inputs. If to the local current expenditures in 1966 of $324 million the earnings of the United States manufacturing subsidiaries in Colombia, reported at $16 million, are added and if sales in the same year (including exports), were $358 million, then, the current foreign expenditures of the same subsidiaries could not have exceeded $18 million. This figure seems completely unrealistic, however, assuming that current expenditure abroad covers the import of many material inputs, the salaries of foreign personnel, and payments for technology transfer, without mentioning taxes paid in the United States.

Moreover, despite the absence of other data, it is difficult to accept the degree of national integration of United States manufacturing subsidiaries in Colombia suggested in the study by the Council on Latin America if one remembers the branches in which USTNCs are concentrated in Colombia according to the study carried out by Harvard Business School. At least two of these branches, the chemical and pharmaceutical and the automotice industries, are characterized by assembly activities with a high degree of imports. The official data from the United States Commerce Department confirms this. Although we do not have detailed data for Colombia, those for the region as a whole for 1962-4 are very revealing. In this short period United States exports to manufacturing subsidiaries in Latin America increased from $506 million to $703 million, and of this total, $402 million and $537 million for 1962 and 1964 respectively represent exports by headquarters of USTNCs to their subsidiaries. These sales increased more than 50 per cent over the same two-year period, from $227 million to $360 million(9). Other interesting data refer to payments for royalties and other technical services related to United States direct investment. In the region as a whole these payments increased between 1957 and 1961 from $70 to 103 million, and by 1968 they grew further to $185 million, reflecting the large expansion of United States investment in Latin American manufacturing.

Thus one arrives at the conclusion that to analyse in detail the operations and financial behaviour of USTNCs and the other foreign-owned manufacturing subsidiaries in Colombia one would need detailed information on the following: (1) the global profitability of these companies; (2) their expenditure on technology transfer; (3) their practices in relation to the purchase of material and non-technological service imports; (4) their policies for establishing the prices of goods imported from the headquarters and of products sold to other subsidiaries of the same transnational system; (5) the amount and the origin of financial resources raised for investment in fixed and working capital, and, (6) their degree of participation in the domestic market and their policies with respect to export possibilities. Without this information, one can hardly estimate the effect of the activities of the transnationals on any economy.

PERU

Given that Peru is less industrialized than Colombia, let us find out what differences or similarities there are between the behaviour of USTNCs in the two countries. The information compiled by Harvard Business School indicates that at the end of 1967 there were sixty USTNCs in Peru, with a total of ninety-eight subsidiaries. Of the sixty USTNCs with subsidiaries in Peru the main activity of thirty-five at the headquarters was manufacturing; seventeen were engaged in commerce, and five in mining. Thirty-five USTNCs engaged in manufacturing had forty-seven subsidiaries; the seventeen commercial USTNCs had eighteen subsidiaries; and the five mining USTNCs had six subsidiaries in Peru. Furthermore, there was a total of twenty-seven subsidiaries which belonged to USTNCs but were engaged in Peru in 'other' or 'unknown' activities.

Apart from mining, still the most important sector of the Peruvian economy, the concentration of USTNC subsidiaries in the manufacturing sector was in relative terms much smaller in Peru than in Colombia. In contrast, USTNC strength in Peru's service sector (finance, commerce, etc.) was relatively greater than in Colombia. It would seem that while Colombia's industrial sector depends much more on United States companies than does the Peruvian, in Peru there is an impressive network of USTNCs in all major sectors of the economy. At least, such was the situation in Peru at the end of 1967 as the result of generous policies toward foreign capital and the prevailing ideology of economic liberalism. On the other hand, in Colombia, several sectors including financial services and agriculture were controlled by nationals.

At the end of the Second World War, half of the twenty-two USTNC subsidiaries in Peru were in the manufacturing sector and the other half in remaining sectors of the economy. In the following period (1947-57) twenty-eight new USTNC subsidiaries in Peru were similarly distributed. As in Colombia, the peak of the new entries (seventy-two) had been reached in Peru during the period (1958-67). Forty per cent of these entries occurred in the manufacturing sector, 30 per cent in commerce and the rest in other activities. The distribution of these new entries was quite different from that which took place during the same period in Colombia, where 75 per cent of the new entries of USTNCs were concentrated in the manufacturing sector.

Although details on the reasons for the differences between these patterns are lacking, one can nevertheless offer the hypothesis that while in Colombia foreign companies took advantage of the process of import substitution, the free trade policy pursued by Peru offered investment opportunities in a wide range of activities, in the absence of the need for the sector importing manufactured goods to advance to the assemblying stage. It is also probable that the reduced size of the internal market, even for non-durable consumer goods, discouraged USTNCs, which then delayed their decision to establish subsidiaries in Peru and, in some cases, did not see particularly attractive opportunities because of the absence of potential local competitors.

Nonetheless, the pace of entry of USTNCs into the manufacturing sector in Peru accelerated. Between 1958 and 1967, forty-seven subsidiaries established themselves in this sector in comparison with twenty-five between 1946 and 1957 and eleven set up before the end of the Second World War. One should also note the vertical integration which occurred between manufacturing (mostly assembling) subsidiaries and commercial services. To what degree the emergence of the subsidiaries in the financial and ancillary services sector was part of the trend toward vertical and horizontal integration will have to be established in a future study carried out in the country itself. However, it is probable that the rapid growth in numbers of foreign companies in the financial sector may have been related to the expansion of international trade in Peru in the sixties rather than to the country's industrial progress.

Concerning the manner of entry, it seems that in Peru emphasis was on the establishment of new subsidiaries rather than on the acquisition of already existing firms, as in Colombia. Furthermore, in Peru there were no mergers of new with pre-existing subsidiaries. All this suggests that, given the level of development achieved by Peru, the USTNCs had to create new productive units because there were relatively few companies eligible for purchase or conversion, the result of the low degree of diversity of the industrial structure in a country dependent primarily on mining and agricultural exports.

As far as ownership patterns were concerned, in 1967 the degree of control of the subsidiaries by the respective USTNCs was even greater than in Colombia. Of the ninety-eight subsidiaries, sixty-six were 100 per cent owned by the headquarters and another twenty-five had a majority control from abroad. In only seven subsidiaries was there any participation by capital other than that of the respective USTNC. It is quite probable that these were joint ventures with non-Peruvian capital established in Peru only recently, except for domestic participation in small companies set up by foreign investors independent of USTNCs.

In Peru the concentration of USTNC subsidiaries in a limited number of industrial sectors was even more noticeable than in Colombia. Of the fifty-seven manufacturing subsidiaries established in Peru before the end of 1967 (forty-seven of these were still in business at that time), twenty-four were set up in chemical and pharmaceutical industries (including soap and cosmetics); twelve in the food industry; seven in automotive and related industries, and six in the metal industry. Of the remaining eight subsidiaries, two were engaged in oil refining and the rest in producing consumer durables. While there was a complete absence of foreign companies in the intermediate goods sector, almost all the USTNC subsidiaries studied by Harvard Business School were engaged in assembly activities.

These characteristics of Peruvian foreign-owned industry suggest that United States capital entered Peru, as it did Colombia, to take over the growing market for finished consumer goods involving the small part of the population with relatively high incomes. Since it appears that backward linkages were not created, one can safely say that the effect of all these enterprises on the industrial structure of Peru, over more than ten years, was minimal. The entrance of USTNCs into Peru, speeded up during the sixties, can hardly be explained by their advantageous position in relation to the domestic entrepreneur in financial and technological terms, except in marketing technology. Rather, it seems to reflect the relative preference of the Peruvian businessman for export agriculture and for acting as financial intermediary. However, room in this last field has become progressively limited for nationals due to the emergence in Peru during the sixties of strong foreign banking groups in the form of subsidiaries or the growing participation of their capital in the nominally national banking system.

As in Colombia, USTNC manufacturing subsidiaries in Peru produced almost exclusively for the domestic market. Furthermore, their participation in the internal market supply grew much faster than industrial production. While the value of the latter grew by 80 per cent between 1958 and 1967 at constant prices (which means at an annual rate of 6.5 per cent), the value of local sales of United States manufacturing companies grew almost four times: from $68 million in 1957 to $245 million in 1966, according to the information of the United States Commerce Department. There are no figures on sales by industrial branches for 1957. In 1966 local sales of processed foods by United States subsidiaries totalled $60 million; those of the chemical and pharmaceutical industry $35 million and of other industries $150 million, including the assembly in Peru of motor vehicles from imported parts.

Although USTNC exports increased from $3 million in 1957 to $39 million in 1966, 80 per cent of the latter came from processed foods. It would be worth while finding out what proportion of the $39 million represented sugar exports since for statistical purposes this product is considered in Peru as a manufacture. The data for other export categories are even less impressive than in Colombia. While in Colombia sales abroad represent 4 per cent of the total sales of United States manufacturing subsidiaries, in Peru they only represented 3 per cent. It is especially interesting to see that the subsidiaries in Peru did not regard it as useful or possible to export any manufactured goods even to the LAFTA (Latin American Free Trade Association) or to neighbouring countries. This is not because of high costs or related factors but because USTNCs with subsidiaries in Peru also have them in almost all the other Latin American countries. The type of products and the general practices of the USTNCs of dividing up the markets explain the absence of Peruvian manufactures in the Andean region.

According to data compiled by the Commerce Department, the book value of direct United States investment in the manufacturing sector of Peru increased from $31 million in 1959 to $96 million at the end of 1968. In other words, it grew at a faster pace than the value of United States private investment in other sectors (with the exception of the category entitled 'others' which most probably included agriculture, financial services and tourism). According to the same source, the net income of United States capital investments totalled $48 million in the period of 1960-8 and the reinvestment of undistributed earnings amounted to $12 million. In contrast to Colombia, here one sees the predominance of net entries of United States capital as opposed to the reinvestment of earnings, despite the fact that the declared profitability of United States companies in Peru was apparently higher than in Colombia (8.6 per cent per year compared with 6.4 per cent in Colombia). However, all these data should not be taken too seriously in view of the fact that, according to another statistical series from the Commerce Department, the earnings of the United States manufacturing companies in Peru reinvested in the country in the period 1960-8 amounted to $18 and not to $12 million.

Once again detailed research carried out by Peru could clear up the reasons for these statistical discrepancies or errors. In any event, the presence in Peru and Colombia of the phenomenon of an inverse relation between the level of total earnings and the proportion of total investments represented by their reinvestment suggests that these concepts are not very useful in analysing the financial behaviour of foreign companies in the region and its effect on the balance of payments of the countries under study. It is worth repeating that in Colombia as well as in Peru there is good reason to seriously doubt the relationship between the reported profitability of a USTNC subsidiary and the global real earnings from its operations seen from the viewpoint of the head office or of the global system.

Since the distribution of United States manufacturing investment in Peru by industrial branches is very similar to that observed in Colombia, it seems reasonable to accept the hypothesis that the growing interest of USTNCs in Peru up to the 1968 revolution reflected their expectation of relatively high earnings, on the one hand, and of an expanding internal market, on the other. Whatever the level of global earnings, it is quite probable that they were relatively higher in Peru than in Colombia perhaps because, except for the food industry, manufacturing activities in Peru consisted to a higher degree in the assembly of imported intermediate goods.

This situation is reflected in the data compiled by the United States Commerce Department. According to these the local current costs of United States manufacturing companies in Peru totalled in 1966 $187 million, their total sales in the same year (including exports) amounting to $282 million. Given that the declared profits from these sales at the subsidiary level, after deducting local taxes, totalled only $10 million, $85 million were to be accounted by expenditures abroad on imports of goods, payments for technology and technical assistance, and United States taxes. As in other cases of the entry into a market in which 'new industries' are highly protected and oligopolistic conditions prevail, the size of expenditure abroad strongly suggests that the actual profits of USTNCs from their operations in Peru are far bigger than those declared by their Peruvian subsidiaries.

CHILE

Unfortunately, no detailed information on the appearance, the manner of entry, the ownership patterns and the distribution by industrial branches of USTNC subsidiaries in Chile is available because the Harvard Business School study does not present separate data on Chile. However, certain data from national sources, Corporación de Fomento de la Producción (CORFO)(10), suggest patterns similar to those prevailing in Colombia and Peru in the case of twenty-two out of the fifty foreign companies which applied for fiscal incentives granted under the law DFL 258 between 1960 and 1968(11). Two-thirds of the twenty-two companies belonged to the same industrial branches in which USTNCs were concentrated in Colombia and Peru during the period 1958-67. Six companies were producing chemicals and pharmaceuticals, five processed food and three metallic goods.

In nineteen out of twenty-two companies studied, there was a majority foreign control of capital at the beginning of their operations, and in fifteen out of nineteen, foreign capital participation exceeded 75 per cent. In eight of the twenty-two companies, foreign participation increased after the start of operations and one-half of the sample (eleven) was 100 per cent foreign-owned by 1968. The degree of foreign capital control did not diminish in any single case. In the majority of firms the managing director was a foreigner and the financial director was a foreigner in all the companies which consumed a high percentage of imported raw materials or intermediate goods.

Of the total of twenty-two companies surveyed, nine were newly formed with imported capital and the rest originated in the expansion of already existing domestic firms. While in half of the cases (eleven companies) new investment went into the expansion of the supply of goods already produced in Chile, the remaining half was dedicated to the partial substitution of imports or the introduction of new products. The sales of all the companies studied (twenty out of twenty-two) grew faster than the industrial product of the corresponding sector. Furthermore almost all the companies produced for the domestic market and only in half of those few which exported significantly did these exports equal 25 per cent of total sales.

Half of the companies (eleven) considered exports to other countries of the Andean Group to be unfeasible since there were already subsidiaries of the same firm in most of the countries of the region. While the other half was interested in principle in production for the Andean market, their managers considered that they would have to install larger production units or modify production processes because their plants were originally designed exclusively for the Chilean market. Only one of the companies surveyed was established specifically for serving the external market.

The results of the local survey on the destination of the production of the twenty-two manufacturing foreign-owned companies, are corroborated by data from the Commerce Department. According to that source, the global sales of United States manufacturing corporations in Chile amounted in 1957 to $51 million and were absorbed exclusively by the internal market. By 1966 the value of their sales reached $84 million, of which $77 million went to the Chilean market; $3 million were exports to the United States and $4 million were exports to other markets. In 1966 the participation by United States Chilean subsidiaries in sales of manufactured goods to the Andean market was still nil.

Between 1959 and 1968 the book value of United States investments in Chile's manufacturing sector increased from $21 million to $65 million. However, the pace of expansion was very slow until 1964. In the first five years of the sixties the value of United States investment increased only from $21 million to $30 million and most of new investments took place in one single year, 1961. Between 1965 and 1968 United States investment in Chilean industry grew rapidly, more than doubling its value between the end of 1964 and the end of 1968 (from $30 million to $60 million). This phenomenon can probably explain the relatively slow growth - in comparison with Colombia and Peru - of the total sales of United States manufacturing companies in Chile between 1957 and 1966. It is probable that the sales grew much more rapidly after 1966, particularly in view of the fact that the acceleration of United States investment in Chilean industry coincided with a similar trend in the commercial sector. While between 1959 and 1963 the book value of the United States commercial subsidiaries in Chile increased only by $5 million, it expanded between the end of 1963 and the end of 1968 by $24 million.

Though available data should be treated with caution, the United States Commerce Department figures do seem to indicate that in the period of the slow growth of the United States manufacturing investment in Chile (1959-64) all new investments were financed with reinvested profits. Later (1965-8) half of new investments ($19 million) originated in the net inflows of new capital and the remainder came from non-distributed earnings. In the late sixties the relative share of undistributed earnings in total income was greater in United States-owned commercial enterprises than in manufacturing firms. On the other hand, imports increased considerably both in absolute and relative terms due to the striking expansion of imports (by industries such as chemicals and pharmaceuticals, metal products and automotive assembly) and of technology payments.

In fact, of the twenty-two foreign-owned manufacturing companies studied in detail, eight imported all their raw materials or intermediate products and another three were importing the main raw materials from their headquarters. All were subsidiaries almost 100 per cent foreign-controlled, established in chemicals and pharmaceuticals, electrical appliances and the automotive industry.

The total earnings reported to the United States Commerce Department and the net income (earnings minus reinvested profits) registered a very slow growth during the whole period 1959-68, partially reflecting the relatively late expansion of United States manufacturing investment in Chile. However, the reported profitability was much higher than in Colombia or Peru (12.5 per cent average annually), perhaps one of the highest in Latin America. Unfortunately, data are lacking for explaining these great differences between the levels of profits in Colombia, Peru and Chile. One possible explanation could be the undervaluation of assets in Chile. Another could be the easy access to local financial resources for working capital resources, which in a highly inflationary situation are usually secured at negative real interest rates. The CORFO study emphasized that in Chile both plant expansion projects and new operations by foreign subsidiaries were financed mainly with domestic resources. In fact, under the law DFL 258, foreign investors had ample access, limited only by their repayment capacity and economic solvency, to credit from the domestic banking system. They were obtaining financing from CORFO, the Banco del Estado de Chile or commercial private banks. A large proportion of the financing provided from abroad took the form of machinery, equipment and accessories generally imported from the headquarters of the investing foreign firm.

INTRA-ANDEAN COMMERCE AND FOREIGN MANUFACTURING COMPANIES

The similarity of the industrial structures of the large countries of the Andean Group, the concentration of foreign companies, in general, and of USTNC subsidiaries as well, in the same industrial sectors (final consumer goods), the dependence of companies on imports of a large proportion of intermediate goods from their headquarters, and the virtual non-existence of export activities explain the almost complete absence of manufacturing trade within the Andean Group despite the participation of its members in the regional trade liberalization programme initiated by LAFTA countries in 1961.

On the other hand, the appearance of LAFTA resulted in rapid trade expansion of the Andean Group with the rest of Latin America (especially in respect to imports) between 1961 and 1967, causing significant commercial deficits in the region. According to the UN-IMF Direction of Trade, while exports to the rest of the Latin American countries by the five signataries of the Cartagena Agreement in 1969 increased from 4.3 per cent of their f.o.b. exports in 1961-3 to 5 per cent in 1964-6, imports by the Andean Group from the rest of Latin America grew in the same period from 8 to 11.2 per cent of their total purchases abroad. On the other hand, the participation of Andean countries in the total trade of the group hardly changed. It represented 2.8 per cent of their exports in 1961-3 and 2.7 per cent in 1964-6. The same occurred with intra-group imports (2.8 per cent of total trade in 1961-3 and 3.3 per cent in 1964-6). As can be seen in Table 11.2, the value of exports of manufactured goods within the Andean Group did not even reach $20 million by 1966-7.

TABLE 11.2. Value of Exports by the Andean Group, 1966 and 1967

(US $ million)

Country	1966	1967
Colombia	8.3	7.7
Chile	6.3	6.1
Peru	2.3	1.3
Ecuador	1.5	1.3
Bolivia	0.1	–
Total	18.5	16.4

Source: INTAL-BID, Exportaciones de manufacturas a América Latina, Series 'Estudio 1', several volumes, Buenos Aires, 1969.

In the case of the leading exporter of manufactures to the subregion, Colombia, 90 per cent of these exports went to Ecuador and Peru; in that of Chile 50 per cent to Peru and Ecuador in 1966 and 75 per cent to the two countries in 1967. Peru exported minimal quantities of manufactured goods to Colombia and Chile. While small Ecuador's exports went almost exclusively to Colombia, Bolivia, as could be expected, exported hardly anything to the area. Great variations in the value of the manufactured goods exported from one year to the next and the shortness of the list of exports indicate that at least until 1967 these transactions were marginal to the main activities of the mostly foreign manufacturing companies involved.

It is perhaps significant that 80 per cent of the intra-Andean manufactured goods trade originated in Colombia and Chile. Moreover, it appeared that only a small part of the manufactured goods exports within the area came from USTNC subsidiaries. In these conditions one could predict that, even assuming that the Andean Group were to abolish tariffs on all consumer manufactures produced in the region by firms controlled to an important degree by foreign companies, it is unlikely that such trade liberalization would result in expansion of intra-zonal trade in manufactured goods. Such an expansion could only occur if the foreign companies present in certain major consumer manufactures branches decided to compete regionally or to differentiate production at the national level in such a way that they could complement each other in a regional market. Meanwhile, as the small number of TNCs operate in the same industrial branches of Colombia, Chile and Peru, it seems more probable that the subsidiaries located in the largest Andean countries will attempt to expand production in order to enter least-developed Bolivia and Ecuador, as long as such a new strategy is in accordance with the interests of their headquarters. Little is known in 1970 about the attitude of these companies to the Cartagena Agreement.

However, all this creates a dilemma from the viewpoint of economic interests of the area, particularly of underdeveloped member countries. In view of the scarcity of investment resources, perhaps it would benefit the region as a whole if the already established industrial companies, including foreign firms, were to extend the scope of operations through exports to the less-developed neighbouring countries. From the viewpoint of Bolivia and Ecuador, such a solution would not seem acceptable. These two countries, attempting to achieve at least the level of industrialization of the larger members of the group, hoped that the Andean Common Market would help them. Thus the interest of Bolivia and Ecuador in the build-up of consumer goods industries was a logical answer to the problem of uneven regional industrial development. Consequently, unless the larger countries of the subregion were willing to offer 'compensation' to Bolivia and Ecuador, by offering them industrial projects in new sectors, both of these small countries would continue to search for themselves for industrial projects in the traditional manufacturing sectors at the cost of all kinds of incentives offered to foreign capital. The magnitude of these incentives could change the attitude of the headquarters of transnational companies already operating in Colombia, Chile and Peru and make it attractive for them to enter peripheral countries of the Andean Group.

Thus in 1970 the regional grouping faces the complicated task of searching for regional instruments which could allow avoidance of the alternatives of:
(1) expanding export trade in traditional manufactured goods from the 'centre' of the region to its periphery (politically unacceptable to Bolivia and Ecuador); or (2) the proliferation in the two poorer countries of small consumer goods plants whose production would have no chance of gaining access to the markets of the three more advanced member countries. Only the harmonization of foreign investment criteria at the regional level and the negotiation of sectoral programmes for industrialization could increase the negotiating power of the smaller members of the group with regard to transnational corporations and prevent a repetition of the experiences of the Central American Common Market where, with quite disastrous results for that regional integration scheme, a race to offer incentives to foreign industry took place during the sixties.

THE POSSIBLE POSITION OF TRANSNATIONAL CORPORATIONS IN THE ANDEAN COMMON MARKET

While the interest of TNCs in the future of the Andean Market seems limited, the situation is somewhat different with regard to those TNCs which are not yet operating in the area or which are at the stage of drawing up investment plans for initially supplying the domestic markets of each of the three larger countries. Business journals with international circulation, produced for the executives of large TNCs, are trying to convince their readers that the signature of the Cartagena Agreement considerably affected the member countries' negotiating position vis-a-vis them and that consequently the transnationals' position in respect to the setting up of new subsidiaries in the area should change substantially.

It is worth recalling that the same business information media had great hopes for the LAFTA in the early sixties. However, in the late sixties they all arrived at the conclusion that, in planning their activities in Latin America, the TNCs should not take the LAFTA too seriously. Thus TNCs interested in entering Latin America are advised to apply in respect to their future investments in Argentina, Brazil or Mexico strategies different from those suitable in the case of Andean Group countries. It is suggested that the future investor in the three largest Latin American countries ought to think mainly in terms of supplying the respective domestic markets, should try to disarm latent 'nationalistic' hostility through accepting domestic capital participation without losing technological control of the new company and, finally, should initiate contingency planning in case markets for the product emerge outside Latin America. It is thought that such contingency planning, especially in respect to the possibility of marginally entering the United States market, would help to limit the area of conflict between the investor and the largest Latin American countries and, in many cases, would help to maximize profits of the global transnational systems.

With regard to the Andean Group, the same sources suggest that a potential manufacturing investor should closely monitor all regional developments and start thinking immediately in terms of new projects for supplying the whole area. One magazine, set up exclusively for the large USTNCs, Business Latin America, published brief studies of the five Andean Group countries with emphasis on their future participation in the Cartagena Agreement. The purpose of the surveys was to offer TNCs a guide to the region, by pointing out the scope of commitments under the Cartagena Agreement concerning trade liberalization and regional industrialization and by providing information on the key institutions and individuals in each country of the area allegedly ready to extend 'friendly treatment' to TNCs interested in taking advantage of Andean Common Market potential. The main points of these and similar surveys published in the United States may be summarized as follows:

(1) The liberalization of intra-Andean trade in the products put on the LAFTA common list and the setting up of a minimum common external tariff on imports from outside the subregion, show that the Andean Common Market is making a much more serious attempt at fostering subregional trade than did LAFTA.

(2) The rapid initiation of a operative programme for the Andean Common Market should receive maximum priority in TNCs which operate or are interested in entering Latin America.

(3) The strategy of TNCs should take into account that there are various ways of protecting the interests of their subsidiaries, whether already established or to be established, through several tariff liberalization mechanisms incorporated into the Cartagena Agreement. Specifically, these mechanisms cover (a) products reserved for sectoral industrial development programmes or complementarity agreements; (b) products still not manufactured in the area but not included in the previous group; and (c) products temporarily exempt from automatic annual tariff reductions.

(4) The TNC should act fast given the tariff liberalization schedule agreed upon in the Cartagena Agreement, since its inclusion in a corresponding tariff

cut group could be of critical importance for that enterprise's future in the Andean Common Market. Thus TNCs operating in industries covered by the programmes of sectoral development should establish 'persuasion contacts' with the governments of potential host countries while those which plan to add new products to the traditional ones should find the best way of having them included in the list of the corresponding group. Others which consider it more important to work within the national protectionism trends than to take advantage of possible opportunities of the expanded market should try to be included in the special exemption lists.

(5) While in the LAFTA the TNCs were in positions to achieve most of their objectives through sectoral industrial meetings, the Cartagena Agreement stipulates that the most important mechanism of integration - the sectoral industrial programmes - will be negotiated by the governments with little direct participation by the private sector. Consequently, contacts with government officials have to be established either directly or through national chambers of industry. This kind of lobbying should not be difficult due to the fact that, despite the commitment to standardize foreign investment treatment, there will be strong competition between member states to attract important new industrial projects. The lobbying should be carefully coordinated within the subregion and some transnational corporations have already put one high official in charge of coordination in the area.

(6) Even those TNCs that have reservations about the prospects of the Andean Common Market, but which operate in Latin America or in the subregion, should periodically reevaluate their Latin American operations to assess the possible effect of the Andean Common Market.

(7) In any event, each TNC with subsidiaries in the subregion should establish 'intelligence services' on the Andean Common Market and constantly inform the head offices of developments in the area so they are in a position to adapt their strategy and corporate tactics to the new situation. The more aggressive TNCs are already sending executives from their headquarters to the subregion to 'help' the governments and chambers of industry to draw up lists of industries interested in special treatment at negotiations of the Cartagena Agreement.

(8) The TNCs should accept that the Andean Common Market will adopt restrictive positions concerning payments for technology transfer. The rest of the code for a common treatment of foreign investment will be flexible and very probably weak.

POSSIBLE APPROACHES TO THE FIRST STAGE OF A COMMON TREATMENT FOR FOREIGN MANUFACTURING COMPANIES IN THE ANDEAN COMMON MARKET

The limited information available on the behaviour of manufacturing subsidiaries of USTNCs in the three major countries of the Andean Group indicates that their contribution to the development of the recipient countries, in terms of their positive effect on the balance of payments, technological advancement and the creation of new jobs was much smaller than one would have gathered from the assessment made by the governments of the capital exporting countries and the declarations of the foreign investors themselves prior to the signature of the Cartagena Agreement. In most cases, foreign subsidiaries in the subregion are located in the consumer durable or non-durable goods industries where the process of substitution offered high and safe earnings.

Furthermore, there is reason to believe that in some cases these companies displaced weak domestic companies.

As was to be expected, the real level of profits is not reflected in the balance sheets of the subsidiaries since they do not take into account profits make by the headquarters from the sale of industrial equipment, payments for technology and technical assistance, and the export of a considerable proportion of material inputs to subsidiaries in the area. To maximize their total earnings, the TNCs try to secure maximum financial control over their subsidiaries and in the case of joint ventures control is achieved through technology transfer arrangements which stipulate the exclusiveness of the technological contribution and the division of markets.

The fact that such practices would have been impossible in the home countries of the transnationals is irrelevant for the Andean subregion. In the industrially advanced countries there are anti-monopoly laws that make it hard to monopolize the market or the know-how. However, these laws do not exist or do not function in Latin America in general, and in the countries of the Andean Group in particular. Even if they did exist, the respective authorities perhaps would not have the necessary manpower to enforce them. Furthermore, there is reason to believe that due to the technological underdevelopment of the subregion, there are many situations, particularly in the chemicals, pharmaceuticals and electrical machinery (generally electrical and electronic equipment) industries, in which the host countries receive in return for considerable direct or indirect payments, out-of-date know-how that could be purchased much cheaper in competitive conditions in other parts of the world, or where technology is sold without strings attached.

The companies' contribution to the balance of payments of recipient countries in terms of foreign exchange does not appear to be impressive either. Most probably their contribution with headquarters resources to the financing of new investments or the expansion of established industrial projects is a great deal smaller than would appear from the statistics of the United States Commerce Department which simply make a distinction between the net inflows of new capital and the reinvestments profits. More detailed studies carried out at a national level would perhaps show that a considerable proportion of the foreign exchange contribution does not originate at the headquarters or the international private capital market, but comes from sources which the capital exporting countries actually consider to be public overseas aid. One important aspect of the much debated question of the origin of resources for fixed investment (which still waits to be cleared up) is to what degree local investment costs of a subsidiary are financed with external or local resources. The CORFO study mentioned earlier suggests that, at least in Chile, there is a widespread preference for the use of local money perhaps because of prevailing inflationary conditions. Nevertheless, the same thing seems to occur under conditions of monetary stability. In Latin America as well as in Western Europe the TNCs rely as heavily as possible on local sources for financing their working capital(12). These practices have become even more widespread throughout the world in recent years as a result of official measures taken by Washington in defence of the United States balance of payments.

Finally, concerning the effect of foreign direct investment on employment, despite the absence of studies on the interrelation between imported technology and employment, it seems that subsidiaries of large foreign enterprises do not adapt their production processes to the factor proportion in developing countries, as claimed by some economists, but instead they adapt them to the market size. In 1966, the manufacturing subsidiaries of United States companies in Colombia employed 36,000 people; in Peru 21,500 and in Chile, 7500. Management personnel in the subsidiaries in the three largest Andean Group countries totalled 1800 during the same year. They employed 4750 professionals and technicians and 58,450 manual workers. These employment figures do not match the participation of foreign subsidiaries in total industrial production in terms of output. Obviously this is inevitable considering that the foreign companies use technologies originally designed for advanced economies with factor proportions differing from those which characterize Latin America. The problem is not so much their lack of interest in adapting the technologies to other factor proportions but the absence of national technological policies and the nature of technological progress itself concentrated in the industrialized countries.

It would be politically naive and totally unrealistic to use criticisms of the behaviour of foreign subsidiaries in the countries of the Andean Group as a basis for a highly restrictive system for foreign manufacturing investment in the future Andean Common Market. The problem should rather be stated in the following terms: how to eliminate the abuses committed in the past by private foreign investment in the area and how to create the conditions under which private capital and foreign technology could contribute to the industrial and economic growth of the subregion. It is very doubtful that the first objective can be achieved through general laws restricting foreign investment, or the second through all sorts of incentives to foreign private capital, in the hope that somehow these incentives would lead to a strong inflow of financial and technical resources from abroad which would stimulate industrial development. In Latin America the evasion of restrictive measures is particularly easy. In turn, where these restrictions show their efficiency, the entry of external private financial resources dries up. It happened in Brazil at the beginning of the sixties.

In order to design a common treatment for foreign investment, one should take as a departure point the fact that the Andean Group as a whole has much to offer to foreign companies in terms of present and potential market. The experience of countries such as Mexico or Australia indicates that foreign companies, including large TNCs, are willing to accept from the host country (in this case a group of countries) conditions which in other circumstances would seem unacceptable, as long as the negotiating process could establish a quid pro quo favourable to both parties.

Under the assumption that the Andean Group can offer to large foreign enterprises a market of considerable size with dynamic prospects and a very attractive level of 'lawful' earnings, and considering that the main objective of a TNC is to maximize its global earnings, one should begin by destroying the myth that the earnings of TNC subsidiaries are lower in Latin America than elsewhere. The myth is kept alive, on the one hand, by the accounting practices used by these enterprises in order to favourably impress the host countries, and, on the other, by the patent lack of capability to refute such assertions shown by local fiscal authorities(13).

In many parts of the world, and particularly in countries which receive considerable amounts of private foreign investment such as Western Europe, Canada and Australia, there is an impressive stock of knowledge and experience on how to deal with the large TNCs. The possession of such experience seems to be the primary condition for establishing a realistic and fruitful dialogue

SKIWP - P

between the countries of the Andean Group and foreign investors, now and in the future. This is probably the field in which the subregion needs more technical assistance than any other. The speeding up of the learning process would require the sending of huge numbers of national technicians presently working on foreign investment to centres for the study of TNCs. These centres have sprung up in most of the advanced countries, particularly in the mother country of the largest number of TNCs, the United States.

What does all this mean in terms of a common treatment? First, one would have to standardize the rules for the fiscal inspection of accounting procedures of foreign manufacturing subsidiaries established in the region. In other words, one would need permanent cooperation between the finance authorities of the five members of the Andean Common Market in order to detect defects in the fiscal systems which permit the completely legal export of indirect profits through inflation of the costs of imported goods and technology. Tolerance of this state of affairs brings with it many serious disadvantages for the subregion: (1) considerable fiscal losses; (2) a heavy burden for the consumer and (3) the absence of negotiating power vis-à-vis future investors. By showing, through their complicated accounting procedures, that their level of earnings is lower than in other parts of the world, foreign subsidiaries create an atmosphere under which it is possible to demand all kinds of privileges, concessions and incentives ranging from an increase in tariff protection to a disproportionate extension of fiscal exemptions. As in many countries internal political considerations do not permit special concessions to foreign capital, concessions are extended to all industry, whether foreign or national, resulting in a bonus for inefficient national industry and in monopolistic income for efficient foreign companies.

The attempts made in Latin America to limit the remittance of profits, mainly in answer to balance-of-payments difficulties, represent weapons which are too crude to solve the basic problem of the entirely legal export of indirect earnings. Unless one considers it useful to encourage the reinvestment of profits at the national and regional level, through preferential fiscal treatment, the foreign companies should have the right to export profits as long as they can prove that an increase in their profits corresponds to their efficiency and that their balance sheet and profits-and-loss statement accurately reflect their income and expenditure and do not include fictitious operations which favour the headquarters.

Once this standardization of accounting control has been established, it will become feasible to carry out the collateral task stipulated in the Cartagena Agreement: that of the general harmonization of fiscal policies(14). As long as there is no way of comparing the respective levels of the real fiscal burden carried by foreign companies in the Andean subregion, a comparison of the nominal levels of such burden does not make much sense. A very high nominal fiscal burden can easily be lower in effective terms than a light nominal burden, as long as there is no way of making a regional comparison of net taxable profits, which are skilfully manipulated by the financial executives of the subsidiaries with the assistance of their headquarters and trustworthy local accountants.

The standardization of accounting control over the activities of foreign subsidiaries is especially urgent in view of negotiations on a common external tariff for goods not produced in the region and for the lists of external products temporarily exempted from intra-regional tariff liberalization. The little one knows about the probable behaviour of foreign companies to which

either one of these two systems would apply suggests that, in accordance with
the global strategy of their headquarters, the subsidiaries interested in
entering the subregion will fight for a relatively high common external tariff,
supposedly as compensation for high costs and investment risks. On the other
hand, the companies interested in preserving their dominant position in the
domestic market of the country where they operate will do everything possible
to be included in the list of products protected by national tariffs until
1985. However, the strategy of the head offices will not reflect the text-
book considerations of the relative production costs in different parts of
the subregion, but will follow the combination of global considerations
related, among other things, to: (1) the presence or absence of sister subsidiaries in the subregion, (2) the probable costs of the readaptation of
existing plants to the needs of the multinational market, and (3) a comparison
between the possible profits resulting from expansion of the market under
extremely competitive conditions and the maximum use of inputs produced in
the region, on the one hand, and, on the other, the present real earnings
derived from the small local markets served by assembly plants using to a considerable extent inputs from their headquarters.

Only through knowledge of the real level of profits made by the transnational
systems from their subsidiaries in the different countries can one establish
a rational basis for a decision by the Andean Group on, first, whether the
subsidiaries interested in the status quo deserve to be included in the lists
of exemptions and, second, what level of external protection should be
offered to foreign enterprises that want to enter the subregional market with
new products.

There is an important reason for insisting that some permanent contact be
established immediately, under the auspices of the authorities of the Cartagena Agreement, between five national offices in charge of the preparation of
lists of exemptions and of the feasibility studies for new projects. From the
viewpoint of future regional industrialization cooperation, there is a danger
of a situation arising in which the feasibility studies will stay in the hands
of private consulting companies, aided by the large transnational manufacturing
companies.

One should assume that these consulting firms will present within a short
period of time an impressive list of industrial projects, both within and outside the sectoral programmes, which could be established in a given country
as long as the proponents can be assured of the support of interested governments in securing 'adequate' regional tariff protection with respect to the
rest of the world. These projects would obviously receive technical assistance
from the TNCs under 'certain conditions'.

Cooperation between the national entities on feasibility studies for the new
industries would appear to be necessary in view of the absence of progress in
this field in the two smaller countries and in view of the political need to
direct some important new projects to these countries. If Ecuador and Bolivia
do not receive technical assistance in this respect from the other Andean
countries and if, as we know, the interest of foreign private capital in them
is minimal, both countries could find themselves without any projects when
the time comes to negotiate sectoral programmes.

These proposals may appear very difficult to transform into a coordinated
regional plan of action, particularly because of the shortage of time. There
exist, however, in the subregion several mechanisms designed independently at

the national level that could help to establish the first phase of a common treatment for the foreign investment:

(1) It seems that in all the countries of the region, with the exception of Bolivia, the introduction of exchange restrictions has led to the establishment of registers of foreign enterprises in order to provide them with foreign exchange for imports, remittances of profits and capital withdrawal. The correct and standardized design of these foreign investment registers, which ought to become mandatory, could simplify the task of bringing to light the practice of foreign manufacturing companies of transferring part of their profits to their headquarters through alleged payments for technology transfer and through overcharging for imported goods.

(2) For the first time in the Latin American history payments for royalties and technical assistance are controlled in the area. The experience of Chile and Colombia in this field is very valuable. Armed with the experience of Argentina and Brazil, trying to do the same thing, and enriched by Japanese experiences, Chile's and Colombia's learning process could serve as a basis not only for the establishment of a common treatment for the explicit expenditure of foreign companies on their account but also for drawing up a basic common contract for technology transfer and technical assistance at different stages of the operation of the enterprise.

(3) There is growing concern in the subregion over the increasing use by foreign companies of local financial resources. This has been accompanied by attempts by Chile and Peru to limit the scope of action of foreign financial intermediaries. Combined concern over both these problems led some governments to the conclusion that once the expansion of foreign banks in the country was checked, somehow the problem of excessive access by the foreign companies to internal financial sources would be solved. However, at least in Latin America, there is no convincing evidence that there is a direct link between the ownership patterns of the private banking system and the respective use of its resources by foreign or domestic companies. An especially interesting case is Mexico where, despite the fact that the whole financial system is in the hands of nationals, the 600 United States subsidiaries have no difficulty in gaining access to local savings. The fact that there has been no conflict between foreign and domestic enterprises in Mexico over this question does not reflect the high degree of patriotism of local bankers, but rather the growth during the sixties of the global availability of resources in the hands of the national financial system. Chile also managed to stop the expansion of foreign banks through the ingenious mechanism of 100 per cent legal reserves on new deposits in foreign banks. However, according to the CORFO study, not only do foreign manufacturing companies have no problems in obtaining private domestic financing for local investment and working capital expenditures, but they have access to official credit under the DFL 258 as well.

If one accepts the premise that the activities of foreign companies should be based on the use of external resources, then it would be appropriate for the countries of the Andean Group to try to harmonize their policies concerning the access of foreign subsidiaries to local financial resources. The achievement of such a common treatment perhaps presents less problems than do other fields. Once it has been agreed that the subsidiaries are not to have access to the official credit of the host countries, it could be stipulated that they must finance all capital expenditures with external resources and then regional ceilings could be set on their internal debt incurred for working capital purposes. This debt could be related to their fixed capital, assets, sales volume, etc.

At this point one should mention one of the many paradoxes that occur in relations between countries which receive foreign private investment and the respective foreign companies. Where it is considered inappropriate that companies controlled from abroad use excessive local financial resources, it is difficult to see the virtues of joint ventures when they have a minority participation of domestic capital and in some cases even when they have a majority control of local interests. It is particularly hard to understand the increasing attraction of these joint ventures for Latin America in the presence of overwhelming evidence that the control of an enterprise does not come from the ownership of 51 per cent of its capital, especially if it is in the hands of a large number of stockholders. It is enough to concentrate the ownership of a minority block of capital in a few hands and to exert administrative and technological control.

Unless there is good reason to hope that the fostering of joint ventures represents the initial stage of a policy leading to the step-by-step 'nationalization' of certain activities, the preference for this system of ownership suggests, under Latin American conditions, several things. First, it could reflect the traditional way of thinking that participation in the ownership can be equated with participation in control. Second, it may represent official interest in offering national groups, which have great economic or political influence, participation in the monopolistic rent accruing to lucrative and efficient foreign companies. Third, it may reflect a purely political move toward concealing the growing transfer of the dynamic sectors of the economy into foreign hands, a situation that antagonizes the nationalist feelings of Latin American societies. However, it does not seem logical to insist, on the one hand, that the foreign investor should give up the use of local savings and, on the other, to foster the establishment of joint ventures. The case in favour of joint ventures is weakened even more when one recalls that the Andean Group considered encouraging the entry of TNCs with the participation of private or mixed private or public capital from the subregion.

To sum up, among several fields where policies on foreign investment in the dynamic sectors should be harmonized regionally the following are perhaps particularly important:

(1) The design of registers for foreign enterprises and the policies aimed at control of their profits in order to make it difficult for TNC subsidiaries to transfer a part of their profits to their headquarters through alleged payments for technology and through overcharging for imported goods.

The elimination of transfer pricing practices would create a strong incentive for the greater use of local or regional raw materials and intermediate products. At present, foreign companies argue that even when local raw materials are available, it is not feasible, due to the absence of economies of scale, among other things, to enter into the production of intermediate goods at internationally competitive prices. However, the absence of evidence that imports of the same intermediate products are carried out in competitive conditions invalidates such an argument, especially in the case of the opening up of a subregional market. Moreover, the problem of economies of scale has not been sufficiently clarified. This concept is used and abused in the framework of technologies designed expressly for the large markets of advanced countries or for large export markets. Another argument in favour of the import of intermediate goods is based on the supposed or actual low quality of goods produced in developing countries. If the public sectors or private enterprises of the Andean region willing to undertake the production of imported intermediate goods were in the position to secure the necessary technology from abroad under competitive conditions, and if governments decided to strengthen technical education at all levels, perhaps the problem of the low quality of intermediate products would become less serious.

(2) The coordination of controls on payments for technology transfer and technical assistance which, as the studies made in Colombia and other parts of Latin America have shown, are subject to many abuses by the transnationals and the 'free' suppliers of technology.

Although most modern technology is controlled by the large TNCs, there is a doubt as to whether these technologies are the most suitable for countries with the development level of the Andean Group. The alleged monopolistic technology concentration in the hands of USTNCs has not been thoroughly analysed. Not only are there alternative technologies in other parts of the world, but the information at hand also suggests that many owners and suppliers of technology in Western Europe and in Japan show more willingness than large USTNCs to adapt technology to the conditions of developing countries(15). The coordination of the control of declared payments for technology should be followed by the search within the Andean Common Market for alternative technologies, if only with the purpose of increasing its negotiating power with TNCs.

(3) The parallel task would be to try to coordinate national legislations on patents and industrial propriety initially drawn up at a time when nobody in Latin America was aware of their direct effect on the cost of imported technology.

In some cases, for instance the chemical and pharmaceutical industry, perhaps it would be worthwhile considering the joint regional cancellation of patent rights whenever the products fall into the category of 'public goods'. It might be useful to study the experiences in this field of Italy, Venezuela and other countries.

(4) The complete restriction of access by foreign subsidiaries to local public as well as private financial resources for the purposes of financing their local investment costs and the coordinated regulation of access by the same companies to local financing for their working capital might be considered.

This second task is particularly difficult since the financing of working capital does not necessarily have to take the shape of direct bank credit. The companies may obtain indirect financing through their local suppliers by extending the time limit for payments for local goods and services according to TNC global financial needs. Given the possibility of the evasion of credit restrictions of this kind, it would be counterproductive to introduce draconian measures that would simply encourage such evasion.

(5) A common regime to deal with the foreign acquisition of domestic firms should be designed.

The available information on Colombia and Peru, together with data gathered by Harvard Business School on Mexico, suggests that during the period 1958-67, a growing proportion of USTNCs found that the acquisition of existing, mainly domestic firms was the best way to enter these countries. In Colombia, of the 104 subsidiaries established during that period, thirty-five were set up through the acquisition of existing local enterprises. Almost all of them (thirty-one) were in the manufacturing sector. In Peru, of the total of seventy-two new manufacturing subsidiaries, twenty-three were the result of acquisition. The Mexican case is particularly interesting since the proportion of new TNC subsidiaries which resulted from the acquisition of existing firms rose from 30 per cent in 1946-57 to over 50 per cent in 1958-67. In the second period 50 per cent (116 out of 227) of new manufacturing subsidiaries entered Mexico through the purchase of local firms. These data suggest that the phenomenon of purchases acquires growing importance with the expansion of the industrial structure of a developing country. However, the mere prohibition of purchases does not seem to lead to positive results. If not supported by other measures, the alternate route for TNCs is to set up a subsidiary in the country in order to use its financial and technological power at a later date to eliminate national competitors from the market. It is not an exaggeration to predict that the creation of the Andean Common Market will be followed by a wave of purchases of weak companies owned by nationals so that they can be used as points of entry into the subregional market.

(6) The coordination of policies towards joint ventures with the clear understanding of the countries of the region that a joint venture would have to comply with certain conditions in order to be treated preferentially in comparison to completely foreign-owned companies must be considered.

On the one hand, many so-called joint ventures in Latin America are only nominally jointly owned. On the other, the indiscriminate encouragement of joint ventures would reduce the possibility of the emergence of regional TNCs established with capital brought exclusively from the area. There is also the very sensitive legal problem of the participation of the capital owned not only by nationals but also by foreign residents of the host country. Excessively liberal treatment towards the capital of residents can offset all efforts to increase national or regional control over the joint ventures.

(7) There is a need to coordinate regionally attitudes toward foreign companies that may alternatively seek the protection of the national lists of exemptions from tariff reductions in order to maintain a dominant position in the countries in which they are established, and those companies which may try to enter the Andean market with new products.

It is hard to offer concrete proposals on the best way to act in this field. It seems, however, that if the matter is left exclusively in the hands of the national governments, which will soon face serious pressures from foreign companies of both kinds mentioned above, the most serious tensions will arise during the multilateral negotiations on the exemption lists and the liberalization of tariffs on new products not included in the programmes for sectoral industrialization.

Finally, one should insist once again that the policies to be implemented to deal with foreign investment must cover not only the possible restrictions or regulations suggested in this paper (particularly, the limitations of hidden but until now legal transfers of the profits to headquarters, the control of declared payments for technology transfer, and the modalities of access to local financing and of acquisitions of domestic firms), but also a range of incentives which the developing countries use to offer to foreign private capital, interested in local manufacturing and related activities.

Leaving aside incentives in the form of tariff protection and quantitative

234   Some Key Issues for the World Periphery

import restrictions, matters which are on the agenda of the Cartagena Agreement authorities, incentives to foreign investment can be classified in seven major groups:

(1) reimbursement of taxes on the imports of raw materials, intermediate products and capital goods;
(2) market monopolies;
(3) fiscal concessions;
(4) official grants and credits;
(5) provision of industrial infrastructure (building sites);
(6) provision of buildings for the plants; and
(7) legal guarantees.

The design of a complete common treatment for foreign investment in the dynamic sectors would have to take into account that ideally all these incentives should be subject to regional coordination. The approaches to the common treatment presented here have only dealt with points that the author considers of particular importance for the achievement of some sort of common agreement on points on which the opinions of the authorities of the Cartagena Agreement could carry sufficient weight at the national level due to the general favourable political atmosphere and the economic priorities accepted in principle in the subregion. However, due to the lack of detailed information, the paper has not dealt with important points such as fiscal concessions, the provision of infrastructure and of physical facilities for future plants, and legal guarantees. It is in this area that there may begin a fierce race to attract foreign investment and urgent social cost-benefit studies are needed at national and regional level, backed up by detailed studies of prevailing legal structures.

Perhaps in these circumstances one should insist that the countries of the Andean Group commit themselves to freezing the level of investment incentives laid down in the respective legislation for a period of two years. Thus, the early agreements on a common treatment that could be achieved within the Cartagena Agreement would represent merely the first stage of the negotiation of a more comprehensive common treatment. At the later stage an attempt would be made to harmonize remaining parts of the treatment, something which - frankly speaking - would be impossible if member states reserve to themselves the right to take unilateral measures in many fields indirectly affecting foreign investment in the Andean region.

NOTES

(1)   Published originally in Spanish in Helio Jaguaribe, Aldo Ferrer, Miguel S. Wionczek and Theotonio Dos Santos, La dependencia político-económica de América Latina, Siglo XXI S.A., Mexico, 1969, pp. 111-46, and reproduced in this volume (Chapter 9).

(2)   For further details, see Raymond Vernon, 'Multinational Enterprise and the Nation State: Project Report from the Harvard Business School, Journal of Common Market Studies (Oxford), Vol. 8, No. 2, December, 1969.

(3)   John W. Vaupel and Joan P. Curhan, The Making of International Enterprise, Harvard Business School, Cambridge, Mass., 1969. The study covers 187 USTNCs engaged principally in manufacturing activities and representing 80 per cent of total U.S. direct investment in manufacturing outside of the United

States and Canada.

(4) These sales patterns are very similar to those found throughout Latin America. According to the U.S. Commerce Department, sales by U.S. subsidiaries in the region as a whole were concentrated in the post-war period in four areas, in decreasing order of importance: chemical and related products, transport equipment, processed foods, and electrical equipment. They represented two-thirds of all local sales of U.S. manufacturing subsidiaries.

(5) While differences may be due to the reinvestment of profits from manufacturing activities in other sectors, there are no data on this subject.

(6) Insisting that the profitability of U.S. manufacturing investments in Latin America is lower than in other regions, a study of the Council of the Americas (Herbert K. May, The Effects of United States and Other Foreign Investment in Latin America, New York, 1970) declares that the acceleration of U.S. investment in Latin American manufacturing which occurred during the sixties reflected 'the basic faith in the future of Latin America' on the past of the large U.S. corporation. No comments are needed on this point.

(7) The Motivation and Flow of Private Foreign Investment, Palo Alto, Calif., 1961.

(8) Herbert K. May, op. cit.

(9) For unknown reasons, the U.S. Commerce Department stopped publishing these data after 1964.

(10) Corporación de Fomento de la Producción, Comportamiento de las principales empresas extranjeras acogidas al D.F.L. 258, Publication Number 9-A/70, Santiago, May, 1970.

(11) For a description of the DFL 258/60, see Sergio Nicolau, La inversión extranjera directa - Caso ALALC, México, 1968, pp. 126-7.

(12) For details on the European case, see David B. Zenoff, 'Remitance Policies of the U.S. Subsidiaries in Europe', The Banker, London, May, 1967. For developments in Latin America in the first half of the sixties, see O.A.S. IA-ECOSOC, El financiamiento externo para el desarrollo de América Latina, CIES/1382, Port-of-Spain, June, 1969.

(13) The author was impressed by the observation made in one of the studies on Colombia by Constantine Vaitsos, that even the chemical and pharmaceutical companies whose implicit earnings from 'technology transfer' represent the multiple of their declared earnings defend to the bitter end the amount of direct payments for technology purchases not for the purpose of increasing their profits but to take away the attention of the official negotiators from the key problem of gains originated in the overcharging for imported inputs. In Mexico the opposite occurs. Foreign automotive companies, for example, 'give away' technology to their subsidiaries, but they do their best to conceal their policies on the inter-company pricing of imported parts. Thus they achieve the dual purpose of creating the image of a benevolent foreign enterprise and of insuring very considerable global profits which the country they operate in finds difficult to identify.

(14) On this point it would be helpful if the Andean countries and the

Cartagena Agreement authorities were to watch very closely the technical work developed within the LAFTA, at the periodic meetings of the Directors of Internal Taxation.

(15) Numerous interviews by the author with top executives of United States manufacturing subsidiaries in Mexico indicate that they find a way to adapt their technology to Mexican conditions and tend to lower their costs only when faced with the danger of competitors from other continents entering the market.

CHAPTER 12
Pacific Trade and Development Cooperation with Latin America*

IN THE late sixties in the wake of the highly disappointing advance of regional economic integration schemes in Latin America and Southeast Asia, the concept of Pacific basin cooperation emerged simultaneously in various major countries bordering on the Pacific Ocean in Asia and in the western hemisphere, particularly in Japan, Australia and Canada.

It led to a long series of Pacific Trade and Development Conferences, sponsored by political scientists and economists of the Pacific area countries and held consecutively in Tokyo (1968), Hawaii (1969), Sydney (1970), Ottawa (1971), Tokyo (1973), Mexico City (1974), Auckland (1975), Bangkok (1977), San Francisco (1978) and Seoul (1980). These periodic academic gatherings dealt extensively with such specific aspects of economic relations within the region as resource endowment, industrialization, foreign trade, foreign investment, the labour market and technology transfer. Moreover, several separate Pacific conferences were held under the bilateral auspices of Chile and Australia. Finally, the Pacific Basin Economic Council, a forum for informal meetings of businessmen representing the major Pacific industrial countries was established in the late sixties.

On the occasion of the Pacific Conference held in Viña del Mar, Chile in September 1970 and again at a Seminar on the End of Hemispheric Isolation in Latin America at Williamsburg, Va., 1976, I presented a Latin American view on trade, investment and technology issues involved in the proposed expansion of economic cooperation within the Pacific basin. Furthermore, I had a chance to participate actively in five Pacific Trade and Development Conferences and was in a way responsible for organizing one held in Mexico City in 1974 on the subject of technological exchanges in the Pacific region. Since an attempt is made in this paper to evaluate the present state of and prospects for Pacific trade and development schemes, it may be helpful to use my 1970 and 1976 analyses as a point of departure(1).

---

*This paper was published in <u>Asia Pacific Community</u> (Tokyo), No. 9 (Summer 1980).

In the early seventies the Pacific region still seemed to belong to the realm of geo-political and strategic concepts rather than, at least as far as Latin America was concerned, to exist as a politico-economic community, although some trade, investment and technology links started developing after 1965 between the southern republics, the western hemisphere and the Far East, Oceania and Canada. Commercial exchange between Latin America and the rest of the region (excluding the United States) was still, however, in the mid-seventies of marginal importance to all parties concerned. While it did not exceed 10 per cent of Latin America's foreign trade, about two-thirds of the commodity flows represented trade with Japan and another 30 per cent with Canada.

Trade between Latin America and the rest of the Pacific region between 1965 and 1975 involved the following commodity groups: Latin America exported primary commodities - minerals from Chile and Peru, mainly to Japan; oil from Venezuela, and bauxite and alumina from the Caribbean to Canada; and tropical agricultural products, including coffee and cotton, from Brazil, Central America and Mexico principally to Japan and Canada. Moreover, some products of Latin America's temperate zone agriculture, such as grains and meat, were exported to Japan and smaller Far Eastern countries.

In the opposite direction, there were Latin American imports of wool and tin from Australia and Malaysia, respectively; of capital goods by major Latin American countries from Japan and Canada; and of consumer durables and non-durables by the less developed Latin American republics, particularly Central American nations, Panama and Venezuela, from Japan, and, in negligible quantities from Hong Kong.

As one might have expected, Latin American trade with New Zealand, and the Far East and developing Asian countries (South Korea, Taiwan, the Philippines, Indonesia and Thailand), and with China and Soviet Asia was practically non-existent, although in the mid-seventies some Latin American countries (Brazil, Mexico, Peru and Venezuela) established trade relations with China. In brief, the major part of the slowly expanding commercial exchange between Latin America and other countries located within the Pacific basin (excluding the United States) involved almost exclusively Japan and Canada and conformed to the overall composition patterns of Latin American foreign trade.

In the first half of the seventies I thought that the general lack of knowledge in Latin America of economic, resource and technological developments taking place in Australia, Canada, Japan and lesser Western Pacific countries was the single most important obstacle to the expansion of the Latin America's tenuous economic, financial and technological relations with other parts of the Pacific region. This lack of information seemed to make very difficult any prognosis about the future economic <u>rapprochement</u> between Latin America and the rest of the region whose role in the world economy was increasing very swiftly. It was clear at that time - at least to me - that, judging by rates of GNP growth, the expansion of their external trade and technological progress, Japan, Australia and Canada together were the third most dynamic subsector of the world economy after the European socialist bloc and the European Economic Community (EEC). Moreover, taken individually, Japan, the fastest growing industrial economy in the world, occupied second place in terms of GNP after the United States.

AUSTRALIA AND CANADA

In comparison with Japan, in view of their relatively small populations, both Canada and Australia seemed to be second-class industrial powers. But their resource bases expanded in the period 1965-75 at an unprecedented pace. Moreover, these two smaller developed Pacific economies grew over the same period at a considerably higher average rate than the economies of most older, free market industrial countries in the North Atlantic area. Their growth, both in terms of GNP and of newly discovered natural resources, prompted the two leading members of the British Commonwealth in the Pacific region to search for new international economic alignments, particularly as a result of their somewhat disappointing experiences with traditional economic and financial links with North Atlantic countries and with United States - and United Kingdom - based transnational corporations (TNCs) that increasingly dominated both the extractive and the manufacturing industries of Australia and Canada.

What I found in 1965-75 in the three Pacific countries, Japan, Canada and Australia, was the common denominator of economic nationalism, present in Japan since its opening to the West a century ago. It was gaining strength in Canada, which lives in the shadow of the power of the United States, and was emerging in Australia, whose historical dependence on British capital and technology was broken by the forceful entry of United States competition. The impression that economic nationalism was gaining the upper hand in these two lesser Pacific powers seemed to be confirmed also by most of the economic development studies and reports that appeared from the late fifties in Canada and after 1965 in Australia.

According to these studies, political and intellectual élites, supported by large sectors of public opinion in Canada and Australia, were showing growing concern with the impact of transnational corporate structures - horizontally and vertically integrated, concentrated in the extractive industries and manufacturing, and operating worldwide - upon the national development of Australia and Canada. Consequently, these two countries were searching for ways and means to impose national economic and social objectives upon those transnational giants without necessarily closing the door to capital and technology under TNC control.

If Japan did not complain about the real, potential, or presumed dangers of foreign-based transnational corporations, it was because Japanese policies diverged fundamentally from neo-classical trade and investment theories. Japan never really opened itself to foreign capital. Two of the factors that contributed to the Japanese economic miracle of the post-war period were the country's ability to mobilize an extremely high internal saving rate (up to one-third of national income) and its ability to adapt to Japanese conditions technology developed elsewhere, while rejecting the traditional proposition that the only way to develop a free market economy was through the package transfer of capital/technology/managerial skill involving the direct participation of foreign private investment.

After the Meiji period, Japan developed its own capital and managerial resources base. It copied foreign technology first, and started buying it selectively afterward - at internationally competitive prices. Only in the seventies did Japan open itself to the outside world by lifting slowly, and again selectively, its restrictions upon the entry of foreign private capital. That policy change, however, did not seem to endanger Japan's economic independence, since it occurred only when Japan became an increasingly important exporter of its own capital, technology and managerial skills, not only to neighbouring countries but also to other developing parts of the world, including the Soviet Union and China.

The demand for raw materials in what might be called the giant Switzerland of the Far East grew by leaps, and Japan's attempts to diversify its natural resource availability overstepped the boundaries of the Asian continent, which had been providing Japan with practically all its primary commodities before and during the Second World War. Already by the late sixties, Australia had become Japan's principal supplier of raw materials, and the two countries' interdependence was increasing. In iron ore, alumina, copper, coal, titanium, zinc, wool, sugar and meat Australia was by far the biggest single exporter to the Japanese market. Moreover, there was little doubt that Australia would become, during the late seventies, the world's largest exporter of a whole range of minerals, particularly of iron ore, aluminium, coal, copper, lead and zinc.

VARIED PERFORMANCES

If the rate of discovery of natural resources in Canada was less impressive than that in Australia, it was by no means negligible in the period 1965-75. Whereas Canadian GNP and foreign trade were growing more slowly than those of Japan and Australia, one would suspect that this was not necessarily due to the resource base which was enormous, but to other factors. The most important was perhaps Canada's continuing dependence upon slowly growing primary commodity markets, such as the United States and Great Britain, and its difficulties in accelerating its manufactured exports because of restrictive policies followed by the large number of United States-owned industrial TNCs that played and continue to play a decisive role in the manufacturing sector and were the major source of technology for Canada.

The structure of the Canadian economy, however, underwent a rapid change in 1965-75. Between 1950 and 1965, a technological revolution took place in agriculture, with the proportion of people working in that sector falling from 21 to 9 per cent, while farm output doubled. Moreover, somewhat belatedly Canada decided to undertake a major scientific and technological effort, largely financed by the public sector. Federal expenditures on research and development, which were expanding at an average annual rate of 10 per cent in the sixties, increased even more in the early seventies.

Thus, in the Pacific area, Latin America faced in the early seventies three major countries (Japan, Australia and Canada) engaged in constant efforts to expand their resource bases (by worldwide joint mining and other ventures for resource-poor Japan), improving their intake of technology (divorced from foreign private capital in Japan), and strengthening their domestic research and development base through generous state support. Despite the worldwide economic recession of the early seventies, all three enjoyed fairly rapid economic growth throughout the mid-seventies. Such a performance would not have been possible without the presence in Japan, Australia and Canada of well-designed educational systems, particularly on the middle technical level, which permitted both a continuous increase in labour productivity and the relatively easy shift of labour from agriculture to more research and development (R&D)-based productive sectors. The impressive economic growth of the three countries proves that the quality of education, technology and resource exploration, together with the abundance of managerial skills, whose presence was patent in Japan and was steadily growing in Australia and Canada, are more important tools for the achievement of growth than the traditional economic policy followed by the earlier industrializers, such as the United States and Great Britain.

It seemed in 1970 and again in 1976 that the pace of human and physical resource development in the major countries of the Pacific area, accompanied by rapid economic growth, would have a healthy demonstration effect on Latin America and help to destroy myths circulating there about the limited availability of natural resources throughout the world; about the impossibility of acquiring technology from outside other than in neatly-organized packages of capital/technology/managerial skills, sold to Latin America by United States transnational corporations; and about the allegedly secondary relevance for rapid growth of major educational and R&D efforts. Consequently, I thought at that time, first, that Latin America would learn a lot of useful lessons from Japan, Australia and Canada, and second, that Latin America's bargaining power vis-à-vis transnational corporations, the major holders of capital, technology and managerial skills, might be strengthened by the diversification of Latin America's commercial, financial and technological ties with the three major Pacific powers other than the United States. I was aware that the actual evolution of these new Pacific basin relations would depend upon a definition, first, of what these three major powers could offer Latin America and what, in turn, Latin America could offer Japan, Australia and Canada. At the risk of separating artificially what are traditionally components of a single package, I treated in my 1970 and 1976 papers the future of intra-Pacific relations under five separate headings: development aid, trade, private capital, technology and information.

DEVELOPMENT AID

In spite of the fact that, together with Scandinavia, Japan, Australia and Canada belonged in the early seventies to a small group of advanced countries whose contributions to official development aid flows, if measured by the aid-GNP ratio, had been increasing much faster than those of the United States, the United Kingdom and most countries of continental Europe, and that, measured in absolute terms, the net flow of resources from Japan, Australia and Canada to developing areas under official development assistance increased from US $240 million in 1960 to over $2000 million in 1975, I was somewhat pessimistic in respect to development aid prospects of these three major countries.

By 1975 it seemed that Latin America could not count on a considerable increase in official financial aid from Japan, Canada and Australia for various reasons. Most of Japan's public capital and technical assistance continued to flow to its Asian neighbours, followed as a rule by considerable amounts of export credit and private capital investment. No substantial change in the distribution patterns of rapidly-growing Japanese official capital aid could be expected because, as is the case of most advanced countries, Japanese development aid has two major objectives: the widening of access to additional primary resources and the creation of new export markets.

The increase of Australian official development aid prior to 1975 was due mainly to the urgent need to support the newly independent New Guinea-Papua, which at that time absorbed 70 per cent of Australia's total capital aid and technical assistance. Since the rest of Australian development aid went to South and Southeast Asia under the Colombo Plan, continuation of the trend was expected.

While the distribution of Canada's growing official aid reflected less immediate economic and political aims than those of Japan and Australia, some two-thirds of Canadian development aid and technical assistance was channeled to India, Pakistan and Sri Lanka. Other priority areas were ex-British African nations (particularly Nigeria and Ghana) and the former British West Indies, where Canada has strong commercial and financial interests. These areas in turn provided Canada with a considerable part of its demand for tropical agricultural commodities.

TRADE RELATIONS

In 1970 and 1976 it was particularly difficult to project future Pacific trade trends from past performance in spite, or perhaps because, of the rapid growth of the three major economies (Japan, Australia and Canada) and of dynamic changes in the patterns of intra-Pacific trade. Much of the new trade in the case of Australia was due to the spectacular expansion of the Japanese economy. Since trade between Australia and Canada, on the one hand, and Japan, on the other, was growing rapidly, there was no reason in principle why trade between the Latin America Pacific countries and their more developed counterparts in the region could not expand as well. The obstacles, however, were formidable and they could not be reduced to distance, the traditional single major obstacle to trade everywhere except in the case of Japan.

While the resource-base 'explosion' was taking place in the Western Pacific (Australia, New Guinea, Indonesia and elsewhere) and in Canada, economic nationalism in Latin America was intensifying, deeply affecting attitudes toward exploitation, management, and international commercialization of raw material, particularly mineral resources. Under these conditions it seemed very difficult to foresee the expansion of traditional exchange of Latin American materials for manufactures from Australia and Canada, countries well-endowed in raw materials, or even for industrial goods produced in raw-material-hungry Japan, unless these three major Pacific industrial powers would decide to invest heavily in export-oriented industrial joint ventures in Latin America. The rapid growth of trade between Brazil and Japan seemed to point in that direction but it proved to be exceptional.

If Brazil allowed its minerals to be shipped in growing quantities to the Japanese market in the seventies, it was because Japan, in association with local interests, invested in Brazilian mining and industry. The presence of Japanese enterprises, not only in the mineral sector but also in export-oriented manufacturing, made it politically palatable for Brazil to accept that a considerable part of its natural wealth was exported with little processing. I postulated both in 1970 and 1976 that other Latin American countries would like to see the kind of foreign investment strategy followed by Japan in Brazil applied to them as well. I thought that in the longer run this might occur, particularly if the Latin American countries neighbouring the Pacific Ocean were integrated into a common market. In the early seventies, however, the industrial and technological backwardness and the size of their individual economies were making the Andean countries less attractive than Brazil for new foreign investment.

Finally, it seemed that in some more distant future Japanese policy patterns that included technical assistance to state-owned heavy industries, and even participation in joint investment ventures with local state enterprises, might be adopted by Canada and perhaps by Australia, helping the establishment of a new intra-Pacific trade relationship in the framework of economic nationalism. I will try to explain later why my expectations were not fulfilled.

NEW MODES OF PRIVATE CAPITAL INVESTMENT

Given poor prospects for official aid from the developed Pacific economies to Latin America in the mid-seventies, and under the assumption that Latin America would finally realize that financing the import bill through expensive export credits only postpones the day of financial judgement, two avenues were left for trade expansion between Latin America and Japan, Australia and Canada: increased purchases of Latin American primary commodities by major Pacific countries, and the appearance of non-United States Pacific region capital in Latin America. This capital would have to enter Latin America in the form of joint ventures for producing raw materials for the investing countries and manufacturing goods for third markets. These measures seemed both in 1970 and 1976 the only solution acceptable to all parties, and offered a strong medium-term stimulus to the growth of intra-Pacific trade and of the Latin American economies.

Japan, the most innovative economy of all, took the first steps along this route in the early seventies. Since the Far Eastern industrial superpower was conscious of Latin America's importance as a resource base and potential export market, the number of Japanese ventures in Latin America mining and manufacturing was on the increase throughout the last decade. While all Japanese official resources going to Latin America until 1970 took the form of export credits, Japanese private direct investment in the region had been increasing albeit slowly after 1960. Already in the mid-sixties Japanese private investment in Latin America represented close to one-third of total Japanese private investment abroad, a larger proportion than in Southeast Asia, presumably because of earlier rapid Japanese pre-empting of attractive investment opportunities in that part of Asia and the persistence of war conditions in Indo-China.

Japanese direct investments in Latin America, which reached a total of perhaps US $1200 million by the end of 1972 and jumped to over $2000 million in 1975, took three major forms: (1) participation in the equity capital of new enterprises mainly in mining and manufacturing management; (2) credits for the acquisition of capital equipment and technology by local enterprises, a technique followed in Latin American extractive industries with repayment taking the form of discounts on the prices of minerals produced for export to Japan; and (3) direct private investment in enterprises (land acquisition for Japanese agricultural emigrants in Brazil) fully owned by Japanese interests. As Japanese sources stated in the late sixties, while the 'aim of investments in Latin America extractive industries is to assure the supply of mineral resources needed by Japanese industries' that of manufacturing investment is 'to promote Japanese exports through assistance to new industrial enterprises interested in the use of Japan-made complete plants, capital goods, raw materials and intermediate goods; in this way Japan is able to protect its participation in export markets or to open new ones'(2). Most investment in Latin American manufacturing was concentrated in the seventies in the automotive and steel industries, although some Japanese investments were made in chemicals and other non-durables, such as textiles, in Central America.

SKIWP - Q

Moreover, the large Japan-based transnational corporations appeared in growing numbers in Latin America as contractors for state-owned projects, particularly steel mills, oil refineries and port facilities. The number of Japanese private missions interested in surveying resources and eventually exploiting them, preferably in joint ventures, also rose. Brazil, Chile. Peru and after 1976 Mexico seemed to offer particular attractions to Japan. Thus Japanese interests in Latin America increased steadily, involving relatively small outlays of foreign capital, sales of technology, capital goods, technical assistance, and the export of newly-exploited raw materials and energy sources to Japan.

The same could be said about Canadian investment, which originally entered Latin America in the first quarter of this century, mainly in public utilities. Latin America was in the mid-seventies the single largest area of Canadian direct private investment abroad. In addition to public utilities, Canadian private investment was concentrated in banking and mining in the Caribbean and Central America and in mining and related metal processing in the Andean countries. The picture over the 1965-75 period was, however, one of disinvestment in public utilities and some expansion in mining, manufacturing and ancillary activities, particularly in wood and paper industries. It was estimated that the flow of direct investment from Canada to Latin America accounted for only a fraction of total Canadian capital exports, which went mainly to the United States and Great Britain.

While by 1975 there were no Australian investments in Latin America, New Zealand occasionally granted the area medium-term credits aimed at financing exports of its agricultural surplus. Since Australia, New Zealand and Canada are capital-importing countries, it was difficult to expect very large flows of their private capital to Latin America even in the long run, unless such investments were necessary to balance trade with that part of the Pacific region.

TECHNOLOGY TRANSFERS

The final question I asked myself both in 1970 and 1976 was what were Latin America's chances for importing untied technology from Japan, Australia and Canada given, first, that the prospects for the inflow of capital to Latin America from the major non-United States countries of the Pacific region other than Japan were limited, and, second, that increasing dependence upon transfers of capital/technology/managerial skills in the traditional package form, involving full or majority control of the package by the capital exporters, was not the best political and economic solution for Latin America.

Endowed with growing economic power, Japan, which itself mastered the art of importing technology separately from capital, did not seem willing to part with its technology without capital and managerial participation. Complaints heard in Southeast Asia about the 'invasion' of Japanese transnational corporations echoed those of Latin America, Australia and Canada about the growing predominance of United States transnational corporations in their respective economies. Yet Latin America's limited experience with Japan between 1960 and 1975 suggested that both Japanese public and private sector attitudes toward providing Latin America with capital, technology and management might be somewhat more flexible than those that seem to prevail in the United States corporate world. Such flexibility was hoped for owing to the fact that Japan did not consider it worthwhile to commit too much in the way of capital resources to a group of developing countries, considered of secondary importance, on the other side of the Pacific basin. Whatever the reasons, the Japanese performance seemed to coincide to some extent with the exigencies of Latin American economic nationalism. Moreover, because of the tradition of adapting foreign technologies in Japan, Japanese technology looked to be more adaptable to Latin American conditions than United States originated technology.

Whatever advantages might accrue to Latin America from an additional trickle of official development aid from the major Pacific countries other than the United States, from the creation of new intra-Pacific trade, from the entry of foreign private capital from the advanced countries of the Pacific region under conditions more flexible than those traditionally prevailing in the hemisphere, and from some injections of technology originating in Japan, Australia and Canada with or without capital participation of these countries, I thought in the first half of the seventies that very tangible benefits could be had just from greater awareness of the Pacific region on the part of Latin American economic policymakers, technical experts and social scientists. I based such expectations on the fact that the three major Pacific countries had found it possible, unlike Latin America, to design and implement policy measures that were diminishing to manageable proportions frictions between the owners of foreign capital and technology, on the one hand, and the host countries, on the other.

In brief, while I envisaged some possibilities for opening Latin America to the Pacific market for capital and technology, it seemed that perhaps the most urgent and most beneficial step for Latin America in the short run might have been to widen communication and information channels with the strangers in the Pacific basin. In brief, I expected a demonstration effect on Latin America of development strategies adopted by Japan, Australia and Canada after the Second World War and the increased trade and investment complementarity within the whole Pacific region, including Latin America.

DISAPPOINTMENT IN 1980

By 1980 most of those earlier modest predictions, expectations and hopes about the possible expansion of economic, financial and technological links between the major advanced Pacific countries and Latin America had proved incorrect. First, relations between Australia and Canada, on the one hand, and Latin American countries, on the other, continued extremely weak. Second, in spite of some academic and business interest in Japan in Pacific basin cooperation, Japanese-Latin American relations continued to stagnate in the face of the very impressive expansion of Japanese trade, capital flows and technological exports towards other parts of the Pacific region, Southern Asia and the Middle East.

This stagnation cannot be explained exclusively by the onset of worldwide economic stagnation in 1974, as witnessed by the general slowdown of the growth rate in advanced market economy and socialist countries. The Pacific basin economies as a whole, and particularly Japan and the Asian newly-industrializing countries (NICs) - South Korea, Taiwan, Hong Kong and Singapore - registered over the preceding decade growth and trade expansion rates higher than the global averages, excluding perhaps the European socialist bloc (until 1978). Japan's steady rise as an economic, financial and political power was unrivalled. In 1978 Japan's GNP stood at 40 per cent of United States GNP, its foreign trade volume became second to that of the United States and its foreign exchange holdings became second to West Germany's. While Japanese economists might contend that the 'Japanese miracle' petered out sometime between 1956 and 1972 or that it definitely ended after the so-called 'oil crisis' of 1973-4, non-Japanese sources do not consider that country's performance disappointing at all and stress Japan's extraordinary resilience to worldwide recessionary developments.

Foreign observers have no difficulties in singling out the factors responsible for the outstanding Japanese performance: the relentless productivity drive linked to amazing technological progress; the integration of industrial with foreign trade policies permitting constant industrial modernization vis-à-vis other highly advanced countries; the conflict-free cooperation between the private and the public sector; and - last but not least - the absence of the burden of military expenditure. It seems paradoxical that this well-integrated package of self-centred 'economic nationalism' policies followed by Japan after its defeat in the Second World War, was largely responsible for its extremely limited economic and financial presence in and development impact on Latin America. While for Australia, Canada and the Asian NICs Latin America hardly existed at all, for Japan it had only marginal economic and political importance throughout Japan's rise to the status of a world economic superpower.

The figures, presented in two tables at the end of the paper, on trade flows during the period 1974-8 between Japan, on the one hand, and Latin America, Australia, Canada and the Asian developing countries, on the other, and on relative changes in the Japanese trade distribution between 1969 and 1978, support the previous statement. In very broad terms, both Japanese exports to and imports from Latin America stagnated in the seventies (even at current prices in some cases) and their share in Japanese global trade declined between 1975 and 1978 from 6.2 to 4.4 per cent in the case of exports and stayed at 3.5 per cent in that of imports. This absolute and relative stagnation cannot be explained just by the steep increase in the costs of Japan's oil imports after 1973. It reflects rather the dynamics of Japanese trade with the Pacific resource-producing developed and developing countries and Japan's political strategy and industrial development patterns. Leaving aside oil, over the period 1974-8 Japan increased both in absolute and relative terms its resource imports from the non-Latin American Pacific basin and other Asian developing market economies. It expanded very substantially also both in absolute and relative terms its industrial edports to all segments of the world economy but Latin America. In spite of the increasing oil bill, Japanese imports from Australia, Canada and the developing economies of Asia and Oceania grew from 18 per cent of total Japanese imports in 1974 to over 25 per cent in 1978. Exports to the same destination stood at 28 and 26 per cent of total Japanese exports in both years. These figures indicate that by the late seventies the economies of Asia and Oceania had become closely integrated with Japan, largely because of the 'resources explosion' in the region and the complementarity between both parties. One has evidence here that trade follows growth and not that growth originates from trade as neo-classical economists postulate.

Many factors worked against the development of sustained Japanese-Latin America relations: the distance, 'resources nationalism' in Latin America and Latin American linkages with the United States economy. While 'resources nationalism' made Latin America a difficult source of Japanese imports, its relatively advanced but unintegrated import substitution process, dominated to a considerable degree by the United States firms, made it a 'difficult' market for

Japan. Under such conditions, Latin America faced a continuous current account deficit with Japan in contrast to the steady surplus with Japan of Australia, Canada and the developing market economies of Asia and Oceania. Such a situation added to financial instability in Latin America and created obstacles to Japanese private capital flows.

JAPAN'S LATIN AMERICAN STRATEGY

Japanese trade and investment policy in Latin America was more conservative than elsewhere not only because of the region's economic nationalism and its overall political and financial instability but also because of self-centred attitudes of Japanese firms not compensated by official policy measures. Japanese strategy in Latin America, which seems perfectly correct from the viewpoint of profit maximization, can perhaps be described in the following terms: import marginally if prices and conditions are better than elsewhere, maximize exports whenever feasible with the assistance of official credit facilities, become involved in joint ventures with as little capital as possible, and keep control over technology. Such is at least the perception of business relations with Japan by most Latin American official and private sources.

It is pointed out, for example, that in spite of numerous Mexican initiatives Japanese trade and investment in that country stagnated throughout the sixties and the seventies. The Japanese showed the first signs of expansion only after Mexican oil resources were 'discovered' by Japan. Consequently, while Japanese investments in Mexico amounted in 1979 to US $180 million and equalled the accumulated value of all prior Japanese investments in that country, Japanese investment projects in Mexico for 1980-82 are reported at close to US $1000 million. It is thought in Mexico that this strong and sudden interest of Japanese manufacturing firms reflects not only the belief in the promising prospects for Mexico's economic growth in the near future but is also related to Japanese direct concern with diversifying its access to oil resources.

All this would suggest that while like all other industrialized countries Japan has an economic strategy for itself, it was unable for more than a quarter of a century to elaborate either a global and mutually acceptable strategy for the developing world or, for that matter, a more limited strategy for its longer-term economic relations with Latin America. In Japanese disinterest in Latin America two factors played an important role: the Japanese success in assuring access to the growing resources in Asia and Oceania, and the wide opportunities for expanding markets for manufactures both in the North Atlantic area and in developing Asia. The protracted and deepening international economic stagnation is changing all the parameters under which Japan was able to operate successfully after the Second World War.

This is perhaps why, as it was reported from Tokyo in early 1980, Japan is engaged in seeking a new set of political and economic policies. This endeavour brings to the surface Japan's renewed political interest in the expanded concept of Pacific basin cooperation, and academic interest in the problems of the so-called Third World(3). The search for new postures has as its background Japan's concern with potential involvement in the latest phase of the conflict between the United States and the Soviet Union which threatens to destroy the delicate balance in Japan's political and economic relations with the latter and China. The search for new solutions is further complicated by the presence of two Japanese schools of thought on that country's future economic growth. One tends to embrace the idea of 'zero growth', while the other wants to assure growth through an increase in military expenditure.

Given Japan's actual economic power position, it is hard to believe that it can avoid taking major global strategic, political and economic decisions that would involve the abandonment of its post-war position to the effect that 'Japan can go it alone' by economic means under the umbrella of United States power and that what is good in the short-run for Japanese business is also good for Japan's longer-term future.

JAPAN'S FOUR OPTIONS

Four major options seem to be available to Japan. Because of its position in world economics and politics none is purely economic and all have strategic and political implications. These options are:

(1) the 'zero growth' strategy;
(2) the support of growth by increased military expenditure;
(3) expanded cooperation in the Pacific region;
(4) Japan's embracing of the proposals for restructuring the world's economy in the light of the most serious impact of the international crisis upon North-South relations.

The 'zero growth' strategy may appeal to some sectors of Japanese society, mostly intellectuals, who may wonder whether reaching United States, Swedish or Kuwaiti *per capita* income levels has any meaning in terms of social and individual welfare. It is, however, under present world conditions an unmanageable and self-defeating strategy. A steep decline in Japanese growth rates would have a most serious negative impact upon the economies and development prospects of Asian and other underdeveloped countries once one accepts that it is growth which is the engine of trade and not vice versa. Consequently, with 'zero growth' Japan could not envisage any sort of peaceful coexistence between an island of prosperity and welfare and the neighbouring Asian poor and stagnating mainland in the absence of Japanese sustained growth. This would be unacceptable. The present quandary of the world economy is largely due to the deceleration of growth rates in the advanced countries through deflationary policies which inhibit growth without being able to deal with inflation. More of the same medicine would lead to international political and economic disaster.

Growth through Japanese expanded military expenditure, appealing for obvious reasons to cold war proponents, would amount eventually to Japanese national suicide. As a conservative but enlightened European commentator put it bluntly in February 1980:

> Nearly all of Japan's Asian neighbors think that heavy Japanese rearmament in the 1980s would be the worst response to America's accusations of a 'free ride'. Japan has done infinitely more for world freedom while spending under one per cent of GNP on defence in the past 35 years than it did when spending 20 times as much in the 15 years before that. All the neighbours fear the introduction of soldiers into Japan's decision process. They recognize that Japan's unprecedented experience as an unarmed great power has been a lesson for other great powers. . . '(4).

Following this line of argument to its final conclusion, one could predict that if Japan's rearmament drive were to contribute to the outbreak of a military conflict between the United States and the Soviet Union, Hiroshima and Nagasaki would look to the survivors - if any - of the global nuclear holocaust as harmless cocktail parties. On the other hand, it is highly likely that the real purpose of pushing Japan along an armaments road has more to do with Japanese competition on the world market than with security reasons.

Expanded Pacific regional cooperation along the lines postulated in the seventies under the auspices of Pacific Trade and Development Conferences but involving more serious Latin American participation has very slim prospects of sustained success, as long as it is divorced from a global approach to international economic difficulties. Under the conditions of the 'resources explosion' (excluding oil) in the Pacific basin, the economy of that region is encountering built-in trends toward commodity surplus output, depressed real prices and speculative violent short-term commodity price swings. The international commodity picture bodes ill to the economies of developing countries burdened with excessive external indebtedness. Only economic recovery in the industrial countries and the stabilization of commodity trade can make less-developed countries (LDCs) problems more manageable. The declining absorptive capacity of developing regions, due to external debt, inflation and the shortage of development financing, makes it highly improbable that these regions, including the major NICs, can expand their markets for manufactured imports whether from Japan or other sources. The protectionist wave in the industrial world and the trade war among its major national components is accompanied by the shrinkage of markets in LDCs(5). Wherever this does not occur, the cost is the increase in external private debt. While in principle, one could still have in 1980-1 some hopes for expanded trade, investment and technology flows within the Pacific basin, they would clearly be only marginal.

The fourth but the only rational longer-term option is Japan's serious participation in restructuring the world economy. Detailed proposals to that effect have been made by the Independent Commission on International Development Issues under the chairmanship of ex-West German Chancellor Willy Brandt(6). What the Brandt Commission postulates on a world scale is a radical change in relations between industrial and underdeveloped countries that has already occurred between rich and poor people in individual advanced countries since the industrial revolution. What is more, the report - aptly entitled <u>North-South - A Programme for Survival</u> - argues that the proposed structural changes and the massive transfer of resources from rich North to poor South is in the North's interest. Since Japan became a part of the richest North in the post-war period, it should take the Brandt Commission proposals seriously if only because in the absence of a basic change in political and economic relations between the advanced and the underdeveloped world, Japan by itself with all its wealth and power will not have too bright a longer-term future. Further thinking along the lines of the proposals for global stimulation of the international economy made, for example, by Masaki Nakajima, chairman of Mitsubishi Research Institute, in 1978 is much needed in Japan and in other parts of the developed Pacific basin.

The Nakajima 'Proposition for the Global Infrastructure Fund' sees the need for a 'Global New Deal' arising both from the failure of post-war Keynesian economic policy to prevent stagnation in the North and the urgency of eradicating poverty in the South. Regarding the former, emphasis is placed upon massive global stimulation as the only viable means of sustaining growth in the context of faltering technological progress, the inflationary bias of strictly national deficit-financed stimulation efforts and the collapse of the Bretton Woods international monetary system.

Specifically, the 'Proposition' calls for a US $500 billion investment between now and the turn of the century in a series of 'super projects', such as massive solar power generation or harnessing sea currents to produce electricity, amounting to an international public works programme. The projects would aim to expand energy and food supply for developing countries. It is estimated than an annual investment of US $13 billion would result in an annual $25 billion multiplier expansion of aggregate demand. Nakajima contends that the inflationary impact of the proposal would be mitigated through the effect of the project on loosening potential tight supply constraints in the food and energy sectors. The 'Proposition' calls for joint OPEC/OECD funding with the suggested US $13 billion annual investment divided among West Germany, Japan and the United States ($5 billion), OPEC ($5 billion) and other industrial nations ($3 billion). These funds would come from public sources requiring a 30 per cent increase in official development aid from the industrialized nations. One wonders why so little has been heard lately in Japan about the Nakajima proposals whereas so much has been said about supporting economic growth via increased defence expenditure, which clearly conflicts with the ideas of Pacific basin trade and development cooperation and with Latin American views of the world.

NOTES

(1)   Miguel S. Wionczek, 'The Pacific Market for Capital, Technology and Information and its Possible Opening in Latin America', Journal of Common Market Studies (Oxford), Vol. 10, No. 1 September, 1971, and 'Latin America and the Pacific Region: Trade, Investment and Technology Issues', in Roger W. Fontaine and James D. Theberge (Editors), Latin America's New Internationalism: The End of Hemispheric Isolation, Praeger, New York, Washington and London, 1976.

(2)   Japan Economic Research Center, 'Experiences and Problems of Latin American Investments of the Private Japanese Sector', Document elaborated for the Sixth Annual Meeting of the Inter-American Economic and Social Council, Port-of-Spain, Trinidad, June, 1969.

(3)   The Pacific Basin Cooperation Study Group, Interim Report on the Pacific Basin Cooperation Concept, Tokyo, 14 November 1979.

(4)   Norman Macrae, 'Must Japan slow? A survey', The Economist (London), 23 February, 1980, p. 11.

(5)   The UNCTAD report on the world economic outlook for 1980-1 warns that the non-oil exporting LDCs as the group will have to engage in restraints on imports because of the combination of declining terms of trade and poor prospects for growth in export volumes. See UNCTAD, Interdependence of Problems of Trade, Development Finance and International Monetary System - World Economic Outlook, 1980-1981, TD/B/783, Geneva, 11 March, 1980 (mimeo.).

(6)   North-South - A Programme for Survival, The Report of the Independent Commission on International Development Issues under the Chairmanship of Willy Brandt, Pan Books, London and Sydney, 1980. See also Chapter 24, this volume.

TABLE 12.1. Japan Trade with the World, Latin America, Australia, Canada and the Developing Market Economies of Asia and Oceania, 1974-8

(US $ million)

	Imports c.i.f.						Exports f.o.b.				
	1974	1975	1976	1977	1978		1974	1975	1976	1977	1978
World	62094	57864	64504	70560	78731	World	55538	55754	67028	804700	97501
LAFTA	2052	1891	2016	2541	2501	LAFTA	3159	2685	2685	3483	3858
CACM	143	194	256	321	237	CACM	255	185	314	466	436
Cuba	442	341	50	63	106	Panama	1018	1134	1304	1328	1445
L.A.	2638	2426	2312	2915	2844	L.A.	4432	3904	4303	4877	4792
of which						of which					
Argentina	230	214	253	419	461	Argentina	443	363	233	300	200
Brazil	662	884	819	947	787	Brazil	1389	926	882	840	1252
Chile	403	258	298	327	367	Mexico	307	347	386	451	639
Mexico	309	212	248	311	356	Venezuela	400	359	563	917	771
	1604	1568	1618	2094	1971		2539	1995	2064	2508	2862
Australia	4030	4160	5358	5285	5299	Australia	1996	1740	2309	2330	2692
Canada	2666	2499	2715	2881	3182	Canada	1589	1151	1552	1708	1871
Asia and Oceania						Asia and Oceania					
LDCs*	14903	10837	14700	15428	17607	LDCs*	12773	12669	14193	17327	23398

*Excluding the Middle East.

Source: U.N. Yearbook of International Trade Statistics, 1978, Vol. I

TABLE 12.2. Distribution of Japan's Trade by Major Regions

(percentages)

	Imports c.i.f.			Exports f.o.b.		
	1969	1974	1978	1969	1974	1978
Developed market economies	53.1	41.7	41.5	52.6	47.7	47.2
LDCs	41.2	53.2	53.7	41.2	45.0	46.0
Socialist countries	5.7	5.1	4.9	6.2	7.3	6.8
US-Canada	31.7	24.7	22.8	31.4	23.3	25.8
Western Europe	9.6	8.0	9.1	10.9	11.5	13.8
Developing Asia	15.8	20.1	22.0	26.4	22.6	23.7
Middle East	12.7	24.6	26.0	3.4	6.1	10.1
Latin America (excl. Cuba)	7.0	3.5	3.5	4.0	6.2	4.4

Source: U.N. Yearbook of International Trade Statistics, 1978, Vol. I

CHAPTER 13

Transnational Corporations in Latin America: Political and Economic Problems*

INSTEAD of attempting again to offer a global overview of trade, investment and economic development in Latin America, I will concentrate on one, perhaps the most important aspect of that broad subject: the economic and political conflicts which arise from the presence of transnational corporations (TNCs) in Latin America. In view of the fact that these conflicts involve not only transnationals and host countries, but also the relations between the host countries and the home countries of the TNCs, I will try, first, to point out and define the problems and, second, to offer some constructive proposals acceptable not only to Latin American countries but to others in which transnationals operate, in order to find a peaceful solution to such conflicts.

It seems that nowadays there is agreement throughout the world that not only do conflicts between TNCs and host countries exist but also that the intensity of such conflicts will increase in the near future. Therefore, some action is needed to defuse them. In a speech on relations between the United States and Latin America, delivered in Houston, Texas on 1 March 1975, the United States Secretary of State, Henry Kissinger, mentioned TNCs as one of the key problems of the hemisphere. In the fall of 1974 a senior economist from the Brookings Institution, Fred Bergsten, ventured an opinion that the possibility of an international conflict around the twin issue of TNCs and national interests could, in the near future, become a central problem of world politics and economics. In Latin America and the rest of the developing world a growing number of policymakers and their advisers and public opinion makers has been expressing similar concern.

Given the magnitude of concern, disagreement still exists between the main TNCs' home countries and not only the developing host countries, but developed host countries as well, with regard to the origin and the nature of these conflicts and the way they should be dealt with. Consequently, TNCs have become the subject of detailed studies and international debates - at the United

---

*This paper was originally delivered as the 1975 Christian A. Herter Memorial Lecture, School for Advanced International Studies, Johns Hopkins University, Washington, D.C. in March 1975, and published in Spanish in Comercio Exterior (México), Vol. 25, No. 4, April, 1975.

Nations, both in New York and Geneva; at the OECD in Paris; and within the recently broken-off 'new dialogue' between the United States and Latin America, in Washington. In all these debates the host countries and many independent experts have directly or by implication postulated the urgent need for drawing up new 'rules of the game' for TNCs, be they in the form of 'rules of behaviour', 'guidelines' or a 'code of conduct'.

In 1974, after the UN Group of Eminent Persons made public a report on the effects of TNCs on development and international relations, the UN Economic and Social Council established the Commission on Transnational Corporations, with the purpose, among others, of making recommendations that could eventually lead to the drafting of a code of conduct applicable to TNCs. One of the purposes of the code would be to protect the interests of the host countries, especially the developing ones. One should add that the United States, the largest home country of TNCs, expressed the most serious reservations about the recommendations of the UN report and its basic assumptions. Apparently, the United States did not share the report's opinion concerning the essentially antagonistic nature of relations between TNCs and host countries, especially in those parts of the developing world where TNC economic power has a very serious impact upon relatively weak sovereignty. It also seems that the United States did not accept the position of the majority of the UN Group of Eminent Persons, who proposed that governments and the international community correct this inequity through measures aimed at increasing the negotiating power of host developing countries <u>vis-à-vis</u> TNCs.

The debate on TNCs that started at the OECD at the beginning of the seventies was suspended for more than two years, and only under pressure from certain European countries and some former British dominions, which act both as host and home countries of TNCs, was it reopened. Since the matter is under consideration at the OECD at the time of writing, it seems premature to speculate on the shape of an eventual agreement among all OECD member countries concerning possible international regulation of TNCs. However, there are reasons to believe that the differences within the OECD with regard to the perception of underlying conflicts may be bigger than expected.

It seems that in the so-called 'new dialogue' between the United States and Latin America and the Caribbean a stalemate has been reached on TNCs. The United States position was set forth by the Secretary of State in his Houston speech in the sense that the United States was prepared to accept:

(1) drawing up a declaration of principles which would regulate the treatment of TNCs and the transfer of technology;

(2) creating intergovernmental systems which would arbitrate investment disputes and take care of problems arising among governments from such disputes;

(3) establishing new measures of cooperation to deal with legal and jurisdictional conflicts relating to TNCs; and

(4) encouraging private enterprises to offer contributions, considered vital to Latin America, in ways that conform to the political and economic needs of the host countries.

The Latin American position on TNCs was elaborated in detail in January 1975 in Washington, just before the 'new dialogue' was broken off as a consequence of the inclusion in the United States Trade Act of 1974 of commercial sanctions against Venezuela and Ecuador because of their membership of OPEC.

Latin America's official spokesman in the 'new dialogue' did not share the United States viewpoint regarding the need for new intergovernmental systems to solve investment disputes. Moreover, the region wished to go beyond a simple declaration of principles which would regulate the treatment of TNCs and considered that the new cooperation measures should take the form of an international agreement in which a coherent set of rules of conduct for TNCs would be spelled out. Finally, the Latin Americans postulated that the general principles covering transnationals, included in the UN Charter of Economic Rights and Duties of the States, must constitute the basis of hemispheric relations in that field.

Article 2(b) of the Charter declares that each state has the right:

> . . . To regulate and supervise the activities of transnational corporations within its national jurisdiction and to take measures to ensure that such activities comply with its laws, rules and regulations and conform with economic and social policies. Transnational corporations shall not intervene in the internal affairs of a host State. Every State should, with full regard for its sovereign rights, cooperate with other States in the exercise of the rights set forth in this sub-paragraph;

Latin American concern over the adverse political and economic consequences of TNCs for the host and home countries and over the unequal distribution of economic costs and benefits of their operations were the background to the 'new dialogue' and the adoption of the UN Charter of Economic Rights and Duties of the States. The Latin American countries, while arguing for the inclusion of TNCs in the agenda of the 'new dialogue', in the fall of 1973 defined their position in the following terms:

> There is a deep concern in the Latin American region over transnational corporations which intervene in the internal affairs of the host countries and attempt to evade national legislation and the jurisdiction of national courts. Transnational corporations constitute a positive element in Latin American development as long as they respect the sovereignty of the host countries and adjust themselves to their development plans and programs.

> Latin America considers it necessary that the United States cooperates to surmount the consequent difficulties or frictions and to avoid those which might arise from the conduct of the transnational corporations that violate the principles established herein.

The 'new dialogue' debates clarified a number of substantive points on the general Latin American position, particularly the following:

(1) the problems which derive from the activities of TNCs in the host country are not limited to the hemisphere but are of an international character;

(2) since the controversial subjects are not only economic, but political as well, they must be dealt with simultaneously;

(3) these subjects do not lend themselves to bilateral agreements between host countries and TNCs; like other foreign investors, the TNCs must accept sovereignty, the legal systems and the jurisdiction of the host countries,

and the host and the home countries must negotiate certain 'rules of conduct' which the TNCs would obey;

(4) the home countries must offer guarantees to the host countries that the 'rules of conduct' agreed upon will be adhered to by the TNCs.

The wide gap concerning the 'rules of conduct' between the viewpoints of the United States and Latin America is clear. The United States considers that the problems are exclusively of a hemispheric nature; it adopts the position that conflicts and difficulties are mainly, if not totally, economic; it insists that intergovernmental mechanisms be established to solve disputes concerning investments; and even though it admits the joint responsibility of the United States and the Latin American host countries for drafting 'principles of conduct' applicable to TNCs, it takes the position that United States power over United States-based TNCs is so limited that at its best the United States could pledge itself to use its persuasive capacity with respect to the implementation of the agreed 'principles of conduct'.

The gap is still wider when one examines Latin American viewpoints more closely. According to Latin Americans, the 'rules of conduct' drawn up through joint hemispheric negotiations, and independently of their legal form, must contain principles specifying that the TNCs:

(1) will submit themselves to the laws and regulations of the country where they are established and in case of a dispute will accept the exclusive jurisdiction of the domestic courts of the host country;

(2) will abstain from any interference in the domestic affairs of the host countries;

(3) will also abstain from interfering in relations between the government of a host country and other states, as well as from disturbing these relations;

(4) will not act as a foreign political instrument for another state nor will they serve as a means of extending to the host countries the juridical dispositions of the home country;

(5) will abide by the policies, objectives and national development priorities of the host country and will contribute positively to their implementation;

(6) will provide the government of the host country with pertinent information concerning their activities to insure that they are conducted in accordance with the policies, objectives and national development priorities of such country;

(7) will carry out their operations in such a way that they result in a net entry of financial resources to the host country;

(8) should contribute to the development of scientific and technological capability of the host country;

(9) will abstain from restrictive business practices;

(10) should respect the socio-cultural identity of the host country.

Allegations that these ten principles contain unfounded implicit accusations

to the effect that TNCs have on occasion undermined economic and political
sovereignty of the developing host countries, could be refuted very easily
with the abundant evidence available in Latin America. Furthermore, it is
not necessary to argue that TNCs are bad or amoral since the problem does not
involve moral values. TNCs, in the same way as other economic units, are not,
as such, moral or amoral. They have their own goals: power, growth and
profits. In specific situations these goals may or may not coincide with
political, economical or social objectives of countries in which the TNCs do
business, or may work against national goals.

For a long time the advanced market economy countries have recognized the
possibility of conflicts between private and social objectives at the national
level. Otherwise, the public regulation of private activities, which as far
as the United States is concerned goes back to the nineteenth century, would
not make any sense. If the possibility of such conflicts did not exist, then
such government agencies as the Federal Reserve System, Securities and Exchange
Commission, Food and Drug Administration or the Justice Department Anti-Trust
Bureau would disappear for want of a role.

The problems which have arisen with TNCs, on the international level, are due
to the fact that these powerful private units function across borders; their
private objectives and goals do not necessarily coincide with those of host
countries; the distribution of costs and benefits favours the home countries
and more equal distribution is hindered by the historically conditioned
unequal relation between TNCs and the majority of the host countries' enterprises.

Without resorting to radical literature, this diagnosis can be easily substan-
tiated. The use as a counter-argument of the alleged phantom of pseudo-
nationalism growing in developing countries is of little use because conflicts
with TNCs also occur in developed countries such as Canada, France, and
Australia. Moreover, nationalism has always existed in the developed world.
The fact that it is now seen more clearly as a global phenomenon may be due
to two reasons: first, the revolution in communications has permitted advanced
societies to become aware of multiple manifestations of nationalism throughout
the world, and, second, the importance of TNCs in global production, trade
and finance constantly increases. As for their growing importance in the
world economy, abundant evidence for this is produced by the most trustworthy
sources, including voluminous and well-documented reports of the United States
Congress.

At the risk of repetition, it seems necessary to reiterate that modern TNCs
differ from traditional enterprises established in a highly-developed country
and dedicated to international investment and trade activities not only
because of the size and geographical scope of their operations. Contrary to
some definitions still in use, the majority of TNCs are more than huge companies with manufacturing units established throughout the world to minimize
production costs and to supply world markets on an integrated basis under
centralized guidance from the TNC's home country. They are no longer manufacturing, mining or banking institutions per se, but enormous conglomerates
of integrated segments horizontally and vertically. Vertical integration
means that the TNC is dedicated to activities which range not only from the
raw materials stage to the production of finished manufactures, but also
include international trade and financing under the same or a different
corporate name. Horizontal integration refers to the fact that a company
carries out manifold activities in different sectors in many countries

simultaneously. Under these circumstances, one specific activity in a given country is important for the TNC only within the limits of its global strategy. Frequently, a certain market situation or a specific activity in a developing country is of marginal importance for the transnational system. Although it is marginal and dispensable, the system will defend it in case of danger or threat because in each instance the power of the whole system and not just its economical viability is at stake.

Thus the TNC may remain in the host country or leave it; continue or suspend production; buy local merchandise or services or import them; invest financial resources or withdraw them from the branch. The TNC enjoys a great degree of independence with regard to what the host country can expect from its operations. To use a literary analogy, the host country viewed by the TNC often seems like a train station or a port of call. The trains or boats, the property of the central system, either stop or pass through, load or unload merchandise and passengers, stay some time for repairs or to refuel, all in accordance with centralized external decisions. It is not difficult to imagine why developing host countries, which during many decades made every possible effort to integrate foreign economic activities of the enclave type into their productive systems and to place them under their jurisdiction, do not calmly contemplate the recent modalities of TNC operations. Although those operations are apparently linked to local productive systems and are formally subject to domestic jurisdiction, they remain out of the reach of the host country in terms of fundamental decisions.

Some well-meaning people who express astonishment at the Latin American arguments with reference to 'rules of conduct' for TNCs may find it difficult to believe that these enterprises do not behave as 'good corporate citizens' abroad. With regard to this matter, one might immediately ask the public regulatory agencies in the United States if the TNCs abide by such rules in their own home country. Furthermore, the issue is not whether or not they behave as 'good corporate citizens' worldwide. Even though they may do so in terms of public relations, it could very well be that in other ways their action conflicts with the political, economic and social interest of host countries. The real bone of contention is the confrontation between the sovereignty of the developing host country and that of the TNC, a confrontation which constitutes an international extension of the battle between the sovereignty of any country or state and large, powerful, private production units. Anyone unwilling to accept the validity of a dictum that 'what is good for General Motors is good for the United States' should not find it difficult to accept equally that what is good for IBM, British Petroleum or Alcoa may not be so good or may even be detrimental to a weak developing country in Latin America or elsewhere.

The first Latin American proposal that TNCs must submit to the laws and regulations of the host country and, in case of a dispute, abide by the exclusive jurisdiction of the local courts, is not in any way radical. Although no one has proposed, as yet, that the activity of a Japanese TNC in the United States should abide by the rules and regulations of Japan, it seems hard for Americans to accept the Latin American position concerning the prevalence of domestic jurisdiction when speaking of the activities of branches and affiliates of United States-based TNCs. The only explanation that can be given for these conceptual difficulties is that they are rooted in a legal way of thinking inherited from the nineteenth century. At that time the world was usually divided into the 'civilized nations' and 'the rest', in such a way that international law, formulated by the former, had a universal value, with or without the consent of the others. According to this somewhat outdated school of thought, not only were all international agreements sacred, including those signed in the sight of the gunboats of a stronger 'civilized' party but all the concessions made by 'civilized governments' to their private entities operating abroad were also valid in the 'less civilized' world for the infinite duration of the agreement. All attempts by 'less civilized' governments to renegotiate existing agreements and concessions were doomed from the start because of their alleged retroactive character.

The proposal which would submit TNCs to domestic jurisdiction has been extended by Latin America to disputes which arise from the persistence of private agreements which stipulate that controversies should be submitted to the courts of the country of origin, of a third country or to international arbitration. In Latin America it is an axiom that only the state can, if it so desires, accept international arbitration and that no private party can have recourse to extra-national jurisdiction.

The second principle, which refers to the fact that TNCs must abstain from interfering in any way in the internal affairs of a host country, is based on the historical experience of Latin America with private foreign investment as well as with its modern form, the TNC. It is not an act of faith but a real fact that TNCs do interfere in the internal affairs of host countries whenever they can, and in particular whenever these countries try to change the pre-established rules for the purpose of regulating the economic activities under their jurisdiction. One can argue that all means are adequate in a case of self-defence, but doubt arises whether the actions of a state which tries to change inadequate 'rules of the game', frequently imposed from the outside, represent an act of aggression or of self-defence. This question can be answered in both ways.

The interference of a huge TNC in the domestic affairs of a country can be direct or indirect, according to the relative strength of the parties involved. The report of the UN Group of Eminent Persons, mentioned earlier, indicates that the action of TNCs in the political field may be less direct and less obvious. In the countries of origin these companies may influence foreign policy and domestic affairs thanks to their great financial strength and their connections, close at times, with high public officials. They can thus exert a lot of pressure on behalf of or against host governments, according to whether or not they receive favourable preferential treatment.

The third principle expands on the previous one. Examples are known, not only in the remote past but also in recent times, of TNCs asking the governments of the home countries to intervene with the host country, through political and economic action, on behalf of the interests of the TNC. Such 'petitions' are often accepted. These situations, handled sometimes with the help of lobbies in the home country, seem to be frequent, despite the fact that they violate the constitution of the host country which forbids a foreign investor from calling for the protection of his government as long as there exist local judicial procedures capable of solving disputes over foreign investment. Situations are known in which economic restrictions and sanctions are imposed in order to benefit TNCs. Similarly, from time to time economic pressures are applied through financial and other international agencies. United States legislation provides two instruments to be used as sanctions against the acts of host countries considered to be contrary to the interests of United States private investors: the Hickenlooper and the Gonzalez amendments to Foreign Aid Acts.

Even though it has been officially recognized that these punitive actions have serious political disadvantages, the listing of Venezuela and Ecuador among the countries excluded from preferential access to the United States market for manufactured goods because of their alleged unfriendly attitude, demonstrated by their joining the OPEC, shows that conflicts resulting from pressures of some TNCs on their home countries persist internationally. Frequently, these conflicts flare up when the host country expropriates a TNC, with resulting controversy over whether the affected foreign company received 'prompt, adequate and effective' indemnization.

The fourth principle forbids TNCs from serving as an instrument of policy of another state. It is related to the well-known matter of the extra-territorial application of the laws of the home country through prohibiting foreign subsidiaries of a TNC from carrying out activities that might be considered illegal or contrary to the national interests of the country of origin. This extra-territorial application of the national laws of the home country can create serious conflicts between a TNC and the host country, which might never have adhered to the international agreements - or which might have denounced or considered irrelevant - the international agreements upon which the action of the home country was based. Such is the case, for example, when the United States invoked the Trade with Enemy Act to avoid commercial exchange with a third party. Another case which Latin Americans keep in mind is that of the extra-territorial consequences of certain legal measures against the monopolies which directly or indirectly affect the activities of foreign subsidiaries and affiliates of United States transnationals.

The fifth principle refers to the obligation of TNCs to abide by the domestic development policies, objectives and priorities of host countries and to contribute to their implementation. This proposal brings up the issue of the actual or potential conflict between the global corporate strategy and the development goals of the developing host country. Latin American countries consider that their economic autonomy is endangered and their ability to attain development goals is weakened because of the obstacles they face when they attempt to control the activities of TNCs in respect to foreign trade, financial and capital movements, cartelization of production and distribution, human resources allocation and technology transfer, among other things. It seems that these fears are not limited to Latin America nor to other underdeveloped regions. They are also present, albeit perhaps in other forms, in some advanced countries where both laymen and experts blame TNCs for the present international economic instability, 'stagflation', and for the futility of the Keynesian 'package' of fiscal and monetary policies when faced with a grave cyclical recession occurring simultaneously in all main industrialized economies. Although there seems to be a difference of opinion about how home countries should treat TNCs, Latin Americans insist that the autonomy of a nation state has priority over the economic autonomy of a TNC.

According to the sixth principle, the economic autonomy of a developing host country cannot prevail over the global objectives of a TNC unless such a country has at its disposal sufficient information about TNC activities not only in aggregate terms but also about their activities country-by-country. The lack of such detailed and direct information hinders effective supervision and regulation of TNCs in the host country, since the country does not have access to the necessary elements to evaluate TNC activities and their fiscal, financial, foreign trade and balance-of-payments consequences. Again, Latin America's position, far from contradicting it, actually follows the line of thinking which is rapidly gaining currency in many advanced host countries.

It insists on the key importance of disclosing corporate information with the aim of establishing quantitative and objective norms to measure both the private rentability and social costs and benefits of activities carried out by those enterprises. A developing host country is at a considerable disadvantage in that respect not only because of the restrictive information policy followed by TNCs, but also due to differences between national accounting systems.

The seventh principle, which postulates that transnationals must make continuous net financial contributions to their host countries, is a consequence of the growing conviction in Latin America that such positive net transfer take place as an exception rather than as a rule. The fact that repatriated earnings often exceed new investments is not considered as proof of the previous assertion. Latin American economists know the difference between the stocks and the flows of financial resources and they reject the simplistic and incorrect way of posing the problem. What is objectionable, however, are the general accounting practices of TNCs in host countries which result in most of the profits of the system being considered as costs of branches and affiliates. In the light of extended practices of manipulating prices of imported and exported goods through transfer pricing and inflated and growing payments abroad for interest, royalties and technical services, few people in Latin America, starting with the fiscal authorities themselves, take the annual balance sheets of local TNC subsidiaries seriously. A still smaller number consider the balance-of-payments figures as a guide to the foreign exchange cost of the operations of a TNC.

Despite the existence of phony intermediaries in off-shore financial centres, which make any investigation of the subject especially difficult, it has been discovered in recent years that in many Latin American countries the unregistered earnings of TNCs, which originate from their local operations, may be many times greater than the profits registered in the annual profit-and-loss statements which may be formally correct. It should be noted that TNCs have had total success in pretending that subsidiaries' profits are below those of local enterprises because of their superb accounting ability. It is hard to put any faith in this image of low earnings, if one assumes that TNCs know how to do business at least as well as local companies, if not better. Whenever TNCs have been forced to disclose financial information with respect to technological transactions between local subsidiaries and other members of the system, it has been proven that a good share of those payments really represent profit transfers to headquarters. This is not necessarily done for fiscal purposes, but often in response to other considerations, such as the advantage for a TNC to be able to demonstrate to its shareholders that it had high profits in the home country. Whatever the reasons, the net financial contribution to the home country is usually negative.

Moreover, the foreign relations of local banking systems are such that, even in the face of all sorts of restrictions on loans to foreign companies or even in the absence of foreign banks in the host country, TNCs have easy access to local credit. This preferential access to domestic credit sources yields substantial dividends, not only in inflationary situations, when real banking interest rates in the host country tend to be close to zero or negative, but also during deflationary periods when domestic credit may be made unavailable for weaker local enterprises.

The eighth principle, regarding the need for TNCs to contribute to developing the domestic scientific and technological capacity of their host countries, is based on the increasing volume of evidence that TNCs in Latin America use technology provided from the headquarters of the global systems and do not seriously undertake any research and experimental development (R&D) in the developing host countries. Statistics on R&D expenditure of the main countries of the region show that approximately 90 per cent is financed by the governments of the respective states. It is true that the lack of R&D effort on the part of local enterprises can be explained by their technological weakness. On the other hand, TNCs are not technologically weak at all; rather, what happens is that the import of technology not only represents good business but also permits the TNC to avoid risks. Furthermore, to justify the concentration of R&D activities in the home country, TNCs use the argument of economies of scale in R&D activities.

From the standpoint of a developing host country, such technological policies have numerous disadvantages. First, since imported technology is transplanted with few or no adaptations to local conditions, it is markedly geared to the extensive use of capital in economies where this productive factor is scarce. Second, contrary to what is generally supposed, technology transfer takes place mainly within transnational systems. Therefore, its diffusion in the economy is very limited. Third, through its lack of efforts at adaptation the technology-controlling enterprise negatively affects the emergence of a local technical capability. Fourth, most of the imported technology can be classified as consumption and not production technology. This can be deduced from the fact that the two largest sellers of technology in Latin America, in terms of registered payments, are two industrial sectors dominated almost entirely by TNCs: pharmaceuticals and motor vehicles. In neither do substantial technological innovations in respect to production processes take place in Latin America. Lastly, the mechanical reproduction of imported technologies by TNCs, with the purpose of satisfying consumer preferences, supposedly autonomous but really manipulated through commercial propaganda, has serious social consequences. Therefore, the traditional transfer of technology through TNCs hardly offers unlimited benefits to Latin American host countries.

The ninth principle, related to restrictive business practices, arises since TNCs operating in Latin America frequently limit the activities of their subsidiaries in the world market through restrictions on exports, controls of distribution, and the allocation of external inputs and financial flows. These practices, followed especially by TNCs long-established in Latin America, are difficult to combat, since they generally arise from an informal network of arrangements for market division within the transnational system. Such practices not only affect the prospects for regional exports from each country, but also limit access to the markets of developed countries. Once again, outside forces interfere with the export decisions and policies of the host countries.

Finally, the tenth principle calls attention to the social consequences, disturbing but often forgotten, of the import by TNCs of commercial propaganda regarding production and consumption patterns which might be appropriate for high-income industrialized countries but which distort the socio-cultural characteristics of the poorer countries and are the cause of social tensions. These patterns also produce a feeling of alienation in vast sections of population. It is quite evident that in the search for profits without regard to social costs the TNCs are the leading agents for demonstrating consumption levels of advanced countries.

Once the Latin American position has been defined in detail, it is difficult to be optimistic about perspectives of closing the gap between 'unequal partners' through a hemispheric dialogue about TNCs. Perhaps a first ray of hope can be seen in the fact that the United States recognizes that the question of TNCs must be dealt with jointly with that of technology transfer. So far these two subjects have been treated separately in the 'new dialogue'. However, they should be considered together, in order that the United States may understand why Latin America objects to the present unsatisfactory technological role of TNCs in developing countries.

It is not easy to foresee significant progress on the main issues of the 'new dialogue'. It is difficult to imagine, first of all, that Latin America will stop pressing for some kind of international regulation of TNCs on a world level rather than just within the hemisphere. Some Latin Americans believe that the United States expects to get some kind of preferential access to the region for the United States-based TNCs, through negotiations concerning 'principles of conduct' within the scope of the 'new dialogue'. It is doubtful, however, that Latin America would accept such special treatment if one bears in mind that for every two United States TNCs there is one European or Japanese, and that the majority of Latin Americans would like to see a greater diversification of sources of private foreign investment.

Neither does it seem probable that Latin America is willing to participate in new intergovernmental systems which would intervene in investment disputes. Although such systems do already exist in international organizations, Latin America decided to abstain from joining them some time ago.

As far as new measures for cooperation are concerned, Latin America looks upon them favourably only if they take into consideration the changes taking place in the relations between industrialized and developing countries. With regard to TNCs, Latin America has already declared its position and expects that the ten basic principles will be examined with the utmost care. Contrary to some interpretations, Latin America does not wish to have a confrontation with the United States over this or any other subject. However, hopes do exist that discussions and negotiations will abandon the level of generalities and become more realistic. It is extremely difficult for Latin America to accept the validity of the general statement that: 'foreign private investment is good under any circumstances' or that 'the technological contribution of transnationals is important because these enterprises believe so'.

One would hope that perhaps one day the United States will reach the conclusion that the imposition of a certain international order upon TNCs not only responds to the interests of host countries, but also to those of the home countries. The power of TNCs not only affects the national interests of weaker host countries, but also the interests of large countries. If any evidence were needed, the so-called energy crisis of 1973-4 offered an excellent lesson to all concerned.

CHAPTER 14

Technology Transfer Through Transnational Corporations*

WORKING HYPOTHESES

THE PURPOSE of this paper is to review the state of knowledge about the transfer of technology through transnational corporations (TNCs) to Latin America and to find the evidence (or lack thereof) for a number of hypotheses contained in the paper written for the OECD in 1973 by Professor C.A. Michalet(1).

While distinguishing between internal and external transfers of technology by TNCs, Michalet notes that most of the existing evidence relates to the activities of United States-based TNCs and their technology transfers to the less-developed countries. Literature on this subject seems to be particularly abundant in Latin America where a number of country case studies has been written in recent years, mostly by local economists. These studies cover the experience of three major Latin American republics: Argentina, Brazil and Mexico, and also of some countries of the Andean Group, particularly Chile, Peru and Colombia. To the knowledge of the present writer, the volume of similar literature on less-developed countries of Asia and Africa is considerably smaller, although studies sponsored by international agencies belonging to the UN family (ECOSOC, UNCTAD, ILO) have been made in order to survey the problems of technology transfer via foreign direct investment in India, Pakistan, Nigeria, Egypt, Lebanon and Kenya.

Some of Michalet's major hypotheses have been selected for checking against the Latin American evidence. The criterion for selection was not so much the relative importance of a given hypothesis, as the availability of quantitative evidence in the literature on the subject. A few words of warning are in order. First, while Latin American writings on foreign direct investment (and TNCs) are abundant, the subject is usually treated with high political content. Second, only in recent years has this literature started to differentiate between the political, economic, social and cultural consequences of foreign investment in general and those of TNCs. Third, a plethora of studies on foreign direct investment and TNCs in Latin America shows no common

---

*This paper was published originally in Development and Change, Sage Publications Ltd. (The Hague), Vol. 7, No. 2 (April 1976).

methodological ground. Fourth, attempts to analyse the nature of technology
transfer to the region arose within the general framework of studies of 'dependence', independent of any critical interest in the behaviour of foreign
private investment in Latin America.

Evidence that such a distinction still persists between the study of general
problems of foreign direct investment (whether positive or negative) in Latin
American economic development, on the one hand, and attempts to analyse problems of technology transfer on the other, can be found in the agenda of the
so-called 'new dialogue' with the United States, prepared at the Bogotá meeting of Latin American foreign ministers in November 1973. The Latin American
governments proposed two items for negotiation with the United States: 'science
and technology transfer' and 'multinational corporations'.

A similar distinction seems to characterize the position of developing
countries in the international agencies. Consequently, problems of technology
transfer are being dealt with by an UNCTAD Permanent Committee on Technology
Transfer, established in August 1974, while the subject of TNCs is entrusted
to a Commission on Transnational Corporations, a subsidiary of the UN Economic
and Social Council, also established in December 1974.

The following nine Michalet hypotheses will be compared with existing Latin
American evidence(2).

(1) TNCs play an essential role in disseminating technological knowledge
abroad; and a great percentage of technology sales by industrially-advanced
countries consists of internal technology trade between TNC parent companies
and their foreign subsidiaries, as is shown by statistics that cover technology
transactions involving United States-based TNCs.

(2) If we are to judge from the comparison of available statistics on payments
for technology transfer received by United States-based TNCs with their
research and development (R&D) expenditure, low-technology industries rank
higher in terms of royalties than those of high-technology. Assuming that
the statistics are reliable, technology-intensive industries thus appear to
transfer little technology to their subsidiaries. When high technology
products are concerned, any transfer of technology is accomplished by the
export of new products rather than by direct investment.

(3) The actual cost of internal technology transfer between TNC parents and
their foreign subsidiaries cannot be measured by capital outflows (payments
of royalties for licensed knowledge trademarks and charges for general technical assistance) that are recorded in the balance of payments of the host
country. Such capital outflows do not include the considerable indirect costs
of intra-firm technology transactions which, under the elaborate internal
accounting procedures of most TNCs, may appear under various headings. Within
the TNCs, there is a marked lack of correspondence between book price and
real price of any internal technology transaction.

(4) TNCs appear to devote more resources to R&D and to innovation in the manufacture of new products than to the introduction of new production processes.
This reflects a strategy which calls for products to be continually changed
in order to meet competition. It also reflects a specific pattern of transfer,
directed more towards the diffusion of technology components incorporated in
new products. Since commercial success becomes the dominant concern of a TNC,
R&D activities which help to adapt the product to the varied tastes of

consumers in different countries are given very high priority.

(5) Patterns of R&D and of technology transfer may become, and in fact are, the subject of conflict between the TNCs and their host countries. The issues at stake include not only balance-of-payments and currency stability considerations of the host country, but also the fact that technology transfer through TNCs tends to standardize production, management and marketing techniques. These techniques generally reflect patterns in force in the most highly-developed countries in which almost all TNCs originate. They may be ill-suited to the economic and social structure of the less-developed countries, endanger R&D activities of local enterprises, and run counter to host country attempts to develop 'appropriate' technologies.

(6) R&D activities of TNCs are highly centralized in the parent companies. Although the technologies thus originated are adapted to 'consumer preferences' in the laboratories of their subsidiaries, this does not represent substantial innovation.

(7) R&D activities of subsidiaries are highly controlled by the parent companies. Even though a new product or process may be discovered in a decentralized laboratory, it will first be launched on the parent company's market. The technology will not be transferred back to the affiliate until several years have passed.

(8) In any event, the R&D burden in financial terms is unevenly distributed between the parent company and its foreign subsidiaries, being to the detriment of the latter as a result of the product cycle. The foreign subsidiaries have to finance new products and processes while deriving no benefit. The TNCs do not promptly transfer their latest technology but prefer to exploit product advantage by exporting.

(9) From the purely technological aspect, the global strategy of TNCs is undeniably a factor generating dependence on the part of the recipient country since domestic 'mono-national' enterprises are not in a position to match the global R&D power of a TNC. In the common case of a TNC subsidiary being established through acquisition or take-over, the R&D activities of the acquired local firm will be integrated into the global R&D system or discontinued altogether.

TNCs IN LATIN AMERICA

The ample presence of TNCs in Latin America is common knowledge. It is also well known that, prior to 1970, most of them were United States-based, except perhaps in Argentina and Brazil. However, the pattern of origin has changed considerably in the seventies since TNCs based in Western Europe and Japan started to appear in growing numbers in the region. It is worthwhile recalling that, according to a Harvard Business School-sponsored survey based on a sample of 187 United States-based TNCs, practically all those present in Western Europe at the end of the 1960s were also engaged in operating subsidiaries and affiliates in Latin America. Of these 187 firms, 185 operated in Western Europe and 182 in Latin America in 1968. Their spread during the period 1952-67 seems to have been more rapid in Latin America than in Western Europe: while forty-one United States-based TNCs entered Europe in that period, their number operating in Latin America increased by sixty. In 1968 the major host country for United States-based TNCs in Latin America was Mexico (162), followed by Brazil (111), Venezuela (107) and Argentina (99). If absolute numbers are significant, in 1968 as many sampled corporations were present in Mexico as in the United Kingdom, figures for Brazil were comparable to those for Belgium and Luxembourg together, those for Venezuela to those of Spain, and for Argentina to the Netherlands.

If we take into consideration the relative levels of economic development and the structure and size of individual national markets in the two regions, it is not surprising that in 1968 considerably more United States-based subsidiaries and affiliates were operating in Western Europe than in Latin America. In West European countries the totals varied from 800 in the United Kingdom to 185 in Spain; the highest and lowest figures for the four Latin American countries were 431 for Mexico and 187 for Argentina

As Table 14.1 shows, in 1968 the distribution by sector of United States-TNC subsidiaries in Western Europe and Latin America showed considerable differences. Historical evidence demonstrates that in Latin America they first entered mining and tropical agriculture and then during the 1950s spread to manufacturing and commerce. The largest TNC subsidiaries in the area are still those engaged in mining and petroleum. During the 1960s, TNC subsidiaries in banking and tourist services appeared in strength.

TABLE 14.1. Distribution of United States-Based TNC Subsidiaries by Sectors, 1968

	Western Europe	Latin America
Manufacturing	2062	1325
Commerce	1142	414
Extractive Industries	27	130
Other activities	772	500
Unknown activities	1077	541
Total	5081	2910

Source: based upon data in J. W. Vaupel and J.P. Curhan, The Making of Multinational Enterprises, Harvard University, Boston, 1969.

Further differentiation is shown by the presence of subsidiaries of United States-based TNCs in Western Europe and Latin America according to industrial branch (see Table 14.2).

During the late 1960s the principal manufacturing areas for United States-based TNCs in Latin America were food processing, chemicals including drugs and cosmetics, electrical appliances, the automotive industry, and petroleum (mainly refining, with the exception of Venezuela). These patterns reflect the first stages of the import substitution-oriented industrialization programmes launched in Latin America in the post-war period(3). While considered as a broad worldwide vertically-integrated industrial sector, chemicals and

TABLE 14.2. Distribution of United States-Based TNC Manufacturing Subsidiaries, 1968

	Western Europe	Latin America
Meat and dairy	88	102
Other food and beverages	188	142
Textile and apparel	28	25
Lumber, furniture and paper	52	39
Chemicals	268	246
Drugs	181	129
Soaps and cosmetics	44	30
Petroleum	168	79
Rubber and tyres	56	45
Stone, clay and glass	78	49
Primary metals	66	52
Fabricated metals	128	59
Farm machinery	19	8
Office and computing machinery	38	17
Other - non-electrical	155	42
Household appliances	24	16
Electronics	107	39
Other electrical equipment	90	55
Motor vehicles	130	74
Other transportation equipment	58	31
Instruments and precision goods	57	20
Other industries	47	26

Source: See Table 14.1.

petroleum involve considerable R&D effort, the same does not apply if we examine the output characteristics of these two industries in Latin America in the 1960s. As happened in the case of other major groups, chemical and petroleum activities in the area produced mainly final consumer goods. In many smaller countries, e.g. Andean Group members and the Central American republics, the real nature of TNC subsidiaries' manufacturing activity was to assemble final products from the raw materials and intermediate goods imported from the parent companies. In a way they were similar to the TNC subsidiaries which were established on the western rim of the Pacific region (between South Korea and Singapore) during the 1960s, with the difference that while the latter produced for export, the Latin American foreign-owned enterprises produced almost exclusively for individual domestic markets.

To a considerable extent this still applies in the major Latin American republics. The first study of TNCs to be made in Mexico shows the following sectors in which concentration is particularly great: tobacco products, automobiles, rubber products, chemicals (including drugs and cosmetics), and electrical appliances(4). In each of these industrial branches the output of TNC subsidiaries exceeds one-half of total domestic output. In the non-durable consumer goods category 30 per cent of output is provided by TNC subsidiaries and affiliates; in durable consumer goods this amounts to 60 per cent; in intermediate goods 32 per cent; and in capital goods 36 per cent. The significance of these figures is evident only if one realizes that more than half of total industrial output in Mexico is accounted for by consumer durables and non-durables, and that, in addition, the average size of TNC subsidiaries represents a multiple of domestically-owned enterprises.

Similar patterns of distribution of TNC subsidiaries by industrial branch and by size relative to domestic firms can be detected in the 1967 data made available by the Harvard Business School survey of Andean countries. In Colombia in that year 90 per cent of the subsidiaries of United States-based TNCs operated in five industrial branches: chemicals and drugs, food processing, automobiles and accessories, office equipment, and petroleum refining. In Peru over 90 per cent of the subsidiaries operated in the first four of these branches. In Chile, according to fragmentary data, most United States subsidiaries operated in three sectors only: chemicals and drugs, electronics, and automobiles. In these three Andean countries the United States-based TNCs represented almost all foreign investment in manufacturing; and for all practical purposes, their subsidiaries did not amount to much more than plants which assembled parts imported from the parent companies(5).

THE TECHNOLOGICAL BEHAVIOUR OF TNCs IN LATIN AMERICA

This extremely brief overview of the presence of TNCs in the Latin American economy has established some basic points of reference from which to evaluate their technological performance in the region in the light of Michalet's hypotheses.

Hypothesis 1

If available financial statistics are used, it is difficult to quarrel with Michalet's view that 'multinational corporations play an essential role in disseminating technological knowledge' in Latin America, and that 'a great percentage of technology sales by industrial countries consists of internal technology trade between multinational enterprise parents and their foreign subsidiaries'. Mexico is the only Latin American country in which a detailed analysis of technology payments abroad has been made which distinguishes between internal technology transactions and arms-length technology sales. In 1971 it was found that:

(1) practically all technology sales (86 per cent of total visible payments) result from manufacturing activities;

(2) 80 per cent of payments for technology transfer in the manufacturing sector, equivalent to close on 70 per cent of total payments, are accounted for by TNC subsidiaries;

(3) the origin of imported technology is basically determined by the home country of the parent company;

(4) more than 50 per cent of technology payments made by TNC subsidiaries correspond to sectors which produce consumer durables and non-durables;

(5) the ratio between technology payments and the value of output is seven times higher in the case of TNC subsidiaries than of domestic firms;

(6) payments tend to increase as percentages of output value with the degree of ownership control of subsidiaries by the parent systems;

(7) payments are closely correlated to the size of the subsidiary; in fourteen of nineteen industrial branches analysed in Mexico the five largest TNC subsidiaries accounted for more than 50 per cent of total payments by foreign-owned firms, and in ten branches the percentage exceeded 80 per cent(6).

The Mexican pattern seems to be confirmed by incomplete information available from Argentina, Brazil and the Andean countries. However, comparison is difficult for two reasons: first, in none of the other countries have attempts been made to disaggregate payments data for TNC subsidiaries and for domestic private and public enterprises; second, samples of payments taken outside Mexico are very small and mostly cover industrial sectors which are completely dominated by TNCs, such as pharmaceuticals and the automotive industry.

While the information collected and analysed in Mexico is very interesting in itself, it cannot be evaluated without information on the type of technology that is acquired and in which sector, and the extent to which technology purchased is both adapted to local requirements (whether in terms of the factor proportion mix or of social needs) and disseminated - either diffused directly or disseminated via the demonstration effect upon the receiving economy.

All these questions must be answered, even if in a preliminary way. Otherwise, the developing countries which receive most of their technology through the TNCs may find themselves in the unenviable position of acquiring inadequate technology at a cost that is higher than the market price. If this were so, such technology transfers would increase rather than decrease the very large gap that already exists between technology-advanced and technology-backward sectors, and would enhance the economic and other power in the hands of the major technology transfer agents, the TNCs.

Hypothesis 2

Michalet's second hypothesis offers considerable difficulty. There is plenty of evidence in Latin America that 'low-technology industries rank higher in terms of royalties than high-technology industries'. Both low- and high-technology industries operate in Latin America; but the statement that 'assuming that the statistics are reliable, technology-intensive industries thus appear to transfer little technology to their subsidiaries' raises more questions than it provides answers. Let us put two Latin American cases, of Brazil and Mexico, side by side. In Brazil during the period 1965-9, more than 90 per cent of technology payments were made by foreign-owned firms in the following sectors: rubber and tyres, electrical equipment, printing industry, textiles and apparel, and machine tools. On the other hand, over 90 per cent of technology payments in agricultural machinery, railway equipment, lumber and furniture, office equipment, beverages, primary metals and fabricated metals were made by locally-owned enterprises(7). In Mexico in 1971, on the other hand, not one domestically-owned segment of twenty-one major industrial branches accounted for a majority of technology payments, while on the average 80 per cent of all technology payments in manufacturing corresponded to those made by TNC subsidiaries. Branches in which the 90 per cent ceiling was exceeded included the following: food and beverages, tobacco, rubber and tyre and automotive industry(8). Thus, while in Brazil we find both the TNC subsidiaries and local firms with high- and low-technology intensity participating in technology transactions abroad, in Mexico the patterns are simpler: the low-technology TNC subsidiaries seem to be the biggest participants in the technology transfer game.

If we look at absolute figures the issue becomes even more complicated: the two largest technology sellers in Latin America in terms of registered payments are both almost completely dominated by TNCs, i.e. pharmaceuticals and motor vehicles. But while the first is a worldwide high-technology industry, very little has happened in the second, technologically speaking, since Mr. Ford's Model T was assembled at Detroit more than fifty years ago. On the other hand, there is no evidence that either of the two industries exports much technology to Latin America, if technology is taken to mean what it is expected to mean: substantial technological innovations involving the change of production processes. Rather, both industries export to the region minor technological innovations which are aimed at product differentiation. Such technology is mostly mechanically reproduced in Latin America for the purpose of catering to the allegedly exogenous 'consumer preference' through the manipulation of commercial propaganda which originates in the TNCs.

It is quite possible, therefore, that the distinction between high and low technology is of little use in understanding the technological contribution of TNCs to the economic development of less developed countries. It is perhaps better to use another distinction introduced by a Canadian economist, Gerald Helleiner, between 'production technology' and 'consumption technology', using as the point of departure Lancaster's theory of demand relying heavily on a product's characteristics(9). While agreeing that the TNCs transfer a considerable amount of 'industrial production technology' to the developing countries, Helleiner notes that they tend to participate only in that segment of the production technology market in which capital-intensive technologies and/or technologies which require relatively large-scale units for efficient operations are employed. Since such conditions are rarely met in developing nations, the transfer of 'production technology' is often replaced by that of 'consumption technology'; this covers not only minor innovations leading to excessive product differentiation, but all sorts of technological 'software' such as new distribution techniques and modern methods of commercial propaganda aimed at the manipulation of consumer preferences. There is some evidence that this applies to Latin America. In Mexico, for example, payments for technology transfer include very large amounts for trademarks and brand names that clearly form part of 'consumption technology'. If this is true, what probably occurs is that for both high- and low-technology industries the sort of technology transfer between developed countries is very different to that between developed and developing countries. This means that for our purposes the distinction between the activities of low- and high-technology industries is not useful. In brief, both groups in Latin America preferably transfer 'consumption technology', whether chemicals with high R&D or automotive industries in which R&D has been low over time.

Hypothesis 3

This hypothesis has been proved repeatedly in many studies of technology transfer to Latin America (see footnote 2 above) and also in the Fajnzylber-Martinez study of the Mexican industrial sector. Vaitsos postulates that in the Andean countries capital flows covering technology transfer in the pharmaceutical and automotive industries represent only a fraction of the total financial flows on 'technology transfer account', most of which are hidden somewhere.

Partial evidence for Mexico is available in a study of technology transfer at enterprise level in four branches of industry: the automotive industry, parts and accessories for automobiles, pharmaceuticals, and intermediate petrochemical products(10). The persistence of the phenomenon of indirect or hidden costs has led Latin American experts to postulate the disaggregation of the 'technology packet' for negotiating purposes. The marked lack of adjustment between the book price and the real total cost of any technology transfer has been widely evidenced in Latin America, both in the case of internal TNC transactions and of arms-length purchases.

Hypothesis 4

Partial confirmation of this hypothesis can be deduced from the discussion of Hypothesis 3. The available evidence suggests strongly that the proposition that TNCs foster R&D activities which help to adapt the product to the varied tastes of consumers in different countries is even more valid in Latin America than it is in the advanced countries. Most of the limited R&D by TNC subsidiaries in Latin America is directed not only to adapting products to consumer tastes, but to changing these tastes.

Hypothesis 5

The patterns of R&D developed by TNC parent companies in the advanced countries very often conflict with the objectives of the host countries. This is not only because technology transfers through TNC subsidiaries tend to standardize production, management and marketing techniques, but because they generally reflect the patterns of consumption which apply in the most highly-developed countries. Independent of any political or ideological bias, there is consensus in Latin American literature that most technologies which originate in the TNC parent companies are ill-suited to the economic and social structure of the developing country and increase the gap between the modern and subsistence sectors. These negative effects are not limited to R&D and its transfer in manufacturing and service activities. The well-advertised Green Revolution in agriculture, which originated in agricultural R&D activities sponsored directly or indirectly by major TNCs, is now the subject of scrutiny in various Latin American countries. Analysis of its impact on Latin American agriculture (and Southeast Asian agriculture as well) provides growing evidence that, by forgetting the socio-cultural characteristics of the peasantry in Latin America and by ignoring socio-economic problems such as the land tenure structure, this sort of agricultural research has an unexpected adverse effect: an increase of the gap between commercial large-scale capital-intensive agriculture and subsistence farming.

Michalet's hypothesis that R&D which is concentrated in the home countries of the TNCs will endanger R&D activities of local enterprises has been largely proven in Argentina, Mexico, and some countries of the Andean Group(11). Helleiner notes that TNCs have no incentive to enter the field of researching for technologies 'appropriate' for developing economies(12). In his survey of the behaviour of United States industry in developing countries, Skinner brings out additional factors which are responsible for the non-adaptive attitudes and distrust of the adaptive capability of local firms: the risk-averting tendency of TNCs and the technological culture patterns prevailing in the United States(13).

Hypothesis 6

This hypothesis is widely supported by evidence from many Latin American countries. As we noted regarding Hypothesis 4, the situation seems to be even more serious: in many consumer durables and non-durables, 'consumer preferences are adapted to new products rather than products being adapted to consumer preferences. A brief study of the experiences of Argentina throws a very interesting light on this subject(14).

Hypothesis 7

There is no doubt that the R&D activities of TNC subsidiaries are highly controlled by the parent companies. However, the volume of 'production technology' in the subsidiaries is so small that empirical evidence does not exist for the hypothesis that if a new product or process is discovered in a decentralized laboratory it will first be launched on the parent company's market. There is slight evidence from Argentina and Mexico that in some branches the laboratories of subsidiaries are used as experimental stations when experiments by parent companies are too costly or are barred by legislation. In the capital goods sector experiments are extended to selling equipment that has not been fully tested by the parent company in order that it may be tested at the risk of the buyer. In this respect some evidence has been collected by the National Industrial Technology Institute of Argentina(15). In Mexico and perhaps in some other Latin American countries, foreign-owned pharmaceutical enterprises test new drugs on local patients- this is made possible by laxity in the application of local legislation, while such experiments are prohibited in advanced countries.

Hypothesis 8

This has been largely proven in major Latin American countries by the administrative regulation of technology transfer contracts: Argentina, Brazil, Mexico, Colombia and Chile.

Hypothesis 9

In Latin America there is rapidly increasing quantitative and qualitative evidence that domestic 'mono-national' enterprises are not in a position to match the global R&D power of the TNCs. This explains why there is growing pressure for the implementation of national and regional policies intended to strengthen local adaptive and productive R&D capability with strong financial and administrative state support. Such pressure has already been translated into the Brazilian Science and Technology Plan, into the initiation of a similar exercise in Mexico, and into the technological common policy decisions in the Andean Common Market.

LATIN AMERICAN POLICIES IN THE FIELD OF TECHNOLOGY TRANSFER

As might be expected in a region that faces persistent balance-of-payments problems, Latin America's preoccupation with technology transfer originated with these problems(16). By chance rather than design, Chile and Colombia, both of which were forced to apply foreign exchange control mechanisms, discovered in the mid-1960s that payments for technology acquired abroad not only represented a considerable portion of the total cost of servicing foreign direct investment, but were growing far more rapidly than other capital account payments. In the 1960s neither Chile nor Colombia witnessed large and continuous inflows of new foreign investment, and their respective treasuries consequently became very concerned. Confidential inquiries made at home and abroad disclosed that, in many cases, technology import payments reflected skilful accounting manoeuvres by foreign firms with the intention of circumventing foreign exchange restrictions imposed upon profit transfer abroad; in other cases, charges were completely out of line with prices in international technology markets.

Colombia sent fiscal experts to Western Europe and to Japan in order to check data collected from the balance sheets of individual foreign subsidiaries and their annual tax declarations with information on technology prices in the advanced countries. These experts brought back sufficient evidence of persistent 'over-pricing' of technology to convince the Executive that it was urgently necessary to establish, at the Treasury-Central Bank level, a Royalties Commission which would scrutinize all requests for foreign exchange for payments abroad for supposed technology imports. At the same time Chile established a similar body known as the Review Commission for Royalty Payments. Both these regulatory agencies were empowered to reject requests for foreign currency in the case of non-substantiated payments. In Chile, moreover, payment ceilings were established for certain industries (ranging from 4 per cent of net sales in the food processing industry to 8 per cent in chemicals); in others (automobiles, electronics and textiles), requests for foreign exchange for technology payments were subjected to case-by-case approval. Chile also restricted the duration of technology transfer contracts to an average of three years.

The success of these two countries in substantially curtailing the outflow of foreign exchange for technology payments had a side effect that was to prove instrumental a few years later in the introduction of more sophisticated technology payment regulation mechanisms in Argentina and Mexico, and in the development of a technological policy in the Andean Common Market, to which both Chile and Colombia had belonged since 1968. This side effect was that government agencies in Chile and Colombia were provided with insight into the nature and content of technology contracts at the enterprise level. Prior to 1967 government experts of Latin American countries, with the exception of Brazil, had no access to documentation which was considered confidential by private parties, allegedly because the trade and technical secrets that it contained might endanger a firm's position vis-à-vis local or foreign competition.

The access to technology contracts, first in Colombia and Chile and later in other Latin American republics, proved to be a necessary condition for an understanding of the characteristics of the international technology trade in less-developed countries, and for the design of national technology import policies. It is perhaps worthwhile to add that the whole exercise would probably not have taken place were it not for the spread in Latin America of knowledge concerning Japan's long-standing practice of screening and regulating technology imports from abroad. In the late 1960s Tokyo, particularly the MITI offices, became a Mecca for Latin American economists who were engaged in the study of policymaking in the transfer of technology field.

Independent of the initiatives taken in 1967 by Chile and Colombia, Brazil had several years earlier started on a similar course, in 1962 introducing legislation which established, in the Central Bank, a registry of contracts related to technology imports and technical assistance agreements. This was done at a time of most serious balance-of-payments difficulties. The 1962 law contained provisions regarding ceilings on technology payments and the duration of individual contracts. Some years later, with the establishment of the autonomous National Institute for Industrial Property, Brazil entered the stage of active search on the international technology markets for 'appropriate' technologies that would be suitable for further adaptation to the country's industrialization programmes. Here, too, the demonstration effect of Japanese policies was clearly visible. It was also easily understandable in view of the long-standing economic relations between the two countries, and the presence of a large body of Japanese immigrants in Brazil, particularly in the industrial triangle São Paulo-Rio de Janeiro-Bello Horizonte.

The occasion to compare notes on the experiences of individual countries in the field of technology transfer policies came in 1969 when the Andean Common Market decided to proceed with the elaboration of a common policy regarding foreign investments. This culminated in late 1970 in the adoption by the six member countries of Decision 24 which covered both foreign direct investment and technology trade treatment. Most Latin American economists working in national technology transfer regulatory agencies, or engaged in academic work in that field, participated in one way or the other in the technical work at the Andean Common Market Executive Secretariat at Lima which led to the drafting of these first regional policy measures. Japan provided some technical assistance for the exercise. Some unorthodox American economists also lent a hand, but the absence of West Europeans was evident.

Decision 24, strongly opposed by United States private investors in the area and particularly by United States-based TNCs, spelled out in detail a common regime for foreign direct and portfolio investment, and gave guidelines for future technological policy in the area. These guidelines placed special emphasis on improvement of the work of existing national registries for technology transfer contracts; on the exchange of information between members of the Andean Common Market; on features of technology transfer contracts, with the aim of strengthening the bargaining power of domestic technology buyers vis-à-vis foreign sellers; on the modernization of national industrial property legislation (patents and trademarks); and on the definition of regional priorities for joint projects involving technological adaptation and R&D activities.

In spring 1973 the part of Decision 24 which dealt with technology was translated into another regionally-binding commitment, Decisions 84 and 86. The purpose of these was to establish regional technology policies in five major areas: technology imports, technology assimilation and adaptation, retrieval of technical knowledge existing in the area, its application to productive activities, and the setting up of a comprehensive regional technological information system. Decision 84 emphasized the need to disaggregate the 'technology package', the objective of international transfers, with the purpose of identifying those elements which lend themselves to local purchases. To that end, technology import requests in Andean Common Market countries were to be accompanied by information permitting the authorities to distinguish between specific product or process technologies (key technologies) and general non-proprietary know-how (peripheral technologies).

In July and September 1971, under the influence of Decision 24 and in response to pressure by the domestically-owned industrial sector, Argentina passed two laws which were intended to reduce foreign exchange outflow for technology purchases by the foreign-owned automotive industry, and to channel the supply of foreign technology under the scrutiny of the National Registry of Licence Contracts and Technology Transfers. This agency, which worked within the state-owned National Industrial Technology Institute, had as its principal objective the evaluation and control of foreign technology acquisitions. It was empowered to revoke transfer contracts if similar technologies were available domestically, if contracts contained export restrictions and tie-in clauses in respect to foreign purchases of capital goods and raw materials, or if they fixed technology or technical assistance prices out of line with the content of licence agreements. The Technology Institute was charged with the elaboration of periodic global forecasts regarding characteristics of the technology trade and R&D activities of local industries, including foreign-owned enterprises. These regulatory measures in the technology field were accompanied by new legislation covering the treatment of foreign investments and of industrial promotion.

What were perhaps the most comprehensive measures for the regulation of technology transfer were introduced by Mexico in February 1973, when the National Technology Transfer Registry Directorate was established within the Ministry of Industry and Trade. Legislation enabling this to be done had been elaborated in 1972 by a group of experts who were fully cognizant of Andean Common Market developments and of experiences with technology transfer in Argentina and Brazil. As in other cases, the legislation reflected preoccupation with the balance-of-payments burden of technology payments which, in 1969, were estimated at $200 million. The Mexican Law on Transfer of Technology and the Use and Exploitation of Patents and Trademarks differed from earlier legislation in Latin America in that it provided that both present and future technological contracts must be approved by the government. The Law not only covered technology transfer contracts with foreign sources, but also contracts between enterprises incorporated within the country. Moreover, it applied to all contracts, independent of whether or not they involved money payments for services rendered. The Law spelled out fourteen reasons why the government might refuse registration and order revision of the contract. The major reasons for refusal were: deviations, as measured in international/comparative terms, between the cost of the acquired technology and its market value; clauses providing for arbitration in foreign courts; excessive duration of a contract; and restrictive clauses in contracts with regard to exports, production, use of complementary technologies, purchase of equipment and raw materials, and similar restrictive business practices.

The proportion of contracts which were successfully registered through May 1974 (64 per cent approved and 36 per cent rejected out of a total of about 1000 new contracts processed) was not a good yardstick for measurement of the ultimate rate of approval. This is because companies which had existing technology contracts were able to choose between offering them for immediate registration, or taking a two-year period in which to make adjustments.

When the legislation came into force early in 1973 over 4000 contracts were outstanding. These were to be processed by the late summer of 1975, so that a complete picture of the characteristics of all contracts submitted for registration would not be available until early 1976. But there are reasons to believe that not all contracts were submitted for registration in Mexico. The only incentive which the law provided for the registration of existing contracts was that a full tax rebate was available to transferee companies on royalty payments. However, if both parties, and particularly a TNC parent system, wished to evade the law, it was almost impossible for the Registry to discover whether a contract existed, particularly if visible payments for technology transfers were not involved. Non-registration by Mexican subsidiaries of TNCs seemed to be rather high, judging by the fact that out of 100 major TNCs with subsidiaries or affiliates in Mexico, some 60 failed to report any technology contracts. All of these insisted privately that parent companies transferred technology to Mexican subsidiaries free of charge.

An analysis of the 300 contracts which were rejected by the authorities gives evidence of the abuses that have become almost traditional in international technology trade(17). Eighty-one per cent were turned down because the cost of technology was found excessive (while the government had not set final ceilings for technology pricing, it considered as reasonable payment, depending on the industry, 1 to 3 per cent of net sales value in food processing, or 6 to 10 per cent in pharmaceuticals); 40 per cent were refused because the contracts were for periods exceeding the legal maximum of ten years; 40 per cent because limits were placed on the volume of production or on sales prices; 26 per cent because the technology importing company was required to turn over to the licensor any patents, improvements or innovations it developed; and 23 per cent because claims under the contract were subject to jurisdiction of foreign courts. As these percentages show, the majority of rejected contracts were in conflict with more than one provision of the law. After rejection they were frequently renegotiated and resubmitted for approval. Very few cases are known in which legislation caused the suspension of technology flows. While foreign exchange savings through cutting down the level of technology payments had been estimated at some US $80 million for the duration of rejected and subsequently revised contracts, some interesting findings can be reported.

(1) The largest and the majority of payments were made by TNC subsidiaries and affiliates.

(2) Payments for trademarks and brand names were larger than payments for either technology or general technical assistance.

(3) In some cases technology payments appeared in the contracts as flat payments for R&D developed at the parent companies.

(4) In certain cases payments for similar technology were considerably higher than those made not only in Western Europe but also in Brazil, for example, where the regulation of technology contracts started ten years earlier than in Mexico.

(5) Patented knowledge was very rarely included in the contracts in spite of the fact that in Mexico TNCs had repatented new products and processes on a massive scale.

(6) With the entry of domestic businesses into partnership with fully-owned foreign subsidiaries and the transformation of the latter into joint ventures, a process actively fostered by Mexican foreign investment legislation, some TNCs immediately tried to raise the cost of technology transfer. These attempts tended to fail due to resistance by the local participants.

(7) Certain amounts of technology payments were directed not towards parent companies but towards financial intermediaries in the tax havens of the

Caribbean or of Western Europe.

(8) The transfer pricing of imported equipment, components, spare parts and raw materials, and the 'reverse' transfer pricing of exported finished goods, were the most difficult problems to be dealt with in view of the total lack of cooperation by the authorities of countries of origin and of destination of traded goods. What very often appeared in foreign trade statistics as triangular trade was mostly a fiction; goods travelled more directly, while trade bills and payments travelled through the most unexpected places.

Notwithstanding all this, no major and only few minor conflicts arose with respect to the administration of the 1972 technology transfer legislation in Mexico. An article on the Mexican experience put it as follows:

> One reason why the Technology Registry has been widely accepted is, in fact, that its directors have been very open to discussion and negotiation with companies. In many cases, civil servants and company lawyers have even jointly thrashed out the criteria now guiding the Registry in its decisions. A recent report to the US-Mexico Businessmen's Committee noted that: to the extent that businessmen and the Mexican Government continue to exert their best efforts to develop economically rational approaches for dealing with the transfer of technology, the Law can become an instrument for the promotion of the transfer of technology inside and outside of Mexico(18).

A major, and perhaps in the long run the most important outcome of Mexican technology transfer regulatory policies, has been the growing awareness in the country that while the proximity of the United States, the strong presence of the TNCs, and the 'easy' access to foreign technology create strong disincentives to local R&D, its negligence has a high indirect cost, both politically and socially. Consequently, in the fall of 1974 Mexico started to elaborate the National Science and Technology Plan for 1976-80. This Plan put the highest priority on the development of adaptive and productive technological capabilities in selected areas of national economic and social interest.

NOTES

(1) C.A. Michalet, 'Transfer of Technology and the Multinational Firm', OECD, DAS/SPR/73.64 Paris (mimeographed). An abbreviated version of this paper appeared in Development and Change, Vol. 7, No. 2 (April 1976).

(2) The major sources for the comparisons used here are: Organization of American States, The Transfer of Technology to Latin America, Washington, D.C., 1972; Aldo Ferrer, Tecnologia y politica economica en América Latina, Editorial Paidos, Buenos Aires, 1974; F.R. Sagasti and M. Guerrero C., El desarrollo cientifico y tecnológico de América Latina, Instituto para la Integración de América Latina, Buenos Aires, 1974; M.S. Wionczek (Editor), Comercio de tecnologia y subdesarrollo económico, UNAM, Mexico, 1973; and the following country studies: Argentina - J.M. Katz, Oligopolio, firmas nacionales y empresas multinacionales; la industria farmacéutica argentina, Siglo XXI Editores, Buenos Aires, 1974; Brazil - N.F. de Figueiredo, A transferencia de tecnologia no desenvolvimiento industrial do Brasil, IPEA/INPES, Rio de Janeiro, 1972; Chile - UNCTAD, Principales cuestiones que plantea la transmisión de tecnologia - Estudio monográfico de Chile, Geneva, 1974; The Andean Common Market - C.V. Vaitsos, Comercialización de tecnologia en el

Pacto Andino, Instituto de Estudios Peruanos, Lima, 1973; Mexico - M. de Maria y Campos, Transferencia de tecnologia, dependencia del exterior y desarrollo económico, UNAM, Mexico, 1968; M.S. Wionczek, Inversión y tecnologia extranjera en América Latina, Editoral Joaquin Mortiz, Mexico, 1971; and M.S. Wionczek, G. Bueno and J. E. Navarrete, La transferencia international de tecnologia - El caso de México, Fondo de Cultura Económica, Mexico, 1974.

(3) For an analysis of post-war Latin American economic strategies, see M.S. Wionczek, 'Latin American Growth and Trade Strategies in the Post-War Period', Development and Change, Vol. 5, No. 1 (1973-4), pp. 1-35.

(4) F. Fajnzylber and T. Martinez Tarragó, Las empresas transnacionales - Expansión a nivel mundial y proyección en la industria mexicana, Mexico, 1975 (unpublished).

(5) For details, see C.V. Vaitsos, op. cit., and M. S. Wionczek, Inversión y tecnologia extranjera en América Latina, op. cit.

(6) Fajnzylber and Martinez, op. cit.

(7) N.F. de Figueiredo, op. cit.

(8) Fajnzylber and Martinez, op. cit.

(9) G.K. Helleiner, 'The Role of Multinational Corporations in the Less Developed Countries' Trade in Technology', Paper presented to the Sixth Pacific Conference on Trade and Development, Mexico City, July 1974, and published in World Development, Vol. 3, No. 4 (April 1975), and K.J. Lancaster, 'Change and Innovation in the Technology of Consumption', American Economic Review (May 1966).

(10) Wionczek, Bueno and Navarrete, op. cit.

(11) For details, see the various essays collected in M.S. Wionczek (Editor), Comercio de tecnologia y subdesarrollo tecnológico, op. cit.; and the recent books by Sagasti & Guerrero and by Ferrer, op. cit.

(12) Helleiner, op. cit.

(13) W. Skinner, The American Industry in Developing Economies - The Management of International Manufacturing, New York, 1968.

(14) G. di Tella, 'La manipulación de la demanda: el problema de las marcas', in Wionczek (Editor), Comercio de tecnologia y subdesarrollo tecnológico, op. cit.

(15) A. Aráoz, 'Importación de tecnologias experimentales', Comercio Exterior, Mexico, May 1974.

(16) For a detailed survey of developments in the field of technology transfer regulation in Latin America, see J. Hodara, 'Apuntes sobre el desarrollo cientifico y tecnológico en América Latina', UN Economic Commission for Latin America, Mexico, October 1974 (mimeographed).

(17) For a detailed evaluation of the working of the Mexican registry, see

M. de Maria y Campos, 'La politica mexicana sobre transferencia de tecnologia; una evaluación preliminar', Comercio Exterior, Mexico, May 1974.

(18) A. Riding, 'Technology Transfer - Mexico Gets It Right', The Financial Times, 24 January 1975.

CHAPTER 15

Science and Technology and External Dependency Relations*

IT is appropriate to look briefly at both the economic history of Latin America and the historical background of the scientific and technological underdevelopment of the region. It does not seem possible to speak of a strategy for technological independence as part of a national, if not independent, at least autonomous socio-economic development, without attempting to identify the roots of the present situation. Such examination must be very general because so far the contribution of scientific and technological underdevelopment to the kind of socio-economic development attained in the region and the impact of that backwardness upon Latin American relations with the advanced countries have not been studied satisfactorily.

Knowledge of the roots of Latin American scientific and technological underdevelopment is so limited that an eminent economic historian of the region, Prof. Stanley J. Stein, who has worked on the initial phase of industrialization in Brazil and on Mexican economy and society at the end of the colonial period, has recently asked a question which is very relevant to the present debate on science, technology and strategies for independence(1).

Recalling that by the mid-nineteenth century Japan, as well as Latin America, started the process of capitalist transformation and growth in very similar conditions, Stein pointed out the totally opposite results of that transformation. Despite having established restrictions on the inflow of capital and foreign entrepreneurs, Japan achieved a process of autonomous development and maximized its benefits from international trade. This, in turn, allowed Japan to become an important economic and technological world power in less than a hundred years. On the other hand, after having chosen the traditional participation in the international division of labour which entailed free imports of consumer goods and equipment, capital and technology, free entry of foreign technicians, businessmen, bankers, mining and construction engineers and even

---

*This paper was presented at the Seminar on Science, Technology and Strategy for Independence held at the University of Campinas, Brazil in December 1977, and published in Spanish in the proceedings of the Seminar, edited by Severo Fagundes Gómez y Rogerio C. Cerqueira Leite, under the title Ciência, Tecnología e Independência, Livraria Duas Cidades, Saõ Paolo, 1978.

rail-workers, Latin America only managed to deepen, during the same period, dependency on world industrial centres in every respect. Stein asks, how can these two radically different experiences be explained?

A partial answer can perhaps be found in a paper written at the beginning of the seventies by a Brazilian sociologist, Helio Jaguaribe, which offers a wide historic panorama of the frustrated socio-economic development and of the scientific and technological backwardness of Latin America(2). According to Jaguaribe, the structural incapability of Latin America to achieve autonomous development, together with what he calls the inability to bring science and technology up to date, is derived from the workings of various factors which affected Latin American societies since their Iberic origins and which, albeit modified, are still felt. During the first centuries of the colonial period, under the influence of the Spanish and Portuguese metropoles, the culture of metropolitan and colonial élites suffered the imposition of a dogmatic orthodoxy and medieval traditionalism, which had been surmounted in the rest of Europe during the Enlightenment. Furthermore, in Latin America this cultural formation, contrary to modernizing scientific and technological advance, was accompanied during the eighteenth and nineteenth centuries by the persistent rigidity of social dualism. The traditionalist and anti-rational cultural formation together with social rigidity converted Latin America into a dualistic society of 'masters and slaves'. That society persisted until and including the first decades of the present century. It was based upon a raw materials exporting economy generating little demand for science and technology inputs. These inputs were provided almost completely during the nineteenth century by the industrialized European countries and more recently by the United States through 'free' trade of goods, capital and technology, subject to consumption by Latin American élites, instead of serving as a starting point for their own scientific and technological efforts.

This contrasted not only with the situation in Japan in the second half of the nineteenth century during the Meiji Revolution, but also with the conditions characterizing the United States throughout the whole last century. The levels of economic underdevelopment and of scientific and technological backwardness in North America - in comparison with Europe - were very similar to those of Latin America during the early part of the nineteenth century. However, North America emerged from this backwardness through changes which did not take place in Latin America because of reasons identified by Jaguaribe. The writings of Prof. Nathan Rosenberg, who has carefully studied as a historic process the interrelations between the development of the United States economy and the scientific and technological progress of American society during the nineteenth century, contain very interesting evidence to the effect that the North-American success had to do very much with the fact that social structures and values offered, early enough, adequate conditions for the integration of originally imported science and technology with the educational and productive systems of the United States(3).

At the beginning of the North American industrial revolution, during the first quarter of the nineteenth century, the dependency of the United States on European technology was perhaps as great as that of Latin America. However, the big difference between the United States and Latin America was that, as a result of the pragmatic and rational attitude towards life, social mobility and open and flexible educational systems, North American society started producing rapidly its own science and technology. This took place if only because differences in resource availability and living conditions on both sides of the North Atlantic created problems to United States settlers and offered opportunities and challenges that for obvious reasons were outside the framework of European experiences. Furthermore, the United States managed to integrate scientific knowledge and technological innovations with the productive process. Thus nineteenth century United States science and technology resulted from a mix of imports and of efforts to experiment and adapt imported knowledge to local conditions and needs. If the same thing has not happened in Latin America, it is because of internal social conditions rather than external factors or dependency relations.

This hypothesis is important in view of fashionable explanations of technological, economic and political dependency of the so-called peripheries in terms of capitalist dynamism *per se* and ill-defined external factors. Although the bases of Latin American underdevelopment and dependency were established firmly during the nineteenth century, their origin goes further back in the past and reflects the enduring colonial heritage(4).

This colonial heritage, together with the consumption-oriented demonstration effect of welfare levels achieved in the industrially-advanced countries at the beginning of the twentieth century, explains to a considerable extent the frustration of the supposedly autonomous Latin American industrialization process. This process was started during the thirties within the framework of an import-substitution strategy. Although this clearly imitated the final period of industrialization in advanced countries, it had very particular characteristics. The authors of this strategy assumed that it was possible to successfully repeat the advanced industrial experience without previously changing the social relations inherited from a society of 'masters and slaves'. It was also erroneously thought that it was possible to industrialize 'in reverse' by starting with final consumer goods industries in the hope that the process of industrialization would later expand more or less automatically to encompass capital goods manufacturing. As historians have shown, it did not work that way during the industrialization of Great Britain, continental Europe, or the United States.

Thus Latin America entered the so-called 'easy industrialization' stage in the thirties without taking account of the obstacles or constraints. The fact that advanced country industrialization took place under very different conditions was not perceived. These conditions included a dynamic agricultural sector; a modern educational system; constant expansion of the internal market; social mobility; and a growing stock of scientific and technological knowledge, produced to a great extent internally.

It was postulated that the industrial process would somehow solve all these problems and would simultaneously guarantee the region's social and political stability. Due consideration was not given to the fact that the static stability which prevailed in societies of 'masters and slaves' in Latin America was totally different from the dynamic stability achieved in the North Atlantic area.

The strategy of imitative industrialization seemed easy to Latin America since it presupposed, among other things, that the region had free access to the technological and scientific advancement accumulated by the centres of the world economy. In fact, initially this was possible, and meanwhile not the slightest effort was made toward improving the quality of human capital available locally or creating organizational and scientific and technological infrastructures. This was possible because the development strategy left the agricultural sector to its own fate, concentrating efforts on the establishment

of manufacturing activities which only reflected the profile of pre-existing
demand. This was defined by two factors: income distribution patterns inherited from the colonial past which reflected a dual society, and consumption
patterns imported from high income countries by the élites of Latin American
societies. Since this stage corresponded to industrial activities which produced consumer goods with a low technology content and low investment requirements per worker and unit of output, no difficulties appeared with respect to
technology or management despite the general underdevelopment of Latin American economies. As Jaguaribe correctly diagnosed, the demand for technological
knowledge during the first phase of Latin American industrial development was
fairly limited and could be satisfied with massive imports of relatively
simple technologies.

The possibilities of easy industrialization ended in Latin America long before
the imports of science and technology led to their adaptation to local conditions or to any massive local production of new know-how. In the following
stage of industrialization which consisted in the appearance of industries of
consumer durables, intermediate products, and, in some cases, capital goods,
the absence of modern indigenous scientific, technological and managerial
knowledge gave way to the progressive denationalization of the domestic productive structure through the increasing inflow of big foreign enterprise -
mostly transnational corporations (TNCs). These companies offered the élites
and the middle classes what they wanted or needed: increasingly diversified
and sophisticated consumer goods and the technical and managerial know-how
for their production and distribution. Due to their technological power, the
big foreign companies also took advantage of the emerging demand for intermediate and capital goods by means of, first, imports from their home countries
and, later, local production within the especially favourable framework of an
import substitution strategy.

Thus the lack of interest of the national élites and of Latin American states
in science and technology as a factor of change, together with the absence of
internal market expansion, imposed unsurmountable limitations upon the industrialization model based on import substitution, a model whose benefits were
reaped mostly by large private technology producers from outside the region.

The socio-political inability to create bases for an extension and a deepening
of internal economic modernization through changes in income distribution, the
technical modernization of primary sectors and massive educational and technological effort, brought about in the sixties feeble attempts to support industrialization with the integration of a regional market(5). This new variant
of an 'easy' industrialization strategy failed because it attempted to export
to the rest of Latin America problems unsolved within the framework of national
societies. As soon as the strategy of regional development failed around 1970,
Latin America returned to the model of traditional participation in the international division of labour, this time attempting to boost exports of consumer
manufactures. However, it was forgotten that the three decades of import substitution, followed by industrialization at the expense of neighbours, had
not achieved modernization or strengthened the productive system in the hands
of nationals. On the contrary, the region witnessed the progressive displace-
ment of nationals, particularly in the manufacturing and modern service sectors, by productive entities controlled from abroad. Given the local scarcity
of capital, management abilities and technological know-how, the new strategy
was, once again, more useful to the latter than to national societies. However, instead of searching for an explanation of this apparently insoluble
situation in the lack of local effort during the period of unprecedented

worldwide scientific and technological advancement, the defenders of Latin American political power patterns found refuge in populist demagogy while intellectuals fell in love with dependency theories(6).

According to Jorge Sábato, an Argentinian scientist, and other students of scientific and technological backwardness in the region, Latin American élites adopted contradictory attitudes(7). Until the mid-sixties Latin America was not even aware of the direct relationship between the failure of industrialization, societal dualism and growing technological and managerial dependency. When growing social pressures raised the issue of a social and economic development model with a more nationalist content regarding the build-up of an indigenous scientific and technological capacity, instead of making an urgent massive national effort Latin American governments focussed their attention on the transfer of technology, in many cases without changing traditional policies toward foreign investment. As a subject of national and international debate, the transfer of technology emerged on the Latin American scene as part of the first attempts to understand the scientific and technological backwardness of the region(8).

For reasons still not clear, Latin America dedicated itself to the search for the liberalization of technological trade as if scientific and technological backwardness, with all its counterproductive consequences for the productive process and patterns of socio-economic development were due to an insufficient supply of external technology. It was conveniently forgotten that, with few exceptions, the growing denationalization of the imitative industrialization process did originate in an absolute scarcity of technological know-how but rather, first, in the weak internal capability to select, assimilate and adapt technologies available outside the region; and, second, in the almost total absence of the capability to use them to produce locally the new knowledge, the process without which neither the United States nor Japan nor Western Europe would have achieved autonomous economic development during the nineteenth century. So it seems that once more Latin America is seeking an easy way out from a rather difficult situation. It is assumed that a certain degree of control of technology imports will open the way to their easier adaptation to the socio-economic needs of the region. However, independently of the short-term advantages of the elimination of numerous financial, fiscal and other abuses which have accompanied the free and indiscriminate import of modern technological knowledge, mainly through large TNCs, the scientific and technological underdevelopment of Latin America will not disappear simply through improved adaptation of imported technologies to internal demand or know-how.

The following reasons for the limited usefulness of the regulation of technological imports - in the absence of other policy measures - should be emphasized:

(1) In Latin America, as well as in the rest of the world the profile of global technological demand is defined by the structure of production and the model of development adopted.

(2) Considering that the private objectives of technology suppliers to underdeveloped countries do not necessarily coincide with the socio-economic and political aims of Latin American societies, it is not, nor can it be by definition, the function of the suppliers, including TNCs, to take care of the restructuring of the underdeveloped productive systems through adjustments in technology transfer mechanisms.

(3) While international private sources of technology dedicate themselves primarily to the production and commercialization of advanced industrial technology, the complicated problematique of Latin American underdevelopment needs solutions for the whole technological universe, including agricultural, social and other technologies.

(4) In view of the fact that proprietary technology originating in advanced countries is used to ensure its owners a participation in usually oligopolistic markets, practices aimed at achieving such an objective limit the process of internal diffusion of foreign proprietary technologies, prevent the creation of local innovative capacity and, therefore, hinder autonomous development.

Without postulating the isolation of an underdeveloped society from foreign privately-produced know-how, it is easy to see that in order to adjust the private objectives of the technology owners, even slightly, to the socio-economic and political objectives of the receiving societies some prerequisites must exist in the receiving society to allow such a 'marriage of convenience' between the two parties. These include the formation of a national policy on science and technology linked to the concept of national development; the internal accumulation of a stock of knowledge concerning national scientific and technological needs; and recognition by the local holders of power of the importance of scientific and technological activities as a factor of change and modernization. Only when these prerequisites are fulfilled will it be possible to achieve a socially useful and politically convenient integration of imported proprietary know-how with the global supply of freely available knowledge.

However, in Latin America these prerequisites are far from fulfilled. First, even in countries which are starting to design national science and technology policies, they are divorced from economic and social policies. Second, the scientific and technological communities are not only weak but composed mainly of people trained in advanced countries, who share the preferences and values of developed societies. Third, the stock of knowledge concerning local scientific and technological needs is limited, full of discontinuities and biased in favour of imitative socio-economic development. Finally, the degree of recognition among the holders of power of the role of science and technology is extremely low, as seen by the total failure of the attempt to design and implement a long-term scientific and technological policy in Mexico.

As a result of the persistence of all these factors, of the divorce between local scientific and technological activities and the educational and productive system, and of the absence of a general scientific and technical culture, the knowledge and know-how produced in Latin America - at a high financial and social cost - is only applied marginally. This waste of local scientific and technological talent stems from not understanding that in underdeveloped countries the supply of scientific and technological knowledge produced internally does not automatically create the required demand. Due to historic and sociological reasons, the small existing global demand is oriented to the highly advanced countries. The fact that national private and public enterprises, together with the Latin American state, have little interest in using internally-produced science and technology has been amply proven. In some cases it occurs because of the excessive prestige of imported knowledge, in others because of fear of risk, and in others because of mistrust of the society in the capacity of local scientists and technologists.

The fashionable notion in Latin America that it will be feasible to change scientific and technological relations with the advanced world through obtaining better treatment from foreign suppliers of technology shows an impressive degree of ingenuity. Nor can other viewpoints which have many proponents in advanced and underdeveloped countries give the hoped-for results. In advanced countries it is generally emphasized that the fostering of science and technology for development amounts to the promotion of modern scientific institutes in underdeveloped societies, together with massive modern technological transfers, preferably through private channels. On the other hand, many spokesmen of the underdeveloped world believe that indigenous science and technology will start flowering once international barriers which hinder access to the progress of the scientific and technological world are eliminated. It is doubtful that these two extreme and simplistic positions will offer any solution to Latin America. Science institutes, massive transfers and the elimination of obstacles to the flow of knowledge will scarcely diminish the dependency of Latin America as long as the capacity of the region to absorb technical know-how and to use it for autonomous development and to produce indigenous knowledge is very weak.

First and foremost, Latin America needs to build its own internal scientific and technological capability. Its achievement will depend more on an international and national long-term integrated effort than on partial initiatives guided by ideological preferences or wishful thinking, closely linked to traditional and anti-rational cultural formation and to social rigidity, both inherited from the colonial period and difficult to surmount.

The scientific and technological advancement of the region will depend more on the creation of strong ties among investigation, education, and the economy than on the volume of imported knowledge and the allocation of financial and human resources to research institutions. In the absence of internal demand for local production of knowledge, a corollary of the absence of scientific and technological culture, the modern research institutes established in Latin America, with or without external assistance, run the risk of premature death or of becoming sources of the brain-drain. At the same time, excessive dependence on massive technology imports through traditional channels fosters the appearance of advanced technological enclaves which perpetuate themselves in the context of general backwardness and increase the social dualism originally inherited from the colonial period.

The attainment of autonomy in the field of science and technology is made difficult due to the weakness of its infrastructure, which in turn reflects the increasing gap between constant advancement in this field in the central countries of the world and the backwardness of the Latin American periphery. It is difficult to postulate scientific and technological autonomy while adequately prepared human resources are scarce; information systems are inefficient; statistical data is lacking; the use of computers follows the patterns of very advanced countries; engineering and consulting services are mostly in foreign hands; the quality of instruments, materials and scientific equipment is low; technical norms are only observed exceptionally; and international cooperation follows priorities and methods established abroad(9). In Latin American conditions all these activities need as much - or more - attention as science and technology, conceived in a restricted manner as the production of knowledge.

Finally, the difficult problem of priorities appears. The scientific and technological gap between the central countries and Latin America is already so big that it is impossible to think of closing it completely. On the other hand, many aspects of the technological and scientific advancement achieved in industrialized countries have no social relevance or application for the region in view of the scarcity of resources, the weakness of the infrastructure and the dissimilarity of needs. Latin American scientific and technological strategies and priorities have to concentrate only on some aspects of world scientific and technological progress. Here it is tempting to postulate a triple strategy: fostering scientific and technological research along the lines of major national social and economic priorities; emphasizing the search for adequate existing local technologies; and directing research to those fields of science and technology of advanced countries where the research dynamics and recent advances indicate the possibility of major discoveries and innovations of wide social relevance.

Thus the progressive construction of the infrastructure and selective support to the production of knowledge and know-how represent perhaps the only way to strengthen the domestic scientific and technological capability of a Latin American country. Its strengthening will bring a slow but constant change in scientific and technological relations with the outside world, weakening little by little the historic situation of dependency when internal demand for knowledge was satisfied almost exclusively from abroad. Only when the relative participation of domestic science and technology in the productive, educational and cultural processes increases to such a degree that it will be, roughly, equivalent to the contribution of imported knowledge will it become possible to speak about autonomous socio-economic and technological development. It is completely illusory to expect that such an ambitious goal can be achieved exclusively through management, regulation and control of foreign-produced knowledge. In summary, for the achievement of national technological and scientific autonomy and socio-economic development, a coherent group of internal measures is needed and not just the imposition of controls at the border.

NOTES

(1)   Stanley J. Stein, 'Introduction' to Roberto Cortez Conde and Stanley J. Stein (Editors), Latin America - A Guide to Economic History 1830-1930, University of California Press, Berkeley, Los Angeles and London, 1977, pp. 3-16.

(2)   Helio Jaguaribe, 'Ciencia y tecnología en el cuadro socio-político de la América Latina', El Trimestre Económico, (México, D.F.) Vol. 38, No. 2, (April-June 1971), pp. 389-432.

(3)   Nathan Rosenberg, 'American Technology: Imported or Indigenous?', The American Economic Review (Menasha, Wisc.), Vol. 67, No. 1 (February 1977), pp. 21-6.

(4)   Stanley J. Stein and Barbara H. Stein, The Colonial Heritage of Latin America - Essay on Economic Dependence in Perspective, Oxford University Press, New York, 1970.

(5)   See Miguel S. Wionczek, 'Latin American Growth and Trade Strategies in the Post-War Period', Chapter 8 of this book.

(6)   For an excellent survey and critique of Latin American dependency theories from a Marxian viewpoint, see Gabriel Palma, 'Dependency: A Formal

Theory of Underdevelopment or a Methodology for the Analysis of Concrete Situations of Underdevelopment?', World Development (Oxford), Vol. 6, No. 718 (July-August 1978).

(7)   Jorge Sabato, 'El cambio tecnologico necesario y posible en America Latina', Comercio Exterior (Mexico, D.F.) Vol. 26, No. 5 (May 1976) , pp. 541-6.

(8)   Joseph Hodara, 'La conceptualización del atraso científico-tecnológico de América Latina: El telón de fondo', México, March 1976 (unpublished).

(9)   With respect to the situation in Mexico, see Consejo Nacional de Ciencia y Tecnología, Plan Nacional Indicativo de Ciencia y Tecnología, México, D.F., 1976.

PART III

GLOBAL PROBLEMS

CHAPTER 16

Bilateral Resource Exploitation Arrangements Between Less Developed and Industrialized Countries*

THE FUTURE shape of bilateral arrangements covering exploration, exploitation and international trade in mineral resources between the resource-rich less developed countries (LDCs) and the major resource-consuming developed countries (DCs)(1), can be perceived with certain clarity only if and when answers are provided to questions that are of deep concern to many people in the DCs. These key questions are:

(1) does the world at large face a period of growing scarcity of mineral resources?
(2) in what sense does the problem of DC access to LDC mineral resources arise?
(3) do LDC demands regarding the future use of their mineral resources conflict with the general objective of world economic expansion or, in other words, what is the 'new international economic order' with respect to non-renewable resources?
(4) what is the actual state of contractual relations between LDC resource-holders and DC resource-users, and is the present tension between the two parties a temporary or permanent feature of international economic relations?

The evidence presented in this paper suggests the following answers:

(1) there is no growing scarcity of global mineral resources;
(2) the problem of access to LDC mineral resources can be meaningfully discussed today only in terms of changing conditions of access and not of free unconditional access;
(3) the future external use of LDC mineral resources as postulated by LDCs does not conflict with the needs of the expanding international economy; moreover, the proposals in that respect incorporated into the agenda of the 'new international economic order' are hardly revolutionary;
(4) the contractual relations between most LDC resource-holders and DC

+This paper was presented at the Ninth Pacific Trade and Development Conference held in San Francisco, California in August 1977, and published in Lawrence B. Krause and Hugh Patrick (Editors), <u>Mineral Resources in the Pacific Area</u>, Federal Reserve Bank of San Francisco, San Francisco, Calif., 1978.

resource-users, as actually practised, have undergone very substantial changes during the past twenty years; these changes started long before the concept of the 'new international economic order' was coined by the LDCs in 1974.

Consequently, along with the changing patterns of international political and economic relations between the LDCs and DCs, future bilateral resource arrangements will result from the continuous process of mutual adjustment interwoven with monetary conflicts of interest. These conflicts will not degenerate into a 'resources war' unless, of course, political and economic relations between the two sectors of the world economy deteriorate into a series of bitter confrontations.

MINERAL SCARCITY

In spite of the fact that both the planet and its resources are finite and exhaustible, it is impossible to marshall any serious evidence in support of the position that the world at large faces a period of growing scarcity of mineral resources. Not only were the alarmist theses of the briefly famous Limits to Growth satisfactorily disposed of by the subsequent wave of political, economic and technological criticism; they have also been contradicted by the findings of two recent inquiries into the longer-term prospects for the world economy, undertaken by the two Nobel Prize laureates, Jan Tinbergen and Wassily Leontieff(2).

According to the Tinbergen study, while the fear of exhaustion of natural resources, together with the measures taken by the OPEC countries, has started international discussions on natural resources in general and on non-renewable resources in particular, an overall shortage of minerals does not appear to be a real danger for the near future. The quantity of metals, minerals and other useful elements contained in the first 1000 metres of the earth's crust and in the seas represents, with the exception of oil, several million, or even several hundred million, times the world's present annual consumption(3).

According to the Leontieff study, the availability of mineral resources - even under relatively conservative estimates of resource endowments and given the uncertainties associated with long-run supply and demand - should not create physical obstacles, in terms of shortages, to the sustained growth of the world economy for at least the next twenty-five years. Obstacles of a technological nature are also not to be expected. On the other hand, the Leontieff group believes that far-reaching internal social, political and institutional changes in LDCs, and significant adjustments in the world economic order, would be of considerable help to assure the world economy a rate of growth comparable to that of the 1950s and 1960s(4).

In the absence of more competent experts on the world economy than Tinbergen and Leontieff, not to mention their large cast of collaborators, the first of the questions may be considered to be answered negatively(5). Thus the world does not appear to be facing a period of growing scarcity.

It is sometimes argued that although the fact that we are not approaching a physical depletion of worldwide resources may be reassuring as regards prospects for medium-term growth of the world economy, this ignores the cost dimension which has significant implications both for the combination of factors used in the production of intermediate and final goods and for the total cost of production of these goods. Furthermore, it is argued that at least some of the literature that deals with mineral resource problems suggests that in recent years resource costs have increased in real terms because the cost-reducing effects of technological changes in mining were unable to offset rising scarcity rents and the increased costs of exploiting less accessible and poorer quality ores. In fact, however, not only is the evidence regarding rising cost trends still very sketchy, but it is based on the unproven assumption that most - if not all - easily accessible and high-quality mineral resources have already been located, have been taken into production, and are approaching depletion. Recent discoveries of extremely rich sulphur and copper deposits in Central Europe, natural gas in France, iron ore in Australia and oil in Mexico, all parts of the planet which were presumably well-surveyed geologically, suggest strongly that the world economy is still very far from that stage. In fact, when only poor quality mineral resources are left which can be exploited only at great expense, technological innovations may be expected to accelerate the substitution of 'cheaper' resources for those showing constantly increasing costs. Such a phenomenon occurs even in the 'very special' case of petroleum.

DC ACCESS TO LDC MINERALS

Does the lack of DC access to mineral resources represent a major obstacle to the growth of industrial economies? The deep concern with this issue may be due to ignorance of the dynamics of resource availability and of the imperative needs for growth in LDCs. Moreover, some do not realize that political realities have changed since the first half of the present century when DC resource-consumers used to enjoy the 'divine right' of free and unconditional access to LDC resources under traditional concessions.

The lack of any clear definition regarding what the right of access should or should not mean may underlie the wider confusion arising from the popular concept of resource scarcity that erroneously equates resources with reserves. Contrary to the popular impression, in part created by the term 'non-renewable resources', mineral resources are not fixed quantities but change over time. Reserves refer to the subset of total resources which are identified (proven, probable or possible), and are recoverable in a given period under existing economic and technological conditions. Consequently, the magnitude of recoverable reserves is constantly changing. Reserves are reduced by downward price changes, increases in costs, expanded availability of substitute materials and by public restrictive regulations. They are at the same time constantly enlarged by new discoveries and by new political, economic and technological developments that make it possible to produce from deposits that could not previously be exploited.

The meaningful appraisal of access to mineral resources at the global or national level is made particularly difficult by information limitations. The only source of detailed data about mineral resources stock (i.e. reserves recoverable at any given time) is the resources industry, which has an incentive to propagate the image of resource scarcity and to magnify barriers to entry into resource exploitation. The exclusive holding of such information is a prerequisite for successful participation in the oligopolistic game of exporting and internationally trading mineral resources(6).

Except for a portion of the ocean floor (and this is only temporarily valid, judging by the slow but steady progress of the UN Conference on the Law of the Sea)(7) there is not a 'no man's land' left on the planet. The issue of free access to the world's non-renewable resources lost its relevance when the political decolonization phase ended in 1975 with the disappearance of the Portuguese colonial empire in Africa. Discussion of conditions of access must take into consideration both global resource availability and the changing modes of resource exploitation practised in the LDCs.

Factors that have a direct bearing upon the security of supply for resource-deficient DCs and the barriers to entry into the resource-rich LDCs of particular relevance include: (1) the expansion of geographic limits to recoverable resources; (2) the emergence and proliferation of independent enterprises ready to provide services to the LDCs; (3) the growing LDC resource policy sophistication, and (4) increased domestic resource usage by the LDCs.

Despite rapid post-war rates of industrial growth, resource availability has more than kept pace with the increase in global consumption. Both political changes (decolonization) and the technological revolution in exploration techniques are responsible for the increased resource availability. This expansion has occurred almost everywhere. In Africa the myth of resource concentration in temperate Eastern and Southern Africa was destroyed by the important discoveries in tropical West and Central Africa and in the sub-Saharan desert region. In Asia the enormous mineral wealth of Soviet Siberia and China, almost unknown only twenty years ago, has been confirmed. Similar occurrences have been registered in the polar and subpolar parts of the Northern Hemisphere (Canada and Alaska). Other instances of change in resource availability have occurred in South America, Southeast Asia and even in Europe (Poland, both Germanies and France, among others), a continent supposedly more than fully explored over the past several hundred years.

Many exploratory techniques which originated directly or indirectly from the space programme have become common knowledge since they were developed not by private industry but by the governments of major powers. In the case of some particularly sophisticated and costly exploration methods, a proliferation of technical supply sources followed. Most people in charge of resource management policies, not only in DCs but also in semi-developed resource-rich nations, are now cognizant of this important development. The rapidly-growing availability of exploration technologies has been just as responsible as any nationalist pressure for the decline of the traditional package of exploration cum exploitation cum export trade of unprocessed resources which characterized the private mineral resource industry until the 1950s.

Then came a fairly recent extension to LDCs of the concept of mineral resources development. Few officials responsible for mineral development in the LDCs are unaware of the important role that these resources can play in the national economy. Their potential contribution in providing employment, in supplying revenues through royalties and taxes, and in providing foreign exchange through exports, is generally better understood in LDCs than may be thought. The LDCs also realize that the infrastructural aspects of mineral exploitation have an important bearing upon the general process of economic and social modernization. The associated development of communications, townships, public utilities, medical and educational services follows on the footsteps of major discoveries and of the development of important non-renewable resource deposits in relatively virgin and underdeveloped areas.

The 'discovery' of the resource management concept led the LDCs one step further. Even the poorest of them want to break from the patterns of agricultural underdevelopment and to diversify their economies, and they now appreciate that mineral resource development cannot be left to incidental foreign initiative. Many realize that domestic capacity to manage resources is necessary not only in order to strike more advantageous deals with foreign private interests, but also to turn mining into a major sector of the economy. To help develop a domestic resource policy capacity, the LDCs have some relatively new alternative sources of information, knowledge and assistance: (1) DC independent consulting firms; (2) survey missions from the socialist bloc, and (3) technical assistance programmes of UN agencies(8). In addition, missions from international financial organizations have improved the LDC tax system, and advisers from former metropoles who are keen to diminish the ex-colonies' dependence on bilateral financial aid have provided important indirect assistance. In this way, external non-private participation in the early operational stages of LDC mineral development (basic mapping, exploration, and evaluation of potential resources) and in the establishment of an institutional framework for development of the mining sector (geological and mining bureaus, state mining corporations, training of professionals, etc.) has become an increasingly important external input into the formation of mineral resources development policy in LDCs. This factor receives little attention from those in the DCs who are preoccupied with the theory that barriers to 'free access' to LDC mineral resources arise from simple 'irrational' nationalism.

The next factor to consider is the growing operational management capacity that has been developed locally in LDCs through the long presence of foreign private mining enterprises. That capacity has been generated by: (1) supervision by local authorities over foreign mining; (2) LDC restrictive policies on skilled labour imports; and (3) the large and increasing gap between the costs of expatriate and local personnel. Consequently, with the possible exception of such places as Zaire or perhaps Papua New Guinea, local participation in operational and, to a growing extent, administrative and financial management of mining operations, has increased dramatically within the past two decades. One example may suffice here. At the time of the Mexican oil nationalization in 1938 the number of local engineers employed by foreign companies hardly exceeded twenty and even the majority of foremen were foreign. When Venezuela bought out foreign oil companies in 1976, no more than fifty top executives were foreigners in the third largest LDC oil set-up in the world. The presence of local resource management capacity at the enterprise level and the well-founded belief of most LDCs that in new mining development projects such capacity can be established in the medium term plays a major role in shaping the new relations between LDC resource-holders and DC resource-users.

Finally, it must be kept in mind that some of the resource-richest LDCs like Brazil, Mexico, Indonesia or Malaysia, have advanced considerably on the road to industrialization. Thus their attitude toward resource exports is becoming conditioned by longer-term industrialization objectives that include manufacturing of industrial goods for export(9).

International mining enterprises have responded to these new factors on the world resource scene by making a conscious effort to loosen their ties with some more advanced LDCs in favour of developing countries that may be more remote but are less politically sophisticated. The future history of post-war mining in colonial or post-colonial parts of the Pacific region may discover some interesting patterns of that search for politically neutral mining resource locations. But the developments reviewed here extended rapidly throughout the LDCs during the 1960s. Consequently, it can be maintained that the 'new international resource order' started to emerge long before the OPEC - with the helping hand of oil transnationals - did what it did in 1973.

In the face of accumulated evidence it is no longer possible to defend the proposition that the DCs have exclusive control of technology, capital and markets, while the LDCs have only raw materials to dispose of. International mining corporations seem to be more aware of the change than do DC governments and academic theorists. This is why some corporations adopt much more accommodating postures vis-à-vis LDC resource-holders than do their own DC governments.

THE NEW ECONOMIC ORDER

Previous observations lead to the question of the rationale of the 'new international economic order' with regard to the resources sector and its compatibility with the needs for international economic expansion. Many volumes have been written on this subject, both by the 'new order' proponents and by its enemies. No agreement is yet in sight. But perhaps the best resumé of the political and economic rationale of that 'new order' has been provided by an African public figure:

> The New International Economic Order is about distribution: the distribution of world production, the distribution of the surpluses derived in any country and the distribution of economic power.
>
> It is about the distribution of production because unless we in the poor countries can produce more of what we need ourselves and play a greater role in processing our raw materials into manufacturing goods before exports and unless the industrialized countries are prepared to admit our manufactures, we will remain unable to meet the basic needs of our people. . . .
>
> It is also about distribution of surpluses, because, unless we can retain the surpluses earned or the goods we produce, then we will remain poor and dependent no matter how much we produce. . . .
>
> Further, a New International Economic Order is about distribution of power At present there are almost no significant formal or informal decision-taking forums in which the Third World has an effective enough voice for its interests to be taken into serious account when decisions are formulated and agreed(10).

This simple, albeit perhaps crudely worded, statement contains a clear message to the DCs in respect of the 'new international resources order'. First, LDCs are aware of their power to control physically a large part of the world's natural resources. Second, the domestic use of these resources and their processing before export should have priority over their export in an unprocessed state. Third, the LDCs aim at increasing their participation in the resource rent - in the Ricardian sense - from resource exploitation and trade(11). Fourth, they have a strong preference for negotiating the new international framework for future resource exploitation on a multilateral rather than a country-by-country or commodity-by-commodity basis.

Such messages should not be treated lightly as irresponsible nationalist aberrations. They come from the rightful holders of an important asset, sometimes their only asset, who are willing to negotiate about the form of its disposal, taking into consideration their national interests. To give priority to their own interests over those of foreign parties has been the DCs' primary rule of behaviour for quite some time. If the LDCs' demand that the rule should be given general application feeds the image of scarcity and sense of insecurity, then that is quite another story. Reactions are much calmer when countries such as Australia or Canada take the same position. In fact, resource nationalism originated in resource-rich but otherwise less opulent developed countries and not in LDCs, which are only latecomers to the game.

Perhaps fortunately for all parties concerned, there is much more to the 'new international resource order' than a search for a more equitable distribution of gains from resource exploitation and trade. If that was its single objective, the situation could easily degenerate into a very difficult zero-sum game. The LDCs posit, however, that the more equitable distribution of mining rent and profits would make sense for them only in a context of dynamic expansion of the worldwide resource economy and of reasonable stability of international resource trade conditions. Such a context changes the nature of the distributional issue into a positive non-zero-sum game. Such games are played internationally all the time.

On the basis of their own historical experience the LDCs believe that the market alone cannot resolve the issues of international distribution of gains, economic expansion and trade stability to the satisfaction of LDC policymakers. The 'once-and-for-all' character of mineral exploitation, the presence of two different actors (a national state and usually a large foreign enterprise), the distinct locations of the asset and of its 'final' disposal, imperfections of markets with a strong tendency toward oligopoly, and vertical and horizontal integration patterns of resource industry, are just a few of many elements that call into question the 'fairness' of the market solution. Issues such as steady resource output expansion and price and income stability for LDC resource-holders can be cared for only by the introduction of elements of international government action into the resource market.

Leaving aside the controversial issue of secular trends in the terms of trade(12), anyone cognizant of the problems of LDC social and economic management knows that the difficulties arising from seasonal and cyclical fluctuations in exportable resource demand make such management extremely difficult, especially during the downswing of the cycle. Recent international agency attempts at financial compensation schemes for primary producers did not prove beneficial because such schemes were not only of limited magnitude but also act _ex post_.

Under the 'new international economic order' the LDCs would like to see the early establishment of _ex ante_ price and incomes stabilization schemes along the lines of Keynes's 1942 commodity plan(13). The LDCs believe, and are not alone in this respect, that there is a need for a world wide long-run stabilization policy in the field of resource production and trade that would take into consideration conflicting interests of producers, traders and consumers(14). Such a policy could only be implemented under real life conditions, however, if its designers and implementers - governments and not private parties - kept in mind that conflicts arise not only among producers, traders and consumers but also among the objectives of growth, stability and efficiency.

Thus the LDCs posit that a realistic global - whether renewable or unrenewable - resource policy would not substitute international public intervention for market allocation, as some people may think, but would have to try hard to conciliate them. Such a policy would not be able to assure the optimal achievement of any one of the three major overall objectives of growth, stability and efficiency in the mineral sector of the world economy. Clearly, it would not be even the 'second best' policy. But as Solow wisely observed, with 'first best' policies absent from real life and 'second best' functioning quite inefficiently in the resources field, risks involved in the attempt to implement what is possible are not too great(15).

These are exactly the limited objectives pursued by the UNCTAD 'integrated commodity program' supported by the LDCs(16). While it covers major foodstuffs and other agricultural commodities, some key world-traded minerals (bauxite, copper, iron ore, manganese, tin and phosphates) form its kernel. A growing number of DC policymakers have reached the conclusion that 'the market for exhaustible resources might be one of the places in the world economy where some sort of organized indicative planning could play a constructive role'(17). As a result there is room for cautious optimism about the future of the UNCTAD scheme. Since its adoption depends upon the political will to reach a compromise and not upon technicalities, it may alleviate at least some of the tensions that characterize DC/LDC resource relations. The DCs concerned with access to resources should in all fairness keep in mind that many measures taken by LDCs during the past two decades to increase their share in resource rent and profits originated from fear of the insecurity of markets and from concern about price and revenue fluctuations.

It is worth noting that the initial hostility towards the UNCTAD 'integrated commodity program' and its central support peice, the common stabilization fund, has been fading away in the DCs perhaps more rapidly than expected. Only recently the UNCTAD scheme was considered in many places either as some sort of 'idiot's delight' or as a grandiose hoax that the LDCs wanted to perpetrate on the DCs for the purpose of destroying 'free market forces' through 'financial subversion'. Except for the indexation of commodity prices the subject is discussed seriously now both by DC scholars and policymakers(18).

CONTRACTUAL RESOURCE RELATIONS BETWEEN DCs AND LDCs

While DC concern with the worldwide extension of 'resource nationalism' received strong stimulus from the so-called oil crisis of 1973, resulting in the subsequent debate on the 'new international economic order', this in no way represented the watershed between the traditional and the innovative approach to the external exploitation of LDC natural resources. The departure from traditional practice had started in the 1950s, accelerated in the sixties and gained an upper hand during the seventies. While old colonial forms of resource exploitation agreements still survive, they have gradually been replaced all over the LDC world by new types of concession. The most innovative aspects of these consist of provisions, first, for the host country's participation in ownership and, second, for its increasing management role in most phases of the resource industry, including, in a few cases, marketing of output abroad(19).

The appearance of the modern resource exploitation concession was the result of a long sequence of slow and gradual changes in the nature of the traditional concession, based originally upon the grant of practically unrestricted rights (for half a century or more) to exploit mining enclaves in a foreign territory.

Under the 'old order', royalties accruing to the LDC in accordance with physical output volume or its estimated export price (a 'primitive' production tax), were sometimes accompanied by nominal land tax on the permanently leased mining property.

Even prior to DC discussion of such topics as the structure of international resource markets, the economic consequences of vertical and horizontal integration, transfer pricing and the like, the LDCs progressively abandoned the practice of relying on royalties as the only or main source of their resource income. This departure from past practice became quite extensive by the mid-fifties, and was in response first to LDC internal demand for financial resources and later to their growing realization that the special characteristics of mineral resource development made it an economic activity that was considerably different from either export agriculture or the first stage of (consumer goods) industrialization. Empirical observations of different operational stages of the resource sector (from exploration to marketing abroad of final product), together with growing awareness of the micro-economic and technological implications of mineral development for the local economy, led to policy measures aimed at progressive integration of foreign-owned and export-directed resource industry enclaves into domestic development.

The measures taken - individually or in packages - at a speed commensurate with differing degrees of LDC skills and bargaining power, included:

(1) replacement of royalties by export taxes and/or income taxes, later combined in some countries in special 'resource' taxation;
(2) revision and tightening up of traditional incentives - tax holidays, accelerated depreciation and depletion allowances(20);
(3) local equity participation;
(4) regulation of export-oriented resource infrastructure (railways, roads and port facilities);
(5) contracting, management and marketing agreements;
(6) joint processing facilities;
(7) provisions for employment and training of local personnel; and
(8) extension of local multiplier effect through local purchasing.

It is sometimes maintained that production sharing and contracting arrangements originated in the early 1960s in Indonesia through the initiative of European socialist countries and Japan to engage in production of agricultural commodities for export, and that only later did they start to cover non-renewable resource exploitation. Recent studies suggest, however, that such arrangements appeared more or less simultaneously in many parts of the LDC world, including Latin America(21). They responded not only to 'resource nationalism' but to technological change in resource exploitation and to institutional change in the structure of markets for 'final' mineral products (22).

Most of the measures that appear in modern contractual arrangements between LDCs and DCs may be broadly divided into financial provisions (such as increased royalties) and economic development provisions (such as promoting linkages with the rest of the local economy). Other measures, particularly some aimed at capturing an increased share of the resource rent, are now being tried, often with a considerable degree of success. Such is the case with tax measures applied by the Caribbean countries in 1975 to aluminium transnationals within the framework of the International Bauxite Association whose worldwide membership accounted for two-thirds of world bauxite reserves and mine output(23).

Implementation of the 'new resource order' has been accelerated - and not initiated - by the 1973 OPEC oil price action because that action in itself was part and parcel of the long process of change and adjustment in the patterns of resource arrangements between LDCs and DCs. The OPEC success inevitably brought other possible forms of cooperative action to the attention of mineral-producing nations. Its demonstration effect led to the setting up of bauxite and iron ore associations, which were looked upon prematurely by DCs as the beginning of a new period of 'resource cartels' that would bring havoc to the 'free working of market forces' in the resource sector of the world economy.

The nervousness of the DCs was due to their non-appreciation of some important facts. First, assuming generously that 'free market forces' did once operate in the resource sector, they ceased to do so in the inter-war period when world production and trade of key minerals became dominated by large oligopolistic corporations, which in many cases substantially controlled not only supply but also demand. The recent so-called 'resource cartels' represented only the LDC countervailing response to these long-established oligopolistic situations. Their purpose was not to confiscate but to transfer the increasing share of economic rents from these corporations to the LDCs. Second, while patterns of global resource availability offer a basis for only few LDC mineral 'cartels'(24), these cartels - if successful in raising prices above long-term market price trends - would create a danger of encouraging the exploitation of new or marginal deposits and, in the longer run, would defeat the objective of the 'resource cartels'(25).

Producer associations perform an extremely useful function from the LDC viewpoint. They strengthen and continue what used to be informal LDC information networks, not only with respect to general world market conditions in specific resource industries, but also with respect to the characteristics of individual production cum export arrangements in different countries. The increased flow of economic and technological information from the DCs and LDCs through non-private channels prior to 1973 was largely responsible in the sixties for the emergence of resource development policy concepts in the LDCs and for their growing resource management capacity. While the post-1973 producer associations have been of limited use in cartelizing resources, they have been of considerable assistance in standardizing LDC positions vis-à-vis international corporations and DC resource-consumers. The role of information as the decisive input in policy formation, long appreciated by the DC private resources industry, has now become recognized by many LDCs.

Thus the dynamics of the world resource situation, multiple factors underlying LDC demands for the 'new international economic order' in search of better equity, stability and expansion of international resource economy; the important micro-changes that have occurred in individual arrangements and agreements between LDC resource-holders and the DCs provide substantive evidence to the effect that the 'new international resource order' has been more rapidly implemented than it may seem on the surface. Perhaps the continuous progress of its implementation has in part been responsible for LDC pressure for accelerating the rate of change.

CONCLUDING REMARKS

This paper suggests that the traditional division of production factors in the resource sector into DCs with exclusive control of capital, technology and markets, and LDCs with only non-renewable resources, became progressively transformed, thus significantly altering the relative bargaining power of the parties involved in resource exploitation and marketing. This is particularly true with respect to technology (assuming that technology covers all kinds of know-how) and markets. In the special case of oil the same can be said about capital.

This new situation may somewhat complicate mutual adjustments between LDC resource-holders and DC resource-users, but it will not make them impossible. Even under conditions of increasing technological capability and LDCs' growing domestic demand for resources, the LDCs cannot follow extremely conservationist policies. They badly need resource export proceeds for financing economic growth and sometimes also for participating in the international power game, and are little interested in a zero growth strategy.

Throughout the debate about the 'new international economic order' the LDCs have demonstrated great interest in trading access to raw materials - under the new conditions of co-participation in most stages of resource development - and for access to markets. As a competent observer of the world economic scene, sympathetic to the LDC position, remarked:

> Outside a few possible special cases, such as oil, LDC bargaining power could best be employed in broadening and improving existing international resources markets; DC commitments regarding freedom of access to their markets and a gradual end of their protectionism must be the necessary price for their gaining access to LDC supplies(26).

Other observers have expressed the belief that the necessary quid pro quo might be found on a lower and less politicized level. Thus a 1974 UN report asserted that in view of the desire of non-oil exporting countries to achieve a substantial and lasting improvement in the prices of their primary commodity exports, and in view of the DC need for an assured supply of essential raw materials and foodstuffs at reasonable and relatively stable prices, 'there should be a common interest in broad supply commitments by exporters and purchasing commitments by importers' under a general commodity stabilization scheme(27).

Given DC refusal to accept the principle of indexation, the trade-off between access to resources and access to markets does not seem possible. But the possible establishment of a weakened version of UNCTAD's 'integrated commodity program' might be of considerable help in smoothing out the bilateral resource negotiations at the country or the enterprise level. What is hardly likely, however, is the acceptance by the LDCs - without change - of the Japanese scheme for resource development cum imports under long-term contracts. In inflationary times such arrangements make little if any sense to LDC resource-holders, even if the contracts were to incorporate ex ante the indexation clauses to which, for obvious reasons, Japan continues to be opposed. The lack of LDC enthusiasm for such long-term schemes can be better understood if one recalls the remarks of a well-known United States authority on international trade that while 'the fear of losing access to raw materials led some DCs to dream of reviving the special relationship with selected LDCs', the LDCs 'have to gain from a multilateral market free of neo-colonial overtones'(28).

Assuming the relatively speedy adoption of the 'integrated commodity program' and some relaxation of quantitative trade restrictions applied to the LDC manufactures and semi-manufactures under special preferential schemes, the question of the future shape of bilateral resource exploitation arrangements between LDCs and DCs can be raised. In general terms they will follow the trends of the past twenty years, which were described aptly in the following terms:

> . . . the new structures have broken the tight link between ownership, control, and financial risks and benefits that was inherent in the traditional concession. Arrangements have been negotiated that have repackaged these elements in ways not feasible under the old structures. Because ownership and control have become important political symbols in most developing countries, new contractual forms have been created to allow greater freedom in allocating ownership, control and financial risks and benefits in ways that satisfy both the economic and new political imperatives. Where a foreign firm is considered important for its financial, technological, or marketing contributions, the new structures permit the negotiation of agreements that grant control and financial arrangements reflecting the bargaining powers of the parties. Ownership can be allocated in a way that makes the presence of the foreign firm politically acceptable in the host country(29).

Considering the relation between LDC resource-holders and DC resource-users, it is quite probable that major changes will take place in both resource exploration and in the marketing of the 'final' product.

The LDCs will pursue to an increasing degree the objective of putting resource exploration and evaluation in the hands of independent enterprises through the use of service contracts. The worldwide proliferation of sources of such know-how provides the LDCs with considerable opportunities in that field. Moreover, independent exploration represents the most convenient and sometimes the only way to obtain information needed by the LDCs for negotiating either exploitation service contracts or joint exploitation arrangements. Decisions that are correct from the resource-holder's viewpoint on the terms of service contracts or on equity participation in the exploitation cum export stage, depend greatly upon the availability of correct information on the size, wealth and geological characteristics of new resource assets, the subject of bilateral negotiations.

There are two reasons for insistence by LDC resource-holders on local processing. First, the increased degree of local processing translates itself into balance-of-payments gains and savings to the domestic economy if it contributes to economies of scale in the domestic manufacturing industry. Second, it expands taxable profits through higher value added. The LDC demand for increased processing of resources at home may be met relatively easily by foreign mining corporations. Not only do they often have ownership links with LDC industrial sectors, but the trend towards a major degree of processing at source responds to their own interests of saving on labour and transportation costs.

Although continued trends in the LDCs toward joint ownership and/or management of non-renewable resources for export can be expected, it is hard to speculate about concrete formulae with respect to the degree of LDC financial involvement. While, on political grounds, LDCs may continue to insist on majority capital participation, they are becoming more and more aware that capital control does not automatically lead to real control of the enterprise. Capital scarcity, together with other considerations, may thus lead some LDCs towards the so-called tripartite arrangements involving co-participation of local public and private capital along with that of foreign investment. In the more advanced LDCs, a limited financial presence in resource development may become attractive to local private industry, whether domestically- or externally-owned, both because it offers direct profits and also because it is the place in which important pricing decisions affecting the domestic industrial sector are made.

It is difficult to state whether such complicated joint ventures will be easy to manage. Their success will depend upon the satisfactory solution of numerous problems with respect to management, technology and the distribution of profits. The history of conflicts within joint United States-Japanese industrial ventures established in Japan in the period 1967-75 suggest that most of them can be solved(30).

An increasing number of LDCs have adopted the position that technology transfers that take place exclusively through foreign enterprises - whether in resource industries or elsewhere - do not offer a satisfactory basis for establishment of domestic technological capability in that they are unduly expensive and contain many clauses that restrict the use of the technology. Consequently, the LDCs will continue to search in all resource exploitation stages for unpackaged technology that is available from foreign private and public sources through alternative channels. This trend will be facilitated by the growing number of alternative technology sources. With respect to pricing technology acquired in packages cum foreign investment, all imported capital goods, the major LDCs will press for the unpackaging of these transactions for negotiating purposes and for the separate pricing of different parts of the package in accordance with market conditions prevailing in the DCs. The long-term objective here is to acquire technology from DCs under the most favoured-nation clause, i.e. not to pay exorbitant premiums for the ignorance of international technology market conditions.

Finally, one can expect that all future bilateral resource contracts involving LDC resource-holders will have to contain clear, unequivocal and fairly detailed general review clauses in order that their content may be periodically adjusted to changing conditions of resource industries, particularly in the light of subsequent agreements entered into by the parties involved. These clauses may provide for periodical reviews (every three to five years) and/or for emergency reviews in the case of pertinent worldwide or local developments. Moreover, the agreed clauses may list all specific issues due for revision. The acceptance by the DC resource-users of such review clauses in all resource exploitation arrangements with the LDCs would go a long way toward minimizing conflict. Some internationally acceptable guidelines with respect to the behaviour of international resource enterprises in the LDCs - one may add as a final thought - might be of help in getting rid of many conflicts that have characterized this sector of the world economy over the past twenty years.

NOTES

(1)   The politics and the economics of oil - albeit highly relevant to the subject of this paper - are not treated here.

(2)   Jan Tinbergen (Coordinator), Reshaping the International Order - A Report to the Club of Rome, Dutton, New York, 1976 and Wassily Leontieff, et

al., The Future of the World Economy - A United Nations Study, Oxford University Press, New York, 1977.

(3) Tinbergen, op. cit. p. 255.

(4) For details see Leontieff, op. cit., pp. 44-9.

(5) By stating that 'total resources are large enough to stagger imagination' the U.S. Society of Economic Geologists' symposium adopted in 1972 a similarly optimistic attitude toward the problems of mineral wealth in the United States. See Eugene Cameron (Editor), The Mineral Position of the United States, 1975-2000, Wisconsin University Press, 1973.

(6) As Robert Solow noted: 'our actual oligopolistic, politically involved, pollution producing resource industry is not exactly what the textbook ordered'. Richard T. Ely Lecture, 'The Economics of Resources or the Resources of Economics', The American Economic Review (May 1974), pp. 1-14.

(7) 'La négotiation d'une convention internationale a progressé', Le Monde, 17-18 July 1977, p. 32.

(8) For details on the last point, see United Nations, Mineral Resources Development with Particular Reference to the Developing Countries, New York, 1970. The document, published three years before the OPEC 'disaster', reported that during the 1960s the UN has organized geological and mineral survey missions to over fifty LDCs, including such exotic places as Afghanistan, Burundi, British Solomon Islands and Madagascar. While some missions failed to transmit knowledge, others succeeded.

(9) Miguel Wionczek, 'Latin American Growth, Trade and Cooperation', Vierteljahresberichte, 68 (June 1977), pp. 107-19.

(10) Amon Nsekela, 'The World Bank and the New International Economic Order', Challenge No. 1 (1977), pp. 78-9.

(11) The DC literature on this subject is not particularly voluminous. See, however, Solow, 'The Economics of Resources', and Helen Hughes, 'Economic Rents, the Distribution of Gains from Mineral Exploitation, and Mineral Development Policy', World Development, Vol. 3, Nos. 11-12 (1975), pp. 811-25.

(12) As W. Arthur Lewis wisely suggests, the solution of this issue should be left in the hands of economic historians. See his The Evolution of the International Economic Order, Research Program in Development Studies, Woodrow Wilson School, Discussion Paper 74, Princeton University, N.J., March 1977 (mimeo).

(13) John Maynard Keynes, 'The International Control of Raw Materials (1942)', Journal of International Economics, Vol. 4 (1974), pp. 299-315.

(14) This point is emphasized in all UNCTAD literature on the subject. For details, see Alfred Maizels, 'A New International Strategy for Primary Commodities', in G.K. Helleiner (Editor), A World Divided - The Less Developed Countries in the International Economy, Cambridge University Press, 1976, pp. 31-52.

(15) Solow, 'The Economics of Resources', op. cit., pp. 6-7.

(16) For the present position of the LDCs, the DCs and the socialist countries on the UNCTAD 'integrated commodity plan', see Dragoslav Avramovič, 'Commodities in Nairobi', Development and Change, Vol. 8, No. 2 (April 1977), pp. 231-47.

(17) Solow, op. cit., p. 13.

(18) For a comprehensive resumé of these debates, see Marina von N. Whitman, Sustaining the International Economic System: Issues for U.S. Policy, Essays in International Finance, Princeton University, 121, June 1977.

(19) David Smith and Louis Wells, Jr, Negotiating Third World Mineral Agreements: Promise as Prologue, Ballinger Publishing Company, Cambridge, Mass., 1975.

(20) The evidence has accumulated the world over that such incentives were unnecessary and often expensive gifts to foreign mining enterprises. See Hughes, op. cit.

(21) Smith & Wells, op. cit.

(22) Anthony Scott, 'The Development of the Extractive Industries', Canadian Journal of Economics and Political Science, Vol. 28, No. 1 (February 1962), pp. 70-87.

(23) For details, see Malcolm Gillis and Charles McLure, Jr, 'Incidence of World Taxes on Natural Resources with Special Reference to Bauxite', The American Economic Review (May 1975), pp. 389-96.

(24) Marian Radetsky, 'The Potential for Monopolistic Commodity Pricing by Developing Countries', in Helleiner, op. cit., pp. 53-72.

(25) See Hughes, op. cit., and Lewis, op. cit.

(26) Carlos F. Díaz Alejandro, 'North-South Relations: The Economic Component', in C. Fred Bergsten and Lawrence Krause (Editors), 'World Politics and International Economics', International Organization, Vol. 29, No. 1 (Winter 1975), p. 277.

(27) United Nations, Problems of Raw Materials and Development, Report of the Secretary General of UNCTAD prepared for the Sixth Special Session of the General Assembly, New York, 1974, p. 16.

(28) Díaz Alejandro, op. cit., p. 278.

(29) Smith & Wells, op. cit., p. 52.

(30) 'Joint-Venture Problems in Japan', The Economist, 14-20 May 1977, pp. 100-1.

CHAPTER 17

Less Developed Countries and Transnational Corporations: Conflicts over Technology Transfer and Major Negotiable Issues*

This paper defines and analyses the conflicts resulting from the present mechanisms by which technology is transferred from transnational corporations (TNCs) to the developing countries. It is hoped that a study of this kind will be of help in solving some of these conflicts to the ultimate benefit of the latter.

There are three main reasons why there is an urgent need to find solutions. First, the available evidence strongly suggests that TNCs represent a permanent feature of world productive structure, particularly in the field of manufacturing. Second, since TNCs are a major worldwide source of modern technology, it is highly likely that most of the technologically underdeveloped countries will continue to depend for quite some time upon technology produced, owned or controlled by these global firms. Finally, developing countries have become increasingly dissatisfied not only with the terms and the conditions of technology transfer through TNCs but also with the results of such transfers.

THREE DIFFERENT VIEWS OF TECHNOLOGY TRANSFER THROUGH TNCs

There are three schools of thought on the role played by TNCs in international technology transfer to developing countries. These three viewpoints may be called orthodox, radical and reformist.

The orthodox viewpoint is shared by TNCs and the governments of major TNC home countries. It maintains that technology produced in the advanced countries is appropriate to the needs of developing countries and that the most efficient and adequate mechanism for transferring this technology is commercially, through TNCs. A statement made by an official spokesman for the United States,

---

*This paper was written in the winter of 1977/78 for the UN Center on Transnational Corporations, and published by the United Nations under the title Measures Strengthening the Negotiation Capacity of Governments in their Relations with Transnational Corporations: Technology Transfer through Transnational Corporations, A Technical Paper, United Nations, New York, 1979.

which is the largest single source of modern technology, summarizes that position:

> Present U.S. policy is predicated on the belief that investment and investment-related activities (e.g. licencing, service and management contracts) represent the most <u>effective method</u> [italics added] for the international transfer of privately-owned technology. The U.S. continues to favour a liberal investment policy with a minimum of government intervention in the transfer of technology process. Such a policy attaches much importance to the maintenance of a sound and predicable investment climate in the recipient country, i.e., an environment which allows a reasonable return on investment and protection of proprietary rights. Without these factors, transfer of privately-owned technology to the developing countries runs the risk of being significantly reduced. Likewise, we believe that the adoption of rigid and unduly restrictive rules could also act as a serious disincentive to technology transfer. In short, the policy is one of support for international technology transfer and development on the part of the private sector, and the development of indigenous scientific and technological capability in the LDCs by the U.S. public and academic sectors(1).

The rationale for this orthodox viewpoint is based on the following propositions. First, most modern technology is available to the developing countries through transfers among TNC members (affiliates wholly or predominantly owned by the parent), because such transfers offer all the necessary combinations of technology components within a complete system of technology development and transfer. Second, technology transfer needed to establish any new productive facility is a complicated process, requiring special knowledge and skills for each stage of the facility's development. Transfer involves, among other things, the mastery of process and product technology, technological support from the source of technological inputs during all the stages of transfer, and a learning capability in the technology-receiving unit. All these conditions can be fulfilled only within a TNC because of the intricate relationship among its affiliates, the markets served, and the technology itself. So, full and successful technology transfers are highly unlikely without majority ownership and probably require full ownership.

The orthodox school insists that the alleged success of TNCs in transferring technology is due not only to their mastery of the whole 'technology package' - from the conceptualization of the project to the marketing of the final product - but also to the fact that this package is closely integrated with management, marketing and financing skills. The 'technology package' covers many stages, including site selection, decision on plant size, plant construction and start-up, continuing operations, and constant product adaptations and changes. Thus it is more than the sum total of the different pieces of knowledge necessary to solve specific technical problems at various stages. The most important 'parts' of knowledge are not embodied in designs, manuals, patents and other written mechanisms of transfer; rather they consist of the accumulated experience of people who run industrial operations on the global scale within a TNC system. It is stressed that such knowledge cannot be acquired in the market separately through licensing, technical literature or imitation.

According to the same orthodox viewpoint, any attempt to unpackage the technology transfer will either fail or result in considerably larger costs to the new productive unit. Most technological transfer literature, apparently reflecting the intense political feelings about foreign investment and foreign technology, tries to separate elements of technology transfer that in actual business practice are usually combined. But this viewpoint considers such theoretical efforts at best misguided. While isolated pieces of technology may be usable at times, full technology transfers and their translation into productive units require an understanding of the environments of both the source and destination of the technology(2).

The orthodox position is based upon a number of premises and assumptions open to serious questioning by technology recipients, particularly the developing countries. Some of the more significant of these are the following:

(1) The world is composed of technologically advanced centres, located in the home countries of TNCs, and technologically backward developing countries.

(2) The technological problems of the developing countries are the same as those of the advanced technology-producing centres.

(3) The international division of labour between technology-producing countries (or rather, global units such as TNCs) and technology consumers is a natural state of affairs that must be accepted by all parties.

(4) TNC control of most modern technologies makes it advisable and unavoidable that the backwardness of developing countries should be eliminated through the adoption of these technologies.

(5) Not only is technology socially neutral, but its external control has no major social or political consequences.

(6) Since technology transfer consists of a physical transfer of knowledge across national boundaries through the establishment of a new productive unit, the welfare of the host country will automatically increase - regardless of who controls this unit - by the amount of knowledge physically transferred to its territory.

(7) The price that the recipient pays for technology is not an issue, for three reasons: first, the price cannot be established because of the complexity of the technological knowledge and its transfer; second, the transfer of technology involves costs far beyond any price its present owner may charge the recipient, and third, technology flows within a TNC offer large external economies to all parties, including the host countries.

Practically all these premises are rejected by the radical school of thought, and most of them are also rejected by the reformist school. Both radical and reformist critics have marshalled considerable evidence to support this position. This evidence is based on theoretical considerations as well as on observation of actual technological behaviour by TNC affiliates, not only in developing countries but also in more advanced countries which, because of their own technological lag, are almost completely dependent upon technology imports via TNCs.

The main tenets of the _radical_ position on technology transfer are:

(1) The present international technological division of labour is not the natural state of affairs but the result of historical developments.

(2) Technological problems of the developing countries are not the same as those of technology-producing centres, because they have basically different social and economic problems.

(3) Because the social and economic structures and problems of developing countries are different, technology available in the advanced countries, mostly controlled by TNCs, is not appropriate for these less developed societies.

(4) The location of all major research and development (R&D) in the advanced home countries confirms that technology transfer by TNCs involves only the physical transfer of modern productive facilities controlled centrally from outside.

(5) Technology is not socially neutral, and the external control of technology has most serious social, economic and political consequences for developing countries. Its mass and undiscriminating import keeps them in a condition of technological dependence by making it unlikely that they will design and produce technologies appropriate to their own needs and conditions.

(6) TNC ownership and control of technology is not only the most important mechanism of these firms' continuing technological domination of the developing countries but also a major source of TNC profits.

(7) The only way that developing countries can break out of this permanent technological dependence is to drastically limit imports of TNC-owned and controlled technology and to turn to inward-organizing broad technology import-substitution programmes. These should not copy advanced technologies but rather involve the design of 'appropriate' technologies and the fostering of technological cooperation and exchange among all developing countries(3).

The radical school offers, among other things, the following evidence to support its position:

(1) The only two countries which have escaped technological dependence in recent years and become political, economic and technological powers despite their initial technological poverty are Japan and the Soviet Union. Both countries - one capitalist and the other socialist - engaged in long-term mass imports of foreign-owned technology rather than foreign direct investment with its resulting loss of ownership and control. This strategy permitted them to build up during the present century their own scientific and technological capabilities and to retain autonomy in using this accumulated and assimilated stock of knowledge for their own needs. On the other hand, all the developing countries that accepted technology imports with private capital investment are today more technologically dependent upon the outside world than ever, since they never developed their own indigenous scientific and technological capabilities.

(2) Technology imports via private capital investment have not alleviated but actually compounded the development problems of developing countries. The internal gap between foreign-controlled technological enclaves and the rest of the society has increased secularly. Whatever appropriate indigenous technology existed before the mass entry of foreign modern technology has been destroyed. Furthermore, mass technology imports have negatively affected income distribution, employment opportunities and the use of domestic inputs for development.

(3) The inappropriateness of advanced country technologies to the social and economic conditions in most developing countries seems to have increased in recent years because:

(i) New 'advanced' technologies are becoming increasingly product-specific because of the growing market for 'luxury' consumption goods in the rich countries;

(ii) Each round of new investment tends to incorporate new capital-intensive technologies;

(iii) The growing technological differentiation of the productive system in the advanced countries leads to more standardized products and to an employment pattern which places much greater emphasis upon specialization of functions;

(iv) Modern firms show a growing tendency to compete in terms of the technical sophistication of their products rather than in the price, relying upon certain sales techniques to ensure consumer acceptance of these 'new' products, and,

(v) The dramatic increase in advanced countries in the scale of production, which is both cause and consequence of the very rapid differentiation of technologies at the production stage, makes production in small developing country markets seem relatively inefficient.

(4) Since technology import costs have become a major drain on the balance of payments of developing countries, their global external dependence continues to increase with no sign of any reversal in the foreseeable future.

The _reformist_ school posits that developing countries need an appropriate mix of technologies and not just appropriate _home-made_ technologies. Such a mix includes modern foreign-produced and controlled manufacturing technology, available chiefly through TNCs. Without import of these technologies, developing countries would not be able to build up their domestic consumer durables and capital goods sectors nor their export manufacturers. TNCs have a useful role to play, provided two conditions are fulfilled: first, that TNC technology imports are directed and controlled by the host countries so as to contribute to the creation of domestic scientific and technological capability and, second, that these technology imports are not considered the exclusive or the most important channel of transfer. Reformists stress that TNC performance in this respect is highly disappointing, because the technological and other objectives of TNCs differ considerably from the national objectives of the developing countries and also because the developing countries have not yet been able to define technological autonomy goals and design policies to achieve them.

Reformists make the following observations in arguing that technology transfers via TNCs are far from an unmixed blessing for the host developing country:

(1) While TNCs play an essential role in disseminating and diffusing technological knowledge worldwide, a large percentage of their technology sales consists of internal trade between parent companies and foreign subsidiaries because of their general unwillingness to license technology to third parties.

(2) Since the available evidence strongly suggests that TNC parent companies get more royalty payments for low-technology industries, the theory of product

cycle would indicate that relatively little new technology is transferred from the parents to their foreign affiliates.

(3) The actual host country cost of internal TNC technology transfers is considerably higher than that recorded in payments of royalties for knowledge and trademarks and financial charges for technical assistance. Recorded payments do not include the considerable indirect cost to affiliates (and thus to the host country) which may not be immediately apparent under the elaborate internal accounting procedures practised by most TNCs. Also, there are some additional costs from restrictions upon the use of this imported technology dictated by the global interests of the TNC parent.

(4) In their strategy of product differentiation, most TNCs appear to devote more resources to lesser innovations used in the manufacture of new products than to the search for new production processes. Furthermore, TNCs concentrate on consumption-oriented rather than production-oriented technology in developing countries.

(5) Technology transfers within TNCs that tend to standardize production, management and marketing techniques generally reflect the patterns of the highly advanced countries, endanger the R&D activities of local enterprises, and run counter to developing countries' attempts to develop technologies more 'appropriate' to their own needs and their factor endowment.

(6) While TNC R&D activities are highly centralized in the parent company, any local activities in affiliates are mostly limited to adapting the final product to consumer preferences and do not lead to any substantial innovation.

(7) Not only have R&D expenditures in TNCs been unevenly distributed between parent and affiliates but worse, foreign affiliates often have to finance new products and processes without deriving any benefit from them, since TNCs prefer to exploit their product advantage by exporting rather than by transferring their latest technologies to affiliates.

(8) The global strategy of TNCs undeniably generates technological dependence in the host country. For one thing, national firms cannot match the global research and development of a TNC. Also, when TNCs expand abroad through acquisitions or take-overs, the R&D activities of the acquired local firms are either integrated into the global system or totally discontinued(4).

Thus the reformist school insists that the TNCs and their defenders equivocally equate technology transfer with the diffusion of innovation within TNCs. However, international diffusion of information and knowledge, defined as the process by which products or products and process technologies, previously unavailable to the recipient country, are diffused across national boundaries, does not represent real technology transfer.

The reformist idea of development does not accept the concept of technological dependence. According to reformists, real technology transfer must include some absorption and assimilation of the technology by the host country in a way that permits the county to utilize the technology on its own and subsequently use it to create new technologies. Mere movement of technology within the same channel (such as parent company investment abroad in a wholly-owned or majority-controlled affiliate) does not constitute transfer per se because it is usually not accompanies by any important technological spill-over to the recipient society. While such spill-over is far from automatic and very often goes against the interests of the foreign technology owner, it can be achieved with the help of appropriate host country policies. As long as TNCs continue to insist that the mere physical movement of processes, machinery, management or products across national borders represents real transfer, conflicts between them and the developing countries will increase.

Reformists insist, furthermore, that the intensity of these conflicts will not diminish as long as developing countries continue to regard the TNC as the major channel of international technology transfer, as many still do. While they might increase the TNC contribution to real technology transfer through long-term technological and development policies, they must also employ alternative channels for enhancing their technological capability: technical literature, training abroad for personnel, exchanges of information and personnel through technical cooperation programmes, imports of machinery and equipment, licensing of proprietary knowledge, industrial espionage, etc. Moreover, developing countries should build their own bargaining power vis-à-vis TNCs by seeking alternative sources of technology among smaller industrial and other firms in the advanced countries. Firms which are not TNCs have important technological resources in sectors such as electronics, scientific instruments, computer software, automotive parts and petroleum exploration, among others. The technological progress made by smaller firms in advanced countries in agriculture and energy and in social sectors such as medicine and health, housing, educational services, etc., should also be kept in mind. Since the developing countries have a better bargaining position with small companies than with TNCs, they can obtain important technology from these sources at more advantageous terms, either through straight purchases or joint ventures. Because of the dynamic nature and entrepreneurial spirit which characterize many of these small firms, their contribution to the development efforts of host developing countries and the magnitude of real transfer may be substantially greater than that obtained through the TNCs, particularly in relation to the degree of dependence and the financial costs involved.

THE SEARCH FOR MAJOR NEGOTIABLE ISSUES

Although most developing countries have technology transfer options other than TNCs, this paper concentrates on how developing country bargaining power in this area can be enhanced so that TNCs may be used as a vehicle to build up domestic technological capability. There are limits, however, to the extent to which this is possible. These are imposed not only by TNCs strategies and preferences for wholly-owned affiliates abroad when export sales of finished products are impossible, but also by such factors as developing country industrialization policies, international industrial proprietary systems, and the technological fixity of production processes.

There are two parallel approaches to be taken in dealing with conflicts over technology transfer: (1) multilateral negotiations to elaborate international rules of the game in the last segment of world trade - technology trade - where no such rules as yet exist; and (2) the national approach, involving a strengthening of the bargaining position of individual developing countries so they can negotiate technology transfer arrangements that would not only offer better terms than in the past, but would also take into account their developmental needs.

The multilateral approach has advanced considerably in the past few years through the UNCTAD negotiations on an international code of conduct for technology transfer. It is hoped that these negotiations will lead to the convocation of a UN Negotiating Conference on the code, perhaps later in 1978(5). Moreover, a code of conduct for transnational corporations, on which the UN Commission on Transnational Corporations began work in 1976, is also expected to occupy itself with, <u>inter alia</u>, (1) contribution by transnational corporations to the scientific and technological development of their host countries and (2) appropriate participation by transnational corporations in the technology transfer to developing countries(6).

Except in some of the larger developing countries, however, there has been much less progress with respect to the strengthening of host country negotiating capacities(7). This lack of progress is due as much to the TNCs' bargaining advantages as to the fact that most developing countries have not yet been able to define clearly the issues to be negotiated with foreign companies. Most of them are far behind the theoretical literature in their conceptualization of these negotiable issues and often adopt positions consisting of a contradictory mixture of the orthodox, radical and reformist viewpoints.

There has been growing concern over the contribution of TNCs to the scientific and technological development of developing countries and over their participation in the real transfer of technology to these countries. This concern was reflected some years ago in recommendations contained in the report of the Group of Eminent Persons on the impact of multinational corporations on development(8), which prepared the way for the establishment of the United Nations Commission on Transnational Corporations. Among these recommendations, the following are particularly relevant:

(1) International organizations should try to revise the international patent system and evolve a system which would reduce the cost of technology provided by TNCs to developing countries.

(2) The host government should carefully evaluate the suitability of any product for meeting local needs before a TNC is permitted to introduce it into the domestic market.

(3) National agencies for screening and handling TNC investment proposals should be responsible for evaluating the appropriateness of the imported technology, assisted by information and advisory services provided by international institutions.

(4) Host countries should require TNCs to make reasonable contributions towards product and process innovation suited to national or regional needs, and should further encourage them to undertake such research through their affiliates.

(5) Host countries should explore ways of importing technology other than by foreign direct investment, and should acquire the capacity to determine which technology would best suit their needs.

In view of our earlier discussion, it appears that six issues of growing concern to developing countries deserve attention in bilateral negotiations between individual countries and TNCs:

(1) The real cost of the technology acquired, as measured by profits, royalties, technical assistance fees and other payments made by affiliates to TNC parent companies;

(2) Conditions imposed by the TNC parent upon the use of technology acquired by affiliates for production of goods for both local and external markets (restrictive business practices, use of trademarks, etc.);

(3) Developing country inability to obtain through TNCs required inputs, among other things technology, capital, management and new external markets, other than through a fully TNC-controlled package;

(4) The relative appropriateness to host country needs of technology transferred from TNCs to their foreign affiliates;

(5) The scope, nature and direction of research and development of TNCs in their host countries; and

(6) The impact of local personnel training and subcontracting by TNC affiliates upon national technological and industrial capabilities.

Until very recently, most developing countries, including such major ones as Argentina, Brazil, India and Mexico, concentrated their attention on ways to reduce the cost of foreign technology, eliminate restrictive conditions on the use by local affiliates of parent company technologies, and unpackage the 'bundle' of technology, management and capital in large, mostly state-sponsored projects. There has been much less attention paid in developing countries to the relative appropriateness of imported technology and the spill-over of TNC technology to the rest of the economy through the research and development activities of TNC affiliates, local training of personnel and subcontracting. Stronger action in these areas would have required the integration of technological and industrial policy, and the integration of these with long-term development policy - a condition which has been largely absent so far, not only in developing countries but in most advanced countries as well.

TECHNOLOGY COSTS

Several larger developing countries, mainly in Latin America, have experienced some success in reducing cost and eliminating restrictions on the use of TNC-controlled technology. That is because from the mid-1960s these countries have had administrative mechanisms for regulating technology transfer in the form of national registries for technology transfer contracts. The establishment of such registries enabled them to collect a large number of transfer contracts, something previously unavailable to national governments. A comparative analysis of these contracts by the authorities of various developing countries revealed general levels of direct technology transfer payments by economic sectors and patterns of restrictions on the use of the imported technology.

This led to the discovery, first, of major individual upward deviations from international patterns of royalty and other technology payments and, second, of major upward differences in payments within sectors compared with payments made by developed countries with a comparable market size and production structure. While the first deviations indicated monopolistic technology pricing, the second suggested general overcharging that developing countries accepted through a lack of information about world technology cost factors.

When faced with convincing evidence of overcharging according to international standards, TNCs have grudgingly accepted the two basic premises of technology transfer regulatory authorities: first, that similar technologies should be similarly priced, and second, that with some adjustment for market size, the most-favoured-nation clause should be applied worldwide to technology transactions in the same way as it has been applied to the international trade in goods and other services. Thus the disclosure to competent national authorities of the prices of imported technology led to numerous fruitful negotiations, ending with considerable decreases in direct technology costs to developing countries.

Serious difficulties arose, however, and will continue to arise, in two situations quite common in intra-TNC technology transfers: first, when technology has been made available to the affiliate allegedly free of charge and, second, when the parent finances its global research and development by imposing a general levy upon all its affiliates.

Considering that one of the major objectives of a TNC is to maximize its global profits, there is no reason to accept at face value the contention that the parent provides any input to its affiliate free of charge. In real life, there are no free lunches nor free technology transfers. 'Free' provision of technology in a TNC system means only that an unknown or undefined cost of technology is charged to the affiliate through indirect channels such as export pricing of inputs other than technology (capital, capital equipment or intermediate goods) and other transfer-pricing practices(9). The fact that once a TNC decides to transform a fully-controlled affiliate into a joint venture (or is forced to do so under host country prodding), it starts immediately charging the new company directly for technology transfer, is not necessarily a sign of an intent to increase profits. In most cases it only means that the previously available internal accounting procedure is being replaced by direct technology cost accounting and payments.

TNCs also contend that the constant flow of technology within the global productive system makes it impossible to price these flows separately, because neither technology cost nor its market value can be defined. But this contention should not be taken too literally by the host country either. Despite their aversion to selling technology outside their system through licensing etc., most TNCs engage from time to time in such operations. When they do so, the pricing of both embodied and disembodied technology does not seem to create unsurmountable accounting or other difficulties. So national regulatory agencies should insist upon the disclosure of additional financial data when TNC affiliates receive 'free' technology from their parent. This will permit the host country to at least estimate the real cost to it of a 'free' technology circulating within a TNC system.

The practice of many TNCs of fixing the affiliate financial contribution to their global R&D effort complicates the task of national regulatory agencies charged with controlling technology costs and prices. First, it is extremely difficult to ascertain whether the outflow of these funds for general R&D exceeds the value of technology actually transferred, although the circumstantial evidence strongly suggests it generally does. Second, since payments are used to finance future R&D activities rather than to cover past expenses, there is no guarantee that such future activities will be of benefit to the affiliate. The product cycle theory says that the foreign affiliate is bound to derive benefits from such future technological innovation only after a very considerable delay. Instead of promptly transferring their latest technology to subordinate members of their system and producing new goods in foreign markets, TNCs prefer to exploit their technological advance by exporting new goods.

Under pressure from the national regulatory agency, a TNC affiliate will consider lowering direct technology payments to the parent to bring them into line with international levels of royalty or technical assistance fees. But it is a much more formidable task to bring about the disclosure of indirect affiliate costs of free technology or to reduce the size of a fixed technology assessment, particularly in case of a very large TNC with a dominant position in the world market. In the first situation it would be necessary to find out the going market prices of individual inputs imported by the affiliate from the parent. The job, though difficult, is not impossible, however, because comparable inputs are sold in the world market at arm's-length by competing producers from the same sector. Furthermore, contrary to TNC contentions, there is no such thing as a completely original and exclusive technology not comparable with anything else, except perhaps in the case of very advanced military research and development which is of little interest to most developing countries. In the case of a fixed technology assessment by a very large TNC using, for example very sophisticated technology from the production of computers, the situation may look almost hopeless from the viewpoint of the host country's regulatory agency. But the recent elimination of the leading foreign computer firms from Brazil without any apparent danger to local industrial development suggests that at least the more advanced developing countries have some room for action in that respect too.

RESTRICTIVE PRACTICES

It seems much easier today than even a few years ago to liberalize the restrictive conditions imposed by a TNC parent upon its affiliates' use of technology, because of the very considerable progress made in identifying these conditions both on the international level and in bilateral technological relations. The clear identification of such restrictive business practices would not have been possible without the work started by the developing countries in 1972 at UNCTAD on an international code of conduct for technology transfer, and without the parallel collection of relevant information by national regulatory agencies in Latin America. At UNCTAD the developing country experts elaborated an impressive list of some forty restrictive business practices applied in technological transactions. While other similar practices may have been discovered by national regulatory agencies elsewhere, all major worldwide practices associated with technology transfer, which adversely affect competition or increase the market dominance of the technology holder, have by now been identified. While normally these restrictive practices are applied in arm's-length technology transfer, a TNC may also impose them upon its foreign affiliates in order to strengthen its centralized control and to maximize global profits. These practices include: territorial market restraints; tying transferred technology to the purchase of goods or services within the TNC system; restricting an affiliate from entering into agreements, involving competing or complementary technology; restrictions on research and development; and restrictions on adaptation or innovation of technology.

The application of these restrictions by TNCs to foreign affiliates harms the host country in several ways. It may seriously constrain the affiliate's export capacity, increase the cost of technology, isolate the affiliate from the broad stream of worldwide technological advance and impede expansion of the affiliate's technological capacity. Some authors insist that estimates of the financial impact of these restrictive practices upon the total cost of developing country technology transfers should also include the costs, or rather the potential losses, arising from the failure to achieve such transfers because of these restrictions.

The experience of developing countries that have tried individually or jointly to eliminate or limit the use of these restrictive practices has demonstrated that once such practices are identified it is relatively easy for the host country's regulatory agency to enforce their partial disappearance if it takes a pragmatic approach. The relative ease of the task is due not to the country's sovereign right to legislate but rather to the fact that most of these restrictive practices are considered illegal in the major advanced countries that are home countries for TNCs and also major sources of technology transfer. So, despite the lack of any formal international agreement outlawing restrictive business practices, there do exist common international standards. Consequently, TNCs are willing to abide by these standards if the host country can prove their violation and if it is willing to act 'reasonably', in the sense of not pressing too hard for full elimination of those restrictive practices that may be of vital interest to a given TNC or may reflect past commitments to third parties.

The clearest example of restrictions that cannot be totally eliminated by a host developing country are territorial market restraints upon foreign affiliates and the tying of transferred technologies to the purchase of goods and services within a TNC system. From the viewpoint of a host country, certain types of market restraints and purchase agreements may be more important than others. Thus it is up to the host country to use a common sense approach in deciding which restrictive practices it can and which it cannot tolerate, without falling unnecessarily into a rigid non-negotiable position. It may be worth mentioning, for example, that after establishing the National Registry for Technology Transfer for both TNC affiliates and third parties, Mexico was able to eliminate from transfer contracts most of the restrictive clauses dealing with exports, production, use of complementary technologies, purchase of equipment and raw materials, etc. Similar success was reported in Argentina and Brazil during the early 1970s before their technology transfer control mechanisms were liberalized under pressure from TNCs.

THE UNBUNDLING OF THE TECHNOLOGY PACKAGE

Transnational corporations' clear preference for providing the package of technology, capital and management and, in some cases, for also opening new external markets through fully-controlled affiliates, represents a much bigger challenge to developing countries than excessive technology pricing or restrictive business practices. TNCs usually insist that because of the complexity of providing technology, production, management and new product distribution in a developing country, all the subsequent stages of setting up, operating and managing an affiliate - whether in manufacturing or other sectors - must be tightly controlled by the parent. The counter-proposition by a host country that a joint venture would serve its interest better misses the central issue: that technology, and not capital participation, is the decisive factor in the control of a modern enterprise. Thus, unless the local partner - be it the state or a private party - has developed its technological capability, the establishment of a joint venture (even with majority control by local interests) will not necessarily reduce its technological dependence upon the TNC parent. At best, the joint venture may result in the appropriation of a part of the economic rent by local participants, and serve some political purpose.

But it will hardly, by itself, affect the nature of technology transfer or the degree of technological dependence.

Once this important point has been clarified, it is worth examining why TNCs insist upon full control of all closely interrelated 'bunches' of technological knowledge needed to establish a manufacturing affiliate. Most, if not all, of these 'bunches' encompass roughly the following eight stages of the process of pre-investment, construction and the putting on stream of a new manufacturing project: (1) feasibility and market surveys prior to the investment decision; (2) determination of the range of available technologies and choice of the most 'appropriate' one; (3) engineering design, involving both plant design and selection of machinery; (4) plant construction and installation of equipment; (5) technology process design; (6) management and operation of production facilities; (7) marketing; and (8) minor innovations to improve the efficiency of the established process.

A TNC engaged in setting up a fully-controlled manufacturing facility in a developing country will insist upon minimal host country interference in technological decisions in these areas, justifying its behaviour by citing the success of the TNC system and its previously established foreign affiliates. Three major considerations can be detected behind TNC insistence on this point: first, TNC control of a given process and product technology gives the final product an advantageous position vis-à-vis the host country and competitors; second, the duplication of technologies, controlled very often through an interlocking system of patents, assures the affiliate of a well-protected, long-term market not only for final products but for most technological and physical inputs needed from its setting-up stage to the end of its productive life; and third, unless the technology used by the new affiliate is basically the same as that available to the rest of the TNC system, the TNC will not be able to reap the full advantages of external economies and operational integration.

Consequently, a TNC has by definition little interest in spreading technical knowledge outside its affiliates or in building up the technological capability of the host country. The real diffusion of technology within the host country might in the long run weaken the foreign affiliates' privileged position by creating local knowledge of technological options and, where there is an expanding market, by increasing the danger of entry by competitors.

There are two exceptions to this TNC restrictive attitude towards the real transfer of its technology outside its affiliates. Technical assistance will be provided, for a price, to local producers of intermediate inputs and to consumers of the affiliate's final products. The purpose of such technical assistance is to strengthen the TNC's market position by tying to the affiliate both sources of local inputs and local consumers of the final product. Thus, the 'satellization' of subcontractors and customers, rather than the expansion of their technological capability per se, is the objective of any foreign TNC affiliate. This point is very often overlooked by a host developing country when it demands that a TNC affiliate increases the local content of its product or establishes wide technical training programmes for its product distributors.

As long as new products are selected for domestic production under the traditional import-substitution strategy (which implicitly defines ex ante technological choices), a host country with weak internal technological capability has little chance of avoiding the perpetuation of foreign-controlled technological and productive enclaves in its industrial structure. Since both product and technological choices are left in fact to the TNC, the host country is in a position to negotiate with affiliates only minor things such as the size and the location of the plant, local participation in plant construction and installation of equipment, and the degree of employment of local personnel. But these issues do not involve major technological decisions nor the unpackaging of different technology 'bundles'. Neither do they involve autonomous decisions by the host country about the social and economic appropriateness of technology, because the technology to be used has been defined by two factors: the decision to produce a given product and the control of the concrete technological option by a TNC.

The TNC involved in setting up a new foreign affiliate or introducing a new product in a captive market is perfectly aware that its technology should be adapted in a minor way to the size of the market and the availability of some local inputs. Very often the affiliate will do this on its own without any prodding by the host country. But when it is a question of major adaptations, involving, for example, the increased use of labour instead of capital, the TNC affiliate will be most reluctant to proceed, even under the pressure of the host country. There are various reasons for this: first, local and global profitability may conflict with each other; second, the adaptation of process technology may involve some risks, whereas capital equipment and related existing process and product technologies seem risk-free; third, machines create fewer problems than human labour, particularly in a relatively unknown milieu; and finally, any major tampering with plant design, selection of machinery and operation of production facilities would certainly affect the full integration of the affiliate into the TNC system.

Only the most developed of developing countries in terms of the size and diversification of their productive system, or countries that will consciously try to build up their technological capability, are able to avoid technological dependence upon TNC affiliates. Even in such cases, attempts at unbundling the technology package will most probably fail at the setting-up stage of a TNC manufacturing affiliate, because at that point the bargaining power of the newcomer <u>vis-à-vis</u> the host country is particularly strong. Faced with demands it considers unreasonable, a TNC may simply forego its initial investment decision, with only minor losses incurred in feasibility studies and market surveys.

The power relationship between a TNC and a host country changes considerably, however, once a foreign affiliate starts operating. Contrary to popular thinking, the establishment of an affiliate abroad puts very serious constraints upon the freedom of a TNC. The possible capital loss from closing down the affiliate's operations represents perhaps the least constraint, since this can almost always be written off for tax purposes by the global TNC system in such a way that the real financial loss is only minimal. Far more important to the parent TNC is the complete loss of a market considered highly promising and the public admission of a major error of judgement that may seriously impair its national image. Consequently, most TNCs are willing to go a long way in accepting the host country's <u>ex post</u> demands before withdrawing from it completely.

It is at that time that the host country is in a position to press for such concessions as a relatively major adaptation of products, the introduction of new products better suited to the local factor endowment, the increased use of local raw materials and intermediate products, and the expansion of R&D

facilities beyond the quality control stage. Some countries such as Brazil, India and Mexico have been fairly successful in this, especially in the durable consumer industry characterized by mature technologies, where the spectre of competition from new local or mixed-capital firms makes the TNCs willing to renegotiate their original technological strategies. Even in these situations, however, the host country should not be overly optimistic as to the magnitude of the technological spill-over from the TNC affiliate to the rest of the economy.

Individual measures, such as unpackaging a 'little bit' of a TNC's technology, capital and management 'bundles' through the establishment of joint ventures, increasing the degree of adaptation of foreign-designed products to local conditions, incorporating certain more labour-intensive processes into the production flows and expanding the use of local inputs may have a number of benefits for the host country in terms of the style of life, employment objectives or balance-of-payments considerations. But all these benefits are most probably marginal, short-lived and of limited relevance for the objective of transforming traditional technology transfer (diffusion of technology within the TNC) into real technology transfer that will strengthen domestic technological capability and diminish technological dependence. Such measures will have lasting effect only if they are supported by a well-defined, long-term domestic industrial policy integrated closely with a policy of building up the infrastructure, human resources and institutions for an autonomous technological effort. This, in turn, depends upon the quality of the educational system and the innovating capacity of the state and the local public and private entrepreneur.

THE APPROPRIATENESS OF TNC TECHNOLOGY TRANSFERS

Another major issue worthy of becoming the subject of bilateral negotiations between developing countries and TNCs is the appropriateness to the host country's needs of technology made available by the TNCs to their foreign affiliates. To claim that many TNC-transferred technologies are not appropriate to the needs of the host countries does not necessarily imply the unreserved acceptance of the radical viewpoint discussed earlier. The development of operative proposals for increasing the appropriateness of TNC-controlled technology runs into a number of serious difficulties because of the confusion surrounding both the concept of appropriateness and the definition of developing country needs. Under the implicit normative assumption that the purpose of development in a developing country should be to fulfil the basic needs of its society, most technologies which TNCs provide to foreign affiliates are not appropriate. They seem less inappropriate, however, under the more relaxed and perhaps more realistic assumptions that: (1) the industrialization process per se represents over the long term the most important way out of underdevelopment, and (2) practically all developing countries are characterized by a considerable degree of openness vis-à-vis the world economy, a trend increased by the emergence of TNCs.

Under this assumption, the appropriateness of TNC-controlled technology would have to be judged by the degree to which it contributes to the broadening of the industrialization process and/or the expansion and diversification of the host country's export trade and the improvement of its terms of trade with the outside world. While TNC-provided technologies are rarely appropriate for the broadening of the industrialization process in developing countries, they are often appropriate from the viewpoint of the second objective. Without the mass entry of TNCs into developing countries, the impressive expansion of developing-country manufactured exports to the advanced countries in recent years would have been impossible. Consequently, one might posit that host countries should try to commit TNCs even more than previously to transfer of technologies that would help potential developing-country manufacturing output enter foreign markets. Such a strategy, however, is not devoid of serious longer-term problems, as the experiences of the Republic of Korea, Taiwan, and other TNC export platforms in Eastern Asia have demonstrated. These experiences strongly suggest that developing-country export objectives may work at cross purposes with other objectives during bilateral negotiations with TNCs unless the export objectives become integrated into a longer-term development strategy involving, at least in theory, a mix of outward- and inward-directed development. Although such a mix of development policies has been successfully practised since the mid-nineteenth century by most of today's advanced countries, even the more developed and larger developing countries seem to be unable as yet to evolve that sort of integrated long-term strategy. Instead, in response to the vagaries of the international business cycle, wars and other external political cataclysms, they try simultaneously every possible partial and contradictory development strategy (expansion of international trade links, import substitution and regional integration) with quite disappointing results.

The other way of judging the appropriateness of TNC-controlled technologies is with respect to the size of the market and the factor endowment. The obvious fact that technological progress depends on the size of the market available to the innovating firms has been discovered only recently, because of the long-standing divorce in developing countries between the economic and the engineering professions. For a long time it had been forgotten that present and, at times, successful attempts to scale down and adapt modern industrial technologies to smaller developing country markets were preceded by about a century of continuous scaling-up of technologies originally invented for the relatively small markets of the United States and Western Europe in the nineteenth century. This scaling-up was necessary so that new technologies could serve markets constantly expanding in response to population growth, transport improvements and rising incomes.

Until very recently the scaling-down of TNC technology to the size of the market was not very fashionable. First, there were the two conventional reasons: (1) the alleged technological fixity and indivisibility of most processes invented in the advanced countries; and (2) the global advantages accruing to the TNC from the reproduction of available technology in affiliates without major adaptation. Another important reason was that because of their lack of technological sophistication, the developing countries themselves for a long time thought that the absence of alternative lower scales of production in the advanced countries reflected some undefined 'natural' or 'scientific' law. They would have been surprised to learn that the archives of many TNCs (as well as independent firms and individual inventors) were full of technological innovations and process and product technologies which had never been put to use simply because they were not required by the market size or the factor endowment in the advanced countries. This naiveté has led developing countries, attracted by the mirage of the easy import-substitution strategy, to accept at face value most TNC arguments that any attempt to tamper with the scales of given technologies would lead to serious diseconomies. It has also induced them to offer TNCs very generous concessions and subsidies in the form of tariff protection in cases where the use of technologies inappropriate to the size of the local market resulted in the construction of plants with excess capacity and unduly high fixed capital investment.

Only in the past few years has the issue of the scaling-down of technology become the subject of more serious discussions, perhaps under the dual impact of the increased technological sophistication of some developing countries and growing international technological competition. The first surveys of the state of the art in scaling-down technology brought unexpected, highly interesting results. They indicated that while the technical and economic feasibility of scaling-down existing product and process technologies is quite limited, it increases considerably if the reduction of scale is accompanies by major adaptation of the product or process. They also indicated that process industries are at present less promising candidates for scaling-down through change and adaptation of technology than mass-production, heterogeneous product industries, because process industries involve more complex design features and require sophisticated scientific and engineering skills both for redesign and actual operation. Heterogeneous product industries offer quite a large range of possibilities for scaling-down and for the partial substitution of labour-intensive techniques for capital-intensive ones(10). These possibilities, which seem particularly promising in such industries as electronics assembly, agricultural equipment, sugar, pulp and paper, and even steel, offer great negotiating opportunities to developing countries in their dealings with TNCs.

THE SCOPE AND NATURE OF TNC RESEARCH AND DEVELOPMENT ACTIVITIES IN DEVELOPING COUNTRIES

As a rule TNCs do not engage in R&D activities in developing countries and may limit such activities even in the advanced host countries of their affiliates. A report by the National Conference Board of the United States estimated that foreign R&D activities of United States-based TNCs in 1971 and 1972 amounted to only about 10 per cent of domestic R&D expenditures of all United States companies out of their own funds (i.e., excluding support by the United States government). These expenditures were made primarily in Canada and Western Europe, with about two-thirds of the total being spent in Canada, the United Kingdom and the Federal Republic of Germany. Only a negligible share of the total was spent in developing countries. Even in the most advanced of these, there are relatively few R&D laboratories, and most of them are concerned primarily with technical services and quality control. A study launched recently by the University of North Carolina with TNC funding corroborates this(11).

The same study noted a gestation sequence of R&D activities in TNCs which is closely tied to market growth and sophistication, to the level and nature of manufacturing activities, and to supporting infrastructure. Though there are some exceptions in which a TNC affiliate entered more serious R&D activities after acquiring a local company with a somewhat sophisticated laboratory, the normal sequence consists of a TNC affiliate's development of a quality control unit within the manufacturing plant and some engineering capability to provide process assistance on the plant floor. At some later point, as manufacturing operations grow in size and sophistication, technical service and quality control activities tend to be organized in a separate laboratory within the TNC affiliate. Eventually, such a laboratory may become the base for process and product adaptation of activities transferred from the parent. The emergence of such primitive R&D laboratories, able to begin rudimentary adaptation of imported process and product technology to local demands and the use of local inputs, takes as a rule some five years. Another five years may be needed to build up the unit in a foreign affiliate to the level at which it has the same capability to adapt process and product technology to local needs as similar facilities in the advanced countries. Thus, under present conditions, some ten years may be needed to create within a TNC affiliate some indigenous research capability that can increase the number of products adapted or processes brought in from the parent company and start some embryonic applied research on its own - provided the TNC parent shows an interest in such activity(12).

The few country studies of developing countries present a similar picture. In India, for example, where most TNC affiliates established R&D units under governmental pressure, these units have not done nor do they plan to do any basic or applied research. They are mainly geared to adaptation and experimental activities related to the environment and the use of local materials. The generation of new production technology is extremely weak, because 'formal arrangements between the parent and the subsidiary have little tendency to allow for any departure from the parent's technology and technical change'(13).

In Kenya there has been a general lack of technical change locally generated by TNC affiliates. These affiliates have also failed to respond to the government's attempts to induce them to develop their own technology. The only government measure to have any impact was the imposition of tariffs, which played some part in inducing the affiliates to increase the number of products assembled locally(14).

The Kenya study ascribed these attitudes of local TNC affiliates to the smallness of the economy and the underdevelopment of its industrial sector. But the discovery of similar findings for Argentina, one of the most industrially-advanced developing countries, cannot be so easily explained away. Although a considerable amount of adaptive and innovative R&D takes place within TNC affiliates in Argentina, very rarely is it used internally. Except for a few cases in which the affiliate achieved increased importance within the TNC system because its R&D achievements were applied by the system as a whole, there is evidence that even when the local affiliate accumulates considerable technological experience in the local market, the successive generation of product and plant designs used locally is decided and worked out by the TNC parent(15).

The Argentinian findings, along with circumstantial evidence gathered in Brazil, Canada and Mexico, strongly suggest that in the more developed of the developing countries and even in some advanced TNC host countries, two types of specialized R&D activities have emerged within the TNC systems. Both fit perfectly the general pattern of centralization in the TNC parent. The first type consists of small local R&D activities aimed at adapting new products or processes to the affiliate's local market. Since these activities are limited to quality control, technical services and miniaturization of the technical norms used in the home country's development and engineering activities, they have only a weak innovation function. The second type of R&D responds to the TNC's need to specialize for world markets. It engages on behalf of the parent in fragmented work of high scientific standard, stays in direct and permanent contact with the parent's central laboratory, and does research of little immediate interest to the local affiliate.

In both cases, the local facility is unable to function independently, in view of its close dependence upon the TNC system and its lack of control over the innovation process. These patterns used in some larger developing countries apparently originated some fifteen to twenty years ago in Canada, host country to the largest number of TNCs in the world. R&D of Canadian-based TNC affiliates (and consequently of Canada as a whole) was described a few years ago as being either non-existent or very sophisticated and highly developed. It is practically non-existent in cases where TNC affiliates operate only support laboratories which serve exclusively as technical service centres to examine why a product may fail to operate in the Canadian market, to help with its adaptation to that market, and to adjust or scale-down foreign manufacturing technology to local conditions. On the other hand, it is sophisticated and highly developed in cases where the parent has set up in Canada an independent R&D laboratory aimed at serving its international research programme. Such an advanced laboratory does not interact with local manufacturing activities. It reports directly to the parent and confines its research to a specific stage of the R&D process. While such an enclave-type of R&D does increase the innovation capability of a TNC, it offers little benefit to the host country, except in the employment opportunities it provides to local highly-qualified manpower(16).

Thus available worldwide evidence suggests that the host developing country cannot expect too much from TNC expansion of local R&D activities. If things are left to 'natural' forces, the affiliate may take fifteen to twenty years to build facilities which will have some rudimentary ability to perform basic and applied research related to problems of the host country. If the host country presses for the more rapid expansion of R&D, and if the affiliate finds highly qualified manpower available locally, it may establish on behalf of its parent a kind of independent laboratory like those presently found in Canada, the United Kingdom or the Federal Republic of Germany. In both cases, the technological dependence of the host country will not be abated.

Perhaps the only way out of this painful dilemma for some larger developing countries is to build up their own national R&D centres in a few important, carefully defined areas, and to impose upon TNC affiliates the obligation to subcontract some of their research projects to these centres and to permit their technical personnel to serve actively as part-time teachers and part-time researchers in their centres. Since such practices have been introduced in some advanced host countries in Western Europe, and in former British dominions (Canada, Australia and South Africa), and since certain TNCs are willing to acknowledge that internal technology transfers within TNC systems fail to increase domestic technological capability, host developing countries may be able to obtain genuine TNC assistance for their national R&D centres and their educational systems.

Such TNC activities are bound to remain haphazard and marginal, however, unless the host countries undertake a major effort towards identifying the potential of TNCs to help national technological capabilities beyond the limits of traditional technology transfer. Useful ideas in this area, involving some of the smaller advanced countries, emerged in the OECD Directorate for Science, Technology and Industry in 1974. The OECD proposed a major research programme on the effects of TNCs on national scientific and technological potentials as a result of their production and transfer of scientific and technological knowledge and their position in the industrial structure of individual OECD countries. The proposed research was to focus on a few important industrial branches and cover the following issues:

(1) The overall pattern of international R&D in each of the selected branches and the relative importance of TNCs in such efforts;

(2) The forms and manners through which the scientific and technological activities of TNCs establish relations with the domestic R&D potential of individual countries, and the consequences and impact of these relations;

(3) The geographical distribution among TNC home and host countries of the TNCs' laboratories, pilot plants and testing centres;

(4) The type of relations that exist between the different R&D units and engineering units identified;

(5) The relations established, if any, between affiliates and local research centres and universities;

(6) The status of nationals employed as research workers and engineers in R&D units of affiliates and independent TNC research centres (level of qualifications, proportion of total staff, place of training, promotion opportunities, participation in advanced training courses outside the TNC system, and circulation within the firm);

(7) In cases where the birth of an affiliate was the result of a takeover or acquisition, whether the R&D activities of the former enterprise have been maintained, increased reduced or suspended; and

(8) The nature and intensity of the flow of technology disseminated in the host economy through industrial and commercial exchanges between TNCs and local enterprises. This would consist of:

(i) An assessment of the exact TNC mechanisms used in the host country to transfer technology between the parent company and affiliates, or between affiliates;

(ii) An analysis of the technology policies followed by the parent and its local affiliates in their relations with competing national firms (patent policies, degree of exchange of information, cross-licensing, written agreements on technology and production); and

(iii) An analysis of the form and intensity of the contractual relations established between affiliates and local forms that supply intermediary products required as production inputs or purchase the TNC affiliates' production.

To date no information is available on the implementation of this OECD research programme, which was presumably related to OECD work on a code of conduct for transnational corporations that ended in mid-1976 with the publication of the OECD Guidelines. Although the project was reported abandoned because of opposition by some major OECD members and many TNCs, its revival at the international level would be of great importance to these developing countries which are negotiating for greater TNC contributions to their domestic technological capability. The importance of such a research programme is due to the fact that individual developing country governments do not seem to have clear answers to such questions as:

(1) The way in which TNCs through patent policies, abolition of R&D in acquired local firms, market dominance, or other business strategies, restrict the

availability of technologies useful to the host country's objectives;

(2) The extent to which, if any, R&D undertaken by the TNCs (whether in the home or host country) and the diffusion of TNC-controlled technology to suppliers and customers contributes to the building up of host country technological capability beyond what is necessary for the TNC's particular business objectives;

(3) The way in which host country policies affect the R&D strategies of TNCs and how they contribute to national objectives of home and host countries;

(4) The relevance to the host country quest for technological capability of the TNC transfer of technology to local firms through subcontracting; and

(5) The extent to which and under what conditions the technological and managerial training of local scientists and engineers by TNCs contributes to host country objectives.

The scant literature on these questions in the developed countries suggests that there is considerable ignorance in these areas worldwide. The fact that TNCs seem unwilling to discuss these problems openly feeds growing public scepticism both in advanced countries and developing countries towards the elaborate and expensive public relations campaigns of TNCs aimed at sustaining their image as 'good world citizens'.

SUBCONTRACTING AND PERSONNEL TRAINING

TNC subcontracting to local firms and affiliates of other TNCs has expanded considerably in the past ten years to provide intermediate inputs for production for domestic markets and for manufactured exports. TNCs are principally motivated by the desire to employ cheap labour, sometimes enhanced by tax concessions and credit subsidies granted by developing countries seeking to alleviate serious and growing problems of unemployment. Most TNC subcontracting is carried out in Mexico, Central America and the Caribbean, chiefly by United States-based TNCs; in the Far East, by United States and Japanese TNCs; and in North Africa, by European TNCs. The TNCs' power in subcontracting arrangements arises from their control of technology and of access to markets (both in developing and developed countries). Such arrangements are particularly common in electronics, automotive components, semi-processed foodstuffs and other consumer non-durables. According to the destination of the final products, subcontracting can be related to exports to developed countries, exports within a developing country's region and import substitution of components manufacturing within developing countries. In Puerto Rico, for example, all local subcontracting by TNCs is related to exports of final consumer goods to the United States. Mexico, on the other hand, represents a case in which intermediate inputs produced by local firms are incorporated into goods exported to the United States and to Latin America - under the LAFTA preferential trade system - and also into products consumed domestically.

Some developing countries regard TNC subcontracting to local firms not only as a factor helping to solve the unemployment problem and improve the balance of payments on current account, but also as an important step on the road to industrialization. On the other hand, TNCs emphasize that subcontracting can, among other things: provide for the transfer to developing countries of second-hand technologies and low-cost and labour-intensive equipment; be based partially on the use of local technologies which at a later stage, with TNC assistance, can be improved and can lead to the emergence of more 'appropriate' local technologies; increase the general level of technological skills of the local labour force, since it involves strict specifications and quality control of intermediate products; result in considerable improvement of organization and management techniques among subcontractors; and, finally, lead eventually to the development of joint ventures. But even if all these indirect benefits are accepted, it still has not been proved that subcontracting in developing countries offers a major channel for the real transfer of technology(17).

One of the few studies on technological aspects of international subcontracting makes the following distinctions among subcontracting arrangements: (1) between independent units in countries at different levels of development; (2) between a local firm and a TNC or its local affiliate; (3) between two subsidiaries of different transnationals in the same country; and (4) between two subsidiaries of the same transnational enterprise in different countries(18). Since none of these arrangements involves, by definition, the creation of new technological knowledge by the subcontractor, their contribution to developing country technological capability is limited to the diffusion of existing knowledge to the subcontracting firms within the limits of traditional TNC technology transfers. Such diffusion tends to consolidate the dominant technological position of the contracting party rather than develop the scientific and technological capabilities of other TNCs. The situation could change in favour of developing countries only if their own governments would offer extensive assistance to local subcontracting firms through: the development of national R&D centres in sectors in which subcontracting arrangements are concentrated; the fostering of product design centres; the provision of financial resources for local R&D activities at an individual firm level, etc. Until now, however, because of their erroneous view of the limited nature of TNC technology transfers, few, if any, developing countries have organized such local technology development programmes.

Most, if not all, TNCs dedicate considerable resources to the training of local personnel at all levels because of the high relative cost of using expatriate personnel and the pressure of host governments for the 'nationalization' of the affiliates' personnel. TNCs claim that these training activities represent perhaps their biggest single contribution to the growth of developing country technological capabilities. Like many other TNC contentions, this assertion should not be accepted at face value. TNCs and their local affiliates train personnel for their own use and take every possible measure - including salary policies - to prevent the 'pirating' of this personnel by competitors, government agencies and the system of higher education. The degree of intra-country mobility of high-level manpower employed by TNC affiliates depends on many factors. A recent study suggests that such mobility is higher in countries with a high degree of competition among TNCs of different nationalities (e.g., South Africa) or in countries whose economic structures has been radically changed by an important discovery of new resources (e.g., Nigeria where oil was discovered), as opposed to developing countries advancing steadily along the path to industrialization with a large presence of TNCs of the same nationality (e.g., larger Latin American developing countries). These findings would suggest that only the participation of TNC personnel in research, training and teaching activities outside the affiliates themselves would represent a meaningful contribution to the growth of the country's autonomous technological capability. It is up to the developing countries to impress upon TNCs the need to expand such activities.

CONCLUSIONS

In line with economic and social development models, most developing countries need an appropriate mix of technologies which includes, particularly for the industrial sector, modern foreign-produced and controlled technology, available mostly (although not exclusively) through TNCs. Imports of this technology are necessary for the expansion of their consumer durables and capital goods sectors and for their production of manufactures for export to advanced countries. The present condition for these imports, via TNC technology transfers, is highly unsatisfactory from the viewpoint of the developing countries: they are expensive and full of restrictive conditions and do not, as a rule, contribute to domestic technological capability.

There are, however, reasons to believe that TNCs could play a more useful role in technology transfer to developing countries provided: first, that technology imports via TNCs were controlled by the host countries in such a way that there was more spill-over of the imported knowledge to the host society, which would, in turn, contribute to domestic scientific and technological capability; and, second, that technology imports via TNCs were not regarded as the most important channels of transfer but were accompanied by other independent transfers. It must be stressed, however, that the technology transfer performance of TNCs has been highly disappointing up to now, not only because mature TNCs prefer to keep their technology under exclusive control but also because the developing countries have not yet been able to define technological autonomy goals, design proper domestic technological policies, and negotiate commitment by TNCs to abide by such goals and policies.

To solve the increasingly frequent conflicts between TNCs and developing host countries over the issue of technology transfer, two parallel approaches are needed: (1) international multilateral negotiations to elaborate worldwide rules and standards for technology trade; (2) bilateral negotiations with TNCs on specific transfer of technology arrangements for the purpose of providing developing countries with better transfer terms and increasing the direct contribution of these transfers to the host countries' domestic scientific and technological capability.

Six major issues arising from traditional TNC technological transfer should become the subject of bilateral negotiations between individual countries and TNCs:

(1) The real cost of the technology acquired, as measured by profits, royalties, technical assistance fees and other payments made by the affiliates to TNC parent companies;

(2) Conditions imposed by TNC parents upon the use of technology given to affiliates to produce goods for both local and external markets (restrictive business practices, use of trademarks, etc);

(3) The developing countries' inability to obtain through TNCs required inputs of technology, capital, management and new external markets, among other things, in forms other than a fully TNC-controlled package;

(4) The degree of appropriateness to the host country's needs of technology transferred from TNCs to foreign affiliates;

(5) The scope, nature and direction of R&D activities of TNCs in the host country;

(6) The impact of local personnel training and subcontracting by TNC affiliates upon national technological and industrial capability.

A number of developing countries has recently been able to bring down the cost of technology transferred via TNCs and to eliminate many restrictive conditions imposed on such transfers. Since such a task has proved possible only when the host country has full knowledge of the content of technology transfer contracts, the setting up of national regulatory agencies such as registries of technology transfers is essential if developing countries hope to negotiate better transfer terms.

In two common situations, however, the task of bringing down the technology cost becomes particularly difficult: when technology is provided to the affiliate from the TNC system allegedly free of charge and when the parent finances its global R&D effort by a general levy imposed upon its affiliates. Nor has it proved possible to eliminate all restrictive conditions imposed on the use of technology imported by affiliates from TNC parents.

The unbundling of the technology package confronts developing countries with much bigger challenges than excessive pricing of technology or restrictive business practices. The idea accepted by many of them that the establishment of joint ventures results in such unbundling and a subsequent decrease in technological dependency is not supported by evidence. Unless the local partner, be it the state or a private party, has developed its own technological capability beforehand, the establishment of a joint venture, even if majority-controlled by local interests, will not necessarily reduce its technological dependency upon the TNC parent. It may lead to an increase in technology costs instead.

Only the most developed of the developing countries endowed with relatively large markets, or those that have consciously sought to build up domestic technological capability, are able partially to escape from technological dependency upon TNC affiliates through a combination of measures: the establishment of joint ventures, and/or increasing the adaptation of foreign-designed products to local conditions, incorporating certain more labour-intensive processes in the production flow, and expanding the use of local inputs. But even such measures, in most cases, will do very little to transform traditional technology transfer (diffusion of technology within the TNCs) into real technology transfer and thus strengthen the host country's domestic technological capability. The more lasting benefits can be achieved only if such measures are supported by a well-defined, long-term industrial policy integrated closely with a national development policy and a policy of building up infrastructure, human resources and institutions for an autonomous technological effort.

While most TNC-transferred technologies are not appropriate for the fulfilment of basic developing country needs, they may be appropriate in varying degrees to the export objectives of the host country. Considering the degree of openness of most developing country economies, these countries should press TNCs for more transfers of technologies suitable for bringing their potential manufacturing output into the markets of the developed countries.

In the case of import substituting activities, there is considerable and growing room for adapting TNC technologies to the size of the local market and to the factor endowment. Although most developing countries are still unaware of these possibilities, recent research in both the advanced countries and the developing countries has shown that there is a considerable increase in the technological and economic feasibility of scaling-down imported product and process technologies if this is accompanied by a major adaptation of the product or process. There is growing worldwide evidence that a new approach to a technological process, in which the various steps in the process are analysed and low-scale operations considered, is becoming more usual - something which would have been considered impossible by the advanced countries and most TNCs even five years ago. These possibilities, which seem to be increasing, particularly in such industries as electronics assembly, agricultural equipment, sugar, pulp and paper, and even steel, offer great negotiating opportunities for developing countries in their future dealings with TNCs.

Since not too much spill-over of technological knowledge from R&D activities of TNC affiliates to developing societies can be expected, these countries should consider building up their own R&D centres in a few important, carefully defined areas. Then they should get TNC affiliates to subcontract some of their research projects to these centres and permit their scientific and technical personnel to participate in them actively as part-time teachers and researchers, in an effort to counteract the tendency for TNC local R&D facilities to become focal points for an internal brain-drain.

TNC affiliates' training programmes for their personnel and technical assistance for local subcontractors are of limited value in building up domestic technological capability in developing countries. Their indirect effects upon the diffusion of technological culture in the developing countries should not be underestimated, however, particularly in dynamic economic growth situations. By creating new job opportunities, these programmes increase the mobility of high level managerial and technical manpower within the country.

NOTES

(1)   Walter B. Lockwood, United States Representative at UNCTAD deliberations on a code of conduct on transfer of technology, 'Transfer of Technology: The U.S. at the UNCTAD Negotiations', in U.S. Policy toward Science, Technology, and Development, Conference on Transfer of Technology: The Future of Regulation, Washington, D.C., April 1977.

(2)   Jack N. Behrman and Harvey W. Wallender, Transfers of Manufacturing Technology within Multinational Enterprises, Ballinger, Cambridge, Mass., 1977, Preface, pp. xiii-xvii and Chap. I, pp. 1-21.

(3) The most recent complete statement of the radical position can be found in Frances Stewart, Technology and Underdevelopment, Macmillan, London, 1977, particularly in Chapter 4, 'Appropriate Technology' and Chapter 5, 'Technological Dependence', pp. 95-140. See also, among others, Norman Clark, 'The Multinational Corporation: The Transfer of Technology and Dependence', Development and Change (The Hague), Vol. 6, No. 1 (January 1975), pp. 5-21.

(4) For more extensive elaboration of these points, see, among others, Chrles-Albert Michalet, ' The International Transfer of Technology and the Multinational Enterprise', Development and Change (The Hague), Vol. 7, No. 2

(April 1976), pp. 157-74, and Keith Pavitt, 'The Multinational Enterprise and the Transfer of Technology', The Multinational Enterprise, John H. Dunning (Editor), Allen and Unwin, London, 1971, pp. 61-85.

(5) The present state of UNCTAD pre-negotiations concerning the code of conduct for technology transfer, which covers not only transfer undertaken by TNCs but all sorts of commercial transfers, is described in UNCTAD, Report of the Intergovernmental Group of Experts on an International Code of Conduct on Transfer of Technology at its Fourth Session, held at the Palais des Nations, Geneva, from 31 October to 10 November 1977 (TD/AC.1/L.5).

(6) 'CTC Intergovernmental Working Group: Chairman's suggestions for an annotated outline of a code of conduct', The CTC Reporter (New York), Vol. I, No. 2 (June 1977), p. 11.

(7) Latin American experiences in the late 1960s and the early 1970s were analysed in detail by the author in 'Notes on Technology Transfer through Multinational Enterprises in Latin America', Development and Change (The Hague), Vol. 7, No. 2 (April 1976), pp. 135-56. See also Chapter 15 of this volume.

(8) The Impact of Multinational Corporations on Development and on International Relations, United Nations publication, Sales No. E.74.II.A.5, pp. 68-70.

(9) The objective of transfer pricing or administrative price setting within a TNC system goes beyond merely assuring that the system exacts maximum profits from the transfer of technology to affiliates. Behind transfer pricing, Vaitsos identified such diverse factors as (a) global tax minimization or tax avoidance; (b) reduction of tariff impact on goods produced in the same country; (c) market control and price setting that impedes entry of other firms; (d) hedging against changes in currency values; and (e) reduction of the risk of host government reactions, trade union pressures and anti-trust and other governmental actions in response to high profitability. For details, see Constantine V. Vaitsos, 'Foreign Investment and Productive Knowledge', in Beyond Dependency, Guy F. Erb and Valeriana Kalab (Editors), Overseas Development Council, Washington, D.C., September 1975, pp. 75-94.

(10) There is growing worldwide evidence that a new approach to a technological process, in which the various steps in the process are reconsidered and redesigned, can produce an economic and low-scale operation - something which would have been considered impossible by the advanced countries and by most TNCs even five years ago. For details see, among others, R.B. McKern, A Survey of Opportunities for Low Scale Manufacturing in Developing Countries, OECD Development Centre, Paris, April 1977; Nicolas Jécquier (Editor), Appropriate Technologies, OECD Development Centre, Paris, 1976; A.S. Bhalla (Editor), Technology and Employment in Industry, I.L.O., Geneva, 1975.

(11) Jack N. Behrman, 'Potential Regulation of R&D Activities Overseas', Conference on Transfer of Technology: The Future of Regulation, Washington, D.C., April 1977.

(12) Ibid., pp. 7-9.

(13) Simitra Chishti, Technical Change and Multinationals: A Case Study on Eight Firms in India, OECD Development Centre, Paris, November 1975, p. 39.

(14) Raphael Kaplinsky, Technical Change and the Multinational Experience: Some British Multinationals in Kenya, OECD Development Centre, Paris, October 1975, pp. 42-8.

(15) Jorge Katz, 'Creación de tecnología en el sector manufacturero argentino', Trimestre Economico (Mexico), Vol. XVL, No. 177 (January-March 1978), p. 181.

(16) Arthur J. Cordell, 'Innovation and the Multinational Corporation: Some Implications for National Science Policy', Long Range Planning (Ottawa), September 1973, pp. 22-9.

(17) Meeting of Experts on International Subcontracting and Reinforcing Developing Countries' Technological Absorption Capacity, Summary Proceedings and Consultants' Reports, OECD Development Centre, Paris, February 1977.

(18) Ibid., Charles-Albert Michalet, 'International Sub-Contracting', pp. 45-87.

CHAPTER 18

The Less Developed Countries' External Debt and the Euromarkets: The Impressive Record and the Uncertain Future*

THE EXPANSION of international trade and investment between 1830 and 1930 and the economic exploitation of the colonial empires would not have been possible without the stimulus of private capital exports and trade finance supplied since the aftermath of the Napoleonic wars by the London and Paris financial markets joined by large United States commercial banks on the eve of the First World War. Without mentioning the vagaries of the international economic and financial cycle in the nineteenth century that on many occasions brought havoc to both owners of lendable funds and borrowers, the absence of any regulation and control of these activities ended with the financial disaster of the 1930s. That disaster consisted of the massive default of European and less developed country (LDC) borrowers (mainly Latin Americans) who repudiated close to one-half of their dollar bond issues and direct loans with the nominal value of over $2000 million, equivalent to perhaps $20,000 million at 1975 prices.

The massive reappearance of private international banks as lenders to the LDCs started in the mid-1950s. But only in the past few years has this phenomenon become the subject of concern in international financial agencies, in the advanced countries and to a lesser extent in the LDCs. The concern has its origin, first, in the overall five-fold increase of LDC external indebtedness from $36,000 million in 1967 to over $200,000 million at the end of 1977; and, second, in the fact that by 1975 international private banks replaced multilateral financial agencies and governments of the industrial countries as the <u>principal</u> source of LDC medium- and long-term external financing.

---

*This paper was written in preparation for the Seminar on LDC External Indebtedness and the World Economy held at El Colegio de México (México City) in October 1977, and published in the special issue on international indebtedness and world economic stagnation, edited by the author, of <u>World Development</u>, Pergamon Press (Oxford), Vol. 7, No. 2 (February 1979).

The private debt of LDCs has been defined here as the financial obligations - with more than one year maturity - of the governments or guaranteed by the governments. It does not include, except when made explicit, the private debt of the private sector in the LDCs.

World Bank figures show that of the total external medium- and long-term debt of eighty developing countries outstanding at the end of 1976 and estimated at $169,000 million, $89,000 million or 52.5 per cent originated with private lenders. Seventy-five per cent of the latter figure (about $67,000 million) corresponded to the outstanding private external debt of the LDC governments or to the private debt guaranteed by them. The remaining 25 per cent ($22,000 million) represented the private LDC debt to private foreign sources guaranteed by the lending countries (export credits) or by transnational corporations.

The figure of $89,000 million underestimated, however, by a very considerable margin, the total magnitude of LDC indebtedness to private external sources. It is thought that LDC short-term financial obligations to external - mostly private - sources were of the order of $50,000 million without considering the IMF drawings. While most of this latter sum consisted of trade credits and was in principle self-liquidating, it is of general knowledge among international debt experts that since the onset of the world recession in 1974 a number of LDCs, including many major borrowers, faced with balance-of-payments difficulties, started using a part of their short-term borrowing for long-term purposes. Under these circumstances, the total external debt of the LDCs at the end of 1976 (excluding genuine short-term commercial borrowing) probably exceeded $200,000 million, out of which the indebtedness with private foreign sources was of the order of $125,000 million, some 60 per cent of the total.

THE EUROMARKETS

This essay will deal almost exclusively with LDC borrowing in the eurocurrency markets over the period 1967-77. This limitation reflects several important factors. First, outside international expert circles much less is known about this type of borrowing than about the LDC debt to multilateral financial agencies and to bilateral direct lending institutions - both private and public. Second, borrowing in the eurocurrency markets has special characteristics absent elsewhere. Third, LDC indebtedness in those markets has been growing at a particularly high rate. Finally, the concentration both by borrowers and lenders in the eurocurrency markets, very similar to that observable in global financial operations between private lenders in the DCs and the LDC public borrowers, gives rise to some very difficult problems. Consequently, an analysis of the LDCs' borrowing activities in the eurocurrency markets may help to clarify a number of major issues related to the general problem of growing LDC external indebtedness and to the future of financial relations between LDCs and the rest of the world economy.

The eurocurrency market is the natural child of post-war domestic financial controls introduced by the United States, Western Europe and Japan. Its expansion was greatly stimulated by the restrictions on foreign lending by domestic banks introduced in the 1950s first by Great Britain and then by the United States, by United States ceilings on deposit interest rates and by Switzerland's bank restrictions in the early 1960s on interest on non-resident Swiss franc accounts. While all these restrictions did not work, additional international liquidity in the form of so-called petrodollars was created by the appearance of large balance-of-payments surpluses in some major oil-producing countries. Some weak and isolated attempts to set up supra-national controls over international capital flows, such as imposing reserve requirements on eurocurrency deposits the way they are applied in domestic banking systems, failed because of the divergence in political and economic interests of major capital exporting countries. Consequently, since euromarket activities are outside the realm of control of both domestic monetary authorities and international official financial agencies, the eurocurrency market became one of the major potential sources of international monetary and financial instability.

From its inception the euromarket registered very high and sustained rates of growth. While its size was estimated in net terms at $15,000 million in 1965, it grew three-fold to $44,000 million by 1969 and expanded once again three-fold to $132,000 million by 1973. This spectacular growth continued. The Bank for International Settlements' net estimates of external liabilities in foreign currencies of banks domiciled in eight European countries which report to that institution put the eurocurrency market in December 1976 at $250,000 million. Another source, the Morgan Guaranty Trust, that includes in the total the estimates of liabilities in foreign currencies of banks outside the BIS reporting area, put the net size of the euromarket at the end of 1976 at $300,000 million. The euromarket continued growing during 1977 and in the early months of 1978. By March 1978 it stood in net terms at close to $400,000 million. Thus it is the second largest financial market after that of the United States. Its total assets are equivalent to over 30 per cent of the assets held by the United States banking system and exceed those of the New York financial market.

Until 1969 United States banks abroad and United States corporations were the most important users of eurocurrency funds. After that date the market witnessed the decline of United States borrowing and the increased use of its resources by private and public sectors of European industrial countries. LDCs appeared as large borrowers from the euromarket only in the early 1970s as the consequence of a combination of various factors: the slow growth of international official lending, the advice received from major industrial countries that LDCs should rely more on private financial resources than on official 'aid' flows, and the rapidly expanding volume of financial resources available at the euromarket.

Many LDCs had been contributing funds to the eurocurrency market since its emergence through placement of their international reserves and privately-held foreign exchange. They were not significant users of these financial resources, however, until 1972. While some eurocurrency bonds were placed by a few LDCs as early as 1968, only after the beginning of the seventies did an increasing number of them start discovering the attractiveness of borrowing in eurocurrencies. Most literature seems to agree that initiative in that respect originated with lenders rather than potential borrowers.

Even when eurocurrency lending to the LDCs had reached a magnitude that gave rise to considerable concern in the governments of some major lenders, the LDCs as a group were still large providers of funds to the euromarket. It is estimated that in September 1976 perhaps as much as $75,000 million (over 30 per cent of total eurocurrency funds) originated in LDCs: some $41,000 million were eurocurrency assets of oil-exporters, $18,900 million were assets of non-oil producing LDCs, and perhaps an additional $15,000 million represented assets held in offshore banking centres on behalf of LDC governments, public and private institutions and rich individuals.

LDC Operations on the Euromarket

The LDC aggregate figures on assets held in the eurocurrency markets are not particularly useful for the purpose of estimating the degree of the net indebtedness of the LDCs to that international financial market. Not only is the overwhelming role of the oil-exporters as contributors to that market obvious, but the remaining LDC deposit holders in the eurocurrency market are in most cases different from those who borrow eurofunds. Moreover, the borrowings of the non-oil producing LDCs in that market grew both rapidly and constantly. In 1976 alone gross euroborrowings of the LDCs, including oil-exporters, were reported at some $17,500 million, or almost 8 per cent of all funds available. Since a significant proportion of eurocurrencies available at offshore banking centres was also lent to LDCs, their use of eurofunds amounted perhaps to one-eighth of total eurodeposits.

For a number of reasons it is extremely difficult to arrive at correct figures concerning the volume of LDC operations with the eurocurrency markets because statistical information about LDC borrowing in these markets appears to be consolidated with that involving LDC direct borrowing in foreign financial institutions domiciled in their home countries. Most large private lenders such as leading United States, British, French and Japanese banks operate both directly with the borrowers and through the eurocurrency markets.

Given that data about LDC annual net borrowing from each of these two sources separately are not available, the only indication of the volume of LDC borrowings from the eurocurrency market can be obtained from information about individual gross commitments by the lending institutions. Announcements to that effect which appear in the international financial press, have been collected, analysed, processed and published since 1974 by the World Bank under its capital market reporting system(1).

These figures, unfortunately, cannot be considered either as complete or final for a number of reasons. Neither should they be looked upon as reflecting correctly the actual net private indebtedness of individual LDC borrowers.

There is no legal requirement anywhere that eurocurrency transactions, whether commercial credits or international bonds, be individually disclosed or announced publicly; thus, available figures are neither complete nor final, being based on private announcements. Moreover, there may be many reasons why a borrower or a lender may not wish to publicize a particular transaction or its terms. Consequently, many eurocredits - perhaps one-fifth - are never publicized. Usually unreported transactions include most loans smaller than $5-10 million or credits extended by one single banking institution. In addition there is a bias toward under-reporting in all major borrowing countries, who account for 75-80 per cent of total transactions. This bias can be explained by two factors: first, with respect to borrowers already well-known in the international financial market, lenders have little interest in announcing or reporting all but the large or more unusual credits; second, with the growth of the external debt, some borrowers may not be interested in publicizing new debt operations except to the parties directly involved.

The euromarket debt figures should not be looked upon as reflecting correctly the size of external public debt to the eurocurrency markets for other reasons as well. First, the information about individual loans that serves as the basis for the aggregate country figures covers exclusively the commitments made by the lenders at the time each loan was signed or announced. Since it does not indicate the volume of actual transactions, the extent of actual drawings, if any, or repayments, it is neither a gross nor a net figure. Nor does it register the cancellation of the borrowing, in total or in part, that may sometimes occur after the signature of the loan. Finally, while the World Bank makes efforts to exclude from its tabulations parts of the borrowings provided by official export credit agencies and parts financed from domestic deposits in the borrowing country, the fact that many transactions take the form of complicated financial packages increases the margin of error in World Bank reporting on international private credits. All these factors also explain why the World Bank's global LDC external debt estimates differ from those originating in other sources such as the Bank for International Settlements or the Morgan Guaranty Trust.

Volume of LDC Debt to the Euromarket

Estimates to the effect that the LDC debt outstanding in the euromarket totalled at least $40,000 million at the end of 1976 fit with available annual data about eurocredit announcements. According to Morgan Guaranty Trust, which runs its own parallel reporting system, LDCs contracted in the euromarket between 1972 and 1976 some $45,750 million or 45 per cent of the total of $108,000 million borrowed in that market by Western industrial countries, the socialist bloc and the LDCs (see Table 18.1). Assuming, first, that a large part of LDC credits announced in 1976 (perhaps $15,000 million) was not disbursed by the end of the same year and, second, that some 15-20 per cent of the earlier credits were unreported, the total of $40,000 million outstanding seems plausible.

TABLE 18.1. Eurocurrency Bank Credits, 1972-6

(US $ million)

	1972	1973	1974	1975	1976
Grand total	6857	21,851	29,263	20,992	28,602
Advanced countries (including socialist countries)	4392	14,569	21,920	9,828	13,115
LDCs	2465	7282	7343	11,164	15,487
Non-oil countries	1532	4531	6276	8264	11,332
Oil-exporters	933	2751	1067	2900	4145

Source: Morgan Guaranty Trust Company of New York, World Financial Markets (monthly).

While many sources, including the World Bank, maintain that the rapid expansion of eurocredits to the LDCs does not yet create major repayment problems, the contrary position can also be defended in view of the considerable shortening of the eurocredits maturity that took place in 1975-6 and also because of increased costs of borrowing. Thus American Express International Banking recalled in March 1977 that not only 65 per cent of eurocredits raised in 1973-6 carried a maturity of less than eight years, but that in 1975-6 at the peak of LDC borrowings, 88 per cent of eurocredits had been for less than eight years(2). Consequently, the burden of amortization of eurocredits, particularly in the case of non-oil exporting countries, would grow rapidly in the following five years. It is estimated that 95 per cent of the eurodebt of all non-oil LDCs will have become due for repayment by 1983. According to American Express estimates, by 1980 over half of the new gross eurocurrency borrowing by LDCs will be dedicated to refinancing maturing LDCs' bank debts. By 1985 for every three eurodollars borrowed, two will be used for eurodebt repayment.

According to World Bank Debt Tables, 1976, while practically all LDCs had some obligations to private creditors of all sorts, five major borrowers were responsible at the end of 1974 for 62.8 per cent of total LDC debt to private sources, ten major borrowers accounted for 78 per cent and fifteen major borrowers for 85.2 per cent of the total.

In view of the weight of eurocredits in private lending to the LDCs (more than half of total lending from private sources comes from euromarkets), the list of major LDC borrowers in the euromarket by the end of 1975 looked very similar to that of major borrowers in private capital markets as a whole.

During the period 1971-5 fifty LDCs (including eight oil-producing countries) raised $29,590 million of eurocredits in the following way: $985 million in 1971, $3027 million in 1972, $7556 million in 1973, $7567 million in 1974 and $10,455 million in 1975. Of this total $7395 million (24.9 per cent) corresponded to eight oil-exporters (Indonesia, Algeria, Iran, Venezuela, Gabon, Ecuador, Nigeria and Saudi Arabia); $16,663 million (56.2 per cent) to 'higher income' LDCs; $2995 million (10.1 per cent) to 'medium income' countries; and only $887 million (2.9 per cent) to 'low income' countries. The remaining $1659 million (5.5 per cent) was committed to a few non-IBRD members such as North Korea, Hong Kong, Cuba and Brunei.

The individual country figures suggest that a very limited number of the LDCs, most of them oil-exporters and larger semi-industrialized countries, use in a significant way private financial resources available in the eurocurrency market. Only fifteen LDCs (Mexico, Brazil, Indonesia, Algeria, Peru, Iran, the Philippines, Argentina, South Korea, Venezuela, Cuba, Hong Kong, Malaysia, Zaire and Panama) borrowed during the period in question more than $500 million each from the eurocurrency market. The volume of borrowing ranged in this group from the high of $5839 million (Mexico) to the low of $523 million (Panama). The borrowing of eight other LDCs ranged from $200 to $500 million and that of an additional four was between $100 and $200 million each. Eurocredits granted between 1971 and 1975 to the remaining twenty-three LDC borrowers appearing on the World Bank eurodebt list ranged between $3 and $67 million, a magnitude of marginal consequence in most cases.

While the degree of concentration of LDC borrowing in eurocurrency markets by countries was already very high in the first half of the seventies it increased even further in 1976. As shown in Table 18.2, in the period 1971-5 the five largest euroborrowers (Mexico, Brazil, Indonesia, Algeria and Iran) accounted for $17,578 million (almost 60 per cent) of a total of $29,600 million; the ten largest borrowers (the big five plus Peru, the Philippines, Argentina, South Korea and Hong Kong) negotiated $23,168 million (over 78 per cent), and the fifteen largest borrowers (the previously listed countries and Venezuela,

Malaysia, Zaire, Panama and North Korea) received $25,978 million (87.7 per cent of the total).

TABLE 18.2. Major LDC Debtors to the Euromarket at the end of 1975[1]

(US $ million)

1. Mexico	5839	⎫	⎫	⎫
2. Brazil	5295			
3. Indonesia	2533	⎬ 59.4%		
4. Algeria	2230			
5. Iran	1681	⎭	⎬ 78.3%	
6. Peru	1680			
7. Philippines	1376			
8. Argentina	974			⎬ 87.8%
9. South Korea	802			
10. Hong Kong	758		⎭	
11. Venezuela	658			
12. Malaysia	641			
13. Zaire	530			
14. Panama	523			
15. North Korea	458			
Total	25,978			
Grand total	29,590			

[1] Publicly announced lender's commitments and not actual borrowing figures.

Source: World Bank, Borrowing in International Capital Markets, 1973-5.

Since this list contains four oil-exporters and seven higher income LDCs, the question arises why many other LDCs, belonging to the same two categories and having presumably a relatively easy access to international private financial markets, did not make use of that access. It is not less interesting to know why those LDCs which used the euromarket credit facilities did it in such a substantial way.

Factors Affecting Borrowing and Lending on the Euromarket

A study sponsored by the OECD of LDC borrowing in euromarkets suggests that there are no simple answers to those apparently simple questions(3). The volume of the LDCs' private borrowing must be related to factors involving both borrowers and lenders. The large volume of transactions took place, as expected, only when borrowers were willing and able to borrow and lenders were interested in lending. Clearly, although private lenders were fairly generous in assessing lending risks of many LDCs, not all potential LDC borrowers were interested in borrowing. Thus, not only did many oil exporters feel that they did not need to borrow, but also some financially hard-pressed non-oil LDCs adopted a very cautious attitude to international private lending facilities.

The study reviewed the record of eleven LDCs ranging from Brazil, the second largest borrower in private capital markets, to marginal borrowers such as India and Kenya. These eleven countries accounted for over $10,000 million of eurocredits, about one-third of total LDC borrowing in 1971-5. The survey, which covered both oil-producers and non-oil LDCs of different per capita income levels, classified the borrowers in three categories: 'eager' borrowers (Brazil, Zaire, Ivory Coast and Panama); 'ambivalent' borrowers (the Philippines, Indonesia, Singapore and Colombia); and 'reluctant' borrowers (India, Kenya and Nigeria). While moved by different considerations in each case, the eight 'eager' or 'ambivalent' borrowers launched sustained efforts to enter into international private financial markets and were successful in their endeavours. The three 'reluctant' countries made a few rather small borrowing operations but abstained from larger and sustained euroborrowing.

Reasons for the interest in each of eight successful cases and reasons for the lack of interest in euromoney in the three remaining ones were of extreme variety. Among four countries that encouraged very actively the inflow of eurocredits, Brazil opened its doors to eurobanks for the purpose of fostering her industrialization programme, while Zaire sought money abroad to augment mining activities. The Ivory Coast borrowed extensively because of persistent balance-of-payments difficulties. Panama sought relatively large eurocredits for the double purpose of financing budget deficits and strengthening her position as a secondary off-shore banking centre in the face of growing competition from other Caribbean banking havens.

Among 'ambivalent' borrowers reasons for ambivalence were many. Remembering the debt crisis of 1969 the Philippines was reluctant to borrow again for quite a time - until 1972. In Colombia earlier miscalculations with respect to the inflationary effect of external borrowing made larger eurocredits the subject of serious domestic political controversies. In Indonesia the political infights within the government prevented the definition of a uniform and coherent policy toward foreign private lenders. In Singapore the policy of attracting eurocredits was influenced by two conflicting considerations. The active interest in making out of the country a major regional financial centre for Southeast Asia was counter-balanced by the need to insulate the domestic economy from the impact of such transactions.

Finally, three countries belonging to the group that abstained from entry into the eurocurrency market were guided by reasons of their own. During the period 1971-5 India raised only one $10 million eurocredit because she believed that borrowing in private markets would negatively affect her access to concessional credits. Because of disappointing experience with the increase in the interest rate on a small eurocredit negotiated in 1972, Kenya decided to abstain from borrowing from the euromarket. Nigeria refused many offers from international private lenders because of a desire to remain independent of commercial lenders and because of a conservative financial policy(4). It may be relevant to note that reluctant attitudes vis-à-vis the euromarket were adopted by countries with a considerable degree of historical influence of British conservative colonial financial management. Obviously, such influence was absent in Latin America and Southeast Asia.

Leaving aside oil-exporters who are good risks anyway, international private lenders demonstrated a clear preference for relatively large and growing 'higher-income' LDCs with stable political systems, a broad mineral resources base (not necessarily limited to oil), well-established permanent contacts with the international banking community, and in the case of the newly independent

LDCs, those on good political terms with the former metropolis. These factors were responsible more for the image of the country's credit-worthiness in the eyes of eurocurrency lenders than refined economic indicators or the quality of domestic economic policy management. The businesslike, largely non-ideological attitude of private lenders showing very little interest in the end-uses of the proceeds from their credits (as long as they believe that the borrower will repay his debts) often contrasts with ideological, moralistic or power-politics motivated attitudes of multinational and bilateral official lenders. These contrasting attitudes seem to be in part responsible for the great expansion of euromoney lending to LDCs in the early 1970s.

Terms and Conditions of Euromarket Loans

The assertion that private lenders seem to have no preference with respect to the use of their funds, as long as the borrowing country responds to their image of 'good risk' and its government is willing to guarantee the loan, is supported by the statistical evidence.

Table 18.3 should be looked upon with some reservations because the data on private eurocredits to private end-users seem to be grossly under-reported. While this table discloses that 90 per cent of eurocredits were used by public sectors of a limited number of LDCs considered to be 'good risks', the actual proportion may be perhaps of the order of 80 per cent. But it is highly significant that, for example, one-sixth of total outstanding eurocredits had as their destination publicly-owned extractive and processing industries in the LDCs, many of which might have some difficulty in raising loans in multinational and bilateral official agencies. Moreover, Table 18.3 suggests that although euromarket intermediaries would prefer to lend for projects rather than for other purposes whenever bankable projects were available, foreign private financial resources were provided rather indiscriminately for general balance-of-payments support, programme loans and project loans.

The Wellons study insists that - at least between 1971 and 1974 - the heavy borrowing of some LDCs in the eurocurrency markets was not the consequence either of shrinking of traditional multilateral and bilateral official sources of credit or of the decline in export proceeds. While this opinion is not applicable to borrowings made after the onset of the recession, it is quite probable that many LDCs found the use of private capital markets attractive in the early 1970s not because they were starved of financial resources but because private loans represented, on the one hand, a relatively easy way out of internal political difficulties that would accompany such unpopular measures as tax reforms and, on the other, provided a means of neutralizing the economic surveillance attempts of international and official bilateral agencies. Moreover, some LDC borrowers also took the position that private borrowing was preferable because it was largely free from cumbersome bureaucratic procedures on the lender's end.

In many LDCs balance-of-payments and budgetary difficulties occurred in 1972-4 not only because export proceeds and fiscal revenues did not grow rapidly enough, but also because expenditures on imports and domestic public - capital and current - spending expanded substantially. Thus, for example, during the short-lived commodity boom of 1972-3, a number of LDCs augmented import bills and domestic public spending considerably under the assumption of the continuation of favourable export conditions. These expansionary policies continued in many LDCs after the recession began in 1974. In the absence of additional

TABLE 18.3. Reported End-Users of Eurocredits to LDCs, 1971–3

(per cent)

Government	36
National	32
State	3
Municipal	1
Public sector	54
General	3
Central and foreign exchange banks	12
Financial sector	12
Extractive and processing industries	17
Utilities	5
Transportation	5
Private	8
General	2
Subsidiaries of foreign corporations	6
Unclassified	2

Source: P.A. Wellons, Borrowing by Developing Countries on the Eurocurrency Market.

financial resources made available in 1975–6 from international capital markets, many programmes and projects (some aimed at increasing employment and social welfare) would not have been financed at all. Consequently, political and social difficulties might have increased. Thus the availability of eurofunds (and of private financial resources from other sources as well) made it easier to sustain the levels of economic activity in some LDCs, levels otherwise untenable or calling for a major domestic effort(5).

The increased participation of LDCs in euromarket borrowing – from 35 per cent of the total in 1972 to 52 per cent in 1976 – was accompanied, as noted earlier, by the growing concentration by borrowers. The explanation of this phenomenon, responsible for the increased worries of financial and monetary authorities in major lending countries, is not difficult. First, only a small number of LDCs that established themselves as 'good risks' in the private international capital markets could continue borrowing. Second, the accumulated borrowing by some LDCs reached such a level by 1974–5 that additional lending even at increasing risks was perceived by lenders as the best – if not the only – way to assure repayment of the earlier debt. Third, many private lenders convinced themselves that the political importance of individual large LDC borrowers, together with high domestic political costs in the lending countries of a probable financial crisis caused by LDC debt default, offered the assurance that the governments of the lenders in cooperation with multilateral lending agencies would somehow bail out unlucky lenders in the case of such a crisis.

Similar reasoning was followed by larger LDC borrowers, some of whom demonstrated a high degree of skill in discreet negotiations with major private lenders about rescheduling part of the debt. Thus, while the notion that incurring large external debt leads the borrowing country into heavy political and economic dependence upon the lenders is essentially correct, the degree of such dependence may be related inversely to the debt size and to the political weight of the borrower in the eyes of the lender's government. The numerical majority of LDCs that abstained from heavy private borrowing consists most probably of two groups: one is composed of many countries that because of their extreme level of underdevelopment and their small size did not have the political and operational means necessary to accumulate large private debts, and another includes only a few countries whose political and economic cost-benefit analysis of their growing indebtedness pushed them along the difficult road of austerity and 'self-reliance'.

A detailed comparison of the terms and conditions under which, according to World Bank data, a sample of seventeen LDCs, including all twelve major borrowers, arranged their eurocurrency credits in the period 1973-5 shows a progressive hardening of these terms that seems to be independent of the behaviour of the cost of euromoney.

In 1973, the first year of the great expansion of LDCs' euroborrowing, the average size of individual operations was of order of $25-30 million, most of the credits were extended by single banking institutions and the terms under which the credits were granted followed rather closely those applied to advanced country borrowers.

Except in the case of a few smaller oil producers who were not interested in borrowing for longer than five-six years, most other LDCs were able to negotiate loan maturities exceeding in many cases ten years and averaging between eight and ten years. Major borrowers such as Algeria, Brazil, Iran and Mexico were able even to arrange larger credits - exceeding $50 million each - for twelve or more years. Moreover, some of these large credits contained grace periods of two-three additional years. Consequently, the maturity structure of the LDCs' private borrowing in eurocurrency markets was in 1973 even better than that of developed countries. While the developed countries' borrowings with maturity up to six years accounted for about 20 per cent of their total eurocurrency credits, LDC borrowings with the same maturity represented only 8 per cent of the total. On the other hand, while eurocurrency credits of the advanced countries with maturities exceeding ten years accounted for only 10.8 per cent of the total, the percentage of the same maturity loans to the LDCs stood at 36.2 per cent.

Furthermore, the range of 'spread' (the margin over LIBOR(6) charged to the borrowers by the intermediaries) paid by the LDCs, particularly by large borrowers widely known in the market, followed closely the 'spread' paid by advanced country borrowers. It is said by some that the modest magnitude of 'spread' reflected the optimistic 'market' assessment of the LDCs' credit standing. Others maintain that the low 'spreads' were results of keen competition for borrowers. New LDC borrowers had to pay more for entrance into the international capital market. While the 'spread' for countries like Brazil, Colombia, Iran and Mexico ranged from 0.5 per cent to 1 per cent over LIBOR, the new entrants (Cuba, Panama, the Philippines or Peru) were paying between 1.25 per cent and 2 per cent, with average loan maturities not exceeding eight years.

The year 1974 witnessed the beginning of economic recession, serious uncertainty about the future of the eurocurrency markets in the wake of the bankruptcies of some lending banks, and a steep increase in eurocurrency interest rates that, after having reached for a brief period the unprecedented level of 14 per cent, averaged for the year as the whole 11 per cent compared with 9 per cent in 1973 and 7.5 per cent in 1975.

While in 1974 the volume of LDC euroborrowing increased by $1000 million only, much less than in 1973 (when it grew by over $5000 million) and in 1975 (by $3000 million), the conditions of LDC borrowing changed drastically to the detriment of most borrowers. Maturities over ten years became exceedingly rare, while those not surpassing six years increased considerably. The additional costs of borrowing - not to mention the jump in the basic LIBOR rates - went up considerably.

'Spreads' that at the beginning of 1974 averaged slightly less than 1 per cent rose to 1.6 per cent-2 per cent in the final months of the year, except in the case of some oil exporters (Iran, Venezuela) and of the particularly tough bargainer (Brazil) which were able to pay less than 1 per cent 'spread' during the whole year. The cost of intermediation for Argentina, Colombia, Mexico, Peru and the Philippines averaged 1.5 per cent and was even higher for Indonesia, South Korea and Zaire, among others. Periods of grace were practically eliminated and commitment, management and participation fees, known in banking jargon as the 'front load', appeared as the rule rather than the exception. Thus, while detailed calculations are impossible, the actual cost of LDC borrowing in the eurocurrency markets increased by the end of 1974 in comparison with 1973 perhaps by as much as 50 per cent and was almost double that charged on 'hard' loans by multilateral agencies and bilateral official sources. Private lending to the LDCs became a very good business for the lenders.

The tendency towards shortening of maturities and increasing the cost of financial intermediation continued in 1975 in spite of the fact that the market became the LDC borrowers' market. Private lending to industrial countries declined sharply for the first time since the emergence of the eurocurrency market - from $23,100 million in 1974 to $20,500 million in 1975.

If the total borrowing in international capital markets increased in 1975 (from $40,800 million in 1974 to $42,700 million) it was due to large expansion of credits both to LDCs and European socialist countries. LDC borrowings increased by close to $3000 million or 30 per cent (to $13,450 million) while those of the European socialist bloc increased by $1600 million or more than 100 per cent (to $2800 million). The major part of new LDC borrowings came, one may add, from oil-exporters. But the borrowing of non-oil producers increased as well, although much less both in absolute and relative terms.

The borrowers' market notwithstanding, borrowing conditions for LDCs deteriorated further. First, credits with a maturity of over ten years disappeared completely and the bulk of borrowing (75 per cent) had a maturity not exceeding six years. Just within the two years between 1973 and 1975 the average maturity for LDC borrowers, including oil-exporters, shortened dramatically: for Algeria, from twelve to seven years; Argentina, from seven-and-a-half years to five years; Brazil, from twelve to six-and-a-half years; Indonesia, from eight-and-a-half years to six years; Iran, from nine-ten to five years; Mexico, from ten to four years; Peru, from nine to five years etc. The 'spread' increased once again. In most cases, whether for large or small LDC borrowers, it averaged between 1.625 and 2 per cent and, in particular, borrowing transactions exceeded 2 per cent. The size of the one-time commitment, participation and management fees increased and the grace periods were almost completely forgotten.

Financial intermediaries explain these trends as the result of the euromarket disturbances of mid-1974 and the increased concern over exposure to risk which emerged at that time. This simple explanation hardly seems satisfactory, however, given the fact that the hardening of terms took place in the borrowers' market and no established LDC borrower, including such doubtful borrowers as South Korea and Zaire, was denied funds. Euromarket financial intermediaries took the line that the growing lending risks could be taken care of by increasing commissions on new credits and by shortening maturities, measures hardly contributing to the borrower's credit-worthiness either in the short or in the long run. It was at this point in late 1975 that some domestic monetary authorities, particularly in the United States, started issuing warnings about certain risky borrowers although some observers were remarking quite cynically that the real financial risks facing the eurobanks were quite limited if only because they were lending not their own but other people's money(7).

The eurocurrency lending to the LDCs not only continued growing in 1975 but underwent quantitative and qualitative changes. The size of individual transactions increased greatly. While in 1973 only fourteen credits, amounting to $100 million or more each (five of them to Algeria), were extended to LDCs, the number of such credits increased to twenty in 1974 (including one single $500 million loan to Mexico) and to thirty-five in 1975. All these big loans amounting to a total of $6800 million and granted in 1975 to Algeria (3), Brazil (6), Colombia, Hong Kong (2), Indonesia (5), Iran, Iraq, South Korea, Malaysia, Mexico (9), Morocco, Peru, the Philippines, Uruguay and Venezuela, were extended by consortia of the largest United States, European and Japanese banks. Although 110 banks from all over the world appear as the leading participants in these giant credit operations negotiated in 1975, the names of a small group of the largest United States, Canadian and European banks repeated themselves with considerable frequency. Bank of America participated as one of the leaders in nineteen cases; Chase Manhattan in fourteen; Citicorp in thirteen; Chemical Bank, Morgan Guaranty Trust, Lloyds Bank and Toronto Dominion Bank in eleven each; etc.

Many factors were responsible for the increased size of LDC euroborrowings from 1975 on. Inflationary pressures and the growth in the supply of funds in the euromarket may be some of them. On the other hand, the repeated participation of a limited number of the largest euromarket intermediaries in these big loans can perhaps be explained in part by problems involving the task of rapidly raising large sums of money and risks arising from financial operations of such magnitude.

The stagnation of demand for funds in the industrial countries, accompanied by the steady expansion of available financial resources in the hands of euromarket intermediaries, brought some changes in terms and conditions of eurocredits to LDCs in 1976 and 1977. Because of high profitability to the lenders of these credits and in the face of worldwide competition for borrowers, both interest rates and bank commissions declined considerably, falling by the end of 1977 to the lowest level since mid-1974. On the other hand, the maturities of eurocredits expanded somewhat. The 'spread' between the actual cost of money lent to LDCs and LIBOR was situated in late 1977 on the average at about 1 per cent. The average maturity of credits rose to about seven years as against five-and-a-half years in 1975.

It should be stressed, however, that only oil-exporters and the new LDC entrants into the euromarket (like India, Tunisia and Jordan) had access to these liberalized credit conditions. Large old debtors (Brazil, Algeria and South Korea, among others) not only were forced to pay high (close to 2 per cent) commissions but faced considerable difficulties in extending their borrowings' maturities. Mexico, where very large oil deposits were discovered, represented a special case: although it was granted unusually long maturities (up to ten years), it had to pay bank commissions at the levels prevailing in 1975-6.

Eurocredits, International Banking and the World Economic System

The continuous and accelerated expansion of the volume of eurocredits to the LDCs started to cause serious concern among certain national monetary authorities, particularly such United States Government agencies as the Treasury and the Federal Reserve Board, only during 1976. Their concern was not so much about the structure of the debt and its burden on the LDCs' economies but about the degree of involvement of major international United States banks in lending to LDCs both directly and through the eurocurrency markets(8).

Perhaps as many as 800 financial entities, domiciled all over the world but concentrated in the United States, Western Europe and Japan, were involved during the seventies in eurocurrency loans to LDCs and some 150 were domiciled in the United States. In spite of the large degree of intra-country and inter-country competition for the LDC clientele as the end-users of international private credits, the degree of concentration on the lenders' side was increasing rapidly. Growing evidence leads to the conclusion that both the United States private banking system and the largest United States banks played not only the dominant but also a growing role in lending operations to the LDCs(9).

Thus, according to Morgan Guaranty Trust, United States banks, whether operating directly from the United States or through the network of eurocurrency intermediaries abroad, accounted by 1976 for some $40,000 million of the $60,000 million of international private bank loans to the non-oil producing LDCs alone. The Federal Reserve System estimated that by the end of 1975 the twenty-one largest United States banks had lent $22,800 million to the LDCs (including oil-producing countries) with $14,500 million, or nearly two-thirds originating in the top six banks: Bank of America, Citibank, Chase Manhattan, Morgan Guaranty Trust, Manufacturers Hanover and Chemical Bank(10).

This predominance of United States-based international private banking in lending to LDCs reflects in part the circumstances in which the euromarket was born in the 1950s as well as changes which occurred in United States commercial banking legislation in the 1960s. Moreover, the following additional factors may be worth mentioning:

(1) the size of the United States banking system as compared with those of competitors in Europe and Japan;

(2) the overwhelming use of the dollar as the international lending currency;

(3) the global presence of United States banks that covers not only financial centres of the developed world but also the Middle East and the majority of LDCs;

(4) the business aggressiveness of United States bankers as compared with much more conservative attitudes towards lending abroad shared by European and Japanese bankers; and, finally,

(5) the disappointing domestic banking profit performance in the United States itself that makes profits from international operations particularly important (in 1976 some 75 per cent of profits made by United States banks originated in their foreign operations).

To the long-standing concern about the impact of unregulated foreign private lending through the eurocurrency market upon the effectiveness of the United States domestic monetary and financial policies, the fear of possible financial risks for the banks themselves was added. It resulted in a series of official warnings addressed in 1976-7 to the United States banking community which pointed out the particularly risky LDC borrowers and the degree of foreign exposure of the leading United States banking institutions. While this official concern diminished in late 1977, the leading international economic journals continued pointing out the overall vulnerability of the euromarket.

Thus, noting that international banking business 'has almost doubled since 1974 to a staggering $650,000 million', The Economist (London) commented in mid-1978 that:

> Domestic banking business in industrial countries has stagnated. As a result, most major national banks now do between a quarter and a half of their business overseas, while for the large Americans the proportion is even higher. The business has got riskier as excess liquidity has forced banks to lend larger sums for longer periods at ever shrinking margins to a handful of major government clients rather than the traditional widespread of corporate customers.
>
> The ability of this new type of borrower to repay, at least on time, has yet to be fully tested. Bank creditors still get the shivers about loans to Peru, Turkey and Zaire. On the deposit side, the concentration of deposits in the hands of just a few oil-rich sheikhs and states with a strong preference for holding their oil surpluses in highly liquid bank balances remains worrying(11).

In the opinion of The Economist, while 'the creation of some kind of supranational authority to supervise the Eurocurrency activities of international banks would not be feasible, or wise', more coordinated action by central banks was urgently needed. Such action should cover at least the adoption of similar systems of collecting information on the international activities of their private banks and of assessing such information, and should put an end to the attempts by those banks to evade control by operating through offshore and bank-haven subsidiaries.

The principal objective of private lenders to the LDCs and elsewhere, obviously including lenders, is to maximize profits at what they consider to be 'reasonable' risks. The achievement of such a private objective, while improving the lending country balance-of-payments position, may be in conflict and, in fact, very often clashes with the major national objective of assuring relative domestic monetary and financial stability. In the light of the continuing expansion of international activities of private banking systems it is easy to understand why monetary authorities would like to see some degree of control over foreign lending activities of banks. Some West European governments perhaps would not mind seeing similar controls applied to their international banks as well.

Nobody seems to know, however, how to approach this problem, in spite of the fact that it is quite clear that in view of the worldwide scope of operations of the euromarkets unilateral controls imposed by individual countries cannot work. Consequently, the United States and some European monetary authorities are coming around grudgingly to the position that attempts to control sources of funds should be replaced by control of the end-use of eurocurrencies, particularly by LDCs. Only multilateral official financial agencies in which the United States and Western Europe have still very substantial influence could achieve this purpose if these agencies were provided with more lending resources both for short- and medium-term balance-of-payments support and for developmental lending.

This reasoning is behind the 'Witteveen facility' established at the IMF, and Western initiatives at the World Bank and the IMF aimed at increasing their resources considerably so that multinational official lending may replace at least a part of private lending to the LDCs, strengthening the position of the Bank and the Fund not only vis-à-vis LDC borrowers but vis-à-vis giant private lenders as well.

The achievement of this objective would be considerably easier if another group of new actors - the oil-producing surplus countries - were not present on the world financial scene. These powerful actors play their own games in accordance with their own objectives which may sometimes coincide but more often are in conflict with the objectives of the three other groups - the DCs, the LDC borrowers, and the international private banks.

CONCLUSIONS

Thus the previous North-South bipolar financial set up (the rich official lenders and 'aid donors' from the North versus the poor borrowers in the South) has been replaced by the four-corner game with active participation of new sources of lendable funds (surplus oil countries) and of giant private financial intermediaries. This new situation makes it particularly difficult to talk about the future role of euromarkets in the provision of financial resources for the LDCs. According to the conventional wisdom, not only are the euromarkets here to stay but they will continue acting as useful international financial intermediaries between DCs and LDCs. Behind this attitude there are two uncertain assumptions: first, that the world economy will resume in the near future its post-war growth; and, second, that this world economic recovery will bring LDC demand for funds into some equilibrium with the supply of loanable resources.

This optimistic position contains, however, some serious flaws. Financial resources available from the euromarkets are loaned - as should be expected - only to those LDCs that are considered 'good' lending risks. The greatly increased indebtedness of most major LDCs which occurred in 1974-6 led, however, to a rapid deterioration of their image of 'good risk' borrowers. Consequently, since mid-1977 for the first time in ten years the potential demand for loanable funds in LDCs is not being matched by the growth of euromarket lending activities not because of the shortage of resources but for other reasons. On the one hand, most LDCs have been forced to cut their growth rates; on the other, some giant private financial intermediaries together with some lender governments like the United States rightly consider that the element of risk involved in lending to at least some LDCs might have unduly increased. If the aggregate LDC borrowing figures do not register these now developments but show continued expansion of credits, it is because private eurolenders were engaged in 1977-8 in a frantic search for new, less indebted clients.

While newly emerging trends in private - including euromarket - lending operations with LDCs may be only temporary, they may also confirm the validity of the often forgotten paradox of private lending: one lends to 'good risks' only and not necessarily to those who need to borrow. If it were so, then even world economic recovery would not guarantee the automatic access of LDCs to private international capital markets in forthcoming years once the lenders run out of 'good risks'.

The situation looks even less promising if such a recovery does not materialize; judging by the forecasts available in the spring of 1978 slow recovery seems more and more certain. Given the size, the distribution and the structure of the LDC external debt, closely related to the private lending operations of the 1970s, the continuation of the world economic recession for several years would clearly put most of the LDC borrowers in the category of 'high risks' for private lenders at a time when the past and present LDC borrowers might need financial assistance from abroad more than ever.

While experts may have differing views on the seriousness of aggregate LDC indebtedness, on the measures needed to keep it manageable from the lenders' viewpoint, and on the debt relief measures for certain specific cases, there is a general consensus to the effect that the LDCs as a group and the major LDC borrowers individually cannot repeat the 'borrowing from the private sources' performance of 1974-6 during the period 1978-80 unless the terms and the conditions of borrowing are radically liberalized. Since such sustained liberalization is hardly on the cards in the international private capital markets in view of the growing image of lending risks, the role of euromarkets in providing financial resources for thw LDCs may well decline substantially in the future independently from the magnitude of lendable surpluses available.

In the presence of continued political opposition in the DCs to official development assistance, accompanied by the reappearance of protectionist trade measures, it is extremely difficult to visualize who will be in a position to fill - under the conditions of a protracted world economic recession - the financial resource gap in the LDCs. In brief, it seems that at no time in post-war history has the future of the LDCs depended as much as at present upon the world economic performance.

REFERENCES

Bank Of International Settlements (1974-7) Annual Reports.

The Economist (1974-8), particular issues.

Euromoney (1975-7) (monthly).

OECD (1977-8) Financial Market Trends (published five times a year).

World Bank, (1976, 1977), World Debt Tables.

NOTES

(1) The World Bank's annual publication World Debt Tables, and its periodical supplements, is the most important single source of statistical information about the external debt situation of the LDCs and the least-developed advanced countries.

(2) The Amex Bank Review (London), Vol. 4, No. 3 (25 March 1977).

(3) P.A. Wellons, Borrowing by Developing Countries on the Eurocurrency Market, OECD, Paris, 1977.

(4) In 1977-8 Nigeria abandoned its earlier attitude and started borrowing heavily in the euromarket.

(5) It was already clear in the late 1960s that at least in Latin America foreign borrowing was generally used as the pretext to postpone important domestic reforms. For details, see M.S. Wionczek, 'El enduedamiento público externo y los cambios sectoriales en la inversión privada extranjera de América Latina', in Helio Jaguaribe et al., La dependencia Politico-económica de América Latina, Siglo XXI Editores, Mexico, 1970.

(6) London inter-bank offering rate.

(7) The Economist (London) 22 November 1975.

(8) At the Paris Conference that ended in June 1977, the US supported by other industrial countries took the position that the general problem of LDC indebtedness did not exist.

(9) See, among others, Andrew F. Brimmer and Frederick R. Dahl, 'Growth of US banking activities abroad', Journal of Finance (May 1975); and Nicolas Sargen, 'Commercial bank lending to developing countries', Federal Reserve Bank of San Francisco Economic Review (Spring 1976).

(10) 'Memorandum on Foreign Assets and Liabilities of US Banks', prepared for Subcommittee on Multinational Corporations by the staff of the Federal Reserve Board, Washington, D.C., 1976.

(11) 'Lenders of last resort to Topsy', The Economist (London), 10 June 1978, pp. 87-8.

CHAPTER 19

Science and Technology Planning in Less Developed Countries: Major Policy Issues*

INTERNAL OBSTACLES TO ADVANCES IN SCIENCE AND TECHNOLOGY

THERE is increasing evidence that the expansion of science and technology (S&T) systems[1] and general scientific and technological advance face many formidable internal obstacles in more advanced underdeveloped countries such as Argentina, Brazil, Egypt, India or Mexico. In the preparatory stages of the UN Conference on Science and Technology for Development (UNCSTD), held in August 1979 in Vienna, these obstacles were identified as related, among other things, to policies and priorities for science and technology, S&T infrastructure, educational and training systems, availability of entrepreneurs and managerial skills, S&T information systems, technological extension services, etc. The fact that these obstacles persist, in spite of increased financial support offered science and technology by the state, assistance extended by international organizations, and local and regional S&T planning attempts, strongly suggests that the task of building up the domestic S&T capacity in LDCs is much more difficult and complicated than it has been assumed in many quarters, both within the United Nations and at the national level.

Practically all major LDCs continue to depend to an overwhelming degree on the scientific knowledge and the technical know-how produced in the advanced countries. In most instances domestic research and development (R&D) activities in LDCs consist of imitative quasi-research in pure and applied sciences, accompanied by very little progress in technological innovation, including fields in which relevant and competent indigenous R&D has been badly needed for quite some time. One of the major reasons for this is that many economic and social problems arising in the context of overall underdevelopment are

---

*This paper was written for the Symposium on Science and Technology in Development Planning organized jointly in Mexico City in May 1979 by the UN Advisory Committee on the Application of Science and Technology to Development (ACAST), the UN Committee for Development Planning (CDP) and El Colegio de Mexico, within the framework of preparations for the UN Conference on Science and Technology for Development (UNCSTD), and is published in the proceedings of the Symposium, edited by Victor L. Urquidi, Pergamon Press, Oxford, 1979.

quite different from those presently facing high-income countries, whether market-oriented or centrally-planned economies. Among other reasons one may mention the working of the international economy and the socio-cultural characteristics of many LDCs.

Consequently, whatever R&D efforts are made locally in the LDCs, sometimes at considerable financial and social cost, they are often largely wasted due to the absence of permanent links between S&T activities and local educational and productive systems. The weakness of these linkages leads to a lack of correspondence between the demand for, and the supply of, internally-produced knowledge and technical know-how.

First, LDC scientists and technologists participate only marginally in higher education activities, even in cases where the few existing R&D centres are physically located at the universities. The unsatisfactory conditions of general, and, in particular, of technical education result, in turn, in great shortages of the kind of technical staff needed to support R&D. These shortages of middle-level human resources for S&T, together with the bureaucratization of the public sector, and the inadequacy of higher education institutions, depress further the generally low productivity of local small and fragmented scientific and technological communities. Moreover, the absence or the weakness of S&T diffusion mechanisms at all educational levels perpetuates the isolation of S&T from society, and impedes the extension of scientific and technological culture outside the small élites directly engaged in research activities.

Second, the demand of the productive system for technical know-how and innovations is satisfied mainly from abroad, even in the most advanced LDCs. On the one hand, productive units, whether private or public, and whether national or foreign-owned, show clear preference for foreign-originated technology because its use involves less risks at the enterprise level than does experimenting with new locally-produced techniques. On the other, the productive system assumes that local scientists and technologists are unable to produce either useful knowledge or the process and product technology which could progressively supplant S&T imports. Thus, from the viewpoint of the entrepreneur, technology imports seem more convenient and profitable than unproven local know-how.

Third, not only do S&T systems in LDCs lack human resources both in quantity and quality, but financial and managerial resources available domestically for R&D continue to be largely inadequate, both in absolute and in relative terms, when the per capita income differences between LDCs and developed countries and LDC needs are considered.

Fourth, the deficient functional distribution of R&D expenditures in LDCs inhibits S&T expansion. While up to three-quarters of financial resources, available mainly from the state, is spent as a rule on salaries and wages of R&D personnel, funds for both hardware and software, indispensable for serious and relevant S&T efforts, are either scarce or misused because scientists and technologists tend to follow the 'overequipment' trends fashionable in some advanced countries.

Fifth, while most R&D institutions - whether located at universities or in the public sector - display a critical lack of researchers, institutional proliferation is the order of the day because of the false self-prestige of their directors. In consequence, very few scientists and technologists dedicate full time to R&D. Even worse, in the face of the general absence of R&D managerial skills, the best brains become rapidly absorbed in S&T administrative tasks, and readily move into other political or bureaucratic activities.

Sixth, S&T development is highly unbalanced both sectorally and by disciplines, with a consequent neglect of very important R&D areas. This reflects two facts: first, the S&T centres and institutional network in the LDCs result from haphazard and uncoordinated individual initiatives and, second, most decisions concerning research areas and priorities are taken by foreign-trained S&T personnel, whose preferences, despite their operative competence, lead them to engage in the kind of research in vogue in more advanced countries.

Seventh, while in most LDCs the supply of so-called pure researchers is larger, for historical reasons, than that of staff interested in applied research and technological innovation, financial resources for basic research are extremely scarce. Because of lack of interest on the part of the private sector in R&D, neither are there sufficient funds for applied research nor for technological development. These activities are concentrated in but a few sectors of the more advanced LDCs, in which the presence of the state and the public sector as the producer of strategic industrial goods and social services is particularly strong. Thus, for example, in Mexico in the seventies petroleum and energy, commercial agriculture, and medicine and health absorbed about one-half of the total financial resources available for S&T. On the other hand, all LDCs - including Mexico - neglected R&D in areas of key importance for balanced and equitable socio-economic development such as subsistence agriculture, non-renewable (except petroleum) and renewable resources, capital goods manufacturing, transport and communications, urban development and housing, etc.

The expansion of S&T activities in LDCs is also hampered by a host of other factors, since whatever weak and sporadic attempts are made to allocate more financial and human resources to S&T, these allocations are neither linked with overall socio-economic planning nor supported by a longer-term S&T strategy and incorporated into medium-term research programmes. Neither LDC political élites nor scientific communities as a rule relate S&T activities with socio-economic development needs. A further difficulty arises because ignorance of this relationship is even greater among domestic entrepreneurial groups.

Contrary to evidence provided by common sense and the experiences of advanced countries, science and technology is looked upon in most LDCs as just a 'new' sector which - it is thought - should receive more support than in the past because of the worldwide technological revolution whose nature and importance are only dimly perceived. This primitive perception of the importance of S&T translates itself into the appearance, from time to time, of S&T 'crash programmes' which are supposed to close that particular gap between LDCs and DCs. These programmes usually amount to little more than sending potential researchers abroad for training, and/or small increases in the budgets for existing R&D institutions. As a rule, however, foreign training is not coordinated with increased allocation of funds for R&D. Nor are efforts made to integrate these 'crash programmes' into overall S&T priorities and objectives. Thus results are disappointing, particularly from the viewpoint of LDC politicians who want to have rapid scientific and technological results. In their absence, the brief periods of official support for S&T are followed by abandonment of crash programmes and by anti-intellectual recriminations against local S&T élites for their alleged betrayal of the country's interests.

Moreover, practically nobody in the LDCs realizes as yet that science and technology consists of a broad spectrum of activities which affect all spheres of national life, and that, in turn, S&T advancement is affected by all sorts of policies in force. Consequently, isolated actions, such as the allocation of funds for improving the quality of human resources engaged in R&D, and the expansion of R&D facilities, may be nullified by non-S&T policies which continue directing weak domestic demand for knowledge and technical know-how toward external sources.

If this happens even in those more advanced LDCs where attempts have been made to engage in S&T planning, it is because most of their non-S&T policies were designed long before the recent half-hearted recognition of the role of S&T in LDC socio-economic development. As no attempts have been made in any LDC to integrate S&T policy actions with economic and social policies, and given that many traditional, particularly economic, policy instruments have a perverse impact upon the objective of building up an indigenous S&T capacity, the results of uncoordinated S&T policy actions in LDCs are highly disappointing. While the conflict between science and technology policy and other policies is particularly visible in the field of LDC industrialization, it can also be discerned in other important sectors, such as agriculture, health services or urban development.

A FRAMEWORK FOR SCIENCE AND TECHNOLOGY PLANNING

This brief survey of major internal obstacles to advances in S&T in the LDCs enables us to define an overall framework for S&T planning. This framework assumes the necessary, but not sufficient, condition of creating in the longer term some sort of autonomous domestic scientific and technological capacity:

(1) S&T planning should be incorporated, whenever possible, into general long-term socio-economic planning or in its absence or weakness should reflect a national development strategy;

(2) its main purpose should be to expand the size and to improve the quality of the S&T system so that it may pursue R&D of relevance to domestic socio-economic needs;

(3) an additional major objective must be the establishment of links between domestic production of knowledge and of technological know-how, on the one hand, and the economic, productive and political systems, on the other;

(4) it must give very high priority to diffusing scientific and technological culture throughout the society or, using economic terms, to creating some degree of preference by local S&T consumers for domestically-produced knowledge and technical know-how;

(5) it must go beyond the sphere of R&D activities, as defined in advanced countries where S&T infrastructure is strong and diversified, and build up S&T infrastructure in the broadest sense, including not only human resources (for managerial, R&D and research-support activities) and the network of R&D centres, but also such R&D support services as diffusion and information gathering mechanisms, recollection and processing of statistics, data computation, engineering and consulting firms, production and maintenance of R&D

equipment and instruments, and technical standards;

(6) it must establish some priorities for very broad R&D areas, taking into consideration not only long-term socio-economic development objectives, but the present and potential availability of human resources; S&T planning will be meaningless if it limits itself to an elaboration of a consolidated list of possible R&D projects which might be undertaken if additional financial resources were available;

(7) it should, under no circumstances, be led by the mirage of autarchic production of knowledge and technical know-how, in spite of the political appeal of such an objective in some LDCs; it should be based on the premise that externally-available knowledge and technology can be, in the medium run, only supplemented with local R&D production, and that the major role of local R&D is to increase gradually the degree of national self-reliance with respect to decisions on the application of knowledge and technical know-how, whatever its origin may be;

(8) except when externally-produced knowledge and technology is unavailable or - albeit available - its application conflicts with major national socio-economic development objectives, S&T planning must give the highest priority to the building of domestic capacity to absorb and adapt S&T produced externally, as a precondition to indigenous production of knowledge and technical know-how;

(9) because the building up of indigenous capacity to absorb, to adapt and eventually to produce knowledge and technical know-how can be successful only if accompanied by the emergence of domestic demand for it, S&T planning must provide for instruments regulating technology imports, instruments that would be applied not only to technology transfer transactions, but to industrial property and direct foreign investment as well;

(10) provisions must be made for establishing permanent planning mechanisms with the full participation of the S&T community and domestic users of technology, mechanisms that would be able to defend themselves against the dangers of bureaucratization; such mechanisms would be in charge of reviewing periodically S&T longer-term strategy; of designing the framework and the guidelines for medium-term S&T plans, and of contributing to the task of the elaboration of R&D programmes for the duration of a S&T plan;

(11) finally, S&T planning must make a distinction between science planning and technology planning, even though it is almost impossible to establish clear limits between scientific and technological activities.

SCIENCE AND PLANNING

Contemporary literature on S&T is full of rather idle speculation about the relationship between science and technology. The little that is known about this relationship is that it is not linear, and that modern S&T systems started, historically, from many different points of the continuum. In the early nineteenth century some countries excelled in science (France and tsarist Russia), while others had relatively little science but experienced considerable technological progress (Great Britain). There were also countries which lacked both (the United States), and where S&T started through technological experiments. Now all these countries are major S&T powers.

It is often maintained in LDCs that advances in science are a luxury which they do not need, or can hardly afford. Voices are also heard to the effect that the only science which should be promoted is that which will result in very rapid technological application of its findings. Both attitudes, which are not only incorrect but socially damaging, originate with pragmatic ignoramuses. The LDCs need good science <u>together</u> with relevant technical know-how for reasons that go beyond the common sense proposition that good science is helpful to the production of technology. Science has other important functions besides supporting the expansion of technical know-how. The most important function, perhaps, is that of providing a base for a general scientific culture, badly needed for an increased degree of overall rationality in LDC societies faced with the most complicated and pressing social and economic development problems. While scientific attitudes are not expected to replace ideologies, the use of ideologies, in the absence of control mechanisms provided by science and rationality, has led in the past, and will lead in the future, to major political and social disasters.

The LDCs must promote science for other reasons as well. Scientific advance is an important source of national satisfaction and prestige, offers permanent linkages to the outside world, and provides socially useful occupations to clusters of scientists which, however tiny, represent the kernel of S&T élites in the LDCs. Disregard for, or the abandonment of, science by the LDCs would clearly result in the permanent emigration of first-class human assets, which would represent a very considerable loss to the society. Such emigration would take place even if an LDC gave the highest priority to technological advancement, because psychological characteristics of researchers, social determinants, and the values involved in the production of knowledge are quite different from those involved in the production of technical know-how. These differences explain why first-class scientists are very rarely first-class technologists, and vice versa, although there will always be exceptions to this general rule. Together with the differing nature of scientific and technological endeavours, and functional differences between science and technology, social and psychological aspects of S&T explain why scientific planning offers a different sort of challenge, and calls for approaches and methodologies different from those involved in technological planning.

It is sometimes maintained that, because of the unpredictability of scientific discovery, science does not lend itself to any planning. The statement is true only in cases where planning attempts to impose upon science short-run criteria aimed at 'assuring' practical and direct application of scientific progress. Since such criteria for science contradict the very nature of scientific discovery and advance, the planning of science in this sense should not even be attempted.

However, the impossibility of establishing 'pragmatic' criteria for science does not invalidate the need for, and possibility of, planning for science in LDCs. Science can and should be planned, first, because of the scarcity of human resources for S&T and, second, because of the infinite choices facing scientific endeavour and speculation. The major objectives of science planning are - in the broadest terms - fourfold: (1) to increase scientific productivity and assure excellence, i.e. to produce good and relevant science at the lowest social cost; (2) to create conditions for an interdisciplinary approach to scientific problems; (3) to advance the frontiers of science in such a way that scientific advance may assist, directly or indirectly, specific applied research and technological development, neglected by S&T effort in the advanced societies; and (4) to support the national educational system at all levels.

Both S&T planners and scientists in the LDCs must be aware, however, that the presence or the absence of possible linkages between pure research and its subsequent application to other segments of the S&T continuum, or to other ends, cannot be determined *ex ante* and that, furthermore, the application of science to the solution of non-scientific problems cannot become the sole criterion for scientific support. History abounds in examples of scientific discoveries that were followed by their non-scientific application only after a delay of many generations. Other great scientific discoveries have never been translated directly into technological progress.

Contrary to some misconceptions, judicious and intelligent science planning does not involve the abdication of scientific freedom by researchers. The task of S&T planners, all of whom must have some experience with the nature of scientific advance, is limited to defining, in very general terms, those wide areas or categories of disciplines in which scientific progress seems more likely than in others, in view of the availability of highly competent human resources and infrastructure, on the one hand, and some sort of balance between accumulated knowledge and the perceived scope of the nature of unresolved scientific problems, on the other. These elements must be carefully weighed - again in very broad terms - against alternative needs for scientific progress in an underdeveloped society. The complicated process of arriving at general priorities in respect to support of scientific activities - in LDCs and elsewhere - should never fall into the trap of absolutist rigidity. Neither should it degenerate into unilateral decisions about the social relevance or irrelevance of specific research projects.

While it seems easy to arrive at an abstract conclusion that research in biology may be more relevant for an LDC than the pursuit of astronomy or topology, translation of such 'priorities' into either support for, or the withdrawal of support from, specific disciplines or - even worse - specific research projects, clearly courts disaster. The most S&T planners in LDCs can expect and hope for is that the combination of human resources available for, and willing to engage in, scientific activities, with financial and managerial resources will produce good science, and that the support of science by the state will increase the socialization of scientific élites, i.e., improve their grasp of the social function of science.

Achievement of an increased degree of social consciousness on the part of participants in local scientific efforts in the LDCs should be considered a great feat in itself. Scientists in LDCs are more 'asocial' than their counterparts in advanced societies, not only because they share certain non-social values and are the product - as anyone else - of faulty LDC educational systems, and victims of the overspecialization which characterizes much modern science, but also because these scientists are often rejected by their own underdeveloped societies.

Armed with very broad guidelines in respect to preferred areas of scientific endeavour established within a flexible framework, engaged in consistent long-term support for scientific infrastructure, and in sustained efforts to diffuse science and a scientific culture, S&T planners in LDCs can expect positive responses from local scientific communities. Good scientists anywhere are clearly able to make a distinction between outside interference with scientific freedom in the name of real or ill-conceived social needs, and the genuine support of science viewed as an important segment of the S&T continuum as related to development.

While science planning cannot be left to scientific communities alone, neither can it be accomplished without their direct participation; responsibility for the planning and programming of research must be left to scientists and their institutions. The role of the overall S&T planners as advisers at these levels is still very considerable. First, they can help in designing longer-term research programmes. Second, they can act as innovators in the institutional field. Their third task would be to devise and implement long-term science support mechanisms, both in supplying research hardware and software, and proposing measures that would make the daily operation of scientific institutes and individual researchers more secure, financially and otherwise. The reasonable working of such mechanisms and measures does not depend on the provision of funds alone, but also on the elimination or alleviation of manifold bureaucratic obstacles present in abundance in any underdeveloped society and also due, in the case of scientific activities, to general ignorance about the importance of S&T vis-à-vis other activities.

In brief, science in LDCs should be underplanned rather than overplanned. Furthermore, the planning should be directed to the outer fringes of scientific endeavour and to its infrastructure and not to the substance of scientific research itself. Clearly, planners should avoid falling into the other extreme of catering indiscriminately to those segments of LDC scientific communities which demand more money from the state but are unwilling to accept any social compromise, claiming to be citizens of the alleged 'free republic of science'.

PLANNING OF APPLIED RESEARCH AND TECHNOLOGICAL DEVELOPMENT

Planning of applied research and technological development in the LDC is another story, involving as it does substantive problems. It also makes imperative a detailed diagnosis of the 'state of art' in respect to technical know-how available from different sources, foreign and local; the degree, if any, of indigenous technological innovation; channels for technology transmission and policy instruments which affect, in any important degree, imports and the local production of technical know-how; as well as the global and sectoral demand for technology. Even when all such information is collected and analysed, planners will still be unable to establish criteria and fix priorities for technology imports, their local adaptation, and the production of technical know-how, unless they can relate these criteria and priorities to a longer-run socio-economic development strategy. In other words, unless national policymakers at the highest level have a clear idea about what kind of society they want to construct, no coherent technological policy is possible. In the absence of a national development strategy the future shape of the society will be decided by technology imported largely on the grounds of its private profitability.

Ideally, technological planning in LDCs should be incorporated into overall socio-economic long-term planning. In most LDCs, however, formal socio-economic planning resembles science-fiction or ritual rhetoric rather than a real national exercise. In such a situation relating technology planning to what some social and political writers call a 'national project' of the future society may represent the second-best, but realistic, solution, because it will perhaps be the only way to permit a first approximation to the overall long-term technological needs of the society in question.

The next task of the planners would be to define and delineate those economic and social sectors whose different functional characteristics decide specific technology needs. In the case of S&T planning in Mexico, for example, long debates on that subject in the mid-seventies involved public policymakers, private sector producers and users of technical know-how, and leading educators. The decision arrived at by negotiation was originally that there was a need to make distinctions among technological policies and priorities in respect to the following sectors: agriculture and forestry, fisheries, manufacturing industry, mining, energy, transport and communication, urban development (including the construction industry and housing), medicine and health, and education. This division of technology by sectors was later found to be in need of refinement because, first, it did not take into account certain strategic economic activities that could only with difficulty fall into the category of a sector; second, it overlooked some important intra-sector differences; and, third, it forgot some 'sectors' which were not productive in the limited economic or social sense. Consequently, the list of technological sectors was amplified by: (1) adding food production which covers the whole range of activities from agriculture to distribution of processed foodstuffs; (2) subdividing manufacturing activities into consumer non-durables, intermediate goods and consumer durables, considered jointly with capital goods; (3) subdividing agriculture into commercial and subsistence agriculture; and (4) establishing a new broad category covering such problems as ecology, renewable resources and natural phenomena.

The elaboration of a similar 'technological map' of the economy and the society is a prerequisite for the following planning stage. Using the systems analysis approach, this involves sectoral diagnosis of technological demand and sources of supply. Such an exercise, for which the best national experts, including scientists, must be mobilized, implies the availability of a considerable body of knowledge on the general state and direction of worldwide technological advance in individual sectors or subsectors, and the collection of detailed information about technical imports (also by sectors), and about the sectoral 'state of the art' in local R&D. As no single national public agency, and no single local R&D institution has such information, this planning stage can only be successful if there is the broadest participation by national experts in each field, preferably on an individual basis.

This stage of technological planning also involves the establishment of a permanent S&T statistical office, able to process detailed information about the national S&T system in terms of its institutional structure, human resources, and R&D programmes and projects in progress or planned. Such an office must work in close cooperation with national agencies in charge of regulation of technology imports, industrial property (patents and trademarks) policy, and the control of direct foreign investment, the latter a major channel for transmission of foreign-originated technical know-how.

The following stage corresponds to the translation of the sectoral diagnosis of technology supply and demand into general R&D guidelines, for a period of at least ten years, to be revised periodically in the light of technological advances both within and outside the country, and in the light of possible changes or adjustments of domestic socio-economic policies. The elaboration of such guidelines would involve the presence of representatives of all major local R&D institutes, and of major technology consumers in both public and private sectors. Eventually, the substantive guidelines - which cannot be considered, however, iron-clad priorities - will indicate possible R&D areas of broad subjects. Such guidelines will have to be treated in a very flexible manner, with the understanding that the reasons for the exclusion of some areas or subjects are threefold: either these R&D areas can be taken care of by technology imports, or they are not highly relevant to the economy and the society in question, or no human resources are available domestically for their meaningful pursuit. Substantive guidelines which are broad in scope and indicative rather than mandatory offer a great advantage for the planning implementation stage: they will permit R&D institutes to work out programmes and projects tailored to both their human resource endowment and their financial and managerial possibilities. They will also permit them to adopt some general criteria with respect to the training of new researchers and the creation of an institutional infrastructure for the more distant future. It is at this point that the possibilities of international S&T cooperation should be explored in detail.

FINAL PLANNING STAGES

The final task of S&T planners, common to both science and technology is to estimate the capacity of the domestic S&T system to absorb additional financial resources in the light of: (1) the possible supply of new human resources and (2) expenditure planned for the expansion of S&T physical and institutional infrastructure. This exercise, which will make use of all the information - both quantitative and qualitative - collected during the planning process, belongs to the planners themselves. It will make it possible to set long-term financial targets for S&T support, and must be done simultaneously from two ends: it must consider the potential availability of total financial resources for S&T, and also the probable costs of (1) maintaining the existing S&T system, (2) training and employing new S&T personnel, and (3) improving and expanding S&T infrastructure over the planning period. Attempts to set broad overall national targets for S&T expenditures - in terms of a proportion of GNP or per capita income - which do not consider the S&T system's financial and human resources absorption capacity, are useless.

At this point S&T planning, in a formal sense, will be accomplished. It will clearly be of little use, however, unless it is followed by an implementation stage, whose description and analysis lies beyond the scope of this brief paper. It is worth mentioning, however, that implementation cannot be limited to the mere elaboration of a sequence of S&T sectoral and institutional research programmes and projects for the duration of the plan. It will have to involve many very important political and substantive decisions in respect to such issues as the shape, and the power, of the permanent S&T plan implementation agency, and its position within the executive branch; legal and institutional changes needed to eliminate possible conflicts between S&T policy instruments and non-S&T policies; and concrete measures aimed at expanding and strengthening S&T infrastructure. The scope and the importance of implementation strongly suggest that institutional arrangements made originally for planning purposes should not be abandoned after the elaboration of a plan. They will have to be redesigned, however, in the light of experiences acquired during the planning process.

Considering the growing global interest in S&T planning and advance in LDCs, it is suggested that the relationship between science planning and technology planning be studied further at international and national levels after the UNCSTD. Such studies should abstain from advocating ex ante the divorce of scientific planning from technology planning in the LDCs. Whereas the present division of labour in international agencies would make such a proposal attractive on the grounds that science and technology deal with 'different things', such a divorce, if implemented, would be very harmful for LDCs. What is needed is global recognition that while, for example, the UNESCO approach to S&T problems, putting most of the stress on science cum culture, is not correct, neither would it be correct to place all the emphasis on LDC technological advance while forgetting science.

NOTES

(1) Defined as the total of scientific, technological and industrial development research centres and the tangible and intangible scientific and technological infrastructure.

CHAPTER 20

The Origins of the UNCTAD Code of Conduct for Technology Transfer*

IT HAS been proposed that, in view of the fact that the present economic order not only does not work properly on a worldwide scale, but also does not do justice to the legitimate interests of underdeveloped countries, it will inevitably be replaced by a new order. The general guidelines for such a new order were established in the UN Charter of Economic Rights and Duties of States, and supported by an impressive and growing array of declarations by international organizations and by resolutions adopted at meetings of Third World countries.

However, progress in implementing the new international economic order has not been very impressive. It is true that during 1975 and 1976 multilateral negotiations started at UNCTAD in Geneva and in the Conference on International Economic Cooperation in Paris on new modalities of international commodity trade, transfer of financial resources for development, renegotiation of the external debt of underdeveloped countries and other important aspects of economic relations between the industrialized world and its periphery. Although the results of these negotiations have been almost nil, there are still some reasons for qualified optimism since all the parties involved are making efforts to avoid a return to the confrontations of the past.

There are many ways of explaining the stagnation of the dialogue on the new international economic order. Perhaps one decisive factor is that North-South negotiations coincided with constant deterioration of the world economic situation, which more and more resembles that of the thirties. Some people may recall two successive world economic conferences, held respectively in 1929, on the eve of the great depression, and in 1933, at its height. These attempts to pose and to solve the basic problems of economic relations within the advanced capitalist world of the time ended in total failure, contributing to the victory of fascism in Spain, Italy, Germany and Japan and opening the way to the Second World War.

---

*This essay was published originally in Spanish in Nueva Política (México), Vol. 1, No. 4 (October 1976-March 1977), the issue dedicated to the New International Order.

Without falling into pessimistic determinism and without accepting fully the lessons of the thirties which have limited validity in 1976, one must insist that the process of building the new international order will take quite a long time. If all goes well perhaps that order will be in force by the end of the century. Perhaps with some exaggeration one might argue that recent declarations and resolutions concerning the new international order present the doctrinal sequence of the order of things which the countries of the world periphery would like to see translated into reality. Moreover, while the Charter of Economic Rights and Duties of States serves as a basic law or a constitution of the new order, studies by Wasily Leontieff and Jan Tinbergen, both Nobel prize winners, offer a profound diagnosis of present and future economic world problems(l). Nonetheless, what is still missing is the translation of the doctrine into a legal structure and the setting forth of rules for its implementation.

As the long history of attempts to establish the international law of the sea convincingly demonstrates new juridical structures, recognized throughout the world, can hardly be drawn up all at once or within a short time. It seems likely that the new structure of international economic law will emerge from a series of partial attempts to codify standards of international conduct in many well-defined and clearly-delimited fields. This demarcation of areas and specific subjects is absolutely necessary despite the close relationship among them. The partial attempts to codify the new order can take the form of legal instruments which differ according to the circumstances: international treaties and conventions in some fields, international regimes or codes of conduct in others.

The political realism necessary to carry out this great task more or less satisfactorily, entails avoiding falling into a trap of apparent inflexibility which characterizes many Third World legal cultures. Within these cultures it is frequently thought to be more important to establish compulsory legal instruments than to adequately administer an agreement based on general consensus. Since there are many perfect laws which are not applied in Third World countries due to the absence of sanctions or simply the bad faith of rulers, it would be counterproductive if the Third World were to follow the same formal course in creating new international economic law.

The establishment of the new international economic order, which will never be perfect, should not be confused with the creation of a millenary world republic, free from the defects which have characterized intra-social and international relations from times immemorial. It would be especially serious if it were thought that the new order can be based on the concept of the general community of interests of all parties, a concept introduced by optimistic eighteenth century philosophers. Rather the new order will be based on the concept of the struggle between the relative power of different participants, an idea originated from more cynical and more realistic observers of political, social and economic relations.

To give a concrete example, I shall present a practically unknown account of progress achieved in negotiating at UNCTAD an international code of conduct for technology transfer. Perhaps this account will teach us that only the adoption of partial and clearly incremental approaches makes it possible to advance step by step towards the implementation of the general postulates needed to change the international economic order. Despite its slowness, such advance is possible only given certain preconditions: the promoters of change must be in a position to clearly define the scope of action; they must

The Origins of the UNCTAD Code of Conduct for Technology Transfer   371

accumulate detailed knowledge about the nature of the problems involved and mobilize the necessary political backing; and they must be flexible and innovative in order to make the most of the margin of initiative available. Adequate control and management of these elements in international negotiations will permit a change in pre-established power relations as well as lead to a general call for a solution to a problem whose existence had previously not even been noticed.

Before dealing with the example it must be stressed that the question of an international code of conduct for technology transfer is not a minor matter. First, modern socio-economic development depends on the availability of technological knowledge and not only on the presence of material, human, and financial resources. Second, the value of world transactions involving the purchase and the sale of technology exceeds some US $20,000 million a year. Finally, international trade in technology represents the only part of world trade in goods and services which has remained outside the scope of international regulations.

The international transfer of technology, defined correctly as a problem of technology trade, appeared on the agenda of the United Nations at the end of the sixties. At that time, however, no-one knew how to deal with it either conceptually or technically. This is evident from the majority of reports prepared at that time by various UN agencies initially put in charge of studying the problems arising from the international patent system, established a hundred years previously by and for the main industrialized countries.

It was Resolution 39(III) adopted at UNCTAD III in Santiago, Chile in 1972 which included the subject of technology transfer, through the initiative of various Latin American countries. During the next few years, between 1972 and 1974, a series of annual meetings of the UNCTAD Intergovernmental Group of Experts on Transfer of Technology took place in Geneva. Year after year the representatives of the industrialized world insisted with repetitive monotony that it was not feasible to establish any rules for international technology trade, for apparently simple reasons. At the same time, the spokesmen of the developing countries expressed their conviction, still very vaguely, that technology transfer, in which they played the role of buyers, should be subject to some kind of international control.

The arguments of the industrialized countries followed four conventional truths. First, supposedly, no-one knew what the technology was really about. Second, in the prevailing state of ignorance nobody possessed the conceptual elements necessary to define technology transfer. Third, there was no need to deal with technology transfer at an international level because technology was presumably circulating freely throughout the world through private channels due to the fact that technological knowledge was mainly produced by private enterprises. Finally, it was suggested it would be dangerous to regulate the transfer of technology to the less-developed world, whose present and future depended on technological knowledge imported from the industrialized world, because such regulation could weaken the interest of the owners of technology in sharing it internationally, obviously at a price.

After more than two years of very arid discussions, partly conceptual and partly semantic, some of the representatives of the developing nations in the UNCTAD Intergovernmental Expert Group came to the conclusion that the Group was not the proper place for preparing international regulations of technology trade for a rather simple reason: the industrialized countries which produced technology were not interested in such an endeavour. In the fall of 1973 these experts from the underdeveloped world decided to transfer the subject from the United Nations to an informal non-governmental forum. This was done to show the industrial countries that it was both feasible and necessary to design a set of rules for technology trade.

The decisive step was taken in Aulanco, near Helsinki, in September 1973, during the annual assembly of an international scientific organization, the Pugwash Conference for Science and World Affairs. The Pugwash movement was created in the late fifties by Albert Einstein and Bertrand Russell to involve the world scientific community in private debate and unofficial negotiation on such politically vital subjects as the atomic race between the Soviet Union and the United States. At the beginning of the seventies the organization, with the membership of about three hundred scientists from all over the world, many of them Nobel prize winners, extended its concern to the problems of development and the growing conflicts between the industrialized North and the underdeveloped South.

It was not difficult to get a mandate from the Pugwash movement to organize a group of experts of different nationalities to study in their personal capacity the problem of technology transfer. A few months later sixteen specialists were invited from the United States, Western Europe, Japan, Latin America and the socialist countries to form this ad hoc group. All were recognized internationally as experts in the field. The meeting of experts was held in Geneva in May 1974. Within one week the first draft of an international code of conduct for technology transfer, later known as the Pugwash proposal, was unanimously approved by all participants.

Very little money was needed to organize that initial meeting. Scarcely $10,000 were spent on financing the trip to Geneva of a dozen people from such places as Buenos Aires, Tokyo, New Delhi, Mexico City and Cairo, without taking into account the minor expenses of European participants. It was possible to get this small sum from Canada and Switzerland, from official and also from private sources.

Experts from two major countries were absent from the Geneva meeting. Despite attempts to secure the participation of someone directly involved in a big United States corporation, apparently no United States businessmen had time for such unimportant matters. A Soviet expert, who accepted the invitation, did not show up either, for reasons unknown. However, two officials of the Soviet mission in Geneva who came to the meeting were politely told that it was a completely private affair and for people expressly invited. They were promised that a copy of the final draft would be sent to the mission. The promise was fulfilled a few weeks later.

The Pugwash draft, signed by fourteen experts, was presented in November 1974 to UNCTAD, upon the official request of Indian and Mexican missions in Geneva. It domonstrated to the Intergovernmental Expert Group that it was feasible to draw up a set of rules for an international code of conduct for technology trade, in comprehensive and adequate legal and technical language. No attempt has been made to impose the draft upon the Intergovernmental Group. Its only purpose was to serve as an example for future UNCTAD debates on the subject.

It was at the next meeting of the Intergovernmental Expert Group held in the fall of 1974 that the first battle took place on the issue of the long-term work programme of the Group. Developing countries at UNCTAD not only now had

The Origins of the UNCTAD Code of Conduct for Technology Transfer 373

evidence that a code of conduct was feasible but they also had accumulated a broad knowledge on how to deal with the problem of international technology trade. However, UNCTAD still did not have an express mandate to start working officially on a draft of a code. The Intergovernmental Group was empowered by the Santiago resolution only to study 'the possibility and feasibility' of such a code of conduct. Once again the meeting of the expert group became the scene of interminable conceptual, methodological, and procedural debates. Some of the large developed countries which opposed the code were still unwilling to give up. Eventually, after having consulted all the members of the Intergovernmental Group, the developing countries realized that through small concessions they would get the backing of a number of small industrialized countries for the establishment of a working group of governmental experts with a specific mandate to prepare a draft of a code of conduct instead of studying its feasibility in general and philosophical terms.

Why did broad international backing for the idea of elaborating a draft of an instrument for the regulation of technology emerge suddenly in the fall of 1974? This occurred because Latin America, Asia and Africa are not the only technology-importing regions in the world. Among the industrial nations there are also many heavy importers of technology: all the smaller West European countries and the former white British dominions - Australia, Canada, and New Zealand. For reasons similar to those of the developing world, once these countries analysed the Pugwash draft they realized that to continue the task at the governmental level was in their own interest. Moreover, socialist countries, which import a lot of technology from the West, also saw potential political and economical advantages in formalizing through an international code of conduct their technological relations with the technology exporters, including large transnationals.

The question of the new mandate for the UNCTAD was submitted to a vote, for the first time in the history of intergovernmental UNCTAD groups and committees. The big industrialized countries that were against the proposal argued that 'gentlemen do not act in such a way' and that unnecessary friction might result from the vote. Expressing its regrets, the Group of 77 explained that what was at stake was not a 'violation of gentlemanly behaviour' but the need to establish a clear mandate which would allow a reasonable way to deal with a subject which the majority of UNCTAD members considered to be important, legitimate and technically manageable. Only four countries voted against the new UNCTAD mandate: the United States, Great Britain, the Federal Republic of Germany and Switzerland. After the vote the Group of 77 did not think it fit to reveal that the main body of arguments in favour of its position emerged from a meeting financed with Swiss and Canadian money. To reveal such details might have been considered highly undiplomatic.

So, with only four votes against it, a mandate to create a governmental experts working group within the UNCTAD to draft a code of conduct for technology transfer was established, to go into effect by the spring of 1975. A few days after this decision the UNCTAD Trade and Development Board managed to transform the 1972 Intergovernmental Expert Group into a permanent UNCTAD commission, acknowledging officially the importance of technology transfer in the area of international economic relations.

In early May, 1975, a few days before the first meeting of the new working group, ten specialists from key Third World countries came to Geneva to prepare for the meeting. Each of them, Latin Americans as well as Asians and Africans, had previously done his homework. Consequently, it was possible in four days to redraft and to expand the Pugwash proposals into a more complete and better structured draft of the code to be used in negotiations with experts from the industrial countries.

The improved draft was officially tabled for discussions by the spokesman of the Group of 77 on the inaugural day of the first meeting of the experts working group. This time the draft consisted of eight lengthy sections dealing with the objectives and principles of a code and its application, national regulation of technology transfer, restrictive business practices, guarantees, special treatment for developing countries, international cooperation and the solution of conflicts. Most of the industrialized countries reacted violently to this completely unexpected initiative by the Group of 77. It was claimed that the expert working group had not been convened to elaborate any concrete draft but just to discuss general ideas on the subject. After a heated and lengthy procedural debate the spokesman of the Group of 77 (and incidentally, the author of this article) quoted from the Oxford and Webster dictionaries, used in Great Britain and the United States respectively, exact definitions of the words 'draft outline' appearing in the resolution that established the working expert group. In this way the procedural debate was brought to an end. The meeting proceeded to a preliminary reading of the draft outline presented by the Group of 77.

Obviously, experts from the industrialized countries were not ready to go immediately to the working meeting that the developing countries' representatives had in mind. At the end of the first meeting of the working group they had only managed to present an outline of the first chapter of their counter draft, covering the principles and objectives of a code. To continue the task, the next meeting of the working group was set for November 1975, on the eve of the first session of the UNCTAD Commission for Technology Transfer. During a visit to Washington in June 1975 a high-ranking official of the United States State Department remarked half jokingly to the author: 'You created a lot of problems for us'. 'What is the problem?' I asked innocently. 'Well, you see, we put our best lawyers at the State and Justice Departments to critically review the Group of 77's draft of the code. They did not find anything which might be objectionable on technical grounds'. The comment was highly complimentary but not surprising. If one wishes to start serious negotiations, one must be able to present one's position in competent legal and technical terms. Obviously, there is always room for political discrepancies and conflicts. But to defend a position with arguments which do not stand up to technical criticism does not lead anywhere.

When the second meeting of the expert working group on the code started in Geneva in the autumn of 1975 the industrialized countries brought with them their draft outline of a code of conduct. Its elaboration started in Washington, in July 1975, with the participation of the different United States government agencies involved in technology trade. The United States draft outline was later presented at the technical OECD meeting in Paris where it was revised and transformed into a joint draft outline of all Western industrialized countries. The socialist countries also found it convenient to convene a group of their experts in East Berlin in September 1975. The socialist draft outline was submitted formally at UNCTAD a year later, in November 1976, when a common position on the code of conduct had been approved at the political level in the socialist bloc.

By the end of November 1975 the necessary conditions were created at UNCTAD for starting international pre-negotiations concerning a code of conduct for the transfer of technology. The pre-negotiations, which lasted just one week, took place in a conference room with three tables. The centre table was taken by Third World experts. The other two were occupied by representatives of the industrialized capitalist countries and the socialist countries respectively. The pre-negotiations were based on two different texts. True, they did not get far, but anyone who had ever participated in international negotiations knows that to start them it is absolutely necessary to have preliminary versions of negotiable texts. If such texts, even of a most general nature, do not exist, then the discussions are rendered irrelevant and superfluous.

The subject of an international code of conduct on technology transfer was submitted in February 1976 for the consideration of the ministerial meeting of the Group of 77 in Manila, which gave its political blessing to the original Geneva draft of May 1975. A few months earlier, during the special meeting of the UN General Assembly held in New York in September 1975, foreign ministers of all three major groups, the industrialized, the socialist and the Third World countries, confirmed the need to continue the preparation of a code of conduct for technology transfer. Their unanimous decision stated that such a code should come into effect during the latter part of 1977. Consequently, during UNCTAD IV in Nairobi in May 1976, the same subject became the only matter on the international agenda of North-South relations on which it was politically possible to achieve agreement on the continuation of negotiations. They were reopened in Geneva in November of the same year. From then on the Group of 77 made every effort to arrive at a single draft outline of a code by the end of 1977, so that a UN negotiating conference could proceed to the approval of the final text in 1978.

So it seems that in the not too distant future we shall see the establishment of an international code of conduct for technology transfer, whose initial take-off involved the expenditure of scarcely $10,000. Perhaps this account suggests that to change the international economic order it is not sufficient to be right nor is it necessary to have financial resources. One must know how to propose technical solutions at an opportune political moment, how to act with persistence and, above all, have the diplomatic savoir faire to be able to generate political backing all over the world.

NOTE

(1) Wassily Leontieff et al., The Future of the World Economy, United Nations, 1976; and Jan Tinbergen et al., RIO - Reshaping the International Order, New York, 1976.

CHAPTER 21

The UN Conference on Science and Technology for Development: Three Essays*

I. SOME QUESTIONS FOR THE 'WORLD JAMBOREE'

LESS than two years before the United Nations Conference on Science and Technology for Development (UNCSTD), understanding of the links between science and technology and the development needs of the Third World is still very slim.

In the advanced countries the position seems to prevail that fostering science and technology for development amounts to establishing modern scientific institutions in the less-developed countries and to massively transferring modern technology to them, preferably through private channels. On the other hand, many spokesmen for the underdeveloped world understand science and technology for development as abolishing all international barriers that hinder their access to the fruits of scientific and technological progress.

It is highly doubtful that either of these two extreme positions offers a solution to the problems of the less developed countries. Scientific institutes, massive transfers and tearing down the barriers to the flow of knowledge will hardly do the trick - because the capacity of the poor world to absorb and to use scientific knowledge and technical know-how in a socially meaningful way is very weak.

What the underdeveloped countries need first and foremost is the build-up of their internal scientific and technological capacity. The achievement of such an objective will depend more upon a long-term integrated international and domestic effort than on piecemeal initiatives guided by ideological preferences or by wishful thinking. This rather simple proposition seems to have been overlooked by many, if not most, of the diplomats, scientists and international bureaucrats participating in the preparatory stages for the UN Conference on Science and Technology.

---

*These three essays were published in The Bulletin of the Atomic Scientists, Educational Foundation for Nuclear Science (Chicago), Vol. 33, No. 10 (December 1977), Vol. 35, No. 4 (April 1979) and Vol. 35, No. 9 (November 1979).

One of the major obstacles to the advancement of science and technology in the underdeveloped world originates in the divorce between local research and development (R&D) activities and the educational and productive system and from the lack of a general scientific and technological culture. Consequently, the advance of science and technology in the poor countries will depend more upon establishing permanent and strong links between the R&D system, education, and the economy than on the volume of imported knowledge and an increased allocation of human and financial resources for research institutions.

In the absence of domestic demand for their output (a corollary to the absence of scientific culture) the modern scientific institutes that are set up in the less-developed countries either wither away or become sources for brain-drain. On the other hand, dependence on massive imports of technology through traditional channels leads to the emergence of advanced technology enclaves in the less-developed countries that perpetuate themselves in an otherwise technologically backward culture.

Given that scientific and technological policy for development in less-developed countries must be a part of overall development policy and must result in the building of bridges between R&D and the educational and productive systems, UNCSTD runs the risk of failing if - as seems to be the case - plans for its organization are left mostly to scientists from the North and bureaucrats from the South.

Many people will react to this gloomy presentation of prospects for this conference by pointing out that it is not either the first or the last global jamboree of little relevance. Others will say that considering the magnitude of financial resources wasted worldwide not only on highly irrelevant but also deeply harmful things such as armaments, spending $20 million every ten to fifteen years on a science and technology assembly is a trifling matter(1).

I would respond that we can hardly afford any more global jamborees on science and technology. Not because they represent a waste of time, human energy and money, but because the gap between the scientific and technological performance of the developed countries and the less-developed countries is growing. It is becoming unmanageable and is breeding internal and international conflicts.

However, if it were well thought out, and well managed, the conference could offer a much needed chance for all parties to arrive at some sort of general consensus about: (1) the preconditions for building science and technology for development; and (2) making international scientific and technological cooperation work better than in the recent past.

If such goals were achieved, the conference might represent an important contribution to the future of two-thirds of humanity who, in the era of intercontinental missiles and interplanetary expeditions, cannot see their basic biological and human needs satisfied.

The job is difficult not only because both developed and less-developed countries seem to be paralysed by short-term political considerations, but also - and more important - because scientific and technological underdevelopment in the less-developed countries is part and parcel of their overall underdevelopment.

In respect to science and technology this means that while most holders of power in less-developed countries have very primitive notions of science and technology and of its societal role, the scientific communities in the less-developed countries are, as a rule, tiny, mediocre copies of their counterparts in the advanced world. Their technological élites are largely under-educated and deficiently organized.

Moreover, most members of these poor societies are now succumbing to frustration because of their constant exposure to the image of wealth and welfare in the advanced countries. These people are being told day in and day out that this has been achieved largely through scientific and technological progress.

In recent attempts to formulate and implement scientific and technological policy programmes in several of the larger less-developed countries, like India and Mexico, many useful insights about the problems have been gained.

In order for a society to have socially relevant science and technology and to use the acquired knowledge and know-how for satisfying its needs, it must have a minimal capacity to define these needs with some clarity. Once defined - and they cannot be defined from the outside - the society will have to undertake several major tasks, such as improving the general quality of human resources; establishing educational systems worthy of that name; modernizing managerial élites (public and private); and assuring - hopefully through democratic means - that political power will not stay permanently in the hands of primitive and unscrupulous politicians (civilian or military).

In brief, the job of organizing science and technology <u>for development</u> (and this is, presumably, what the Conference is about) is not a question of money, haphazard institution-building or external assistance. It is a question first and foremost of internal social transformation involving a long and strenuous domestic effort that will give results only in the long run.

Since, however, the basic needs of underdeveloped societies cannot be satisfied without scientific and technological inputs and are perceived as urgent by a growing number of people, the less-developed countries need a lot of help from the outside. However, such help will be mostly useless if it takes the form of strictly scientific and technological cooperation. Since there cannot be science and technology worthy of that name in a social vacuum and under repressive political conditions, cooperation in science and technology must be linked with the goal of accelerating social transformation in the less developed countries.

To maintain that international scientific and technological cooperation or assistance is neutral amounts to propagating dishonest myths. According to its content, cooperation may either retard or help social transformation.

The job of building up science and technology for development is doubly difficult. First, the scientific and technological backwardness of most less-developed countries is much greater and deeper now than the backwardness that characterized (in pre-socialist times) relatively recent entrants into the mainstream of scientific and technological progress - the socialist countries. Contrary to many beliefs, based upon ignorance or prejudice, the Soviet Union before 1917, Poland and Hungary before 1945 and China before 1948 were quite advanced in all possible respects, including science and technology, in comparison with most of Latin America, Africa and Asia of the present day. Among other things, their élites had scientific and technological culture and tradition, two important ingredients of progress in science and technology.

The second difficulty arises from the absence of social transformation in the underdeveloped world. We all know that scientific and technological progress achieved in the advanced countries over the past 200 years followed rather than preceded social transformation. While obviously the scientific and technological progress of nineteenth century Europe and the United States had its impact upon the direction of social transformation, only in the past fifty years has the sheer magnitude and weight of science and technology become the decisive factor in that transformation.

In most of the less-developed countries, social and political conditions are very much different from those in today's advanced cojntries - whether West or East 100 or fifty years ago. Social transformation is not only largely absent but attempts to promote it are suppressed. Only a boundless optimist can detect positive social transformation today in the poorest part of the globe, South Asia; in the richest, the Middle East; or in the part in between, Latin America, overwhelmed presently by military dictatorships.

Organizers of the Conference managed to leave such basic issues as the less-developed countries' relative scientific and technological backwardness and absence of social transformation out of the agenda of the meeting. Instead the Conference is expected to offer a global overview of the progress of science and technology in the less developed countries and to discuss obstacles to its growth.

Time-consuming and costly mechanisms are being set up to produce elaborate national papers evaluating the scientific and technological progress in some 100 poor countries, and offering ideas about future policies and actions on national, regional and international levels. The wisdom contained in these papers is expected to be distilled by regional UN commissions and other offspring of the rapidly growing UN family, and then to be discussed jointly with the eminent leaders of official delegations.

I can hardly wait to read papers on the scientific and technological progress and policies of Honduras, Paraguay, Ecuador, Senegal, Gabon, Zaire, Bangladesh, Nepal and Afghanistan, written by local wise men. Speaking about the part of the world I know better, I am more curious to learn from official domestic sources about the progress in these fields in countries such as Argentina, Uruguay or Chile, where in recent years conscientious and well-organized efforts have been made by patriotic thugs to destroy local scientific and technological communities. Their efforts have resulted in the mass exodus abroad of some of the best human resources available in these countries.

What can non-governmental groups of scientists and technologists with high international reputations and moral solvency do with respect to the gloomy prospects for UNCSTD? One alternative would be to forget the whole thing and continue cultivating our own gardens. Another, perhaps more decent, is to establish contacts with other similar groups also preoccupied with preparations of that conference, for the purpose of exerting joint pressure over its organizers. The pressure would aim at dedicating at least a part of the 1979 jamboree to discussion of the real issues, not to the presentation of self-congratulatory official reports.

All these real issues are related either to internal causes of scientific and technological backwardness of most of the less-developed countries - the absence of social transformation - or to the inadequate conceptual framework of traditional international cooperation. Some of the major issues are related to both.

The topics are plenty and few of them have appeared in the now-forgotten declaration on International Cooperation for Development, approved at the September 1975 special session of the UN General Assembly. A list of major topics might cover the following questions:

(1) What kind of local, social and political conditions are necessary for building science and technology in the less-developed countries?

(2) What kind of educational systems may make the job of building science and technology in the less-developed countries not only possible but socially useful?

(3) Can science and technology be meaningfully developed in the less-developed countries without participation of the productive systems?

(4) What purpose, if any, is served by the mushrooming national science and technology councils in the less-developed countries in face of the backwardness of political structures?

(5) What should be the characteristics of national science and technology plans, not limited to a purely decorative exercise?

(6) What kind of technology transfer do less-developed countries really need? And what makes the difference between real and spurious transfer?

(7) What sort of institution-building, in the science and technology sector, should the less-developed countries engage in without running the risk of bureaucratizing amd finally killing the tiny existing scientific and technological systems?

(8) Who is responsible for the growing brain-drain from the less-developed countries - rich imperialists abroad or power-holding thugs at home?

This list is suggestive of many useful exercises that should be undertaken to develop an emergency action programme aimed at saving UNCSTD from a premature, and perhaps not totally deserved, death.

NOTE

(1) The UN budget for UNCSTD is of the order of $15 million, according to preliminary estimates.

II. SCIENCE AND TECHNOLOGY FOR DEVELOPMENT

As the time approaches for convening the 1979 UN Conference on Science and Technology for Development (UNCSTD) in Vienna next August, the predominant mood is one of malsise. Most of the criticisms - and the source of this malaise - involve the institutional mechanisms which were established for the Conference.

Its secretariat is widely criticized for 'not providing more of the analytical tools required for discussing how to handle science and technology for development'(1). The governments of the less-developed countries (LDCs) come under fire for not showing much interest in Conference preparations. In most cases, they are leaving the work on the national papers, which are expected to represent the core of that global meeting, 'to institutions and individuals of little weight in the political, economic and cultural life of the country'(2). Nor do the advanced countries appear to be very interested.

Although I subscribe to most of these criticisms, I do not propose to add more fuel to that particular fire. Instead I will attempt to address some major underlying issues responsible for the very uncertain prospects for the meeting.

These may be divided into three categories:

(1) the present state of the world economy, which largely explains the industrial countries' lack of interest;

(2) the socio-political background of LDC attitudes toward science and technology, which explains the excessive bureaucratization of their preparations; and,

(3) the modus operandi of the United Nations system by which the UNCSTD Secretariat functions.

A brief analysis of these three issues strongly suggests that the widely-expected failure of the Conference has been assured beforehand by forces which cannot be controlled by UNCSTD institutional mechanisms themselves.

While many scientists and some technologists may not see any connection between the world economy, science and technology and the prospects for the Conference, a direct connection exists. Indeed, the problem starts here.

Growing evidence suggests that the advanced countries have recently - since 1970 - entered a stage of protracted economic stagnation accompanied by increased uncertainty about the rate of future advances in science and technology, (S&T).

The decline in the growth rate of advanced countries has seriously affected growth prospects in most of the less-developed countries (excluding a few fortunate oil-producers). Even these low LDC growth rates are sustained only by increasing financial dependence upon the advanced countries and the few oil-producers, a dependence reflected in the continuous expansion of the LDC external debt at rates clearly unsustainable in the longer run. Briefly, in the midst of a major international economic crisis, the dependence of LDCs on the overall growth of advanced economies is greater than ever.

Some radical social scientists suggest that the LDCs should 'delink' themselves from the advanced sector of the world economy and become self-reliant, but no one has been able to offer a reasonably coherent political and economic model for such 'delinking' and 'self-reliance' in trade, finance and technology. The fact that socialist countries - including China - have been expanding their relations with the world economy because of their need for more trade, more finance and more technology, suggests that the design and implementation of such a model might be extremely difficult.

Certain disquieting developments which feed the uncertainty about future S&T progress, particularly with regard to industrial innovation, should be considered in the framework not only of general economic stagnation but also of power politics. The attempts by many major Western countries to close the technological gap with the United States provoke growing United States fears of losing its lead in technology(3). Both developments may have most serious negative consequences, not only for technological interchange among Western advanced countries but also for the less-developed world.

Knowledgeable people of many nationalities seem to agree, first, that the present unprecedented level of socio-economic welfare enjoyed by the advanced industrial societies has been largely due to the concentration and the exceptional rate of Western S&T progress over the past 100 years; and second, that, as demonstrated by the post-war emergence of West Germany and Japan, a causal relationship can be established between S&T advances and international changes in the distribution of political power. Nevertheless, discussion of the present and the future is gloomy.

General consensus exists about the growing economic and S&T competition among the United States, West Germany and Japan. Many link this with the uncertain future of the world economy and with each country's internal necessity to defend its share in that economy which is presently expanding much more slowly than in the past quarter-century. Many envision the emergence of technological protection measures as a corollary to the increasing wave of trade protectionism. Some also relate the trend toward technological protectionism to signs of the slowdown in S&T advance which, in turn, seems related to overall economic stagnation(4).

As proof accumulates that neither economic growth nor S&T advancement is automatic, preparations for the biggest global encounter on science and technology for development coincide at least in the industrial West with deep and increasing uncertainties about the future of growth, of science and technology - and of development as well. Worse still, neither economists nor S&T practitioners seem to possess analytical tools that explain what has been happening lately both in the world economy and in global S&T advance.

These uncertainties for the less-developed countries cannot be resolved by questioning the importance of growth and the relevance of S&T advance, as they may in more developed societies. At their present income and welfare levels the latter may forego more economic growth and live quite comfortably with their slowly expanding stock of S&T, provided they use it in socially more meaningful ways.

This static recipe does not offer, unfortunately, a satisfactory solution for LDC problems. First, the nature of international economic relations is such that the persistent slowdown in the growth rate of the advanced countries will ruin whatever limited prospects the LDCs may have of alleviating their overall social and economic misery. Second, the nature of S&T relations among advanced countries suggests that because of economic stagnation and the dynamics of power politics, access to science and technology in the less-developed nations may suffer further limitations.

Thus Western Europe's lack of interest in UNCSTD and the United States' apparent inability to commit itself to any concrete programme of assistance may be explained more simply than was supposed

If the major advanced countries are so concerned with their relative technological positions; if they believe that technology is the key to economic and hence to political power; and if, finally, world economic prospects are highly uncertain, then at least in the short run, these countries would have no reason to promote the rest of the world's access to proprietary technology, or to assist the less-advanced states in building up their S&T capability.

Indeed, given the static international economic situation, one might ask why the industrial countries would foster competition when too much competition already exists. The beggar-your-neighbour attitude would strongly favour not only trade protection but 'technological defence' as well. All this does not bode well for either the disadvantaged nations as such, or for the success of the Conference.

To explain the LDCs' lack of genuine political interest in science and technology on the eve of UNCSTD, we must recall how their governments became involved in these matters. The explicit interest of these countries, especially those more developed in science and technology, dates only from the early 1960s. It followed the belated discovery by economists from advanced countries that technology is an endogenous factor in economic growth, at least as important as capital, labour and physical resources.

The 'discovery' of science and technology by the LDCs can also be related to: (1) advancing industrialization; (2) their economists' penchant for macro-planning exercises; (3) the confidence of technocrats that science and technology can be fostered without the interest of the private - either domestic or foreign - sector; and (4) the influence of some parts of the UN system such as the Advisory Committee on Applications of Science and Technology (ACAST) and the UN Office for Science and Technology, as well as international agencies like UNESCO and UNCTAD (and the OAS in the case of Latin America).

Most probably each of these factors contributed to the creation, some ten years ago, of government agencies in Latin America and major Asian LDCs known as national science and technology councils whose purpose was to design S&T policies(5). In the late 1960s some of these countries, bent upon rapid industrialization, created additional policy instruments to regulate technology imports and modernize national industrial property legislation. All these initiatives were based on the assumption that the coalition of state, national S&T communities and local, private industrial technology users would support policies which expanded domestic capability and related it to national development needs.

The seventies demonstrated that with very few exceptions (Brazil and India perhaps) these expectations were too optimistic. Proponents of autonomous scientific and technological development found it extremely difficult to mobilize state, domestic entrepreneurs and scientific communities for their cause. Governments in these countries proved to be relatively unknowledgeable about S&T problems; domestic entrepreneurs found nothing wrong in a profitable coexistence with technological dependence; and weak local scientific communities responded with suspicion to what looked like bureaucratic interference with their liberties.

Consequently, the national science and technology councils were bogged down in marginal bureaucratic activities. Without high-level political support attempts at planning for science and technology withered away and the expected <u>rapprochement</u> between the scientific community and the users of S&T did not occur. Both private enterprise and the public sector continued importing foreign technology indiscriminately and on a large scale, and the infrastructure for S&T remained weak and disjointed.

The impact of the international economic crisis on the disadvantaged nations, which augmented their dependence upon foreign private interests and resources, made progress even more difficult. In the wake of mounting social and economic difficulties, the states started losing interest in science and technology while foreign and domestic private sectors, under the banner of free economy, launched a subtle but vigorous campaign against public intervention in that domain.

These developments led to the progressive dismantling of most of the S&T policy instruments in Argentina, Mexico and Peru over the past few years. They also explain why the majority of those citizens in the less-developed nations with distinguished careers in the field of S&T policy abandoned their own countries for international agencies.

Further evidence supporting these assertions can be found at an international meeting on science and technology, where most LDC delegates side with the pre-1960 school of uninitiated diplomats and bureaucrats. This sorry state of affairs was visible also at the first two UNCSTD preparatory conferences, held in January 1977 in New York and in February 1978 in Geneva. At both the preponderance of third secretaries from permanent UN missions was far from accidental, indicating the present political attitudes to science and technology in most disadvantaged nations.

Facing all sorts of short-run crises and difficulties, the top policymakers of these countries found the meetings expendable. Foreign and domestic private interests supported their position.

Under these adverse conditions no miracles could be expected from the UNCSTD secretariat even if it were manned by the best available experts. Moreover, UN institutional mechanisms established for the conference have been handicapped from the beginning by the <u>modus operandi</u> of the UN system which, like a medieval monarchy, has few characteristics of a rational operation.

The Conference - like all other global conferences - was established on the margin of the UN system. While institutional expediency defined the form and the mandate, intra-UN political considerations dictated the choice of its secretary general, who started his reign with unequivocal gestures aimed at ascertaining his own feudal sovereignty. These gestures hardly endeared him to the competing UN lords, who reciprocated this 'unilateral declaration of independence' with a hands-off position <u>vis-à-vis</u> preparations.

In the diplomatic language of the UN system, all these events can be described as 'absence of harmonized United Nations policy on science and technology'. The degree of this absence is evident in a report of the <u>ad hoc</u> Working Group on Policy for Science and Technology within the UN system(6).

According to this report:

>   the United Nations system at present is composed of a wide spectrum of activities in science and technology under widely different systems of

planning and implementation and with insufficient coordination among the parts, . . .

there is also a need to ensure that greater harmonization, compatibility and complementarity be achieved between policies in the field of science and technology at the national level and those at the level of the United Nations system at large, . . .

in the absence of clear, consensual definition regarding what constitutes a 'science and technology' category, no detailed quantitative assessment can now be made of the utilization of the currently available resources for science and technology in the United Nations system(7).

This <u>sotto voce</u> description of the actual management of science and technology issues within the UN system explains the intellectually unsatisfactory level of most of the documentation elaborated for the conference, the disappointing results of regional preparatory meetings, and the confusion surrounding the issue of 'science and technology and the future' - point four of the Conference agenda(8).

It could hardly be otherwise. Many authors of these documents and reports have had very little exposure to actual science and technology <u>for</u> development problems. Except for members of the Advisory Committee on Applications of Science and Technology, individual contributions to scientific and technological advancement are largely unknown. Furthermore, many bureaucratic interests are in conflict. The lessons of direct experience with science and technology, whether in research or policymaking, are thus replaced as the source of inspiration by earlier UN documents and resolutions, 'sacred texts' which by saying little can satisfy everybody.

Considering the absence of 'harmonized United Nations policy on science and technology', the obvious attitudes toward cooperation in the advanced countries, and those toward science and technology in the LDCs, only inveterate optimists and dreamers expect anything substantive and relevant to emerge from the deliberations at UNCSTD.

Does this mean that $15 million (the reported budget of the UNCSTD Secretariat) and additional large sums that will be spent by official participants represent pure waste? Not necessarily.

While the documentation and the reports from the debates will probably prove inconsequential, the preparations for that Conference are prompting many groups of concerned citizens all over the world - scholars and non-scholars alike - to answer questions of science and technology policy in the context both of development and underdevelopment. These independent initiatives have already expanded our scant knowledge about these extremely important global issues. Such initiatives deserve to be encouraged both before and particularly after the fact, if only because in the world of power politics and international and national bureaucratic games, free inquiry about the forces that are shaping our future is very badly needed.

NOTES

(1)   Jon Sigurdson, Welcoming remarks to the Lund seminar on 'Technology, Science and Development in the Changing International System' (31 May-2 June

1978, quoted in Lund Letter, No. 6 (July 1978).

(2) 'National Papers - into the Final Stretch', Lund Letter, No. 5 (May 1978).

(3) See, as evidence, the following excerpt from an article datelined Washington, D.C., International Herald Tribune, Paris, 18 April 1978: "For decades, every new technology or its product seemed to have Made-in-U.S.A. stamped on it, from instant copying and instant photography to advanced computers, nuclear reactors, oral contraceptives, synthetic fibers and jet airliners. . . . Things have changed. There is concern in the White House and Congress, in industry and universities, that the United States is losing its technological lead". As reported by the same newspaper on 2 November, President Carter's concern over a decline in technological innovation in the United States led to a cabinet level review and to a memorandum asking a presidential aide to defend in the Congress all research and development programmes contained in the budget for fiscal year 1980.

(4) The slowdown in S&T advance should be understood not as the decline in the rate of scientific discoveries but as the slowdown in the application of S&T for the production of goods and services and for the increase in welfare.

(5) Eduardo Pablo Amadeo, 'National Science and Technology Councils in Latin America - Achievements and Failures of the First 10 Years', Paper presented to a Seminar on S&T Policy Issues in Latin America, Florida International University, Miami, April 1978.

(6) ACAST, Report of the Ad Hoc Working Group on Policy for Science and Technology within the United Nations System, E/AC.52/XXIV/CHP.2, June 1978.

(7) ACAST, ibid., pp. 10-11.

(8) See, for example, UNCSTD, Recommendations of Expert Group on Agenda Item 4 of Conference Agenda, EMI/CRP.2/Rev. 2, November 1977.

III. UNCSTD WAS NOT A TECHNICAL FAILURE. . . .

Half-way through the UNCSTD deliberations in Vienna The Economist (London) ventured a prediction that:

> Conceivably something other than rhetoric may come out of the current United Nations jamboree on science and technology for development at Vienna. But probably no more than an extra dollop $200-300 million is to be channeled through existing United Nations agencies over the next two years. That will not be much for a conference that will itself cost an estimated $50 million by the time it winds up at the end of August(1).

This prediction was correct. Despite two weeks of negotiations, little substance can be detected in the final text of the UNCSTD Programme of Action, with the exception of an agreement to establish such a fund, based upon voluntary but regular contributions. Initially it is for the two-year period 1980-81 and is to be administrated - upon the insistence of the Western industrial countries – by the United Nations Development Programme. The rest of the fifty-page Programme of Action is divided into three parts: strengthening the scientific and technological capacities of developing countries; restructuring the existing pattern of international scientific and technological relations, and strengthening the role of the United Nations in the field of science and technology and the provision of increased financial resources. Such phrases are rhetoric even though expressions like 'target area' are used for each of these parts.

In fact, no targets whether international, regional or national were agreed upon in Vienna; no concrete commitments were made either by developed or developing countries; preparations for an operational plan for carrying out the Programme were left until a later date, as were decisions about scientific and technological activities and policies within the UN system. Thus, while the UNCSTD cannot technically be described a failure, its contribution to the international mobilization of science and technology for development is minimal. This may sound harsh, but it reflects the reality of the situation more than the painfully negotiated final agreement known as the Vienna Programme.

The UNCSTD, the largest and the most expensive UN jamboree of the seventies, was not a technical failure because no major participating party had any interest in confrontation; and this despite the threatening sounds coming from the Group of 77 in successive meetings of the UNCSTD Preparatory Committee and in the first week of the UNCSTD itself.

The Group of 77 did not want any new confrontation with the industrial countries because of its weakness, division and limited political and technical competence. The Declaration on Science and Technology for Development, adopted at the ministerial meeting of the Group of 77 held in Bucharest on the eve of the UNCSTD, was described in the UNCSTD general debate by the Soviet spokesman as a 'romantic' statement. Since one can hardly deal with real issues of science and technology from 'romantic' positions, 'romanticism' cannot have been the only reason for the Bucharest Declaration.

One of the reasons was perhaps the perceived need to bypass many issues related to the sorry state of science and technology in the world periphery, and to avoid further division and self-incrimination. As far as science and technology for development is concerned the Group of 77 is not a bunch of angels. The misery of their general level of scientific and technological development is not simply a result of colonial and neo-colonial influences, or of the depressing state of world economic relations. Some members of the Group of 77 may be poorer than others, and some are extremely poor, but many of these societies' technological problems originate from a wrong social allocation of resources. This is demonstrated by income distribution patterns and expenditures on arms and other 'consumption' goods, and cannot be explained by an absolute lack of resources.

The Bucharest Declaration states that the Group of 77 is firmly convinced that:

> Science and technology must become a fundamental resource for increasing production for the rational and efficient use of raw materials and energy, for preserving and improving the environment, and for enhancing the quality of life, and to achieve these ends, the ability to harness modern science and technology is essential.

If the Group of 77 were really serious about these matters, its members would have made their case for international funding of science and technology for development at UNCSTD much more convincing. They would have firmly committed themselves to the development of their scientific and technological capacity through their own efforts. Instead they merely asked for $2000-4000 million of external funds. They insisted on the creation of a 'global information system', and proposed the establishment of an intergovernmental coordinating committee under the UN General Assembly. Acceptance of concrete commitments on the part of the Group of 77, however, would have meant a lot of painful soul-searching, urgent domestic reforms, and allocation of more locally-available resources for science and technology. It might also have meant a critical reappraisal of fashionable and easy solutions to the problems: a questioning of the assumption that money and free worldwide access to scientific and technological information compensate for the dramatic backwardness of science and technology in most of the members of the Group of 77. Money and freedom of access might be of some help, but only so long as they are not seen as automatic guarantees of painless scientific and technological advance towards the heaven of general welfare or the paradise of power.

The advanced countries had reasons of their own for not raising similar issues at UNCSTD. They are passing through the most painful crisis of the post-industrial era and are unable to see their way out of it. Fortunately for them, but for them alone, the crisis is occurring within the framework of institutional and social arrangements at the national level, introduced or expanded after the Second World War. At the price of the constant inflation these offer certain safeguards to protect national standards of welfare from the corrosive impact of the crisis. Nevertheless, exposed to growing domestic political and social tensions, the developed countries are attempting to isolate themselves from international transmission of the crisis through all sorts of protective policies. These include defence of their national scientific and technological potential, and development of their capabilities in the same field.

Since both science and technology are badly needed in a world characterized by competition for power, international trade and domestic welfare, it is indeed 'romantic' for the Group of 77 to expect large transfers of technology from the industrial countries, particularly now, just for the sake of international morality and justice.

Relations between the advanced countries and the members of the Group of 77, are highly politicized particularly after the confrontation that took place at UNCTAD V. The industrial nations therefore - whether capitalist or socialist - were not in a position at UNCSTD to tell the 'romantics' of that Group what they really thought about their Programme of Action. They were unwilling to send them home without anything. The political cost of confrontation in Vienna was perceived by the advanced countries as too high in comparison with the small concession contained in their counter-proposal for a UNDP science and technology fund. Everybody knew, moreover, that the Group of 77 would accept any face-saving device or programme as long as it would involve the provision of some new money.

There were other actors at UNCSTD interested at least in preventing it becoming a technical failure if not in any more positive outcome, namely the hundreds of higher-level UN bureaucrats from all over the world (mainly from New York, Geneva and Paris, not counting the 500 who came from Geneva to service the meeting). The status and power of the UN bureaucracy depends on steady quantitative expansion of the system. Before UNCSTD the bureaucrats were already divided over the issue of who should take care of science and technology at the UN after the Conference. Although the strong and unprecedented bid by UNESCO to take over the matter failed, the statement by its Secretary General at the general debate suggests that intra-UN conflicts around that and other issues are very serious indeed: 'Regarding institutional arrangements, the United Nations system is a polycentric system. No agency is subordinated to another or to the United Nations itself'(2).

But granting that the degree of polycentrism practised within the UN system long ago passed the stage of what might be considered a reasonable division of labour and functionality, UN bureaucrats were united in Vienna on the issue of giving more power to the UN for science and technology. This was independent of the kind of work that might be called for, designed, or recommended by member governments. Consequently, the UN bureaucracy was a natural ally of the Group of 77 in terms of the financial and institutional arrangements contained in its draft Programme of Action and supported by the Bucharest Declaration. Thus, since the UN bureaucracy also shared the desire to avoid technical failure, it was avoided in Vienna to the partial satisfaction of all concerned.

Thus a solution assuring elimination of the danger of a 'technical failure' was available in Vienna from the start. And if the compromise was not achieved on the first day, it was due to the ceremonial nature of the gathering rather than to the existence of conflicts.

By the beginning of the second and final week of UNCSTD everyone, except for a few scientists, was relieved and reasonably satisfield. Political actors on one side were talking in glowing terms about 'the seed money' for future science and technology for development, while those on the other end of the negotiating table were complaining sotto voce about the cold reality which was forcing them to accept a 'few crumbs from the rich man's table'.

Le Monde (Paris) described the UNCSTD as a relative victory for the developing countries(3). But the question of whether it was a success in substantive conceptual and policy terms must unfortunately be answered in the negative. Paradoxically perhaps, the Conference was on the whole much worse than some - albeit not many - parts of UNCSTD preparations.

First, the fact that the Vienna meeting was not a serious high-level political conference, contrary to the claims of some official participants, indicates that at the national level science and technology is very much divorced from serious politics. This is particularly true of countries of the Group of 77, even if their delegations were led by high officials of the ministries of education, of the science and technology councils and so on. Since these bodies are secondary actors in domestic politics, serious political discourse and international bargaining in Vienna was subject to the most serious limitations.

Second, the UNCSTD did not offer any major conceptual progress, despite the fact that some sections of the final Programme of Action were written in more precise and clear language than previous international declarations in that field. This is particularly true in respect of the role of domestic scientific and technological capability in development, and the existing pattern of international scientific and technological relations. But on the whole supporting documentation for the Vienna Programme of Action is confusing, vague and conceptually weak. The same things have not only been said before, but have been expressed in better and more convincing ways. Reference can be made here, for example, to the so-called Sussex Manifesto of 1970 on the role of science and technology in developing countries during the UN Second Development Decade(4), and to some reports of pre-UNCSTD ACAST seminars.

The intellectual sterility of the UNCSTD exercise can nowhere be seen better than in its treatment of the agenda item 4 on science and technology for the future. Presumably this was to form a core of the Vienna conference. Instead it became a pain in the neck of the UNCSTD secretariat, of the legion of outside consultants and the sizeable contingent of scientists present in Vienna. It is no secret that neither the UNCSTD Secretariat nor official participants in the five successive meetings of the UNCSTD Preparatory Committee had any idea of how to handle the beast. A common sense approach would have suggested that since the entire Conference was to deal with science and technology for the future and not for the past a most serious inquiry was needed on the dynamics of scientific and technological advance, and of expected social change. Such an inquiry would have paid close attention to the frontiers of science and technology and their possible interrelations with worldwide developments in the next few decades. But in spite of the mushrooming of the so-called sciences of the future, nobody at the United Nations was willing or able to touch the subject. Eventually, and at a very late date in the game, in the winter of 1978-9, the UNCSTD secretariat parcelled out the job to an impressive number of social scientists, despite their almost complete lack of contact with the frontiers of science and technology.

The two separate reports were presented at Vienna as two parts of the same study, under the respective impressive titles 'Dynamism and Development' and 'The Critical Point'. Since the two philosophical exercises were not read in Vienna, but the agenda point was still pending, a working group was improvised to dispose of the matter. They had the brief to produce a short text to be adopted at one of the final UNCSTD plenary sessions, after the 150 speakers in the general debate had finished their marathon. Towards the end of the UNCSTD a highly disappointing text emerged from the working group amidst comments that since it was not adding anything new to the debate it should be forgotten. Some knowledgeable but cynical UNCSTD participants intimated that the official delegations were not particularly keen about debating the subject of the future since it did not lend itself to any draft resolution.

Whatever happened formally during the final plenary meeting of UNCSTD, science and technology for the future, the frontiers of science, and other similarly important subjects all sunk in the agitated waters of the Vienna jamboree without making a ripple. No better proof is needed that UNCSTD was a failure than the fact that it did not in any serious way take up the issue of science and technology for the future.

NOTES

(1) The Economist, 25 August 1979, 'Talking technology in Vienna', p. 54.

(2) UNCSTD Press Release STD/10A, 21 August 1979, UNESCO States Views in General Debate.

(3) Le Monde, 'Un nouveau dialogue Nord-Sud', 2-3 September 1979, p. 1.

(4) Report of ACAST, UN Dept. on Economic and Social Affairs, New York, ST/ECA/133,1970 reprinted by the Institute of Development Studies, University of Sussex, IDS Reprints 101.

CHAPTER 22

A Diagnosis of Past Failures and Future Prospects of the New International Economic Order*

Within less than five years after the official launching at the United Nations in the fall of 1974 of the North-South dialogue on the New International Economic Order (NIEO), this 'dialogue' reached a complete stalemate on all - both major and minor - issues. Considering this highly disquieting, an attempt has been made here to throw some light on three broad questions: (1) what has been happening with the NIEO negotiations; (2) what are the underlying issues behind the deadlock; and (3) whether there is any way out of the present stalemate.

The author assumes that the New International Economic Order is needed not because the traditional order is wicked, immoral, or unjust, but because in the long run it does not bring real benefits to anyone, due to its inadequacy in rapidly-changing international political, social, and economic conditions. The best proof that the old international economic order is inadequate is that it has led thw world economy into chaos and stagnation.

In spite of the voluminous and ever-increasing literature on the subject(1), the NIEO has not yet been defined satisfactorily. As an ideal political programme of the LDCs, perhaps it cannot be defined at all; and as a dynamic set of multiple objectives obtainable only through difficult multilateral negotiations, perhaps it should not be defined. The broad areas that badly need a substantial revision of the traditional rules of the global political and economic game have been identified in official UN documents and elsewhere. They include such key international issues as trade in raw materials and manufactured goods, technology and energy, flows of public and private capital across borders, and the international monetary system(2). To this impressive list the question of international control of the natural resources potentially available in the seabed and in space through recent technological advances

---

*This essay was written for the Seminar on the Future of the New International Economic Order held in Mexico City in January 1979 under the joint auspices of the UN Institute for Training and Research (UNITAR) and the Centre for Economic and Social Studies of the Third World (CEESTM), and published in Development and Change, Sage Publications Ltd. (The Hague), Vol. 10, No. 4 (October 1979).

should be added.

A considerable number of technically competent schemes and policy proposals reflecting the general philosophy of the NIEO now exists in all the abovementioned fields. Most of them have been elaborated not by the Third World 'radicals' but by academic experts from the Western developed countries, acting in their personal capacity or as staff members of international organizations. Many proposals go back to the ideas that circulated in the West in the thirties and the early forties. Some are associated with the name of John Maynard Keynes. Since the opposition of the major advanced Western countries, on the one hand, and the frequent lack of consensus among the LDCs themselves on the other, have kept the most recent NIEO initiatives from being implemented, it may be worthwhile to present a full list of specific deadlocks:

(1) The Integrated Commodity Program, supported by the Common Fund, which was proposed by UNCTAD to eliminate extreme price fluctuations in the principal ten to eighteen raw materials and foodstuffs produced largely by the LDCs - thereby assuring the latter a certain degree of export proceeds stability - reached an apparent impasse at the end of 1978 after two years of unsuccessful negotiations during which the programme's sponsors scaled it down considerably because of its alleged heavy financial implications(3). Only in 1979 and for the purpose of heading off a new North-South confrontation at UNCTAD V in Manila, did Western developed countries and the Soviet Union with its allies sign the framework agreement on the Common Fund. The agreement itself is still to be drafted by an UNCTAD interim committee and as a well-informed source commented ' . . . ominously both the Americans and the Russians immediately indicated they found the package unsatisfactory'(4). While in 1976 the developing producer countries were calling for a $6 billion fund to bring order to the commodity markets, this has been bargained down to $400 million for market stabilization with the so-called 'second window' to finance marketing and export promotion. In Manila all major industrial countries dismissed that 'second window' as unnecessary(5).

(2) Individual commodity negotiations, which were to cover some fifteen products under the UNCTAD IV agreement reached at Nairobi in 1976, and were supposed to pave the way toward the Integrated Commodity Program, have made practically no progress; only one commodity agreement - on sugar - has been renegotiated in the three years that separated UNCTAD IV from UNCTAD V(6).

(3) When multinational trade negotiations under the General Agreement on Tariffs and Trade (GATT), known as the Tokyo Round and concentrated mostly on non-tariff trade restrictions, ended in mid-April 1979 virtually all the developing GATT members abstained from initiating the final agreement. While the results of the negotiations may give LDC manufactures somewhat better access to developed country (DC) markets, growing DC protectionism - particularly in the field of consumer goods, which account for the major part of LDC manufactured exports - more than offsets any Tokyo Round achievements(7). Almost certainly the 'informal' or 'voluntary' export restrictions negotiated outside of GATT would have hit LDCs even more severely were it not that a large part of their manufactured exports originate in the affiliates of transnational corporations (TNCs) or in LDC firms subcontracted by TNCs to produce parts and/or to assemble final products for export to the DCs(8).

(4) The flow of official development assistance from international agencies and under bilateral arrangements is declining in real terms and as a percentage of the GNP of developed countries, not only because of worldwide inflation

but also because of the growing service burden on the outstanding LDC debt(9).

(5) Concomitantly with the declining role of official development assistance and the stagnation of the flow of private capital to LDCs, the role of private banking in the development financing of the LDCs continues to increase, and the LDCs' total long-term (over one year) liabilities to international private banks exceeded in 1978 those to official multilateral and bilateral financial agencies. Despite the growing LDC external public debt, which (including short-term commercial debt) was estimated at the end of 1978 at some $400 billion, no agreement has been reached at UNCTAD or elsewhere on common rules and criteria for possible debt renegotiations; such renegotiations, which are growing in number, take place on an *ad hoc* case-by-case basis, because both the lenders and the richer developing countries prefer to negotiate on debt individually(10).

(6) The debt-relief measures agreed upon in early 1978 for the poorest LDCs, which transformed official loans into grants and donations, have not been put into practice by some major DCs, including the United States, presumably because of domestic legislative difficulties.

(7) At the World Bank and the IMF, the periodic discussions about replenishment of the Bank's resources and expansion of the Fund's quotas are proceeding at a slower pace than ever in response to conservative domestic financial and monetary considerations and to the excessive global liquidity of the eurocurrency market, which cannot be controlled by the national monetary authorities of the major DCs and which was estimated in early 1978 at over $700 billion.

(8) No progress has been reached and none is in sight on the subject of linking Special Drawing Rights (SDRs) with development financing.

(9) The orderly functioning of the international monetary system proved at least as difficult (if not more difficult) under flexible exchange rates as under the previous fixed rates, as demonstrated by the extreme exchange-rate fluctuations in 1978. The defence of the United States dollar programme, announced by President Carter on 1 November 1978, and the agreement on a European currency unit (ECU), reached in Brussels one month later by seven out of nine members of the European Economic Community, did not eliminate the acute concern about the future of international money markets: some experts claim that 'the international monetary system is a disaster area'(11).

(10) UNCTAD negotiations on the international code of conduct for technology transfer, opened in 1975, reached a deadlock in November 1978 on the key issues of its legal character and its implementation machinery; they were expected to continue in the fall of 1979 after UNCTAD V(12).

(11) Even relatively less-important international agreements such as the UNCTAD Code of Conduct for Maritime Conferences, adopted in 1975 after several years of negotiations, have not been implemented; the European Common Market countries dropped their opposition to that Code only at UNCTAD V in Manila as a 'good will' gesture towards the LDCs.

(12) Finally, notwithstanding the large volume of rhetoric at international and regional levels on the concept of national or group self-reliance, the LDCs have made minimal progress in regional economic and technological cooperation even though perhaps only a dozen of them can look forward to some

degree of individual quasi-autonomous development(13).

Since the underlying philosophy of the NIEO programme is essentially reformist and aims at improving existing mechanisms of international relations rather than changing them, it seems strange that the developed countries, which presumably subscribe to liberal economic norms, should place so many difficulties in the way of implementing the NIEO. To the contrary, they should be interested in the progressive reform of a set of international economic relations that are increasingly inadequate for meeting their own objectives. As was pointed out recently,

> . . . a number of the key elements of the NIEO program have clear stabilizing effects on the existing economic system and, in the long run, their implementation may possibly even give the kiss of death to the pursuit of vigorous restructuring(14).

Thus, although implementation of the UNCTAD Integrated Commodity Program would not affect the long-term interests of the DCs in security of access to raw materials, it might help greatly in the management of international and domestic business cycles. Increased official financial assistance to LDCs and the improvement of its terms and conditions would expand the market for DC manufactured exports. The more orderly functioning of the international monetary system would not only eliminate undue private speculation against weaker currencies, including the dollar, but would lower the barriers against international flows of capital to the LDCs, which are generously endowed with natural resources, land, and labour, but short of capital and technical know-how. A code of conduct for international technology transfer would set the rules of the game for the only part of international trade left completely outside the realm of regulation and surveillance; moreover, through its contribution to LDCs' domestic technological capability, the code might help to alleviate serious international tensions arising from worldwide technological disequilibrium. If the developed countries - both capitalist and socialist - would consider their own longer-term interests, many obstacles to the revision and modernization of the traditional economic order could be overcome with relative ease. Instead, the Western DCs concentrate on fending off their short-term problems, and the socialist advanced countries continue disclaiming any responsibility for the results of the 'exploitative excesses of the capitalist system'. Since the LDCs are not helpful either, the obstacles to the NIEO appear enormous.

The LDCs are not helpful on a number of counts. First, under the guise of defending their individual sovereignty, in NIEO debates they were able to divorce the question of international reform from that of the new domestic economic and social order. The fact is, however, that the equity of internal political, social, and economic relations in most LDCs leaves much to be desired, to say the least; nor has anyone been able to explain how greater equity in international relations can translate itself into more equitable domestic social and economic welfare in the LDCs in the absence of a commitment by the present rulers of these countries to social and economic reforms. The dense fog surrounding these uncomfortable issues at the United Nations affects NIEO credibility and cuts serious limitations upon the support the NIEO might receive from the more progressive sectors of public opinion in developed countries.

Second, the common front of LDCs in NIEO negotiations, inspired in 1974-5 by the success of OPEC, is crumbling. While growing conflicts and friction among the LDCs are commonly attributed only to the DCs' political manipulation, they are perhaps also due to two specific but rarely mentioned factors: pronounced disparities in the size and development levels of members of the Group of 77; and the impact of the present world economic crisis upon individual LDCs(15). While the emergence of LDC interest in the NIEO coincided with the final years of the relatively satisfactory, albeit unequal, post-war performance of the world economy, the progressive deterioration of world economic conditions in the seventies led many LDCs on the double road of populist policies at home and 'third-worldism' at the international level. With the general defeat of populism in Latin America and Southern Asia, followed by a return to conservative domestic social and economic policies, the LDCs' support for cooperation on the NIEO at the United Nations and elsewhere was superseded by pragmatic approaches to immediate external difficulties(16).

Since the advanced countries have always preferred conservative pragmatism and special relations of a unilateral type, individual dialogues reappeared on the international scene, eroding the support for the NIEO in most major and middle-sized LDCs. The intense flirtation between industrial countries and the so-called NICs - in OECD parlance, 'the newly industrializing countries' (Argentina, Brazil, Mexico, India and some export-oriented Far East Asian countries) - offers evidence in this respect. Japanese interest as a silent partner in the Association of South East Asian Nations (ASEAN) and France's support for the economic reorganization of black Africa can be understood only within this political framework. In a world in which the Western industrial countries adopt 'beggar-your-neighbour' and 'sauve-qui-peut' attitudes, it may be unrealistic to expect the much weaker LDCs to act otherwise.

The intra-LDC conflicts and friction, together with the failure of populist 'reforms' and the LDCs' disenchantment with the lack of progress on the NIEO front, led inevitably to the decline of the LDCs' capacity to negotiate with the advanced countries at the United Nations and elsewhere. As the major LDC capitals became less interested in the long-term objectives of the NIEO, the political and technical level of LDC negotiators in international fora deteriorated. The parallel bureaucratization of the international agencies themselves compounded the difficulties. In brief, the responsibility for the NIEO stalemate does not fall exclusively upon the shoulders of 'heartless neo-colonialists'.

Additional complications also arise from the fact that there are more actors in the NIEO game than is generally assumed. Confrontation and negotiations involve not only the developed capitalist countries, the Group of 77, and the socialist states (including as a separate player, China), but two other groups of actors: - transnational corporations, and the members of the incipient global public system consisting of both UN and non-UN international agencies and their regional and subregional extensions. These new actors entered the international policymaking process in the past twenty years. It would be an error to consider, as some do, that they reflect a new global private conspiracy, in the first place, or express a new global public power, in the second.

While differing functionally from national states, both TNCs and international public agencies are in many senses similar to them. Like national states, they vary in size and development level and are endowed with different degrees of power. Also like national states, these newly-emerged players have four major objectives: survival, security, welfare, and power. While only welfare has an explicit - albeit partial - economic content, economic issues are implicit and at times important factors in the remaining three objectives. Moreover, all categories of players, old and new, have in common that they can function only if and when they consist of hierarchical structures whose members are bound by underlying loyalties to the respective structures.

According to conventional radical wisdom, TNCs not only represent the last stage of economic imperialism but they are the tail that wags the dog - the advanced capitalist state structures. Moreover, it is assumed that they are not only bent upon the economic exploitation of our planet through the maximization of profits and hence the accumulation of political power, but also that they provide the ideological underpinning and support for the capitalist forces fighting against the advance of socialism. Allegedly acting as sort of joint chiefs of staff in the anti-socialist crusade, TNCs are said to be particularly mischievous in the LDCs by interfering in their economic, financial, social, and political life and by forging all sorts of chains that make it practically impossible for the new or old weak LDCs to fulfil their national objectives. This line of reasoning, which represents 'scapegoatism' in its purest form, leads easily to the defeatist but nonetheless comfortable conclusion that the NIEO cannot be achieved until TNCs and capitalism itself are banished from the world forever(17).

It may be more useful to assume simply that, in trying to fulfil their own objectives, TNCs interfere with all other actors on the international scene and interfere more with weak than with stronger nation states. Once it is accepted that among the TNCs important but sometimes conflicting objectives represent not only economic power but also the survival, security, and welfare of their 'citizens', it becomes easier to understand the TNCs' otherwise confusing international behaviour. Thus, since they are deeply interested in survival, they enter willingly into arrangements with socialist states that exclude external proprietary control of economic activities in these countries; long-term security considerations induce them to accept co-ownership and co-production formulas in many non-socialist states, which would have been unthinkable only a quarter of a century ago; finally, welfare (and growth) considerations largely explain the TNCs' strong and sustained participation in scientific and technological advances.

On the other hand, the conflicts between the objectives of the TNCs and those of other actors on the international scene often bring untold headaches not only to the governments of LDCs but to those of the DCs as well, as demonstrated by the international monetary problems faced by Washington. Furthermore, the quasi-autonomous behaviour of the TNCs may lead to the emergence of new international coalitions similar to OPEC. It is difficult to judge, for example, which is more dependent - OPEC on the TNCs' worldwide distribution of oil, or the 'seven big sisters' and large oil 'independents' on OPEC. At present new coalitions arise from certain common export interests of TNCs operating in the newly industrializing countries and of the LDCs that are in a position to expand manufactured exports to developed industrial markets. As a matter of fact, in the world of growing protectionist pressures, certain TNCs may well be among the few allies available to some LDCs in international trade policy.

Given their strong position in the world economy, the TNCs' relations with the NIEO cannot be reduced, as many believe, to one single item of the long NIEO agenda - a code of conduct for TNCs. Whether one likes it or not, the presence of TNCs affects most of the NIEO agenda. Consequently, little progress will be made on that front unless some new <u>modus vivendi</u> is arrived at through negotiations between NIEO proponents and this set of international private actors. Unfortunately, present developments in the LDCs are not particularly conducive to such a new modus vivendi which depends largely upon an increase in the LDCs' bargaining power. Overpowered by the apocalyptic vision of the strength and inflexibility of the TNCs, and disenchanted with the NIEO, most LDCs have recently surrendered whatever new bilateral economic order they were able to establish for TNCs in the past decade.

This brief survey of the NIEO players would not be complete without an overview of the international public agencies that centre on but do not limit their range of action to the UN system. This system itself has undergone a very considerable evolution since its establishment in San Francisco in 1945 by fifty signatories of the UN Charter. Contrary to the belief of some idealistic souls, the UN system is not the expression of a new global power, or a world government in its initial stage. Composed of the secretariat, a dozen specialized semi-autonomous (and, in the financial sector, even completely autonomous) agencies, regional commissions, and other permanent or ad hoc bodies and expert groups, it reflects the spontaneous and, at times, very chaotic expansion of the agenda of international relations.

In spite of having faced for the past twenty years a permanent financial crisis and having been burdened by a sizeable external debt, the UN system manages somehow not only to survive but to marshall and to manage increasing financial and human resources. It gives employment to many thousands of people stationed all over the world. It has established hierarchical structures and expects from its personnel some sort of basic loyalty as 'international civil servants'. Its strength comes not only from its global ideology but from its growing bureaucracy.

The UN system started as a mostly political body dominated by the West, particularly by the United States, and progressively became an open-ended permanent 'global assembly' for treatment of almost any subject. The interests of its over 150 member states are represented not only by permanent diplomatic missions in New York, Geneva, and elsewhere, but also by different national groups in the secretariats of the system. These secretariats are described by critics as a multi-headed bureaucratic hydra, or a sort of medieval monarchy, or a special kind of an inefficient transnational public corporation. Whatever its shortcomings and the similarities of its behaviour to that of other actors on the international scene, the successive failures of attempts to reorganize the United Nations in the past fifteen years strongly suggest that the system is not only unique, but that it is perhaps the best available in the international public realm.

Unfortunately, the system's productivity, efficiency, and impact upon world affairs, which have never been optimal, are declining. Moreover, its shortcomings seriously affect the prospects for the NIEO. Most, although not all, of these shortcomings are directly related to the system's main objectives – survival, security, welfare, and power – which are basically the same as those of other internationally active social groups. Other impediments arise not only from the fact that the people who man the system often happen to have divided loyalties and very specific individual interests, but that in some instances the international civil service is still a concept rather than a reality.

Using the language of the literature on transnationals and empires, the UN system, at its centre and also in its affiliates, branches, agencies, and dependencies, is run in the broadest terms by three categories of people: globally thinking moralists, skilful political operators and non-imaginative bureaucrats. Over time, the system has had a more than proportionate increase in the numerical participation of operators and bureaucrats in response to the dynamics of the system itself, the expansion of its geographical scope of influence, and the way it recruits its personnel. These trends have been strengthened by the fact that the system offers political, financial, and individual security to people who outside the realm of international public bureaucracy might have a tough life. All these factors together, plus many others, are at the heart of what is known to many insiders and outside observers as the crisis of the UN system.

Contrary to some beliefs, this crisis reflects not only the behaviour of nation states but the system's internal problems. Some of these might be mentioned as affecting particularly the system's ability to deliver international services of intermediation and conflict resolution:

(1) the detachment of 'global policy strategists' from real life, which recalls the attitudes of global military planners in the military establishments of major national powers;

(2) the concomitant tendency to consider verbal expressions of negotiated partial agreements 'in principle' (declarations, resolutions and reports) as the equivalent of action;

(3) the interpretation of such 'action' by individual agencies and units in terms of their particular short-run interests, which results in the unending process of intra-system bureaucratic negotiations and severely affects the quality and the relevance of substantive work, including studies, reports and policy-oriented initiatives(18);

(4) the replacement of innovative action by repetitive exercises along the lines of fashionable global subjects; and

(5) the extremely low priority assigned to the implementation of agreed decisions, under the pretext that implementation is a matter to be dealt with exclusively at the national level.

The actual NIEO negotiations are as much affected by these major shortcomings and limitations of the international public system as by the conflicts of interest among the nation states and their groupings, and by the global activities of TNCs. In spite of the volume of work done over the past years on reorganization of the UN system, these shortcomings have not been studied in sufficient detail. Moreover, it is both curious and symptomatic that NIEO proponents pay little attention to them. Instead, they concentrate on such issues as the representation of different countries and regions in the secretariats of international public agencies and the voting formulae in the agencies themselves.

Thus, for example, it is hopefully assumed in many places that if only more people from LDCs were working in international public agencies and if the voting rules in such bodies as the World Bank and the IMF were adjusted to new political realities, the international system would improve its performance in favour of LDCs and consequently the NIEO would progress at a more rapid pace. There is no evidence available as yet that would lend support to these general propositions, which may be considered as necessary but by no means sufficient conditions for NIEO advancement(19). A more persuasive diagnosis states that:

> . . . the NIEO is impeded by institutional proliferation and the lack of a coherent and coordinated approach to the economic and social agenda at both international and national levels, and by the failure of the international secretariat to inspire confidence and analyse progress(20).

In summary, the considerable degree both of overlapping and conflict among the objectives, structures, and loyalties of the three major categories of actors - nation states, transnational corporations, and international agencies - on the international scene greatly complicates the decision-making process with regard to the NIEO. It is only against the background of the maze of relations among multiple categories of international actors, with their individual and group objectives and particular loyalties, that the difficulty of organizing the New International Economic Order can be understood. If the task were limited solely to the interaction of nation states, perhaps it would be easier to accomplish. The relatively smooth and 'peaceful' working of the international system between the Napoleonic wars and 1914 offers circumstantial but not convincing evidence in this respect(21). It should be remembered, however, that in the nineteenth century 'concert of nations' less than ten nation states really counted and that the total of independent of quasi-independent national entities did not exceed forty.

Thus, both in international and national social and economic matters, the world is doing much worse than at any time since the early thirties in terms not so much of absolute performance, as in measuring performance against expectations. In the developed market-oriented Western societies, a quarter-century of post-war rapid material progress resulted in general expectations of full employment, job security, and individual high-level consumption as part and parcel of basic human rights. In the industrialized socialist societies, which in terms of individual consumption are less than twenty years behind the Western capitalist world and which provide their members with employment and job security as a matter of course, expectations put increasing emphasis on the weakest part of the package - individual consumption and political rights. In the underdeveloped periphery, the demonstration effect of the two different packages of social and individual welfare available in the advanced world is resulting in the spread of a highly idealized vision of the optimal society. This vision is a composite version of the most attractive elements of the capitalist and socialist worlds. Its instant objectives are full employment, job security, high-level consumption, and individual freedom.

This idealized vision conveniently forgets, first, that it took the capitalist West some two hundred years to arrive at its present stage of technology-based prosperity; and, second, that it took the Soviet Union, the centrepiece of the socialist system, over a half-century to leave behind the state of general backwardness which, it should be added, at no time could have been compared with the underdevelopment characteristic of most of the periphery, particularly in ex-colonial Africa and Asia. This idealized vision of the 'best of all worlds' forgets, also conveniently, the historically high social cost of building modern capitalism in the West and the socialist welfare states in Eastern Europe. Serious social and economic historians of Western Europe between 1789 and 1870, of the United States between the Civil War and 1914, and of the Soviet Union between 1917 and 1953 are aware of these uncomfortable 'details'.

On the one hand, there is the high overall level of welfare reached in the
advanced capitalist and socialist countries, with the aid of recent intense
scientific and technological advances; on the other, there is the general level
of poverty, hunger, and unemployment, the concurrent lack of basic political
human rights, and the rising level of minimal expectations in most of the LDCs.
Considering the challenge offered by the foregoing, the present world performance is quite disappointing. Notwithstanding the rhetoric of interdependence
and international cooperation, the objectives of survival, security, welfare
and power are fostered by traditional means and unilateral policies, whether
nationally or within and by international public agencies and transnational
corporations. The failures at a national or - in a shrinking world - a tribal
level are particularly striking. The frustrations of national social and
economic policies both in the DCs and the LDCs represent a measure of a general
global crisis.

While academics and some politicians in the advanced North talk about the need
to replace the concept of growth by one of development and there is increasing
talk about the urgent need to 'do something' about global basic needs, short-
run policies in the developed countries fail to assure even growth in the
North itself. A passive consensus seems to be emerging both in capitalist
and socialist countries to the effect that the economic growth rates of the
past twenty-five years cannot be maintained(22).

Much time, money, and human energy has been dedicated to elaborate rationaliza-
tions of the thesis that rapid economic growth is no longer possible, or
feasible, or advisable, since the basic human needs of the advanced societies
have been (almost) fulfilled, and since growth is also limited by existing
physical resources. In the DCs there has lately been concern about basic
needs in the underdeveloped peripheries and the suggestion that the latter
return to agricultural pursuits and 'small-is-beautiful' types of technology
as their defence against the excesses of industrial civilization. Advocates
of such a policy tend to overlook the increasing underutilization of production
capacity in the advanced countries and they also find it convenient to keep
silent about the misuse of a large part of these facilities for purposes alien
to the peaceful application of capital, labour, and natural resources for
development. Many spokesmen for the LDCs and the NIEO skirt the same issues
when dealing with developments in their own spheres of influence.

In brief, we are facing a declining growth rate, worldwide inflation, open and
disguised unemployment, mounting indebtedness, monetary crises, and the rising
social tensions and the progressive bureaucratization of societies and international structures. The only activity that seems to prosper is the product
of the search for national security and power through the arms race(23). And
the world being what it is, the arms race becomes contagious. These same LDCs
that clamour for a new economic order based upon better international morality
and equity, do their utmost to reallocate power to themselves by increasing
their own military capability. The elimination of military dependence through
the establishment of local military industries and, whenever possible, of
nuclear strike capability is quite fashionable in many major LDCs(24).

The NIEO points out as its supreme objective harmonization of the interests
at national and international levels of the developed and underdeveloped parts
of the world economy. This objective is expected to be achieved through negotiations within the context of economic growth, social development, scientific
and technological (S&T) advances, and political accommodation. Unfortunately,
however, not only are the forces of economic growth missing in the capitalist

West and in the underdeveloped South, and perceptibly weakening in the socialist East, but it becomes more and more difficult to discern at either the global or national level the dynamic factors required for advances in S&T.

With growth rates in the Western developed countries declining steadily, and with those in the socialist and the underdeveloped countries sustained, to some extent, through external borrowing for anticipated consumption(25), there is worldwide concern about the slowing accumulation rate of scientific discovery and technological innovation(26). Given this trend, and in the light of the uncertain future of the world economy and each country's need to defend its share in the world economy and trade, many people foresee the emergence of technological protection measures, as a corollary to the increasing wave of trade protectionism. In the highly industrialized economies, the slowdown in the application of new science and technology for the production of goods and services and for higher welfare is explained by the vicious circle of the fall in investment followed by a fall in the application of S&T for development. In the socialist countries, which seem to live increasingly on Western technology, bureaucratic overcentralization os held responsible. Finally, in the LDCs science and technology are subject to the combined effect of local social and cultural constraints and of inadequate types and channels of technology transfer from advanced Western countries.

Consequently, the weakness of the S&T contribution to the development needs of the LDCs compounds social tensions deriving from antiquated political and economic structures, from glaring welfare disparities between advanced industrial centres and backward peripheries, and from widening welfare gaps within the underdeveloped societies themselves. Since there are almost no international and national conditions conducive to carrying on the NIEO negotiations within the framework of a positive non-zero-sum game, the political accommodation of conflicting interests becomes extremely difficult, if not impossible.

Some people consider that North-South economic issues are the key global problems to be faced by the world during the rest of the twentieth and the early twenty-first century. This chapter has made an attempt to demonstrate, however, that these problems have been accompanied and complicated by other, no less important, global issues: military and security problems between the East and West, exacerbated by the trend toward military independence in the South and by nuclear proliferation; North-South political problems caused by the rise of nationalism; conflicts between TNCs and nation states on the issue of control and distribution of earnings from productive, mainly industrial, activities; and problems in the international public system, including the United Nations, with regard to the sovereignty of the nation states.

Any strategy for the NIEO must take account of the links between all these global issues. In other words, in addition to the explicit interdependence between problems of trade, development finance, technology, and the international monetary system, which form the NIEO agenda, there is the implicit interdependence between the military and political issues on the one hand, and the social and economic conflicts, on the other, whether global, regional or bilateral. Acknowledgement of these two types of interdependence does not necessarily mean that all these issues can be negotiated as a single package. The failure of the Paris Conference has demonstrated that even negotiation of the NIEO package by itself is highly difficult.

A clear vision of the interdependence of all major global issues is needed to move the NIEO from its present stalemate, resulting not only from lack of political will on the part of the advanced Western countries, but also from the internal short-run difficulties of the LDCs, and the inefficiency of international bureaucracy. The stalemate is also due to the absence from the negotiating table of two other groups of actors: the socialist states, which account for about one-third of the world economy, and the transnational corporations, which represent about one-half of international trade.

By their absence from the NIEO debates, as was the case at the Paris Conference, and by their passive participation elsewhere, the socialist states also work against their own long-term interests. It is one thing to reject responsibility for the past; it is another not to participate - or to be excluded from - the process of negotiating the shape of the future. Moreover, breakdowns in the existing political and economic order, like the post-war developments in Southeast Asia or the present crisis in Iran, are a threat to all countries, including socialist ones. Chaotic regional or local situations can easily turn into confrontations among the nuclear superpowers. Thus progress on the NIEO front requires the permanent presence and the active participation of the socialist segment of the world economy.

Although complaint about the absence of TNCs from the negotiations may sound almost treasonable to NIEO proponents, no serious negotiation should deal with one of the major parties to the dispute through intermediaries or by proxy. In the present century this sort of approach was attempted without success in many political conflicts between nation states. The long delay in the recognition of the Soviet Union between the two World Wars and the exclusion of China from the United Nations for a quarter-century after 1948 are perhaps the most conspicuous examples of the divorce between diplomacy and reality. If the TNCs not only exist but are so powerful that, according to some, they are the tail wagging the dog (the nation states), then the TNCs must be recognized as an important element of international power relations and dealt with accordingly.

Recognition of the TNCs by the international community of nation states might not only lead to solution of some of the conflicts arising from the TNCs' presence, but might also permit a better definition of the concept of sovereignty in terms of the interests of both the nation states and the community of nations(27). While it is clearly up to the experts in international law to search for and, if necessary invent, adequate legal formulae to give TNCs worldwide recognition as international actors, the present confusion as to TNCs' rights and obligations vis-à-vis nation states is not particularly helpful to the NIEO.

Two major groups of nation states perpetuate various myths concerning the TNCs. On the one hand, the DCs, in which transnationals originate and which provide the base for their global activities, claim that they do not have enough power to deal with these omnipresent entities. On the other hand, the LDCs, which have infinitely less power than do the DCs and which are affected more than anyone else by TNC operations, hope that TNC power can be curtailed by some sort of a legally-binding international convenant that TNCs would obey in spite of not being a party to it.

Both positions are difficult to defend. Although the DCs have considerable power over their TNCs, this power is limited by, among other things, the concept of national sovereignty particularly dear - for good reasons - to the weaker nation states. At the same time, it is highly unlikely that LDCs will increase their power over TNC activities in their territories through an international legally-binding agreement unless provisions are made for its implementation. Since an agreement among the nation states on the TNCs would transcend in many important instances national borders, no such agreement can be implemented without the participation of all the parties concerned. Participation of TNCs in the NIEO, which has not yet been explored is as important as the participation of socialist countries in the NIEO negotiations.

The interdependence between the NIEO and the other global issues identified above has been recognized in some theoretical writings but not in the practice of policymakers of nation states. Within the international public system this recognition has given rise recently to a stream of general declarations by consensus, solemn unilateral or group statements, and world 'plans of action' whose practical value is extremely limited. In some circles, particularly in the North, such general declarations are often accompanied by a recommendation to postpone any action on the NIEO because other important matters such as the big powers' military and security problems must be dealt with first. It has been stated repeatedly that the NIEO can only be taken care of after West and East have advanced significantly toward disarmament, thereby making available large resources for the solution of the global problem of underdevelopment.

Recognition of the relationship between the East-West armaments race and NIEO failures is important for the developing world. Any developing country or group of countries that uses for its short-term benefits the military and political tensions between the capitalist and socialist blocs damages the prospects for a change in the economic relations between North and South. On the other hand, any LDC that diversifies its political and economic links, whether with developed or developing countries, contributes in the long run to the NIEO by diffusing the bipolar power relationship and strengthening the trend toward plurality of development models. In other words, a rational dynamism in East-West relations, which depends not only on the superpowers and their respective allies but on the LDCs as well, might make it possible to modify what now appear to be non-negotiable positions on specific NIEO issues.

Once it is recognized that the NIEO cannot progress in the present climate of military tension between East and West, it becomes clear that any accommodation to and conflict resolution of other global issues - nationalism, the distribution of earnings from TNC activities, and sovereignty - would represent a net gain for the NIEO.

A question frequently raised is whether the NIEO should be negotiated as a package or in parts. Some maintain that multilateral package negotiations are easier both for DCs and LDCs because they offer trade-offs between possible gains and losses involving specific issues and particular groups of nation states. The experiences of the Paris Conference do not support the 'package deal', not because the conference ended in failure, but because the reasons for the failure cannot be attributed exclusively to the DCs.

A multilateral international negotiation of many issues at the same time can be successful only if a reasonable combination of trade-offs is perceived and accepted by the principal negotiating groups and also within each major group of negotiating nation states. In Paris, while the industrial West demonstrated little, if any, interest in compromise solutions of individual items and of the package as a whole, the LDCs were no more willing to trade off among themselves the possible gains and losses accruing to their different subgroupings from different parts of the package.

Rhetoric notwithstanding, the extent of disagreement on the major NIEO issues among the LDCs, disagreement papered over by some ingenious negotiating formulae, was equal to that prevailing among the advanced countries. Since the Paris Conference, it has haunted the Group of 77 in its intra-negotiations on many specific issues, including the Integrated Commodity Program, LDC indebtedness, and others. The persistence of these disagreements, which in Paris were submerged behind the 'common front' adopted against the rigidity of leading DCs, represents perhaps the biggest single threat to the NIEO future. The threat is compounded by the silent support of the more advanced LDCs - the so-called NICs - to the campaign conducted by some industrial Western countries that dispute the existence of a Third World.

Meaningful multilateral 'package' negotiations, with the participation of over a hundred nation states, are impossible not only politically but in terms of the logistics of the negotiating process. Add to this the difficulties of defining and agreeing upon the trade-offs within the Group of 77, as well as the difficultues experienced by the theoretically equal sovereign co-actors in delegating the authority to negotiate, and there remains the second best solution - the separate negotiation of major NIEO agenda issues in different fora.

There is no doubt that in such disjointed negotiations the LDCs are severely handicapped by limited technical capacity at the individual country level. Consequently, the Group of 77 needs for its NIEO negotiations a secretariat similar to the OECD arrangement available to the Western industrial countries. Such a NIEO secretariat would be useful, however, only if accompanied by improved performance of the international public system and particularly of the secretariats of the United Nations and its agencies both on a technical and political level.

Improvement of UN performance should be understood as the restoration of the system's only valid function - as a competent intermediary in the highly complex situations involving the respective numerical majorities and minorities of member nation states. The UN system and other international public agencies should foster innovative actions designed to strengthen the negotiating capacity of the LDCs and, at the same time, to improve the role of the secretariats as 'honest middlemen' and 'interlocuteurs valables'. Otherwise, the UN system, its extensions, and other parallel structures run a double risk: first, of losing whatever international relevance they may still have; and, second of transforming themselves into aimless conglomerations of the newest 'new class', without any power to influence world developments. The dangers of such a drift toward international irrelevance and oblivion should not be underestimated, particularly by those at the top of the international public system.

Any serious debate on the NIEO and its future should not be limited to a repetition of earlier debates on the pros and cons of specific technical solutions for specific substantive issues arising from the traditional economic relations between North and South. Such debate must deal with the issues underlying the present deadlocks and the progressive stagnation of negotiations. It is not enough to agree that the issues are complicated and the negotiations difficult, and that it may take many decades to adjust the present economic order to the changing political order and to the rapidly increasing needs of the world's backward peripheries.

It is time to acknowledge that the NIEO, which is necessarily a complicated, difficult and long-drawn-out process, will not be achieved - at the present pace of negotiations - even by the end of the next century. Such a prediction violates, however, the whole dynamics of human history. Between 1875 and 1975 the world has changed dramatically despite all sorts of obstacles arising from the teachings of conventional wisdom and from the short-term interests of the actors present on the international scene at that time. Not only is there no doubt that the world will have changed again by the year 2075, but there are reasons to believe that the change will be more profound than in the past. Blocking the NIEO will not stop the process of change, which should not be equated with the nineteenth century's optimistic liberal idea of unending progress; on the other hand, present attempts to foster the NIEO may help to make this process less unruly, less painful and more rational.

NOTES

(1) Among relevant recent books are: Jagdish N. Bhagwati (Editor), The New International Economic Order: The North-South Debate, M.I.T. Press, Cambridge, Mass., 1977; Karl P. Sauvant and Hajo Hasenpflug (Editors), The New International Economic Order: Confrontation or Cooperation between North and South, Westview Press, Boulder, Colorado, 1978; and Roger D. Hansen, Beyond the North-South Stalemate, McGraw Hill Book Co., New York, 1979.

(2) One of the earliest but still one of the best contributions on the NIEO, a report of a group of experts appointed by Commonwealth Heads of Government at their meeting in Kingston, Jamaica in May 1975, identified eight major NIEO issues: commodity arrangements; trade liberalization and access to markets; economic cooperation among developing countries; food production and rural development; industrial cooperation and transfer of technology; the transfer of resources; invisibles; and international institutions. For details, see Toward a New International Economic Order, Commonwealth Secretariat, London, August 1975.

(3) The history of negotiations through UNCTAD IV can be found in Dragoslav Avramovic, 'Commodities in Nairobi', Development and Change (The Hague), Vol. 8, No. 2 (April 1977), pp. 231-48.

(4) 'Common Fund - Mountain in Labour', The Economist (London), 24 March 1979, p. 108.

(5) Noting that 'the non-oil producing developing countries have been caught between the hammer of rising oil prices and the anvil of higher machinery costs', another politically non-suspect source, the Financial Times added that the prices of raw materials and commodities 'are not only falling in real terms, but are being held down by powerful Western consumers who need to keep production costs down while raising their own workers' living standards'. Brij Khindaria, 'UNCTAD in Manila', Financial Times (London), 8 May 1979.

(6) An Associated Press cable from Geneva, published in International Herald Tribune (Paris) on 13 December 1978 and quoted here in its entirety, describes well the situation prevailing in this field: 'Nations that produce and consume natural rubber failed after four weeks of negotiations in Geneva to reach an international trade agreement. The United States was blamed for the impasse, and a United States official conceeded "it is fair" to say Washington

prevented an accord. Separately, in London, talks on a revised international pack for cocoa were also at an impasse, with the United States apparently taking a hardline'.

(7) For a quite realistic appraisal of present trends in North-South trade, see a speech of Olivier Long, Director General of GATT, before the European-Atlantic Group (London), 7 November 1978, GATT Press Release 1223. According to Long, 'four years of recession and stagnation were necessary to make people understand the degree to which the markets of the developing countries contribute to sustain the industrial activity in the developed countries. . . . There is the need now to translate this novel recognition into a more energetic change of the North-South relations'.

(8) See, among others, Gerald K. Helleiner, 'Manufactured Exports from Less Developed Countries and Multinational Firms', The Economic Journal (Oxford), No. 329 (March 1973).

(9) Miguel S. Wionczek (Editor), LDC External Indebtedness and the World Economy, El Colegio de Mexico and the CEESTM, Mexico, 1978.

(10) For details, see a special issue of World Development (Oxford), entitled 'International Indebtedness and World Economic Stagnation', Vol. 7, No. 2 (February 1979).

(11) Dragoslav Avramovic, 'Developing-Developed Country Negotiations: Recent Experience and Future Prospects', OPEC Review, (Vienna) (June 1978), p. 54.

(12) Miguel S. Wionczek, 'Prospects for the UNCTAD Code of Conduct for the Transfer of Technology', Mazingira (Oxford), No. 8 (1979).

(13) Constantine V. Vaitsos, 'Crisis in Regional Economic Cooperation Integration among Developing Countries: A Survey', World Development (Oxford), Vol. 6, No. 6 (June 1978), pp. 719-70.

(14) Karl P. Sauvant, 'The Poor Countries and the Rich - a Few Steps Forward', Dissent (New York), (Winter 1978), p. 54.

(15) 'If the economic upheavals are buffeting powerful industrial countries, they are taking an even heavier toll among developing countries, particularly among the poorest of them', 'UNCTAD in Manila', Financial Times (London), 8 May 1979.

(16) A paper by I.H. Abdel-Rahman, 'North Africa and Middle East: Economic and Political Issues', presented to the Conference on the NIEO held in Mexico City in January 1979 notes that one gets the general feeling in this region that the countries, individually and collectively, have too many pressing problems of their own to spare attention for the new international order as proposed globally. This observation is applicable to the rest of the underdeveloped world as well.

(17) For one of the most penetrating critiques of such views see Gabriel Palma, 'Dependency: A Formal Theory of Underdevelopment or a Methodology for the Analysis of Concrete Situations of Underdevelopment', World Development (Oxford), Vol. 6, No. 7/8 (July-August 1978), pp. 881-924.

(18) The overburdening of the international public system with these intra-negotiations, under the guise of coordination among different units, resulted in the shift of substantive work almost exclusively to ad hoc expert committees and outside consultants.

(19) It is unfortunate that international academic meetings on the NIEO do not dedicate more attention to the decision-making processes at the United Nations and the non-UN international public agencies.

(20) Robert W. Gregg, Obstacles and Opportunities in the Establishment of the NIEO in the Field of Decision-Making Structure and Processes of the United Nations, Resumé of a paper submitted to the UNITAR Conference on the NIEO, Mexíco City, January 1979.

(21) Arthur W. Lewis, The Evolution of the International Economic Order, Research Program in Development Studies, Woodrow Wilson School, Discussion Paper No. 74, Princeton University, Princeton, New Jersey, March 1977 (mimeo.).

(22) On the immediate prospects of the world economy, see, among others, UNCTAD, Interdependence of Problems of Trade, Development Finance and the International Monetary System - World Economic Outlook, 1975-9, Geneva, TD/B/712, 17 August 1978. Moreover, growth targets are being revised downward continuously not only by the DCs but also in the socialist part of Europe. Growth rate for the U.S.S.R., Czechoslovakia, and Poland were expected to be 5.4 per cent, 4.9 per cent and 2.8 per cent respectively in 1979, as against 10 per cent or more a year in the previous quarter-century.

(23) See, among others, Economic and Social Consequences of the Arms Race and of Military Expenditure, Up-dated Report of the Secretary-General, United Nations, New York, 1978.

(24) See the Stockholm International Peace Research Institute (SIPRI) annual surveys on worlds armaments and arms trade. The interest in 'national military independence' is not necessarily limited to rightist military governments. A recent report from Greece may be enlightening as it refers to the political platform of the Panhellenic Socialist Party of Andreas Papandreou: 'Greece already produces a great part of the ammunition it needs, and by the end of the year will be assembling its own armoured personnel carriers. Missile-carrying motor-vessels are being built under license from the French. . . . If and when Mr. Papandreou comes to power, he promises that Greece will produce at least 80% of its armaments'. 'A Survey of Greece', The Economist (London), 16-22 December 1978, p. 67.

(25) See 'Comecon's Consuming Lust', The Economist, (London), 9 December 1978, pp. 81-2.

(26) Miguel S. Wionczek, 'Prospects for the UNCSTD - Three Underlying Issues', The Bulletin of the Atomic Scientists (Chicago) (April 1979), and Chapter 21 this volume.

(27) On this point, see Raymond Vernon, 'Multinationals: No Strings Attached', Foreign Policy (Washington) No. 33 (Winter 1978-9), pp. 121-34.

CHAPTER 23

What Can be Done (If Anything) With the Brandt Report?*

IMPACT OF THE BRANDT REPORT

THE BRANDT Commission started its work in December 1977, the final version of its Report was written (after earlier unfruitful attempts to put together some conflicting drafts and proposals) in the late autumn of 1979, it appeared in English in mid-February 1980 and it was commented on briefly and with certain sympathy by the international mass media shortly afterwards. The commission's work coincided with the most turbulent period of recent economic history, marked by steady deterioration not only in North-South relations but also in world economic conditions. Thus one can hardly be surprised that most immediate United States and European comments argued that while the contents of the Report were worth reading and most recommendations sounded reasonable, the timing of its release was highly unfortunate. That timing was not of the Brandt Commission's making. The Report saw the light when the interest of Western industrial countries in the problems of the underdeveloped South reached the lowest point since the end of the Second World War due both to serious domestic economic difficulties in advanced countries and to the revival of the cold war between the two superpowers.

Neither should one be surprised that although the document was reported to be the subject of conversations between the Presidents of Austria and Mexico during the latter's visit to Europe in May 1980, not much was heard on either side of the North Atlantic about the Brandt Report during the spring of 1980. The United States mass media and public opinion were fully absorbed by an electoral campaign, the steep deterioration in the domestic economy and, marginally, by the issue of the hostages in Iran and the Afghanistan conflict. Over the same period, European mass media and governments were occupied with no less depressing economic news from their side of the Atlantic; the protracted EEC squabble between London and Brussels; and French and West German manoeuvres aimed at reestablishing political and strategic contacts with the Soviet Union without endangering the North Atlantic alliance. In this highly

---

*This paper was presented at the Seminar on the North-South Dialogue and its Impact on Latin America, Porto Alegre, Brazil, 7-10 August 1980, and is published in <u>Third World Quarterly</u> (London) (January 1981)

tense international, regional and national context there was clearly very little room for North-South problems and even less for a serious study of the Brandt Report and its policy implications.

The Commission's decision to suspend all activities after the Report's appearance in English, the delays in its publication in other languages, and the usual difficulties that befall distribution of any book by publishers devoid of a worldwide distribution network compounded the problem of the Report's diffusion outside English-speaking countries.

Whatever the combination of reasons for it might be, the fact is that six months after its release outside circles close to the Commission itself the Brandt Report was mostly known through second-hand references and was largely unknown to Third World opinion-makers. In Mexico, for example, a country reasonably well incorporated in the international English-speaking information network, by mid-June 1980 not more than half-a-dozen copies of the Report had reached the hands of people involved or just interested in international political and economic matters. If the Brandt Commission's proposals were hardly perceived in Mexico by the summer of 1980, the situation could not be expected to be any better in most other leading Third World countries.

Informal contacts with centres of international diplomatic activity strongly support this appraisal of the very limited impact of the Brandt Report on worldwide public opinion. It is reported that the general attitude toward the Report among Third World diplomats in New York, Geneva and elsewhere, is not exactly enthusiastic and that in some high places the Report has been looked upon as just another updated 'Pearson report'. Moreover, it may be relevant to note that the widely extended idea that the Report represents the line of thinking of the World Bank and its outgoing President has never really died. Since the World Bank is not exactly 'loved' in some LDCs and since - in ideological terms - it is perceived in various quarters as the extension of United States financial and political power, the identification - however incorrect - of the Report's recommendations with Mr. McNamara is not always politically helpful. Something similar could be said about the opposite perception of the Commission's work in some circles as allegedly reflecting - because of its Chairman's political affiliation - the thinking of the European Social Democratic movement.

Informal, albeit somewhat more technical, comments from the oil-producing countries also seem to be somewhat critical. Some of these sources question the Brandt Report because - it is said - it does not do full justice to the OPEC position in the present energy conflict and on the whole does not present convincingly explicit proposals on monetary reform. The same commentators are of the opinion that the Report depends too heavily upon the industrial countries (particularly the United States) vision of the so-called oil crisis. Moreover, it is added, the document glosses over what the same sources consider to be the highly negative role of the large energy (formerly oil) transnationals while emphasizing unduly the share of responsibility of the oil-producers in the energy crisis. The perception that the Report is both 'too Western' and 'too political', to the detriment of both its technical level and its political credibility as a neutral exercise, does not seem to be limited to countries of the Middle East oil group. It can also be found among some Third World diplomats and politicians from the non-oil exporting countries who had a chance to read the Commission's final product shortly after its appearance on the market.

What Can be Done (If Anything) with the Brandt Report?   413

THE INTERNATIONAL CONTEXT

The Report's policy recommendations reappeared on the international, mostly European, scene shortly before the summit meetings held in Venice towards the end of June 1980. There is circumstantial evidence that this second wave of interest in the Brandt Commission's work was prompted by a combination of various factors: first, the agenda of the second Venice summit meeting that included energy, monetary problems, trade and relations with developing countries was very similar to the table of contents of the Brandt Report; second, the political confrontation between the United States and the Soviet Union subsided somewhat as a consequence of West European intermediation; third, starting in April 1980 the world economic picture deteriorated rapidly (or perhaps around that date the seriousness of the situation on both sides of the Atlantic started to be perceived more clearly); and fourth, there was not enough evidence that preparations for the Venice summit meeting in key capitals were adequate given the overall situation.

The Venice summit meetings took place amidst gloom engulfing the whole Western world once the conclusion was reached that 'something had gone wrong' with the United States economy in April-May 1980. At the beginning of the summer a rapidly-growing number of experts and commentators in the United States and Western Europe started to draw comparisons between the 1979-80 international economic scene and the events of the early thirties. The column of a leading United States economic commentator, Leonard Silk, published under the title 'Dancing on the Titanic?' in The New York Times ten days before President Carter's trip to Venice, offered a sample of the general feeling. Commenting on both United States domestic developments and prospects for the international economy, the article ended with the following frightening reflection:

> Are we dancing a jig on the deck of the Titanic? Economic forecasting is an unreliable art. Economic events need to be managed, since they can not be divined, but the public is apprehensive that the political managers have lost control of events(1).

The Declaration of the Venice Economic Summit meeting (25 June) did not convince anybody that events were under control. Commenting on that document with heavy irony The Economist noted that the distinguished participants promised (in one terse sentence) to study the Brandt report:

> as if it had been sprung on them on the summit eve, rather than been on sale in the world's bookshops for several months(2).

In the opinion of the same conservative British journal, the leaders of the Western industrial powers:

> are not going to indulge in the sort of Keynesianism which Brandt could have made respectable - some pumping out of funds to poor countries so that they can keep up their purchases of manufactured goods. Nor did they give more than stilted encouragement to the IMF to carry that job out more effectively. They were not even prepared to support the idea of a mini-summit at which the poor would also have a voice(3).

With the flood of news about the deepening recession in the United States and the United Kingdom and its rapid extension to all other Western industrial countries (in mid-July it was reported from Tokyo that even Japan would be affected), there was overwhelming evidence that the Western industrial world is suffering from synchronized protracted recession, the most serious of the whole post-war period. Its gravity is compounded by the fact that it is imposed upon longer-term trends of structural stagnation.

World Economic Outlook - A Survey of the Staff of the IMF, released in Washington one day after the end of the Venice meeting, offers proof that those who still believe that these events are just another 'normal' cyclical downturn are mistaken. The paper, the first of its sort in IMF history, starts with the greatest understatement of the year: 'The world economic picture is rather grim'(4). Even at this juncture Western governments continue to abstain from policies of domestic stimulation because, as The Economist stated bluntly, 'conservative slogans are in fashion' everywhere in the North Atlantic region. Information available from the socialist bloc, through such sources as the UN Economic Commission for Europe in Geneva, indicates that perhaps for different reasons the European socialist economies are also suffering the heavy impact of stagnation accompanied by inflation. The annual rate of growth declined in that region in 1979 to about 3 per cent and no improvement is in sight for 1980 and 1981. Finally, negotiations on North-South issues between the industrial countries and the LDCs are completely paralysed. On the eve of the UN General Assembly special session on North-South issues to be started in August 1980, prospects for the 'global dialogue' and the formulation of a new international development strategy are grim as well. At the UN final preparatory meeting of global negotiations held in New York between 20 June and 5 July no agreement was reached either on the special session's agenda or the procedures, because - as LDCs insist - at the last moment the Western industrial countries went back to the non-negotiable positions defended throughout the previous year.

Those who still see some light on the horizon or who do not see quite so grim a picture yet recall that in 1974-5 the LDCs' import demand saved the world economy from a major crisis, and express hope that world trade may mitigate recessionary trends somewhat. This line of wishful thinking is offered by the IMF Outlook, whose experts are aware that, given the grim prospects for the industrial economies for 1980 and 1981, the severity and the duration of the present economic crisis will depend to a very considerable extent on the import behaviour of the LDCs. The IMF Outlook forecasts that the oil-exporters will increase their imports by 20 per cent in 1980 and by slightly less in 1981 and that import demand by the non-oil LDCs will still rise by 4.5 per cent in 1980 after having increased 8 per cent in each of the previous two years. But it is not quite clear why imports (and the GNP) of the non-oil LDCs should continue growing unless these countries are provided very soon with external financial resources of the magnitude suggested by the Brandt Commission but considered impossible in Western capitals. In the absence of such transfers most LDCs will have to forego imports and growth for the sake of paying in 1980-1 about one-third of their total accumulated financial obligations to industrial countries. By the end of 1979 the non-oil LDCs had publicly guaranteed debts of US $250 billion and their non-guaranteed private external indebtedness was estimated at another US $150 billion. In brief, in 1980-1 non-oil LDCs will need close to US $300 billion for the double purpose of rolling over the existing debt and covering current account deficits. While in 1980-1 the foreign exchange costs of the debt service and amortization (including private debts) for these countries will be of the order of US $150 billion, their current account deficits for 1980 are estimated at US $68 billion and at US $78 billion for 1981. Whereas the solution of this simple financial puzzle defeats imagination, the complete standstill in respect to international action suggests a high probability that 1980 will

What Can be Done (If Anything) with the Brandt Report?   415

see the most serious international financial crisis since the thirties.

PROPOSALS OF THE BRANDT REPORT

With such short-term prospects, the Brandt Report's proposals must be looked upon not in the context of the international economic picture as it was perceived in Western capitals and by the Brandt Commission members in late 1979, but in the context of the rapidly accelerating crisis in the middle of 1980. Since the Brandt Commission's mandate, written in 1977, was to deal with North-South problems and not with the problems of the North, the Brandt Report was built upon the double assumption of the general viability of the economy of the North and of the general adequacy of domestic economic policies of the North. The assumption proved to be wrong. Writing his introduction to the Report in mid-December 1979, once the Report was ready to go to press, the Chairman of the Commission himself expressed serious misgivings about these key assumptions, by stating that:

> the present economic difficulties of the rich nations are more serious than those of past recessions and economic crises(5).

and hence:

> it would be dangerous and insincere to suggest that they can be overcome with the conventional tools of previous decades(6).

Given the extreme seriousness of global economic difficulties and worldwide persistence of conventional policy tools, the following comments on the six major groups of the Brandt Report proposals are in order:

(1) Commodity Trade and Development

The Report's recommendations follow closely both the demands of the Group of 77 and the policy proposals defended by LDCs at the UNCTAD since the mid-seventies with little success. The recommendations do not fully endorse the original UNCTAD Integrated Commodity Programme. For the sake of reaching an agreement with industrial countries, that programme was abandoned by LDCs after UNCTAD IV in favour of a relatively small Common Fund which at present can count, at the most, on some US $500-600 million collected through voluntary contributions of commodity importing and exporting countries. With a Common Fund of the size finally agreed on in the spring of 1980 not much could have been expected, even under the relatively normal conditions still prevailing in international commodity trade in 1978-9. Under 1980-1 conditions the Fund can hardly have any impact at all on the LDCs' economies for two reasons: first, the downward pressures on most commodity prices, foodstuffs excepted, are not only growing but accelerating in response to the decline in global demand; second, the increase in commodity processing, marketing and diversification is simply impossible in view of the shrinkage of international markets, accompanied by the persistence of tariff and non-tariff barriers on semi-processed commodities from 'new sources', i.e. traditional non-processed commodity LDC exporters. In the present situation, looking at commodity trade from the viewpoint of long-term estimated financing needs and availabilities is not particularly helpful unless support is also given to the original Integrated Commodity Programme and its far-reaching financial implications. What seems to be more urgent than some piecemeal commodity financing in a stagnant world is restoring demand for commodities in industrial countries, or, in other words, stimulating their domestic growth.

(2) Energy

The international energy strategy under an emergency programme (1980-5) proposed by the Brandt Report looks like a counterpart of the commodity trade and development section in the sense that, while the commodity proposals try to meet some LDC demands by going beyond the present UNCTAD agreement on the Common Fund, the energy programme goes clearly in the opposite direction in the attempt to satisfy the industrial West. Although it is impossible to quarrel with the Report's main conclusion that an accommodation between oil-producing and oil-consuming countries is extremely urgent, the conditions for such accommodation contained in the Report suggest strongly that the 'oil crisis' is considered by the Brandt Commission mostly from the viewpoint of Western industrial oil-consuming countries. This reflects perhaps the heavy participation in the Commission's work of many experts and advisers who see world problems through European eyes.

The extreme dependence of Europe on imported oil can hardly be questioned. What can be questioned, however, is the Report's fascination with oil and not with energy, and its assigning responsibility for the oil crisis 'equitably' to oil-producing and oil-consuming countries when, under reasonable energy consumption policies, there would perhaps not have been an oil crisis at all. Under such reasonable energy consumption policies and in view of the impressive technological progress achieved in the seventies in the field not only of alternative energy sources but of non-conventional hydrocarbons, there should be no room for the panic surrounding the issue of the 'oil crisis' in certain major Western industrial countries which are neither resource- nor technology-poor but whose progress toward a multiple source energy policy is disappointingly slow. Evidence abounds that the global oil question is not necessarily a resource problem but a technological and energy policy problem. If it were otherwise, Japan, the extreme case of an energy resource-poor country, would have been in total financial and economic bankruptcy by now, almost one decade after the first oil crisis of 1973-4. The relative buoyancy of the Japanese economy and the country's considerable success in adapting its energy consumption patterns to the change in the world oil supply suggest that the oil crisis mainly affects those industrial economies whose general economic management is poor or has been incapacitated by political deadlocks arising from severe conflicts among powerful domestic interest groups.

Accommodation between oil-producing and oil-consuming countries would perhaps be easier if the Brandt Report had offered the international community a package proposal of policy action that would include some measures aimed at:

(1) giving more serious attention to the oil-producing countries' quest for the gradual substitution of non-conventional hydrocarbons, first, and other alternative energy sources afterwards, for conventional oil as an energy source;

(2) submitting for international consideration a set of guidelines for the transition period from oil to multiple energy sources in the industrial economies;

(3) assuring levels of energy production in industrial countries concomitant with their resource bases and technological capabilities;

(4) incorporating in the accommodation process, and through common agreement, those multinational energy (formerly oil) enterprises whose control of modern energy technology and of non-oil energy resource bases in industrial countries permits them to dominate not the oil supply but the energy policy decision-making processes both in Western industrial countries and on a global basis;

(5) providing the non-oil producing LDCs (through international financial institutions) with investment funds for the development of available energy resources, including – but not limited to – hydrocarbons;

(6) linking the international energy emergency programme directly with the reform of the international monetary system, with special emphasis on such key issues as the impact of inflation transmitted from the industrial economies to the rest of the world and the orderly recycling of oil and other financial surpluses throughout the world.

Obviously, such an alternative international energy emergency programme would involve disposing of a series of myths underlying the vision of the 'oil crisis' through Western industrial eyes, including the widely-held beliefs that: (1) the earth is running out of oil; (2) all the present world difficulties, including inflation, are due to the OPEC; (3) the exclusive profiteers from the global man-made hydrocarbon shortages are the oil-producing countries; (4) multinational energy corporations are both innocent bystanders in the present global energy mess and helpful midwives in the process of the appearance of new energy resources in the LDCs.

(3) Industrialization and World Trade

The Brandt Report's proposals related to this major group of international economic issues are weak when compared with those addressed to the issues of commodity trade and development and energy. The Report's tendency to balance recommendations directed to the industrial West with others for LDCs is reflected in a brief text on manufactures appearing as a part of 'A Programme of Priorities' (the section on 'Tasks for the 80s and 90s') which summarizes key policy recommendations as follows:

> The North should reverse the present trend towards protecting its industries against competition from the Third World and promote instead a process of positive, anticipatory restructuring. Industrial adjustment policies affect other countries closely and should be subject to international consultation and surveillance. The codes established by the GATT Tokyo Round which concluded in 1979 will be useful if they are acted upon forcefully, but further work is necessary to link temporary safeguard restrictions to genuine adjustment policies. Developing countries should beware of their own protectionism, which affects the competitiveness of their exports, and curtails the opportunities for trade among themselves which is an essential element in their mutual cooperation(7).

There are substantive and operative problems in such a presentation. While at first sight the text seems to be well balanced and its contents sound reasonable on the whole, it creates the impression that the matters under consideration can be taken care of by a series of minor adjustments to existing international trade policies and mechanisms. Unfortunately, the reality is considerably more difficult to handle than the Report's diagnosis would suggest.

First, at the time of a trade war raging among major industrial countries – witness the cases of steel, motor vehicles, electric domestic equipment, chemicals and petrochemicals, and (everybody's) textiles – promoting industrial exports from LDCs is a herculean task. Second, the multilateral and non-discriminating application of General Agreement on Tariffs and Trade (GATT) codes negotiated at the Tokyo Round cannot help the South. These new codes were negotiated among industrial countries and for industrial countries with the aim of arriving at a sort of armistice in the midst of serious protectionist fights waged by non-tariff means. Although the codes offer some quid pro quo to industrial countries, they unilaterally limit their markets to LDC manufactures (through policing LDCs' export-oriented subsidies, to give an example). The non-discriminatory application of the new GATT codes among the industrial countries themselves, if and when achieved, might offer them a respite in the present protectionist weather, but it would only increase LDCs' export trade difficulties. Not only does equality among non-equals amount to inequality, but also, of late, this trade inequality between the North and the South has increased a great deal because of the protracted world economic stagnation which was followed by the present steep cyclical downturn. Third, the trials and tribulations of the General System of Preferences and its uncertain future, particularly in the European Economic Community, are only glossed over in the Report. Fourth, the case for a possible merging of GATT and UNCTAD at some later, undetermined date has not been presented convincingly. Even more than before the Tokyo Round, the GATT has become a 'rich countries' club' while UNCTAD has remained one of the few important UN agencies able to defend long-term LDC interests. Under these conditions a marriage between these two bodies can hardly be appealing to any of the parties involved. Finally, definitely too little attention has been given to the key problem of the necessary broad industrial adjustment at a national level in industrial countries. The lack of progress in that respect due to internal political obstacles has been largely responsible for the present worldwide stagnation and the confrontation between North and South. Unless such a rather painful adjustment takes place and is supported by an internationally coordinated policy designed to stimulate the Western industrial sector of the world economy, no prospects can be envisaged for the recovery and expansion of world trade under conditions favourable to the industrialization objectives of LDCs.

(4) Transnationals and Technology

This group of recommendations forms a very coherent set if one considers that, short of very radical changes at global and national lev el, the LDCs will have to establish a better modus vivendi with transnational corporations (TNCs). Not only is there a shortage of savings and capital in the Third World, but these giant private productive units are also a major source of technology, management and marketing skills which are in very short supply in most LDCs. While the Report emphasizes that such a modus vivendi involves action at both international and national levels, it ascribes particular importance to national measures for policing and regulating TNCs and for increasing the LDCs' bargaining capacity vis-à-vis TNCs in respect to the conditions of capital and technological capability as well. International codes of conduct for TNCs and technology transfer are endorsed and so is the design of effective national policies for LDCs in both fields, with the emphasis on technology. These codes should be supported, the Report states, by intergovernmental cooperation with regard to tax policies and monitoring of transfer prices, harmonization of fiscal and other incentives among recipient developing countries, and forceful technical assistance of international public agencies in science and technology matters.

It is perhaps in this specific field of North-South relations that the difference between the Brandt Report and the ten-years-older Pearson Report is particularly striking. The Pearson Report was hardly aware of deep conflicts between the objectives of TNCs and those of the developing host countries and of the crucial role of technology transfer in development. While it shows considerable improvement over the work of its predecessors, the Brandt Report still shuns, however, some major conclusions about what LDCs must do to be able to use technology imports for building up their own scientific and technological capability. Without long-range science and technology planning and without linking effectively domestic R&D efforts with their productive and educational systems the LDCs will continue to be at the mercy of TNCs as large and indiscriminate importers of often useless and socially disruptive foreign technologies.

(5) International Monetary Reform

International monetary reform and development financing proposals, presented in two separate chapters, are the crucial part of the Brandt Report recommendations. Some observers might say that the Report's position on world monetary management problems is quite radical, particularly when it is borne in mind that nothing less is recommended than the increased participation of LDCs in management and decision-making at the IMF, the bulwark of orthodox monetary approaches to world economic problems. It may be worth noting that the Report is less explicit on the same point when it analyses the World Bank's performance in the chapter on development financing.

In brief, the Report proposes a new monetary order through the establishment of a new international currency which might take the form of an improved Special Drawing Right (SDR) (supported with an appropriately designed 'substitution account'), the implementation of the 'SDR link' idea, the increased stabilization of the international floating exchange system, and the use of IMF gold as an interest subsidy on loans to the poorest LDCs. The success of all these measures would largely depend - it is stressed - upon the reaching of an agreement at the IMF and elsewhere (perhaps at the OECD in the first place) on an adjustment process that would not increase contractionist pressures in the world economy and put greater responsibility for payments adjustment on surplus countries.

So far so good, but one is reminded immediately that at the time of the Brandt Report's writing, all nations but a few oil surplus countries became deficit countries (at least for the duration of the present recession). This uncomfortable reality would lead to the conclusion that under the present conditions the issue of international monetary reform is linked directly not only with that of development finance but also with the international energy problem. This triangular linkage has not been recognized as yet by world financial and economic experts, because of, among other things, the institutional departmentalization of closely interrelated problems. Otherwise (to give striking example) the close interdependence that exists between the 'substitution account' and the recycling problem would be easily seen. Although the triangular linkage is briefly acknowledged by the Brandt Report, unfortunately the document does not dedicate enough attention to its policy implications. On the contrary, the Report accepts perhaps as inevitable continued treatment of the three major problems (monetary system, development finance and energy) with <u>separate</u> sets of measures in <u>separate</u> places and institutions.

Such an approach did not work and does not work. International monetary reform is kept alive only by the largely unsuccessful efforts of the Group of 24 at the IMF. Development finance is in the hands of the World Bank (and regional banks), the OECD, the OPEC Special Fund, and, of course, international private banking. Finally, after the demise of the North-South dialogue at the Paris Conference in mid-1977, global energy problems have not been handled anywhere. Moreover, the prospects of their being handled within the framework of the global negotiations at the UN look more and more uncertain. Under such conditions one really wonders whether an international monetary reform is possible at all through the piecemeal approach, which is also accepted implicitly by the Brandt Report, even if each and all technical proposals supported by the document appear to be very useful on their respective merits.

The Report correctly recalls that the extinct Bretton Woods system reflected the economic and political relations of the time and insists that:

> reform of the world monetary system is urgent and must address itself to the following issues: exchange rate regime, the reserve system (the creation and distribution of the international means of payments or liquidity); and the adjustment mechanism as it affects the countries issuing reserve currencies, surplus countries and deficit countries(8).

But then the Report forgets to probe deeper into the political feasibility of the new 'power sharing' and leaves largely unanswered many tough questions: Does not monetary reform imply a basic change of thinking about 'national interests' and development? Would a reform of the world monetary system under the umbrella of the refurbished IMF work in the absence of a thorough reorganization of the whole package known as 'international economic order'? Is the present-day IMF any more obsolete than other mechanisms of international financial and economic cooperation that emerged at the end of the Second World War? Is the International Monetary Fund the place where a broad monetary reform affecting the distribution of political power might be conceived, designed and implemented once the participation of developing countries in the decision-making of the IMF had been enlarged, as the Report recommends? Are ministers of treasury and presidents of central banks, known both in industrial and developing countries for their conservative attitudes, endowed with a broad enough vision to reorganize the present monetary chaos?

Thus, while the Brandt Report's monetary proposals may seem radical when compared with the present unworkable state of affairs, in the final analysis they fall between two stools: they are too radical for the national establishments in most industrial (and many developing) countries and not audacious enough to deal with the problems of the eighties. Somehow it does not occur to political leaders, financial wizards and economics professors of the North that between Bretton Woods and 1980 as much time has passed as between 1910 and Bretton Woods - thirty-five years. Would the institutions established before the Sarajevo conflict have worked in 1945?

What Can be Done (If Anything) with the Brandt Report? 421

The biggest final criticism that can perhaps be made of the Brandt Report's section on monetary reform is that it does not establish strong and convincing links between international monetary management and global economic management issues. The weakness of such links can be perceived in the Report's final section dealing with development finance.

(6) Development Finance

The centrepiece of the development finance proposals of the Brandt Report is its call for the creation of a new institution, a World Development Fund, which would strengthen the structure of development lending and represent a new start in North-South relations. The proposed Fund, it is stressed, would not be an alternative to the reform and restructuring of existing institutions but their complement. It would be financed by a new system of universal and automatic revenues made available for world development by all countries - West, East and South. It would meet the quantitative and qualitative gaps in the present development finance structure and at the same time complement the lending of the World Bank and the IMF. Its long-term programme lending would help the disbursement of World Bank projects held up by the shortage of domestic resources, as well as to keep countries from reaching a crisis situation in which they would have to go to the IMF for balance-of-payments adjustment finance.

The proposal must be viewed as the institutionalized conclusion of a set of recommendations aimed at: (1) substantial increase in the transfer of financial resources to LDCs; (2) enlargement of the flow of official development finance; (3) improvement of the volume and the terms of lending by international financial institutions; and (4) expansion of multilateral finance for mineral and energy development. Not only does the World Development Fund proposal present a convincing case for a substantial increase in the transfer of resources to LDCs but the Brandt Report makes it clear that such worldwide action can only be successful if the Fund is depoliticized from the very start: the funding would have to come automatically from *all*, including socialist, countries; the LDCs would have an increasing role in the decision-making and management of international financial institutions; and, moreover, political conditions would be eliminated from the operations of multilateral financial institutions.

Most probably, once all these conditions were fulfilled, the new international transfer of resources system would perform its function of maximizing global growth and welfare much better than the system inherited from Bretton Woods. But the passage from the old system to the new one would involve not only change in development finance conditions but also the discarding of all the premises and objectives underlying the whole exercise for the past thirty years in the same field. It is not an accident that international financial institutions were established not in San Francisco's 'brave new world' weather of 1945 but in the more sheltered surroundings of Bretton Woods by two world powers of that time - the rapidly-declining British Empire and its successor, the United States. Consequently, the way in which the international development finance system operated multilaterally and bilaterally in the post-war period can hardly be considered disfunctional, illogical or sinful. It served its function of maximizing the power, growth and welfare of *its* sponsors to whom other members of the Western industrial community were willingly co-opted. It worked with relative efficiency as long as complications resulting from the West's shrinking role in the global economy and policy did not arise.

Looked at without malice or emotion, the Bretton Woods-inspired international financial system is clearly antiquated today. The question remains whether it can be reconstructed by the change of heart of its authors and sponsors, as the Brandt Report intimates and hopes. Unless such a highly unlikely change takes place, the World Development Fund will neither be established nor will it be able to fulfull its two new functions, as defined in the document, of meeting quantitative and qualitative gaps in the present development finance structure, and <u>at the same time</u> complementing the lending of the World Bank and the IMF. It could help even less - contrary to the Report's expectations - to keep LDCs from reaching a crisis situation in which they have to go to the IMF for balance-of-payments adjustment finance. It is hard to imagine that Western industrial powers would be willing to mobilize independent resources which would eventually undermine the position and the power of the IMF.

While the substantial increase in the transfer of net resources to LDCs and the meaningful enlargement of the flow of official development finance seem impossible under present international political and economic conditions, an improvement of the volume and the terms of lending by international financial institutions through measures suggested by the Brandt Report has been taking place slowly both at the World Bank and the IMF. Whether such marginal improvements are adequate to deal with the problems at hand is another story, particularly since the Law of the Dragging Feet seems to dominate the work of international bureaucracies. According to that Law, discovered by <u>The Financial Times</u> of London on the occasion of the Hamburg IMF meeting in May 1980, it takes about a year to have any small reform initiative accepted for discussion at international financial institutions and at least two years for such an initiative to be approved by which time it has lost its original usefulness.

SUMMARY

This necessarily superficial analysis of the contents of the Brandt Report could be ended with the following concluding summary remarks:

(1) The Report's major finding to the effect that the South is sliding into a hell of stagnation, increased poverty and growing socio-political tensions is correct.

(2) The Report contains a large number of proposals for the reform of North-South economic relations, none of them - except the idea of a World Development Fund - completely novel or original; but since the majority of them represents a radical departure from the conventional wisdom that dominates Western industrial capitals, they merit attention; they might improve somewhat the relations between the industrial North and the underdeveloped South.

(3) The Report's proposals on the energy issue are an exception to the document's general approach - they are biased, reflect mostly the oil-importing countries' viewpoint and do not pay due attention to the legitimate interests of the oil-producers.

(4) Attempting to keep a neutral stance in the North-South conflict and for the sake of 'political pragmatism', the Report's proposals taken as a whole fall between two stools: they are too radical for the national establishments in most industrial (and many developing) countries but are not audacious

enough to deal with the global problems of the eighties.

(5) Since the issues related to a reform not only of the IMF but of both the international monetary system and the development finance system have not been thought through, it is forgotten that the absence of any reform is closely linked with and arises from world power politics.

(6) The Report does not recognize fully the role of international bureaucratic structures and transnationals, powerful actors who are not just rational intermediaries in the global economy and politics but have their own interests distinct from those of the nation states.

(7) The Report's vision of the world economy and its recommendations have been overtaken by events. With the deepening international economic crisis, the Brandt Commission's main argument that the South must be helped by the North for moral reasons is no longer valid (assuming that it was valid at some other time). The North must help itself to get out of the combination of structural stagnation and the finance, investment and trade cycle. The only way to solve these problems is to arrange for the transfer of large idle financial resources to the South. The global stimulation of world economy, which might take the form of a World Development Fund, is in the best _immediate_ economic interest of the industrial countries and should not be considered as an aid to the poor. The world economy will not recover from its present slump without a thorough reorganization of trade, finance and technological relations between the North and the South.

(8) It is quite probable that it will take much longer than can be afforded to convince Western leaders of the urgency of restructuring North-South relations; if that were the case such restructuring would take place _after_ and not before an international economic crisis of the magnitude and intensity of that of the thirties. The danger of a Third World War cannot be lightly dismissed but, fortunately, the world political picture is very much different from that of the thirties in spite of the frightening arms race supported by the uncontrolled military technological advance of the two former superpowers.

NOTES

(1)   Leonard Silk, 'Dancing on the Titanic?', The New York Times, 13 June 1980, p. D.2.

(2)   'Getting away from it', The Economist, 28 June 1980, p. 13.

(3)   Ibid.

(4)   IMF, World Economic Outlook - A Survey of the Staff of the International Monetary Fund, Washington, D.C., May 1980, (released 26 June 1980), p. 3.

(5)   North-South. A Programme for Survival, The Report of the Independent Commission on International Development Issues under the Chairmanship of Willy Brandt, Pan Books, London and Sydney, 1980, p. 12.

(6)   Ibid.

(7)   Ibid., p. 272.

(8)   Ibid., p. 207.

Name Index

Alemán, M. 6, 8, 32, 39, 41, 78
Avila Camacho 5, 37

Bergsten, F. 253

Calles, P. E. 3, 36, 37, 38, 42, 70
Cárdenas 4, 37, 74
Castillo, C. M. 191
Cosio Villegas, D. 28

Díaz Ordaz, G. 32, 35, 41, 43

Echeverría, L. 34
Enriquez, O. R. 77

Felix, D. 143

Helleiner, G. 272

Jaguaribe, H. 284

Keynes, L. M. 394
Kissinger, H. 253

Loentieff, W. 296, 370
López Mateos, A. 81

Madrazo, C. 43
Michalet, C. A. 265
Molina Enríquez, A. 68

Nakajima, M. 249
Nyerere 197

Obregón 69

Pearson, F. S. 66
Pearson, W. 66
Porfirio Diaz 36, 49, 51, 66, 67
Prebisch, R. 144

Rodríquez, A. 73
Rosenberg, N. 284
Ruíz Cortines, A. 8, 41, 78

Sábato, J. 287
Silk, L. 413
Singer, H. W. 104
Skinner, W. 273
Solow 302
Stein, S. J. 283
Sunkel, O. 167

Tinbergen, J. 28, 296, 370

Vernon, R. 54

Subject Index

Agriculture
  in Mexico 20
  trade liberation, Andean Common Market 158
Agrupaciones patronales 40
Alliance for Progress 19, 155
Alternative international energy programme 416
American and Foreign Power Company 71
American investment in Mexico 54
Ancien régime 36
Andean Common Market 154
  achievements and prospects 157
  common treatment for foreign manufacturing companies 225
  intra-Andean commerce and foreign manufacturing companies 221
  technological policy 275, 276
  towards a common treatment for foreign private investment 207
  transnational corporations in 223, 270
Applied research in LDC 364
Appropriateness of TNC technology transfers 325
Argentina
  research projects 130
  technology transfer policies 277
  TNC research and development 328
Asian developing countries 245, 246
Australia, Latin American trade with 239

Balance of payments in Mexico 35
  impact of transfer of foreign technology 98

Bank for International Settlement 341
Bank of America 351
Banking in Mexico 51
Bilateral resource exploitation 295
Brandt Commission 249
Brandt report
  commodity trade 415
  development finance 421
  energy 416
  impact of 411
  industrialization and world trade 417
  international context 413
  international monetary reform 419
  transnationals and technology 418
Brazil
  export of manufactures to advanced countries 159
  import-substituting industrialization 145
  research projects 130
  technology transfer policy 276
  trade with Japan 242
  U.S. research on development in 132
Bucharest Declaration 388
Business Latin America 224

Caciques 38
Cámara Nacional de la Industria de la Transformación 68, 79
Camelot Project 134
Campesinos 38, 39
Canada, Latin America trade with 238, 239
Caracus Protocol 153
Cartagena Agreement 157
Caudillos 36

Central America Bank for Economic
    Integration 186
Central America Common Market 149
  drift into disaster 151
Central America Regime for
    Integration Industries 185
Chase Manhattan 351
Chemical Bank 351
Chile
  research projects 130
  technology transfer policies 275
  U.S. transnational subsidiaries in
    219
Citicorp 351
Colombia
  research projects 130
  technology transfer policies 275
  U.S. transnational subsidiaries in
    210
Comisión Federal de Electricidad 74,
    75
Comité par el Estudio de la Industria
    Eléctrica Mexicana 78
Commission on Transnational
    Corporations 254
Commodity trade
  Brandt report 415
  external demands 155
Common Fund 394
Common market in Central America
    149
Consumption technology 272
Contractual resource relations
    between DCs and LDCs 302
Corruption, elimination in Mexico
    35
Cost-benefit for foreign investment
    in Mexico 56
Cuba conflict, effect on Mexico 82

Debt, less developed countries 339
Debt-relief measures 395
Democratization from above 44, 45
Demographic growth in Latin
    America states 139
  research on impact of 136
Dependence
  external financial relations 167
  science and technology 283
Developed countries, access to LDC
    minerals 297
Developing countries, scientific
    and technological backwardness
    110
Development, UNCSTD 377, 381, 387
Development aid, intra-Pacific
    relations 241

Development finance, Brandt report
    421
Development planning 134
Development research problems in
    Latin America 123
Domestic investment in Mexico 31

East Africa Common Market 194
East Africa Currency Board 197
East-West armaments race,
    relationship with NIEO 405
Economic Commission on Latin America
    128, 144
Economic development, consequences of
    scientific and technological
    underdevelopment 89
Economic élites in Mexico 39
Economic growth in Latin America,
    regional differences within
    major indicators 140
Economic growth model in Mexico 40
Economic nationalism
  Pacific countries 239
  versus external financial dependence
    177
Economic policies in Mexico 3
Educational system
  links with research and development
    117
  in Mexico 92
  science and technology in LDC 381
Electricity industry in Mexico 50,
    65
  nationalization 80
Employment, effect of foreign direct
    investment 226
Energy, Brandt report 416
Eurocredits, international banking
    and world economic system 352
Eurocurrency Bank Credits 343
Euromarket
  factors affecting borrowing and
    lending 345
  LDC borrowing 340
  terms and conditions of loans 347
European currency unit 395
Exchange restrictions 230
Exploration technology 298
Export promotion in Mexico 35, 36
Export taxes 303
External credits in Mexico 13, 18
External debts of less developed
    countries 339
External dependency 167, 168
  science and technology 283
  versus economic nationalism 177
External public indebtedness 158

Subject Index

Federal Government Administration Agencies, participation in public investment in Mexico 7
Fiscal reform in Mexico 35
Foreign borrowing in Mexico 34
Foreign capital position in Mexico 51
Foreign investment in Mexico 49
  in electric power industry 66
  in industry 98
Foreign private investment
  common treatment for in Andean Common Market 207
  in Latin America 167, 172
Free trade zone in Latin America 149

General Agreement on Tariffs and Trade 394, 418

Honduras - El Salvador war 150
Hydroelectric plants in Mexico 66

IMF, *World Economic Outlook* 414
Immobilisme 42
Import-substituting industrialization 141, 286
Incentives for exporters in Mexico 36
Income distribution
  in Latin America 135
  in Mexico 33
Indexation 305
India, transnational corporations research and development 328
Industrial complementary agreements 154
Industrial integration 201
Industrial structures in Latin America 1955 and 1968 146
Industrialization
  in Latin America 284
  in Mexico 32
  world trade, Brandt report 417
Industrialization policies, impact on science and technology 116
Integrated commodity programme, UNCTAD 302, 305, 394, 396
Integration industries 188
Intermediation 350
International mining enterprises 299
Intra-territorial trade imbalances 195
Investment

foreign private, Andean Common Market 207
private foreign capital 167
Investment Commission in Mexico 9
Investment in Mexico 1930-60 6, 7

Japan
  autonomous development 283
  economic independence 239
  foreign technology 103
  Latin American strategy 247
  Latin American trade with 238
  participation in world economy 248
  private capital investment in Latin America 243
  national cohesion 93
  technology independence 314
  trade 1974-8 251, 252
Japanese transnational corporations in Latin America 244
Junta de Cartegena 158

Kampala-Mbale Agreement 194
Kenya
  Kampala-Mbale Agreement 195
  transnational corporations research and development 328

Labour unions in Mexico 39
Labour stratification 92
Labour strikes in Mexico 42
LAFTA 149
  irrelevance for Latin American development 152
  trade expansion with Andean group 221
Land reform in 1937 75
Latin America
  development research problems in 123
  external public indebtedness and sectoral changes in foreign private investment 167
  growth and trade strategies in the post-war period 139
  import-substituting industrialization 141
  Japan's strategy 247
  Pacific trade and development cooperation with 237
  political and economic problems of transnational corporations in 253
  regional differences within major indicators of economic growth 140

430   Subject Index

  regional trade integration   148
  research methods and personnel   129
  research needs and priorities   127
  research on   131
  science and technology and external
      dependency relations   283
Latin American common market   148
Latin American Free Trade
    Association   190
Law for New and Necessary
    Industries   54
Less developed countries
  developed countries access to
      minerals   297
  external debt and Euromarkets   339
  NIEO   393
  resource exploration arrangements
      with industrialized countries
      295
  scientific and technological
      policy for development   357,
      377, 381, 387
  technology transfer from TNCs
      311
Limits to Growth   296
Lloyds Bank   351
Loan maturities   349

Manufactured goods, export from
    Latin America to advanced
    countries   159
Manufacturing, participation in
    GDP in Latin America 1950-70
    145
Manufacturing industry in Mexico
  American investment   55
  foreign private investment   51,
      98
Market allocation   302
Market critics   147
Market size, scaling down of TNC
    technology   326
Mexican Petroleum Institute   115
Mexico
  American investment   54
  consequences of scientific and
      technological under-
      development   89
  economic development   31
  economic planning 1933-63   3
  economy   45
  electric power industry   65
  export of manufactures to
      advanced countries   159
  foreign investment in   49, 51
  Investment Commission   9
  Japanese investments   247

  plan of immediate action 1962-4   17
  Plan Sexenal   3
  Planning Bureau   16
  political situation   36
  productivity of science expenditure
      115
  Public Investment Bureau   15
  reasons for underdevelopment   109
  research projects   130
  science and technology planning   109
  technology transfer regulations   277
  transnational corporations in   269
  U.S. research on development in   132
MEXLIGHT   81
Mineral resources
  availability   296
  bilateral exploitation   295
Mining industry
  in Latin America, foreign investment
      175
  in Mexico   50
Ministry of the Presidency in Mexico
    14
Monetary reform, Brandt report   419
Monopoly of technology   102
Montevideo Treaty   149
Morgan Guaranty Trust   341, 351
Multilateral industrial licensing
    mechanism   189

Nacional Financiera   80
National Council for Science and
    Technology   110
National Electric Code   70
National Institute of Agricultural
    Research   115
National Power Commission in Mexico
    69
National Public Service Defence
    Confederation   72
National science and technology
    councils   100, 384
National Water Resources Law   72
Nationalization
  of electricity industry in Mexico
      73, 80
  of petroleum industry in Mexico   5
Natural resources exhaustion   296
New international economic order
    295, 300, 369, 393
New international resource order   300
Newly industrializing countries   397
  in Asia   245
Nicaragua, levies on regional imports
    152
Non-renewable resources   297
North-South dialogue, Brandt report
    411

Subject Index 431

North-South – A Programme for Survival 249
OECD Directorate for Science and Technology in Industry 1974 329
Oil crisis 416
Oil exporters, euromarket 342
One-party system in Mexico 36
OPEC 304
  Brandt report 412
Pacific Basin Economic Council 237
Pacific trade and development cooperation with Latin America 237
  development aid 241
  private capital investment 243
  technology and information transfers 244
  trade relations 242
Partido Nacional Revolucionario 36
Partido Revolucionario Institutional 39
Patents 94, 95, 277, 318
Peru, U.S. transnational subsidiaries in 216
Petrodollars 340
Plan of Immediate Action 1962-4 17, 19
Plan Sexenal 3
  electric power industry 73, 74, 76
Planning Bureau in Mexico 16
Planning for development in Mexico 25
Presidential cycle in Mexico 35
Presidential Resolution in Mexico 15, 16
Price and incomes stabilization scheme 301
Private banking in LDC 339, 395
Private capital investment, intra-Pacific relations 243
Private foreign investment
  Andean Common Market 207
  Latin America 167, 172
  Mexico 51, 52
Private investment in Mexico
  1930-60 6, 7
  1962-4 21, 22
  in industry 32
Private saving in Mexico 35
Private sector participation in research and development 116
Private wealth 32
Producer associations 304
Production technology transfer, TNCs 272
Project-by-project approach in Mexico 19

Proposition for the Global Infrastructure Fund 249
Public agency spending controls in Mexico 35
Public foreign indebtedness 167
Public Investment Bureau in Mexico 15
Public investment in Mexico
  1930-60 6, 7
  1939-59 12
  1941-58 18
  1959-61 and 1962-4 19, 20
Public services, foreign investment 176
Pugwash movement 372

Recession 413
Regime for Integration Industries 185
Regional economic integration 200
Regional investment policy 201
Research
  freedom 92
  needs and priorities in Latin America 127
Research and development
  in LDC 358
  links with educational system 117
  in Mexico, financial resources 111
  transnational corporations 266, 273, 327
Research units in Mexico 115
Resource availability 297
Resource cartels 304
Resource exploitation, between less developed and industrial countries 295
Resource management 298
Resource nationalism 246, 302
Resource taxation 303
Restrictive practices 321
Royalties 97, 101, 275, 303

Science, UNCSTD 377, 381, 387
Science expenditure productivity 115
Science planning in LDC 357
Science policy in Mexico 110
Science and technology development in Mexico, permanent planning process 114
Scientific underdevelopment
  in Latin America 283
  in Mexico 89
Social transformation, scientific progress 380
Socialist states, absence from NIEO debates 404

Soviet Union, technology
    independence 314
Special Drawing Right 419
State development bank securities
    34
Statistical data in Latin America
    130
Structuralist critics 147
Subcontracting by TNC 331
Sulphur mining in Mexico 50

Tanzania 197
Tariff protection 56
Tax evasion 35
Technical-managerial class 44
Technological dependency of Mexico
    94
Technological maps of the economy
    365
Technological underdevelopment
    in Latin America 283
    in Mexico 89
Technology
    TNCs, Brandt report 418
    UNCSTD 377, 381, 387
Technology costs 319
Technology package 312
    unbundling 322
Technology planning
    in LDC 357, 364
    in Mexico 110
Technology Registry 279
Technology transfer 287
    intra-Pacific relations 244
    Latin American policies 274
    negotiable issues 317
    payments 96
    restrictive practices 321
    TNCs 265, 311, 325
    UNCTAD code of conduct 369
Textile industry in Mexico 71
Third World, Japanese interest in
    247
Tied credits 34
Toronto Dominion Bank 351
Trade integration 141, 148
Trade liberalization 185
    Andean Common Market 157
Trademarks 277
Transfer pricing 231, 279
Transnational corporations 54
    Andean Common Market 210, 223, 225
    Brandt report 418
    code of conduct 318
    commission on 254
    Japan-based, in Latin America 244

LAFTA 156
    in Latin America, political and
        economic problems 253
    local personnel training 332
    NIEO 398
    OECD guidelines 330
    in Pacific countries 239
    recognition of 404
    research and development in
        developing countries 327
    restrictive practices 321
    subcontracting 331
    technology package 312, 322
    technology transfer 265, 311, 325
Tripartite arrangements 307

UNCSTD 357, 377, 381, 387
UNCTAD 394, 395
    code of conduct for technology
        transfer 369
    integrated commodity programme 302
Underdeveloped countries, lessons
    from Mexican science and
    technology plan 117
Underdevelopment in Mexico 109
    science and technology 89
Universities in Mexico, research
    and development in 110
United States
    investment in Latin America 174
    investment in Mexico 53
    research on Latin America 131
Untied States banks, LDC loans 352
United States transnationals
    in Andean group countries 210
    common treatment for in Andean
        Common Market 225
    in Mexico 54
    political and economic problems
        253
    technology transfer to LDC
        265

Venezuela
    Andean scheme 154
    research projects 130
Vienna Programme 388

Witteveen facility 354
World Development Fund 421
World International Bank, support of
    electricity industry in Mexico
    83